BRANDAN KEARNEY'S OFFICIAL CINEMA ON CINEMA AT THE CINEMA READER VOLUME 1 2010-2018

Written and Compiled by Brandan Kearney

A Drag City Book | Chicago

On Cinema and its related projects are produced and distributed by Adult Swim.

Please visit adultswim.com or the [adult swim] app to enjoy the complete On Cinema *library.*

Special thanks:
Eric Notarnicola, Andrew Porter, Sascha Stanton-Craven, Matt Harrigan, Mike Lazzo, Jonathan Roig, Drew Kordik, Tak Boroyan, Ayaka Ohwaki, Caroline Bader, Cynthia San, Ben Berman, Dan Longino, Michael Giambra, Santiago Pedroza, Gabe Patay, Abigail Keever, Jenna Keller, David Zwick, Eric Bader, John Maynard, Danya Levine, Dave Kneebone, Joe Randazzo.

DC749

Copyright ©2019
All rights reserved.

©&℗ 2019 Drag City Incorporated

All rights reserved. No part of this book may be reproduced in any form or by any electronic or mechanical means, including information storage and retrieval systems, without permission in writing from the publisher, except by a reviewer, who may quote brief passages in a review. Request to make copies of any part of this work should be mailed to:
Drag City Incorporated
Permissions Department
P. O. Box 476867, Chicago, Illinois 60647-6867
or e-mailed to: info@dragcity.com

Drag City web address: www.dragcity.com

Library of Congress Control Number: 2019936546
isbn: 978-1-937112-32-5

Design Director: Alan Smithee
Layout Assistant: Dan Osborn

Second Edition

TABLE OF CONTENTS

INTRODUCTION: TIM HEIDECKER vii
INTRODUCTION: GREGG TURKINGTON viii

SEASON 1 1

SEASON 2 13
   FIRST ANNUAL OSCARS SPECIAL 21

SEASON 3 29
   SPECIAL PRESENTATION: FIRST ANNUAL CHRISTMAS SPECIAL 42

SEASON 4 43
   SECOND ANNUAL OSCARS SPECIAL 55

SEASON 5 63
   DECKER: CLASSIFIED 73

SEASON 6 81
   THIRD ANNUAL OSCARS SPECIAL 87
   DECKER: PORT OF CALL: HAWAII 99

SEASON 7 109
   GREGG TURKINGTON'S DECKER VS. DRACULA 116
   DECKER VS. DRACULA: THE LOST WORKS 126
   FOURTH ANNUAL OSCARS SPECIAL 128
   DECKER: UNCLASSIFIED 133

SEASON 8 141
   OUR CINEMA OSCARS SPECIAL 162

SEASON 9 167
   DECKER: UNSEALED 183
   DECKER: MINDWIPE 191
   ELECTRIC SUN 20 TRIAL 199
   FIFTH ANNUAL OSCARS SPECIAL 220

SEASON X 225

APPENDIX I: THE FILMS OF JOE ESTEVEZ 247

APPENDIX II: DEKKAR LYRICS 248

APPENDIX III: GREGG TURKINGTON ON CINEMA 251

INDEX 253

INTRODUCTION BY TIM HEIDECKER

Movies are not that important.

They are a minor distraction from daily life and the toils and sacrifices strong minded people must face each day as they persevere through many trials and troubles against all odds. I have faced these challenges each and every day and I try and make the world a better place through my example and more importantly my deeds. This is self evident and obvious to most, if not all.

The *On Cinema At The Cinema* show was a minor project in the list of many things I am more proud of and continue to develop as I grow as an artist, entrepreneur, community leader and inspiration to so many. This book needlessly chronicles the many reviews we gave over several years but more importantly it shines a light on the many more important elements of my life, including the number one rock group, Dekkar, the hit EDM group DKR as well as the hit television show, *Decker*.

I have very little respect for those who mire themselves in the muck of knowing useless trivia and pointless data about movies, and unfortunately this book is peppered in with wasted ink and pulp. We worked hard with the publisher to extract these pages, or at least make them easy to remove for the vast multitudes of readers who wish to avoid such uselessness. Unfortunately, we were unable to perforate these sections so you will be required to use a little extra force to extract these pages. Or you can just avoid this book completely! There are so many other things you can be doing with your time.

All the best,
Tim Heidecker 2019,
Whaleman 2020

INTRODUCTION BY GREGG TURKINGTON

Movies have surpassed comic books, television, sports, and video games as the great American past time. But it's not just America, it's the whole world that loves movies.

With the popularity of movies it was natural that people would seek expert opinions in order to make informed decisions about which movies to see, and which movies to skip. Thus, *On Cinema At The Cinema* was born. Quickly it became the #1 rated movie review show. As the show's resident expert I have brought my knowledge to the table and educated countless viewers about classics like Humphrey Bogart as well as current movies and information that could be used to make decisions on movie-going or building a home library. I have singlehandedly built and maintain the world's largest collection of movies, the Victorville Film Archive, which will open its doors to the public one day soon. I also started *Our Cinema* which was an alternative show that provided information and expertise when the co-host of *On Cinema*, Tim Heidecker, was undercutting my ability to present this information in the *On Cinema* format. The "Popcorn Classics" segment and "On Cinema On Location" from *On Cinema* have won numerous awards and educated movie buffs about important information that was inaccessable to them through traditional outlets. I was among the first group of critics and insiders to view *Sully*, at a VIP screening in Hollywood.

I also found myself in the *Guinness Book* recently when I watched 501 Movies in 501 Days, the first and only film buff/expert ever to do so. The feat will never be duplicated.

I also became the first movie critic and expert to star in a major motion picture when I starred in Marvel's *Ant-Man* which made over a half a billion dollars at the box office (beating classic movies like *Casablanca* and *Citizen Kane*) and has never spawned a sequel. I also wrote and starred in *Decker Vs Dracula* which marked the big-screen return of James Dean (*Rebel Without A Cause, East of Eden, Giant*).

A book about movies would hopefully stick to the subject at hand: movies. There would be no need for discussion of music or medical issues. Raw data and information about the movies is what book buyers have always wanted. Not needless distractions. Hopefully the author of this book can stay to the subjects at hand and not give in to pressures from certain outside parties whose interest in movies is low, and whose knowledge of movies is even lower.

So grab 5 bags of popcorn and sit down to watch a movie, and read this great book which hopefully collects my opinions, ratings, and reviews in one place for movie historians to enjoy.

Yours in movie expertise,
Gregg Turkington
(Dale from *Ant-Man*, Jonathan Kington from *Decker*,
World Records Book record holder for watching 501 movies in 501 days,
head archivist and CEO of the Victorville Film Archive)

SEASON 1

EPISODE 101
'The Man With the Iron Fists' & 'Flight'

Air date: December 1, 2012
Running time: 6:59 minutes

In this debut episode, Tim Heidecker introduces his new web series, *On Cinema at the Cinema*. Unlike film critics who focus solely on blockbusters, Tim reveals that some of the movies he reviews may not be worth watching at all! In that same spirit of openness, he admits they are still "working out the kinks" in this first episode.

Without further ado, Tim welcomes "film buff" Gregg Turkington, who joins him to discuss the martial arts epic *The Man With the Iron Fists*. Gregg's palpable excitement compels him to mention cast member Lucy Liu before Tim has had a chance to give viewers his synopsis of this "karate kind of movie" set in "feudal China." Tim's annoyance at this interruption soon passes, and they are back on track to review the film.

Tim extols first-time director RZA for being able to "get so much footage" into this rollicking action film. For his part, Gregg observes that leading man Russell Crowe "is always gonna be someone to watch ... and this film is no exception."

In summary, Tim gives *The Man With the Iron Fists* four bags of popcorn and one soda. As a diehard Russell Crowe partisan, Gregg ups the ante with five tubs of popcorn and two sodas. That minor disagreement aside, they are very much on the same page with their love of this movie — especially since Gregg adopts Tim's rating as his own during the recap at the end of the episode.

Next up is *Flight*, starring Kelly Reilly and directed by Robert Lee Zemeckis of *Back to the Future* fame. In what is perhaps the emotional high point of the first season, Tim proclaims that this "phenomenal" movie is his Oscar pick for best picture. Gregg singles out supporting actor John Goodman for special praise and proposes renaming him "John *Great*man."

In a more philosophical vein, Gregg and Tim reflect on how similar the performances of Denzel Washington and Russell Crowe are in quality. "The great actors are all kind of the same in a way," Gregg muses. "They have that kind of talent, and they know how to use it."

Tim's rating is five bags of popcorn and two sodas, meaning that *Flight* narrowly edges out *The Man With the Iron Fists* as this episode's top movie pick.

Gregg's initial rating is four bags, plus an extra bag awarded in honor of John Goodman. He also awards the film a candy bar, causing Tim to worry that the rating system is getting too confusing. Gregg addresses this concern during the ratings recap by giving *Flight* five bags of popcorn, plus an extra bag in honor of John Goodman, for a grand total of six.

With the reviews out of the way, it's time for Gregg's first-ever installment of his popular *Popcorn Classics* feature, which spotlights highlights from his matchless collection of VHS tapes. Gregg makes a strong critical case for *Multiplicity*, a Michael Keaton vehicle with a running time of 117 minutes. In this lost classic, Keaton plays a construction worker who gets cloned. Gregg theorizes that if Keaton could be cloned a hundred times in real life, this "national treasure" would be able to appear in more movies, which would benefit all of us.

Tim says he'd also like to see this approach taken with Keaton's co-star Andie MacDowell, but Gregg cautions him that her number of clones would need to be capped at 50 based on her comparatively lackluster career.

Did YOU notice...?

- Although Gregg says John Goodman should be renamed John Greatman, he refers to him as John Goodman later in the episode.

EPISODE 102
'Skyfall' & 'Lincoln'

Air date: December 4, 2012
Running time: 6:24 minutes

Appearing for the second time as Tim's special guest, Gregg is starting to feel at home. "Great to be back in my seat!" he says. Tim points out that the seat is actually meant for any guest who appears on the show. Gregg can't argue with that.

Skyfall provides a noncontroversial change of topic. As Tim observes, this late but worthy entry in the James Bond canon features the master spy "doing what he does best — spying and whatnot." Gregg concurs: "There has not been a James Bond movie that is not a 10 out of 10," he says, and *Skyfall* is "right up there with the best of them."

At first, Tim feels unable to give *Skyfall* more than four tubs of popcorn, on the grounds that he's not a huge fan of the Bond films and would "rather watch other movies." However, he eventually gives it his maximum rating of five bags of popcorn because it's "great." Gregg also awards it five bags, but packs them tightly, ladles on extra butter and adds 100 sodas.

Tim is eager to move on to the discussion of *Lincoln*, the latest film by his favorite director, Steven Spielberg. He informs us that this historical drama is "one of the great movies of all time" and "doesn't stop giving back." Although Gregg agrees wholeheartedly that it's "one of the best" movies about Lincoln, it's still "not as good as the James Bond film."

Tim presents *Lincoln* with his maximum rating of six popcorn bags, plus three sodas. Gregg shells out four bags and a roll of Lincoln pennies. In other words, both films are very highly recommended but "for different reasons."

This episode's Popcorn Classic is *Murphy's Romance*, a 1985 romantic comedy with James Garner and Sally Field, which "doesn't really work" because "there's no chemistry" and "the age difference is a little too vast." But since it's widely available in dollar bins, Gregg recommends we "give it a chance."

The film's title leads to a timely discussion of "Murphy's Law," which states that *anything that can go wrong, will go wrong*. Gregg illustrates this maxim with an anecdote about his first VHS copy of *Murphy's Romance*, which didn't play properly. It took him two years to find another copy. And when he finally watched it, he didn't enjoy it very much!

In the ratings recap, Tim gives *Skyfall* its original four bags of popcorn. *Lincoln* keeps its six bags, but ends up with only two sodas. (Given Tim's stated love of the movie, this is more likely due to forgetfulness than conviction.)

At this point, Gregg notices the maximum rating has changed from five bags to six. After reiterating that *Skyfall* deserves five bags, he reduces his own rating of *Lincoln* to three and pushes Tim to reduce *Lincoln* to the lawful maximum of five. When Tim responds that the actual maximum is six, Gregg gives *Skyfall* an extra bag.

Wrapping up this unusually contentious episode, Tim urges us to "make sure you go see at least one or two of these movies this weekend."

ON CINEMA ON HOLLYWOOD LEGENDS

Steven Spielberg

Steven Spielberg may be **Tim Heidecker's** favorite director, but he's hardly alone in that! Wherever movies are treasured, Spielberg's classics are sure to top the list: **Jaws**, **Jurassic Park**, **E.T.**, **A.I.**, **Lincoln**...and the list goes on!

Few other directors can match the range of styles Spielberg has mastered, from entertaining "popcorn movies" to thought-provoking films that change how you look at our life. That's just one reason Spielberg is acknowledged by most as the "King" of modern cinema. Long may he reign!

Did YOU notice...?

- *Murphy's Romance* was produced by Columbia Pictures, which was owned at the time by The Coca-Cola Company. The movie accordingly features frequent uses of the word "Coke" in its script, as well as multiple Coca-Cola signs in the background.

EPISODE 103
'Twilight, Part II' & 'Anna Karenina'

Air date: December 4, 2012
Running time: 6:11 minutes

Tim gets the ball rolling by introducing his "big special guest," film buff Gregg Turkington. Gregg delivers a personal message of thanks to all the viewers who have sent cards and letters asking him to appear on the show more often.

The first film up for review is *The Twilight Saga: Breaking Dawn — Part 2*, which Tim hails as "another one of these vampire movies." He found it "romantic," "very scary at times" and "really well made." Drawing on his expertise as a film buff, Gregg lauds the film's "misty and murky" cinematography. "You can tell that they shot a lot of this stuff in the woods," Tim declares.

Based on these positive elements, Tim and Gregg both award *The Twilight Saga: Breaking Dawn — Part 2* an appreciative four bags of popcorn. Gregg emphasizes that for a better viewing experience, it helps to have seen the original *Twilight* film so you'll understand the things that are supposed to be happening in the sequel.

Continuing with the episode's stated theme of "chick flicks," Tim introduces *Anna Karenina* as "an adaptation about Russians from a book." He affirms that the film "is about Anna Karenina" and is "very well done, well made." Gregg speculates that the movie "wouldn't have been possible to make a few years ago when we were at war with Russia and there was that whole thing."

This "groundbreaking" historical importance is one of the factors that lead Gregg to name *Anna Karenina* as his official Oscar pick: "This is the type of movie that Oscar loves to reward, and what greater reward *would* there be than to get an Oscar?" In light of these and other facts, both reviewers give *Anna Karenina* a solid five bags of popcorn.

In addition to this aesthetic unanimity, this episode is notable for the inaugural appearance of Gregg's *On Cinema On Location* featurette, which combines real-time *cinéma vérité* footage of famous film locations with tidbits of little-known movie trivia that Gregg has collected over the years.

In this debut segment, Gregg takes us to a "cemetery lake" in the greater Los Angeles area where crucial scenes from the comedy *Hot Shots!* were filmed. Comparison shots show how little this scenic location has changed since its glory days.

The episode wraps up with an uneventful recap of the ratings for *The Twilight Saga: Breaking Dawn — Part 2* and *Anna Karenina*, during which Tim and Gregg remain in lockstep critical agreement.

EPISODE 104
'Red Dawn' & 'Life of Pi'

Air date: December 4, 2012
Running time: 7:08 minutes

It's Thanksgiving, and Tim kicks off the festivities by introducing "a very cool guest" by the name of Gregg Turkington. In a deeply personal preamble, Tim opines that Thanksgiving is a great time for watching movies, because families are gathered together and household chores can be put off or ignored completely.

Today's first movie is *Red Dawn*, an up-to-date remake of the classic 1984 "what-if" thriller about Russians who attack the United States of America and get more than they bargained for. As Tim notes, the remake switches the enemy to North Korea and delivers "a lot of tension, a lot of action." Gregg tries to put in a good word for the original, but Tim favors the new and improved version: "I always prefer the remakes because it's a better movie, and you can tell."

Tim gives *Red Dawn* a generous five bags of popcorn but no soda. Gregg is somewhat less impressed, parceling out a mere four bags and a cup of plain water.

Tim notifies would-be holiday moviegoers that the film's title is *Red Dawn*, not *Red Don*, which sets the stage for his revelation that *Life of Pi* has nothing to do with dessert. "It's *p-i*, from math," he clarifies.

This leads to an unexpected bonus discussion of private investigators in cinema. Tim would love to see a movie titled *Life of P.I.*, but Gregg reminds him that this concept was already explored by Chevy Chase in *Fletch*. Tim recollects that it was also pioneered by "Bogie, from the Bogie movies."

Getting back to business, Tim describes *Life of Pi* as a "weird" movie with "a philosophical touch to it." Gregg quips that because it features so many animals, it should have been called *Animal House 2*! Kidding aside, although Gregg likes the *Fletch* movies better, he "would still recommend" *Life of Pi*. While it probably wouldn't satisfy people looking for "a sports movie," it's sure to please everyone else.

Tim thinks it will "win Oscar," but Gregg worries that it's a little too "weird" to receive this honor. Tim gives it four bags of popcorn, period. Gregg gives it five bags as well as "some sort of strange snack" like "crackers wrapped in seaweed."

Time once again for *Popcorn Classics!* On this special holiday segment, Gregg digs deep into his archives and pulls out *Twilight Zone: The Movie* (1983).

First, a word of warning: This movie should not be confused with the *Twilight* film reviewed in Episode 103. In reality, *Twilight Zone: The Movie* "is sort of the original *Twilight* saga" because it came from an old TV show, whereas the *Twilight* movie came from "a popular series of books."

Having cleared this up, Gregg alerts us that *Twilight Zone* stars Dan Ackroyd and the tape can be found on the eBay website, where you only have to pay for movies if your winning bid is accepted.

In the recap (or "remake"?) of Tim's *Red Dawn* rating, the movie gets four bags of popcorn and a soda. *Life of Pi* is upgraded to five bags of popcorn and two sodas. Gregg bestows four bags on *Red Dawn* and five on *Life of Pi*, and exhorts us to "watch them both if you can."

ON CINEMA ON HOLLYWOOD LEGENDS

Humphrey Bogart

When you add up his countless gifts to the moviegoing public, it's no shock that **Humphrey Bogart** was born on Christmas Day. He is best known for **The Maltese Falcon** and its unofficial sequel, **Casablanca**. But in reality, he appeared in 84 Golden Age movie classics, all of which are now of interest due to the involvement of film history's beloved "Bogie." He was also a founding member of the original Rat Pack, later portrayed by **Don Cheadle Jr.** and others.

Bogie took "the big sleep" in 1957, leaving the world of cinema "in a lonely place." Only 40 years later, he was named the number-one movie legend of all times by **Entertainment Weekly**, beating out still-living heartthrobs like **Leonardo DiCaprio**, **Richard Gere**, and longtime Bogie fan **Woody Allen**, whose own movie **Play it Again, Sam** was a tribute to Bogie's signature line.

EPISODE 105

'The Frozen Ground' & 'Universal Soldier: Day of Reckoning'

Air date: December 4, 2012
Running time: 5:06 minutes

In his opening monologue, Tim thanks viewers for their support of On Cinema at the Cinema.

"Just happy to help," he says.

He also welcomes his special guest, Gregg Turkington, who is glad to be back.

After a long pause, Tim tells us The Frozen Ground is "a serial killer movie."

"With a twist," Gregg clarifies.

Gregg goes on to say that "serial killers are not funny business"; rather, they are "a segment of society that should be eliminated."

That said, he endorses The Frozen Ground as a "thought-provoking" film that "keeps you on the edge of your seat."

Tim seems to be feeling poorly, but he rallies long enough to give The Frozen Ground four bags of popcorn.

Gregg does the same.

On prompting from Gregg, Tim introduces Universal Soldier: Day of Reckoning, but he is clearly preoccupied and doesn't have much to say about it.

Gregg jumps in to stress that this "action film" is "a thriller" and "probably not for the faint of heart." He gives it five bags of popcorn and a can of Red Bull.

This is Tim's cue to share his own opinion of the film, but despite gentle nudging from Gregg, he breaks down in tears.

Gregg gives both films five bags of popcorn in a game attempt to keep the show moving forward.

Unfortunately, Tim is still sobbing even as the title credits for Popcorn Classics roll.

Gregg starts to reach for this week's classic VHS tape but then decides against it.

Instead, he signs off a bit awkwardly: "Keep on watching, and enjoy the movies."

Tim is still sobbing as the cinema lights go down.

EPISODE 106
'Playing for Keeps' & 'Hyde Park on the Hudson'

Air date: December 7, 2012
Running time: 6:26 minutes

In this "webisode," Tim's guest is Gregg Turkington, who says it's "good to be back in my chair."

Playing for Keeps is a special movie for Tim because it stars his favorite actor Dennis Quaid. He describes it as a "really great coming-of-age sort of movie about soccer," which dishes out "a lot of great romance, comedy and sports." In a personal aside, he divulges that "it really took the edge off for me." It's not clear if this is a reference to his unexplained emotional breakdown in Episode 105.

Gregg didn't know anything about *Playing for Keeps* before seeing ads for it, but he "flipped" for it and is already planning to add it to his library. Tim and Gregg both give it four bags of popcorn, but Gregg tosses in a hot dog "because that's what you'd eat if you went to see a sporting event."

In a continuation of the presidential biopic theme from Episode 102, Tim introduces *Hyde Park on the Hudson*, which showcases funnyman Bill Murray as the late President Roosevelt. This movie "has a lot of great heart to it," according to Tim, and was "well done."

This sparks an interesting conversation on the status of Roosevelt's legacy today. Tim submits that Roosevelt was "one of our first presidents." Gregg is skeptical, but he concedes that Roosevelt was "one of the best" and "Bill Murray's one of our best actors." Therefore, "it makes sense that they would come together in this picture."

Though he thought Murray would "ham it up a little more" for this part, Tim feels the performance will earn the beloved comedian a long-overdue Oscar. Gregg speculates that if Oscar had a Best Actor award for comedies, "Bill Murray would have a whole mantelpiece covered with these things."

Tim says "it will be Oscar's sweet revenge" if Murray "wins Best Actor when he was not nominated for other movies."

Now it's time for a new installment of *On Cinema On Location*… or is it? Gregg reminds Tim that they have not yet rated *Hyde Park on the Hudson*. Tim doesn't appreciate this interruption. But after a brief pause to collect himself, he forges ahead with the scheduled segment.

This time around, Gregg has used his sleuthing skills to locate the iconic hotel from *Moment by Moment*, a 1978 romantic drama featuring a young John Travolta and Lily Tomlin at the very top of their game.

Gregg provides some dramatic context for his hand-shot footage, detailing the central role this vintage location played in the amorous ups and downs of the characters' lives.

We've had to wait a bit longer than usual for the *Hyde Park on the Hudson* ratings, but they do not disappoint: Tim gives it five popcorns and two sodas, and Gregg gives it five popcorns and "as many Oscars as you can give: director, film, actor, actress, screenplay. And even the score was quite good."

Did YOU notice…?

- U.S. President Franklin Delano Roosevelt stood 6'2" tall in stocking feet. But Bill Murray was only 6'1" in *Hyde Park on the Hudson*, putting him closer in height to John F. Kennedy.

EPISODE 107
'The Hobbit' & 'Les Misérables'

Air date: December 13, 2012
Running time: 5:01 minutes

Christmas is right around the corner, and Tim has some glad tidings for film buffs: "Film historian" Gregg Turkington is back in the guest chair, and he "knows a lot about movies and is a lot of fun to talk to."

As if to prove Tim's point, Gregg gives us a one-word review of *The Hobbit*: "Finally!"

Delving a bit deeper into the Tolkien mythos, Gregg argues that it's the character of Bilbo Baggins that "really makes this movie rock and roll." Heralding Baggins as "a sort of personal hero," he confesses that "to see him fully realized like this, it makes your heart skip a beat."

Tim marvels at the film's expert special effects, especially those relating to "the people that are tiny, short, small hobbits versus the tall humans."

They both recommend watching *The Hobbit* in the world-class IMAX format. As Gregg says, "It's like you're there in Middle-Earth with Bilbo and the gang."

Tim takes things one step further by predicting that *The Hobbit* will win the Oscar for Best Picture. Director Peter Jackson comes in for special commendation: "If Michael Jackson is the King of Pop, Peter Jackson is the King of Movies."

Tim awards the film six bags of popcorn and six cups of soda. Gregg sticks with the traditional maximum rating of five bags, but throws in "a big hobbit-hug."

Moving right along, *Les Misérables* gets an enthusiastic five bags of popcorn from Tim and a noncommittal "four or five or whatever" from Gregg.

This week's Popcorn Classic is *18 Again!*, a 1988 fantasy starring George Burns and Red Buttons, which Gregg calls "a delight for all ages."

ON CINEMA ON HOLLYWOOD LEGENDS

Bilbo Baggins

Long before he met 'King of Movies' **Peter Jackson** and starred in The Hobbit, **Bilbo Baggins** was the narrator of J.R. Tolkien's Lord of the Rings trilogy, which consists of **The Hobbit** and the three-volume **Lord of the Rings** cycle.

In Episode 107, Gregg calls Bilbo 'a personal hero,' and it's true that they have a lot of 'hobbits' in common!

But in reality, there is one big difference: Bilbo 'hates adventure' and would rather stay 'at home,' whereas Gregg loves adventure. For example, he likes nothing better than to sit on the couch with a tub of popcorn and lose himself once again in the adventures of the one and only **Bilbo Baggins**!

Could this be real-life evidence that 'opposites attract'?

EPISODE 108
'Zero Dark Thirty' & 'Monsters, Inc.' (3D reissue)

Air date: December 21, 2012
Running time: 8:39 minutes

Gregg is just about to start his third month as *On Cinema*'s special guest. As he nears this milestone, he's clearly feeling more confident about promoting the unique expertise he brings to the table, which includes "giving some insights and behind-the-scenes information on some of the new movies."

Tim introduces *Zero Dark Thirty* as "a documentary about the hunt for Osama bin Laden," who is "one of the original bad guys in cinema, and the world." Before getting to the movie itself, he gets younger viewers up to speed with some crucial historical context about "the death of bin Laden," who was "killed in action after we spent years hunting him for the murder of 9/11."

Gregg questions whether the film is actually a documentary in the traditional sense of the word, sparking a debate on the nature of cinematic truth. Gregg claims *Zero Dark Thirty* is more of a dramatization than a documentary, while Tim proposes that these words mean pretty much the same thing. Eventually, Gregg brings the discussion back down to earth with the observation that "it's a great film either way."

Thinking back to comedian Bill Murray's dramatic turn as President Roosevelt in Episode 106, Tim wonders if Sacha Baron Cohen might have been a better choice to play Osama bin Laden. He has "Indian-looking features," Tim observes, and he "could've gotten that sort of perfect mix of comedy and tragedy that makes for great movies."

Gregg suggests Cohen might also have given audiences a clearer idea of what bin Laden's daily life was like before his death, a sensitive issue the movie largely passed over in silence.

These quibbles aside, Tim is certain *Zero Dark Thirty* will be a strong Oscar contender. Gregg suspects it will only be nominated for minor awards like Best Costumes. Accordingly, Tim gives it three stars and Gregg gives it four, at which point they switch the ratings back to popcorn bags.

Although *Monsters Inc.* is technically a re-release, which *On Cinema* normally wouldn't cover, it is technically a new film because it was re-released in 3D, making it fair game. Tim gives very high marks to this bold reworking of a classic film, but Gregg feels it's technically a re-release and is therefore the same movie we've seen "a million times" on TV. Thus, he sees "no reason, really, to go to the theater."

"See, I think you're wrong there," Tim says. "I think it is important to go see this movie on [sic] theaters." He gives the film three popcorn bags to drive his point home. Gregg gives it five, but stipulates that you should simply watch it at home on video. When Tim challenges him on this point, he clarifies

that the 3D wasn't working properly at the theater he visited, and parking was expensive.

Tim states that viewers would have a better time seeing *Monsters Inc.* in the theater with friends and "a great crowd." Gregg counters that you can invite friends to your home, along with "the neighborhood kids." Besides, staying home is a good response to issues like the gas crisis, which is what brought us Osama bin Laden in the first place.

Tim defiantly ups his rating to five bags of popcorn and two sodas. Gregg downgrades his rating to five bags of *microwave* popcorn and a couple bottles of Coke that can be doled out to neighborhood children in little paper cups.

"We agree to disagree," says Tim. "But I think we both agree: Go see *Monsters, Inc.* in the theater this weekend."

Things are getting tense at this point, so it's just as well that *On Cinema On Location* is cued up and ready to roll. This week, Gregg dishes up a "sad, somber" episode "in memory of Bela Lugosi," the original Dracula. In what is probably the emotional high point of the season, Gregg pays his respects to Mr. Lugosi from directly outside the actual vicinity of the apartment where the great actor was found to have died.

In the ratings recap, both reviewers give three popcorn bags to *Zero Dark Thirty* and five to *Monsters Inc.*, which Gregg continues to insist should only be viewed at home.

EPISODE 109
'Jack Reacher' & 'Cirque du Soleil: Worlds Away'

Air date: December 21, 2012
Running time: 6:43 minutes

As this "webisode" gets underway, special guest Gregg Turkington has a personal message for fans of *On Cinema at the Cinema*: "Good to be here and to be part of the *On Cinema* Family, and celebrating another successful episode."

Tim salutes the viewers for their enthusiasm and mentions that many people have written to thank him and Gregg for hyping *The Hobbit* in Episode 107.

This week, Tom Cruise bounces back from the success of *Mission Impossible* with *Jack Reacher*, a crime drama about homicide detectives and snipers that Tim thinks "sounds pretty good" and Gregg calls "an instant classic." Gregg is especially pleased to see Cruise getting attention for his "fine" acting instead of appearing yet again in "the scandal sheets."

Tim reminds us that Tom Cruise is one of his three favorite actors, along with Robert De Niro and "the director Steven Spielberg." He consequently gives *Jack Reacher* six popcorn bags and six sodas. Gregg sticks with the official maximum of five bags: "For me, that's the highest you can give." No sodas for Gregg, though, because this is "a popcorn movie."

Tim introduces the Cirque du Soleil film by offering some background on this real-world circus act, which was filmed for this movie so it could be enjoyed "on demand" beyond the classical circus context. "I loved it," Tim gushes.

Gregg also loved it, not least because it gives you the chance to enjoy Cirque du Soleil anytime, anywhere, without going to Las Vegas to see one of their real-time performances.

Tim initially gives the film five stars, and then amends it to five popcorn bags, and finally settles on four bags because "it is a bit long" and "some of it is in French." Gregg initially gives it four bags, but then — since he "can't recommend it highly enough" — settles on five bags and a cotton candy.

Today's Popcorn Classic is Warren Beatty's *Dick Tracy*, but no sooner does Gregg pull it out than Tim commands him to "put the *Dick* back in your pants." Tim has brought in a "surprise" Popcorn Classic of his own: *Star Trek IV*.

It soon becomes obvious that Tim has an ulterior motive. He and Gregg have had a long-running historical dispute on the *On Cinema* podcast, stemming from Gregg's conviction that *Star Trek II* is the film in which the *Star Trek* gang travels backward in time to visit San Francisco.

Tim hopes to end this debate once and for all by reading him the box of *Star Trek IV*, which allegedly describes the *Enterprise* crew's time travel back to "1986 San Francisco and a world of punks, pizza and exact-change buses."

Gregg's counterargument has two main thrusts. First, the *Star Trek* crew's *actual* home is space, so it makes no sense to say they're going "back" to a city on Earth. Second, he claims Tim's VHS box is missing the hologram "security seal" that would verify it as an authorized copy of the film.

"You probably have a copy of *Star Wars II*," he quips. "That's not something they would sell at a real store here, because you go to jail for piracy."

Tim begs the audience to write to Gregg and let him know that *Star Trek IV*, not *Star Trek II*, is the movie where everyone goes to San Francisco.

For his part, Gregg contends that Captain Kirk et al. traveled to San Francisco in *Star Trek II: The Wrath of Khan*. In *Star Trek IV*, "they go home into space, where they came from."

Tim remains unconvinced. And unfortunately, the episode ends before the debate can be settled.

ON CINEMA ON HOLLYWOOD LEGENDS

Tom Cruise

From his debut in **Risky Business**, to his all-time great performance in **Jack Reacher**, Tom Cruise has always been nothing if not a man for all seasons.

Today, Tom and wife **Nicole Kidman** are certified Hollywood royalty, with many official five-baggers under their belts both separately and in tandem. And that's no accident! They are both hard workers in addition to their undeniable talents in every type of role, on-screen and off. **Tom Cruise** has many, many fans, but few are more dedicated than **Tim Heidecker**, who named his second-born son after this first-class leading man!

EPISODE 110
'Parental Guidance' & 'Django Unchained'

Air date: January 8, 2013
Running time: 8:46 minutes

It's the last episode of the season and the first of the new year, and Tim and Gregg have dressed up in suits and ties for the occasion. In his opening monologue, Tim speaks directly to the audience's heart, stating that it has been an honor to educate them on movies and he has had "a lot of fun" putting the show together. He is grateful to the cast, the crew and his frequent guest, Gregg Turkington.

Gregg also has a personal announcement to share: He will soon be "teaching film history classes at some of the local community centers in the area."

With these formalities out of the way, Tim hops on board the new Billy Crystal vehicle, *Parental Guidance*. He appreciates that this holiday-friendly film was able to "combine family values with comedy in a way I haven't seen since *Monsters, Inc*." [Episode 108] In other words, this is "Billy Crystal at his best."

Gregg praises the strong rapport between Crystal and his co-star Bette Midler, which adds up to "a recipe for family fun."

If there's any flaw with this movie, it's the title. Tim reckons it should have been called *Three Amigos* owing to the irrepressible comedic chemistry between Midler, Crystal and Marisa Tomei. Gregg thinks it would've been "funny" if the movie had been rated R despite being called *Parental Guidance*. That's a bridge too far for Tim: "Not my kind of humor."

Tim gives the movie a judicious six bags of popcorn and two "glasses" of soda. Gregg tries to deliver his own rating, but Tim cuts him off so they can proceed to *Django Unchained*.

Both reviewers rate this Western film as "very violent" — so much so that Tim feels it was a mistake to release it for Christmas. Nevertheless, he calls it "one of the best movies I've seen all year" and awards it four bags of popcorn. Gregg gives it five bags of popcorn and a toy pistol filled with soda.

To round things out, Gregg and Tim go on to recap the best and worst movies of the year. Not surprisingly, Gregg's favorite film was *The Hobbit*. [Episode 107] "It was my favorite film of the year even before I'd seen a frame of it," he admits.

As much as Tim also loved *The Hobbit*, he's leaning toward a "dark horse": Tom Cruise's *Jack Reacher*. [Episode 109] The "great review" he gave it a week ago notwithstanding, a subsequent viewing has convinced him that it's both "Tom Cruise's best movie" and "the best movie of the year."

The worst movie, according to Tim, was the James Bond-themed *Skyfall*. Although he "loved" some of the action scenes, there were "too many moments where I was confused about what was going on." Because Tim believes movies should always be "fun" and never "confusing," he has no choice but to award *Skyfall* zero bags of popcorn.

Gregg defends *Skyfall*, which he views as the best of the Bond movies: "If you don't like this movie, you don't like James Bond."

Tim berates Gregg for challenging his pick for worst film instead of making his own selection. After some deliberation, Gregg chooses *Jack Reacher*, primarily on the grounds that it's "not a good film." When Tim remarks that Gregg gave it a rave review just last week, Gregg explains that he has seen it again since then and realized that "it's amateurish, it's junk."

As the debate escalates, a flustered Tim surmises that Gregg is trying to get back at him for his negative comments about *Skyfall* and proposes that they "disagree to disagree."

The season finale of *On Cinema On Location* provides a special treat for fans of 1999's *Blast from the Past* — a classic romantic comedy limelighting the talents of Alicia Silverstone, Brendan Fraser and Sissy Spacek. Through a combination of dogged research and gut instinct, Gregg has tracked down the house in Southern California where Ms. Silverstone's iconic character "Eve" once lived.

In a perfect world, this human-interest feature would end the episode and the season on an up note. Sadly, there seems to be some lingering resentment between Tim and Gregg due to their conflicting picks for worst movie.

On Cinema On Line

8:07 AM - 10 Jan 2013
I awake, while @greggturkington sleeps peacefully, unknown to him #TheHobbit snub. Today will be a hard day for him.

9:43 AM - 10 Jan 2013
I HAVE NEVER EVEN HEARD OF AMOUR. YET IT STOLE NOMINATIONS MEANT FOR THE HOBBIT. ##PAYOLA #SCANDAL #RIGGEDAWARDS #CORRUPTION #BILBOLIVES

9:51 AM - 10 Jan 2013
WHAT IF THEY HELD AN OSCAR CEREMONY AND NO BODY WATCHED? #HOBBITHEADS

10:04 AM - 10 Jan 2013
DOES ANYONE KNOW IF THERE IS A WRITE-IN OPTION ON THE OSCAR BALLOT? HOBBIT COULD STILL WIN

ON CINEMA ON CINEMA
ON CINEMA ON CINEMA
ON CINEMA ON CINEMA
ON CINEMA ON CINEMA
ON CINEMA ON CINEMA
ON CINEMA ON CINEMA
ON CINEMA ON CINEMA
ON CINEMA ON CINEMA
ON CINEMA ON CINEMA
ON CINEMA ON CINEMA

SEASON 2

EPISODE 201
'Side Effects' & 'Identity Thief'

Air date: February 7, 2013
Running time: 7:23 minutes

Tim starts the second season off with a bang by introducing his guest, Gregg Turkington, as "one of the experts on film."

Tim thanks his audience for their staunch support of the first 10 episodes, and Gregg gives a special shout-out to all the viewers who have been calling for Tim to "increase my appearances on the show." Tim, however, is confident that Gregg is already "well represented."

And with that, we're off to the movies! *Side Effects* is "a prescription medication story about a woman who abuses drugs." Tim went to see it because it starred Channing Tatum, and he was not disappointed: "I loved it."

Gregg calls it "frightening" and "a modern-day *One Flew Over the Cuckoo's Nest*." Tim seconds this view and goes on to make a difficult personal revelation: The movie had a lot of "resonance" for him, he says, because he was recently "diagnosed with having several blood clots in my brain."

Now, he is facing an epochal decision: Should he have an operation for blood clots in his head? Gregg says yes: "You gotta get the operation!" But Tim's doctor says there are other options, including "waiting it out." Gregg counsels Tim to "get another doctor, because that's dangerous."

Obviously uncomfortable discussing these issues on the web, Tim reiterates that his medical woes have made him better able to appreciate *Side Effects*, particularly as it relates to "the whole idea of the medical industry and drugs and Obamacare." Armed with this new insight, he gives the film six bags of popcorn and two sodas, not just because it is "a classic" but also because it is "one of the great American movies of all time."

Gregg shares Tim's high opinion of this dramatic tale: "I don't have a tumor, but I loved the movie." He can't give it six bags being as "the scale only goes up to five." But he throws in a get-well card for Tim and encourages him again "to get this tumor removed." Tim responds that his illness is "none of your business."

After this exchange, Tim is clearly eager to move on to a lighter topic, namely *Identity Thief*, a comedy about identity theft directed by Jon Favreau.

Tim applauds the movie for the universality of its themes: "We've all been down this road before; we've gotten our identities stolen." Better yet, "it's a very funny movie" thanks to the participation of Melissa McCarthy, who is "one of the original funny ladies of cinema right now." He remarks that Ms. McCarthy "almost reminds me of a modern-day Lucille Ball, in that sort of sense of being a comedienne."

Gregg is in full agreement. Having "laughed all the way through" this comedy, he gives it five bags of popcorn and "some of those little chattering teeth." Tim allows the movie only four bags due to its inclusion of "moments that were boring."

The first Popcorn Classic of the season is Steve Martin's *A Simple Twist of Fate*. Gregg acclaims it as "a good movie" and very much "worth seeing" for anyone who wants "to see what it's like for Steve Martin when he's not excelling in a role."

"It'll definitely fill the couple hours that it takes to watch the movie," Tim concurs. In conclusion, Gregg recommends sitting though the film "if you've got nothing better to do."

During the ratings recap, Gregg again expresses his concern about Tim's "tumor." Tim argues that he does not actually have a tumor. On the contrary, he has "several blood clots that doesn't [sic] necessarily have to be operated on."

Before signing off, Tim reminds us that *Identity Thief* is his pick for the "must-see movie of the week."

Did YOU notice...?

- After the end credits, Gregg can be heard telling Tim that he needs "a better doctor" because "it sounds like you went to a vet."

EPISODE 202
'A Good Day to Die Hard' & 'Escape from Planet Earth'

Air date: February 14, 2013
Running time: 7:25 minutes

This episode begins on a somewhat confusing note, as Tim's guest, Gregg Turkington, welcomes viewers to "our program" and Tim responds by saying, "Welcome to *my* program."

More generally, this episode is unique in that it focuses exclusively on what Tim and Gregg call "popcorn movies." This crowd-pleasing genre is a personal favorite of Gregg's, and Tim has to calm his excitable guest down so he can introduce the films in his usual way.

In order to "spice things up" for this all-popcorn movie episode, Tim has brought two cups of actual popcorn to the set. Unfortunately, Gregg finds the snack "a little stale."

Today's first popcorn movie is *A Good Day to Die Hard*, the latest installment in a beloved franchise that needs no introduction. Tim's synopsis foregrounds the all-important involvement of Bruce Willis as well as the presence of "two women."

The episode then takes a nostalgic turn as Tim recalls his first encounter with the original *Die Hard* film: "Bruce Willis was on shows called *Moonlighting*. But here he is! And it was a big success when it came out."

"And it's still good," Gregg observes. Although some people worry Willis is getting too old for the *Die Hard* role, Gregg doesn't see things that way: "Let's keep him in the throne. This is a good series."

"And that's why I hate [James] Bond!" Tim exclaims. "Because Bond kept changing who Bond was." By contrast, "Bruce Willis has always been 'Die Hard' and always will be."

Needless to say, this is not a challenge a lifelong Bond-head like Gregg can take lying down. The crucial difference, as he sees it, is that "with Bond, they're always improving on it." This approach ensures that "each Bond is better than the previous Bond." Also, the Bond films have been "going on for 60 years," and "you can't have someone who's 90 years old who's James Bond."

Tim is skeptical: "It doesn't make sense to me how you can have the same character with different looks with the same name." This train of thought is derailed when Tim chokes on a popcorn kernel and has a coughing fit.

Once he recovers, Tim gives *A Good Day to Die Hard* an authoritative five bags of popcorn as well as "five bags of my own private collection" of popcorn, resulting in an unprecedented rating of 10 bags.

Gregg limits himself to the traditional maximum rating of five bags but also dispenses "a goblet of the finest champagne" so he can "toast Bruce Willis and the whole *Die Hard* gang."

The episode's second and final popcorn movie is *Escape from Planet Earth*, an animated cartoon voiced by Brendan Fraser. In what may well be the emotional high point of the season, Tim describes how the film "chilled and thrilled" him.

Tim's reaction is no coincidence, because from his perspective, *Escape from Planet Earth* is a triple threat: "Sci-fi is my favorite kind of movie, but also comedy and animated films are my favorite kind of movies." Having taken all these factors into account, Tim concludes that *Escape from Planet Earth* is "one of my films of the year."

Gregg also loved the film, with one reservation: The director could have made better use of Fraser's talents by filming him instead of using animation. "People like Brendan Fraser," he claims. "And it's kind of weird to be looking at a cartoon when you could be looking at the real thing."

Tim upholds the director's artistic decision to animate Fraser's role, which he says was "not a mistake." But Gregg still feels it was "the wrong choice" because Fraser "is not Mel Blanc; he's not a fat slob you don't want to look at."

For Tim, this is the last straw. He knocks the popcorn tub out of Gregg's hand: "I'm not letting you say that kind of crap on my show!" He again defends Fraser's animated character on the grounds that the movie wouldn't have worked otherwise. When Gregg offers no response to this counterargument, Tim gets annoyed and leaves the set early.

EPISODE 203
'Snitch' & 'Dark Skies'

Air date: February 21, 2013
Running time: 11:34 minutes

This week, Tim welcomes guest Gregg Turkington back to the set of *On Cinema at the Cinema*. The cordial mood is short lived, though, as Gregg once again interferes with Tim's attempt to read his opening remarks. "Just let me get through my card," Tim says. "You've seen these shows before. You've seen how this works."

Once Gregg has been subdued, Tim introduces *Snitch*, which gathers Dwayne "The Rock" Johnson and Susan Sarandon together to tell a modern-day story about drug dealers. Tim "liked it a lot" and categorizes it as "a very, very great film."

Gregg appreciates the film's "interesting" depiction of the "drug underworld." But he can't in good conscience endorse it over *The Hobbit*, [Episode 107] which is probably still playing in a few second-run theaters.

Tim notices a potential flaw in this advice: "Some of these cheaper theaters are not gonna have the 3D abilities to show *The Hobbit*." Gregg responds that this would still be preferable to watching the film "on your computer at home." Therefore, he urges viewers to take advantage of their "last chance" to see *The Hobbit* "as it was meant to be seen."

Returning to the topic of *Snitch*, Tim gives it a respectable four bags of popcorn, plus two bottles of soda. Gregg also gives it four bags, plus a bonus bag "for being so realistic and gritty."

This brings us to *Dark Skies*, an outer-space horror film that Tim could not finish watching due to "an emergency." He awards it an interim three bags of popcorn, with the stipulation that he will likely raise the rating to four or maybe even five bags after he sees the whole thing.

Gregg, who did watch the entire film, has no qualms about awarding it five bags. He also hints that it would be more helpful for the audience if Tim gave the movie "five half-full bags" to indicate that his review is a work in progress.

Next, Tim ushers in Gregg's brand-new special feature, entitled *On Cinema Presents Popcorn Classics BTC*. Gregg explains that "BTC" stands for "Behind the Curtain." In layman's terms, this means that in each segment, Gregg will interview one of the famous faces known to us from the world of cinema.

In this debut segment, Gregg talks to Joe Estevez, whose lengthy list of world-class credits includes *Apocalypse Now*, *Dr. Spine*, *Necronaut*, Martin Sheen and many more.

Gregg breaks the ice by asking Joe a classic "film buff" question: "What actors should win the Academy Award?" After clarifying that Gregg is speaking generally rather than asking for a prediction, Joe gives the nod to the immortal Humphrey Bogart, star of the Bogie films [Episode 104] and so many others.

Asked to name his "personal top 10" of his own films, Joe cites *South of Reno* (1988) and several others. As the interview wends its way onward, we learn that movie studios will sometimes send valuable sealed tapes and DVDs of completed films to the actors who starred in them, and that Joe doesn't care for butter on his popcorn but loves it with plenty of salt.

Back on the set, Tim rates the segment as "interesting" and hails Joe Estevez in particular as a "nice guy." He's also curious whether Gregg can give us a peek "behind the curtain" of the making of his latest featurette: Did he uncover any secrets or surprising facts about Mr. Estevez?

After giving the question some thought, Gregg reveals that he and Joe had an "off-camera" conversation about the actor's favorite soup and salad bars, which include a regional chain called The Soup Plantation.

ON CINEMA ON HOLLYWOOD LEGENDS

Joe Estevez

Look up the dictionary definition of 'versatile' and you may well find a photo of **Joe Estevez**. With hundreds of films to his credit, Joe has played perhaps every possible cinematic role. But few have earned more acclaim than his dual role as **President Davidson** and **President Davidson Jr.** in the **Decker** franchise — a feat few actors would attempt, let alone succeed! As a child, Joe met **President Dwight D. Eisenhower** at the 1959 White House Easter Egg Roll, which undoubtedly helped him to bring his own presidential portrayals to fruition.

As a longtime Hollywood insider, Joe is also a valued **On Cinema** commenter on movies.

EPISODE 204
'21 and Over' & 'Jack the Giant Slayer'

Air date: February 28, 2013
Running time: 8:11 minutes

Perhaps to head off any possible misconceptions, Tim introduces himself as "the host of my own show, which is *this* show." He then introduces his guest, "film expert" Gregg Turkington.

Before getting to this week's movies, Tim addresses a very sensitive personal issue. First, he thanks his audience for the messages of concern and support he received after Episode 201, during which we learned he has "several blood clots" in his brain.

To Gregg's visible dismay, Tim then announces he has decided *not* to undergo surgery. Two factors influenced this decision: His doctor's "suggestion," and the availability of "homeopathic medicine" and other supplements.

He ends with a strong emotional plea to his viewers: "Let's not worry so much about my health, and let's worry about movies — whether or not movies are good."

This segues into a discussion of *21 and Over*, a comedy about medical students who have to take a test the next day. In Tim's opinion, this movie includes "funny drinking jokes" and "people getting messed up," interspersed with a whole host of "funny situations."

Gregg acknowledges that *21 and Over* is "funny," but he worries it may encourage alcohol abuse. On the other hand: "If you watch old *Flintstones* cartoons, they do things that they would never do in real life." That being the case, he "strongly, strongly" recommends the film.

For Tim, falling "completely in love with the movie" was partly a matter of necessity: "I am going through a period where I need a good laugh, and laughter is the best medicine."

Gregg proposes that "surgery, too, would be good medicine," but Tim rejects this remark as "not appropriate." He goes on to award *21 and Over* five bags of popcorn.

Gregg is certain that if the movie had been titled *National Lampoon's 21 and Over*, "it would've been a five-bagger." He gives it five bags anyway, "because I think that the world does need a laugh." He also awards it "a shot of Jagermeister"; this mischievous comment gets big laughs from Tim.

Speaking directly to Hollywood, Tim stresses the need for a sequel to *21 and Over*, which would ideally focus on the main character's later life as a doctor. Gregg's suggested title is *Doctor 21*.

The remaining film is *Jack the Giant Slayer*. This live-action fairy-tale fable was directed by the improbably named Bryan Singer, who Tim jokes should be named Bryan *Director*.

All kidding aside, Tim "loved" this film "so much" that he "wished it could've gone on and on and on." Indeed, he cites it as evidence that we live in a cinematic Golden Age comparable to the one our grandparents enjoyed back when *Gone With the Wind* was in all the theaters. Little wonder, then, that he gives *Jack the Giant Slayer* six bags of popcorn and adds "make them *giant*-sized!"

Gregg gives it five bags, and then five more, for a total of 10. He also reflects on how lucky he is to have a job where he not only gets to watch great movies but also gets to provide the public service of informing others about how great they are. Tim is impressed by this thoughtful view of the critic's role in society: "I just didn't think about it in that way until now."

This episode's Popcorn Classic ties in well with *Jack the Giant Slayer* in that it's called *My Giant*. In this comedy, Billy Crystal plays a man who meets a totally different man who is "double his size."

Tim is positive the film's "giant" was created with CGI, much like *Lord of the Rings*. He cannot accept Gregg's claim that this illusion was achieved by putting "the world's shortest actor, Billy Crystal," next to "the world's tallest actor."

Gregg casts doubt on Tim's theory by asserting that CGI wasn't pioneered until *The Phantom Menace* (1999). Unfazed, Tim repeats that *My Giant* derives its visual power from "special effects": The "giant" stands closer to the camera than Billy Crystal does, which makes him appear taller. Then, the special effects team fixes their mismatched shadows in post-production.

Gregg's counterargument is drowned out by the *On Cinema* theme music.

EPISODE 205
'Oz the Great and Powerful' & 'Dead Man Down'

Air date: March 7, 2013
Running time: 6:37 minutes

Tim gets this show on the road by introducing himself, *On Cinema at the Cinema*, his guest, Gregg Turkington, and finally Sam Raimi's *Oz the Great and Powerful*.

Gregg is very excited about the release of this prequel to *The Wizard of Oz* "because those of us who are Oz freaks have been waiting since 1939." On a more somber note, he laments the "burden" this long delay has placed on Oz fans — especially those who "passed on" while waiting for "the next chapter" in the Oz saga to come out.

Although Gregg loves the movie, he has one major problem with it: "I miss the Munchkins!" He is well aware that most of the Munchkins fell ill and died in the decades after 1939. But nevertheless, "one of the original Munchkins is still alive and he's going around the country signing autographs." As Gregg sees it, "to not include him in this movie after he's been an ambassador for Oz all these years is kind of a slap in the face."

He also regrets the fact that Judy "Dorothy" Garland's dog Toto doesn't appear anywhere in this film, despite playing an outsize role in the 1939 sequel.

Tim grants the film a paltry four bags of popcorn due to the absence of Munchkins. Gregg gives it zero bags, but with a twist: He will fill Toto's basket from the original classic film with popcorn and eat from that. Since this basket is roughly equal in volume to five popcorn tubs, this is technically an official five-bagger!

Dead Man Down is a showcase for Tim's "favorite current young actor" Colin Farrell. Tim and Gregg agree that Farrell is "always in classics," perhaps because "he doesn't know how to make a bad movie." Farrell's latest classic is no exception: Tim gives it five bags of popcorn and three sodas, and he also names Farrell as his Oscar pick for Best Actor.

Gregg gives it five bags and throws in a can of "mace spray" to ward off "the shady characters" who populate this dark film.

At this point, Tim announces a new feature called *60-Second Soapbox*, which will focus on "serious" issues "outside of film and cinema."

In this kickoff segment, he addresses a vexing question: "What is the role of government in our lives?"

Tim's initial plea for lower taxes and fewer regulations uses up only 45 seconds, but he is able to round out the segment with a last-minute proposition that we "make a promise to our seniors."

During the end credits, Gregg argues that Tim should not be adding political commentary to *On Cinema*, which had previously been a bone of contention on the *On Cinema* podcast series. Tim takes an opposing view, arguing that he "feels good" about the segment.

EPISODE 206
'Carrie' & 'The Incredible Burt Wonderstone'

Air date: March 14, 2013
Running time: 9:26 minutes

After Tim welcomes his guest, Gregg Turkington, the two critics reminisce about the unusually high quality of the movies on offer in the first few months of 2013.

For the sake of balance, Tim also lauds the films released in 2012 as "some of the best movies I've seen in a long time." Gregg singles out *The Hobbit* [Episode 107] as an especially impressive release. Tim names *Jack Reacher* [Episode 109] as another cinematic high water mark, but Gregg has to admit he was "not as big of a fan" of that film.

Switching gears, Tim introduces *Carrie*, a modern-day remake of *Carrie* (1976). As always, Tim favors remakes on principle, because they give directors "the chance to perfect" a film over time. The first *Carrie* was great, he says, but the second *Carrie* is even better! "Maybe the third time will be the charm," Gregg speculates.

Tim asks for Gregg's review, but Gregg would prefer not to talk about the film for fear he'll give away its surprise ending. You need to "watch it yourself," he says.

Tim feels it should be possible for Gregg to offer a general opinion of the film without spoiling the ending. Gregg is willing to let on that *Carrie* is a "horror movie" and is "frightening," but he insists viewers really do need to watch the ending for themselves: "I don't want to give it away."

Tim tries to bring up some plot elements this film shares both with the 1976 film and with the best-selling Stephen King novel from 1974, but Gregg promptly shuts this discussion down to avoid ruining the film's "truly memorable ending."

Tim gives *Carrie* four bags of popcorn. Gregg refuses to issue a rating: "I'll let you wait and see what I give it," he says. When pressed to rate the film immediately, Gregg declines on the grounds that the rating could provide "a little bit of a clue" as to how the film ends.

Under continued questioning, he avows that he "loved the movie." All the same, he will not tell the audience how many popcorn bags it deserves, as he doesn't want to "spoil it for them with spoilers."

Eventually, he compromises by giving it five bags but placing them out of sight behind a curtain. He also throws in a handful of "hot cinnamon candies" in recognition of the movie's "hell theme."

The Incredible Burt Wonderstone is a comedy about dueling magicians, starring Tim's favorite comedic actor, Jim Carrey. Tim found it "very funny" and "sweet," with "a good heart to it." In short, "it's definitely one of my favorite movies of the year, definitely my favorite Jim Carrey movie."

Tim gives the film five bags of popcorn. Not to be outdone, Gregg awards it five bags of popcorn, each of which contains an Oscar for Jim Carrey in commemoration of his "all-time best performance."

Tim then recounts how he was inspired by *The Incredible Burt Wonderstone* to buy "a little beginner's magic kit" from Toys R Us. Although he was dismayed to find that the kit didn't include "some of the tricks that were in this movie," he is still grateful that "because of movies like this, you get exposed to different kinds of culture."

Gregg insinuates that Tim's magic act might be a "fun segment" to replace the more political *60-Second Soapbox* feature, but Tim begs off because he's "not good enough yet."

This week, Gregg's Popcorn Classic is *The Mod Squad*, a mystery drama about juvenile delinquents who fight crime. He reports that this "flashy" and "fun" movie "was a TV show back in the day" but has since been "hipped up."

Before he can complete this thought, Tim pushes Gregg's film aside to promote his own VHS copy of *Dennis Miller Live*. His reasoning is that "sometimes we get hyper-focused on these movies," even though videos can bring many other types of entertainment into our homes.

Being as the show is called *On Cinema*, Gregg stands by his selection of *The Mod Squad* as a Popcorn Classic. But Tim dismisses the film as a "remake," lamenting that "all we do is remakes lately!"

Tim contends that Miller "makes you feel smarter just by listening to him" due to his frequent use of "references" that are very "specific." He also cites Miller's high ratings from *The Wall Street Journal*.

Gregg takes a contrary position, dismissing Miller as a stale purveyor of "15-year-old jokes" about "Bob Dole." He also continues to maintain that Miller's stand-up tape is "not a movie."

The episode ends in an impasse, with Gregg asserting that *Popcorn Classics* is his segment and Tim countering that *On Cinema* is his show.

EPISODE 207
'The Croods'

Air date: March 21, 2013
Running time: 8:27 minutes

Tim gets things underway by thanking his audience for letting him host *On Cinema*. He also gives the website a shout-out for hosting it. Finally, he introduces his guest, Gregg Turkington, who congratulates him on producing "a great season" so far.

This week, only one movie is up for review: *The Croods*, a prehistoric CGI film drawing on the combined voice-acting skills of Nicholas Cage and others. Tim says that although *The Croods* "starts from a place of sadness" because their island was destroyed, it's "a lot of fun," "beautifully drawn" and "one of my favorite movies of the year."

The Croods made Gregg feel "warm all over" and was "a lot of fun." In something of a departure, he even brought "a couple of family members" to see *The Croods*. Despite not being "professional critics," they too "liked this movie."

Tim sees Gregg's family anecdote as strong evidence of the film's mass appeal. It's a movie "by the people, for the people," and you don't have to be a "hooty-tooty" film buff to appreciate it. He also gives high marks to Nicholas Cage's "distinctive voice." Gregg confirms that "we're lucky to have him."

Digging a little deeper into the facts behind the film, Tim confides that he has always wondered what it was truly like "back in the caveman days": "Not just what we see from *Flintstones*, but actually what was it like?"

From Tim's perspective, *The Croods* "bridges the gap": It's "not like a documentary, but it's not as silly and ridiculous as *The Flintstones*." With all this in mind, Tim gives it a celebratory five bags of popcorn.

Gregg gives it five bags as well, only the bags are hollowed-out stones "like they would've done on *The Flintstones*."

Next, Tim announces that "this is a very special episode" because it marks the debut of a new featurette called *Stump the Buff*. The object of this segment is to stump "esteemed film expert" Gregg Turkington (the "Buff" of the title) with a difficult piece of movie lore. But it's not all fun and games, because ThingX.com will donate $500 to the American Cancer Society for "every question that Gregg gets right"!

Unfortunately, Gregg misses all of these tough questions due to their tricky wording. Perhaps most surprisingly, he misidentifies Giuseppe Rotunno — the cinematographer for Robert Altman's 1980 *Popeye* — as Andrew Dunn, even though Dunn wouldn't work with Altman until 2001's *Gosford Park*. Gregg also misspells Richard Dreyfuss's name, among other technical errors.

As a result, no money goes to the cancer charity. This disappoints Tim because he thought that as a film buff, Gregg would've been able to get all the answers right.

FIRST ANNUAL OSCARS SPECIAL
Live Broadcast from Hollywood's Biggest Night

Air date: March 24, 2013
Running time: 1:49:54

Live from Hollywood, "the Capital of Oscar," a new gold rush is on as Tim and Gregg prospect for Oscar gold.

But it's also a somber occasion, as Tim recently cut the tip of his finger off while fishing. Gregg recommends the supermarket as a safer source for fish, but Tim says he fishes mainly to relax. "Doesn't look very relaxing," Gregg observes.

Tim and Gregg raise a toast to Oscar!

What Does Oscar Have in Store?
Gregg is sure this year's Oscars will be "great," because 2012 was "a great year for movies." Though *The Hobbit* wasn't nominated, Gregg predicts it will win eight awards through write-in votes, turning Oscar on his head in a night of unforgettable television.

Tim predicts that host "Seth MacFarlane's gonna come out and say, 'I believe I'm not the man for this job.'" He will then ask if anyone is willing to take over, and Billy Crystal will seize the helm just as the Academy planned all along.

A James Bond tribute is on tonight's Oscar menu, and Tim's hoping this means the long-running franchise will finally call it quits. Since *Skyfall* was "the most successful Bond movie to date," Gregg thinks it's far more likely the Bond quota will be upped to two films per year.

A Glimpse Behind the Oscar Curtain
Gregg's first filmed segment takes us to Hollywood's Dolby Theatre, giving us a rare glimpse through the glass doors and into the theater itself — empty now, but soon to be filled with expectant crowds.

Stump the Buff!
Next up, it's a clash of the Oscar titans as Tim and Gregg play *Stump the Buff*. If Gregg can answer just three questions correctly, he will win a backup VHS copy of Pia Zadora's *The Lonely Lady*.

Sadly, he flubs the first question on how many Oscars *Lord of the Rings* received, because it's not clear whether Tim was asking about Oscar categories or the total numerical number of statues handed out. He misses the other questions on similar technicalities.

80 Years of Oscar Glory
To prove "you don't have to be a millionaire to build a great Oscar collection," Gregg has brought some classic VHS Oscar winners in a milk crate.

With most of these titles selling for pennies on the dollar, he explains, there's no excuse not to have the full 80 years of Oscar glory at your disposal!

Meanwhile, Tim needs some ice for his "throbbing" finger because the discomfort is making him "sick." For now, he's gulping down champagne to dull the pain.

Gandalf's Defeat
We're off to the races, as the Oscars get underway with the *On Cinema* team in hot pursuit!

Tim's first prediction proves to be a flop, as Seth MacFarlane refuses to yield the stage to Billy Crystal. But all is forgiven, because MacFarlane did "a good job" that included William Shatner in an "awesome" dance sequence.

Gregg would like to see the dance segments cut in favor of more film clips, for the benefit of people who can't necessarily afford a movie ticket.

In a major upset, Christoph Waltz takes Best Supporting Actor, edging out unnominated write-in candidate Sir Ian McKellen of *The Hobbit* fame.

Tim has gotten some ice, which is helping his finger. He's also taking Percocet and washing it down with plenty of champagne.

I, Candy
Gregg brings us an interview with one-time Oscar nominee Candy Clark, who provided the "eye candy" in George Lucas' one-and-only *American Graffiti*. Later in her career, she visited the same dentist as Gregg, leading to her surprise guest appearance here tonight.

Candy Clark, near-miss pick of 1973's Oscar litter.

John Aprea leaves his mark on Gregg's VHS collection.

Although she did not walk away with an Oscar, Ms. Clark recalls the enjoyment she had in Hollywood's Golden Age with the likes of Jeff Bridges.

To Gregg's dismay, she is unconvinced *The Hobbit* will win through a write-in campaign. She thinks *Argo* or *Lincoln* is more likely to have its eyes on the prize.

Tim is disappointed by this segment, which didn't provide much insight into Ms. Clark's close encounter with Oscar.

Coming In on a Wing and Aprea
The Best Actress award is another blow for Gregg, as Cate "Galadriel" Blanchett's write-in bid for *The Hobbit* was not enough to drag her to the finish line ahead of *Silver Linings Playbook*'s Jennifer Lawrence.

But all is forgiven as a certified Oscar legend joins the set: *The Godfather II*'s very own John Aprea! Mr. Aprea wasn't nominated for any of the film's 12 Oscars, but he's more than happy to sign Gregg's slipcased double-VHS edition of the film.

And the Oscar for Best Oscar Goes to…
Tim is annoyed that Oscar's James Bond tribute did not actually mark an end to the venerable spy franchise. With the "old" Bond squatting on valuable cinematic real estate, will there be enough room for up-and-comers like *Jack Reacher*?

Tim also charges that Seth MacFarlane "sucks" and "ruined the whole night." The host should have been Billy Crystal, who gets "the Oscar for Best Oscar."

As Gregg argues that the Oscars should be presented in a movie theater — to show respect for the medium that birthed them — Tim is pouring champagne into the can of Coke his producer made him drink to sober up.

Tim has gotten his fill of Oscar's musical numbers, which are "stupid." Although Gregg feels it's important to honor Oscar-caliber songcraft, he agrees with Tim that enough is enough.

"I can't believe I fucking lost my finger," Tim says. "You wanna see it?" He unwinds the bandage. "You can see the bone." He begins weeping and rushes to the bathroom.

Kirk Douglas: A Man for All Seasons
Gregg takes advantage of Tim's absence to remind us that Kirk Douglas is overdue for a Lifetime Achievement Award.

As Tim stumbles back onto the set, the TV shows Peter Jackson holding an Oscar, leading Gregg to announce incorrectly that Jackson has won Best Director for *The Hobbit* in a surprise upset.

Tim creates a new drink called the Oscar Special, which entails spilling champagne into a cup of popcorn. Soon after, he falls unconscious and starts snoring. While Tim is indisposed, Gregg gives us some inside info — *inside the Oscar envelope*, that is, as he elucidates the all-important role of Price Waterhouse Cooper in keeping Oscar's plans secret until the last possible second.

A Perfect 10
Tim is awake and apologetic: "The champagne got the best of me tonight." He congratulates Anne Hathaway for a well-deserved Best Supporting Actress win. He also congratulates Seth MacFarlane for hosting the Oscars.

Tim takes a viewer's question from Twitter: "How drunk are you on a scale of 1 to 10?"

"10," Tim estimates. This reminds Gregg that the 1979 Bo Derek/Dudley Moore vehicle *10* is a rare instance of a film named after a number.

VHSOS
After a commercial break, Tim comes back alone. Having vomited, he's feeling a little better, but he remains too "depressed" to watch the Oscars.

"I wanted this to go well for you for to watch this," he tells his viewers. "And I apologize." He falls sobbing to the floor and throws up into Gregg's milk crate full of VHS tapes.

A Signature Accomplishment
Gregg has returned, and Tim apologizes again for "not feeling well." He also apologizes to Gregg for vomiting all over his Oscar tapes. Happily, most of the

Oscar's festivities prove to be too much for Tim.

tapes were backups, because Gregg keeps sealed originals of all Oscar titles. But he does expect Tim to replace them!

Tim pulls out Gregg's freshly autographed copy of *The Godfather II* and wipes the vomit from the cover. "That one is fine," he says.

Tim offers Gregg the sandwiches.

Unfortunately, while trying to clean it, he erases John Aprea's signature.

"I'm gonna go now," Gregg says.

An Offer Gregg Can't Refuse
Tim calls Gregg's cell phone and asks him to return for the post-Oscar wrap-up. Gregg complains that Tim is turning the show into "an advertisement for alcoholism." He also wants Tim's assurance that his Oscar collection will be replaced: "It doesn't make me feel very good to see *Forrest Gump* covered in your champagne and Frito-Lay vomit."

To win Gregg over, Tim offers to make him On *Cinema*'s official co-host. Gregg challenges him to repeat this offer so *On Cinema* viewers can record it for posterity.

"Come in and I'll tell you to your face," Tim says.

The Year of the Co-Host
Gregg is very excited and already has plans for taking the show in "new directions." But Tim cautions him that there's a distinction to be made between co-hosting the Oscars special and co-hosting *On Cinema* itself. That's a red flag for Gregg, who urges viewers to send in their recordings of Tim's actual offer.

Tim tries to change the topic to the Oscars, but Gregg isn't having it. He wants a year to prove himself as co-host; if it doesn't pan out, Tim is free to replace him.

Tim prefers to leave it up to the audience: "What do you guys think?" Gregg is willing to abide by the verdict of a popular vote.

After hearing from the public, Tim has a new offer: Gregg will get a one-year trial as co-host, beginning in 2014.

Gregg isn't sure the show will run that long, which makes Tim wonder if he should look for a co-host "who believes in the future of the show."

Gregg questions whether Tim can find a replacement who will tolerate being vomited on. He adds that although Tim is "a great host," he lacks real-world movie expertise. But Tim challenges Gregg's own expertise, given that his Oscar crate contained a tape of *Remember the Titans* rather than the monster Oscar hit *Titanic*.

Tim declares that "2014 is the year of the co-host," according to his interpretation of Twitter's wishes.

"See you guys in 2014," Gregg says as he rises to leave. Tim follows him off the set, and they continue to bicker. Only after Tim promises to make him the co-host immediately does Gregg return to his chair.

Ang in There!
Tim congratulates Ang Lee on winning Best Director. He also thanks Gregg for co-hosting tonight's special.

Gregg thinks Quentin Tarantino should have won for Best Director, which reminds Tim that his bloody fishing accident would make a great Tarantino film: After catching a bass weighing about 8 pounds, Tim attempted to clean it with a "very sharp" boning knife and cut about half an inch from his right index finger.

Gregg reminds him again that Costco membership provides safe and easy access to fish.

Oscar's Folly
Next, it's the moment the whole night has built toward: Best Picture! Will a write-in campaign reward Bilbo Baggins for his "unexpected journey," or will some lesser character slither away with the titular Hobbit's "precious" Oscar? That's just what happens as *Argo* snatches the Oscar from Bilbo's paws, leaving Gregg shaken.

"I guess we'll remember 2013 as the year Oscar jumped the shark," he says. He recalls that in 1977, *Star Wars* suffered a similar snub. Apparently, the Academy has learned nothing since then!

A Great Job
As a consolation prize, Tim names Gregg *On Cinema*'s Best Guest of 2012 and awards him an authentic *On Cinema* mug. He asks for a speech.

Rising to his feet, Gregg eloquently expresses how important movies are to him. Being promoted to co-host would honor his personal commitment to cinema, he says, whereas Tim's "Best Guest" award is "a slap in the face" — especially when accompanied by a low-quality mug "no one wants to buy."

Again, he asks the audience to submit their videos of Tim declaring Gregg the co-host.

Tim tries to appease him by presenting him with a party-sized sandwich tray. Because the sandwiches are full of olives, which Tim knows his frequent guest doesn't like, Gregg rejects it.

"Thanks, Tim, for doing a great job," Gregg says bitterly.

EPISODE 208
'GI Joe: Retaliation' & 'Temptation'

Air date: March 28, 2013
Running time: 5:57 minutes

This week, Tim's guest is Ayaka Ohwaki, a foreign exchange student who has traveled all the way from the island nation of Japan to stay with Tim and his family. When Tim asked Ayaka if she would come on his show to provide "a foreign perspective" on the world of movies, she gladly consented, leading to her special guest appearance today!

G.I. Joe: Retaliation is an action-packed thriller that weaves Bruce Willis, Channing Tatum and Dwayne "Rock" Johnson into a tangled web of international intrigue depicted from a patriotic military point of view.

With all this going for it, you'd expect Tim to love this film… and he does! There's little more to be said, except that this is "another great G.I. Joe film" that gets "five bags of popcorn."

Ayaka gives it one bag of popcorn and five cups of soda. This confuses Tim, because they went to see the film together and Ayaka "seemed to enjoy it."

"I'm just not a big fan of popcorn," she confesses. Tim reminds her that "the popcorn isn't to be eaten — it signifies the rating, like a star." In response, Ayaka grants the film four stars, which Tim translates into four bags of popcorn.

Tim wants to know what it was like for Ayaka to watch an American movie without subtitles. "I didn't understand at all," she says.

Next up is Tyler Perry's *Temptation: Confessions of a Marriage Counselor*, which also stars Kim Kardashian. Although Tim felt this was "not his favorite kind of movie," it was still "funny" and "OK." Because it was also "very well made," he gives it a respectful four bags of popcorn.

Ayaka gives it three bags of popcorn and three cups of soda. Asked to clarify this rating, she grades the movie as "average."

In the latest installment of *On Cinema Presents Popcorn Classics BTC*, Gregg interviews Jimmy McNichol — Kristy's brother and a fine actor in his own right — on his 1981 car chase adventure *Smokey Bites the Dust*.

Jimmy makes it known that his wife is an avid collector who owns three copies of this film. On behalf of the fans, Gregg asks him for an inside tip on the best places to find this collector's item. Jimmy thinks the internet would probably be their best bet.

He also provides an insider's perspective on *Smokey*'s proven status as a Popcorn Classic: It has a lot of "thrills," he says, due to the "chasing cars and crashing." Stepping back to take a broader view of the Tinseltown industry, Jimmy predicts DVDs will get even smaller as technology marches on.

Last, Gregg lands himself an official *Popcorn Classics BTC* scoop: Jimmy plans to follow up his 1978 hit "He's a Dancer" with an all-new album of musical material later in 2013.

Back on set, Tim and Ayaka thank Gregg for a job well done.

ON CINEMA ON HOLLYWOOD LEGENDS

Ayaka Ohtani

Originally born in Japan, **Ayaka Ohtani** first met **Tim Heidecker** when she stayed with his family as a visiting foreign exchange student. Since that time, she has left a warm and lasting mark on the **On Cinema Family** as an occasional co-host and purveyor of **Popcorn Classics**. Later in life, she made her acclaimed dramatic debut in the **Decker** miniseries, more than holding her own against veteran actors like **Joe Estevez** while also coping with the challenges of young motherhood.

However, this classic **Cinderella** story is not without its sometimes tragic side, as Ms. Ohtani has also faced many personal hardships and tough decision points both at home and abroad. Today, Ayaka lives happily in Japan with her husband and young daughter.

On Cinema On Line

5:48 PM - 29 Mar 2013
Not everyone has #filmexpertise

5:56 PM - 29 Mar 2013
#OnCinema has been and always will be MY show. not yours, get it? chill on the hate. #goodfriday

6:01 PM - 29 Mar 2013
Yes, and Star Wars was George Lucas's movie, but we all know what happened when Alex Guiness left the series.

6:05 PM - 29 Mar 2013
you scored 0-5 on the Stump the Buff game. some film expertise. keep this up if you wanna be banned.

6:11 PM - 29 Mar 2013
And i have gotten 5 out of 5 when the cameras weren't rolling. And when the questions weren't tricks to "save money". #greed

6:12 PM - 29 Mar 2013
OK, bye @greggturkington! You are now not welcome on the show! #bye! #blocked #badfriday

6:14 PM - 29 Mar 2013
BANNED by @timheidecker because I told the truth he rigged Stump The Buff to save money and not pay it out to cancer, I KNEW THE ANSWERS

6:15 PM - 29 Mar 2013
send me youtube videos of your #oncinema auditions! I will need a guest for next week!

6:17 PM - 29 Mar 2013
Great, without expertise the show is no better than listening to some jerks talking about movies while using a urinal.

EPISODE 209
'The Company You Keep' & 'Jurassic Park'

Air date: April 4, 2013
Running time: 7:37 minutes

"Acclaimed film buff" Gregg Turkington returns to the guest seat for this special episode, which includes a sneak peek at the one and only *Jurassic Park*.

Tim tells Gregg he did a great job speaking with Jimmy McNichol in Episode 208. Thinking back over the interview, Gregg recollects that he had a lot of fun "getting to know Jimmy" and "talking to him about some of his work."

"I honestly didn't know who he was," Tim says, "so it was neat to learn about a new guy."

Unlike Jimmy McNichol, Robert Redford needs no introduction, and he's back this week with *The Company You Keep*. Tim sums up this "thriller" as "another film by Steven Soderbergh." He gives it "high marks" as well as four bags of popcorn and a glass of soda.

Gregg liked *The Company You Keep* because while you're enjoying the movie, you're also wondering if you're learning something from it. "That's a nice combination," he says. In addition, the film was "exciting," so Gregg gives it five bags of popcorn and puts them on "a runaway freight train."

Of course, when you're talking about excitement, nothing tops *Jurassic Park* — especially when it's in 3D! Gregg is glad they didn't "tinker" with the original film: "This is the same *Jurassic Park* that you know and love, but it's in 3D now." Thanks to this cutting-edge technology, it's "really frightening" when all the dinosaurs "come out at you."

Tim breaks in impatiently to say that "we all know what happens in *Jurassic Park*." After all, this "great" movie is "one of the greatest movies Steven Spielberg ever made." One thing is bothering him, though: If they shot the film in 3D, why didn't they release it that way the first time around?

"You don't want to second-guess Steven Spielberg," Gregg responds. "He's the master."

Tim can't argue with that. In fact, he has prepared "a tribute to Steven Spielberg" for that very reason. But before we can get to it, Gregg unveils a surprise of his own: He recently went to a flea market and bought Tim a rare Spanish-language edition of *El Parque Jurásico* (*Jurassic Park*).

Gregg explains how it works: "When you put this in your video player, you think you're watching *Jurassic Park*. And then it's wild — every line of dialogue is totally in Spanish!"

He offers this tape to Tim as a "tribute" in honor of "all you've contributed to *On Cinema*." Tim soon realizes he can't read the box due to its use of the Spanish language. "That's the beauty of it!" Gregg interjects. "It's so familiar yet so different, and that's why I think you'll have fun."

With no time left in the episode, Tim signs off.

Did YOU notice...?

- At the beginning of the *Jurassic Park* review, there is a technical glitch: This segment of *On Cinema* was supposed to be presented in 3D, but it's not working properly.

On Cinema On Line

 8:27 PM - 30 Apr 2013
Hey @timheidecker, remember #TheCroods? They make tofu now! It might be good for your tumor. I bought some for you.

 7:37 PM - 6 May 2013
Wondering if @TimHeidecker got #TheCroods tofu I left on his porch?

EPISODE 210
'Oblivion' & 'Scary Movie 5'

Air date: April 21, 2013
Running time: 7:28 minutes

Dispensing with the usual pleasantries, Tim tells us bluntly what's on his mind: "It's been a tough week." Therefore, Gregg Turkington will be doing the heavy lifting in this episode.

Although he's a bit nervous, Gregg makes his way through the show's intro with a little help from Tim's trusty cue cards. That leaves him with just two films to discuss, the first of which is the "science fiction movie" *Oblivion*, starring Tom Cruise and Morgan Freeman.

Gregg found *Oblivion* "a little strange," but he's sure fans of *Star Trek* and *The X Files* will find themselves at home in the brave new world portrayed by Cruise and Freeman. Because this movie is "the real deal," he gives it five bags of popcorn and puts a ring around each one "like the planet Saturn."

Tim loved the movie, and he also loves Tom Cruise and science fiction, so naturally he enjoyed watching all three "with my family."

Gregg asks how Tim's family is doing and whether his tumor [Episode 201] has "gone down in size." Tim says he doesn't have a tumor. In reality, his problem is "blood clots," which have now "doubled" to reach a total of "12."

Gregg reminds him that he could have gotten surgery, just as Gregg himself advised back at the beginning of the season. But Tim says "that ship has sailed." In an understandably gloomy mood, he prompts Gregg to continue with the reviews.

And with that, it's all hands on deck as "Lindsay Lohan, Charlie Sheen and the whole *Scary Movie* gang" bring us *Scary Movie 5*. As Gregg says, "you know what you're in for" with the latest entry in this venerable horror-comedy franchise: "a lot of laughs, a couple of little chills, a little fright here and there, and a little eye candy in the form of Miss Lindsay Lohan."

Any way you slice it, *Scary Movie 5* offers viewers "a good time," and that's why Gregg gives it five bags of popcorn.

Tim didn't have a chance to watch this movie, because he has been "spending time saying goodbye" to his loved ones. He has also been going through his "storage room," looking at "old pictures" and other "stuff" he must prepare to leave behind.

Gregg suggests that *Scary Movie 5* could offer Tim a welcome distraction from these sad duties. But because "time is so valuable to me right now," Tim can't spare any of it for this film. Gregg assures him that despite its title, *Scary Movie 5* is a comedy; the laughs might do him some good.

Tim prefers to revisit old favorites at this difficult time. He has been seeking out "movies that make me feel good, that I'm comfortable around."

On top of which, he "was never a big fan of the *Scary Movie* franchise," because "it's junk." Also, the people responsible for these films are "the worst" because they're "profiting off of gore" as well as "horror and people suffering." At this final stage of his life, Tim would much rather watch something uplifting, like *The Sound of Music*.

He thanks Gregg for "filling in" on this episode. His voice trembling, he also sends a special thank-you to Ayaka Ohwaki, [Episode 208] "who was such a big part of this season for us."

Gregg again urges Tim to seek surgical help with his tumor. Tim disagrees both with Gregg's description of his blood clots as a tumor and with his optimistic outlook: "There was a very small window in which surgery would have been appropriate, and that window has closed."

"It was closed by you and your idiot doctor," Gregg fires back. He believes modern surgery offers real hope and could allow Tim to "get back to reviewing movies" without any further "erratic episodes."

Tim counters that because we no longer live in the "Dark Ages," there's no reason to submit to a "barbaric" practice like surgery in 2013.

In closing, Tim compliments Gregg for his work on the program and expresses the hope that "we made a small difference." He has one last message for the *On Cinema* Family: "Remember me whenever you go to see a movie."

"Especially if you go to a movie about a stubborn person that won't get surgery when they need surgery," Gregg says. "Definitely think of him then."

On Cinema On Line

11:28 AM - 26 Jun 2013
I have decided to get the surgery #clots #oncinema

1:09 PM - 26 Jun 2013
I'm glad that my expert advice extends beyond movies to medical care! Good riddance to bad tumors. This is great news!!!

1:12 PM - 26 Jun 2013
Fingers crossed that there is cable TV in the hospital that @timheidecker is headed to. #Movies would make the long recovery time go quickly

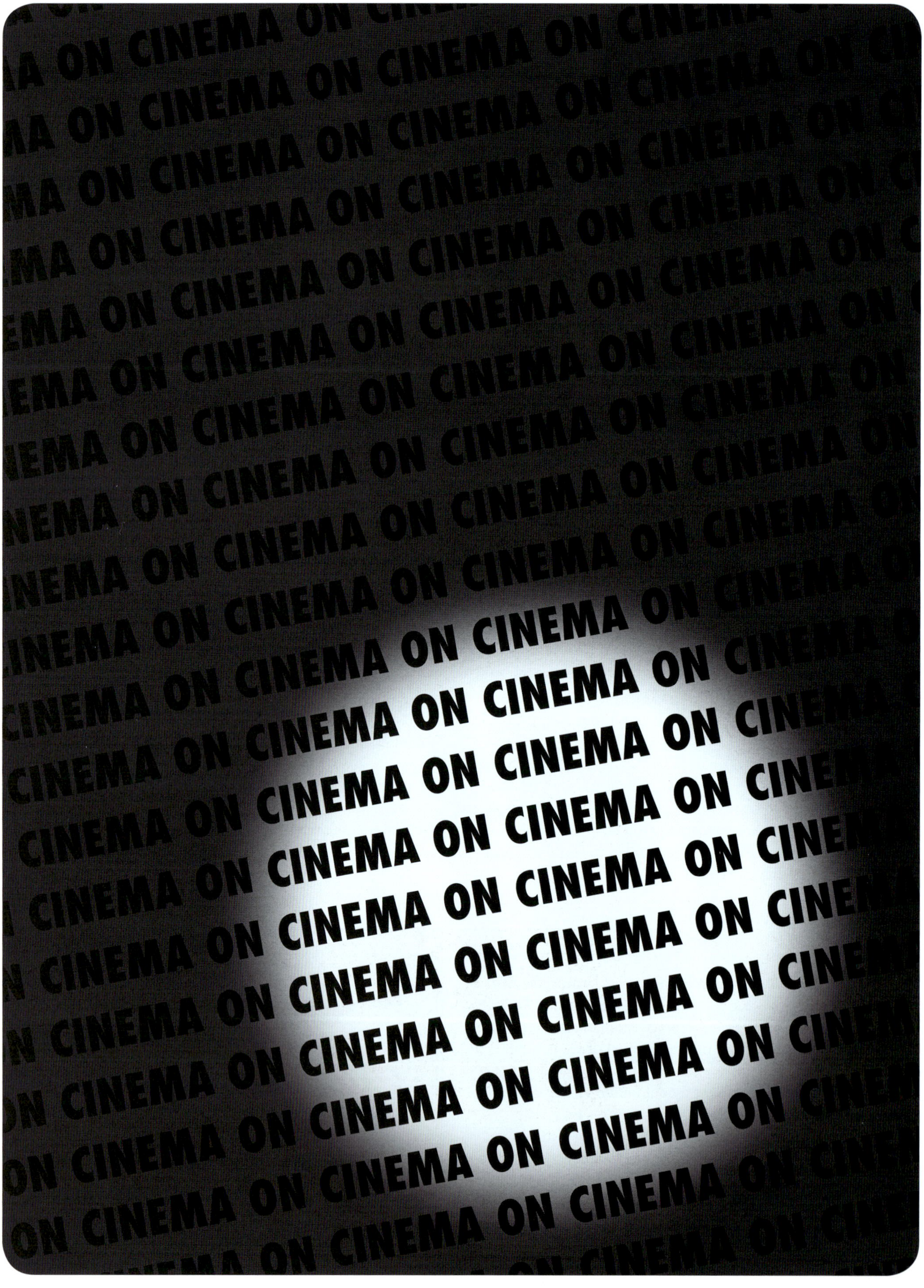
CINEMA ON CINEMA

SEASON 3

EPISODE 301
'The Lone Ranger' & 'Despicable Me 2'

Air date: July 7, 2013
Running time: 10:30 minutes

With the top of his head swathed in fresh white bandages, Tim welcomes us — and this week's guest, Gregg Turkington — to the newly minted third season of *On Cinema*.

Dressed for summer fun in a shirt that's "Hawaiian in style," Tim says "aloha" to Johnny Depp's *The Lone Ranger* and its comely co-star Helena Bonham Carter. This modern twist on a classic Western hero brings Tonto, The Lone Ranger and all the rest back to life for a new generation. Speaking candidly as a longtime Western fan, Tim calls it "one of my favorite movies of the year" and "a lock for Best Picture."

Gregg pegs it as "a cool movie" and gives Disney props for "branching out" from their tried-and-true animated fare. He and Tim also commend Johnny Depp for confounding audience expectations by playing Tonto rather than the Lone Ranger. Tim gives the film "as high a score as you can give," which in this case is six bags of popcorn and five bags of soda.

Gregg gives *The Lone Ranger* his personal maximum rating of five bags. He deducts one bag due to the absence of Tim Burton in the director's chair but restores the bag because "Johnny Depp was just so good." He includes a chocolate heart for Depp, which he changes, on reflection, to a chocolate horse.

Before moving on to *Despicable Me 2*, Tim confides in his viewers about the purpose of his bandaged head. In a monologue that arguably stands as the season's emotional pinnacle, he reveals that he did in fact undergo brain surgery for his deadly blood clots.

Though he often worried that he "was gonna be passed away," he is happily still with us. But his recovery came at a steep emotional cost: Tim's wife "didn't believe in the surgeries," and when he went through with them anyway, she sought and received a divorce.

Concerned, Gregg presses his friend for more details: "Was it cancer, or what?"

"It was blood clots," Tim replies, adding that they have now been "surgically removed." Gregg thinks the clots should have been tested for malignancy, but Tim sticks to his belief that blood clots and tumors are unrelated.

Although he's on the mend, he faces a long and painful recovery. According to his doctor, he's not even supposed to be hosting *On Cinema*, which could be why he's having "a lot of pain" in his head. On the bright side, he is taking "herbal supplements, which are doing the trick for sure." He thanks the *On Cinema* Family, and Gregg, for their support and "well-wishings."

Despicable Me 2 is a stylish cartoon film made with the voices of Steve Carrell, Al Pacino, Steve Coogan and Russell Brand as the villains. Tim loved the first movie, and this one is no exception: It's "fun and funny," suitable for "children" but also enjoyable for "adults who love good movies."

Tim and Gregg were especially impressed with Al Pacino's stellar voice work in this unexpected comedic turn. Even though Pacino has earned more than his share of Oscar nominations in the dramatic realm, Gregg has a hunch this daring role may just net him another.

Despicable Me 2 snags four bags of popcorn and five cups of soda from Tim. Gregg gives it five bags of popcorn and six of mixed candy.

Next, *On Cinema*'s brand-new *On Birthdays* segment covers everything happening in the world of celebrity birthdays. This first installment is a huge one, as none other than Tom Cruise is turning 51. In his celebration of Cruise's career, Tim applauds the actor for "all" his movies, but specifically for *Jack Reacher*. [Episode 109] Tim hasn't had a chance to see Cruise's latest film, *Oblivion*, [Episode 210] but he's sure he "will love it."

Gregg's Popcorn Classic is *Two Weeks Notice*, a romantic comedy with Sandra Bullock and Hugh Grant. Tim is annoyed because he'd hoped Gregg would choose a Tom Cruise film for the occasion, but all that is forgotten as he notices the red tape on the bottom of the VHS box.

Gregg explains that this is his "new coding system," which helps him to navigate his collection and keeps people from stealing his valuable tapes. At Tim's request, he summarizes the clever numbering system. Unfortunately, Tim has a hard time following it because his head is hurting a lot, and he's also having trouble seeing and hearing things.

EPISODE 302
'Grown Ups 2' & 'Pacific Rim'

Air date: July 14, 2013
Running time: 6:34 minutes

After introducing his guest, Gregg Turkington, Tim gets straight down to business with an up-close, in-depth look at Adam Sandler's *Grown Ups 2*, which also stars Chris Rock and company. Tim submits this comedic "last-day-of-school movie" as Exhibit A in his case that "the great Adam Sandler has returned."

He loved how the prequel, *Grown Ups 1*, combined "summer comedy" with "some pretty gross-out comedy-style humor," and he's also happy "to see that *Saturday Night Live* gang coming back together" for *Grown Ups 2*. As far as Tim is concerned, that's more than enough to earn the latter film five bags of popcorn.

Gregg loves the movie too, but he has a small problem with the title. For safety's sake, it should be called *Grown Ups Only*, because the "raunchy" humor in this movie is definitely *not* for immature viewers. That quibble aside, Gregg loved it! He gives it five bags of popcorn, plus an empty bag to throw up in during one of the movie's many "gross-out" sequences.

In Tim's synopsis of Guillermo Del Toro's *Pacific Rim*, Earth is attacked by aliens and defended by humans from inside of robots. Even though the cast of this "sci-fi movie" comprises "a bunch of nobodies," Tim found it "very interesting." Nonetheless, it receives only two stars because "it's not very interesting" and "Tom Cruise should've been in it."

Gregg reminds Tim that Tom Cruise wasn't in the original *Alien* either, but that movie is still a five-bagger, much like *Pacific Rim*. Gregg "loved this movie" and is looking "forward to many more in the series."

Having being persuaded by Gregg's "good point," Tim awards *Pacific Rim* an extra two bags, for a bragworthy grand total of four. Despite this change of heart, he puts Hollywood on notice that "we are not gonna keep seeing movies if it's not gonna have big movie stars."

In an eloquent rebuttal, Gregg points out that "today's nobodies are tomorrow's stars." He illustrates this theory with a real-world example that is very much in Tim's wheelhouse: "If you saw *Risky Business* when it first came out, you'd say, 'Oh, who's Tom Cruise? I never heard of him.' Well, he went on to become one of the biggest stars of his generation."

Tim is unmoved, because Cruise "was already a big TV star" by the time of *Risky Business*. Getting back to *Pacific Rim*, he insists that even Tom Hanks would've been a more suitable replacement for Tom Cruise than the actor Del Toro picked.

Gregg tries a different tack, arguing that as beloved stars grow old, sicken and die, "you need a new generation to replace them." One way to accomplish this is by giving younger actors "a chance in movies" like *Pacific Rim*, which Gregg "loved." But Tim feels that young people with adequate star power are already widely available; Channing Tatum is just one example of a relative newcomer who could successfully have filled in for Tom Cruise in *Pacific Rim*.

This week's Popcorn Classic pits Harrison Ford against Anne Heche in *Six Days, Seven Nights*. Gregg reports that Ford "delivers" in this "action-romance," which makes the picture "exciting" to watch. Put all these factors together, and you've got "a fun package."

Tim remembers *Six Days, Seven Nights* as "a big flop," but Gregg says that on the contrary, it was "a critical darling." The problem, he says, is that "it didn't appeal to all audiences, because it sort of brought back the old *Casablanca* style of moviemaking." For this reason and others, Gregg "absolutely can't recommend this movie highly enough."

Before Tim signs off, Gregg has a surprise for him. He has had a couple of official *On Cinema* uniform shirts made. One is embroidered with Tim's name, and the other bears Gregg's. Tim finds it difficult to verbalize his appreciation for this gift.

EPISODE 303
'Turbo' & 'Red 2'

Air date: July 17, 2013
Running time: 10:35 minutes

Tim's surgical wounds are healing nicely under his new hat, but he still has difficulty pronouncing the words. He is accompanied this week by his guest, Gregg Turkington, who "is here to provide expertise" and is looking sharp in the official *On Cinema at the Cinema* co-host shirt he bought for Tim last week.

Tim alerts viewers that the new *On Cinema* collector's mug is now open for business. One side of this mug is hashtagged #TGFC, or "Thank God for Coffee" — an old saying of Gregg's that Tim has adapted to the internet age. (The mug can also be used for soup.) Shortly thereafter, Tim accidentally breaks the mug as the result of a mishap while putting it out of sight.

Turbo is "a 3D animated movie" that "opens today" and stars "Burt Reynolds' son." It's about a "freak accident" to a "garden snail" that helps it win the Indy 500 drag race. For Tim, "this movie had everything for me" as it ran the gamut from "great adventure" to "comedy." While he would have preferred a NASCAR-themed race, "Indy 500 is the best as well." He awards it five bags of popcorn and five cups of soda.

Gregg loved *Turbo* for its "unique take on the race theme." In most such stories, he explains, a turtle is the beneficiary of the old adage that "slow and steady wins the race." But here, the winner is a snail! It's this kind of attention to creative detail that separates the four-baggers from the five-baggers, and Gregg places *Turbo* firmly in the latter camp. He throws in a saltshaker "because that's how you kill snails in your garden." That said, Tim and Gregg both agree that the lovable hero of this film should *not* be killed with salt.

This reminds Tim of something else he loved about the movie: "I never knew what was going on." He enjoyed this "air of mystery" and appreciated that the filmmakers "didn't treat me like a child" by making the movie overly comprehensible.

Gregg was also confused by *Turbo*, mostly because the promotional email made it look like the title was *Turbo 3* rather than *Turbo 3D*.

At first, Tim is exasperated by this anecdote. But then his manner softens. He has not been sleeping well due to the painful recovery from his head surgery. Because he's unable to sleep on the accustomed side of his head, he's "not getting any sleep."

Gregg says, "If you hadn't broken the coffee glass, I'd get you a cup of coffee."

Unlike *Turbo 3*, *Red 2* is an actual sequel made by Bruce Willis. In this one, the stellar cast includes Willis himself and is joined by Anthony Hopkins (*Hannibal*), John Malkovich (*Being John Malkovich*), Catherine Zeta-Jones (Michael Douglas of *Fatal Attraction* fame), and Mary-Louise Parker (*The Assassination of Jesse James by the Coward Robert Ford*).

Tim speculates that if you "put all these people in a room" and had them "talk about the weather," you would still have "a great movie." Gregg thinks *Red 2* is an even better movie than that, thanks to its "action sort of scenario."

In Tim's opinion, *Red 2* is also better than *Red*, which is very high praise considering that the original film starred Bruce Willis, who is one of Tim's faves. This "action-adventure" has "a lot of humor" and "a lot of heart," and is quite possibly Tim's "favorite movie of the year." He gives it five bags of popcorn and two sodas.

Gregg warns us that there's "a lot of violence" in *Red 2*, but unlike real-world violence, it "serves the plot" of this movie about "assassins." Therefore, he gives it five bags of popcorn and five packages of Band-Aids "for all the blood that is spilled in this great movie."

Next, Tim introduces Gregg's new segment, *On Popcorn*. This is a consumer taste-test quiz that pits the most popular brands against one another to identify the one that's best "for you, the viewer." In this debut episode, Gregg's guest is *On Cinema* host Tim Heidecker.

Gregg briefly goes over the ground rules: Tim will try all the popcorns and then rate them on a scale of zero to five videotapes. Orville Redenbacher and Pop Secret wind up in a photo-finish tie, edging out the Gelson's store brand in this tough face-off.

EPISODE 304
'The Wolverine' & 'Blue Jasmine'

Air date: July 24, 2013
Running time: 10:53 minutes

Tim is looking and feeling better this week, and all his hair has grown back. But after introducing his special guest, Gregg Turkington, he admits he has a confession to make: "I got back into this too quick."

Gregg immediately reaches out to his friend: "If you need a break or something, I'm always happy to host the show."

The Wolverine showcases Hugh Jackman in his titular role as the brooding hero of the *X-Men* comic book. In this installment, The Wolverine (Jackman) "makes a voyage to modern-day Japan" for what might turn out to be the fight of his life.

Tim was annoyed by the cast of "no-names" — Mr. Jackman excepted, of course! — and their hard-to-pronounce names. Despite these flaws, he "loved" this "great action movie," earning it five bags of popcorn.

As a dyed-in-the-wool "X-Head," Gregg deems this "the *Gone With the Wind* of Wolverine movies," not least because "it's a long movie." Although you may need a "pillow" for your "back problems," and some "cups of coffee," the good news is that "this one goes on and on in the best possible way." Gregg gives it five bags of popcorn, plus 10 cups of coffee so you can stay awake.

Next, it's the return of a very different type of cinematic superhero as Woody Allen gets "back in the saddle" to do what he does best in *Blue Jasmine*. The mere mention of the legendary director's name earns a round of applause from Gregg, as Tim congratulates this national treasure on "his 101st" movie.

Blue Jasmine skillfully dissects the ups and downs of "fashionable New York" as a "housewife" undergoes "an acute crisis." Tim says this is yet another "instant classic" from "one of the greats" and "one of the masters." It's also Tim's standout Oscar pick for Best Picture.

Getting personal for a moment, Tim gives us an intimate peek behind the *On Cinema* curtain: He "used to go to" movies like *Blue Jasmine* with his "wife," but their recent divorce has left a "vacuum" in his existence. Happily, Gregg has stepped up to fill this void, accompanying Tim to the movies for "the first time" to see *Blue Jasmine*. Tim confides that the two critics had "a nice dinner" at Carrabba's, a classic Italian restaurant in Southern California where they both live.

After seeing *Blue Jasmine*, he and Gregg "ended up talking a lot about other Woody Allen movies." As a result, Tim "learned a lot about" his friend. This touching anecdote reminds Gregg that what makes Allen so unique is that other directors "are making the movie from the wallet, but he's making it from the heart."

Tim appreciates this "insight." But more than that, he appreciates "the time" Gregg spent with him on their night out, during which Tim sometimes became "a little emotional" due to the "relationship issues" Woody Allen explored so deftly in *Blue Jasmine*.

Gregg is emphatic that such issues are the great director's "particular interest." If you go to "the Bruce Lee movies," you will see "some karate." In much the same way, if you go see a movie by Woody Allen, "there's going to be some moments from the heart."

For Tim, *Blue Jasmine* is such an obvious "six-bagger" that there's no need to "waste time giving it our review." Instead, he awards it six bags of popcorn and moves on to a brand-new segment entitled *On Cinema Presents Stars on Directors*. In this debut episode, workhorse thespian Joe Estevez [Episode 203] sits down with *OCP Stars on Directors* co-creators Tim and Gregg to share his views on the director's art as seen through the lens of the actor.

This week, the director under discussion is the great Woody Allen. Joe's stance toward Allen is first and foremost one of respect: More than "anybody else in making movies today," Allen is "the genius that he is." Asked to place Allen on the official list of top-10 directors, Joe puts him close to the absolute top, in a number-three slot where he is second only to "Hitchcock."

If this is really the case, Tim asks, why do Woody's films "always come out to be flops"? Joe assumes this is due in part to the difficulty of assessing Allen's legacy while alive. "After he passes, if he ever does, we can be very objective about his work," Joe says, at which point we'll see that he was "incredible." Joe has further thoughts on Mr. Allen's output that he shares with us in this powerful segment.

As the end credits roll, Tim and Gregg plan another movie night, and Gregg offers to bring leftovers from Carrabba's.

EPISODE 305
'The Smurfs 2' & '300: Rise of an Empire'

Air date: July 31, 2013
Running time: 9:20 minutes

Tim's back in the saddle with another episode of his "on web" movie reviews, and Gregg Turkington once again joins him as the show's resident guest expert.

Today, the dreams of children of all ages come vividly true as *The Smurfs 2* hits the Silver Screen. Overall, Tim is astounded by "the embarrassment of riches" to be found in 2013's avalanche of "sequels and animated sequels." Buoyed by the talents of "the late Jonathan Winters" and Christina Ricci, *The Smurfs 2* may well be the pick of this litter so far.

This "complicated story" about "Smurfs" was "one of my favorite movies," according to Tim. He loved the first Smurfs movie, and this one, and he predicts these films will keep being made because they've "got a lot of heart and a lot of soul." For now, he gives *The Smurfs 2* an encouraging four bags of popcorn.

Gregg was relieved that all the "loose ends" from *Smurfs 1* were "tied up" in this "great movie." More generally, he was glad to see the TV world of the Smurfs expanded yet again for the big screen, where he hopes it will "become a regular presence."

Brooding on what might have been, Tim recollects that the late Jonathan Winters died before the film was completed. Tim and Gregg agree that although Winters' "sad" demise did not affect the film's quality, it may well result in blockbuster ticket sales as bereaved moviegoers rush to the screen to see what all the fuss was about. It's also a matter of respect: As Gregg observes, "people are going to want to say goodbye to Jonathan Winters in a classy way."

Taking a tactical perspective, Tim ponders the Academy's likely response to this loss. Gregg has previously called for the establishment of a Best Comic Actor award, [Episode 106] and this film bolsters his case. The difference is that in this instance, "the death of Jonathan Winters" could finally "spur" the creation of this award. If that happens, Winters would be "the perfect role" to receive this honor.

Tim does his part to make this happen by naming Winters as his own pick for a posthumous Oscar. He and Gregg both give *The Smurfs 2* five bags of popcorn, and Gregg throws in "five blue popsicles" for the Smurfs.

Shifting the action from the timeless world of Smurf Village to Stone-Age Greece, *300: Rise of an Empire* continues the thrill-heavy yarn that first appeared in *300*, where it was acclaimed by Tim as "one of my favorite movies."

He is less keen on *300 II*, which he calls "disgusting" and "a disgrace to movies" due to the absence of *300*'s leading man Gerard Butler. He gives it four bags of popcorn to commend its emphasis on "action." However, he finds it intolerable that the sequel was made without Butler, who was demonstrably "still alive" at the time of filming, as evidenced by his supporting role in *Playing for Keeps*. [Episode 106]

Gregg objects to these "amateurish" remarks: "Whether a character leaves or stays isn't really how you review movies."

Tim still decries the film's lack of "star power," especially when compared to the dream-team lineup of *Smurfs 2*. Gregg reminds him that once upon a time, in a galaxy far, far away, "no one had ever heard of" Mark Hamill, Carrie Fisher or Harrison Ford. And yet, *Star Wars* "went on to be the most beloved movie of all time." In the interest of fairness, Tim should give *300 II* "a chance" to do the same!

Gregg drives this point home by giving the film an inarguable five bags of popcorn, plus 300 "little bits" of caramel corn.

Popcorn Classics, anyone? This week, it's Christmas in July as Gregg schools us on Michael Keaton's holiday-centric *Jack Frost*. Before getting started, he has a yuletide message for all those Scrooges who say you can't enjoy a Christmas movie in the summer: "The good Christmas movies are movies you can watch year-round." This rule most definitely applies to *Jack Frost*, which is "one you should see."

Gregg also has a "historic" personal connection with this film. He is proud to announce his campaign to get into the *Guinness Book of World Records* by watching "500 movies in 500 days," which he kicked off by watching *Jack Frost*. Because he needs to verify his viewing for the Guinness board, he asks viewers to make themselves known to him if they see him in the theater. He is also accepting movie suggestions from anyone who wants to have a hand in this unheard-of effort.

Tim wraps things up with a reminder to "go see *Smurfs 2*," which is his "official recommendation" for the episode.

On Cinema On Line

5:00 PM - 31 Jul 2013
the world is watching. #500MoviesIn500Days

6:58 PM - 31 Jul 2013
Thinking of you tonight, @greggturkington - you might say we are the reVIEWS Brothers!

11:54 PM - 31 Jul 2013
#500movies500days excited for my friend. Would be cool to be a part of history.

EPISODE 306
'Percy Jackson: Sea of Monsters' & 'Elysium'

Air date: August 7, 2013
Running time: 6:59 minutes

Tim embarrasses himself during the introduction to this episode when he refers to it as "a podcast" by mistake. His guest, he informs us, "is Gregg Turkington."

There are only two movies this week, but Tim needs to rush because he will "have to leave very soon for a doctor's appointment." He will also be visiting his lawyer.

In the meantime, *Percy Jackson: Sea of Monsters* stars "a bunch of no-names again," as one of Poseidon's sons embarks on a race against time to recover the Golden Fleece from its titular sea of monsters.

For Gregg, this mythic film was "kind of like *The Hobbit* underwater: *Hobbit Meets Jaws*, if you will." He "really liked it" and hopes there will be more to come. He gives it five bags of popcorn and "a cup of water in which you can drop a plastic Hobbit."

Tim didn't see this movie, but he gives it five bags anyway because he trusts Gregg's "opinion" of its quality. Gregg confirms that Tim's assessment of this "fantastical and fantastic" movie is right on the money.

In *Elysium*, Matt Damon and Jodie Foster find themselves "set in the year 2154," where wealthy people live in space and the rest of us are stuck on "the ruined Earth." As such, this sci-fi film combines "action" with "a message about equality." Tim was less than thrilled with the "liberal kind of thing" Matt Damon inevitably brings to the table, and he also decries the movie's "negative attitude toward blacks."

Gregg saw *Elysium* as more of a "popcorn movie," without any of the baggage that spoiled it for Tim.

Looking more closely at his cue card, Tim realizes he didn't see *Elysium* either. He gives it five bags of popcorn regardless because he likes science fiction.

"I'm sorry," he adds. "It's just been a hard week for me to get out and see movies." He explains that he's moving out of his home and that he must see the doctor "every two days" for medical testing.

Gregg rebukes Tim for his lack of commitment to the cinema. As he sees it, "a lot of the actors in these films have problems," but they "do their job." Eventually, "you end up with a good movie out of it."

In today's installment of *On Birthdays*, Tim sends birthday wishes to *Signs* director M. Night Shymalan. In a dispute with someone off-camera, he reiterates that he needed "an extra month" away from *On Cinema*. He can't "move heaven and earth to see all these movies" while also recuperating from his blood clot surgery, especially when he has just moved away from the nearest movie theater locations.

Speaking of which, Gregg has a new edition of *On Cinema On Location* on queue. This time, we're off to Excelsior High School in Los Angeles, which once again did double duty as Rydell High School for the making of *Grease 2*. In fact, some of the high-energy musical numbers performed in this memorable film were filmed on the exact site of this school building, not far from where Gregg was standing!

The episode ends on a tense note, with Tim slapping the cue card out of Gregg's hand for talking in an overly familiar manner to the audience. He then storms off the set.

ON CINEMA ON HOLLYWOOD LEGENDS

Johnny Depp

As all diehard movie buffs know, **Johnny Depp** is synonymous with director **Tim Burton**, who has shepherded the flamboyant actor through no fewer than nine certifiable five-bag classics. But there's so much more to the story! For instance, Depp also displayed his swashbuckling side throughout Walt Disney's **Pirates of the Caribbean** franchise.

Even fewer realize that Johnny is a gifted guitarist who has lent a helping hand to music greats from **Oasis** to **Aerosmith**. But as all true movie buffs know, the real, tried-and-true Depp magic only happens when Tim Burton is at the helm. By the same token, a Tim Burton movie without Depp is virtually a contradiction in terms. That's why movie fans across the globe are hoping for many more years of both!

EPISODE 307
'Kick-Ass 2'

Air date: August 14, 2013
Running time: 10:33 minutes

In this episode, Tim gets the ball on the road by apologizing for his behavior on the last episode. In hindsight, it was "unacceptable" to say he "hadn't seen" *Percy Jackson* and *Elysium*. [Episode 306] In reality, he did see both films, but he "was under a lot of stress" due to his "health and personal life."

On the bright side, he has some good news about his health: "I'm in good shape." He apologizes again to his viewers, and also to this episode's special guest, Gregg Turkington.

"No apology necessary!" says Gregg. "It's just fun to be here."

Tim asks Gregg for the current status of his "500 Movies in 500 Days" campaign. [Episode 305] As it happens, Gregg is optimistic that he will soon be "the newest entry in the *Guinness Book of World Records*." In just 15 days, he has already watched 19 movies, which puts him well on the way to becoming "part of history."

Tim offers to help Gregg watch at least some of the *Indiana Jones* trilogy later that night as part of their burgeoning "bromance." [Episode 304]

But for now, it's all eyes on Jim Carrey and *Kick-Ass 2*. In the sequel to Carrey's previous entry in this laugh-out-loud superhero franchise, the titular hero teams up with ordinary citizens to hit crime right where it lives — in our funnybones!

Unlike last week, Tim actually went to see this movie. And when it was over, he "stood up to say 'Thank you, Jim Carrey.'" Even though he was "lost" and "completely disoriented" throughout *Kick-Ass 2* — perhaps because he never saw the original *Kick-Ass* — he "still loved the movie."

Gregg loved it just as much, but he takes issue with its "controversial" title, which he worries may lose the film "half of the audience segment right away." He suggests *Kick-It* as a family- and box-office-friendly alternative title.

Tim gives this "very disorienting film" five bags of popcorn and one soda. Gregg gives the movie itself five bags of popcorn. The title gets zero bags because of its offensive connotations.

For this episode's episode of *On Cinema On Location*, Gregg has "gone to San Francisco." The reason soon becomes apparent: As we recall from Episode 109, Gregg and Tim disagree about which *Star Trek* movie revolved around a time-travel visit to San Francisco. Gregg aims to settle the dispute once and for all by beaming down to the City by the Bay in search of clues.

As Gregg welcomes us to "the site of San Francisco's famous *Star Trek II* filming location," he stands on the literal corner where all the action took place. A cutaway to a vintage still from the movie confirms that this is the precise spot where Captain Kirk and Spock once stood. Yet another shot, taken from a different angle and featuring several other Enterprise crew members, clinches the deal. Case closed!

Or is it? As Tim sees it, Gregg's footage "didn't prove anything." He simply misidentified footage from *Star Trek IV* as footage from *Star Trek II* to create the cinematic illusion that the San Francisco visit occurred in the earlier film.

Tim has one more ace up his sleeve: An *On Cinema* fan sent him a copy of the 1986 paperback novelization of *Star Trek IV*, and the back cover asserts that Spock and friends "must journey back in time to 20th-century Earth."

Gregg says this is "not an official book," but Tim gloats that it was written by none other than Leonard Nimoy, the original Spock. Gregg counters that "Nimoy has made a whole career of doing things that 'kind of' relate to *Star Trek*."

Tim responds that the book is very clearly "based on" the movie. Gregg accepts this, but he has a different interpretation of "based on." He theorizes that the four *Star Trek* movies have been combined in a single book, just as *The Hobbit* book encompassed all three Hobbit movies.

Tim finds a reference to visiting San Francisco in the book. But as it comes on page 59, this appears to support Gregg's position, as does the title *Star Trek IV*, which could be interpreted to mean "all four *Star Trek* movies." Gregg complains that the book obviously had to cut a lot of detail from the movies, which is why he can only give it two bags of popcorn.

For Tim, this is the final straw. He tells Gregg, "I don't think it's a good match to have you on the show anymore" because he "can't handle this much conflict in my life right now." He announces that he will find a new guest for next week. In the meantime, "Gregg Turkington is no longer part of the show."

On Cinema On Line

12:39 PM - 14 Aug 2013
The show I helped create is going in a different direction. Too bad! In the meantime, watch for me in the #GuinnessBook. #500MoviesIn500Days

4:46 PM - 14 Aug 2013
I wish @greggturkington the best and hope he wins the #500MoviesIn500Days challenge.

6:24 PM - 14 Aug 2013
When #500MoviesIn500Days makes national headlines, I'll be sure and thank everyone BUT Tim Heidecker. His show will be off the air by then.

6:25 PM - 14 Aug 2013
Hey @WilliamShatner please tell @Timheidecker he made two mistakes. Star Trek II was set in S.F.--not IV. Also--firing me from #OnCinema.

6:36 PM - 14 Aug 2013
I'll be back with my new show #OurCinema as soon as I can find a theater and a camera. In the meantime keeping busy with #500MoviesIn500Days

12:07 PM - 16 Aug 2013
The Great Disaster of 2013 will be @timheidecker next week on #OnCinema when he realizes he has no expertise on the subject

8:07 PM - 17 Aug 2013
Was going to watch "The Terminator" tonight, and then I realized how much the title reminded me of @timheidecker. #unjust #firing

10:15 PM - 17 Aug 2013
Not wading in the @greggturkington bullshit anymore! Focusing on new exciting guests for #OnCinema ! Big things coming!!! #future

EPISODE 308
'The World's End' & 'The Colony'

Air date: August 21, 2013
Running time: 6:36 minutes

This week, Tim welcomes an electrifying special guest: veteran actor John Aprea! Because Mr. Aprea "has been in movies," Tim is excited to have unrestricted access to "his expert opinion on film." John is excited as well; he hopes to return to On Cinema "every week."

In other exciting news, Ayaka Ohwaki [Episode 208] is back as Tim's co-host. And this time, it's personal: She and Tim are "officially seeing each other"! John congratulates Tim on his new relationship and calls Ayaka "adorable."

The World's End is about five longtime friends who must band together to save humanity from the titular "world's end." Tim "loved this movie," which was "very funny" and "a lot of fun." Adding to the enjoyment, the inclusion of "scary parts" along with the laughs turned the film into "a real rollercoaster." For Tim, giving this movie anything less than five bags of popcorn would be critical malpractice.

John "liked it a lot," though perhaps not as much as Tim. He appreciated that "it moved," and he enjoyed its "different elements," which ranged from "scary" to "funny." All things considered, this "good movie" gets a creditable four bags of popcorn from John.

Ayaka gives it five bags and gets a shout-out from Tim for being "right on the money." John defends his harsh four-bag review, stressing that five is a very high rating and should be "tough" to get.

In *The Colony*, Laurence Fishburn, Bill Paxton and other survivors of the Ice Age must join forces to save the titular "colony" from "a threat more savage than nature." For Tim, giving this "great action-adventure movie" five bags of popcorn is the ultimate no-brainer.

Ayaka gives it five bags as well, and John gives it an enthusiastic "five plus." Tim advises viewers they've got two great choices for movies this weekend. He himself will probably not be going to the movies, though, because he and Ayaka are going to shop for furniture at Ikea.

Speaking of Ayaka, she is the brand-new host of *Popcorn Classics*. Her expert pick this week is *Airheads*, a 1994 comedy about rock-and-rollers on a mission to get their song on the radio (and an early milestone in the careers of Adam Sandler and Brendan Fraser).

Ayaka calls this "a fun rock 'n' roll movie" and specifies that "you don't have to think anything — just watch!" Tim and John also endorse this certified Popcorn Classic as "worth a look."

"It's been a lot of fun doing this episode with you guys," Tim tells John and Ayaka. He is happy to have "an expert on the set" in John, and Ayaka rounds out this cinematic dream team by being "smart and pretty and full of life."

Tim again thanks his guests, noting that although this has been "a tough year," he's now "coming up for air." As the show ends, they head out for drinks at Carrabba's.

ON CINEMA ON HOLLYWOOD LEGENDS

John Aprea

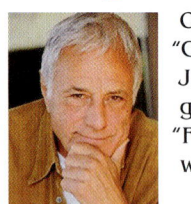

One of the one-and-only original "Godfathers" of American cinema, John Aprea is also a member in good standing of the On Cinema "Family," as his "mob" of loyal fans will attest!

With talents ranging from guest slots on the official On Cinema Oscar Special to his dramatic role as Decker's patriotic **General Cotter**, Mr. Aprea makes excellent use of the skills he learned trodding the boards not just in world-class blockbusters like **The Godfather: II**, but also in all-time box-office faves like **The Seven-Ups** and **Stepford Wives**. John was born in Englewood, New Jersey, and has appeared in many films.

On Cinema On Line

2:10 PM - 21 Aug 2013
I am taking the high road here. But "NOT Cinema" stole my Popcorn Classics segment. Any attorneys who are fans of the real On Cinema?

2:14 PM - 21 Aug 2013
u really wanna go after me who has connections with actor from Godfather? do the math, things could get dangerous for you.

2:20 PM - 21 Aug 2013
Your threats mean nothing. I have been studying judo during my time off. Bring it on! #cowardlylion

2:23 PM - 21 Aug 2013
Tim wouldn't know a key grip from an ice cream cone. No expertise there. And his hosting skills have really deteriorated

2:24 PM - 21 Aug 2013
On Cinema II The Ayaka Years is the worlds worst sequel. #flop

2:20 PM - 23 Aug 2013
Hey @RichardDreyfuss any interest in being a guest on #OnCinema ?

2:22 PM - 23 Aug 2013
Hey @Harry_Styles are you in LA? Would u be a guest on #OnCinema ? My GF is big fan!!! ❤️❤️❤️❤️

3:12 PM - 23 Aug 2013
Hey @richardroeper would love to have you on as a guest for #OnCinema ! DM ME ASAP!!

3:27 PM - 23 Aug 2013
Hey @richardroeper, I would stay away from that OnCinema show, they treat their guests poorly, and they don't respect expert opinions.

3:16 PM - 23 Aug 2013
Hey@FrancisFordC would love to have another member of "the family" on as a guest for #OnCinema ;)

3:19 PM - 23 Aug 2013
Hey @_RobertDeNiro_ I recently had your Godfather costar John Aprea on #OnCinema - would love to have you on as well #offeryoucantrefuse

1:18 PM - 24 Aug 2013
Haven't heard back from any celebs to guest on #OnCinema next week. You deserve the best so I will keep trying!!! #staypositive

4:47 PM - 24 Aug 2013
Hey @MickJagger big #freejack fan! Want to be a guest on #OnCinema ? We shoot in Hollywood, CA!!

11:29 AM - 26 Aug 2013
#OnCinema was never about the guests. It was about helping YOU decide which movies to see!

11:31 AM - 26 Aug 2013
was always happy to have @greggturkington on the show. I just mean we don't need celebrities for #OnCinema to be a hit!

12:52 PM - 26 Aug 2013
I just got off the phone with Ayaka who has reached out on behalf of @timheidecker. I'm pretty busy with #500moviesin500days. Who knows.

12:56 PM - 26 Aug 2013
For those who are keeping track, I am on pace to make history. In fact, I'm now one movie ahead of schedule. #500moviesin500days

12:57 PM - 26 Aug 2013
congrats!! Rooting for you!

12:57 PM - 26 Aug 2013
Experts don't grow on trees.

1:01 PM - 26 Aug 2013
we are shooting a new ep tomorrow. Wanna come down to set for old time's sake? Could use a buff.

12:56 PM - 26 Aug 2013
Let me think about it.

1:05 PM - 26 Aug 2013
Honestly @greggturkington who even cares about minor plot details in Star Trek movies? I'm more into Star Wars and #hobbit anyways.

3:12 PM - 26 Aug 2013
any news?

10:12 AM - 27 Aug 2013
OK @timheidecker, what time do we shoot today?

10:15 AM - 27 Aug 2013
Awesome! Calling you now. Thanks Gregg.

EPISODE 309
'One Direction: This Is Us' & 'The Getaway'

Air date: August 28, 2013
Running time: 11:01 minutes

This week sees the return of Ayaka Ohwaki as Tim's special guest. Tim announces that he and Ayaka are "doing very good" as a couple and that "she is getting me into athletics now."

As an exclusive treat for longtime fans, Tim has another surprise — Gregg Turkington is back! It's Tim's belief that having "two guests" will result in "more of a round table kind of show." He says that so far, "people are loving it."

Tim acknowledges that he and Gregg recently had "a little disagreement." [Episode 307] But they "worked it out" with a bit of assistance from Ayaka, who helped them both to see that "relationships are not just about who's right and who's wrong."

Getting back to the movies, Tim introduces *The Getaway*, starring Ethan Hawke as the mysterious man behind the wheel in this "getaway car chase movie." Tim reveals that "two nights ago," he and Ayaka "snuggled" and "had the popcorn" as they watched this "great movie," resulting in a joint five-bag rating from each of them.

Gregg was less impressed. Because *The Getaway* was "not a great movie," he can only give it two bags of popcorn.

Tim shrugs off this disagreement as "no big deal" and moves on to the episode's centerpiece film: *One Direction: This Is Us*, a musical documentary celebrating one of Ayaka's "favorite groups." Ayaka has gotten Tim "addicted" to the music of this "British pop sensation," so he gives this "great movie" five bags of popcorn. After Ayaka gives it six bags, Tim adds two large bottles of soda to his rating for good measure.

Gregg has two problems with this film. First, it's "not really a movie." On the contrary, "it's a concert by a kiddie band." As such, it's not suitable for review by *On Cinema*. It would, however, be fair game for a show called *On Terrible Music*.

Second, the movie consists almost entirely of "jerks playing awful music," and *On Cinema* "has never been a show for concert movies." Gregg accordingly gives it zero bags of popcorn, adding that in his opinion, the film is "a black hole that sucked all the popcorn out of the world" and "into a void."

Tim and Ayaka both see Gregg's outlook as "sad" and "negative." But Gregg believes film critics have a responsibility to provide viewers with "informed opinions about films" instead of "parroting what our girlfriends say."

Tim counsels Gregg to "go talk to somebody" because he clearly has "other issues going on." He also wonders why he did Gregg the "favor" of bringing him back on the show.

Gregg says that in reality, Tim did *On Cinema* a favor by including "someone who knows something about movies."

"I'm trying to be nice to you," Tim informs Gregg, even though "nobody here likes you."

For this week's *Popcorn Classics*, Gregg had initially planned to present Nicholas Cage in *The Family Man*. But he was forced to change his plans after digging through Ayaka's purse in the green room and finding the VHS tape of *Airheads* she championed as a Popcorn Classic in Episode 308. The video box shows evidence of poorly removed red coding tape [Episode 301] that marks it as coming from Gregg's library.

"This is why I set up this system," he says. "To prevent thieves!" Asked to account for the video being in her possession, a sheepish Ayaka says she "found it in a box" in Tim's room. But Tim swears he's never seen it before.

Gregg complains that his copy of *Airheads* has been "ruined" by the unauthorized coding tape removal and will need to be replaced. He reproaches Tim for "giving my segment to someone else who then is stealing my property and marring it."

Under hostile questioning from Gregg, Ayaka accuses Tim of tearing off Gregg's coding tape. Tim denies this: "She's lying," he tells Gregg. He apologizes to Gregg for the damage to the video, and he warns Ayaka that she has been "disrespectful to the show" and has "a lot of explaining to do." He vows to "get this figured out" when the show returns "next week."

EPISODE 310
'Riddick'

Air date: September 4, 2013
Running time: 9:15 minutes

Tim welcomes us to the last episode of Season Three by apologizing to us for the previous week's episode.

After introducing this week's guest, Gregg Turkington, he breaks the news that his former *On Cinema* co-host and romantic interest Ayaka Ohwaki "has returned to her homeland of Japan because of a visa issue." Although Ayaka was "a sweet girl," Tim has come to feel that "the age difference and the cultural difference" between them "was just too vast."

Gregg declares that Ayaka "was not really an expert in movies." Tim confirms this assessment, and he also makes a solemn on-air promise that when he finds out who vandalized Gregg's copy of *Airheads*, "there will be hell to pay."

Luckily, Gregg has already tracked down a new copy of the film for only four dollars. Tim graciously offers to cover this unexpected expense out of the *On Cinema* budget.

With this "old news" out of the way once and for all, it's time to talk *Riddick*. Boasting Vin Diesel and "an alien race of predators," this sci-fi action "hit" is "one of those great franchises like *Indiana Jones* and *Jack Reacher*," according to Tim. Gregg brings up a few other such franchises, including *Star Wars*, *The Hobbit*, *James Bond* and *Harry Potter*.

Tim sees *Riddick* as yet another example of "the little engine that could," because it's a "movie that everybody believed in enough to happen." He gives it four bags of popcorn and a gallon of soda.

Gregg places it among the top three Vin Diesel movies. He echoes Tim's rating, but he replaces Tim's soda with a fifth bag of popcorn and tacks on "an iron fist, because this movie is exciting."

That's it for this season's reviews, because as Tim makes clear, "there's no other movies this weekend." Instead, he touts the *On Cinema* 2013 movie app as well as the infamous *On Cinema* mug. [Episode 303]

Gregg gives us "a brief update" on his bid to enter *Guinness Book of World Records* history by viewing 500 movies in 500 days. With 465 days to go, Gregg has watched 51 movies, putting him ahead of the curve by 16 films.

He gives us a sneak preview of the three movies he viewed most recently — all of which were chosen from his enormous personal library — and comments that "it does take money" to pay for movies, popcorn, parking and other moviegoer must-haves.

To help meet these expenses, Gregg has created "a Kickstarter campaign" that allows well-wishers to become "part of history" by donating to the online *#500MoviesIn500Days* fund.

Though "your name won't be in the *Guinness Book of World Records*," you will receive "a certificate of thanks and other goodies" when Gregg reaches his goal. He will also be selling signed copies of the movies that earned him this recognition, each of which will come with an authentic photocopy of the *Guinness Book* page that honors his achievement.

Tim ends this sometimes tumultuous season on a warm note, thanking Gregg for his many contributions to the show, and even more importantly, for his "friendship."

On Cinema On Line

1:09 PM - 27 Sep 2013
Hey @greggturkington @Carrabbas this weekend?

2:05 PM - 27 Sep 2013
Been busy? You completely ignored my invite to drop by for movies the other night. Sorry cant make it to @carrabbas--too busy.

2:13 PM - 27 Sep 2013
didn't see invite sorry not always checking my feed. next time!

5:07 PM - 11 Oct 2013
Nice garage sale score today!!! Works out to only 20 cents a movie, for five classics!!! #movies

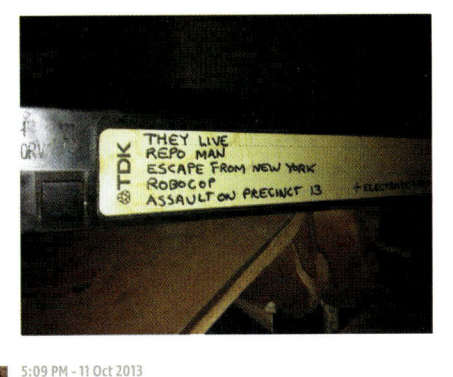

5:09 PM - 11 Oct 2013
how's quality?

5:30 PM - 11 Oct 2013
Real nice! Come by for a movie marathon! Let's watch all 5.

SPECIAL PRESENTATION
First Annual Christmas Special

Air date: December 18, 2013
Running time: 10:52 minutes

Live and on camera for the first annual *On Cinema at the Cinema Christmas Special,* Tim is joined by his guest, Gregg Turkington, who mischievously wishes us "Happy Hobbit-days."

This irreverent greeting reminds Tim of a topical story he read on Glenn Beck's *The Blaze*: At the City Hall in Cleveland, Ohio, "they are not letting them use the manger there for display." That doesn't seem right to Tim, who rhetorically asks, "What country is this?"

He also gives a shout-out to Jeff Stringer, a loyal viewer who recognized him at a "Liberty Rally" both men recently attended in Texas. After realizing he was face to face with the host of *On Cinema*, Mr. Stringer brought Tim to "a cowboy store" and bought him a pair of authentic Texas cowboy boots, which Tim is pretty sure were made from ostriches.

Switching gears, it's time for *The Hobbit: The Desolation of Smaug*. Tim "loved" this movie about the Hobbit's risky search for hidden dragon gold in the Misty Mountains; he gives it five bags of popcorn and is unwilling to budge on that point. Also, he is sure this new installment of the Hobbit legend "will win the Oscar," unlike the previous one.

Gregg confesses he was "a little disappointed in it," but only because "it didn't come out earlier." Seconding Tim's Oscar prediction, he recounts a recent dream in which Santa Claus leaves the North Pole and comes to Earth to deliver a holiday greeting, only to stand revealed as Bilbo Baggins himself. Gregg thinks this dream would be "a cool promotion for the movie, or for Christmas itself" if it were put on film.

Back in the real world, Gregg gives *Hobbit II* five bags of popcorn and throws in a hundred bags more for good measure. Tim won't go quite that far, but he does give it an emphatic 10 bags.

Needless to say, these are very big shoes to fill for Tyler Perry's *A Madea Christmas*, which also stars Larry the Cable Guy in a rare holiday mood. Gregg felt "distracted" throughout Perry's film because his mind was "still on *The Hobbit*." Even as the Madea story inched toward its inevitable climax, he "kept seeing Bilbo" in his mind's eye and "wondering how the whole trilogy is gonna end."

Tim gives *A Madea Christmas* five bags of popcorn because it's technically "the first black Christmas movie." He thinks it's "great" that in the years following the release of the "white" film *A Christmas Carol*, "every race has their own movie" to help them enjoy the Christmas season.

Gregg gives it five bags of popcorn, plus a pair of special blinders "to stop you from seeing or thinking about *The Hobbit* during this movie."

A special holiday edition of *Popcorn Classics* follows. Today's film is *Christmas with the Kranks*, a holiday sidesplitter that benefits from a "hilarious" Tim Allen and an equally "hilarious" Jamie Lee Curtis, to say nothing of Dan Ackroyd, Jake Busey, and Cheech & Chong's very own Cheech Marin.

Tim offers a special tip of the holiday hat to Dan Ackroyd, "who really tears it up" in a movie Gregg calls "an instant family classic."

Giving is the reason for the season, as evidenced by the new annual *On Cinema Gift Exchange* segment. Because Gregg is a film buff, Tim has gotten him a thoughtful gift: A new Blu-Ray player! Gregg can't figure out where the VHS slot is until Tim clues him in that this cutting-edge player doesn't have one.

Tim has also gotten him some top-rated discs to go with his new machine. The shelves of Gregg's film library are built for VHS tapes rather than Blu-Rays, but he figures he can "maybe put them in storage or something." All in all, he's grateful for Tim's "nice" and "cool" holiday presents!

Gregg returns the favor by giving Tim an official *On Cinema at the Cinema* baseball cap, made specially for this holiday occasion. He also gives Tim a matching *On Cinema at the Cinema* shirt, which includes the show's title as well as Tim's name.

Gregg would like Tim to put the hat on right away, but Tim prefers not to mess up his hair, bringing this holiday episode to a close.

On Cinema On Line

2:16 PM - 19 Dec 2013
Very proud to be associated with #HobbitMania. #HappyHobbitdays to everyone.

3:44 PM - 19 Dec 2013
#HappyHobbitdays hashtag is very disrespectful @greggturkington it's #merrychristmas

12:40 AM - 20 Dec 2013
The movie theater is my church.

SEASON 4

EPISODE 401
'Lone Survivor' & 'Her'

Air date: January 8, 2014
Running time: 6:48 minutes

Tim cracks the seal on the first episode of *On Cinema*'s fourth season by thanking his viewers for their interest in his health. He reports that he's "feeling great," and the doctors say his blood clots are gone for good. His only remaining concern is "a sort of tingling numbness" in his hands and feet.

This week's guest is Gregg Turkington, who identifies Tim's symptoms as an early warning sign of diabetes. But Tim is not too worried about having this disease of "old people." He thinks it's more likely to be a problem with his diet.

Tim hurries Gregg onward to the review segment, because he has a medical appointment as soon as he's done shooting.

Lone Survivor is a real-life military dramatization based on Mark Wahlberg as a Navy Seal who must track down the Taliban leader.

The cue card refers to Wahlberg as the "only member of his team to survive" this dangerous mission, causing Tim to inadvertently give away the ending. "We gotta kill the spoilers from these cards," he tells the off-camera *On Cinema* crew.

But even with the spoiler, this is "a terrific movie." It secures five bags of popcorn and two bags of soda from Tim.

Gregg "really liked" this "unofficial sequel to *Zero Dark Thirty*." [Episode 108] He wishes Osama bin Laden could've reprised his role from the earlier film, however, because he was "very interesting as a movie villain." That disappointment aside, Gregg gives this "good movie" five bags of popcorn, plus one turban in honor of its Middle Eastern desert setting.

"God bless the troops," Tim adds.

Next, Spike Jonze returns to the *On Cinema* arena with *Her*, a near-term science fantasy about a lonely man who falls in love with an operating system voiced by Scarlett Johansson. Gregg awards the movie an extra point for its verisimilitude, given that "so much of what people do nowadays is on computers."

Drawing on his vast trove of movie knowledge, he also pegs *Her* as "an unofficial remake" of "Al Pacino's classic *S1M0NE*," a 2002 sci-fi film about a computer-generated movie star who hits the big time in Tinseltown. This new twist on an age-old theme garners *Her* five bags of popcorn from Gregg, along with a red ribbon for the titular character's hair in order to "humanize" her.

Tim loved *Her*, though not as much as he once loved his ex-wife [Episode 301] or Ayaka Ohwaki. He allots it five bags of popcorn and one soda.

Turning his attention to Gregg's "500 Movies in 500 Days" viewing challenge, Tim asks how things are going. In response to viewer demand, Gregg has "put together a segment" addressing this very question.

In this "behind-the-scenes look at a world record in the making," Gregg shows us how he must "scour the world" to gather suitable movies for his campaign. Although he spends plenty of time haunting the retail bins where videocassettes are found, he also gives us an expert how-to tip: classic VHS tapes sometimes turn up where you least expect them, such as the sanitation area at a Valero gas station.

The lesson? Young or old, great movies are where you find them! And with a little financial help from his supporters, Gregg is confident he will "carve out" his "place in history" by watching no fewer than #500MoviesIn500Days.

Back on the set, Gregg estimates that he's already four movies ahead of the schedule that would allow him to set this official world record.

Tim cuts this announcement short and once again bemoans Gregg's tendency to "hijack the show" with his personal film segments.

Episode 402
'The Nut Job' & 'Ridealong'

Air date: January 15, 2014
Running time: 8:04 minutes

Tim extends a warm welcome to regular *On Cinema* guest Gregg Turkington, who is very happy to be back on the set after taking "a little bit of a break" to focus on "setting a world's record" by watching an unheard-of #500MoviesIn500Days.

Tim is not as excited as Gregg to be on this week's episode, because he has been having "a lot of pain" in his right foot. Removing his authentic ostrich-hide boots and his bandages, he shows us his red, swollen and "very tender" foot. He leaves his boots off in order to "let this breathe while we talk."

To assuage viewers' concerns about his foot, Tim verifies that his nephew has already referred him to an acupuncturist. In fact, Tim will undergo his first treatment tomorrow!

Like Brendan Fraser's controversial *Escape from Planet Earth*, [Episode 202] *The Nut Job* animates Fraser's leading role in this cartoon about a squirrel who seeks redemption in the big city.

Tim champions *The Nut Job* as "a great movie." He's glad to see Brendan Fraser back on the Silver Screen, and he also extols the "beauty and "sex appeal" of Fraser's "hot" co-star Katherine Heigl.

Gregg concurs with Tim that *The Nut Job* is a great animated cartoon, in which the stars are not actually visible except for their voices, as anyone who saw the movie would know.

Tim is surprised to learn the film was a cartoon: "The technology now is so good that some of these animated movies look like real life." But as Gregg sees it, the presence of talking squirrels is a reliable indicator that you're watching an animated film. He also says Tim could've "looked at the movie poster" on his way into the theater.

Tim stacks *The Nut Job* up against *Who Framed Roger Rabbit?* in its combination of animated and real-world elements: "Was it animated or was it not? I don't know."

He *does* know that when he hears Katherine Heigl and Brendan Fraser speaking, "it do reminds me of who they are." It's possible this caused him to "daydream a little bit during the movie" about the erotic chemistry between Fraser and Heigl. If so, his loss is Hollywood's gain, as he gives the Tinseltown honchos some free advice: "Put them two in bed together!"

Glancing down at his foot, Tim worries that he should "go to the emergency room" in case he has "gangrene." Gregg reassures him that this is an unlikely diagnosis: "I think you have diabetes."

Whatever the case, they both agree that Tim's suppurating foot doesn't smell very good.

The next movie is *Ridealong*, directed by Tim Storey. This causes Tim to reflect that if they ever made "a biographical picture" of his own life, "you'd call it *Tim's Story*."

Gregg jokes that in actuality, "you'd call it *The Nut Job*." This is no laughing matter for Tim, who reminds Gregg that as "a guest on my show," he needs to "watch yourself" and "show respect for being here."

Ridealong stars rap pioneer Ice Cube in the saga of an unexpected marriage proposal that shakes things up at the Atlanta Police Department. It reminded Tim of *Ferris Bueller's Day Off* in the way it said, "Let's see how much we can cram into a movie in terms of 24 hours."

Although Gregg also noticed "a lot of action" in this police film, "there's more to it than that." For one thing, he finds it ironic that "you would cast Ice Cube in a movie that's this *hot*." This quip earns a rare chuckle from Tim. Gregg gives the movie five bags of popcorn and a tray of ice.

Tim liked *Ridealong* "a lot" — so much so that he "went to see it again" to distract himself from "the pain happening in my leg." He gives it five bags of popcorn.

That's the cue for *Popcorn Classics*, and today Gregg bids a fond *bonjour* to *Forget Paris*, a romantic 1995 comedy with Billy Crystal and Debra Winger. He tries to compare it favorably to *When Harry Met Sally...*, but Tim's inflamed foot keeps getting in the way of the video box. Even so, Gregg vows he "will always remember" *Forget Paris*.

As the lights go down, Tim calls security on Gregg: "I need him out of the building right now, because he just called me a nut job."

On Cinema On Line

7:25 AM - 16 Jan 2014
Congrats to #hobbit2 for best picture nom! #OscarNomination

7:49 AM - 16 Jan 2014
Hooray!!! I knew it would get the nod! How many noms in total? This is the year of The Hobbit!!!

7:56 AM - 16 Jan 2014
Wait where are you seeing this? CNN has a different list.

7:59 AM - 16 Jan 2014
Chill out - #hobbit2 got the nom. @cnn as usual got things wrong.

8:02 AM - 16 Jan 2014
The Oscars is not about #movies anymore. Clearly other forces decide who to nominade.

8:02 AM - 16 Jan 2014
Everyone who saw The Hobbit (millions if not more) expected it to win the award

8:05 AM - 16 Jan 2014
They need a dumpster on the side of the stage at the #Oscars for the "winners" to put their awards in. It was rigged. The Hobbit was best

8:11 AM - 16 Jan 2014
found the #OscarNoms list. it was on http://movienews.com

8:13 AM - 16 Jan 2014
I hope that's the real one. The CNN one can't be right.

8:17 AM - 16 Jan 2014
For once I see why you always scream about CNN. That was a major mistake if Movie News is right

12:20 AM - 17 Jan 2014
Prediction: no one will ever name their baby boy "Oscar" ever again. Meanwhile babies named Bilbo, Gandalf, and Peter Jackson, up by 100000%

7:55 AM - 18 Jan 2014
I had a nightmare that the #Hobbit received no Best Picture nominations. And I never woke up from it! #horror

ON CINEMA ON HOLLYWOOD LEGENDS

Dr. Luther San

Originally from Sebastapol, Calif, **Dr. San's** career as a holistic healer got a real 'shot in the arm' when he came on the air to help **Tim Heidecker** cure a nagging foot problem with traditional holistic alternative medicine.

In later years, Tim and Dr. San had many 'ups and downs' as Dr. San guided him through life milestones like marriage, child-rearing, overcoming illness and addiction, unlocking the hidden keys to creative inspiration, running a successful small business, and learning the importance of **forgiveness** and acceptance.

Through it all, Dr. San has always been guided by a deep desire "to create something beautiful." For Tim in particular, it is this positive spirit of **optimism** that makes Dr. San a forever irreplaceable member of the **On Cinema Family**.

EPISODE 403
'I, Frankenstein' & 'Gimme Shelter'

Air date: January 22, 2014
Running time: 7:10 minutes

Tim's guests this week include Gregg Turkington and professional acupuncturist Dr. San, who has been treating Tim for a variety of health issues including a badly inflamed foot.

As part of his services, Dr. San "has been monitoring" Tim "for the past 24 hours." At Tim's invitation, the medico briefly sets forth the healing principles that make acupuncture the right tool for the job when it comes to Tim's diseased foot.

Based on the appearance of Tim's tongue and pulse, Dr. San has diagnosed him with an "overactive" liver, which is known in the industry as "liver fire." Dr. San's goal is to "smooth the liver so it doesn't mess up your digestion." When Tim wonders if this is a "holistic" approach to his foot infection, Dr. San confirms that it is: "Completely."

The medical theme continues into the review segment, as *I, Frankenstein* tells the familiar tale of the mad doctor's unholy creation. Per Tim, this "must-see" horror thriller depicts the Frankenstein monster "as you've never seen him before," which more than justifies its five-bag rating.

Gregg places this "great movie" alongside other "great series" like *Star Wars*, *Star Trek* and "the Bond pictures." As a "Frankenhead" or "Frankenfreak," Gregg can be trusted to rate each new chapter in the Frankenstein saga highly, especially when they're in color like this one. And that's just what he does here with his rating of five popcorn bags and "a couple of those bolts that Frankenstein has in his head."

Frankenstein is a fable of medical arrogance gone wrong, which gives Tim the perfect opportunity to get Dr. San's expert opinion on how "medicine is being mismanaged" in our own day. In response, the professional healer laments the overprescription of "heavy meds to balance out emotions," which may well be "killing the artists of the future."

Gregg reminds Tim that his show is called *On Cinema*, not *On Alternative Medicine*, and takes him to task for having "another Dr. Frankenstein sitting beside you" and "ruining our show." Tim and Dr. San counsel Gregg that acupuncture would ease his "stress" and "anger."

Brendan Fraser is back in the flesh for *Gimme Shelter*, a gritty sexual drama about a pregnant girl who runs away only to find that Fraser is her real father. Tim "loved this movie," which was "very confusing at many points" and also suffered from substandard performances (with the obvious exception of Brendan Fraser). The inclusion of "two funny scenes" makes this a worthy four-bagger.

Gregg is unsure whether he should be reviewing this "interesting movie" or talking about "medicinal leeches or some other quackery." Addressing viewers who may have "accidentally stumbled upon this show because you're interested in finding out about movies," he suggests they "turn the channel" because "that's not what we do on this show anymore." Putting those concerns aside, he gives *Gimme Shelter* five bags of popcorn.

Tim wants it known that as *On Cinema*'s host, he can "take it in any direction" he wants, and he currently finds acupuncture "a very interesting subject." Although he still loves movies, he doesn't see why they can't also discuss other topics. And since Dr. San's presence on the set is medically necessary, it's logical to involve him in the conversation.

Gregg is skeptical that Dr. San needs to monitor Tim's vital signs, considering that the groundbreaking film critics Siskel and Ebert "both had serious medical conditions" but didn't keep their doctors on hand while reviewing movies.

"If they had, maybe they'd be alive today," Tim points out. He proceeds to say that he doesn't care what Gregg thinks and declares that Dr. San is now "a permanent member of the *On Cinema* Family." He urges the audience not to "discount alternative medicine," particularly now that "typical medicine" has become "part of Obamacare." He doesn't have to pay insurance for Dr. San's therapy, he notes, "because I have to pay for it on my own." This is his own modest way of living out his conviction that "health care is a privilege; it's not a right."

As the lights dim, Tim tries to reason with Gregg about Dr. San's healing powers: "This guy is gonna get me better." Gregg complains that he has not been allowed to give his "popcorn ratings." Tim relents and orders the lights turned back on. Gregg then gives *Gimme Shelter* five bags of popcorn and "two certificates from the American Medical Association, debunking Dr. San."

EPISODE 404
'On Alternative Medicine on Cinema'

Air date: January 29, 2014
Running time: 7:07 minutes

His face marred by infected acupuncture sores, Tim encourages his fans to "forget Obamacare" and pursue wellness on their "own terms" by embracing "acupuncture" and "natural green medicine using herbs." Once again, Dr. San is on the program to give his perspective on the healing arts. Gregg Turkington is also here "to talk about movies a little bit later."

Tim assures Dr. San his treatment is helping with "whatever you're talking about there with the liver and everything." [Episode 403] He asks the physician whether the sores on his face are "natural," and Dr. San confirms that these inflamed blemishes are the result of the "toxins" fleeing Tim's body. "They're expressing themselves," he says.

Tim feels like a teenager with acne, only "zits don't hurt this much." He thanks Dr. San for "getting me back in the best shape of my life" and asks what "preemptive" steps he can take to prevent a recurrence of blood clots. Dr. San promises Tim he will "tonify your blood" and "smooth your liver *chi*."

Tim repeats that "one thing I love about acupuncture is that it's not something insurance covers." This gives him the God-given freedom to pay for it himself under the doctrine of personal responsibility. "If you have health problems, see an acupuncture," he advises us.

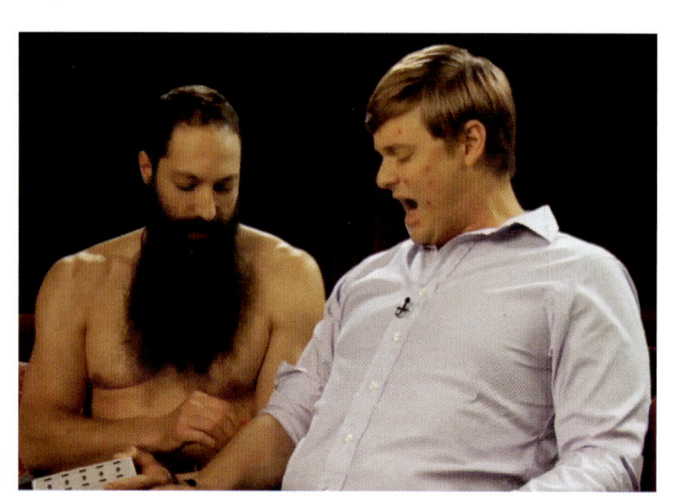

Returning to the "glib, light world of Hollywood," Tim introduces *That Awkward Moment*. Gregg interrupts him to claim that this is a movie "starring Dr. San and Tim Heidecker," which depicts "the awkward moment" when "a movie review show is ruined by quackery."

Tim tells Gregg his editorial comments are "not necessary" and provides his own synopsis of this knockabout comedy in which New York's wildest bachelors struggle to keep it real. Tim calls this "a funny, funny, funny, funny movie" for a total of five bags of popcorn.

Gregg also "liked it a lot," in part because it has a "good cast." He gives it five popcorn bags and throws in "a couple of dirty acupuncture needles" like the ones that "caused Tim to have infected sores on his face."

Labor Day stars Kate Winslet and Josh Brolin. Tim's summary is interrupted by the painful current Dr. San is sending into his arms through his electrified acupuncture needles. Tim asks the specialist to remove the needles temporarily so he can continue his review.

After he recovers, Tim proclaims that he "loved" *Labor Day*, which "should be up there with all the greats." It gets five popcorn bags and two sodas.

Gregg considers *Labor Day* "a serious movie" about "what happens when you pick up hitchhikers." He hopes the events depicted in this "cautionary tale" will never be visited upon *On Cinema* viewers. He gives it five bags of popcorn.

Gregg has a new edition of *On Cinema On Location* queued up, which reprises his well-received visit to the "cemetery lake" where *Hot Shots!* was first filmed. [Episode 103] When Tim questions why Gregg didn't film a new segment, Gregg responds that Tim has clearly stopped caring about "people that are interested in movie criticism." Having turned *On Cinema* into a "medicine show," Tim is certain to "lose 999 percent of the audience" anyway, so "what does it matter?"

Tim takes "great offense" at Gregg's remarks, which are "disrespectful" to him and to Dr. San. Gregg says, "I don't really care about Dr. San." Tim answers in kind, stating that he doesn't care about Gregg or his opinions. Furthermore, he doesn't care "what the audience thinks" of the show's new direction, because "the audience knows that I know what I'm doing, and this is what they should be watching."

Gregg concludes the episode by declaring that *On Cinema* has evolved into "a great show" for those who want to "learn how to get an infected face" from "dirty needles."

EPISODE 405
'The Lego Movie' & 'Robocop'

Air date: February 5, 2014
Running time: 6:06 minutes

Tim apologizes to the audience for his unsightly appearance; he has "what they call a Stage III infection" on his face due to Dr. San's use of unsanitized needles. This news earns a rueful chuckle from Gregg, who suspected all along that Dr. San's needles were "dirty."

Tim has come to question Dr. San's medical *bona fides*. He adds that "if anybody out there knows where he is, I need to speak with him," as do Tim's lawyer and the police. Furthermore, he hopes Dr. San will be "found and arrested and prosecuted and put in jail."

With Dr. San exposed at last as a charlatan, Tim and Gregg are excited to get "back to movies." *The Lego Movie* parlays the popular plastic building toy into a cinematic *tour de force* turbocharged by the voices of Channing Tatum, Liam Neeson, Morgan Freeman and many more. A feverish and semicoherent Tim gives this "movie about Legos" three stars.

Gregg posits that Tim is missing something special about this film. It's not just about Legos; "it's about creativity and the things you can make with Legos," such as the film itself. He says "this could end up being another franchise like Bond that has legs," which is "funny because it's called Lego."

Gregg gives it five bags of popcorn and "five big grocery bags filled with little Lego pieces so you can make your own Lego movie at home."

This reminds Tim of the "Leggo my Eggo" catchphrase, and Gregg agrees this was "a funny ad campaign" for this "waffle or pastry sort of thing you'd have for breakfast."

Robocop is back in 3D as Tim introduces a stellar cast featuring Gary Oldman and Robocop. Gregg says "there's nothing new as far as the story" in this high-tech remake. Being as there has never been a sequel to the first *Robocop* film, he questions why they would want to tell us the original tale all over again. On the other hand, if you loved the first movie, "you're probably gonna love this twice as much!" Gregg gives it his "highest recommendation," which in this case is five bags of popcorn and "a little miniature robot" offered as "a keepsake of the experience."

It's been a while since we've gotten a bulletin on Gregg's "500 Movies in 500 Days" bid for *Guinness Book* immortality. It turns out that when he checked his mailbox "this morning," he was "delighted" to find that "some of the top names in film have sent in their well-wishes." For proof, he plays a video of actor Jimmy McNichol [Episode 208] affirming his solidarity with Gregg's effort. Afterward, Gregg tells Tim how nice it is "to be recognized by your peers."

Tim announces that he will not appear on the show next week because he's "going in for a series of operations" and his doctor has prescribed a period of "no work." He offers Gregg "the position of host for next week."

Gregg is happy to accept: "That sounds neat!" To ensure that the show runs smoothly, Tim promises to provide Gregg with "movies" as well as a guest "who knows what they're talking about."

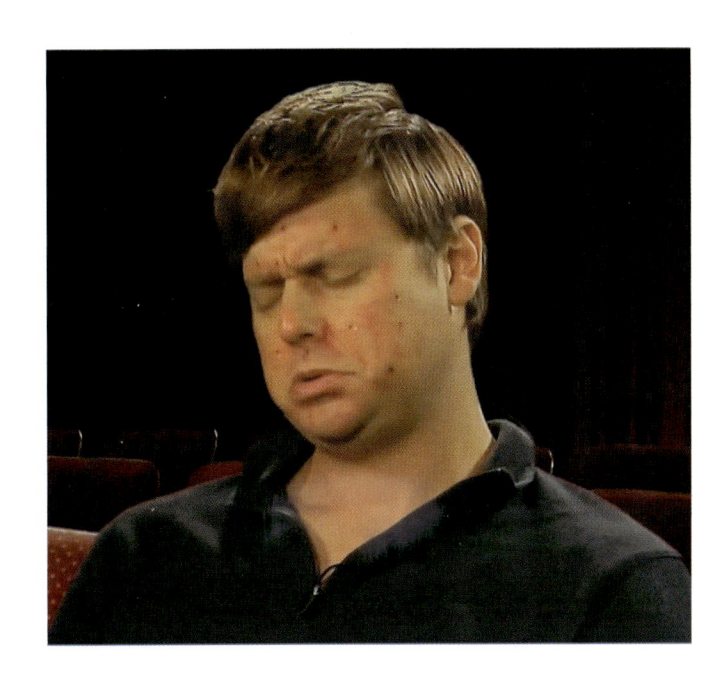

On Cinema On Line

11:18 AM - 5 Feb 2014
"@lordgnarington: @greggturkington didn't do his homework there are 2 sequels to Robocop, a mini-series and a tv series." G is this true??

11:24 AM - 5 Feb 2014
I know about those--they're not official sequels. Just movies "inspired by" the 1st Robocop. They don't count.

11:25 AM - 5 Feb 2014
i honestly don't know if I want this kind of slip up to happen next week. considering my options.

11:26 AM - 5 Feb 2014
It's not a slip-up. I knew about those "tribute" movies. They are not true sequels.

11:27 AM - 5 Feb 20144
@greggturkington bullshit.

11:27 AM - 5 Feb 2014
reevaluating my offer to have you host next week. will need to talk to the #OnCinema family.

11:34 AM - 5 Feb 2014
Your last casting choice, Dr San, was a big mistake. I think the viewers deserve better. I am ready to do the job! #expert

8:02 AM - 6 Feb 2014
please help me decide. should i still let @greggturkington host. #greggyes or #greggno

9:48 PM - 6 Feb 2014
A #greggno vote is a #DrSanYES vote. Please vote thoughtfully. Let @timheidecker know.

8:48 PM - 6 Feb 2014
Still mulling the @greggturkington hosting decision. Votes are leaning against. Tough call for me.

5:31 PM - 7 Feb 2014
The @greggturkington hosting decision will come on Monday. Your opinions have been noted.

7:45 AM - 10 Feb 2014
Good morning. This Wednesday @greggturkington will host #oncinema - this is all I will say on the matter. Now I'm off to the virgin isles.

11:21 AM - 10 Feb 2014
Glad the votes favored me in a landslide. Have a great trip! Get well soon. Hope you get #JackReacher as an in flight #movie!

11:28 AM - 10 Feb 2014
Hey @IanMcKellen would you be a guest on the top rated web movie review series "On Cinema" this Wednesday? We are #HobbitFriendly

11:30 AM - 10 Feb 2014
Hello @Martinfreeman Would BILBO BAGGANS be a guest on the top rated web movie review series this Wednesday? We are #HobbitFriendly

11:29 AM - 10 Feb 2014
as I told you on air we are booking the guest. stop bothering these people and using our name.

8:05 PM - 11 Feb 2014
good luck @greggturkington - The world is watching.

Gregg shares his movie expertise with Professor Larry Turman.

EPISODE 406
'The Girl on a Bicycle' & 'Endless Love'

Air date: February 11, 2014
Running time: 6:15 minutes

While Tim recuperates from a "series of operations" for his stage III face infection, fill-in host Gregg Turkington takes charge of "the top show in movie criticism today." With new titles and a sleek contemporary jazz theme, Gregg is on track to rebrand *On Cinema* as "the newest and hottest, most innovative film/cinema commentary review program on the web."

Gregg's guest is "fellow film expert" Larry Turman, who is best known for his Oscar-nominated production work on Dustin Hoffman's *The Graduate* and other fan favorites. Eager to establish his qualifications as an *On Cinema* guest right off the bat, Mr. Turman plugs his "master's program at USC's film school" and boasts that "I see a lot of movies."

Gregg is thrilled to have a chance to chat about foreign films with a USC-approved film professor. First up is *The Girl on a Bicycle*, which examines a sophisticated Franco-Italian romantic mixup through the eyes of an "international cast." Gregg says this classic plot device is "a ménage à trois, as they say in foreign films." Though this was definitely "not a Bond movie," Gregg felt "it had its charms." It gets five bags of popcorn.

Professor Turman "didn't like it" much, rating it as a mere three-bagger from his expert perspective. Delving into his thought process, he notes that Woody Allen's *Blue Jasmine* [Episode 304] is more his idea of a five-bag film.

Endless Love updates the *Romeo and Juliet* myth, making this classic tale of star-crossed love intelligible for a new era. Gregg calls it "fun" and "a little painful at times." He gives it five bags of popcorn. Mr. Turman scoffs at this: "Jesus, you're some critic."

Next, Gregg enlists the professor's expert assistance with *Popcorn Classics*, which focuses this week on Sean Connery's *Medicine Man*. When Larry does not remember this film, Gregg has to remind him that this "unforgettable" film "was sort of an instant classic at the time."

After Mr. Turman challenges Gregg's stance as "a purported expert," Gregg pulls out the list of movies he has watched so far in his record-setting bid to view 500 movies in 500 days. He's up to 127 movies already!

Mr. Turman advocates a different approach to cinema: He only wants to watch movies he thinks he will enjoy because they're likely to be good. Here, Gregg finds a bit of common ground with the irascible expert by specifying that he too prefers "good" movies.

"Nobody loves a bad movie!" he exclaims. "Fortunately, they don't make a lot of bad movies." Indeed, this is one of the things that define cinema as "a fine art," unlike music, which produces "a lot of bad songs."

"We seem to disagree," Larry tells him.

Gregg defends his theory: "You have to love movies, I think, to be in this business."

"You should do what I spent 40 years doing, making movies," Turman responds. Gregg says he's "not qualified" for that work. "You're talking like you're qualified!" Larry fires back.

Gregg tries to move on, but Larry wants to pin him down on why he's qualified to host a movie review show. Gregg cites his possession of "one of the biggest video libraries in the state," which is the fruit of "15 years" of labor spent "collecting movies." He also explains the "brilliant" coding system he uses to keep tabs on this "historic archive." [Episode 301] Turman concedes that Gregg is "an expert in filing."

Gregg concludes by telling his august guest that it's been nice to have "a peer" on the show — particularly one whose "expert opinions" have helped Gregg to "cover it all" in this episode. He draws a stark contrast between Mr. Turman and Tim, noting that the latter "shows up and takes his shoes off and shows people welts and things on his legs" while talking about "acupuncture" and other "quackery."

As the cinema lights dim, Mr. Turman seems glad the episode is over and he can leave.

On Cinema On Line

12:14 PM - 12 Feb 2014
If @timheidecker isn't busy reading websites on curing cancer using corn, he should check out the non-stop kudos coming my way for hosting!

3:56 PM - 13 Feb 2014
your so-called "triumph" is a disaster. very low numbers and 12 thumbs down.

1:05 PM - 14 Feb 2014
I'm not concerned with numbers. I'm concerned with presenting quality film criticism and expert opinions.

7:47 PM - 17 Feb 2014
hey @greggturkington i'm back and feeling great! my guest dropped out for this week. can you come by? fun #movies!

7:50 PM - 17 Feb 2014
Yes! Thank you Tim.

EPISODE 407
'Pompeii'

Air date: February 19, 2014
Running time: 8:24 minutes

Longtime viewers can breathe a sigh of relief this week, as Tim's facial sores have healed and he's back in the reins of On Cinema.

He thanks last week's fill-in host and this week's guest, Gregg Turkington, for taking the saddle during the previous episode. "That was a lot of fun," Gregg tells him. Tim also thanks all the fans who wrote in to tell him that they missed him and "the way that the show should normally be."

In a fun segment, Tim details his experiences visiting St. Thomas in the "Virgin Isles," where he "got a whole sort of a rehab" that included penicillin for his stage III face infection. He embarked "on a whole new regimen" that entailed "a new haircut, new threads" and quality time with the many "cool people" he met on his Caribbean getaway. The end result? Tim feels "so much better now!"

He also has some bad news: Gregg was "right" when he guessed that Tim has diabetes. [Episode 401] He has come to terms with the reality that he will be "living with" this diagnosis going forward. He has also been "checking out a new website called CureYourself.com," which offers simple tips for overcoming diabetes with flax seeds, which are "very high in helping the blood work properly."

Pulling out a bowl of flax seed, Tim demonstrates how he has been dosing himself with "two big spoonfuls of flax seed every day."

Gregg doesn't think the flax will help, but Tim guarantees that "if you overdose on flax seed, it actually reverses some of the side effects of diabetes." As proof, he cites the fact that he already feels "100-percent better" due to this "wonder drug."

Tim thanks Gregg again for his "fine job" as the fill-in host and asks how Gregg liked working with film legend Larry Turman. Gregg responds that Mr. Turman "had some interesting opinions" but also "had some of his facts wrong." In Professor Turman's defense, Gregg acknowledges that this is typical of "so-called academics" who "aren't really film buffs" and thus "don't understand cinema." While Gregg would not invite Turman "back on the show," he deserves credit for doing "the best that he could."

This surprises Tim, who found that in a recent poll of On Cinema viewers, "Larry Turman ranked number-one on the list of all-time favorite guests of the show."

Gregg concedes that Turman "was definitely an improvement over Dr. San or Ayaka." But he remarks that the poll "wouldn't have included the hosts — people like yourself or myself." Tim denies that Gregg's status as a guest has changed because he briefly acted as the host. Gregg disagrees on the grounds that presidents continue being referred to as such even after they've left office. The same "protocol" applies here, he argues.

Today's movie is Pompeii, which spotlights Tim's "favorite actor Kiefer Sutherland." In this historical biopic, a gladiator rescues the woman he loves from an unwanted marriage in the shadow of the Vesuvius disaster. Tim identifies this "Pompeii movie" as a film "about volcanoes," but Gregg believes it's also "kind of a gladiator movie." Although it doesn't rise to the level of Russell Crowe's Gladiator, Gregg still gives it five bags of popcorn and "a couple baskets of dried volcanic rock."

Tim, who loves "volcano movies," gives it five popcorn bags and a soda. This reminds Gregg that he recently watched Joe Versus the Volcano as part of his "500 Movies in 500 Days" world record. He also discloses that his "only copy" of the list of films he's screened so far, which he needs for submission to the Guinness judges, vanished after he pulled it out to impress Larry Turman. Tim reassures him that "we'll find it."

Today in Popcorn Classics, Gregg spices up the proceedings with a "twofold" Popcorn Classic: He has brought in a home-recorded VHS tape of The Hobbit — which is otherwise not available on video — as well as a package of Jolly Time popcorn. He advises viewers to tape The Hobbit off HBO, "get the popcorn" and settle in for "a fun night."

Tim talks up his own Blu-Ray edition of The Hobbit, which includes commentary by King of Movies Peter Jackson. But Gregg says he would prefer to leave such "scrap" scenes "on the cutting room floor" and "watch the movie the way it was intended to be seen."

As the episode ends, Tim takes Gregg to task for bringing "homemade" movies to the show. Gregg protests that on the contrary, The Hobbit was made by a major studio.

EPISODE 408
'Welcome to Yesterday' & 'Non-Stop'

Air date: February 26, 2014
Running time: 10:22 minutes

Tim is joined by his guest, Gregg Turkington, for a preliminary look at *Welcome to Yesterday* (a.k.a. *Almanac*). This film stars "a bunch of no-names" who play "a group of teens" who find themselves trapped in a time-travel adventure. Tim hails this "sci-fi, fun, friendly movie" as "a classic time-machine movie." However, it would've benefited from the proven star power Tom Cruise or Mel Gibson could've brought to the lead roles. He gives it five bags of popcorn anyway, "because it is about time travel."

Gregg warns us that *Almanac* is "a little scary" due to the inherently scary nature of time travel as a concept. He gives it five bags of popcorn primarily because it's "probably the best time-travel movie I've seen since *Back to the Future 3*."

Non-Stop is a high-stakes aviation mystery that tosses Liam Neeson and the "very pretty" Julianne Moore into a deadly melting pot on board a speeding airliner. Tim calls this "terrific" thriller "the best movie I've seen in a long time" and cheers leading man Neeson "for doing these movies all the time." It gets six bags each of soda and popcorn.

Gregg found this "dark" film "pretty frightening," in part because "it wasn't the comedy that *Airplane!* was." He gives it five bags of popcorn and "a cell phone so you can call 911 if that ever happens to you."

Tim asks viewers to show their appreciation for Neeson's performance in *Non-Stop* and other films by writing to the company that produced the film. His suggested text: "Thank you, Liam Neeson, from the *On Cinema* Family."

On a personal note, Tim says he's "at a place in my life" where Tom Cruise and Tom Hanks are at risk of losing their top spots on his "list of all-time favorite actors" to Liam Neeson. "You've got some competition on your ass," he tells the veteran actors.

Gregg is more impressed with stars like Roger Moore, who originally made his mark as one of the top three actors portraying James Bond, but Tim cuts this argument short on the principle that the Bond movies are "junk."

This week on *Popcorn Classics*, Tim is exasperated that Gregg's copy of *The Slipper and the Rose* is another home-recorded tape. "We're gonna get in trouble from the MPAA," he says, referring to the official film industry organization that prohibits the unauthorized copying of classic films like this one.

Gregg is less worried, because "the only way to get this movie is to tape it off television," leaving him with little choice in the matter. But Tim feels the generic tape box looks "unprofessional" and "amateur" and instructs Gregg "not to do this any more."

Gregg worries that this restriction will result in "a lower quality of selections," but Tim is certain "no one wants to see this old musical junk" in any case.

Moving on, Tim has "big breaking news for *On Cinema* fans": Tim has been making his own movie, starring Tim and written, financed and directed entirely by himself. Now, he's ready to share "an exclusive clip" from this "international spy thriller called *Decker*."

In the clip, U.S. President Davidson (Joe Estevez) summons Special Agent Jack Decker to the Oval Room of the White House to face the looming crisis of a nuclear-armed Iran. A contemptuous Decker reminds the president that "I told you assholes to watch out for Iran, and you didn't listen to me."

President Davidson tells him immediate action is needed: "Otherwise, we're gonna have World War II, nuclear style." He directs Decker to "go to Teheran" and "assassinate every fucking Iranian you see." Decker is willing to take this dangerous assignment. "But not for you — for the American people."

The president wishes him good luck. "Luck is for pussies like you," Decker sneers. "All I need is this gun."

Back on the set, Tim asks Gregg how many bags of popcorn the clip deserves. Gregg finds the question irrelevant since the *Decker* scene is "just a home movie, and you don't review things like that on our show."

Tim responds that these are just "theoretical scenes that we're gonna be presenting to investors next year." But Gregg remains skeptical, not least because the CGI interior "didn't look like the White House at all."

On Cinema On Line

7:10 PM - 27 Feb 2014
I am planning a dramatic, show-stopping, #OnCinema Oscar Special finale that will be talked about for YEARS.

7:12 PM - 27 Feb 2014
The finale to Sunday's #OnCinema Oscar Special is going to blow your mind. My biggest production yet. Don't miss History being made.

6:11 PM - 28 Feb 2014
I have goosebumps thinking about my surprise finale to our #OnCinema Oscar special on Sunday night. It is going to be SPECTACULAR. #movies

5:13 PM - 1 Mar 2014
just booked a HUGE guest for tomorrow. an oscar nominee! #OnCinemaOscars

5:14 PM - 1 Mar 2014
and apparently @greggturkington has a big surprise in store. looking forward to it. #OnCinemaOscars

12:44 PM - 2 Mar 2014
When #TheHobbit wins Best Movie award tonight make sure you are sitting down, with a box of tissues nearby. It will be emotional.

ON CINEMA ON HOLLYWOOD LEGENDS

Larry Turman

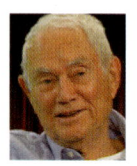

Lawrence Turman is an American film producer and amateur cineaste whose credits include **The Graduate**, **Heroes**, **Short Circuit**, **Mass Appeal**, **The Thing** (1982), **The Thing** (2011), and Ringo Starr's **Caveman**. Notably, Starr first met his wife, **Barbara Bach**, on the set of **Caveman**, which was filmed in Mexico.

Before taking the life-changing role of **Lana** in **Caveman**, Ms. Bach played the comely KGB agent **Anya Amasova** in 1977's **The Spy Who Loved Me**, which marked **Sir Roger Moore's** third **Silver Screen** appearance as the one and only **James Bond**.

Mr. Turman was born in 1926.

SECOND ANNUAL OSCARS SPECIAL
Live Broadcast from Hollywood's Biggest Night

Air date: March 4, 2014
Running time: 1:59:03

This year, Oscar Night is introduced by W. C. Fields (as impressioned by Mark Proksch), who then introduces Tim and Gregg.

Gregg is reveling in his status as co-host, and he's so excited about *The Hobbit II*'s Oscar chances that he's dressed in a "Hobbit-ween" costume patterned on Bilbo Baggins' outfit. He has also invited some fellow Hobbit-heads down as guests of the show.

Tim, who loves Oscar Night, is feeling "positive." In the festive spirit of Billy Crystal, he performs a new original song called "Oscar Fever."

Gregg's Hobbit pipe is a distraction, so Tim takes it away from him. He then demonstrates *On Cinema*'s new "Info-Touch Wall," an interactive screen with all the Oscar facts right at its fingertips.

A Look Behind the Oscar Scenes
Gregg has done some legwork to get behind-the-scenes footage of Oscar Night preparations. He transports us to Hollywood's Dolby Theatre for a sneak peek through the glass doors and into the empty room where Oscar's show-biz lightning will eventually strike.

Will Oscar Smile Upon Bilbo?
Although *Hobbit II* was not nominated, Gregg thinks it's a shoo-in as a write-in for Best Picture. He also anticipates that the Best Original Screenplay gold will go to *The Lone Ranger*.

Tim speculates that a lot of this year's nominees are films "people don't like to see" because they "are not blockbusters" like *Riddick* and *Despicable Me 2*. Could this be why Billy Crystal has given up hosting the Oscars? Tim guesses yes.

He tries to cut to Professor Larry Turman, who's down on the red carpet, but the video feed won't work.

Alarmingly, Tim predicts the current conflict in Ukraine will lead to "a nuclear world war" within two months. He pledges to monitor this dangerous situation throughout the night.

Even though Tim's Oscar Night drinking caused problems last year, he intends to continue drinking because "we are on our way out" due to nuclear war. Further, Tim is "in control of myself," has "never been happier" and is very healthy thanks to his "constant flax intake."

Gregg asks W. C. for his Oscar picks. "*Poppy*, by me, 1936," says the incorrigible funnyman. When asked for a more recent picture, he chooses *Gravity* because its special effects were "stupendous."

Tim asks W. C. if he also does a Jim Carrey impression. "That I do," says the comic legend. "He's one of my favorite young moon cows." After nailing Mr. Carrey, W. C. pays tribute to Mae West and others.

A second attempt to get Larry Turman on the line fails, causing Tim to throw his champagne glass on the floor and curse at the crew.

Ellen Swings and Misses
Tim suggests that instead of hiring Ellen DeGeneres, Oscar could've crowdsourced hosts from the audience.

"It's best to have a professional host when you're putting on a broadcast," Gregg argues. "Not somebody who's gonna have a tantrum and throw things."

They do agree that Ellen DeGeneres doesn't have what it takes. "So far, we're off to a terrible start," Tim says. However, Gregg promises to save the night with "a big, bombastic, spectacular finale."

Tim's Story
Tim screens an original film of his "Oscar fantasy," in which Joe Estevez and John Aprea tread the boards to announce that Tim has won the Oscar for *Tim's Story* (directed by Tim Storey), beating out Tom Hanks, Tom Cruise, Robert De Niro and Jon Voight.

In his lengthy acceptance speech, Tim consoles Cruise for not winning for *Jack Reacher*, reminds America that "you don't have to listen to Obamacare," and shares a tender moment with his wife, Julianne Moore.

Gandalf Snubbed Again
Everyone is unhappy that Jared Leto edged Sir Ian McKellan out for Best Actor. But Tim is far more disturbed by the deteriorating state of affairs in Crimea. "If I had my way, we would be pressing the button and Moscow would be obliterated," he says.

Tim sarcastically thanks Gregg for wearing a "stupid Hobbit costume" and lets him know "the entire crew has been laughing at you behind your back."

Gregg thanks Pink Elephant Liquors for supplying the alcohol that is already making Tim "completely incoherent."

Tim has ample reason to drink heavily, as he sees it. A text from a friend alerts him that Putin is about to make his move: "We are done for, probably by the end of the week."

Tim's "Oscar Fantasy" strikes Oscar gold!

A Stroll Down Oscar's Memory Lane

In a segment called *Down Oscar Memory Lane*, Gregg and Tim salute early Oscar winners like *Wings* (1928), which had to vie for Oscar gold despite a lack of CGI and other modern technologies that can give films visual interest and "mask the shortcomings."

Estevez on Decker

Joe Estevez turns up to give his actorly perspective on the Oscars. "What is it like working on *Decker*?" Tim asks.

"It's terrific," Joe says. To drive this point home, Tim premieres a brand-new scene in which President Davidson is confronted by Decker in the secret presidential elevator. Decker discloses that while torturing a 12-year-old in Tehran, he stumbled on a scheme to assassinate Davidson using a mole within the Secret Service. To stop this plot, Decker needs all the Secret Service files, and Davidson needs to "wear a fuckin' wire."

Back on the set, Joe has a gift for his co-star: A small container of flax seed, long prized for its healing properties!

Gregg has a question from viewers: "What's it like shooting scenes for a movie that you know will never be completed or will never air?" Tim forbids Joe to answer.

Meanwhile, special guest Charlie Chaplin (Mark Proksch) displays the silent-era quirks that made his "Little Tramp" character a national byword.

After Joe offers his personal Oscar predictions, Tim asks him for an insider's peek into the Oscar galaxy. "There's a lot of jealousy," Joe reports.

Tim wants to know some details about Gregg's finale. "It sort of encompasses a hundred years of film history into just a few seconds," Gregg hints.

Stump the Host!

It's time now for a new twist on an old segment as Gregg plays *Stump the Host!* If Tim can answer just three out of five tough movie questions, Gregg will donate $1,000 to the charity of Tim's choice.

Tim correctly identifies the producer of *Casablanca* and the star of 1932's *Dracula*, but he misses the number of Oscar nominations *Pretty Woman* received and the two-letter abbreviation of the international mutual aid fellowship Gregg thinks Tim should join before hosting another Oscars special.

A Salute to Oscar's Martyrs

Tim salutes "Oscar's lost heroes" in the form of "people who have passed on and died." These include Alan Ladd, Albert Dekker, the gifted Inger Stevens and *On Cinema*'s own Charlie Chaplin.

After this somber remembrance, Tim threatens to throw Mark, Joe and the Hobbit-heads off the set if they won't stop talking in the wings. He also threatens to throw Gregg off the show "unless you start picking up your game and talking about something people care about."

Charlie Chaplin tries to lighten the mood by calling the Oscar Special "a jolly good show." But this only prompts Tim to lament Gregg's "dumb choice" to invite "this loser" to perform Golden Age Comedy impressions. Gregg rejects this negative spin, claiming that Mark's segments are preferable to another appearance by "your acupuncturist, Dr. San."

Oscar's Folly: The First Century

As Tim calls for more champagne, Gregg presents a new segment entitled *When Oscar Got It Wrong*, which is based on a successful Facebook post. He notes that *The Wizard of Oz* never won an Oscar even though 1998's *Shakespeare in Love* did. He also thinks 1981 should have been an Oscar tie shared between actual winner *Chariots of Fire* and the unrivaled Popcorn Classic *Raiders of the Lost Ark*.

Tim does his best to cut this exhaustive segment short, even tearing up one of Gregg's cue cards. But Gregg persists right up to the advent of *The Hobbit II*, which hangs in the balance tonight.

When Oscar Met Sally...

After the break, Tim and Gregg are joined by the unforgettable Sally "Hot Lips" Kellerman of *M*A*S*H* legend.

Sally brings us back in time to the 1970 Oscar awards, where a young Sally Kellerman found it "exciting" not just to be nominated but also to sing onstage with then-pop divas Petula Clark and Burt Reynolds. She then recalls how she had to stand like "a wooden Indian" to prevent her breasts from popping out of her dress.

Tim objects strongly to the "upset" in which Sally's Oscar went to Helen Hayes. "I'm glad she's dead," he adds.

"I'm glad she's dead now, too," Sally sighs, "so she doesn't have to hear that."

She goes on to detail how she parlayed a TV acting career on the *Star Trek* pilot into a big-screen Close Encounter of the Oscar Kind when she was offered the legendary "Hot Lips" role by Bob Altman of *M*A*S*H* fame.

This mention of *Star Trek* piques Gregg's interest. He asks Sally if she knows which *Star Trek* film was set in San Francisco. Unfortunately, she hasn't seen these films.

"Thoughts on Ukraine?" Tim asks. "I don't have a clue," Sally answers. Even so, she firmly dismisses Tim's theory that "nuclear war is upon us." Gregg sides with Sally: Viewers should "think about *The Hobbit* and not dwell on fantastical situations."

Gregg also lets Sally know that although Tim is "a good guy," she should be wary if he ever contacts her about "a movie called *Decker*" because it's "not really a real movie."

*Sally Kellerman of M*A*S*H pleads for calm in the face of Putin's Crimean aggression*

An Oscar Night "Hobbit-hug" from Peter Jackson.

Tim, however, urges Sally to make her own choices in life, just as she did when she worked with the uncompromising Robert Altman.

Playing the "Fields"
Gregg interviews Mark on the art of the impressionist while Tim samples some Chinese-style food from show sponsor Red Flower.

Gregg asks Mark what kind of movies W.C. Fields would make if he were still alive. Mark presumes he'd favor "buddy comedies" along the lines of *48 Hours*.

"Do you think alcohol is what killed W.C. Fields?" Gregg wonders.

"Oh, absolutely." Gregg advises Mark to pass this news on to Tim.

We also learn that the life of a Fields impersonator typically entails working along the Grapevine and in towns like Pixley, with a strong focus on "old folks' homes" and "hospice care."

Tim spits a mouthful of Chinese food onto the floor. "There's something off about that," he mutters.

A Hobbit-Head's Oscar Fantasy
Gregg has made his own Oscar fantasy film, which shows Peter Jackson receiving the Oscar he earned for *The Hobbit II*. In an personal cameo reminiscent of Hitchcock, Jackson gets a congratulatory Hobbit-hug from none other than Gregg himself!

On stage, Jackson thanks "Hollywood's number-one film buff, Gregg Turkington," promising him that "you will always be the number-one Hobbit-head in my book."

The Return of Oscar Fever
Tim does a reprise of "Oscar Fever" by popular online request. Unfortunately, he has to vomit halfway through.

Mark performs an extended W. C. Fields juggling-and-dance routine as Gregg tries to help Tim sober up offstage.

You Gotta Close Big
Back in the host seat, Tim complains that the 2014 Oscar crop consists of movies of no lasting consequence. In the meantime, Putin "is playing chess with the world." Unless the USA launches a first strike, Tim says, Russian missiles will soon take out New York and other major targets.

Switching gears, he asks Gregg for some info on his surprise finale.

"You gotta close big," Gregg says. With this rule in mind, he has been working "for the past few weeks" on what is "probably the greatest finale to any variety special, any awards show ever presented."

"I promise you that you will not be disappointed," he promises.

"The finale for the human race will be in the next six weeks." Tim says gloomily between mouthfuls of Red Flower's donated noodles. "It'll be atomic bombs."

And there's more bad news in store, as both Peter Jackson and *The Hobbit II* have been snubbed by Oscar. Although initially dismayed, Gregg concludes that "it's all part of a setup" for *The Hobbit III* to sweep the awards in 2015.

Viva El Oscar!
Tim has a list of thanks, which include "my hero from 10 years from now — me," as well as God, Vladimir Putin, and Harry Truman for "being the first fuckin' guy to drop nuclear bombs on the world." He then introduces "Gregg Turkington's stupid surprise."

Gregg counters that in fact, the finale is "the culmination of all my years as a film expert."

Laboriously hoisting a red curtain, Gregg reveals "500" VHS tapes from his personal collection, which have been arranged on end in a curious pattern.

"This one's for Bilbo!" he cries. "This one's for Peter Jackson. Viva el Oscar!" He knocks one tape over, which eventually causes most of the others to fall down. Viewed from above, the fallen tapes spell out "OSCER."

"Gregg Turkington's big surprise," Tim grumbles. "Oscar with an E."

"It's spelled both ways," Gregg says. Tim rejects this theory and speculates that if he'd spelled the word with an A, all of the tapes would've fallen over.

"I thought it was pretty neat," Gregg says glumly. He walks out.

"I want to thank Gregg Turkington for embarrassing himself in front of a live TV audience," Tim says. "He is no longer part of *On Cinema*. He's done."

"Feast your eyes on Hollywood, California!"

57

On Cinema On Line

11:21 PM - 2 Mar 2014
Reviews worldwide are in. "Gregg's sensational staged Oscar tribute finale was the highlight of an uneven broadcast"

11:23 PM - 2 Mar 2014
Oscer can be spelled Oscer OR Oscar as I told Tim and as anyone can see on the internet. Hundreds of examples of both.

9:33 AM - 4 Mar 2014
it's #Oscar not #OSCER

ON CINEMA ON HOLLYWOOD LEGENDS

Peter Jackson

Peter Jackson originally hails from New Zealand but nevertheless feels very much at home in the misty realms of **Middle-Earth** where he has made a world-class name not just for himself but also for **Bilbo Baggins**, **Gandalf** and all of the other fantastical creatures he brought to unforgettable life in his blockbusting **Lord of the Rings** and **Hobbit** franchise movies.

An all-time favorite of film buff **Gregg Turkington**, Mr. Jackson is a serious film buff in his own right and often cites **Lord of the Rings** (1978) as a major inspiration for his own **Hobbit** movies, which have sold millions worldwide to date and continue to do so at the time of this writing.

Though often snubbed by Oscar, Mr. Jackson has received a star on the **Hollywood Walk of Fame**, which can be seen at 6801 Hollywood Boulevard.

EPISODE 409
'Need for Speed' & 'Walk of Shame'

Air date: March 5, 2014
Running time: 8:03 minutes

Tim's guest, Gregg Turkington, seems even happier than usual to be appearing "on what I think is becoming one of the most valuable resources on the web."

Need for Speed is a revenge-driven race car thriller featuring Michael Keaton of *Jack Frost* fame. [Episode 305] This "great film" was one of Tim's "favorite movies of the year."

Just as important, it brings Aaron Paul (TV's *Breaking Bad*) to the big screen as an undisputed "movie star." This is a crucial development at a cultural moment when people have been saying that TV shows like *The Sopranos* and *Mad Men* "are better than movies." Now, the shoe is firmly on the other foot as "movies like *Need for Speed* come out and everyone jumps for joy because they are better than TV shows."

He gives the film five popcorn bags and two sodas. Gregg, who likes "action and adventure and things like that," gives it five bags of popcorn, period.

Walk of Shame stars Elizabeth Banks, James Marsden and Tig Notaro as an unexpected one-night stand turns the career woes of a TV news anchor upside-down. Gregg dings this "great movie" for being "a little bit unrealistic" and "a little bit insincere, plot-wise." Those issues aside, he "loved it so much" that he "can't knock it," making it a shoo-in for his coveted five-bag rating.

For Tim, the film was reminiscent of the 2005 Johnny Cash biopic *Walk the Line*. That's just one of the "many different coincidences that happen in movies," he reasons, since there are "only so many words" you can use in titles.

Next, Tim has created a brand-new segment called *Movie History*. In this first installment, he goes back in time to uncover the real facts about "the death of VHS."

Through Tim's research, we learn that in 2006, New Alliance Cinema released a VHS edition of David Cronenberg's *A History of Violence*, which would prove to be the last significant film ever released in this format. "So that's the end of the story there, when it comes to VHS," he concludes.

Gregg defends his preferred format, declaring that he "buys 30 or 40 movies a week on VHS." Tim reminds Gregg that top-rated new films like *The Hobbit* and *Jack Reacher* are not available on video. But Gregg points out that you only have to tape such films to enjoy them in the VHS format. That's far preferable to the situation with Blu-Rays, which don't allow you to record movies like *The Hobbit* off the television. The argument ends in a draw, as Tim says Blu-Rays have superior image quality and Gregg rejects this claim as "debatable."

Tim then announces that by popular demand, he will host a new episode of *Stump the Buff*, a "quiz contestant show" in which Gregg must correctly answer tricky questions about movie lore. This time around, Gregg has a shot at a $1,000 cash payout if he can answer just three out of five questions, or $2,000 for all five. Tim will show him five movie stills, and Gregg must provide the titles.

In the first round, Gregg easily gets *Gone With the Wind* correct, but only after misidentifying it as *Casablanca* on his first try, which counts as a failure. In the second, he misses *The Godfather II* due to a technicality involving sequel titling protocols. His luck improves as he spots the house from *Guarding Tess* and one of the people from *Just the Way You Are*, leaving him only one correct answer away from raking in Tim's $1,000 jackpot.

The last still shows James T. Kirk and Captain Spock standing near San Francisco's Golden Gate Bridge. This is a true "Sophie's Choice" for Gregg, as he must either reaffirm his deeply held conviction that this image comes from *Star Trek II: The Wrath of Khan* or debase himself by providing Tim's expected answer of *Star Trek IV: The Voyage Home* in order to win $1,000.

Star Trek II is Gregg's answer, which Tim predictably calls incorrect. When Gregg challenges Tim's reasoning, Tim stands firm: "I fired you from the show last season because of this."

"And you brought me back because you were wrong," Gregg says. The bickering continues, but the episode ends without any clear resolution to the conflict.

EPISODE 410
'Muppets Most Wanted'

Air date: March 12, 2014
Running time: 6:46 minutes

As *On Cinema* prepares to lay its fourth season to rest, Tim "appreciates all the support" he has received from the *On Cinema* Family in recent weeks: "I'm just blessed to have the audience that we have."

He also thanks his guest, Gregg Turkington, for his "support" throughout the season. "I wouldn't miss it for the world!" Gregg exclaims. "Season finale!"

Due to a glut of special features and guest appearances, there's only time for one movie this week. But it's a hot one, as Ricky Gervais and Salma Hayek confront Big Bird and the gang in *Muppets Most Wanted*.

For Tim, this movie is "as good as Muppets can get." In layman's terms, that means it gets five bags of popcorn and five cups of soda. Gregg says the film works for adults and is "perfect for kids." He gives it five bags of popcorn, along with "five newly bundled newborn babies."

With the last of the season's must-see flicks out of the way, it's time to visit once again with Joe Estevez. [Episode 203, *Decker* film clip] It's not all fun and games, though: Joe has a new book out called *Wiping Off the "Sheen,"* which documents "a long conversation" about this life spent on the front lines of the actor's art. In addition to his new book, Joe hypes Tim's as-yet-unfinished *Decker* movie, acknowledging that it "pleasantly surprised" him.

"We'll see if he finishes it," Gregg says.

For the season finale of *Popcorn Classics*, Gregg delivers "an unexpected comedy." In 1992's *Baby Boom*, Diane Keaton "inherits a baby" in a surprise plot twist that leads to "a lot of fun" for viewers. This is an ideal pick for Tim, who loved Ms. Keaton "in all the Woody Allen movies."

Tim is ready to end the show right there. But Gregg wants to introduce a brand-new segment he's "kind of excited about," called *Tim's Mailbag*. He created this feature to give *On Cinema* fans a chance to get answers about the show direct from the source.

Gregg opens the big mail sack at his feet and hands Tim the first letter. It was sent by loyal viewer Tammy Smith of Kenner, Louisiana, who wants to know Tim's favorite movie. After giving it some thought, Tim settles on *Jack Reacher*. [Episode 109]

The very next letter Gregg pulls out comes all the way from Japan. To Tim's amazement, it turns out to be from his former *On Cinema* co-host and love interest, Ayaka Ohwaki.

Gregg is almost bursting with excitement as he waits to find out what Ayaka has been up to lately. "Why don't you read it out loud for the viewers?" he asks.

As Tim reluctantly reads the letter, we learn that Ayaka is pregnant with his child: "Can you believe it?" she writes. "You're going to be a father!"

Tim looks badly shaken as the lights go down, but Gregg can't seem to stop laughing.

On Cinema On Line

1:06 PM - 14 Mar 2014
actively seeking a new guest for #OnCinema Season 5. will literally work with anyone else besides @greggturkington - he is a rat.

1:08 PM - 14 Mar 2014
mark my words - you will never see me and @greggturkington in the same room together - much less a movie review show. he is dead to me.

1:28 PM - 20 Jun 2014
According to @timheidecker, I will not be part of the new season of #OnCinema. Trying to get clarification but he won't give any reason.

1:30 PM - 20 Jun 2014
Not sure how @timheidecker intends to proceed with #OnCinema without the show's resident expert. The show cannot stand on its own.

1:35 PM - 20 Jun 2014
"Lights! Camera! Action!" is meaningless without a #movie expert to make sense of it all. @timheidecker is not a movie expert by any stretch

6:42 PM - 20 Jun 2014
The world needs more #movies less #quack doctors and #phony hosts.

2:38 PM - 17 Jun 2014
Why don't they show #movies at restaurants? It's always some sports game that no one cares about on the big screen.

3:40 PM - 26 Jun 2014
no chance @greggturkington returns to #OnCinema

3:54 PM - 26 Jun 2014
Unless I receive something official through the mail or FedEx saying otherwise, I will report to work as usual July 2. #movie

10:18 AM - 27 Jun 2014
@scorsesemartin any interest in being a guest on a serious film review web show? we shoot in LA next wed. thanks, tim #OnCinema

10:20 AM - 27 Jun 2014
@leonardmaltin any interest in being a guest on a serious film review web show? we shoot in LA next wed. thanks, tim #OnCinema

10:20 AM - 27 Jun 2014
@ebertchicago any interest in being a guest on a serious film review web show? we shoot in LA next wed. thanks, tim #OnCinema

9:27 AM - 30 Jun 2014
Hollywood is full of empty promises and false expectations. struggling today. #OnCinema

9:29 AM - 30 Jun 2014
@greggturkington please let me know your schedule this week at your earliest convenience. thanks.

11:03 AM - 30 Jun 2014
@greggturkington i need to know what's up with you. #OnCinema

11:07 AM - 30 Jun 2014
@greggturkington email me asap. #OnCinema

12:20 PM - 30 Jun 2014
OK.

1:20 PM - 30 Jun 2014
i wrote you back but it bounced back to me. Is this a joke to you? #OnCinema

6:18 PM - 30 Jun 2014
I'm having trouble with my internet, I need to upgrade. Please try again, or better yet, CALL.

6:48 PM - 30 Jun 2014
Just watched Star Trek 2 for the dozenth time. Pretty cool to see Spock on the streets of San Francisco. #MovieClassics

10:42 AM - 1 Jul 2014
apologies have been accepted. welcome back @greggturkington

11:17 AM - 1 Jul 2014
I accept your apology.

11:17 AM - 1 Jul 2014
huh?

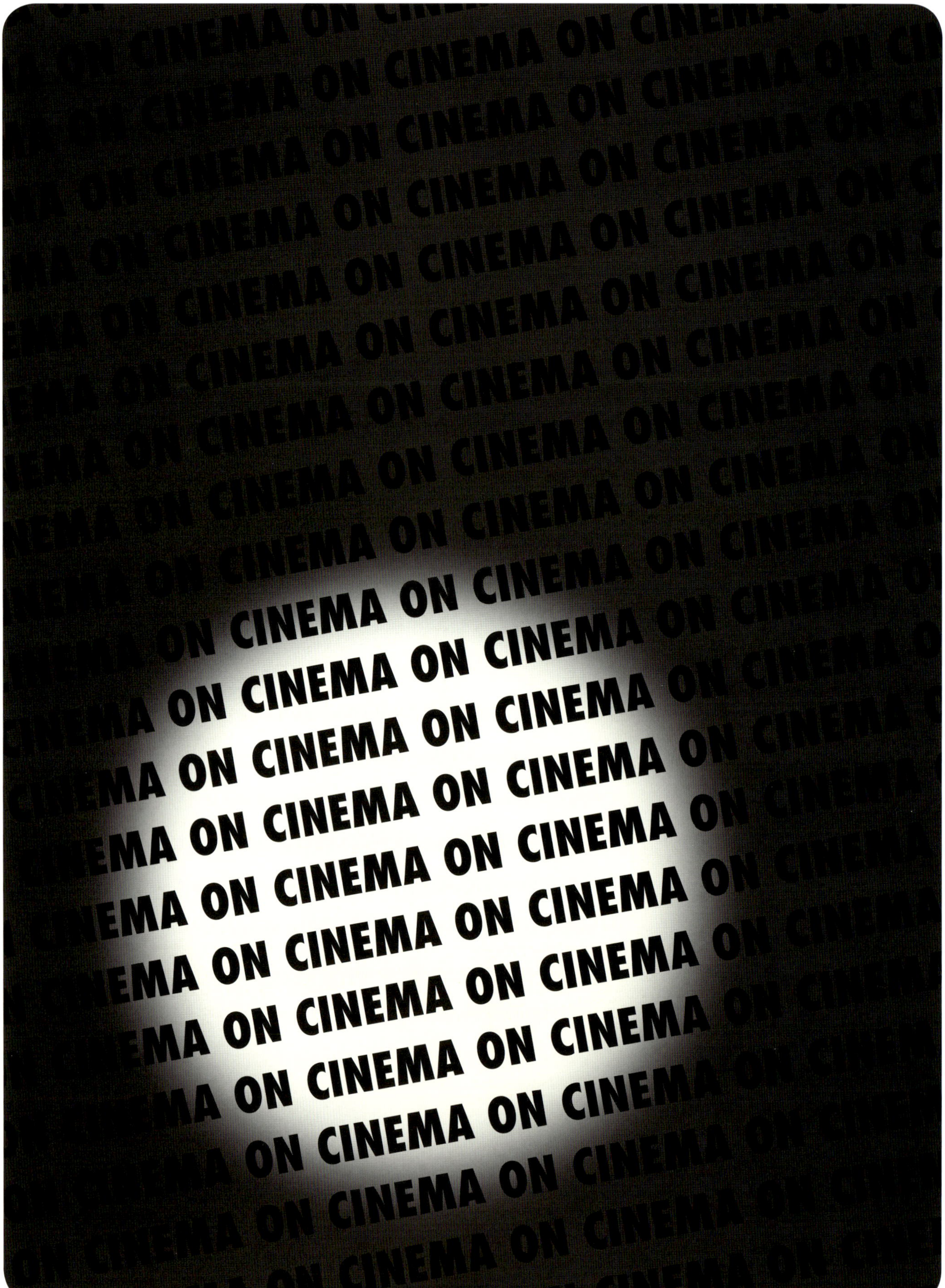
CINEMA ON CINEMA

SEASON 5

EPISODE 501
'Deliver Us From Evil' & 'Tammy'

Air date: July 2, 2014
Running time: 9:46 minutes

It's the dawn of a new season, and change is in the air: Tim has grown a beard! He introduces his first guest of Season Five, Gregg Turkington, who's glad to be "back in the seat."

Tim asks Gregg for a rundown of his between-season doings. The big news has to do with Gregg's record-shattering "500 Movies in 500 Days" project: Gregg is "still plugging away at it" and "getting there." Unfortunately, he lost his list of the 127 movies he'd already watched, so he had to start over. But he has now surpassed the original list by reaching 141. And if he ever finds the earlier one, he can combine the tallies!

As for Tim, he has "relocated to Jackson Hole, Wyoming," and bought a new Kawasaki motorcycle, which is "one of the best motorcycles there are." He needed to get away from "the whole Hollywood scene and the L.A. lifestyle," both of which were preventing him from connecting with nature and "with some of the rights that I have as a patriot."

Commenting on Tim's beard, Gregg says, "You look like Orson Welles." He adds that Welles played Nostradamus, who had "the gift of predicting the future." Gregg wishes that he, too, could foresee the future, "'cause then I'd know when the new *Hobbit* movie is coming out."

Tim and Gregg weren't able to review some of the summer's biggest blockbusters, so Tim reads a list of only the five-baggers. These include must-see entries from stalwart franchises like Captain America, the X-Men and Godzilla, as well as essential one-offs like *A Million Ways to Die in the West*, *Neighbors*, *Blended* and *21 Jump Street*.

Returning to the present, *Deliver Us From Evil* shows how a New York City cop and a Catholic priest put aside their differences to fight demonic possession. In Tim's opinion, this "horror movie" is "very frightening" and "very scary." He gives it five bags of popcorn.

Gregg "liked it a lot," praising it for being like *The Exorcist* if it were "set in New York City." He gives it five "scary" bags of popcorn and says, "Don't go see it late at night."

Tammy stars Melissa McCarthy, Susan Sarandon and Dan "Elwood Blues" Ackroyd in a comedy about a jilted wife who hopes to overcome her emotional anguish by taking a road trip with her alcoholic grandmother.

Tim says, "I laughed my ass off, pardon the French." He gives it six bags of popcorn and three bags of soda.

Gregg is excited to see Ackroyd "back on the screen" as the nation marks the 35th anniversary of *The Blues Brothers*. Although Ackroyd is "not doing the Elwood Blues thing completely" in *Tammy*, "it's hard to get that out of your mind."

Gregg found this "distracting." Also, the film doesn't have "enough music," despite Ackroyd's proven harmonica prowess. These faults aside, it's "a very, very funny movie."

Gregg would gladly give *Tammy* six bags of popcorn, but because "our scale only goes to five bags," he tops out at the maximum. But he throws in a "toy harmonica" so "you can learn how to play like Elwood Blues."

To introduce this week's Popcorn Classic, Gregg dons a hat and a pair of sunglasses, both of which are not unlike the ones worn by Dan Ackroyd and Jim Belushi in their *Blues Brothers* heyday. The film, of course, is *Blues Brothers 2000*, starring Ackroyd and John Goodman.

For Tim, this rips open an old wound: Goodman "is not a Blues Brother," he says, and "Jim Belushi should've been offered that part." Gregg protests that Ackroyd and Belushi "were never real brothers; they were Blues Brothers," and "you can have other Blues Brothers in life." He calls this a "blues movie" that "will cure the blues," and says "it's better than the original."

Before ending the show, Tim has an important announcement to make. But first, he asks Gregg to remove his "embarrassing" Blues Brothers hat. It turns out that the *Decker* film clip featuring Tim and Joe Estevez [Episode 408] will be expanded into a miniseries and "is coming to web television this summer."

EPISODE 502
'Dawn of the Planet of the Apes' & 'And So It Goes'

Air date: July 9, 2014
Running time: 11:13 minutes

A freshly clean-shaven Tim finally addresses viewer concerns about the letter he received in Episode 410 from his former girlfriend and short-lived *Popcorn Classics* host Ayaka Ohwaki.

Citing the "paternity dispute with her and myself," he aims to "clear the air" by announcing that the issue was resolved "in a way that was, I think, mutually beneficial for all parties concerned." After he sent Ayaka "the money that she would need" for an unspecified "procedure," her "problem" was "taken care of."

He assures us that "as a member of the pro-life community," he still believes deeply in "those ideals." However, "when push comes to shove" and you are personally affected by a situation like this one, all options "have to be on the table."

"We are here to have fun and talk about movies," he concludes. "I don't want personal stuff to influence this show."

This week's guest, Gregg Turkington, enthusiastically supports Tim's new stance: "That's what I've always said!" Tim says, "I'm finally on the same page with you on that."

In this week's movie news, Gary Oldman pays a visit to the *Dawn of the Planet of the Apes*, where the titular apes must battle the human survivors of the deadly disease that killed all the humans, with control of the very Earth at stake. Tim says this "sequel to a prequel" of the original *Planet of the Apes* story "is smarter, better, bigger, smarter, faster, funnier, more exciting, scarier than" either of those earlier films.

Tim expects this "fantastic movie" to "win Best Picture." But Gregg hopes it doesn't, as a win could be "a sign it's the last one in the series." He would like to see "another 10 *Planet of the Apes* movies" before they kill the franchise with this honor. For the same reason, he hopes "Bond never wins Best Picture." Tim sees little danger of this happening.

Offended, Gregg insists "the final Bond *will* win Best Picture." But Tim objects that "there's never gonna be a final Bond" as long as "dumb sheeple" like Gregg "keep going and buying into that crap." In conclusion, he gives *Dawn of the Planet of the Apes* five bags of popcorn and two sodas. Gregg gives it five bags of popcorn and a banana cream pie, "because apes do like bananas."

And So It Goes brings *Godfather* alumna Diane Keaton and Michael Douglas back together for a comedy about a selfish realtor who must learn to find room in his life for a granddaughter. Because this "very funny" Rob Reiner film is "the funniest film of the year," Tim gives it five bags of popcorn.

Gregg confirms that "this is a funny movie." What's more, "Rob Reiner is long overdue for an Oscar," making this his pick for Best Picture. He gives it five bags and an Oscar statue.

Tim tells Gregg his new hometown of Jackson Hole has just "one movie theater." They also don't have Starbucks, which has gotten Tim into the "homebrew coffee scene." He is unhappy to be back in Hollywood, where "all they have is Starbucks." All in all, Jackson Hole offers "a better lifestyle."

Gregg thinks Tim is overlooking three very important factors: "Lights, camera and action!" Unlike Jackson Hole, the Hollywood region has "movie magic." Tim rejects this elitist outlook, not least because the original Han Solo, Harrison Ford, is a fellow Jackson Hole dweller.

Tim trots out a brand-new segment called *On Cinema On Guests*, which will help us to "get to know the guests of *On Cinema*" and to understand "why they are such huge cinema buffs." The first episode features "one of our resident film buff experts, Gregg Turkington."

Tim has bought Gregg a nice new suit for this special segment, which takes place in front of a green screen. Instructing Gregg to look directly into the camera, he holds up a VHS copy of *Honey, I Shrunk the Kids* and asks the buff if he's ever seen it.

"Of course!" Gregg says. "That's a collector's item. Where'd you find that?" Next, Tim asks if Gregg would be able to advise him on organizing video collections. "Yeah," Gregg answers. "When it comes to movies, I'm the master of codes!" Wrapping up the interview with his puzzled guest, he asks Gregg where he was born. "I was born in Los Angeles," Gregg reveals.

Back on the set, Tim thanks Gregg for his candid interview. "You were telling me off-camera you were just recently in the hospital for a couple of weeks," he mentions.

"Yeah. During the hiatus, I was," Gregg verifies as the cinema lights dim.

EPISODE 503
'Jupiter Ascending' & 'Planes: Fire and Rescue'

Air date: July 16, 2014
Running time: 10:45 minutes

This week, Tim has "a big announcement" to make. As we learned in Episode 502, he has been enjoying "a nice, quiet, peaceful lifestyle" in Jackson Hole, Wyoming. He loves the clean air, and he's been "eating a lot of bison, which of course is so rich in amoeba acids." Recalling that his guest, Gregg Turkington, was "recently in the hospital having some organ removed," he urges the film buff to "think about living in a clean air space like Jackson Hole."

He then remarks that while visiting the On Cinema Facebook page, he found some "essays that Gregg Turkington wrote."

"I really thought they were terrific," he tells Gregg. "And I started thinking about, well, what is the one area of the entertainment industry that I don't have a foothold in?" The answer turns out to be "publishing." With that aim in mind, he offers Gregg "a book deal" for "a collection of your essays on film." Gregg is enthusiastic about this idea.

Tim is also working on his own volume called Hog Shots, "a coffee-table photo book" compiling iPhone pictures of Tim sitting on motorcycles. As soon as he's made "a ton of money on that," he will publish Gregg's "Hollywood movie book."

Gregg wonders what will happen "if Hog Shots isn't that popular." Tim is sure of his book's success because "if you look the numbers of motorcycles sold every year, it's astonishing." Also, he hopes "to get Tom Cruise for the cover, posing on his bike."

Because photo books can be costly to produce, Gregg suggests it might be better to do the film book first, "and then you can use those funds maybe to do a second movie book, or maybe Hog Shots." But Tim is "pretty confident Hog Shots is going to be the number-one book in America."

Gregg is less sanguine: "I just don't think people care that much about photos of motorcycles in parking lots." Tim looks forward to proving Gregg wrong about the success of "Heidecker Publishing."

Until then, though, it's all about the movies. Sean Bean and Mila Kunis light up the sci-fi screen in Jupiter Ascending, as "a young destitute human woman" is marked for death by a futuristic "Queen of the Universe" in what Tim calls "an exciting, fascinating superhero sci-fi movie."

Gregg forewarns viewers that this film "is not at all realistic; these are not things that happen normally in your day-to-day life." Still, it can be good to "live in a fantasy world for a few minutes," especially when "Mila Kunis provides the eye candy." On these terms, Jupiter Ascending delivers the goods. He gives this "fun popcorn movie" five bags of popcorn.

Tim "loved this movie," but he will only allow it three bags "because it's not an Oscar contender." Gregg sees this more as the Academy's problem than the film's. Accordingly, he dispenses an extra two bags, "which we can slide over to your three bags of popcorn so that we each gave it five bags of popcorn." Tim dismisses this proposal, but under continued critical assault from Gregg over his "bad rating," he ups his total to five bags.

Planes: Fire and Rescue is "another animated Disney movie" about a washed-up racing plane that redeems itself by fighting fires. Tim calls it a "fun action film" that works equally well for children and adults. He knows this firsthand, because "my son and I watched this together when he was out visiting last week." He gives it five bags of popcorn and two bags of soda.

Gregg is confused by Tim's story, but he rallies long enough to give the movie five bags of popcorn and "one of those little captain's badges that they used to give to kids on the flights."

In the latest On Cinema On Location, Gregg is transported through the magic of movies to "Jerry's house" from 1977's Oh, God! comedy starring the late George Burns and the late John Denver. The house itself is being fumigated, so it's not directly visible. But you can still see the iconic trees and the nearby street that appeared in the original film.

Back on set, Tim announces that Decker will launch on July 17. As the lights go down, Gregg asks for more details on Tim's child. He learns that Tim has a 15-year-old son from a previous marriage. Although they had been estranged, the lad has been visiting Tim regularly in Jackson Hole.

On Cinema On Line

3:02 PM - 17 Jul 2014
@greggturkington please show support and tweet link to #Decker #oncinema

3:58 PM - 18 Jul 2014
People should stick to things they're good at.

7:38 PM - 18 Jul 2014
I'm proud of what we have accomplished with #OnCinema. No need for side projects.

7:46 PM - 18 Jul 2014
What, like #500MoviesIn500Days ??

8:44 AM - 19 Jul 2014
#500MoviesIn500Days isn't a side project. It's a once in a lifetime opportunity to set a world record and promote #OnCinema

Episode 504
'Wish I Was Here' & 'Hercules'

Air date: July 23, 2014
Running time: 9:36 minutes

With the right side of his face badly abraded, and his right eye swollen shut, and his right hand swathed in bandages, Tim explains that he recently suffered "an accident" while riding his Kawasaki motorcycle. [Episode 501]

In an affecting monologue, he recounts how it happened. Shortly after completing "our final scene on *Decker*," Tim attended a "wrap party" for the miniseries. On the way home, he "stopped in at a Walmart" to replace some of the undergarments he'd left behind in Jackson Hole. "Because I'm on my motorcycle," he says, "I can park in the handicapped spot up front." But no sooner did he do so than "some old bitch" came out to tell him he couldn't park there.

After advising this interloper to "shut up," Tim got off his motorcycle in order to "go at her." Sadly, his "boot got caught in the saddlebag," causing him to fall over the bike onto his face, which in turn caused the bike to fall on top of him.

"So the bike wasn't even moving?" Gregg asks.

"No, it was stationary," Tim confirms. Nevertheless, he fractured his wrist, "dinged up" his face and "tore something" in his eye. The eye injury is especially problematic because he was already "legally blind" in his left eye. As a result, "I cannot see."

Fortunately, he watched today's movies prior to his accident. But Gregg will need to read the cue cards.

Wish I Was Here stars Kate Hudson as the long-suffering wife of a father who reconnects with his inner self through the homeschooling movement. Tim "liked this movie a lot" because it was "introspective" and "almost like a fairy tale." It gets five bags of popcorn.

Gregg felt "it was more realistic than a fairy tale": Although it depicts dwarfs, they aren't like the ones in *Snow White*. Because it was also "very interesting," he gives it five bags of popcorn and "an Oscar nod."

Tim agrees, naming it as his pick for Best Picture and predicting it will be "a blockbuster" along the lines of *Avatar*. Gregg also awards the film "two nickels" for being "down to earth."

Hercules boasts Dwayne Johnson (a.k.a. The Rock) and John Hurt in what Tim characterizes as "a movie about Hercules." Because he loves "anything with Hercules," Tim gives this "perfect summer movie" five bags of popcorn and recommends it to anyone who seeks "fun popcorn adventure with great special effects."

Gregg praises The Rock for overcoming the popular misconception that he is "not an actor" and predicts that the former WWF legend may be wrestling with Oscar in the very near future. He gives *Hercules* five bags of popcorn and "two souvenir rocks."

Like all of Woody Allen's masterpieces, *Magic in the Moonlight* gets an automatic five bags of popcorn from *On Cinema*. Instead of reviewing this classic film, Tim introduces a new segment entitled *Gregg Turkington's Celebrity Backlot*. In this first installment, Gregg visits the Warner Brothers studio backlot in Burbank, which he "snuck into in order to try and track down Joe Estevez." Gregg hopes that as a Woody Allen expert, Joe will be able to contextualize the film within the larger context of the Woody mythos. Spotting Joe across the lot, he asks the veteran actor for his honest opinion of "Woody's new movie."

"I'll tell ya, anything that Woody Allen does is absolutely fantastic," Joe says. "And his new movie certainly isn't an exception."

"Do you think Oscar is in the cards for Woody?" Gregg asks. "Always!" Joe replies. "Never discount Woody when it becomes Oscar time."

Back on the set, Tim compliments Joe's "very interesting perspective on Woody" and ushers in the latest segment of *Popcorn Classics*. This week, a tough-as-nails Nick Nolte goes head to head with the bad guys in *Q & A*, which Gregg calls a "shoot-'em-up, district attorney type of movie" from the director of *Serpico*, *Dog Day Afternoon* and *Network*. Even though Gregg found it inferior to all three films, he says it's "worth a look if you happen to run across it."

As the lights dim, Tim needs to be helped out of his chair so he can get to yet another medical appointment.

EPISODE 505
'Guardians of the Galaxy' & 'Get On Up'

Air date: July 30, 2014
Running time: 8:26 minutes

As this episode gets underway, Tim is wearing dark glasses to protect his injured eye. Having "lost the sight" in this eye and with "very diminished sight abilities" in the other, he's grateful for the availability of rides through the popular internet service Lyft. He's also happy to see this week's guest, Gregg Turkington.

Although he can't read his cue cards, he has an earphone that cues him on what they say. In this way, we learn that Chris Pratt and Vin Diesel are among the actors appearing in *Guardians of the Galaxy*. Tim finds it hard to hear his cues, but the gist of the plot is that an "American pirate" is pursued by a "manhunt" after a stolen "orb" is "coveted by the village."

Tim regards this film as "one of those great action movies from Marvel." It "sounded great" — especially "the sounds of the action" — and he "loved hearing everybody talk about what was going on in the movie." He gives it five bags of popcorn and two sodas.

Gregg raises concerns that because Tim watched *Guardians of the Galaxy* while legally blind, he's "only seeing half the movie." He questions whether the sightless Tim should be reviewing movies at all.

"I find that offensive," Tim snaps. He proclaims that "anybody, no matter what their predicament, should be able to see the movies that they want to see." He confirms that *Guardians of the Galaxy* is actually "great for blinds."

Gregg disagrees: "You don't want a deaf person reviewing albums for *Rolling Stone*." In his view, Tim should've taken some time off to regain his vision.

"We're not on that kind of schedule," Tim says. He directs Gregg to proceed with his own review: "Don't worry about my situation."

Gregg calls *Guardians of the Galaxy* "fun" and says its cast of characters is "kind of a thrill" compared to "old" heroes like Superman and Batman. He liked the movie a lot, adding "I'm glad I could see it" because "that makes all the difference." He gives it five bags of popcorn and "a cane for the blind."

With help from the buzzing voice in his earpiece, and despite Gregg's attempts to speed things along by reading the cue card himself, Tim eventually lets us know that the next film is *Get On Up*. As Tim puts it, this biopic details James Brown's rise from "stream [sic] poverty" to the "all-time" heights of success.

Tim "loved" this movie, even though it's "not my kind of music" and "B.B. King is about as black as I get." In that respect, it reminded him of "that movie about another blind black man, Ray Charles." In conclusion he asks, "Who knew so much about music as did James Brown and all this stuff he went through?" He gives it five bags of popcorn.

Gregg enjoyed the film's "Oscar-worthy" cinematography as well as its many "visual elements" that will "stick with people long after the last song." He gives this "very, very excellent movie" five bags of popcorn and throws in a CD of James Brown's greatest hits.

Next up, it's *On Cinema On Location*, as Gregg ventures back into the *Oh, God!* universe [Episode 503] to pinpoint the precise intersection where John Denver's car filled with rain in a modern-day miracle wrought by the late George Burns in his titular role of God.

Afterward, Tim challenges Gregg on whether there is sufficient audience demand for more than one *Oh, God!* location feature. Gregg is positive there's "a lot" of public interest in this film's locations.

On Cinema On Line

> 9:37 PM - 24 Jul 2014
> Tears in my eyes as I read all the wonderful comments about the excellent ep 2 of #decker

> 9:38 PM - 24 Jul 2014
> Too many people to thank who made #decker happen. Wish we could have had time for full credits to show my appreciation.

> 9:39 PM - 24 Jul 2014
> And by the way, #Decker is just getting warmed up. ;)

EPISODE 506
'Teenage Mutant Ninja Turtles' & 'Into the Storm'

Air date: August 6, 2014
Running time: 7:30 minutes

Except for a nasty scab near his right eye, Tim's head is healing nicely. He tells his guest, Gregg Turkington, "I'm so glad to 'see' you again." Thanks are due to "everyone at Hollywood Presbyterian's eye department," who restored vision to both of Tim's eyes and left him feeling "glad to be healthy."

In response to audience demand, Tim provides an update on the progress of his cycle-themed photo book, *Hog Shots*. [Episode 503] The project is being held up by a scheduling conflict with planned cover model Tom Cruise, who has not yet responded to any of Tim's communications. The clock is running out, as Tim has already pre-sold 10 copies of this title to Chapman's Books in Jackson Hole, based on Cruise's proposed appearance on the cover.

Appealing directly to Cruise through the democratic medium of the internet, Tim warns the actor he's in danger of "missing out on a great opportunity." He asks Cruise to let him know if he won't be able to do the cover shoot, so Tim can "move forward" with another star. If that happens, Tim worries that "it's going to start affecting the reviews I give your movies."

Teenage Mutant Ninja Turtles reboots the original 1990 debut to deliver an up-to-the-minute modern remake starring Whoopi Goldberg. Tim "loved this movie," especially as seen through the lens of his "20/20 eyes." He gives it five popcorn bags.

Turning to his uncharacteristically silent guest, Tim asks for Gregg's opinion. "I don't really want to say anything about it," Gregg tells him. "Because anything I say might end up in an episode of *Decker*."

This complaint relates to an incident in Episode 502, when Tim conducted a "weird" interview with Gregg in front of a green screen. After viewing the most recent episode of *Decker*, Gregg realized that Tim had inserted him into the episode as CIA Special Agent Kington, presenting his out-of-context interview answers as Kington's dialogue.

Tim claims this is a standard practice in the film industry. "You don't understand how Hollywood works," he charges. Gregg reproaches Tim for not seeking his permission: "I didn't agree to be a part of *Decker*, and I wouldn't have agreed to it!"

He stipulates that if he *were* to be part of the show, he'd want to be an actual actor rather than "some weirdo character" cobbled together from *On Cinema* interview footage.

Tim reassures him that his "CIA analyst" character plays a "cool" and "important" role, and Gregg "should be proud of that." Addressing the issue of the "stolen" footage, Tim alleges that "as soon as you walk onto this set, anything you say or do is mine." He adds that he's "using things responsibly, and you know that."

Gregg still objects to having no foreknowledge of his role in *Decker*. Tim asks Gregg if he wants to be edited out of the episode, and Gregg says he would.

"I can't do that," Tim tells him. "It's already aired." He maintains that his use of the footage is fair game since Gregg "agreed to be part of the *On Cinema* Family."

"Being part of a family doesn't mean being raped by Dad," Gregg responds.

Tim reiterates that "everything you do is mine." If Gregg doesn't want to appear in *Decker*, he can leave: "Walk off, and I don't ever want to see you again!"

As Gregg departs, Tim angrily asserts "his constitutional rights to use whatever footage" he pleases under "the Freedom of Information Act." His use of Gregg's footage was "freedom of speech" and "freedom of self-expression" protected by Article I of the Constitution. "I can back that up to the Supreme Court if I need to," he tells Gregg, now offscreen, "and you know it."

He insists what he did with the disputed footage was "something perfect and beautiful": "I made you into a great actor. And you'll see, people are gonna be running up to you asking you for parts in the next movie. You'll be the next Forrest Gump." In summation, he says, "I did what was right for this show."

"It has nothing to do with this show," Gregg protests from the wings.

This provokes a furious tirade from Tim. "I will go to bed sleeping every night, knowing I did the right thing for this show!" he screams. "I did the right thing for *Decker*! I did the right thing for me! You can go fuck yourself!"

On Cinema On Line

10:49 AM - 7 Aug 2014
Hey guys - @greggturkington is still a bit down about the #decker situation. It would mean a lot if you let him know how good he was.

7:05 PM - 8 Aug 2014
Thanks for all your support during this time. #movies

EPISODE 507
'Let's Be Cops' & 'The Expendables 3'

Air date: August 13, 2014
Running time: 8:54 minutes

Despite last week's conflict over Tim's use of doctored interview footage to include Gregg as a character in *Decker*, Gregg is once again this week's guest.

Tim thanks viewers for "tuning in to *Decker*," observing that he's "almost getting more positivity about *Decker* than" *On Cinema*. This is logical, in a way, because whereas *On Cinema* merely reports on movies, "*Decker* is a movie, or a miniseries."

"I'm glad you're part of it now," he tells Gregg.

"It's a cool show!" Gregg enthuses. He was admittedly "skeptical at first," but he's been getting "a lot of letters and a lot of comments from people," which has helped him to rethink his stance.

"There's things about it I would've done differently, that you should've done differently," he tells Tim. "But being in something with Joe Estevez is kind of a cool feather to have in your cap."

Tim accidentally ends the show early by saying "thanks for watching." As soon as this technical glitch is sorted out, we're off to see the movies! In *Let's Be Cops*, Damon Wayans Jr. and his college buddy dress up as cops to put one over on the Albanian mafia. Tim didn't see it, but Gregg says it's "a typical summer comedy" with "flashes of brilliance." He gives it five bags of popcorn, as does Tim based on Gregg's rave review. Gregg throws in a couple of mini donuts "because cops love donuts."

The Expendables 3 is summer blockbuster fare that leaves no stone unturned, boasting a mix-and-match cast that includes Sylvester Stallone, Wesley Snipes, Jet Li, Mel Gibson, Harrison Ford, Tom Cruise, Arnold Schwarzenegger and so forth. As Gregg puts it, "The gang's all here!"

In this thriller, the titular Expendables must face their toughest enemy yet — themselves! — as they go up against a former founder of the Expendables, with a little help from a new and tech-savvy generation of this dying breed.

Tim says this is "not your grandparents' *Expendables*"; new life has been breathed into the hoary franchise by "the hip-hop generation, web-enabled generation 2.0." Finding it to be his "favorite version of *Expendables*," Tim makes an Oscar prediction: "It won't win, but it should win."

Because this is "Schwarzenegger's baby," Tim gives him five bags of popcorn, and then doles out another 10 bags for the movie itself.

Gregg gives it five bags of popcorn and "two little pills that people think are probably steroids but in fact it's just vitamin C, because I think people unfairly accused Schwarzenegger of using that."

He then draws some unexpected parallels between this Tinseltown colossus and *Decker*, which Gregg feels could be turned into a feature film if Tim would "expand on it a little bit." Tim admits these similarities are no accident, as the first two Expendables movies "were honestly an inspiration for me when writing *Decker*."

Gregg supposes the "intrigue" depicted in the Bond films must also have been on Tim's mind. But Tim says these elements actually came from *Jack Reacher*, the *Jason Bourne* movies and Liam Neeson's *Non-Stop*. [Episode 408] Tim claims all those films "are better than Bond," which is "shit." This disagreement notwithstanding, they both give *The Expendables 3* five bags of popcorn.

Next, Gregg takes us on location with *On Cinema On Location*. This week, *Oh, God!* fans rejoice as Gregg follows up on his previous *Oh, God!* segments by visiting what he presumes is the iconic supermarket formerly staffed by the late John Denver.

Tim has already asked Gregg to stop highlighting locations from this classic metaphysical comedy. Although one *Oh, God!* segment was fine, he says, doing three is "ridiculous." He accuses Gregg of "bumming me out" and "ruining the show."

"I have half a mind to jump on my Kawasaki and head back to Jackson Hole and not even finish out this season," he scowls.

"You'll get on your Kawasaki and fall right off before you even put your key in the ignition," Gregg contends, referring to an accident that befell Tim back in Episode 503.

After an awkward pause, Gregg tries to introduce a new installment of *Tim's Mailbag*. But Tim says there's no time. To Gregg's consternation, he tells us to "stick around for a new show directly after this," called *On Cinema After On Cinema*.

On Cinema On Line

10:47 AM - 14 Aug 2014
"oh god" is right. Tell @greggturkington we've had enough of his "Oh God!" segments. #moveon

An Official Statement
From Tim Heidecker

As a country we are in crisis mode. It's obvious fact I don't need to stayed here but I will to begin my thought. My rant by extreme outrage at the state of things in this country. When I conceived of the idea for Decker it was based on my frustration hatred and fear of the direction this country is going in. I don't see us turning back unfortunately it seems as if we had crossed the Rubicon. Even if the politics of changed we still must realize that there is too much politics dividing us and then there is too many special interests whether it's Wall Street big government or the interests of teachers unions and unions that keep us from being coming a great country again. where have our values gone? Where are the things that made us who we were as a country? Do we even know who we are anymore? There's almost nothing I can do to change this that is why through the show Decker which was a hit on the Internet one of the first television miniseries to become part of an online web series experience I intended to show an example to America and the president that there is a way to behave properly as the greatest country on earth there's nothing that can stop us from becoming that again if only we carefully look at the example I've tried to put forth in my show Decker.

It's not hard to look at the original documents that our founding fathers created. I'm talking about the Constitution. And the Declaration of Independence. Those were the founding fathers documents that told us how to run the country. Those are the documents that we need to search for again and find the answers that will answer the problems we have as a country. It's not rocket science it's simple look at the documents know them know what the Constitution says about our rights and freedom.

Decker is the most important project I've ever been a part of it's exactly what I meant was meant to do as an artist writer producer director. It's amazing program to watch but it's even better when it's written in a book form that you can read. Why? Because you can continue to read it back-and-forth and don't have to see the video of music with all the titles and all that stuff. You can skip to any chapter and read that part.

Central Intelligence Agency
DO NOT COPY/CONFIDENTIAL
Filed March 8, 1998
CASE FILE SUBJECT:
Operative CO483
SPECIAL SUPERAGENT
LEVEL 18 Accesses

Agent Name: Jack Dicker
Code Name: Decker
Aliases: Decker, Fightman
D.O.B.: February 3, 1976
Gender: Male
Nationality: American
Laterality: American
Height: 6'2"
Weight: 195 lbs.
Vision: 20/20
Blood Type: O Negative
Eye Colour: Blue
Hair Colour: Blond
Relatives: Mother, unknown; Father, unknown; Spouse, unknown
Marital Status: Single
Children: 0
Languages: English, Spanish, french, Russian, Uzbeki, Farsi, Japanese, Portuguese, Chinese (Cantonese), Swahili, Korean, Esperanto
Telephone: (202) 555 0191
Mobile: (202) 555 0191
Email: ak47hoopdreams@earthline.net

Home Address: 1570 Bellagio Dr., Beverly Hills, CA 90210
Postal: PO Box 69 144 Broadway, New York, NY 10001

LICENCES
- Firearms
- Vehicle
- To Kill

SPECIALIST FIELDS
- Firearms
- Hand-to-Hand Combat
- Explosives
- Survival in Extreme Environments
- Mind Manipulation

Super agent Jack Decker's place of birth is unknown. At age 12, was recognized as having superhuman congintive and physical abilities and was tagged by the CIA as a potential contributor to Internal Affairs as well as Special Operations. He began to train in close-contact combat, Goju Ryu Karate, sniper rifle marksmanship, Capoeira, Kung-fu, and any and all firearms. Decker revealed himself to be an exceptional asset, but his renegade attitude has gotten him into trouble at agency. He does not listen to anyone else's rules but his own, and has been known to question any and all authority. His superiors have described him as rebellious, handsome and badass. Use caution with this man.

DECKER: CLASSIFIED
Book 1

EPISODE 1

U.S. Special Agent Jack Decker is deep in the hill country of Afghanistan, taking out the Taliban one man at a time.

He meets up with Abdul, a terrorist turncoat whose stolen *jihadi* briefcase may well turn the deadly tide of the War on Terror. Abdul found the mystery briefcase in the office of his Taliban paymaster. There's just one problem: The briefcase is locked! Decker wants to shoot it open, but Abdul warns him this will make it blow up. "You must break the code," he hisses.

Just then, President Davidson calls Decker's cell phone from the White House. Decker briefs the president that he's hit "the mother lode" of Taliban intelligence. "Bring it back here to Washington D.C. at once," the commander in chief barks.

Before heading stateside, Decker thanks Abdul for risking his life to help the USA defeat terrorism. He promises that in return, America will bring "safety and security" to Abdul's own troubled nation.

"My pleasure," Abdul tells him. A U.S. helicopter lowers a rope and Decker is airlifted to safety. But for how long?

EPISODE 2

Decker is back in America with a stolen Taliban briefcase that might just contain the secret plans for an Islamic Bomb.

Decker has little time for red tape.

"I'm the master of codes!"

On arrival at the White House, Decker is confronted by angry protesters who want to "treat Arabs fairly." "Why don't you guys get a job?" he snorts.

In the Oval Room, President Davidson is fretting over his poll numbers as usual. But Decker gets his full attention by showing him a briefcase containing "a plan to destroy America." There's just one catch: The briefcase is protected by a complex three-digit code. If opened in any other way, it will blow up the White House, laying waste to 200 years of proud American history.

Decker has a better idea: They need to call in a master codebreaker from the CIA. President Davidson tries to thwart this plan with typical bureaucratic red tape, but he changes his tune when Decker jams a pistol against his head: "Do you want your brains splattered on the desk, or are you gonna call that CIA guy?"

Will this cowardly president find the intestinal fortitude to do what's right? To be continued!

EPISODE 3

With Decker's gun at his head, the hapless president has no choice but to get the FBI's master codebreaker, Special Agent Jonathan Kington, on the videophone. Time's running out, so Decker gets right to the point: "We need you to crack this three-digit code as soon as possible."

"That's my area of expertise!" the code expert verifies. It's no easy task, but with very few seconds to spare, Kington arrives at the solution. The suitcase is open! But the fight is far from over: "These plans are worse than I thought," Decker grimaces. Something must be done. But what?

EPISODE 4

The secret of the briefcase is laid bare, and it's not pretty: The Taliban will attack the nation's Superbowl in one week's time. Adding insult to injury, they plan to blow up New York's Central Park "today."

Decker's ready and willing to stop this attack dead in its tracks, but President Davidson isn't so sure that's a good idea: "Maybe we should just surrender," he whines. He asks Kington's opinion, but the patriotic code master sides with Decker.

russian - Русский

Добро пожалавать у Блю-Ватер -Туг-оф-Вар

Вид спорта Таг-оф-вор (перетягиван
себя дома в Дэшвуде, Онтарио, Кан
состоит из мужских и женских и
день включает 32 участника.
Представители многих поколений в
спорта, участвуя и болея ежегодно
В 1982 году некоторые фармеры, жи
Концессион) создали совместный к
Содбустерс". В округе они были о
менее клуб распался в 1986 году и
участников клуба. В 1992 году о
инициативе Ерика Фрайтера и полу

ع مشکلات اعضا، و بوجود
عضا، بتوانند ساعاتی از اوقات
ود گذرانده و با حشر و نشر با
هند . به منظور نیل به اهداف
گیرد ؛
هایی بصورت دایمی و یا موقت

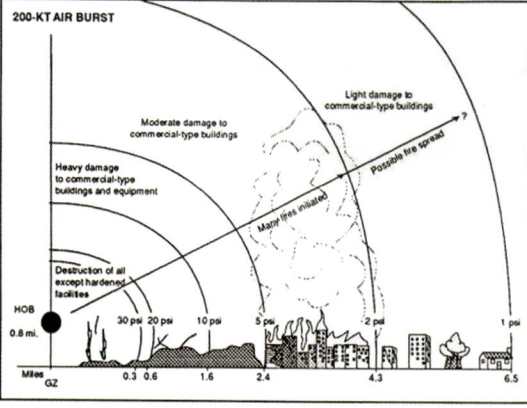

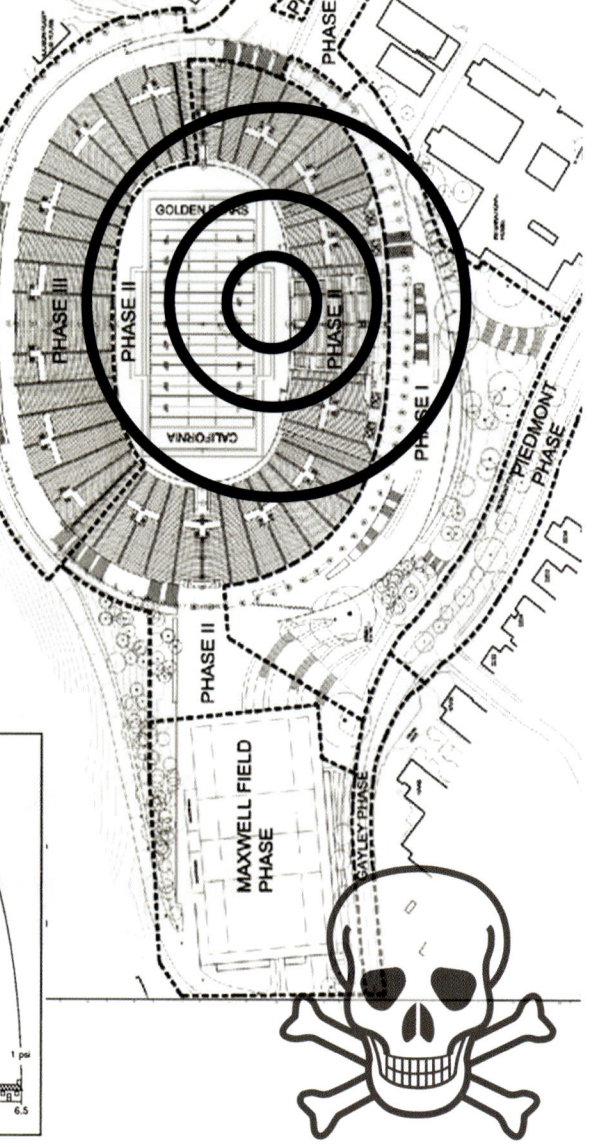

And not only will you and the city of new york be killed,

Defeated yet again, the president agrees to let Decker save the day. Leaping onto his motorcycle, Decker races north on a white-knuckle do-or-die ride to Ground Zero: New York City!

Arriving at the park, he looks for clues. The Taliban's doomsday weapon must be hidden somewhere. But where?

Suddenly, a robed figure in a turban catches his eye. Abdul, supposed friend of the United States, is placing a state-of-the-art mini-nuke in a nearby trash can. In a flash, Decker realizes he was set up!

"It's Allah's will!" Abdul shrieks. "I tricked you!" Decker lunges for the bomb, and the two men struggle for the fate of the city until Decker gets his powerful hands around the traitor's neck. "Die, you piece of shit!" he roars.

Abdul lies dead, but the time bomb is still ticking. With all his strength, Decker flings the device skyward. It explodes safely in the upper atmosphere, forming a patriotic stars-and-stripes display.

EPISODE 5

BACK HOME IN AMERICA, the president thanks Decker for saving the nation from the terrorist attack on New York.

But Decker is not appeased by these words of flattery. He derides Davidson for failing to use his constitutional powers to defend the homeland with force, the only language terror will ever understand: "Don't you realize that as commander in chief, you have the power to bomb these people back to the Stone Age?"

He sneers that Davidson cares more about the lecture circuit than he does about the terroristic chickens now coming home to roost. Stung by the justice of these remarks, Davidson offers to resign on the spot and appoint Decker president in his place. But as a man of action first and foremost, that's a trade-off Decker can never make.

President Davidson then offers him the Congressional Medal of Honor, which Decker *does* accept. He also lets Decker borrow Air Force One so he can take a much-needed vacation in Hawaii.

"Mr. President, you'll never get my vote," Decker scowls. "But you have my respect."

And with that, Jack Decker is off to take a well-deserved rest in Hawaii.

Or is he?

President Davidson announces the death of Abdul to America.

EPISODE 508
'Sin City: A Dame to Kill For'

Air date: August 20, 2014
Running time: 9:37 minutes

Tim introduces his guest, Gregg Turkington, who promptly congratulates him "for a successful season of *Decker*." Gregg confesses that his initial skepticism about the show has been outweighed by positive comments from emails, Twitter and others. "It's pretty satisfying," he muses.

He gives Tim a bouquet of flowers, a bottle of champagne and a framed copy of *Decker*'s first review.

Tim is overcome with emotion as he describes how "a really hard couple of years" culminated in "an honor" of "seeing *Decker* hit the Silver Screen." Turning to Gregg, he says, "I wouldn't have done it without you."

Curious about what Season 2 holds in store for *Decker*, Gregg asks Tim to share some spoilers: "Can you give us a little bit of a preview about what my role will be, and what's gonna happen with the whole gang?"

Tim says that having established the *Decker* universe in Season 1, "it's time to bring in the big guns" in the form of "real actors." As for Gregg's character, Agent Kington, Tim doesn't necessarily see him "continuing into the future of the series," because the show has already "played that card."

Gregg feels that as the "expert on operations in the CIA," Kington is integral to the storyline. Tim says that although he doesn't want to give away major plot points, Decker's enemy in Season 2 "is the CIA," the apparent implication being that this renders Kington obsolete.

Furthermore, Tim recently received "some nice email from Timothy Hutton, who wants to be a part of *Decker 2*."

"That'd be cool to work with him," Gregg says.

"I wouldn't get your hopes up about *Decker 2*," Tim cautions him. Thanking Gregg again for his "really sweet" gifts, Tim moves on to *Sin City: A Dame to Kill For*. In this retooled sequel to the classic original, Mickey Rourke meets Jessica Alba and Bruce Willis en route to Sin City. Tim loved the "noir quality" of the "dark" first film, which gets five bags of popcorn.

Gregg rates the sequel to this film as "good," noting that "if you've seen the original, you know what to expect." He complains that like many sequels, this one makes the error of eliminating "one of the key actors" from the debut film. *Back to the Future 2* is one such example: Without Crispin Glover, the movie was "a flop." Similarly, *The Phantom Menace* disappointed global audiences by leaving Mark Hamill out of the cast. Gregg is worried *Decker 2* may join this shameful list of also-rans if Tim doesn't bring his character back.

"I wouldn't compare yourself to Mark Hamill," Tim objects. "You were a bit player — almost a glorified extra."

"Mark Hamill started out as an extra in things," Gregg says. He boasts that he's been getting a lot of "fan mail," but Tim claims these letters are "all in the same handwriting," a charge Gregg disputes by emphasizing that some of the letters were written "in cursive."

Asked for his review of *Sin City: A Dame to Kill For*, Gregg gives it five bags of popcorn, but also stresses that "it's a cautionary tale of how you can screw up a movie by not honoring people who have made something what it is."

This week, *On Cinema On Location* goes on location to "the schoolhouse from *Oh, God!*" Making good on his threats from the previous episode, Tim stops the tape in the middle and announces he's canceling the segment. He directs Gregg to fill the blank airtime with a Popcorn Classic.

On this week's *Popcorn Classics*, Gregg gives the nod to Meg Ryan's *I.Q.* "Swear to God you've done that one before," Tim breaks in. "That was *Q&A*," Gregg tells him. Eventually he concedes it may be a repeat recommendation, but he still lauds the "comedic genius" of Walter Matthau and the rest of the cast.

Tim calls this segment "a bummer." As the lights go down, he seizes the bottle of champagne Gregg gave him, calling it "junk" and vowing to "drink the whole bottle."

EPISODE 509
'The November Man' & 'Jessabelle'

Air date: August 27, 2014
Running time: 6:48 minutes

As the title music fades, Tim complains of a hangover that "feels like jackhammers going in your head." This is the result of his visit to "a biker bar" filled with "very cool guys." He introduces this week's guest, Gregg Turkington, and tells us again that he "had a big one last night with the guys — my motorcycle guys."

"Did you tell them about your accident?" Gregg asks.

"No," Tim mutters. But he did tell them they are welcome to sleep on his floor when they're in Jackson Hole. Also, in this same spirit of camaraderie, he "got a tattoo."

The November Man stars Pierce "Bond" Brosnan in a larger-than-life CIA assassination drama with international implications. Gregg says it "sounds like Decker." Tim doubts this is a coincidence, because "Hollywood's sorta perking their ears up" at the success of his miniseries.

Gregg sees The November Man as part of a natural progression that runs "full circle from Bond to Decker to Pierce Brosnan, James Bond." But as usual, Tim firmly rejects any suggestion of a Bond influence on Decker.

Despite Brosnan's involvement, Tim "liked this movie a lot," especially its use of exciting elements such as "good intrigue" and "adventure." He gives it four bags of popcorn.

Gregg "loved it" but admits that "it's just hard sometimes to focus when you watch a movie with an ex-Bond, because you're thinking about past Bond glories." That's particularly true of this film, because Pierce Brosnan is Gregg's "favorite Bond." Had he "been completely absorbed" in The November Man, he'd be able to give it five bags of popcorn. Since "that's not the movie's fault," he gives it five bags of popcorn anyway.

In the "ghost movie" Jessabelle, a woman's recovery from "a horrific car accident" is her portal to a new world of supernatural terror. Although "it's not as good of a movie as I would've liked," Tim has "gotta hand it to the director for making a great film." He gives it five bags of popcorn.

Gregg didn't like it as much as Whoopi Goldberg's Ghost, which is "the gold standard of ghost movies." Granted, Jessabelle "does have its moments" (including some that are "scary" and "frightening"), but this is mostly just a matter of ghosts being inherently frightening: "That's the last thing you want, is to be haunted by a ghost."

Apropos of which, he confesses that he himself was "haunted by the ghost of James Bond" while watching Jessabelle, having watched The November Man "earlier in the day." However, "when I did keep my focus, I liked what I saw."

He gives Jessabelle five bags of popcorn, plus a "primitive ghost outfit" fashioned from a white sheet with eye-holes cut into it.

Tim starts to introduce Popcorn Classics, but Gregg surprises him by instead presenting an unscheduled new episode of On Cinema On Guests. This is a segment Tim originally created to help viewers get better acquainted with the film experts they see each week on On Cinema (or to trick Gregg into playing a character in Decker, depending on your perspective).

This week, Tim's former co-host and onetime love partner Ayaka Ohwaki is in the proverbial hot seat, as Gregg interviews her remotely through the magic of video phone calls. While Ayaka tries to soothe the baby in her arms, Gregg tells her that because she was "one of our most popular guests," he wants to give us "an update" on her current activities.

"I've been busy with my baby," she says. "You know, Tim and I have a baby now." She reports that she "named him Tom Cruise" after Tim's favorite actor.

Tim — who believed Ayaka had aborted the baby at his request — hasn't returned her calls "or anything," she says. "But he sent me money, so I bought a ticket to go back to America." In addition to wanting Tim to meet his child, she misses America and also Gregg.

"We'd love to see you here!" Gregg tells her.

"Yay! See you guys soon," she exclaims.

Back on the set, Gregg is alone. "Tim had to go and make a phone call," he explains. "See you next week!"

On Cinema On Line

8:46 AM - 28 Aug 2014
After I make history with #500MoviesIn500Days, what next? A road trip where I watch the 1st #Hobbit Movie once in each of the 50 US States!

1:03 PM - 29 Aug 2014
#Movie critics who can't back their opinions up with expertise are useless. You need to know the #classics! #Casablanca #KramerVsKramer

EPISODE 510
'Dark Places' & 'The Green Inferno'

Air date: September 3, 2014
Running time: 6:46 minutes

Tim welcomes loyal viewers to "the final episode of *On Cinema*" with the unwelcome news that "it's been a tough couple of weeks for me." He vows that as soon as the shooting ends, he will get on his motorcycle and return to his home in Jackson Hole, Wyoming. "We'll see if I ever come back," he says, as he wants to get back to "simple living," "bison jerky" and "friends."

This week, Gregg Turkington is back, and the subject is *Dark Places*, a film featuring "no-names" of the sort Tim is "sick and tired" of watching on the big screen. "Get Tom Hanks in there," he demands.

The movie shows how a secret society of crime fighters brings a troubled woman back to the scene of the crime. Tim "couldn't bear to watch this movie." It contained "too much kid stuff in it," which he "can't handle that right now." Furthermore, he's "up to his ears in shit" as a result of the "demands" constantly being made on him by people wanting "this and that."

Despite these hardships, he continues to "sleep good at night knowing that I did what I thought was right."

"You sleep good at night because you haven't done *anything*," Gregg says. He reveals that he had to shelter Ayaka after she showed up "crying her eyes out because you won't let her into your place." Ayaka is now sleeping on Gregg's couch, and the constant "screaming" of her baby [Episode 509] makes it "hard to watch movies."

Tim says Ayaka "shouldn't have come" to America. "She wanted you to meet your child," Gregg reminds him.

"I told exactly her what to do with that kid nine months ago," he responds. Ayaka made the choice not to do this, he says, and now she must live with it. As for Tim, he's heading back to Jackson Hole and the "people I love."

"You can be with her if you want," he tells Gregg. "You can raise that child." As Tim sees it, "the kid could be at the bottom of the ocean for all I care." He sent Ayaka money, and what she chose to do with it was her decision, not his.

Gregg objects that Ayaka spent Tim's money on "baby food, hospital bills and "a flight for her and the baby to come out and see the baby's father."

Tim is unmoved: "She's not an American citizen and she does not have the rights that you and I have."

Gregg argues that the baby is an American citizen due to Tim's parentage, but Tim disputes that the baby is his, alleging that "she's been sleeping around."

On the positive side, Gregg says that when Ayaka arrived at his apartment, the missing "500 Movies in 500 Days" list turned up in her suitcase. Gregg has already gotten up to 200 movies on his new list, and now he can add the first 127 films back in for a grand total of 327. This means he will finish up the challenge in December, at which point he'll "see "everybody at the *Guinness Book* induction ceremony."

Tim make it clear he will not attend this event. Instead, he will be busy riding his motorcycle.

"And that's the end of *On Cinema*," he announces. "Because I'm done with this." He calls the program a waste of his time as well as Gregg's, though he guesses Gregg "will probably jump off a bridge without" the show. But whatever happens, Tim needs to "get away from the people that are creating negativity in my life."

"Like yourself," Gregg comments.

Tim begs to differ: "I'm a perfect person. The people around me are flawed and full of shit." He urges the *On Cinema* Family to make up their own minds about movies from here on out: "Who cares what I think?"

"What about *The Green Inferno*?" Gregg asks.

"Didn't see it, don't care. It's crap." He adds, "There are more important things in life than movies."

"Yeah, like taking care of your baby," Gregg says. In the ensuing silence, he gives *The Green Inferno* five bags of popcorn.

"Yeah, well, it's your show now," Tim answers. "You're the host of *On Cinema*." And with that, he walks off the set, seemingly forever.

On Cinema On Line

11:53 AM - 14 Dec 2014
Dec 17 is the day I complete my #500moviesin500days @GWR record setting attempt!! Coincides BEAUTIFULLY with release date of @TheHobbitMovie

11:57 AM - 14 Dec 2014
Bittersweet that @TheHobbitMovie saga is coming to end the same day I enter Guirness history #500moviesin500days #worldrecords

12:50 PM - 16 Dec 2014
Less than 48 hours 'til #TheHobbit! Camped out waiting for fellow #hobbitheads to join me!!! #500moviesin500days

12:20 AM - 17 Dec 2014
Anyone want to talk? #alone in line for the #hobbit

12:35 AM - 17 Dec 2014
It's been a long night.

8:52 PM - 17 Dec 2014
As 10:00 approaches and I prepare to set the #500moviesin500days record I wanted to thank all my supporters in this impossible quest.

8:54 PM - 17 Dec 2014
Thanks especially #oncinema's @timheidecker

10:51 PM - 17 Dec 2014
BAD SITUATION internet jerks prepaid for the Hobbit 10 pm screening SOLD OUT , rushing across to buy a ticket at the box office, total BS

10:53 PM - 17 Dec 2014
accident on Van Nuys Blvd has clogged up traffic this is a nightmare still 14 mins away

11:10 PM - 17 Dec 2014
should have gong to earlier screening but wanted to make history at stroke of midnight, ch

11:10 PM - 17 Dec 2014
What next you need reservations to buy popcorn?!

11:14 AM - 18 Dec 2014
After being unable to get into the #Hobbit due to unfair online ticketing policies, I returned home after midnight and set a new record:

11:24 AM - 18 Dec 2014
For those interested in knowing, #500 was "The Burbs" and #501 was "Soapdish". The record was set at 4:27 am PST. #501Moviesin501days

11:17 AM - 18 Dec 2014
#501Moviesin501days outdoes #500moviesin500days and I could not be more proud to submit this infomation to the #GUINESSBOOK

11:17 AM - 18 Dec 2014
Thank you for all who showed concern and support and now is the time to celebrate with a #movie! Going to see the #Hobbit at last at 2:25

6:09 PM - 18 Dec 2014
Third #Hobbit is best yet. Break out the popcorn and mark my words--it will sweep the #Oscars and go on to be the biggest-grossing film ever

On Cinema On Line

7:15 PM - 12 Jan 2015
FINALLY a show where movie expertise is the main attraction! Get ready for the Feb. premiere of "Gregg Turkington's On Cinema At The Cinema"

12:51 PM - 21 Jan 2015
just want to wish my old friend @greggturkington good luck as he prepares to HOST the new season of #OnCinema i truly wish him the best.

8:13 PM - 21 Jan 2015
Thanks, Tim! I'll do the show proud, as we focus more on #movies than ever before!

9:26 PM - 1 Feb 2015
good luck this week @greggturkington #OnCinema #bigshoes

11:28 PM - 3 Feb 2015
i will be watching @greggturkington 's #OnCinema like. a. hawk. tomorrow.

6:26 PM - 3 Feb 2015
Everyone wonders who my new #expert #sidekick will be in the new season of #OnCinema. The best-kept secret in #Hollywood. Find out tomorrow!

7:57 AM - 4 Feb 2015
at the Jackson Hole Starbucks waiting for @greggturkington 's #OnCinema to show up online... where the hell is it gregg?

8:00 AM - 4 Feb 2015
while I wait for #Oncinema to show up I guess i'll get another coffee so they don't ask me to leave.

8:06 AM - 4 Feb 2015
"Good things gone to those who wait". Ironing out a technical glitch. Up in moments!

8:09 AM - 4 Feb 2015
unprofessional bullshit

8:09 AM - 4 Feb 2015
as predicted, you are smearing #OnCinema 's good name. shame on you for this.

8:14 AM - 4 Feb 2015
Does anyone know who to contact for tech support for web video compression settings? Or if you know anything about it, message me.

8:15 AM - 4 Feb 2015
unbelievable

8:18 AM - 4 Feb 2015
Not at all. Even billion-dollar airlines are a few minutes late sometimes. Excited for you to see the new improved On Cimema.

8:22 AM - 4 Feb 2015
and the award to biggest snafu of the year goes to.... @greggturkington

8:25 AM - 4 Feb 2015
for being a FEW MINUTES late? The award actually goes to the guy who falls off a stationary motorcycle and ends up on the ER.

8:29 AM - 4 Feb 2015
"Patience is bitter, but its fruit is sweet." Tweet your favorite patience quotes to @timheidecker while we work out last few tech glitches

8:41 AM - 4 Feb 2015
my only hope is that this unreasonable wait will be worth it

9:22 AM - 4 Feb 2015
@greggturkington does the new #OnCinema even exist?

10:56 AM - 4 Feb 2015
Finally! OK, watching now...

SEASON 6

EPISODE 601

'Jupiter Ascending' & 'The Spongebob Movie'

Air date: February 4, 2015
Running time: 7:36 minutes

The first season of *Gregg Turkington's On Cinema at the Cinema* is underway, and Gregg makes no bones about the topic of the day: Movies!

Acknowledging that some viewers may hold preconceived notions based on earlier incarnations of *On Cinema*, Gregg certifies that his new program will be "going a little more into the world of expertise" than former host Tim Heidecker did.

That's no easy feat, because in the past, Gregg was *On Cinema*'s card-carrying film expert. Now that he's the show's full-time host, he needs a new expert — preferably "someone who could fulfill that role better than anyone."

That "someone" turns out to be a pre-recorded tape of Gregg himself, as seen through a dual-action VHS player/TV perched atop a cardboard box in the guest seat. As the host, all Gregg has to do is press his remote, and his guest relates how he recently set a new world record for watching movies.

The pre-recorded Gregg tells us he had originally planned to earn a permanent spot in the *Guinness Book of World Records* by watching 500 movies in 500 days. In the end, he "did it one better, by watching 501 movies in 501 days." Now, it's just a matter of "hearing from the Guinness folks," which is likely to happen "pretty soon."

The first film up for review is *Jupiter Ascending*. [Episode 503] Speaking as the host, Gregg notes that Mila Kunis and Channing Tatum star in this sci-fi movie. Speaking as his guest, Gregg endorses *Jupiter Ascending* as "kind of the epitome of the popcorn movie" and recommends it to fans of *The Matrix*. He gives it five bags of popcorn and "a souvenir keychain from *The Matrix*."

Speaking as the host, Gregg raves that *Jupiter Ascending* is "really a lot of fun." Expanding on his videotaped remarks, he gives it five bags of popcorn.

Did YOU notice...?

- That wasn't W.C. Fields you were watching in *Golden Age Comedies!* That was gifted Fields impersonator Mark Proksch turning in a performance so true to life, it would fool Fields' own closest friends, such as comedy greats like Mae West, Charlie Chaplin and the late Stanley Laurel.

Departing from outer space, we splash down in the underwater world of *The Spongebob Movie*, which transports the titular deep-sea hero out of the watery depths and onto dry land through the movie magic of live-action CGI.

Speaking from the VHS player, Gregg embraces Spongebob as "an American institution" who is finally "on the big screen where he belongs." He gives it five bags of popcorn, along with a Spongebob cup that can be used to hold drinks or even "a handful of popcorn."

In response to this pre-recorded commentary, Gregg brings up the "interesting trend" of "television shows or cartoons expanding into being feature films." As he sees it, this is "something we should keep our eye on for the future."

As host, Gregg gives *The Spongebob Movie* five bags of popcorn. Combined with his rating as a guest, that's a total of 10 bags from Gregg.

Next, Gregg has a new feature for "movieheads." This feature will replace *Popcorn Classics*, as Gregg finds it too difficult to produce these segments while hosting the show.

Golden Age Comedies With W.C. Fields takes an in-depth look at the best and the brightest in cinematic laughs. Filmed in authentic black and white, and sporting his trademark straw boater and cigar, "your old pal W. C. Fields" gives a shout-out to *Home Fries*, which stars "two lovers and a pregnant Drew Barrymore" as "two love-bugs" who "get into it," much as the late Mr. Fields himself "used to" with his "leading ladies."

Although this "great movie" might be "too risqué for the little ones," Fields calls it "one of my favorites." However, he's quick to admit that "I never watched a movie I didn't enjoy." He looks forward to being back "next week and every week" and he thanks Gregg for opening "this exciting new chapter in W. C.'s career."

Back on the set, Gregg gives himself kudos for creating a show "that introduces movie criticism for all to enjoy." On video, he thanks his host, Gregg Turkington, for having him on the show.

STATEMENT ON GREGG TURKINGTON'S ON CINEMA AT THE CINEMA

I have now watched the first episode of Gregg Turkington's On Cinema at the Cinema — and here are my thoughts:

How dare he? how dare he take what was once mine and drag it through the mud like this? i am beyond outraged that he has the gaul to literally destroy my only child. And the on cinema family should be just (if not more) outraged. It's disgusting what Gregg has done. And do you know what? it's not going to be tolerated.

Gregg has shaken the hornet's nest with this sham/show — and now the hornets are going to strike. I'm going to have to do something I never thought i'd have to do — and it's going to be painful. Stand by for more as the story develops, as the news might say — I am truly sorry that the on cinema family has to go through this. I really wanted all the best for Gregg — I don't know what the future is for on cinema — it's a sad day.

All the best,

Tim Heidecker
Jackson Hole, WY

On Cinema On Line

12:54 PM - 4 Feb 2015
To issue this unwanted statement is extremely rude. I stood by you during the Dr. San era--you made that fraud a GUEST!

12:55 PM - 4 Feb 2015
I will let the ratings and the positive tweets speak for themselves. Sour grapes from Wyoming is not an edict from above!

9:42 AM - 5 Feb 2015
let's get #ISISwithTim trending aka: I Stand In Solidarity (with Tim)

10:39 AM - 5 Feb 2015
If you support the new On Cinema and not Tim's whining and bullying, hashtag #CHRIST (Can Heidecker Really Insist on Silencing Turkington?)

10:41 AM - 5 Feb 2015
You must choose: #ISISwithTim or #CHRIST. There is no middle ground. Let's get #CHRIST trending.

6:56 PM - 6 Feb 2015
Finally got @greggturkington on the phone. Long talk. I think we're on the same page about #OnCinema moving forward.

6:57 PM - 6 Feb 2015
Obviously we both want what's best for the show

12:17 AM - 8 Feb 2015
@timheidecker had some good suggestions for things I could be doing better. This season of #oncinema is going to be great. #host #expert

12:56 PM - 8 Feb 2015
To be clear--it is my understanding that @timheidecker is returning to #OnCinema in an advisory/behind-the-scenes role. I welcome his advice

12:59 PM - 8 Feb 2015
Don't expect any major changes--just a few tweaks to make this season a "10 out of 10".

12:35 PM - 8 Feb 2015
So long Jackson Hole… It's been… Interesting.

8:30 AM - 9 Feb 2015
Back in LA and ready to #CarpeDiem with @greggturkington #OnCinema

11:30 AM - 10 Feb 2015
Fixed the issues with the remote control from last week. Excited to film tonight!!! #oncinema

11:42 AM - 10 Feb 2015
Tim is helping out with some ideas, and sound issues. I learned a lot last week and am ready to make a flawless episode 2!

EPISODE 602
'50 Shades of Grey' & 'Kingsman: The Secret Service'

Air date: February 11, 2015
Running time: 12:07 minutes

This week, *Gregg Turkington's On Cinema at the Cinema* has a brand-new host: Tim Heidecker, former host of *On Cinema at the Cinema*!

Tim introduces his first guest, former *Gregg Turkington's On Cinema at the Cinema* host Gregg Turkington, and thanks him "for being on my show."

Tim says "this has been a wild several months." In a searingly emotional monologue, he says he doesn't want to get "too emotional," but he does need to "bring everybody up to speed." This will result in "a long show" as well as "a somewhat painful show."

To begin with, Tim recently had a personal epiphany: "I do not belong in Jackson Hole with the filth [and] trash that live there." Visitors should also steer clear of the town due to its "bad people," who include close friends of Tim's that turned out to be in the KKK (although Tim "didn't know that when I was hanging out with them and doing business with them").

After fleeing Jackson Hole, Tim saw an episode of *Gregg Turkington's On Cinema at the Cinema*: "It dawned on me that where I belonged was what I had given up" when he moved to Jackson Hole "to live amongst these terrible people."

Tim is grateful to Gregg for coming back to "be the expert that he is on this show," and he applauds himself for recognizing himself as the rightful host of *On Cinema*: "I am the father of the *On Cinema* Family, and the father has come home, much like the classic Bible tales of Abraham and Moses and Jesus Christ himself. I have come back, and my flock is now amongst us."

Tim asks Gregg to share his own thoughts on "this experience."

"I kind of thought it was gonna go on longer," Gregg reflects.

Tim is curious whether Gregg's brief tenure as host gave him "a little more perspective on the work that goes into what I do." Gregg concedes that Tim's job is tough, though not as tough as doing Tim's job while also providing expert commentary and producing segments like *Golden Age Comedies With W.C. Fields*. "I was actually doing more than you've ever done on this show," he says.

Tim is just happy things are back to normal: "All things come back to the center, as my guru says." In related news, Tim's *Hog Shots* book "is not happening," even though he took out "a very large small business loan from the federal government" to publish it. Instead, he used the money for a timeshare in Hawaii. This is where he will shoot *Decker 2*, as it will allow him to attract a higher caliber of talent, such as Colin Firth or F. Murray Abraham. The future of Gregg's character, Agent Kington, remains up in the air.

For Tim, *50 Shades of Grey* was "almost a porno in my book." This "sexy thriller" was "full of nudity and sex of all kinds," including "dirty sex" and "pornographic sex." Nevertheless, he "loved it" and gives it five bags of popcorn "and five cold glasses of soda to put between my legs."

Gregg sees *50 Shades of Grey* "more as a kind of romance." Suggesting that it might be a good Valentine's Day film, he gives it five bags of popcorn and "five little chocolate hearts" in "a heart-shaped gift box."

In *Kingsman: The Secret Service*, Michael Caine and Colin Firth put the SPY back in eSPIonage as the generation gap exacts its toll on Caine's classic Secret Agent Man persona. Tim wonders if this movie is another "tip of the hat" to *Decker*. Gregg is quite sure it's more than that, given the title's similarity to the name of his own character, "Kingston."

To be fair, he presumes that Tim himself was "tipping his hat to Bond" when he wrote *Decker*. Tim disagrees, crediting *Jack Reacher* as his primary inspiration. Both critics see the *Decker* influence as a net positive; as Gregg puts it, "It reminds you of how much we really appreciate Decker's appearance on the action scene."

Tim "loved this movie" enough to give it five bags of popcorn and a soda. Gregg gives it five bags and a videotape containing five episodes of *Decker*, "because these guys have learned a lot from it, and it shows."

Gregg wants to run the latest installment of *Golden Age Comedies*, starring world-class Fields impersonator Mark Proksch, but Tim says "that contract doesn't mean anything to me" and the segment will not be continuing. However, because Mark is already in his suit in front of the green screen, he relents and allows the segment to proceed.

Today's Golden Age Comedy is Vanessa Williams' *Soul Food*, "a fun family romp" that takes care to "dish up the laughs." In closing, Mark thanks Gregg for giving him the chance to do this "short-lived" segment, during which he "had a lot of fun" in his role as the legendary comic W. C. Fields.

ON CINEMA ON HOLLYWOOD LEGENDS

Mark Proksch

It is often said that no one truly dies until they are forgotten! **Mark Proksch** was living proof of this adage, having made it his life's mission in life to spare the immortal legends of Golden-Age Comedy from this undeserved fate. From the **Three Stooges** to the **Four Marx Brothers** to the-one-and-only, irreplaceable **W.C. Fields**, Mark brought all of them back to vibrant life — and then some!

But Mark had his dramatic side too, appearing as the wily Arab terrorist **Abdul** in countless episodes of **Decker** and also risking his own life to bring classic scenes from **Jaws** to vivid life in honor of the anniversary of **Jaws 2**. As a beloved and never-to-be-forgotten member of the **On Cinema Family**, Mark also did his best to make the **Victorville Film Center** and **Six Bag Cinema** successful. His many fans are eager for his return to the On Cinema screen as soon as he can!

On Cinema On Line

7:05 PM - 11 Feb 2015
I AM #FATHER I AM #KING I AM #BACK

1:51 PM - 11 Feb 2015
Golden Age Comedy w/WC Fields will hopefully be back. I'm very proud of my work as producer of that segment and feel it had great potential.

1:53 PM - 11 Feb 2015
I support @TimHeidecker, let's give his new direction a chance. I hope he learned that viewers want #movie talk, not personal issues.

1:54 PM - 11 Feb 2015
I remain as committed as ever to #movies. I will continue to provide #expertise to all of you, and thank you for your support.

1:55 PM - 11 Feb 2015
I think @timheidecker was premature to pull the plug when my last episode had the highest ratings & the best reviews in #OnCinema history

1:56 PM - 11 Feb 2015
I am getting a lot of complaints about the changes he has made and I am powerless to change them back, please direct those to @timheidecker

4:32 PM - 14 Feb 2015
@m_proksch sorry things didn't work out, but would love to have you be a part of the #OnCinemaOscarSpecial

4:43 PM - 14 Feb 2015
Okay! Thanks! FYI- I have other impersonations!

4:45 PM - 14 Feb 2015
anything other than W.C. Fields. that bit doesn't work for us.

4:35 PM - 14 Feb 2015
@GovMikeHuckabee just checking to see if you got my message about Oscar Special. looking forward to speaking with you. respectfully, tim

EPISODE 603
'Hot Tub Time Machine 2' & 'McFarland USA'

Air date: February 18, 2015
Running time: 9:49 minutes

Tim is deeply moved by the "outpouring of love and appreciation" that greeted his return as the host of the now retitled *On Cinema at the Cinema*. [Episode 602]

Today, Tim's guest is Gregg Turkington, who's thankful for the tidal wave of support he got during his one-episode stint as the host of *Gregg Turkington's On Cinema at the Cinema*. [Episode 601]

Tim has recently been "getting readjusted into the L.A. lifestyle." That includes settling into a North Hollywood apartment with his new roommate, Gregg Turkington. He's grateful for the opportunity to "bunk up" with *On Cinema*'s resident film buff and discloses that they've "been watching a lot of movies together."

They've also been "talking about this *Decker* show, which is happening" and "is coming along OK," apart from Tim's "writer's block" that has affected some of the "plot points."

Hot Tub Time Machine 2 yokes *Animal House* alumnus Chevy Chase in tandem with many others, as Lou is saved from an assassin's bullet with a little help from his friends. Tim is "happy they made this one" because it ties up all the "mysteries" from *Hot Tub Time Machine 1*. "It's a very funny movie," and "it's also a quality movie," so it gets five bags of popcorn and two tubs of soda.

Gregg champions the first *Hot Tub* film as "the *Airplane!* of our generation — just a comedy that everybody loved." Eventually, *Airplane 2* was released, "which filled us in on what those guys were up to." In much the same way, *Hot Tub Time Machine 2* brings us up to speed on "what happened with some of the characters" we came to admire in the prequel. He gives it a grateful five bags of popcorn, plus "a little container of chlorine" to kill all the germs in the hot tub water.

Also revving its engines at the starting gate this week is *McFarland USA*, which boasts none other than Kevin Costner at the wheel. Tim enjoyed this film's "interesting story" and "dramatic themes." However, he notifies Kevin Costner fans that it's an atypical Costner offering in its focus on sports.

Gregg says it is in fact "a typical Kevin Costner movie," citing *Field of Dreams* as a classic "sports movie" and indicating that Costner "got sidetracked" for a time from the sports pictures that made his name. Now, "he's come back to what he does best," which is "what the world's been waiting for." Gregg celebrates Costner's return to the fold with five bags of popcorn and five baseballs.

Tim cites this rating as a perfect example of Gregg's cinema expertise: "This is why I have you on the show." He goes on to say that "when I get it wrong, I'll admit when I'm wrong." He's been working on this by visiting Values.com for its "motivational, inspirational messages," one of which is "know when you're wrong and admit when you're wrong."

Tim accordingly steps up to the plate and admits he "goofed" on *McFarland USA*. He makes Costner his Oscar pick in an attempt to make amends. He also gives the movie six bags of popcorn "and my appreciation and my thanks."

In this spirit of reconciliation and amity, Tim introduces a new segment of Gregg's popular *On Cinema On Location* segment, which was canceled in Episode 508 due to its fixation on the *Oh, God!* movies. Gregg is taking no chances this time; instead, he takes us to "the tunnel from *Decker*," through which "John [sic] Decker rides his motorcycle during the credit sequence of the web series *Decker*."

Tim is pleased and more than a little touched by this segment: "That's neat to get a perspective on that." Gregg explains that "after the whole *Oh, God!* thing," he "wanted to start this season of *On Location* off on a good foot."

Tim thanks Gregg for being "such a fan of *Decker*" and asks if he'd like to help write the new season. He adds that if Gregg wants to "come back and play Kingsman," he's welcome to share his "idea for how that would work." Gregg says he has "a lot of ideas for Kingston's character" and "would love to come on board."

A handshake seals the deal, and Tim tells Gregg to "get ready" for a trip to Hawaii, because "we're gonna be going there quite a bit!"

On Cinema On Line

6:13 PM - 17 Feb 2015
You won't believe Sunday's #OnCinemaOscarSpecial grand finale! My special guest will have everyon talking--a true Oscar-winner movie legend!

9:47 PM - 20 Feb 2015
Why did the Oscar Academy hire 5 new employees today? To deal with the extra processing time for all the write-in votes. #HobbitBestPicture

THIRD ANNUAL OSCARS SPECIAL
Live Broadcast from Hollywood's Biggest Night

Air date: February 24, 2015
Running time: 2:16:42

This year, it's "Oscar Fever 2.0" as Tim's theme song gets a live reboot from the On Cinema Marching Band. Tonight, this malady will be shared by musical guest Mike Huckabee and gifted impressionist Mark Proksch. No wonder they call it Christmas for Tinseltown!

Tim welcomes his friend, roommate and co-host, Gregg Turkington, to present his own take on the Oscars through the lens of a certified film buff. Gregg has made an Oscars Special cake, but he drops it while trying to get a closeup.

Tim thanks his co-host for being part of this special night. Taking Gregg's hand, he leads the *On Cinema* Family in a prayer thanking "Lord Jesus Christ" for yet another opportunity to discuss Oscar Night online. He also prays for the strength to find forgiveness if things go wrong.

Tim has got the Oscar Fever.

What's On Oscar's Menu?
In the last Oscar show, Tim was "a little disappointed" by Gregg's finale. This time, Gregg has a finale "no one could be disappointed by." On the contrary, it will "make international headlines" as "one of the all-time legends of Hollywood" returns to the "public limelight."

Tim acknowledges his past problems with Oscar Night drinking. This year, he's bought some organic champagne, which he assumes is non-alcoholic. Because he has a cold, he's also dosing himself with Mucinex cough syrup.

Asked for his Best Picture prediction, Gregg drops a little inside knowledge. This year has only eight nominees because two are still under wraps: *Annie* and *The Hobbit 3*. Gregg's sources say *The Hobbit 3* has already edged out all other contenders in its enchanted quest for Oscar gold.

Tim is annoyed that the Stallone/Schwarzenegger double-threat prison drama *Escape Plan* was snubbed. Gregg comments that this is not a snub so much as an inherent flaw of the Oscar system. If the Academy switched to a monthly award, movies like *Escape Plan* could get the real-time recognition they deserve.

After a technical glitch, Tim castigates the *On Cinema* crew as "lowlife losers." Concerned that his initial prayer to God may have "bit me in the ass," he rips off his crucifix. "Fuck God," he snarls.

Reaching for his champagne glass, he says, "Bad news, everybody. This is full of booze." He finishes the bottle and chases it with a slug of Mucinex.

Behind the Scenes at the Oscars
Next, Gregg has put together his traditional behind-the-scenes feature on Hollywood's Dolby Theatre, home of the Oscars. We get a familiar glimpse of the Oscar Wall of Fame and then a peek into the now-empty room where Oscar will soon make his final decision.

Tim frets that this feature has become "redundant" and counsels Gregg to "get some new energy in there."

The On Cinema Movie Awards
The first-ever *On Cinema* movie awards center on underdog titles that were "shafted" for whatever reason by Oscar. This year, the host is Kim Delgado of *BeetleBorgs* fame. The Best Supporting Actor award goes to Sir Ian McKellan, edging out Joe Estevez, Mark Proksch and Gregg Turkington of *Decker*. Gregg accepts the award on Sir Ian's behalf.

Back on the set, Tim asks Gregg to contemplate the "worst-case scenario" in the form of "an attack on the Oscars tonight" by a terrorist group like ISIS or Charlie Hebdo. Gregg's feeling is that because many popular filmmakers don't get invited to the Oscars, an attack could be "a blessing in disguise" for them.

"If you were an ISIS combatant, and you were able to sneak into the Academy, who would you go after first?"

"I'd have to wait till the Oscars are over and see if anyone defeats *The Hobbit*," Gregg says.

A Moe-tivational Speech
Tim introduces *On Cinema* veteran Mark Proksch, former star of *Golden Age Comedies With W.C. Fields*. Tim recalls how that segment "created a tremendous negative response" because "nobody wanted to see W.C. Fields anymore." Today, Mark will be portraying The Three Stooges instead.

Speaking first as Moe Howard, Mark traces the roots of today's moving picture violence to early cartoons such as Tom and Jerry as well as to the Stooges themselves. "The context of the actual movie, it changes with each generation," he observes, adding the high-pitched whinnying sound that was once the calling card of his brother Curly Joe.

"I died in 1975," he concludes, ending our reunion with the great Moe Howard.

On Location on Middle-Earth
Gregg presents a very special edition of *On Location* from the fantastical realms of Middle-Earth, home of Bilbo Baggins and shooting location of the six-film *Lord of the Rings* trilogy.

"This is the very area where Bilbo Baggins did his magical tricks," he says, standing outside an authentic Hobbit house to "experience life as they did back in Tolkien's time." Sadly, our visit to Bilbo's stomping grounds ends early due to a technical glitch.

Call Me Ayaka

After an exclusive peek at the trailer for *Decker: Port of Call: Hawaii*, Kim Delgado reappears to present *On Cinema*'s award for Best Actor to Tim for his performance as Decker, which beat out Pierce Brosnan, Martin Freeman and Tom Cruise in a classic Tinseltown upset.

Gregg is curious about "the voting protocol" for these awards, but Tim doesn't have time to explain due to a commercial break.

On returning, we learn that Mike Huckabee will not be appearing after all. This is a major blow to Tim, who angrily informs the former governor that he no longer has his backing for president.

With Huckabee not available for an Oscar medley jam session, Tim takes to the ivories himself with a song dedicated to his estranged girlfriend, Ayaka Ohwaki. He also includes his cell phone number on the screen so she can call him. His phone starts ringing midway through the song, but all the callers are men.

On Cinema On Directors

Gregg has a new pilot segment, *On Cinema On Directors*. This week, his guests are *Yes Man* director Peyton Reed and *Decker* director Tim Heidecker.

Peyton describes how he was inculcated with a love of film by his parents, parlaying a Super 8 camera into a directing gig that eventually led to his appearance on this show. For his part, Tim describes the need to "seize the moment" that will make the images in your head real.

Gregg asks for tips on getting top performances out of actors. Tim brags that he's fortunate to work with "one of the best actors in the business" — himself! When working with Gregg, however, he had to resort to "mind tricks" to coax a good performance out of him.

Peyton singles out Gregg's performance — which Tim created with a phony interview and green screen techniques — as superb. To have filmed Gregg without letting him know he was playing a character, Peyton says, was "a kind of genius."

For Oscar picks, Tim elects *Escape Plan* while Peyton gives the nod to *Boyhood*. Gregg remains certain *The Hobbit 3* will win a write-in campaign. But as a member of the Academy, Peyton says that "by the time the nominations are out, it's really impossible to have a write-in category." Under badgering from Gregg, he concedes that it's "not impossible" for *The Hobbit 3* to bring home the proverbial bacon for Oscar.

Gregg next asks Peyton what he would've done differently if he'd directed *Decker*. Peyton pointedly declines to answer this "slippery slope" question.

This irks Tim, who doesn't see why Peyton would need to do anything more than hail *Decker* as "the best movie I've ever seen." After some cross-talk, Peyton strongly implies *Decker* could have used "a few less motorcycle-riding shots."

Calling the interview "a setup," an enraged Tim demands to know how Gregg knows Peyton and why he brought him on the show. It turns out Peyton and his casting team had been looking for "exciting new people," and they felt Gregg's "terrific performance" as Kingston made him "perfect" for the role of "Dale" in the upcoming Marvel film *Ant-Man*, starring Paul Rudd, which wrapped while Tim was in Jackson Hole.

Tim is shocked by this news. "Why didn't you ask me to be in the movie?" he asks. As Peyton presents his theory that the "specific part" in the *Ant-Man* story was better suited to Gregg, Tim gets up and leaves. "Happy Oscars," he says. "I gotta go."

Ant-Mania!

Tim comes back alone to say that Gregg set him up: "What he did to me was as much a disgrace as you can do to a man." He laments that he has been "thrown under the bus" not just by Gregg, but also by "Mike Hucklebee" and the *On Cinema* technical crew.

Gregg is welcome back on the show, and will still be allowed "in my house." But "Peyton Reed will never get a bag of popcorn in my book for any movie he makes," due to his lack of artistic vision in casting Gregg in *Ant-Man*. "Gregg Turkington is gonna fall flat on his face in that movie," he predicts.

There's No Business Like Joe Business!

Kim Delgado is back with the *On Cinema* Lifetime Achievement Award for those "who have made an indelible impact on movies past, present and future." Tonight's winner, Joe Estevez, has done more than his part to earn this award, having been in at least 285 movies including 1974's *The California Kid* and others.

Over a lengthy montage of classic scenes, Joe shares thoughts of a life spent in service to the fine art of the actor's craft. Then, Tim presents him with the formal award, sponsored by Chaplin's Chili. Tim and Joe hug, and in this emotional moment Tim calls Gregg on stage to apologize. "Congratulations on being in a movie," he tells his co-host. "The reason I cast you in *Decker* is because I think you're a good actor, OK? So it makes sense that that asshole put you in his movie."

Oscar Heaven

Tim opens a new bottle of champagne in celebration of "Oscar heaven." Even though Mark is wearing his Larry Fine wig and trying to eat, Tim commands him to don his Chaplin duds and impersonate the "Little Tramp" in honor of Chaplin's Chili: "Take that stupid Larry wig off and do Charlie Chaplin, asshole."

Mark gives it the old college try, but Tim cuts the segment short to focus on a

Larry Fine was one of the original Three Stooges.

sartorial gift from Joe Estevez: It's a dickie, which Joe hopes will come back into fashion as the "Decker."

Afterward, Mark returns as Larry Fine. "I died in 1975 of a stroke," he tells fans, but not before becoming something of a "counterculture" icon. He also tips us off that the Stooges "always used rubber hammers" for safety's sake. Tim thanks Mark for "killing it" as Mr. Fine.

Tim is still getting lots of annoying male callers pretending to be Ayaka, but he can't figure out how to turn his phone off. Gregg buries it in the popcorn machine to mute the sound.

Look Who's Tolkien!
Tim makes Gregg aware that so far, *The Hobbit 3* has not done well: "Let's say — worst-case scenario — *The Hobbit* doesn't win. Where does that put you?"

Having gotten inside information, Gregg's not worried about a *Hobbit* loss. His biggest fear is that with the Hobbit storyline exhausted, there will be no more Hobbit tales to tell.

Fortunately, his attention was brought to a book called the *The Silmarillion*, authored by no less an authority than J.R.R. Tolkien. Gregg picked up a copy for himself and one for Tim because he sees it as the future of the franchise. To make his case, Gregg reads a lengthy paragraph at random, asking viewers to imagine they're watching it in a cinema. He expects the 50 to 150 *Silmarillion* movies Peter Jackson will make over the next 40 years to surpass James Bond as "the most successful franchise in movie history."

Meanwhile, Tim has fallen unconscious and is drooling on himself.

Tim's Big Night
Kim Delgado presents the *On Cinema* award for Best Director to Tim for his work on Season 1 of *Decker*. Because Tim is still unconscious, Gregg accepts it in his stead.

When Tim wakes up, he expresses his gratitude to the *On Cinema* Academy for his award. He also denounces Michael Keaton for daring to "chew gum during the Oscars."

The award for Best Screenplay also goes to Tim. "This is better than an Oscar," he says. "I don't give a shit about Oscars." As if to prove his point, the Best Picture award goes to *Decker*, leaving *The Hobbit*, *Escape Plan* and all the rest in the dust.

Shame on Hollywood!
Tim is angry that *The Interview* was "thrown under the bus" by not winning Best Picture: "Congratulations to Seth Rogen for having the *cojonos* to put that movie out whether or not they were gonna get attacked by Charlie Hebdo or not."

Tim performs a reprise of "Oscar Fever," this time accompanying himself on bass. Halfway through, he throws his instrument down in disgust: "Fuck you, Mike Hucklebee, you've ruined my night." He also complains that he "got diarrhea from that Chaplin's Chili shit."

Oscar announces *Birdman* as Best Picture, dismaying Tim and enraging Gregg, who feels this movie is "just a play that got filmed accidentally."

"Shame on Hollywood," Tim says.

Back in the Tinseltown Saddle
Tim is excited to find out more about Gregg's special mystery guest.

"Throughout movie history there have been some legends," Gregg tells him, naming Humphrey Bogart as just one example. "But there's one legend whose star shone brighter than any, and for many years he has been out of the public eye." But now, this mystery man is ready to come back to the spotlight!

Walking over to the red curtain, Gregg pulls it open slightly to reveal an old man who turns out to be none other than the legendary James Byron Dean!

Though long believed dead, the title of his new book clears up that misconception once and for all: *I'm Still Alive: Why I Faked My Own Death to Escape the Trappings of the Hollywood Star System, Fame and Fortune*.

Tim is skeptical: "I thought this asshole died about a hundred years ago." Gregg rolls a reel of clips from James' matchless career.

Asked by Gregg to tell the audience how he faked his own death, Dean confesses that after his car accident, "I just laid very still."

Tim still can't quite accept that James Dean is really alive. "Would you submit to a DNA test?" he asks the actor.

"Oh yes," Dean replies. He goes on to say that he's been doing "a lot of theater" recently. But at the same time, "being an actor wasn't really that deep for me. I could be a philosopher if I wanted to. I could go into politics."

"Do you think you'd ever make a comeback as an actor?" Gregg asks. Dean says he's been considering getting back into Shakespeare and might even consider "a musical version of *King Lear*."

Tim doesn't see why Mr. Dean would choose to come on *On Cinema*'s Oscar Special when he could've attended the

The unheralded return of the one and only James Dean.

official Oscars: "This all smells like rotten fish," he says, as does Dean himself according to Tim.

"Read the book," Gregg tells him. Tim again demands a blood sample from the frail actor. "I'll take it myself," he threatens.

Calling Dean "a fraud," he orders the elderly man off the set.

As Mark and Gregg escort him gently to the wings, Dean calls Tim "a goddamn stupid son of a bitch" and hurls his original *Rebel Without a Cause* pocketknife in Tim's direction. "Get him off my set," Tim screams, throwing a chair at Dean.

"That could cause me damage," Dean says. "I could sue his ass. I'll be running your show in a couple weeks!"

"Bring it on, asshole!" Tim responds, throwing another chair at the Hollywood legend.

As Gregg apologizes to James Dean for Tim's "rage problems," Tim cuts to cutting-edge footage of Mark Proksch impersonating all Three Stooges at once.

ON CINEMA ON HOLLYWOOD LEGENDS

James Dean

No list of the greats is complete until it has been amended to include the name of **James Byron Dean**. One of the major stars of the 1950s in such films as **East of Eden**, Dean's promising young life was long assumed to have ended at James Dean Memorial Junction near **Cholame, California**, where he suffered a fatal crash in his sports car and died of serious internal injuries including a broken neck.

Decades later, he stunned friends and foes alike by revealing that he had faked his own alleged death in the tell-all story **I'm Still Alive: Why I Faked My Own Death to Escape the Trappings of the Hollywood Star System, Fame and Fortune.**

Though he is no longer a young man, Mr. Dean still loves acting and brings an Old World gravitas to classic roles like **Dracula** and as a member of the **Decker** franchise. It is reasonable to say that the whole world is waiting to learn what this "Giant" of the Silver Screen will do next!

On Cinema On Line

4:43 PM - 14 Feb 2015
Hey @timheidecker, I take it all back. Just saw what you said on-camera after our #OnCinema segment. You're a disgrace.

1:39 PM - 23 Feb 2015
@MrPeytonReed who cares what you think? I can get in any movie I want. Try me.

1:46 PM - 23 Feb 2015
Good luck with that. Why not spend some time @values.com ? Also, maybe stop drinking.

1:46 PM - 23 Feb 2015
Hello @joshuatrank I am a big fan and would love to act in your new movie. Please DM me to set that up.

4:53 PM - 23 Feb 2015
"@joshuatrank: @timheidecker Let's do this." Awesome. Excited to work with you. Let's make movie magic.

7:31 PM - 23 Feb 2015
@greggturkington @MrPeytonReed just got cast in a major motion picture that will blow your "little" movie out of the water.

8:28 PM - 23 Feb 2015
Congratulations, Tim. I'm sure you'll be great. Break a leg.

7:19 AM - 24 Feb 2015
Shit List (updated)
1. @GovMikeHuckabee 2. @MrPeytonReed 2. Fake James Dean 3. Tech crew...

10:06 AM - 24 Feb 2015
Tim, read the book before you falsely claim that was "fake" James Dean. I'm paying to have DNA testing done to clarify this.

10:09 AM - 24 Feb 2015
I will be selling authentic #JamesDean autographs for $5.00 each in order to fund DNA testing to prove he is still alive.

I'M STILL ALIVE

WHY I FAKED MY OWN DEATH TO ESCAPE THE TRAPPINGS OF THE HOLLYWOOD STAR SYSTEM, FAME AND FORTUNE

by JAMES DEAN

PRINTED BY REBEL WITH A CAUSE PUBLISHING

EPISODE 604
'Focus' & 'Lazarus'

Air date: February 25, 2015
Running time: 8:31 minutes

Tim introduces his guest, Gregg Turkington, who is also his roommate. "We've been spending a lot of time together," Tim tells Gregg. "I've literally been around you pretty much 24/7."

This quality time has included several visits to Hawaii for the shooting of *Decker: Port of Call: Hawaii*. "It has been so much fun," Tim says. It has also been "an interesting experience" living with Gregg, a real-world "movie buff" who has been driving Tim "a little nuts" by "constantly watching movies." In order to "have some peace and quiet," he recently turned Gregg's bedroom into his own private "studio apartment."

Gregg is fine with this arrangement, apart from the fact that he can no longer get into his bedroom to access the classic videotapes he stores there. Tim offers a one-step solution: "Get all the movies out of the bedroom, and that way you don't have to ever get in there."

Focus stars Will Smith in a romantic crime film about a pair of grifters whose biggest heist is each other's hearts. Tim says *Focus* "is a very appropriate title for a movie that's very sharp and in focus." It gets five popcorn bags and "five drinks of soda."

Gregg also finds the title "interesting," given that the movie is so "focused on the story." Further, Will Smith deserves an Oscar. He gives it five bags of popcorn and "a little plastic microscope as a keepsake."

Donald Glover treads the boards in *Lazarus*, a.k.a. *The Lazarus Effect*, a horror thriller in which the dead return to life with powers they never imagined. Tim thought it was "a fun movie" that allows you to play "what-if games" like "what if Frankenstein came back to life?" He loved the performance by Donald Glover, or possibly Danny Glover: "Whoever it was gave top-notch work." He gives it five bags of popcorn.

Gregg considers *Lazarus* a timely film, because "coming back from the dead is a topic that's interested people for decades." Classic characters "like your Frankensteins and your Wolf Man and Mummy" are already on the public's radar, and "Lazarus could fit right in with that whole crowd." He awards it five bags of popcorn, plus "a four-leaf clover" for luck, so "that *Lazarus* continues on" as "a popular series."

Speaking of a popular series that has been brought back to life like Lazarus, this week's *Popcorn Classics* focuses on the resurrection of the late Peter Sellers' beloved Inspector Jacques Cousteau, who has been reanimated by Roberto Benigni in *Son of the Pink Panther*.

Gregg discloses that W. C. Fields had been tapped to review this film on *Golden Age Comedies* before Tim "killed" the segment. Referring to Tim as "my little chickadee," Gregg enumerates "a couple issues" he has with *Son of the Pink Panther*: First of all, the box depicts a rating of three stars, "when it's clearly a five-bag-quality movie." But "other than that, it's perfect!"

Tim says this is why he prefers to use bags of popcorn for ratings — it's "a little bit more interesting and a little more colorful."

"That's how I felt about *Golden Age Comedies*," Gregg says, but Tim cuts this discussion short.

He tells us that while browsing Values.com, [Episode 603] he learned an important life lesson: "I need to express myself from my heart."

With this wisdom in mind, Tim has a heartfelt message for Ayaka Ohwaki, his former *On Cinema* co-host and the estranged mother of his child: He is "so sorry about how things went down between us," and he would like to "keep getting in touch" so their relationship will be "meaningful and full of love."

Since he is now "in town," he views it as Ayaka's responsibility to contact him: "You are the mother of my son, Tom Cruise Heidecker, and I want to be a part of his life." He notifies her that "if we get back together, we could become the power couple of Hollywood."

"Where are you guys going to live?" Gregg asks. Ignoring this question, Tim keeps pleading with Ayaka to return to him.

EPISODE 605
'Chappie,' 'The Second Best Exotic Marigold Hotel' & 'The Coup'

Air date: March 4, 2015
Running time: 9:58 minutes

In observance of "Decker Day," Tim has worn his official Decker outfit to the set of *On Cinema*. Also on hand for the looming premiere of *Decker: Port of Call: Hawaii* are *Decker* stalwarts President Davidson (Joe Estevez) and Special Agent Kington (Gregg Turkington). Tim makes it clear that although he is dressed as Jack Decker, the opinions expressed in his movie reviews are entirely his own.

Tim is "in a great mood" because shooting *Decker* has been "so much fun." Even better, "Ayaka and Tom Cruise Heidecker, my child, are back in my life" and all three of them are now living in Gregg's apartment.

"It's a madhouse over there," Tim sighs. "Jumping into the deep end with the fatherhood stuff has been wild." On top of that, he and Gregg have had to make many trips to the beautiful island kingdom of Hawaii to shoot this season of *Decker*, which seems to come as a surprise to fellow cast member Joe Estevez.

Chappie stars Hugh Jackman and Sigourney Weaver in a dystopian coming-of-age film about a stolen "robo-cop" who gets reprogrammed by the bad guys in South Africa. Even though it was "different," Tim greatly enjoyed this "great sci-fi-style movie with robots and everything." His rating? Five bags of popcorn, two bags of soda.

Gregg also "really liked this movie." The long-overdue presence of *Alien* star Sigourney Weaver was especially welcome: "It's been a long time since they made a new *Alien* movie," he says, so it was "pretty cool" to see this "unofficial sequel." He gives it five bags of popcorn.

The Second Best Exotic Marigold Hotel was reportedly directed by American football legend John Madden, with Dame Judi Dench and Sir Richard Gere heading a solid-gold cast in which the owner of an eccentric hotel (Dev Patel) gets married in a traditional Indian ceremony. Tim "loved" this "rom-com, old-person, chick-flick kind of movie with a lot of old people in it." It gets five bags of popcorn and five bags of soda.

Gregg found it interesting that the film upended the tradition established by sequels like *Rocky II* and *Jaws 2* and "incorporated the fact that it was a sequel into the title." This daring approach "could usher in a new era" of creativity in movie titling. He gives it five bags of popcorn or, following the film's lead, "the fifth bag of popcorn."

The third best *On Cinema* movie review this week stars Pierce "007" Brosnan in *The Coup* (a.k.a. *No Escape*). This is a political thriller depicting the heroism and heartbreak of rebellion and romance in the fury and ferment of a Southeast Asian revolution, which Tim didn't get a chance to see because he's been busy with *Decker*. He gives it five bags of popcorn anyway: "I love everything that these actors have been a part of."

"If you're a Bond-head, you'll watch anything Pierce Brosnan does," according to Gregg, and he himself is living proof: "I loved it because of that." Having actually watched the movie, unlike Tim, he doles out five "more informed" bags of popcorn. He throws in "a golden gun" as "a tip of the hat to the Man With the Golden Gun, Mr. James Bond."

Before the lights go down, Tim puts in one last plug for the season premiere of *Decker: Port of Call: Hawaii*, with special thanks to Gregg for co-writing "selected sequences" and to Joe for playing "the evil President Davidson."

On Cinema On Line

6:47 PM - 5 Mar 2015
time for YOU to get back to work. need more pages...

6:52 PM - 5 Mar 2015
Just taking a short break, I have 3 pages for you that are ready to shoot. #Decker2

6:53 PM - 5 Mar 2015
bring them now. we are on set waiting.

6:59 PM - 5 Mar 2015
On my way in 10 minutes

3:56 PM - 9 Mar 2015
why no writing credit for @greggturkington in the opening credits?

3:56 PM - 9 Mar 2015
@greggturkington you didn't contribute to the first few eps.

3:56 PM - 9 Mar 2015
what time is flight back to Los Angeles tomorrow?

3:57 PM - 9 Mar 2015
8 am - leaving condo at 6am

8:43 PM - 11 Mar 2015
thanks to @greggturkington for his creative help with #Decker - he's very good at writing scenes, i think.

EPISODE 606
'In the Heart of the Sea' & 'Cinderella'

Air date: March 11, 2015
Running time: 7:34 minutes

Fresh from the tropical milieu of *Decker 2*, still clad in a Hawaiian shirt and periodically scratching a painful itch on his arm, Tim introduces his guest, Gregg Turkington. He reports that the two of them have been "commuting back and forth between here and Hawaii three or four times a week."

Before getting to the all-important movie reviews, Tim has some more good news about his family: "Ayaka has come back to me with my son, Tom Cruise Heidecker, and we are all a happy family living at the Turkington residence."

He also promotes his son's acting career, showing off a headshot of the infant, who he claims is "such a natural." He asks "anybody out there watching in the biz" to "give ol' Tom Cruise Heidecker a shot."

Former *Happy Days* director Ron Howard once again pits man against nature in *In the Heart of the Sea*, a thrilling deep-sea narrative based on real-world nautical events. Tim thought this "seafaring movie" was "good," and "a great opportunity" for Ron Howard to move beyond *Happy Days*. He gives it five bags of popcorn and a bag of soda.

Gregg, who seems very tired, says he would much rather watch *any* movie than *Happy Days*, which was stolen from *American Graffiti* in any case.

Tim agrees to disagree: "I think *Happy Days* would've happened whether or not you had *American Graffiti* or not." In the ensuing debate, a frequently yawning Gregg pays homage to *American Graffiti* for giving director George Lucas a chance to foreshadow the type of conflict he would later explore so successfully in *Star Wars*. As for *In the Heart of the Sea*, it gets five bags of popcorn and "five rubber duckies" so you can recreate the movie in your bathtub.

Cinderella is world-class Shakespearean actor Kenneth Branagh's innovative live-action entry in the long-running *Cinderella* franchise. Tim and Gregg both "loved this movie," which included "the golden slippers and all the rest" (although Tim couldn't help but take "a little Sleeping Beauty of my own during some if it"). Kenneth Branagh is Tim's Oscar pick for best director, making this modern-day fairy tale "a classic five-bagger."

Gregg says that although the Cinderella fable has historically become "something for children," it retains aspects that are "very adult." This version "kind of delved into that a little bit," so children should be made to understand this is "not a cartoon."

This reminds Tim that while visiting the bathroom for longer than usual, he left his son, Tom Cruise, in front of *The People's Court*. "I have a lot of children's movies that you can show him," Gregg protests. "You don't have put him in front of that."

Tim says he'll do that next time. But this time, "I didn't want to go through the process of getting your shit out of order."

Gregg was hoping to present a new Popcorn Classic, but Tim needs to shut the episode down early so they can catch their flight back to Hawaii.

EPISODE 607
'The Divergent Series: Insurgent' & 'The Gunman'

Air date: March 18, 2015
Running time: 7:27 minutes

It's Family Day on *On Cinema* as Tim rolls out the red carpet for three very special guests: dependable film buff Gregg Turkington, one-time *Popcorn Classics* host Ayaka Ohwaki and — in his show-biz debut — Tim and Ayaka's young child, Tom Cruise Heidecker!

As the infant cries and squirms in Ayaka's arms, Tim remarks that due to his constant travels between North Hollywood and Hawaii, "this is literally some of the only few hours I have to see my family."

Before proceeding to the reviews, Tim asks if Ayaka can give the baby "something to shut him up for a bit."

In *Insurgent*, a woman struggles to tear apart a powerful alliance of inner demons that threatens her society. Tim honors this "action film that I enjoyed watching" by giving it five bags of popcorn.

Gregg regards *Insurgent* as "pretty cool." Its "action plots" with "terrorists and spies and all that sort of stuff" reminded him of "our own *Decker*," though it was "not as good." Still, it was "a good break from everyday life," so he gives it five bags of popcorn.

Sean Penn returns to the movie screens in *The Gunman*, where he plays an international spy who is racing against time to clear his name before the clock runs out. Tim found this film to be similar to *Decker* in its focus on spies and spying. He gives it five bags of popcorn because it's "one of the great movies of the year" and a likely "Oscar winner."

Tim wonders if Ayaka has any updates for the *On Cinema* Family, and she tells us she "got a job as a receptionist" for Dr. Luther, who is a "holistic healer." In other Heidecker family news, Tom Cruise's headshots [Episode 606] are still circulating as Tim attempts to get his perpetually crying son's acting career off the ground.

Finally turning to Gregg, Tim requests his opinion of *The Gunman*. Gregg "thought it was good," but he thinks there's better entertainment to be had "if you turn nightly to *Decker*." While *The Gunman* "has its place," viewers should "wait until this season of *Decker* is done with" to watch it, so they "don't get confused." He gives it a provisional five bags of popcorn, provided it's watched only after seeing *Decker*.

On Cinema On Location is next, and this time Gregg shows us the hilly terrain that will feature in an exciting upcoming scene from *Decker*, in which "the treacherous Abdul meets his maker at the hands of President Decker."

Back on the set, Tim is furious that Gregg "blew the ending" of *Decker 2* by revealing an important plot point. Realizing his error too late, a badly shaken Gregg apologizes profusely.

But the damage is done: "I'm gonna have to rewrite the ending," Tim says. He and Gregg will have to fly back to Hawaii immediately to shoot a new season finale, which Tim will write in the plane. As they hurry to catch their flight, Ayaka and Tom Cruise Jr. are left alone in the dark cinema.

On Cinema On Line

11:07 AM - 18 Mar 2015
Hey #OnCinema family please don't watch the On Cinema On Location segment in today's episode

11:29 AM - 18 Mar 2015
Rewriting and reshooting to make #Decker ending great.

12:02 PM - 18 Mar 2015
I feel awful about my slip. Hopefully not everyone noticed. Or... if you want, I could help you write a new one.

12:11 PM - 18 Mar 2015
no I've got it covered.

7:16 PM - 18 Mar 2015
I've forgiven @greggturkington I hope you can too. Let's #moveforward #Decker

10:54 PM - 18 Mar 2015
Thanks and I know that no matter what, #Decker is going to make #movie history!!!!!! Let's get back to Hawaii!

EPISODE 608
'Get Hard' & 'Home'

Air date: March 25, 2015
Running time: 6:45 minutes

Tim and his guest, Gregg Turkington, are exhausted from flying repeatedly between Los Angeles and Hawaii. Also, Tim is sick from eating "disgusting" airline food. But that's not gonna stop them from reviewing this week's top new movie releases!

Will Farrell is ready to rumble in Ethan Coen's *Get Hard*, about a convicted millionaire who takes lessons from a black person on the etiquette of prison survival. Tim "liked this movie a lot." Gregg calls it "a classic comedy circa 2015" and specifies that it stars "Will Farrell, of course."

Tim suspects Gregg didn't actually see the film, and Gregg confirms that due to a late *Decker* shoot, he "wasn't able to see the whole thing."

"And yet you have an opinion on it," Tim snorts.

Gregg points out that Tim didn't see *Get Hard* either. "How am I supposed to see the movie if I've gotta direct and I'm on the camera the whole time?" he protests. Affirming that "somebody between the two of us needs to find a way to see these movies," he reprimands Gregg for failing to be that person: "You're not carrying the weight that I need you to carry on this show."

Gregg contends that they can't do *On Cinema* and *Decker* at the same time. "Yes, we can," Tim snaps. "And we're proving that we can!" Since they will be flying to Hawaii as soon as they're done shooting this episode of *On Cinema*, Tim instructs Gregg to watch *Get Hard* on arrival so he can review it next week.

Gregg defends himself by asserting that he did watch *Home*, whereas Tim didn't see either movie. But Tim rejects this argument: "I don't have to see *Get Hard* to tell you that it's a five-bag comedy." He gives it five bags of popcorn.

Home puts the inimitable voices of pop divas Rhianna ("Rehab"), Jennifer Lopez ("Let's Get Loud") and Steve Martin ("King Tut") front and center as a young animated girl teams up with a cartoon alien to save Earth from the very real threat of an alien attack.

Tim had no time to see this movie due to the stresses of producing *Decker 2* and the inconvenience of having "a son who's not well." He gives it four bags of popcorn "because it's not my kind of movie."

Gregg gives *Home* five bags because "it's great" and "you're never gonna go wrong with Steve Martin," who has "done a lot of movies." He drowsily adds that he saw *Sextape* starring Cameron Diaz on a recent plane flight; he was surprised by this, because "it's pretty explicit." Disturbingly, an old man across the aisle kept looking over Gregg's shoulder to "see the nudity."

This week's Popcorn Classic is a wisecracking Jack Nicholson in *Man Trouble*, which also stars Ellen Barkin. Because Gregg only "bought it last week," he hasn't "had a chance to see it."

This enrages Tim, who knocks the tape out of Gregg's hand and upbraids him for shirking his duties: "Don't come on here and talk about movies you haven't seen!" He threatens to kick Gregg off the show if he doesn't start watching all the movies.

On Cinema On Line

5:13 PM - 27 Mar 2015
my credit card bill for all our Hawaiian flights is due, can you leave me a check? Just put it on the Sandra Bullock shelf.

5:15 PM - 27 Mar 2015
Sorry forgot to give you the total. $7308.25.

5:17 PM - 27 Mar 2015
promote the series don't use this site for petty expense reports.

7:20 PM - 29 Mar 2015
I should start a business in Honolulu where I take tourists around to see Decker locations and share stories from the filming. #OnLocation

7:22 PM - 29 Mar 2015
not without kicking up to me you won't. Stay in line. And be at airport ON TIME tomorrow.

EPISODE 609
'Furious 7' & 'Woman in Gold'

Air date: April 1, 2015
Running time: 10:15 minutes

Having taken some time to reflect, Tim wants to apologize for "the last few weeks" of *On Cinema*, which have "not been fair to the audience" or to "the *On Cinema* Family." Since then, he and his guest, Gregg Turkington, have "sort of hit our stride" when it comes to reviewing the latest critical picks.

But first, Gregg has some unfinished business from last week: his official review of Will Farrell's *Get Hard*. He watched this "prison film with a heart of gold" while in Pearl City, Hawaii, and found that it was "very much in the vein" of classic racially charged comedies like *Silver Streak* and *Trading Places*. Indeed, "in this film, Will Farrell has cemented his role as the Gene Wilder of our generation." He gives it five bags of popcorn.

Before we get to the reviews, there's some *Decker* news to report. Tim has had "a blast" working with Gregg on the second season of his popular show. They are heading back to Hawaii "tonight" to shoot the rewritten finale. Tim thanks "everybody" for taking the time to watch *Decker: Port of Call: Hawaii: Operation Rescue the Island*.

"I haven't see a script yet for the final scene," Gregg says. "So I'm as curious as the viewers."

Tim is "still tweaking it," and he also wants to "keep it under wraps" to heighten audience anticipation for the "surprise ending," especially since Gregg accidentally gave away the previous surprise ending. [Episode 607]

Furious 7 blends Vin Diesel, Dwayne "The Rock" Johnson and the late Paul Walker, who gave his all for this sequel by dying during the shoot. Tim thinks *Furious 7* should be called *Lucky 7*, "because this was lucky enough to be one of my favorite movies of the year." He gives it seven bags of popcorn.

Gregg claims "it's sad" Paul Walker "never got to see this movie," because "he would've liked it."

Ever the optimist, Tim says "the good news" is that Mr. Walker died "doing what he did, which is driving very fast." Since "that's what this movie celebrates," this was "a wonderful way for him to go." For those of us who are left behind, it's also much better than hearing that he died from "slipping on ice and breaking his neck."

"Or some sort of cancer," Gregg agrees. He contrasts the Walker case favorably to the situation with George Burns, who died at 100 years of age only to leave us wondering if it was really worth it: "Did we actually enjoy the last few movies he made?"

Tim compares Walker's workplace fatality to the martial arts legend Bruce Lee's death from a deadly blow to the abdomen: "That's the way to go," he says wistfully. He himself would like to die in the role of Jack Decker — perhaps while parachuting, or possibly while driving too fast like Paul Walker used to.

Gregg gives *Furious 7* five bags of popcorn and a "commemorative gold cross in honor of Paul Walker."

Speaking of gold, *Woman in Gold* stars Helen Mirren as a Jewish "octononagerian" who must battle the legal system to get Hitler's paintings back from the government. Tim says this "sad movie" left him tearful "in the same way that the passing of Paul Walker did."

Thanks to Values.com, [Episode 603] Tim has learned that it can be important to "check in with your emotions every once in a while." Thus, he's not ashamed to acknowledge that he cried when he found out the Jews were not only persecuted, but "some of their gold was taken, too."

When this film was first announced, Gregg figured it was the long-awaited sequel to Gilda Radner's *The Woman in Red*. After reading a description, he concluded that this was a "different film." He does not recommend taking "small children" to this film "unless you're trying to teach them something about history." Helen Mirren, of course, is "kind of a national treasure." He gives *Woman in Gold* five bags of popcorn doused with plenty of "golden butter." Tim gives it five popcorn bags and six sodas.

Tim dedicates Episode 609 to Paul Walker, whose name should be changed posthumously to "Paul Driver," "because that's what he loved doing, is driving cars fast." "Paul Turbo" would also work for Tim.

Gregg protests that "they'd have to go fix the credits for all the movies he made." But Tim feels there's no need to reinvent the wheel: "They did that with the old *Star Wars* movies when they added Jabba the Hut to all the different scenes." Furthermore, "it's a neat way to show some respect."

Signing off, Tim and Gregg thank the people of Hawaii for their hospitality throughout the filming of *Decker 2*. Tim compliments them as "really nice people for natives."

EPISODE 610
'Ex Machina' & 'The Moon and the Sun'

Air date: April 8, 2015
Running time: 5:22 minutes

In this very special season finale, Tim is joined by his former *On Cinema* co-host and current live-in partner Ayaka Ohwaki, who is filling in due to "a last-minute guest cancellation."

Tom Cruise Heidecker is not on the set this week because he's spending quality time with Ayaka's mother, Mikeii, who is visiting from far-off Japan.

Now that *Decker 2* has wrapped, Tim reports that he and his family have finally had a chance to spread out from Gregg Turkington's master bedroom and "use the rest of the apartment," which has been "really nice."

Ex Machina follows the fortunes of a beautiful yet intelligent robot woman who must fight to hang on to the values that make her human. Tim, who "loved this movie," gives it five bags of popcorn. It gets the same rating from Ayaka, who found it "exciting."

In *The Moon and the Sun* (a.k.a. *The King's Daughter*), James Bond star Pierce Brosnan and Oscar winner William Hurt fit together like the proverbial heavenly bodies of the title as France's dastardly Louis XIV of France plots to steal "a mermaid's life force."

Tim calls it "one of the best mermaid movies I've seen since *Splash*." In fact, it reminded him of *Splash*, "because of the mermaids." He gives it five bags of popcorn and five bags of soda.

Ayaka only gives it three bags: "I don't really like mermaids," she explains.

Ayaka's final Popcorn Classic of the season is *The Hangover Part II*, which she and Tim recently watched on iTunes. She champions the film as "really fun."

After an awkward pause, Tim hints that there's something even bigger than movies on his mind: "I'm sweating now," he says, "because I know what I gotta do."

Turning to Ayaka, he declares that they've been "going together now for a while," and he is very happy with the relationship — especially now that they've taken over Gregg's entire apartment. Looking once again to Values.com for emotional guidance, he says, "If you've got something you love, hold on to it as hard as you can."

Going down on one knee before Ayaka, he takes a ring from his pocket and asks for her hand in marriage. In a touching moment, she accepts: "I'm so happy!" she says as they hug. Offstage, the *On Cinema* crew cheers as the lights go down on this heartwarming scene.

DECKER: PORT OF CALL: HAWAII
Book 2

EPISODE 1
Jack Decker is in Honolulu for seven glorious days of "R&R" and "T&A." But it's not all fun and games: Is it worth it to keep saving the USA, he wonders, when it won't save itself by defending its own liberty against the tyranny of liberalism?

Also, it's not just the Taliban that threatens U.S. interests; there's a new kid on the block named ISIS. Decker knows he will face these murderous threats all too soon. But for now, he needs to relax!

But his relaxation is short-lived, as President Davidson dials Decker's cell phone to say he will soon be visiting Hawaii to do what he does best: give speeches! He'd like to have dinner with Decker, but the agent already has plans: He's going to a party for his best and most trusted friend, Lanoi Arnold.

Decker warns the president not to call him again. But what he doesn't know is that in a secret island cave, Islamic radicals are planning their most daring attack yet.

EPISODE 2
Decker drops in at the newly renovated tiki bar run by his oldest and dearest friend, Lanoi Arnold. Lanoi mentions that the president is about to give a speech, but Decker is only interested in the local cuisine: "I'm not talking about the local food, either," he grins, slyly eyeing an authentic Hawaiian beach beauty.

At Lanoi's request, Decker takes to the karaoke stage and gets the bar on its feet with a sing-along rendition of his original ballad, "Our Values Are Under Attack."

The chickens come home to roost.

But it's not all fun and games. In an undisclosed cave location somewhere deep within the Island Kingdom, the Islamists are getting ready to make their big play. And this time…the target is President Davidson himself!

EPISODE 3
President Davidson is visiting Hawaii at taxpayer expense to address the National Association of Special Interests. Watching Davidson's speech from his stool at Lanoi Arnold's well-appointed tiki bar, Decker mocks the president for "kowtowing to the special interests."

Within moments, heavily armed Arabic men attack Davidson's speech with assault rifles and abduct the impotent president from his podium.

Standing before the TV microphone, one of the gunmen pronounces these chilling Arabic words: "We have captured your president!" With that, he puts the USA on notice that with Davidson under their control, the Taliban will seize Hawaii and use it as their base for a direct attack on America itself.

"It's like Pearl Harbor 2.0 all over again," Decker broods. "I guess this vacation's over." He tries to call the CIA, only to learn that the Taliban forces have jammed the island's cell phone signals.

EPISODE 4
Decker finally gets a call through to CIA headquarters, home of Special Agent Kington. To his surprise, the master codebreaker is out of the office, having traveled to Hawaii on "a secret mission."

Is the turncoat Klingston working with the terrorists? Shocking as it seems, no other explanation fits the facts!

Because he has classified access to the "homing device" attached by law to every CIA agent, Decker is confident he can find and neutralize Kington using GPS technology. The question is, will it work?

Jumping into his GPS-equipped white convertible, Decker follows a winding path to Kingston's exact coordinates.

Meanwhile, at an above-top-secret location somewhere on Hawaiian territory, Kington feverishly connects two yellow cables with a male-to-male RCA coupling adapter. "And now, my plan will be complete," he boasts.

Is Decker already too late?

EPISODE 5
It's 0500 hours, and Jack Decker is running out of time as he speeds toward double agent Kington's compound in the far northeastern corner of the tropical island nation.

Pulling into Kington's driveway, he leaps over the door of his convertible to save precious seconds. Emptying his revolver into the doorknob in case it's locked, he kicks his way into Kington's lair and confronts the turncoat in the act of sorting his VHS tapes.

"Decker, don't shoot!" Kington pleads.

"I always knew you were a traitor," Decker bellows. "And now it looks like the chickens have come home to roost."

Kington discloses that in addition to being a code expert, he is "one of the top film buffs in the world." He is visiting Hawaii to duplicate his VHS collection so he'll have backups of classic films like *Sommersby*. In fact, he visits Hawaii once a year to duplicate his world-class film archive, calling it "the perfect vacation."

Decker slowly lowers his gun. "I thought you were working with the Taliban," he grunts.

"No," Kington assures him. "Just dubbing tapes." After briefing Kington that the president has been abducted and the island has fallen to Taliban extremists, Decker asks for the code master's help.

President Davidson to Appear at Special Interests Fundraiser

The White House announced President Davidson will travel to Honolulu on Monday and deliver remarks on the National Association of Special Interests. The president's speech is closed to the public.

HONOLULU — President Davidson has generally refrained from mixing business and pleasure on the golf course. On vacation here in Hawaii, he has mostly hit the links with the same circle of longtime friends and White House aides he usually pals around with. Until Wednesday, when a newbie joined the Nirst Noursome.

The White House said Banjo, along with aides Joe Paulsen and Mike Brush, was playing with the president on the course at the Marine Corps base at Kanehoe Bay. Turns out Najib was in town on his own getaway, and it is not unprecedented for Davidson to do a golf summit with a world leader. Last year in Hawaii, he played with New Zealand Prime Minister John Key. (In 2011, Davidson famously played a round with House Speaker John A. Boehner at Andrews Air Force Base that did not exactly lead to a good working relationship off the course.)

Davidson has established perhaps a better working relationship with Najib, after making the first visit by a sitting U.S. president to Malaysia in nearly half a century last spring. It was unlikely they had an in-depth discussion of their foreign policy agendas on the course, however, but perhaps focusing instead on trying to avoid the sand traps.

In a statement, the White House said: "The two leaders took the opportunity to discuss the growing and warming relationship between the United States and Malaysia. The president said he looked forward to working with Prime Minister Najib in 2015, during Malaysia's chair year of the Association of Southeast Asian Nations."

President Davidson to give Speech, Attend fundraiser in Hawaii on Wednesday.

"Of course I'll help you," Kington nods, tossing aside a copy of The Inspectors. "Looks like this vacation is over!"

EPISODE 6

DECKER HAS A PLAN to stop the Taliban. "I need to establish a perimeter around the island," he resolves.

Kington worries the insurgent forces will spot Decker's boat and blow it up. But Decker already has that angle covered! The agents jump into Decker's convertible for a white-knuckle ride to the North Shore, where Decker's secret jet-ski lies in wait.

At the same moment, President Davidson is trapped in an undisclosed cave with the Taliban madmen. They have put him behind bars, more like an animal than the so-called leader of the free world.

Even though he's tied down, he can hear the terrorist masterminds talking about Decker. Soon, he learns that someone close to Decker is a mole! The president does his best to write this information down on his hand. But it's no use: The terrorists notice his effort and wash his hand clean with a rag from a nearby bucket.

"You can't do this to me!" the president yelps. But he's not talking to special interests now, and his voice falls on deaf ears. "Where are you, Decker?" he whimpers.

EPISODE 7

ARRIVING AT HAWAII'S fabled North Shore, Decker moves to establish a perimeter per CIA protocol. It's a nice day for a jet-ski ride, despite what the climate alarmists would have you believe. But Decker's mind is focused only on danger.

In the meantime, Kington checks out a sidewalk sale conducted by a veiled woman in a black robe. He compliments her fine taste in VHS cassettes. Realizing she has a film buff on her hands, she pulls a scarce copy of Paul Reiser's Bye Bye Love from under her table. Kington is prepared to pay handsomely for this little-known collector's item!

"This is complimentary for you, being a film buff," she hisses in heavily accented English. That's an offer Kington can't refuse! He heads home on the double, eager to code and catalog this rare find.

"He took the tape," the foreign woman chuckles. "Or should I say — the bait?"

Decker calls Kington's cell phone to brief him on his reconnaissance findings: The terrorists have taken over the island!

Unknown to Decker, Kington is not the only one hearing these words. Deep inside the videocassette of Bye Bye Love, a sinister red light is blinking steadily.

EPISODE 8

DECKER AND KINGTON are regrouping at Lanoi Arnold's tiki bar, which is undergoing some much-needed renovations. When Decker heads to the bathroom, his trusted friend Lanoi takes the opportunity to get acquainted with Kington. "What are your hobbies?" he asks.

"I'm a special agent trained in breaking codes," Kington divulges. "But my *real* passion is that I'm the world's biggest archivist of videocassette movies!" He briefs Lanoi that he's currently aiming for Guinness Book gold as the first person ever to watch 500 movies in 500 days.

For his part, Lanoi recounts how he and Decker served in the Green Berets together. Although he's always trusted Decker, he's starting to have some doubts: "I think he's a double agent, maybe for the Taliban."

Kington shoots this theory down: "He's the truest American you'll ever meet." As proof, he tells how Decker saved Central Park from a Taliban mini-nuke.

EPISODE 9

KINGTON CONTINUES BRIEFING Lanoi on Decker's takedown of the wily terrorist Abdul. "He's the bravest man I know," Kington concludes. "And the president feels the same way."

"I guess I'm wrong," Lanoi concedes. Just then, Decker returns from the bathroom with a question for Kington:

Decker debriefs President Davidson.

"What does Hawaii remind you of?"

"Movies!" the film buff answers. But the correct answer is Vietnam: They will have to fight the Taliban "from the inside out" using "jungle guerrilla warfare techniques."

Kington has one of the world's biggest collections of "Vietnam-related movies." Could watching them help with tactical planning? Decker thinks it's worth a shot.

EPISODE 10

BACK AT KINGTON'S BASE, the agents are studying Good Morning, Vietnam, one of Robin Williams' first important dramatic roles and a personal favorite of Kington's. "The whole cast is great," Kington gushes. "It's a classic."

But Decker worries that the sands of the clock are running out: Outside, the Taliban is blowing up the island's crucial infrastructure. That clinches it: It's time to rescue President Davidson and bring America back to the greatness that is in its national DNA. "That should be our mission right now, is to save President Davidson, as much as I disagree with his policies," Decker growls.

Kington can't argue with that.

EPISODE 11

IN A CAVE SOMEWHERE beneath the island of Hawaii, President Davidson languishes in captivity as his terrorist captors plot their long-dreaded next move: "First Hawaii, then California!"

Suddenly, Decker strolls into their lair. One extremist raises his machine gun, but Decker swiftly terminates them both. "Party's over, shitheads!" he snarls.

As the *jihadis* bleed out, Decker throws open Davidson's cage. Jamming his gun against the president's forehead, he demands to know how many secrets the weak-kneed leader handed over to the Taliban. "I didn't tell them anything," Davidson blubbers. "I didn't know anything!"

"Tell me everything you heard!" Decker thunders. Sweating bullets as he looks down the gun's pitiless muzzle, Davidson finally spills his guts: The Taliban has placed a mole close to Decker!

With that, Decker lowers his gun and prepares to exfil the president stateside.

As he heads back to the Oval Office, Davidson worries whether Decker can save the island in time to avert disaster.

EPISODE 12

It's 0500 hours at Decker's lookout post. Below him, searing red fireballs rise from the ravaged landscape as the Taliban zealots make good on the promises of their murderous ideology. "The terrorists have taken over the island," he realizes.

Meanwhile, at the White House, President Davidson places a video call to Decker. "What's the situation like there in Hawaii?" he asks. Decker explains that due to Davidson's weakness, the Taliban is now threatening the whole country.

"Sometimes I wish you were president," Davidson whines. "Then we would never have gotten into this mess."

The slack-spined president wants to send in the troops, but Decker helps him see the tactical disadvantage in that zero-sum game. Instead, Klingson and Decker will use guerrilla warfare strategies to drive the Taliban insurgency off the island.

But has time already run out?

Decker confronts his most trusted friend, Lanoi Arnold.

EPISODE 13

Back at Kington's base, the master of codes is content to wait for "the calvary." But Decker knows that he himself is the only one who can save the island in time.

The first thing he needs is an "eye in the sky." To this end, he has created a satellite of his own devising that, once orbited, will pinpoint all the terrorist nerve centers.

Kington wants to run Decker's satellite through government safety tests, but Decker refuses to leave Hawaii's fate up to the D.C. bureaucrats. He needs to get his satellite into the ionosphere on the double, for only when he has "eyes in the sky" will he be able to smoke out the full extent of the terrorist network. This will in turn give him strategic dominance of the kinetic conflict space through an "eyes in the sky" vantage point.

From Klingson's base, Decker heads due south across the water and rides a parasail into the lower ionosphere to launch his satellite.

With the satellite orbiting and calibrated, Decker now has a real-time "eye in the sky" to spotlight the Taliban bases. But will he find them in time?

EPISODE 14

On the beach at 0500 hours, Decker and Kington reconnoiter to discuss the next stage of Operation Save the Island. Decker's satellite shows a terrorist base just beyond the mountain. The only catch is, it will require a zipline to infiltrate.

"It's too dangerous," Kington protests. "It would be a suicide mission!" Seemingly forgetting the eternal need to "sacrifice bravery in defense of our country," Kington argues that it might be better to surrender…until Decker brings him to the Pearl Harbor memorial site to honor a few brave men who did just that.

Here, among the hallowed graves that lie beneath the proud flag that still flies high above the solemn scene below, Kingston gradually comes to a new understanding of what it means to fight on the side of freedom.

"Kington, there's something I've never told you," Decker tells him. "My grandfather died fighting in the Battle of Pearl Harbor." Indeed, his brave grandfather's dog tags still lie beneath these icy tropical waters. At that moment, Decker realizes it's up to him to dive in and bring 'em home!

Deep underwater, Decker finally comes face to face with the missing dog tags and the truth of what his grandfather's legacy really means.

EPISODE 15

Decker makes his way through the humid jungle to an abandoned CIA zipline that was closed by President Davidson to protect Hawaiian tree frogs.

"The only endangered species we have to worry about is us — humans!" Decker scoffs. As he sees it, an aerial zipline approach will enable him to achieve strategic dominance of the terrorist camp right when they least expect it. But unknown to him, he has a surprise in store!

EPISODE 16

President Davidson tries to call Decker. The line is busy, so he calls Agent Kington instead, interrupting the film buff in the middle of a classic movie.

The president wants to know where Decker is. Kington briefs him that the daring patriot is "traveling along the old abandoned CIA zipline route."

What Kington doesn't know is, his copy of *Bye Bye Love* is transmitting this sensitive intel direct to Taliban HQ. Now, Decker's life is very literally "on the line"!

EPISODE 17

After a daring zipline journey, with grenade launchers and IEDs bursting in air all around him, Decker makes a white-knuckle landfall near the terrorist camp.

He expects to have the all-important element of surprise, but the shoe is on the other foot as he is unexpectedly confronted, disarmed and abducted by five armed fanatics who were clearly expecting him.

Someone tipped them off. But who?

EPISODE 18
KINGTON ENTERS a Honolulu multiplex at 0500 hours. Meanwhile, Decker is in a tight spot: locked behind iron bars, chained by one hand to a massive rock, and guarded by two Taliban militants!

Pulling out his cell phone, he places a discreet call to Kington. Even though he's in a movie theater, this is one interruption the film buff is willing to tolerate!

Kington helps Decker find the lock's serial number and then uses his training to calculate the combination. Without a moment to spare, he gives Decker the numbers. But will the lock really open?

EPISODE 19
KINGTON'S CODE WORKED! Decker is free, and he has one last score to settle. Two terrorists rush him and go down with a fatal bullet between the eyes. A third loses his nerve and drops his weapon.

Decker needs answers, but the defiant Islamic militant won't talk. Pulling out an American flag and wrapping it around the fanatic's face, Decker decides to give him a taste of the Taliban's own enhanced interrogation methods. "Welcome to the water park," he quips.

It doesn't take much waterboarding to crack even the toughest Taliban nut, and this one is no exception. He's ready to tell Decker who he works for. But will Decker be ready to listen when he finds out it's his oldest friend, Lanoi Arnold?

"He works for the Taliban," the terrorist verifies. "He needed the money for renovations for his bar."

It's not easy for Decker to accept that his best friend has joined the Taliban. But with time running out, he has no choice. As thanks for this information, he lets the terrorist borrow his gun to commit suicide. With visions of a martyr's paradise dancing in his head, the jihadist fires a deadly bullet into his own brain.

Easily gunning his way out of the Taliban stronghold, Decker jumps in his Mustang and prepares for one last showdown with Lanoi Arnold.

EPISODE 20
IT'S TIME FOR DECKER to face facts: His best friend, Lanoi Arnold, has sold out to the Taliban. Thanks to his eye-in-the-sky satellite, detecting Lanoi's location is the easy part. But will Decker have what it takes to do whatever it takes to bring Lanoi to the justice he deserves?

Arriving at Lanoi's tiki bar, Decker draws his gun and soon comes eye to eye with his so-called friend. Lanoi is impassive, even as he looks death in the eyes in the form of Decker's gun. "We've been expecting you," he snickers.

Decker is overcome with emotion as he trains his weapon on his oldest friend. "I thought I could trust you," he frowns.

"You took the bait hook, line and sinker," Lanoi taunts him. Decker demands to know how Lanoi got inside information on Decker's activities: "Is it Klingston? Is he the inside man?"

"No, it's not Kingston." Arnold smirks. "He loves America too much."

But Kington does have one deadly Achilles' heel: "He loves movies too much!" Lanoi recounts how he hid a microphone in a VHS copy of *Bye Bye Love* and tricked Kington into taking it home. As a result, Lanoi has been one jump ahead of his old friend all along.

Standing toe to toe with his most trusted friend, Decker can't bring himself to pull the trigger. Instead, they will go head to head in *mano y mano* combat, each using his Green Beret training to defeat the other. Only when one man lies dead can the other arise as the victor!

Lanoi is ready for it: "Let's do this."

Every dirty trick in the book is deployed as these two men fight not just for life itself, but for two opposing ways of life that can never coexist. Finally, Decker gets his hands around his friend's throat. "Die, you son of a bitch," he hisses.

Moments later, Lanoi lies lifeless beside his tiki bar. "I can't believe I had to kill my best friend," Decker sobs, remembering the good times they had together in happier times. But deep down, he knows this tragic outcome became inevitable as soon as the turncoat Lanoi dared to join up with the Taliban.

Sadder but wiser, Decker takes the long drive back to Kington's headquarters to settle one last score.

On a secluded beach at 0500 hours, Decker begins unloading a cargo van filled with boxes of VHS tapes taken from Agent Kington's lair.

Kington arrives and demands an explanation. "There's a bug in one of these tapes," Decker explains as he carries a box of rare titles to a roaring firepit. "I have to destroy the entire collection."

"Tim, no!" Kington yells as Decker feeds his tapes to the hungry flames. Kington makes a valiant effort to save his compromised collection, but the frantic film buff is no match for Decker's grim determination. Soon, his prized tapes are reduced to harmless cinders.

Later, President Davidson tells America that Hawaii is free and announces a national parade in Decker's honor.

During the parade, Decker gets a cell phone call from Abdul, the wily terrorist he only thought he'd killed. Shockingly, Abdul is still alive and is back in Central Park to finish the deadly job he started.

For Decker, the parade is over! He orders his driver to head to New York.

Decker destroys Kington's collection of bugged videocassettes.

On Cinema On Line

5:30 PM - 13 Apr 2015
Interesting how @timheidecker has become what he hates the most--a terrorist.

5:33 PM - 13 Apr 2015
Decker had some great moments mostly due to the writing and cast like @James_Mane. But destroying a irreplaceable movie archive is not right

5:36 PM - 13 Apr 2015
Maybe for the next season of the TV show Decker can team up with ISIS to flood the Library of Congress. But viewers will have moved on.

5:40 PM - 13 Apr 2015
I'm moving on too. Next season of #OnCinema Tim and Ayaka will review their iTunes purchases but no one will be watching.

5:46 PM - 13 Apr 2015
The $8800 @timheidecker owes me for funding Decker travel expenses with my Visa card will be addressed outside of this public forum

6:15 PM - 13 Apr 2015
FYI i only burned the tapes for the plot to make sense, an ending i had to rewrite thanks to you.

6:15 PM - 13 Apr 2015
and I only did so because i knew you had dubbed all the tapes so i didn't think it would be a big deal.

9:10 PM - 13 Apr 2015
I wasn't dubbing--I was acting. I'm not Kingston. I don't dub tapes. I buy back-up copies. Which you also burned most of.

6:19 PM - 13 Apr 2015
that's all I have to say to you for now @greggturkington - good luck on another meaningless quest. #50MoviesIn50States

9:06 PM - 13 Apr 2015
Two entries in the Guinness Book is far from meaningless. What will you get in there for? Biggest polluter of Hawaii beaches?

7:48 PM - 13 Apr 2015
Also @greggturkington 's writing on #Decker sucked and he was not easy to work with. I doubt we'll work together again.

7:57 PM - 13 Apr 2015
If you consider yourself a member of the #OnCinemaFamily you will do what's right and #shunGregg

9:14 PM - 13 Apr 2015
Join the #OurCinemaFamily instead. No bullying from a terrorist/rageaholic...just pure #movie criticism from experts and buffs

8:03 PM - 13 Apr 2015
@m_proksch Let's meet soon to talk #OnCinema and #Decker future.

8:03 PM - 13 Apr 2015
Wow! If love too! Thanks!

8:05 PM - 13 Apr 2015
you are ready to be a star but we'll need to do a lot of work to get you there. Hope you have the guts.

8:06 PM - 13 Apr 2015
absolutely do! Thanks again!

7:41 AM - 14 Apr 2015
Idiots supporting @greggturkington have officially backed the wrong horse. #OnCinema & #Decker will be stronger without him (and you)

9:21 PM - 13 Apr 2015
For those who asked, I called my landlord and I don't think @TimHeidecker will be there much longer, he is not on the lease.

7:43 AM - 14 Apr 2015
might want to look up imminent domain there, chief.

11:05 PM - 14 Apr 2015
@timheidecker is an #abusive dad to the #OnCinemaFamily. Say NO to bullying, and YES to #movies and #expertise. #OurCinema is coming! #NBC

11:50 AM - 28 Apr 2015
My pledge to you: #OurCinema will concentrate 100% on MOVIES. Not unrelated personal #issues!

12:24 PM - 28 Apr 2015
have you forgotten? I gave you a chance at your own show & you fell flat on face. History WILL repeat itself. #BanOurCinema

2:39 PM - 27 May 2015
Signing a deal this afternoon for "Our Cinema". 60 episodes. Network.

On Cinema On Line

9:00 AM - 29 May 2015
Days ago I received a call from an employee at a movie rental store in Victorville, CA. The shop had a 10' x 20' storage locker full of VHS.

9:09 AM - 29 May 2015
It is an incredible acquisition and I am literally breathless with excitement. Many five-bag titles were included.

10:13 AM - 4 Jun 2015
This copy of "Mrs Winterbourne" looks unplayed!

8:51 PM - 26 Jun 2015
In Victorville this weekend finishing cataloging all my duplicate copies. At least 100 movies I have in triplicate! It's like a #museum here

8:25 AM - 25 Jun 2015
ANT-MAN is officially completed, and I can't wait for you to see it.

1:24 PM - 26 Jun 2015
folks, @greggturkington is in the JAPANESE version of Ant Man. not the US version. everyone can calm down.

1:25 PM - 26 Jun 2015
it makes more sense now. no way @MrPeytonReed would have used him in US version for such a big movie.

11:14 PM - 27 Jun 2015
For the record: @greggturkington is in ALL versions of ANT-MAN. His performance will go GLOBAL. @timheidecker is in NO version of ANT-MAN.

4:28 PM - 29 Jun 2015
So curious how you're going to phrase your apology to me when I see you.

4:34 PM - 29 Jun 2015
@MrPeytonReed u do not have final cut and if Gregg is in premiere version it will likely be cut before public sees it.

4:34 PM - 29 Jun 2015
The digital prints have shipped, my friend. Every country in the world will see @greggturkington's performance in ANT-MAN.

11:20 PM - 14 Jul 2015
Congrats to @timheidecker for his cameo in the unofficial #FantasticFour remake. Will keep my eye out for it! #movies

9:05 AM - 15 Jul 2015
I was the first #movie critic to act in a #major movie. Too bad #GuinnessBook doesn't care about who was the #second! Congrats @timheidecker

1:01 PM - 15 Jul 2015
The future holds many treasures for supporters of #OurCinema

7:42 AM - 29 Jul 2015
@greggturkington before making any #OurCinema deals we need to speak. please call me when you can, thanks. -t

11:39 AM - 30 Jul 2015
Great productive talk with @ABCNetwork about #OurCinema today. A few details remain to be hashed out.

11:41 AM - 30 Jul 2015
@greggturkington @ABCNetwork did you get my voicemail or not? Imperative that we speak.

11:49 AM - 30 Jul 2015
I don't have the voice mail option on my phone, can you try calling later after 2? In the middle of filing project

12:38 PM - 30 Jul 2015
who did I leave message for. I smell BS

1:30 PM - 30 Jul 2015
Can someone help Gregg set up his voicemail so he can hear my messages?

6:48 PM - 3 Aug 2015
@greggturkington wanted to invite you to premiere of Fantasmic Four but they are sold out, can only bring myself. sorry.

7:51 PM - 3 Aug 2015
No problem! You spent $15,000 to be in the movie, the least I can do is spend $15 to see it!

6:49 PM - 3 Aug 2015
word on street is Fantasmic For is 10 times better than ant man was. i guess it's just a better movie?

7:53 PM - 3 Aug 2015
Word in the #movie theater is just the opposite. I trust #movie buffs over people who live on the street.

On Cinema On Line

2:05 AM - 5 Aug 2015
Caught a sneak-peek screening of #TheFantastic4 and I have to admit, I'd give it a Fantastic FIVE bags of popcorn. Congrats @timheidecker

8:15 AM - 5 Aug 2015
appreciate it but AGAIN you are not authorized to use bag system until you re-sign with me. Just call me.

7:34 PM - 5 Aug 2015
RT if you agree @greggturkington should the right thing and return my phone calls!

10:51 AM - 6 Aug 2015
In a production meeting for #OurCinema today and tomorrow. What's your question?

4:55 PM - 7 Aug 2015
@greggturkington if you're free this weekend come by the apartment for some dinner or something? Ayaka and T.C. would love to see you.

10:53 PM - 7 Aug 2015
I would rather meet elsewhere. Would you guys want to meet me at @Maggianos. I have some free time before #OurCinema starts.

6:22 AM - 8 Aug 2015
@greggturkington @Maggianos sorry trying to keep TC on a diet of whole oats and nutrition can we do @panerabread?

10:04 AM - 8 Aug 2015
@timheidecker @panerabread OK see you there at 1:00

10:12 AM - 8 Aug 2015
@greggturkington @panerabread who said 1? Either 11am or 3pm

10:15 AM - 8 Aug 2015
Sorry can't make 3 pm, have #OurCinema business to deal with this afternoon. 1 or 130 is all I can do

10:18 AM - 8 Aug 2015
@panerabread fine. Not Ayaka and TC then. (Nap time) move meeting back to @Maggianos then?

10:33 AM - 8 Aug 2015
@timheidecker @panerabread @Maggianos Yeah I would prefer Maggianos, last time at @PaneraBread it was stale.

12:34 PM - 8 Aug 2015
See you in a few minutes. Just leaving @ABCnetwork #OurCinema meeting right now.

12:35 PM - 8 Aug 2015
@greggturkington @ABCNetwork who has a meeting like this on Saturday? I smell BS.

12:36 PM - 8 Aug 2015
Soundstages here are open on the weekends. I smell BS too! BIG SUCCESS for #OurCinema!

1:12 PM - 8 Aug 2015
@greggturkington WHERE THE FUCK ARE YOU

1:38 PM - 8 Aug 2015
sorry went to @panerabread by accident. There soon!

3:17 PM - 8 Aug 2015
Good meeting with @greggturkington and GREAT food thanks @Maggianos !!!

5:10 PM - 8 Aug 2015
@timheidecker You're so welcome! Thanks for stopping by!

4:02 PM - 8 Aug 2015
@timheidecker @Maggianos Nice to see you and I will think about what you said

8:41 AM - 27 Aug 2015
BREAKING NEWS: @greggturkington will be returning to #OnCinema - we both reached an agreement on terms.

7:50 AM - 31 Aug 2015
meeting with @greggturkington to sign agreement for S7 of #OnCinema ! will post document when signed. will make a lot of people happy.

8:30 AM - 31 Aug 2015
Can we meet tomorrow morning? I'm meeting with some HobbitHeads today to discuss a possible event.

8:54 AM - 1 Sep 2015
hey @greggturkington meet you at @panerabread at 10am. bring a pen! ;)

10:13 AM - 1 Sep 2015
We signed! Great meeting with @greggturkington ! will post document asap. thanks all. #OnCinema

10:25 AM - 1 Sep 2015
I am happy to report I am returning to #OnCinema as all my conditions have been met. More #movie reviews and special segments this season!

ON CINEMA ON CINEMA

ON CINEMA SEASON 7 TERMS SHEET

The following is a list of terms agreed upon by Tim Heidecker and Gregg Turkington, in order to secure Mr. Turkington's involvement with Season 7 of On Cinema at the Cinema. These terms are binding and any deviation or breach of terms will result in Mr. Turkington's departure from On Cinema at the Cinema with no legal or financial obligations. These terms will be made public and available to the "On Cinema Family" so as to create accountability and due diligence in accordance with said agreement.

- "On Cinema at the Cinema" is about MOVIES and MOVIES ONLY. Discussion of Personal matters and outside projects will be kept to a minimum.

- Gregg Turkington will be referred to as "Gregg Turkington, from The Victorville Film Archive."

- The "Popcorn Bag Rating System" is a scale that goes from One (1) bag of popcorn (very poor quality film) to Five (5) Bags of Popcorn (Extremely high quality film.)

- Gregg Turkington will be allowed to produce and include up to Eight (8) outside segments during the season, including but not limited to 'On Cinema On Location', 'Golden Age Comedies', and 'Treasures of The Victorville Film Archive'."

- Gregg Turkington will immediately cease any development, writing, producing or presenting of the show "Our Cinema" for Internet, Television, Podcasts or other distribution methods.

- Tim Heidecker agrees not to destroy, mutilate, vandalize, burn or damage in any way any part of Gregg Turkington's award-winning film collection and/or library (Victorville Film Archive.)

- Tim Heidecker agrees to hand over full, creative control of the web-series "Decker" to Gregg Turkington. Gregg will direct, write and producer the 3rd season for a period of One (1) year and/or Twenty (20) Episodes plus an additional Two (2) hour special.

- Tim Heidecker agrees to continue to portray the role of Special Agent Jack Decker during during Gregg Turkington's tenure.

_____ DATE 9/1/15
TIM HEIDECKER

_____ DATE 9/1/2015
GREGG TURKINGTON

SEASON 7

EPISODE 701
'Ant-Man' & 'Fantastic Four'

Air date: September 9, 2015
Running time: 12:02 minutes

It's Lucky Season 7 of *On Cinema*, and Tim's very first guest brings a high-stakes jackpot of movie expertise to the dealer's table. Gregg Turkington is back!

"I didn't think I'd be back this season," Gregg admits. He "had a deal in place with ABC" for *Our Cinema*, but a number of "sticking points" caused him to put this project on hold and "get back to *On Cinema*."

Tim recognizes that Gregg and many viewers "were upset about the way I handled your collection" in the *Decker 2* season finale. Although this is "water under the bridge for us," some viewers still don't understand Tim's side of the dispute: "I believed in my heart that what I was setting aflame was dubs of those movies." Nonetheless, he apologizes.

Gregg compares Tim's destruction of his collection to visiting "the Louvre with a flamethrower and destroying all those great paintings." He adds that although he was "upset" when Tim did this, because it was "not cool," he is "over it now."

Also, he has some good news: A fan alerted him to a video store in Victorville, California, "that decided to discontinue the VHS format and rent only DVDs." These tapes had been "gathering dust" in a "storage locker" until the owner decided to save money on storage fees by donating them to Gregg.

Now, Gregg has moved to Victorville to catalog and sort the collection, which he has named the Victorville Film Archive. "It's about five times as big as my previous collection," he says, and "every single movie that you burned has been replaced. In many cases, in triplicate!"

Tim calls this "one of those almost-too-good-to-be-true happy endings, which I'm proud to be a part of."

Time now for the latest news from the Heidecker clan. Ayaka is "doing great," and Tom Cruise is entering "the terrible twos" despite being barely one year old.

As for Tim, he's been focusing on musical self-expression due to the success of "Our Values Are Under Attack," which was the number-one (in the sense of being first) musical download from *Decker 2*.

Since Tim is so "gifted musically," he will take "the next few months" to "work on that almost exclusively." Fans awaiting *Decker 3* need not fear, though: Tim is turning the franchise over to Gregg, who "will be directing and writing and producing the entire affair."

In making this decision, Tim was guided — as he so often is — by the example of Steven Spielberg. This great director has the ability to "create a universe in something like *Jurassic Park* or *Jaws*" and then hand the sequels off to "smaller people." Tim is excited to see where Gregg goes with the series.

Gregg makes it plain that he has no intention of tinkering with a proven formula. Taking his cue from the Bond movies, he intends to stick closely to "the concepts that make *Decker* such a successful series."

Finally, Tim and Gregg turn their attention to a pair of very personal films. *Ant-Man* stars Gregg Turkington and others in what Tim summarizes as a story that "doesn't matter" and "didn't make sense."

Gregg reminds him that *Ant-Man* was "number one for several weeks." But he recuses himself from commenting further on his own film because "it would be unfair."

Tim feels that on the whole, *Ant-Man* was "a miss." In fact, he's puzzled that the studio "decided to put this one out" instead of "keeping it locked up in a vault." Calling it "a trainwreck" and "one of the worst movies I've ever seen," he goes on to "shame the studio and everyone involved for allowing real trash to come out and deceive the wonderful filmgoing audience."

He also condemns the actors — "even the small parts" — because "every member of the cast was horrible." He gives *Ant-Man* just one bag of popcorn — "a sad and lonely bag with no salt, no butter and many unpopped corn at the bottom of the bag" — though in truth, this is "way more than it even deserves."

Next up, *Fantastic Four* stars Tim Heidecker and cast in the familiar origin story of these DC Comics superheroes. Tim gives this "quintessential popcorn movie" six bags of popcorn for hitting "a home run."

Gregg says that "although the beginning's a little bit slow," it turned out to be "one of the best superhero movies" ever made. He "completely understands" why Tim "would pay $15,000" to secure a cameo "vanity role" in which he was given "a fantastic four lines."

Tim interrupts by threatening to have the *On Cinema* crew throw Gregg off the set. As the lights go down, Tim continues to insist that he did not pay director Josh Trank $15,000 to appear briefly in *Fantastic Four*. Gregg challenges this narrative by claiming he overheard the phone call.

EPISODE 702
'Black Mass' & 'Maze Runner: The Scorch Trials'

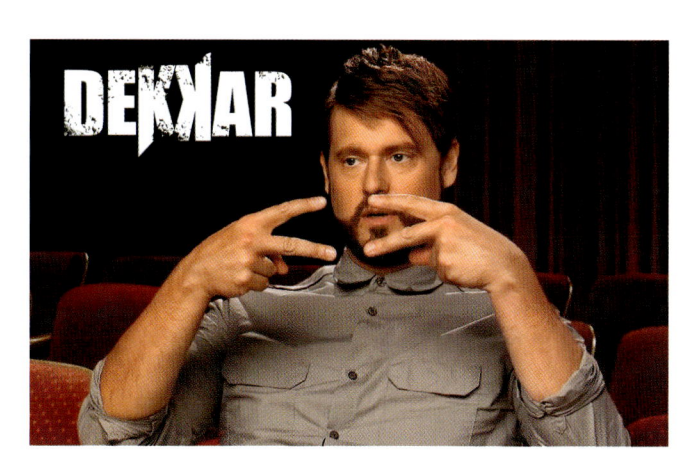

Air date: September 16, 2015
Running time: 10:07 minutes

Lucky Season 7 continues with a winning hand: It's a full house as Tim welcomes his special guest, Gregg Turkington of the Victorville Film Archive. In his new role as director of the VFA, Gregg has been "slaving away" to get "literally thousands of movies" cataloged and coded for ease of use.

Asked for an update on Season 3 of *Decker*, Gregg confirms that "all the episodes are written." Also, most of the cast is "in place," and "we're building sets right now." In a hint of things to come, Gregg says the third season will feature "the most exotic locale yet."

Not to be outdone, Tim offers even "bigger news": "With the support of my family and my friends, I'd like to announce the formation of my first-ever band, called Dekkar."

Gregg can't figure out why Tim would name his band Dekkar "when there's an existing movie series called *Decker*." Tim responds that it's "a different spelling" and "Decker" is an integral part of his name. Gregg sees a potential snag: If *Decker* fans "see a CD, they're going to think it's a soundtrack to one of the *Decker* movies." But Tim is confident the different logo and spelling will distinguish his established "hit action series" from his brand-new "progressive rock music" group.

In related news, Dekkar will be heading into the studio shortly to record their debut three-song EP.

Black Mass lures Johnny Depp and Benedict Cumberbatch into the real-life lair of Whitey Bulger, "the Mafia guy from Boston who became an FBI informant." This mob-themed organized crime drama reminded Tim of *The Godfather*, *Goodfellas*, *Married to the Mob* and other films that help us imagine "what life might be like in the *Costa Nostra*." He gives it five bags of popcorn and one soda.

Gregg "liked" this "very serious look at a real problem in America," but he frets that "Johnny Depp was wasted" in his role as an old businessman. Depp is "much more suited to fanciful characters" that "wear velvet gowns" or "a strange cap." Casting Robert Duvall in this old-man role would've freed Depp to play a properly "flamboyant" character, such as animated cereal mascot Cap'n Crunch, "a talking cat" or perhaps even "a giraffe that comes to life as a person."

Gregg gives *Black Mass* a punitive four bags of popcorn for "wasting Johnny Depp's time and our time as well." But then, because he "liked the movie so much," he reinstates the missing bag for a perfect five-bag rating.

In the new *Maze Runner* movie, the titular heroes face "unimaginal [sic] obstacles" as they hurtle down the open road of a desolate landscape from the future. Tim considers this film to be "emblematic of the *Maze Runners* series" in its fidelity to "the characters." He rewards it with five bags of popcorn and five cans of soda.

Gregg thinks *Scorch Trials* is an example of "what Hollywood sometimes gets wrong," in that this sequel took a very long time to come out: "You don't want to keep people waiting *too* long," he says, "because then they might move on to something else." In this case, however, the risky gamble paid off: The film was "excellent," if "a little scary."

Tim agrees that he would not take little Tom Cruise Jr. to this film. On the other hand, he *would* take his wife, Ayaka, to see it on a date night, because when you have a child, it's important to "keep that flame alive" (as Tim and Ayaka recently did by going to see *The Lego Movie* at a second-run dollar theater).

Gregg gives *Scorch Trials* five bags of popcorn, plus a whistle so you can get help if you're ever stuck in a maze.

In honor of the season's ongoing Lucky 7 theme, Gregg has arranged to do a "lucky dip" for this week's *Popcorn Classics*. In plain English, this means Tim must close his eyes and pick a movie from a plastic bag filled with bona fide Popcorn Classics from the Victorville Film Archive. This week, the lucky winner is *Our Song* — a prime example of the cinematic riches to be found at the VFA. Since Gregg hasn't actually seen this movie, Tim pulls out *The Bodyguard* instead, tying things up neatly for *Popcorn Classics* and this episode.

On Cinema On Line

8:44 AM - 22 Sep 2015
Hey @timheidecker call me asap, found something at picnic this weekend

8:50 AM - 22 Sep 2015
still recording. will see you on set.

EPISODE 703
'The Intern' & 'Hotel Transylvania 2'

Air date: September 23, 2015
Running time: 7:51 minutes

Tim hurries onto the set, where his guest, Gregg Turkington, is already waiting and anxious to speak to him about something.

Tim was running late because until "about 15 minutes ago," he was at Axiom Studios in San Juan Capistrano finishing up the demo recording of "Empty Bottle" by his new band, Dekkar. [Episode 702] The studio is run by a musician named Axiom, whom Tim met at Guitar Center. Axiom recorded and mixed the song, and he even played drums and helped Tim with "some of the orchestration."

Because this was "one of those rock 'n' roll weekends," Tim also got his ears pierced. That combination of work and play resulted in "this incredible piece of music," which Tim predicts will be "a number-one song on *Billboard*."

Gregg wants Tim to tell viewers how to hear the song online, so they can "get to the movies."

However, Tim is more interested in Dekkar. Waving his CD-R of "Empty Bottle," he says, "We're not gonna talk about movies today. We're gonna listen to music, and we're gonna appreciate the work I did this weekend." He hands the CD-R to the crew, and the world-premiere of "Empty Bottle" gets underway.

Tim enjoys the music, often singing along with the lyrics or his own guitar solos. Gregg mostly looks uncomfortable. Once the song finally fades, Tim asks Gregg how many bags of popcorn the track deserves.

"I think instead of spending the weekend making that music," you should've come to the picnic that you were invited to by Ayaka's boss, Dr. Luther," Gregg responds. Gregg *did* go to Dr. Luther's "wellness picnic," and now he's curious if Tim has ever met his fiancé's boss "that she's been working for a year and a half."

Tim hasn't met Dr. Luther, but Ayaka "spoke kindly of him."

Reaching behind the seat, Gregg pulls out "a candid photo" of Dr. Luther. Saying "he looked very familiar to me," he hands the photo to Tim.

At first, Tim assumes Gregg has "photoshopped" the image. But Gregg swears it's an authentic photo from the picnic.

After examining the photo further, Tim reaches a shocking conclusion: "*That's Dr. San!*"

"I know," Gregg tells him.

Angrily holding up the photo, Tim calls Dr. San "the most wanted man in America" and notes that "he fooled me and he fooled our audience." He complains that his "soon-to-be-wife," Ayaka, has been "working as a secret agent, almost" by consorting with the fugitive healer.

Gregg defends Ayaka against this charge: "I don't think she knew anything about Dr. San."

Tim turns his pent-up anger against Gregg: "I've been looking for this asshole since [sic] for two years, and you're telling me he's been right under my nose the whole time? *Get the fuck out of here!*"

"I didn't have anything to do with it," Gregg protests. Tim continues screaming at Gregg for telling him "my wife is working for Dr. San." He demands that the crew turn the lights off.

"I'm sorry," Gregg says as the cinema darkens.

Did YOU notice...?

- Gregg wore his *Ant-Man* shirt to Dr. Luther's Wellness Picnic!

On Cinema On Line

2:22 PM - 23 Sep 2015
Not happy about today's On Cinema. This is not why I returned. @timheidecker has violated the principal tenet of our agreement. #movies

7:50 AM - 24 Sep 2015
broaden your horizons. Accept life as it comes to you. Life is not just about movies FYI

7:00 PM - 25 Sep 2015
movies enrich life

EPISODE 704
'The Martian' & 'Sicario'

Air date: September 30, 2015
Running time: 9:03 minutes

This episode begins with a video montage that tells the story of Dr. Luther San's transformation from a "healer" who was treating Tim's foot problems with acupuncture, to a despised fugitive, to his fiancée Ayaka's mysterious employer, "Dr. Luther." The title sequence ends on a note of hope, as the show is titled *On Cinema at the Cinema Presents The Dr. San Forgiveness Special*.

True to the theme of Lucky Season 7, this episode is another 24-carat full house: Tim and Dr. Luther San are here, of course, but also on set are Gregg Turkington and *Decker* star Joe Estevez, who will be moderating this public quest for reconciliation.

Tim explains why he was so surprised when Gregg told him Ayaka was working for Dr. San: He assumed Ayaka had been referring to him as Dr. Luther-san, "as a Japanese woman would."

Addressing Dr. San, Tim says, "I had been one of your patients, and you had been treating me for various diseases that I had." Because Tim's "initial reaction to the acupuncture had been negative," he "overreacted." This soon led to "a falling out" between himself and Dr. San, which Tim characterizes as "one of my biggest regrets"

"I'm really sorry about the reaction that expressed itself on your skin," Dr. San tells him.

"That's why we're calling this the forgiveness hour," Tim says. "Because we all have made mistakes." He emphasizes that his stage III face infection was not the result of Dr. San's unsanitized needles. The problem was rather that Tim "had come into the process from an impure place."

Dr. San confirms Tim's diagnosis, attesting that he uses only "pure" 14-karat gold needles because it's "impossible for them to be dirty."

"We're not here to place blame," Tim says. "We're here to forgive and move on." He expresses his gratitude for Dr. San's "great relationship with Ayaka," and he's also happy Dr. San will be treating his son, Tom Cruise Jr., "who has his own set of health problems." He feels "so much more relief now" to have "the great doctor on my side again."

Next, Tim asks Dr. San to shed some light on the problems with vaccines. The doctor observes that "it's tricky bringing up a kid these days in today's modern world," due to "so many opinions and voices coming from all around," including the drug industry: "They're brainwashing us, making us convinced that we're gonna go extinct as a species unless we get all these vaccinations."

Tim has a strong personal interest in this topic, as Tom Cruise Jr. had been getting "vaccination shots" before Dr. San informed him that "millions of children in this country are dying every day" from this controversial treatment.

In conclusion, Tim asks Dr. San's forgiveness for "the way I sort of threw your name through the mud." Dr. San says, "My forgiveness is all yours, and I accept your forgiveness, and it feels really good." In an emotional moment, Tim and Dr. San clasp hands and reaffirm their commitment to each other as doctor and patient.

Dr. San also has a peace offering for Tim and the *On Cinema* audience: It's a colorful pamphlet "about vaccinations and about how much harm they cause in this world." Tim thanks the doctor for this "incredible" document and vows to "take Tom Cruise off all that stuff, starting today."

Dr. San applauds Tim's decision on the grounds that it's best to let our bodies "do their thing." Tim is excited to embrace this philosophy, which promises that "you don't have to go to the doctor anymore" provided you "follow the words of Dr. San."

So great is his confidence in the medico that he is having Dr. San live with him and Ayaka for "the next couple weeks and trying to get Tom Cruise up to 100 percent." He looks forward to "the energies bouncing off each other" as Dr. San takes his place in their home. The two men hug.

Gregg is eager to present *Popcorn Classics*, having driven 90 miles from Victorville, but Tim says there's no time because Dr. San is going to play us a song. In the show's spirit of forgiveness, he assures Gregg that *Popcorn Classics* will open the show next week and will feature not one but two movies.

As Gregg dejectedly leaves the set, Dr. San takes out a flute and plays his haunting "Song for Peace" for Tim and Joe.

People assume that vaccination is the best choice for protection against health concerns - *but that's not true.*

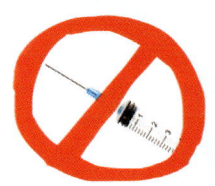

Please look inside to learn about the dangers of vaccination - and to discover the beauty of Healthy Healing and the Natural Alternative

Wait!
Before It's Too Late:
Don't Vaccinate!

A healthy, safe, natural path to good health and peace of mind is within your and your family's reach.

Healthy Healing
and the Natural Alternative:
Just Say No to Vaccination

Open your mind to close your pain

What is vaccination?

vac-ci-na-tion (vak'se-na'shen) n.

1. Inoculation with a vaccine in order to protect against a particular disease.
2. Intentionally injecting the body with unnatural substances in an attempt to cure conditions that can actually be treated with much more natural, healthy methods, so long as the body's mind and soul are ready and open to experiencing something alternative - and beautiful.

What are the dangers of vaccination?

For starters:
- autism
- multiple sclerosis
- SIDS
- shaken baby syndrome
- overwhelming the immune system
- promiscuity and immoral behaviour
- intaking unnatural substances
- encouraging government intrusion

What is Healthy Healing and the Natural Alternative?

Here are some options:
- accupuncture
- meditation
- natural vitamins
- organic bovine colostrum supplements
- avoid foods with added sugar
- quality sleep
- natural infection to strengthen the immune system

What are the beauties of Healthy Healing and the Natural Alternative?

Protection and treatment against disease - the safe and natural way! Honest, pure, and true, whether you're protecting you or your loved ones, you won't have to worry about dangerous, unnatural substances in your bodies.

EPISODE 705
'Pan' & 'Steve Jobs'

Air date: October 7, 2015
Running time: 9:25 minutes

Tim thanks viewers for "bearing with" last week's *Dr. San Forgiveness Special* and also for making it "one of the highest-rated episodes in *On Cinema* history."

As promised at the end of that episode, this one starts out with an installment of *Popcorn Classics*. Having once again traveled all the way from the Victorville Film Archive to share his knowledge of cinema history, special guest Gregg Turkington pulls out *Blue Streak*, starring Luke Wilson as "a master jewel thief" whose plans to retrieve "the hot rock" from "a construction site" don't always go as planned. Gregg lionizes this 1999 thievery-themed comedy as "one of the all-time great Popcorn Classics."

Having gotten Gregg's segment "out of the way," Tim goes directly to *Pan*, "a Peter Pan movie" that transports Hugh Jackman into a thoroughly modern take on the timeless world of Never-Never Land. Recognizing that "Peter Pan just didn't come out of thin air," he is happy to finally see "that origin story that we've all been looking for" of history's original costumed superhero. Tim "liked this movie" and gives it five bags of popcorn.

Gregg was skeptical at first: "Of all the franchises to reboot, why Peter Pan?" But once he watched it, all the missing pieces fell into place: The reboot was "a stroke of genius, because this is one of the best movies of the year." Because *Pan* is "nothing short of a miracle," it "will give you a second lease on life." He gives this "delight" five bags of popcorn and "a jar of Peter Pan-brand peanut butter."

The mention of this product reminds Tim that "Dr. San has gotten rid of all chemically induced foods" in the Heidecker household. Dr. San's disapproval very definitely extends to Peter Pan peanut butter, which is full of "corn syrup" according to Tim. Gregg disputes this, arguing that the peanut butter is "fine."

Steve Jobs is a timely biopic about "the computers of Steve Jobs." Not knowing much about the late Apple founder, Tim was intrigued to learn that he died due to "similar issues that my son's dealing with right now, with his liver or his kidneys or something."

He was also intrigued by Jobs' habit of wearing "black turtlenecks that Decker usually wears." He suspects that "in a way," director Danny Boyle and actor Michael Fassbender may have been "giving a little nod to Decker himself." If so, Tim expects to see more black turtlenecks in movies as this attitude takes hold. In the meantime, *Steve Jobs* gets five bags of popcorn for being "one of the classic movies of our generation."

Gregg says "film buffs should rejoice" over *Steve Jobs* because it's the first biopic in history to use the subject's "full name as the title of the movie." He reckons that if the film had been called *Jobs*, people would assume it was "a screwball comedy." To avoid this misconception, Hollywood used the full name, which "inadvertently pioneered a new style of naming biographies." Therefore, *Steve Jobs* deserves five bags of popcorn and "some melted apple butter."

Next, Gregg has a *Decker* update (which, he stresses, is not a *Jack Decker* update): "We have shot most of the scenes for the first four episodes." Tim hasn't been on the set yet and is looking forward to shooting all his scenes next weekend. Gregg promises that everything is "plotted out," and the shoot will not be a "slipshod" production like *Decker 2*. Further, the episodes will begin airing just one week after Tim's scenes are shot and edited into the existing footage.

Although the title remains under wraps, Gregg tantalizes us with its official abbreviation: *D3 DVD*.

On Cinema On Line

10:39 AM - 1 Sep 2015
happy to report Joe Estevez is returning for season 3 of Decker. #dreamteam. 20 new epsidoses and 2-hour finale.

10:48 AM - 8 Sep 2015
Decker III is going to be a big hit and win awards

8:07 PM - 10 Sep 2015
Hey @TimHeidecker would you be interested in a paid acting job for little Tom Cruise Heidecker? I have some info for you. Meet @TCBY 11am?

8:07 PM - 10 Sep 2015
@tcby sounds good. see you then.

10:44 AM - 28 Sep 2015
Shooting Decker 3 today and it feels like this is going to be the one that puts the franchise into the top tier with Bond, Star Wars, etc.

10:45 AM - 28 Sep 2015
The quality level is much higher than Decker Hawaii, and we are making more use of modern moviemaking technology.

10:49 AM - 28 Sep 2015
Thematically very different than Hobbit but we have reached that level of quality with Decker 3. But clearly our franchise will continue!

GREGG TURKINGTON's DECKER vs. DRACULA
Book 3

Episode 1

PRESIDENTIAL SECRETARY Ayaka greets Jack Decker as he arrives for a meeting with President Davidson. Decker stops to admire her infant son: "Maybe one day he'll become an agent like Jack Decker," he chuckles.

Marching into the president's lair, fresh from defeating al-Qaida *mano y mano* in the hills of Bora Bora, Afghanistan, Decker demands to know what his commander in chief wants.

First, the president apologizes for his typically weak response to the Hawaiian terror plot. But Decker has no patience for this doublespeak, having long ago made it clear what Davidson needed to do: Close the borders, follow the Constitution, and use strategy to defeat terrorism at any cost. "You failed on all three fronts," Decker snarls.

President Davidson folds instantly under this onslaught and promises to resign on television that very night.

Seconds later, a phone call races across the presidential hotline with news that shakes Davidson to the bone. "Something terrible has happened," he bleats.

"Your fundraisers can't find enough money in their coffers to pay for another term?" Decker jeers.

But the laughter dies on his lips when he learns that in reality, the newest threat America faces is one of history's oldest: "Dracula, also known as Nosferatu."

Long thought to be dead, this spirit of eternal evil lives on and has concocted his most dangerous scheme yet: He has joined forces with the Wolf Man, the Mummy and Frankenstein to create a doomsday machine also known as the Destructicon, which will destroy the entire world in just 48 hours.

Decker is ready and willing to confront Dracula head to head then and there, but the president directs him to stay at the White House and "head up operations." Agent Kington can easily go in Decker's stead, since he's already in Transylvania for a monster movie convention.

Decker rogers this plan: "Kington is a good man." In the meantime, the Oval Office will serve as the command base for covert U.S. counterinsurgency operations against Dracula and his cronies.

Meanwhile, deep within Castle Dracula, the vampire chuckles as he puts the finishing touches on his Destructicon.

Agent Kington secures the perimeter of Castle Dracula.

Episode 2

AGENT KINGTON is in a top-secret U.S. military transport helicopter, flying over the Transylvania Mountains in search of Dracula's castle. The pilot locates the target and briefs Kington on his clandestine mission: He must enter the castle, defeat the age-old vampire, and neutralize his world-threatening Destructicon.

Kington parachutes down to the gloomy grounds of Castle Dracula. Back at the White House, Decker and President Davidson get a video call from the agent saying he's ready to make his approach.

Decker wishes he had been assigned to this dangerous task: "My money's on Dracula. Kingston doesn't have a chance!" But the president believes the Master of Codes is America's "only hope" and wants to give him a chance to prove his worth.

Having penetrated the perimeter of Dracula's lair, Kington opens his satchel and removes a large wooden cross and some garlic. Climbing the stairs to the castle, he knocks boldly at the door. It opens, but no one is there!

Watching on the radarscope, Decker identifies threats in Kington's vicinity. He advises Kington to "take the target out" immediately. President Davidson questions these bold tactics, but Decker swiftly shuts him down: "The time for capitulation and kowtowing down to what Dracula's requests are has passed." It's time to "make America great again" by taking the fight directly to Dracula!

That's exactly what Kington is planning to do as he walks through

At long last, Agent Kington meets up with Dracula.

116

Abdul makes an unexpected proposal.

the eerily decorated foyer. "Is anybody home?" he calls. A split second later, in another room, the door of a coffin swings open and Dracula himself emerges!

Kington draws ever closer to the nerve center of Dracula's operation, demanding that he "come out and face the music."

Suddenly, the two men are face to face. "I was expecting you," the vampire hisses. He introduces his associates, the Wolf Man and Frankenstein, who step forward to protect their ringleader.

But Kington is not cowed: "By order of the United States President of America, you are under arrest." He insists that Dracula and his henchmen hand over the keys to the Destructicon. Otherwise, he will have no choice but to deactivate it by cracking its numeric access code.

Dracula defiantly refuses to negotiate with Kington. He is only willing to talk to President Davidson. In the meantime, the notorious Wolf Man shows Kington to his room — a lonely prison cell deep within the eternal walls of Castle Dracula!

Episode 3

AT THE WHITE HOUSE, the president is falling prey to panic even as Decker orders him to "man up and take charge of the situation." Despite his hatred of Big Government, Decker makes an epochal decision: He will stay in the White House as acting president in order to monitor the theater of operations, and Davidson will deploy to Transylvania to lock horns with Dracula and rescue Kington.

Sitting in the darkened Oval Office, Decker is well aware that if Dracula wins, the resulting crisis for America will happen on his own watch as acting president. "I hope Davidson doesn't capitulate to Dracula," he mutters.

President Davidson reluctantly climbs aboard Air Force One and prepares to meet America's immortal nemesis on his home turf of Transylvania.

Back at Castle Dracula, the vampire and Frankenstein are looking forward to destroying the world in just 48 hours unless they can somehow be stopped.

Meanwhile, just outside their lair, it is now President Davidson's turn to take the spine-chilling walk up the forbidding staircase that from time immemorial has led the unwary traveler to Castle Dracula.

Inside, Dracula, flanked by the Mummy, welcomes his new guest. But the vampire's old-world politesse is wasted on Davidson, who demands then and there to know where Kington is being held.

"He's resting comfortably in one of our master suites," the fiend intones.

Davidson berates Dracula not just for threatening the world, but also for making a deadly error: "You have made an enemy out of the greatest superpower that this planet has ever seen."

Dracula is unimpressed. He gestures to the Mummy, and seconds later the president is forcibly abducted. "Help, Decker!" the hapless president snivels. "If you can hear me, please!"

Acting President Decker sits in the Oval Office, angrily watching this scene unfold. "He was tricked!" Decker fumes, pounding his granite-hard fist on the presidential desk. "He fell into the rabbit's nest again." Ayaka does her best to calm the seething agent.

Next morning at 0600 hours, Decker gets an unexpected phone call from Abdul, his deadliest foe, whom he had long believed to be dead only to learn he was still alive.

Abdul has a highly unusual offer for the United States: "The Taliban and al-Qaida network has been monitoring Dracula's movements for quite some time," he briefs Decker. "We feel that he poses a threat to our interests and our oil fields."

With Dracula poised to end the world, Abdul believes it's time for the United States and the terrorists to put aside their differences and fight the vampire together.

"No thanks, Abdul," Decker spits. "I will never work with terrorism!"

But then, Abdul reminds him that Earth is "our planet's only home."

Decker can't argue with that. "Abdul, you've got a deal."

Meanwhile, Dracula is angling for a diabolical deal of his own as Agent Kington and President Davidson pace the floor of a dank prison cell hidden somewhere deep within the unhallowed bowels of Castle Dracula.

President Davidson capitulates to Dracula and the Mummy.

EPISODE 706
'Goosebumps' & 'Bridge of Spies'

Air date: October 14, 2015
Running time: 7:40 minutes

Tim introduces his guest, Gregg Turkington, who identifies himself as "the writer, director, producer and co-star of *Decker vs. Dracula*." Gregg reminds Tim that he needs to get back on the *D3 DVD* set to finish shooting the season. But Tim stalls him, saying "there will be a major announcement regarding" *Decker vs. Dracula* after the review segment.

Jack Black stars in *Goosebumps*, which brings a juvenile horror writer's imaginary beings to life-threatening reality on the big screen in small-town Maryland. Tim calls this "a great horror comedy for kids" and gives it the maximum five bags of popcorn.

Gregg also "loved it." It felt to him like "an unofficial Tim Burton movie," which naturally left him pining for the whimsical presence of Johnny Depp. But "on its own merits, it was fantastic." It gets five bags plus "the phone number of Tim Burton so we can get him involved next time."

To show the respect due to *Bridge of Spies* director Steven Spielberg, Tim stands up to deliver his review of the Master of Cinema's latest masterwork. Unfortunately, this leaves only his midsection visible to the camera, so he has to sit back down. Although Tom Hanks and Alan Alda face plenty of suspense in this "Cold War spy thriller," there's no suspense at all about Tim's rating of a Spielberg film: This is a quintessential, slam-dunk five-bagger!

Gregg also gives *Bridge of Spies* five bags, minus "a few kernels per bag" because this "courtroom drama" has no classic alien characters like E.T., which is incongruous in a film by the Master of Science Fiction.

Speaking of suspense, it's now time for Tim's major announcement: "*Decker vs. Dracula* has been canceled, by me."

He apologizes to any audience members who couldn't avoid seeing the first three episodes of this "disaster." He gripes that Gregg not only "pissed all over" the *Decker* franchise, but he also "shit on it" by showing "absolutely no respect for the universe that I created." He's sorry he ever entrusted Gregg with writing a script worthy of the *Decker* brand, especially now that Gregg has "turned it into a mockery" by bringing Dracula into the proceedings.

Gregg tries to take issue with this viewpoint, but Tim cuts him off: "Shut up, or I'll punch you in your mouth."

Tim also complains that Gregg "showed blatant disrespect for America" and "American values" by depicting "the capitulation of Decker to the Taliban" as they team up to battle the global Dracula menace.

"Wait and see how it turns out," Gregg implores him. But Tim insists this is not an option, because the program has been canceled and he will never return to the film set.

Gregg charges that Tim's beard is far more inappropriate than the supernatural subplot: "You're the one that shits all over" the series, he says, "when you show up on the set with a dyed black beard that Jack Decker would never wear."

Tim responds that his beard is not dyed: "It's how my hair comes in." He also charges that Gregg has "no idea" what he's doing. Turning *Decker* over to Gregg was "the biggest mistake" of Tim's life; the "negative reactions" to the show are unprecedented.

Gregg challenges this claim on the grounds that the reactions he's heard have been positive. "Then you're not looking on the right places," Tim says. He also accuses Gregg of fraud for putting James Dean on the screen in the central role of Dracula, even though Dean is long dead. Gregg says that on the contrary, Dean's "return to the Silver Screen" is "one of the special things" about his show. There's been "a lot of buzz" about the actor as *Decker vs. Dracula* takes its place in the pantheon of stellar James Dean vehicles.

Tim counters that this is a "bad buzz" from "angry and upset" viewers and forbids Gregg to work with any of the *Decker* characters again. Gregg then threatens to create a new show called *Becker*, which will feature "President Donaldson."

Tim is adamant: "In the parlance of your horror movie language, RIP to *Decker vs. Dracula*."

Gregg is defiant: "Then in the language of horror movies, *Becker vs. Dracula* rises again from the crypt."

"If you want to work on *On Cinema*, you don't touch the *Decker* franchise ever again," Tim tells him. He then walks off the set, leaving Gregg sitting in the darkness and muttering about the amount of hate mail Tim will soon be receiving.

On Cinema On Line

2:09 PM - 14 Oct 2015
i will not be speaking about my decision at this time.

8:12 PM - 14 Oct 2015
No one agrees with @TimHeidecker's decision. For a man who claims to hate ISIS and Taliban, he behaves very much like them, destroying art.

8:14 PM - 14 Oct 2015
sometimes you just gotta do what you gotta do.

8:15 PM - 14 Oct 2015
It is unthinkable that @TimHeidecker would prematurely pull the plug on history--the return of James Dean to the silver screen.

8:16 PM - 14 Oct 2015
Becker Vs Dracula is an option we are exploring. There is a lot of uncompleted footage for this season that is completed already.

8:28 PM - 14 Oct 2015
Good thing @TimHeidecker wasn't involved with #StarWars or #JamesBond or #BackToTheFuture or those would've been shut down prematurely too.

7:39 AM - 15 Oct 2015
nothing personal against @greggturkington - but my decision is final. had to stop the bleeding. #OnCinema #DecisionPoints #HardChoices

8:47 AM - 15 Oct 2015
OPEN LETTER TO @timheidecker: DIG DOWN DEEP AND DO WHAT'S RIGHT. BE A MAN OF YOUR WORD AND LET @greggturkington CONTINUE WITH DECKER3DVD.

10:09 AM - 15 Oct 2015
I don't take my marching orders from you or any other members of the #hollywoodelite

9:51 AM - 15 Oct 2015
You can be sure that Taliban Tim has no plans to remove Dekkar's garbage music from the web anytime soon.

10:07 AM - 15 Oct 2015
Convinced @adultswim and @YouTube to take down #decker3 !!! The removal will happen Monday! Good riddance!

10:30 AM - 15 Oct 2015
Even God had to sacrifice his only son. #decker3

1:14 PM - 15 Oct 2015
The weak part of Decker Vs Dracula was @timheidecker. Unprepared, unprofessional, and unable to get through his lines.

1:21 PM - 15 Oct 2015
"Our Values [freedom of expression] Are Under Attack [by Taliban Tim Heidecker and his censorship]".

1:27 PM - 15 Oct 2015
I am in touch with my lawyers, you had better put the 3 episdoes of DvD back on air or face lawsuit

7:55 AM - 16 Oct 2015
of course it was painful to do this to my friend @greggturkington but life is not a cakewalk and i do forgive him for his mistakes.

11:42 AM - 16 Oct 2015
Taliban Tim please reconsider

6:51 PM - 16 Oct 2015
Hey just had a great call with Gregg and we are all good! #decker3 will be pulled on Monday. Thanks all!! TGIF!

6:57 PM - 16 Oct 2015
This is not true. I did not talk to you today.

10:13 AM - 17 Oct 2015
Good morning @timheidecker. I am hereby asking you as a friend and loyal part of the #OnCinema family, to please leave #Decker3DVD online.

8:55 PM - 17 Oct 2015
I have a new idea for a compromise. 12 new eps of DvD, you only have to appear in 5 of them. Decker wipes out Isis in ep6

9:06 AM - 19 Oct 2015
Good news! #Decker3 is now offline! thanks everyone!

9:50 AM - 19 Oct 2015
and your name is officially "MUD". Congrats on mirroring the Taliban in your own life. #FreeDvD will be trending by 5 pm.

9:52 AM - 19 Oct 2015
Taliban Tim believes DvD doesn't meet his high "quality standards"??? Sorry Tim but we've all heard "Empty Bottle". Your standards are low.

12:02 PM - 19 Oct 2015
the #FreeDvD movement is a flop just like #Decker3 was.

12:20 PM - 19 Oct 2015
#JamesDeanHeads, #DraculaHeads, #FreedomHeads, #ClassicHorrorHeads, and #DeckerHeads all agree: BRING BACK DECKER VS DRACULA #FreeDvD

7:45 PM - 19 Oct 2015
I use the power of #forgiveness to understand that I asked to much of @greggturkington - I learn more every day #DrSan

A statement regarding Decker vs Dracula:

I just had an INCREDIBLE session with Dr. San! He has been monitoring my blood levels and energy counts for the past few weeks and wonderfully managing my stress! I am grateful to him for his wisdom! He has also been working with my son, Tom Cruise Jr and managing and treating his multiple health issues using advanced bio-energy therapy.

Dr. San recognized that the very small amounts of negative energy which has been generated by my decision to pull DvD from the Internet is setting back the hard work Dr. San has been doing to get Tom Cruise Jr well. In a very intense 7 hour family health workshop Dr San (no fan of Decker vs. Dracula, believe me) urged me to practice not only on forgiveness (something I am becoming a master of) but kindness, grace and acceptance. We all must accept some things in life as they are presented to us. We are not gods and have to allow life to happen as it happens. Simply put: It is what it is.

Therefor I have decided to restore the 3 episodes of Decker vs Dracula (warts and all) to youtube.com and www.adultswim.com without further comment.

Sincerely, Tim Heidecker

EPISODE 707

Episode 707: 'Jem & the Holograms' & 'The Ghost Dimension'

Air date: October 21, 2015
Running time: 10:13 minutes

This week, Tim kicks off his new show, *On Cinema at the Cinema*, which will feature discussions on movies with "a variety of guests."

Because this is the Lucky Seventh Episode of Lucky Season 7, viewers will strike it rich with "a special casino-themed show" that will include "games" and help them to reflect on "how lucky you guys are to be with us every week."

From off-screen, Tim's first guest, Gregg Turkington, suggests "there's probably no one watching" since Tim canceled *Decker vs. Dracula*.

Tim introduces Gregg as "Mr. Sour Grapes himself." In response, Gregg points up the irony of calling the show lucky, when the audience is unlucky enough to be subjected to "gambling" and "personal problem discussions."

"Incorrect," says Tim. In fact, the games will take place after the movie reviews.

Gregg announces that since it's "game time," everyone should "get on Twitter and tweet at Tim Heidecker, 'Bring back *Decker vs. Dracula*, because we all loved it.'"

Tim is unwilling to submit his decision to "the court of public opinion": "What matters is quality, and that's why we'll never see another episode of *Dracula vs. Decker*."

Jem and the Holograms stars Molly Ringwald "from the Molly Ringwald movies" as a young girl becomes a music superstar by believing in her dreams. "This is a classic," Tim says, "and in my opinion, one of the great classics of all time." He gives it five popcorn bags.

Gregg calls it "kind of *A Star Is Born* scenario but with animated characters who now come to life." He gives it five bags too.

Paranormal Activity: The Ghost Dimension is the latest entry in this popular ghost franchise. Tim plans to keep watching these films for as long as Hollywood keeps making them.

Based on his experience with *Decker vs. Dracula*, Gregg is skeptical: "You'd pull the plug after the third episode," he says, "so that people never found out how they ended."

Tim really enjoyed the "spine-tingling" *Ghost Dimension*: "I love a good horror movie!"

"Like *The Dr. San Forgiveness Special*," Gregg mutters. "That was a horror movie."

In his defense, Tim argues that the *Forgiveness Special* was much better than trying to "reboot" Dracula, who is just "this old tired guy in a tuxedo."

Returning to the topic of Tim's beard, Gregg alleges that it was "a disaster" for the Decker character, as was Tim's "piss-poor performance" in the titular role. Adding insult to injury, Tim went on to "pull the plug and have a tantrum like a crybaby" just because viewers overwhelmingly preferred *Decker vs. Dracula* to *Decker 2: Port of Call: Hawaii*. He worries that "professional jealousy" is "destroying this franchise."

Tim salutes Dr. San for giving him a powder called "Relax," which Tim takes twice a day to counteract the "negativity" and "vitriol" Gregg exudes.

"What's more negative than pulling the plug on a show that all these people depend for their livelihood and to be entertained by?" Gregg asks.

Tim is feeling "calm and at peace" despite Gregg's attacks and again recommends Dr. San's relaxation powder to the audience. Gregg strongly objects to the notion that instead of watching and enjoying *Decker vs. Dracula*, viewers should "take some weird drugs from some quack doctor who's been discredited."

Tim wants to move on to "the fun games." But Gregg says fans in "the James Dean forums" are furious at being denied the late actor's first performance since 1955.

Tim gives Gregg a stark choice: Play the game, or go back to Victorville. Gregg elects to finish the episode.

In a new *Stump the Buff* segment Gregg must answer questions pertaining to lucky number 7. Gregg misses most of the questions on technicalities, such as having a wrong word in the title of *Seven Brides for Seven Brothers*.

The last question is "What is the lowest-rated film in *On Cinema* history?" Gregg says, "It was that One Direction documentary that you and Ayaka went to." [Episode 309] But Tim's answer is *Ant-Man*, causing Gregg to get up and leave.

With Gregg gone, Tim pulls out some "In the Money" scratchers. He wins $1,000 on his first try, making Lucky Episode 7 a real-life case of truth in advertising.

EPISODE 708
'Autobahn' & 'Scouts Guide to the Zombie Apocalypse'

Air date: October 28, 2015
Running time: 6:01 minutes

This week, *On Cinema* has an edgy new theme song: Dekkar's "Empty Bottle." It also has an edgy new guest: Dekkar drummer, guitarist and producer Axiom is in the house!

In a candid discussion, Axiom affirms that it's "awesome" to be a guest on *On Cinema*. Tim says he was supposed to go to Axiom's studio "to do a final mix on 'Empty Bottle.'" Unfortunately, because his son, Tom Cruise Jr., was "a little under the weather," Ayaka told him, "You're not leaving."

Axiom came to Tim's rescue by bringing "a mobile rig" up to the North Hollywood area, enabling them to work on the track without distractions. He plays the new mix, as he and Axiom discuss the rationale for boosting the bass to get a rebooted modernistic "hip-hop" sound.

They spend some time discussing Axiom's recording software, which is "a professional one" that "costs a lot of money." Axiom has been working on music since he was a child. He even has an official record label back home in Italy, which is his home country.

That's the segue to an important revelation: Axiom will be releasing a Dekkar album! "I'm now signed on Axiom Recordings!" Tim crows. He looks forward to Dekkar being "the number-one band in America as soon as that record comes out."

But first, a little background: Tim and Axiom "met at the Guitar Center" while looking for recording gear. The two musicians "kind of clicked" after Axiom "wanted to help" Tim, who seemed like he "didn't know that much about all that gear." The rest, as they say, is history!

Autobahn (a.k.a. *Collide*) stars Anthony Hopkins and Ben Kingsley in a romantic drug-heist thriller that neither Tim nor Axiom had a chance to watch because they were too busy remixing "Empty Bottle."

Tim wonders if they should get other musicians to bring Dekkar to the live stage, but Axiom says backing tracks are also an option. Either way, there's no doubt Dekkar will soon go on tour, because the band is "really good."

Scout's Guide to the Zombie Apocalypse allegedly marks the dramatic debut of Patrick Schwarzenegger, Arnold's son. Although he didn't find time to see it, Tim "liked this one a lot." He gives it five bags of popcorn. Axiom didn't see the film either, so he withholds judgment for now.

Tim thanks Axiom for filling in and sharing his thoughts on this week's top films. He's excited to sign his contract with Axiom, after which they can "go to Chateau Marmont" to celebrate.

"Welcome to the new machine," Tim says. "Rock 'n' roll 2.0: Dekkar!" He foresees being hailed as a member of the "greatest rock groups in the world" and to "playing Wembley Stadium."

He also breaks some inside news: "Empty Bottle" will be the band's premiere single!

"You heard it here first," he confirms.

On Cinema On Line

12:28 PM - 2 Nov 2015
@timheidecker called me this morning but I didn't answer. Afraid he might start singing "Empty Bottle"!

7:15 PM - 3 Nov 2015
@greggturkington please please call me it's an emergeny #OnCinema

EPISODE 709
'Spectre' & 'The Peanuts Movie'

Air date: November 4, 2015
Running time: 9:26 minutes

Today, former *On Cinema* host and frequent *On Cinema* guest Gregg Turkington is "filling in for our usual co-host, Tim Heidecker." Gregg says "there's been a family emergency with little Tom Cruise Heidecker," which required Tim to go to the hospital. Gregg wishes Tom Jr. "the best of health" during this difficult time.

Standing in what appears to be a dimly lit storage locker full of cardboard boxes, Gregg identifies a second emergency that befell the show this week: "When Tim left, he didn't leave me the passcode to get into the studio." Luckily, "that emergency has been squashed," as Gregg generously "consented to shoot the episode here at the Victorville Film Archive." The dark, narrow, cluttered space "is just the screening room, where we dub the tapes." He promises to show us around the actual Archive later in the episode.

In the meantime, he's excited to be able to review *Spectre*, which he has "been looking forward to all year." This James Bond spy thriller "stars, of course, Daniel Craig" as the titular Ace of Spies, who must uncover "the terrible truth behind Spectre."

Gregg assumes Bond needs little introduction to the *On Cinema* Family, since the program is "a known refuge for Bondheads." As such, they will already be aware that "Daniel Craig is possibly one of the best Bonds yet." Further, "this is "the best of the Daniel Craig Bond movies" and "possibly of all the Bond movies." He forecasts that it will be the first Bond film to win an Oscar for Best Picture, "but not the last." He gives it five bags of popcorn, plus "a Styrofoam coffee cup that you would have in your car, but it secretly has a tracking device, 'cause that's what Bond is great at: gadgets!"

Because Tim is at his ailing son's bedside, Gregg has arranged to create "a sort of estimated or projected rating for him." He's sure Tim will "love this movie" since "it's very similar to his own *Decker*," so he gives it five more bags on Tim's behalf.

In *The Peanuts Movie*, Snoopy and his team "take to the skies to pursue their arch-nemesis." Gregg says the plot will be familiar to readers of "the Peanuts cartoon." The main difference is that "great characters" like Pigpen and The Red Baron take on "kind of a 3D" appearance that is "not as flat as some of the old Peanuts movies." Apropos of which, he takes issue with the title: "This is not *The* Peanuts movie, it's *A* Peanuts movie."

On the whole, Gregg "loved this movie." His only reservation is that John Goodman should've been cast as the voice of Charlie Brown. That misstep costs it one bag of popcorn, marring what would otherwise be an undisputed five-bag review. Putting that disappointment aside, he gives it five bags of popcorn and five bags of peanuts.

Tim's projected rating is five bags of popcorn, plus two Milky Way bars for little Tom Cruise Heidecker, who Gregg trusts will get to see the film once he recovers.

Next, Gregg has a special "Victorville Archives edition of *Popcorn Classics*." Walking out of the "Screening Room" storage locker to the "Archive" storage locker next door, Gregg lifts the door to reveal numerous cardboard boxes.

This week, Gregg debuts a new *Family Ties* segment, in which he looks at "the ties that bind a family of actors." This time, the focus is on comedienne Goldie Hawn and her comely daughter, comedienne Kate Hudson.

For the Hawn segment, Gregg pulls out the romantic comedy *Swing Shift*. Much of his review is drowned out by a passing train. But we do learn that *Swing Shift* exposes "the roots of Kate Hudson's comedic timing, which she learned from her mother."

The Hudson segment shines a proverbial spotlight on *How to Lose a Guy in 10 Days*, which Gregg hopes we get a chance to see some time.

Signing off from in front of the screening room, Gregg once again sends good thoughts to Tom Cruise Jr.: "Get well soon, buddy!" He invites us to come back next week, when *On Cinema at the Cinema* will welcome "your new host, Tim Heidecker."

EPISODE 710
'Rings' & 'By the Sea'

Air date: November 11, 2015
Running time: 12:16 minutes

Returning to the set that in happier times hosted *The Dr. San Forgiveness Show*, a tearful Tim forewarns viewers that "today we're not gonna be talking about movies."

Bravely choking down his emotions, he continues: "We're going to be talking about my son, Tom Cruise Heidecker, who passed away over the weekend."

He introduces a "wonderful panel" consisting of Dr. San, Axiom and Gregg Turkington. Gregg says that although he doesn't "usually get choked up about too many movies," the loss of Tom Cruise Jr. "feels as bad as" classic tearjerkers like *Old Yeller*, *Brian's Song* and *Ghost*. He offers to console Tim with "a care package" of films from the VFA: "I don't mind giving them to you; I have duplicates of a lot of these titles."

Tim is touched: "Thank you for that. Thanks for being here." He asks Gregg to say a few words in remembrance of Tom.

"He was really good to work with," Gregg recalls. "Just a really good kid." He very much wishes "they could have done more scenes together" in *Decker vs. Dracula*.

Tim turns next to Axiom, who says "it's a pleasure for me to be here." Tim thanks Axiom for having offered "unbelievable words of support," noting that "when you're in a band, you're like brothers."

"Yeah, exactly, so I want to support you." Axiom replies. "I don't really know what to say."

Tim then turns to his medical adviser, Dr. Luther San, who has been living at the Heidecker household for the past several weeks. "From my own eyes, I could see you tried everything," Tim assures the naturopathic healer.

"I'm just so sad," Dr. San sighs. "I wish there was something else we could've done." He relates how he and Tim "cleansed the house" and "went foraging for all the herbs ourselves." They also "tried magnets" on the ailing tot, which Dr. San hoped would "pull the iron in his blood back into alignment." Tim attests that the doctor even spent time "burning sage."

"And that just got rid of all the negative spirits," Dr. San says. "I really don't know what else we could've done."

"You could've taken him to a real doctor," Gregg suggests.

"I did what I was trained to do," Dr. San answers. He adds that "most people" who go to the hospital get sick there.

"He was already sick," Gregg points out. That being the case, a hospital visit would've been preferable to treating the child with "the magnets from the fridge."

"It's nobody's fault," Dr. San concludes. He urges all of them to "stop pointing fingers at each other."

Tim believes two primary factors were involved: The vaccinations that Ayaka endorsed and the black mold in Gregg's former apartment. Dr. San concurs, citing Tim and Ayaka's use of highly toxic chlorine bleach to kill the mold.

Tim shows a montage of touching on-screen moments with his son, compiled by the *On Cinema* team. Afterward, he asks Gregg where he thinks Tom Jr.'s acting career was headed. Gregg says Episode 18 of *Decker vs. Dracula* included a role that would've been "a bit of a stretch," but he's sure Tom Jr. would've nailed the scenes "if he had lived to do them and the show hadn't been canceled."

"Thank you for saying that," Tim responds.

Vowing to "quickly do the movies," Tim introduces *Rings*, which is "a *Ring* horror movie." He hasn't seen it, but he encourages us to "check it out."

By the Sea stars Brad Pitt and Angelina Jolie. Tim missed it due to "funeral arrangements," but Gregg thought it was "very good." He gives it five bags of popcorn, as does Tim.

Tim confesses that at first, he wasn't sure if it was a good idea to do this show. "But I think by talking about it — getting it out — you kinda get a chance to heal," he says. You can also "reflect on life" and the possibility of "a master plan out there." He asks Dr. San to repeat his beautiful words from the funeral service.

"When a bolt of lightning strikes in the forest, some of the trees burn down," Dr. San intones. "And you just kind of let the fire burn, and some of the trees end up standing."

"And we're standing today and honoring Tom Cruise," Tim says. In that spirit, he performs "Farewell, Tom Cruise" in memory of his son, accompanying himself on bass. Axiom and Dr. San join in on flute and tambourine. At the song's end, Tim thanks the *On Cinema* Family for their condolences.

As the lights go down on Lucky Season 7, Tim and Axiom discuss the worldwide success of Eric Clapton's "Tears in Heaven."

Tom Cruise Heidecker
2014-2015

TomCruiseHeidecker@gmail.com

Dear On Cinema Family,

Thank you for your kind words, and sympathies during this trying time. T.C. would be so honored you cared so deeply.
Special thanks to Dr. San & our new friend Axiom for being there for us, everyday in every way.

Love, Ayaka Heidecker

DECKER vs. DRACULA: THE LOST WORKS

Although *Gregg Turkington's Decker vs. Dracula* was canceled, we can reconstruct a possible story line from the existing script as well as stills from never-before-used footage. Here's an all-too-brief look at what movie history might've had in store for fans.

Terrorist leader Abdul, who betrayed the United States yet again, escapes in a motorboat.

Kington confirms that Decker only pretended to make a deal with Abdul to fight Dracula.

With only one second left to spare, Kington cracks Dracula's deadly Destructicon code.

Dracula raises the Three Stooges from the dead, but they turn against him and drive him into exile.

President Davidson announces that Dracula can no longer be a threat to our world.

Kington (right) and Decker receive commendation for their vital role in defeating Dracula.

President Davidson gives Kington full access to the Library of Congress Film Archive.

Special Agent Kington will return in **Decker vs Dracula: the feature film**

Much of the real story remains untold, as it awaits official unclassification!

On Cinema On Line

8:49 PM - 23 Feb 2016
@m_proksch I'm considering inviting you back for #OSCARSPECIALIV but you HAVE to up your game.

9:38 PM - 23 Feb 2016
Anything you need!

9:45 PM - 23 Feb 2016
do not cross me or this will be your LAST special. Take it to the next level.

9:59 PM - 23 Feb 2016
Wouldn't dream of it! Point taken!

7:42 AM - 25 Feb 2016
hey @greggturkington will need to know TODAY if you are in or out for #OSCARSPECIALIV

11:16 AM - 25 Feb 2016
IN! At rehearsal now for the finale. Promise you will LOVE it!

7:09 PM - 27 Feb 2016
I would rather be an #expert in #MOVIES than in #hashtages. cc: @timheidecker

7:11 PM - 27 Feb 2016
just be an expert in doing what I want/say and we'll be good.

7:43 AM - 28 Feb 2016
My pledge to you is this: I will not drink a drop tonight / we will have no technical problems / very limited and short breaks

10:36 AM - 28 Feb 2016
And let's pledge to keep the special movie-centric this year!

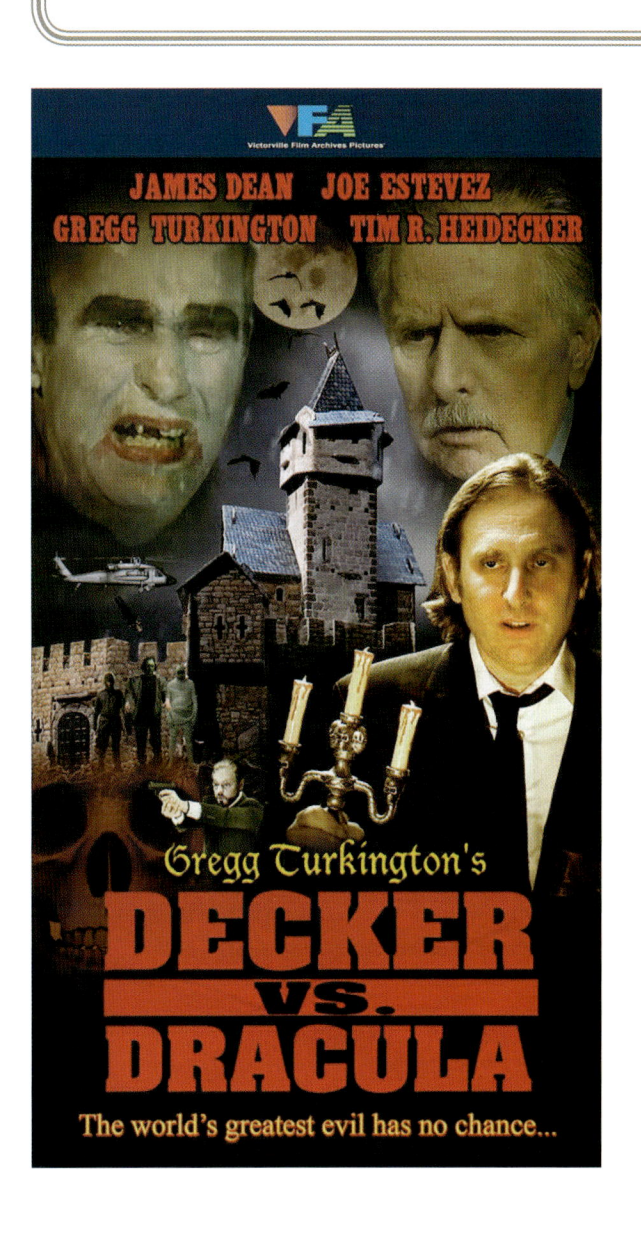

JAMES DEAN   JOE ESTEVEZ
GREGG TURKINGTON   TIM R. HEIDECKER

Gregg Turkington's
DECKER VS. DRACULA
The world's greatest evil has no chance...

ON CINEMA ON HOLLYWOOD LEGENDS

Axiom

A gifted songwriter, producer and multi-instrumentalist, Axiom emigrated from his native Italy to San Juan Capistrano, Calif., to make the most of these talents. A fateful meeting with **Tim Heidecker** at **Guitar Center** gave his career the push and the guidance it needed, culminating in the formation of **Dekkar** and **DKR** and the composition of the #1 download hits "Empty Bottle" and "MT-BTL 2.0."

It also resulted in a lasting friendship! While it lasted, Axiom could always be counted on as Tim's right-hand man on and off stage, to make the sacrifices needed to keep Tim and the band at the top of their game where they belonged.

FOURTH ANNUAL OSCARS SPECIAL
Live Broadcast from Hollywood's Biggest Night

Air date: March 2, 2016
Running time: 3:05:21

Tonight's Oscar Night gets off to a hard-rockin' start with Dekkar's alternative-prog-grunge version of "Oscar Fever."

Afterward, Tim apologizes for his behavior on the last Oscar Special and promises "a dry set" and "a positive, great show." He's feeling happy, having finally found out "who I am" after "searching for him my whole life."

Tim's guest is "friend of the show" Gregg Turkington, who will help out with "some of the expertise stuff."

"You didn't tell me that you were bringing Dekkar to the show," Gregg glowers. Tim feels that since it's his own show, he was under no obligation to do so. He orders Gregg to "cheer up" and also invites him to apologize for *Decker vs. Dracula*, "which was a big flop."

"I'm really, really sorry that we didn't get to do all 20 episodes," Gregg says.

What's in the Cards for Oscar?
In other *DVD* news, James Dean will undergo a live DNA test on tonight's Oscar Special. "We're gonna find out once and for all whether or not he's James Dean or not," Tim notes, clearly hoping to unmask the legendary star as a fraud.

Tim also has a surprise to unveil: While visiting the Rainbow Room on the Sunset Strip with Axiom and Manuel, he was surprised to see "bad boy Johnny Depp" walk in. After a brief chat, Depp promised to stop by the Oscar show.

Gregg is excited: "That would make up for bringing Axiom and Dekkar," he says.

Tim gives out a shout-out to Chaplin's Soup and Subs for their sponsorship. Their spokesperson Hank claims that after the success of last year's sponsorship, Chaplin's Chili was bought out by Levisons Acquisitions. "We still have great items," Hank says, including "a three-bean, three-alarm chowder."

Raising the sensitive topic of Gregg's traditional Oscar Night finale, Gregg promises he will deliver "the biggest spectacular finale in *On Cinema* Oscars Special history."

"Well, your competition's not very strong," Tim reminds him.

Turning to Oscar, Tim and Gregg agree from the get-go that a write-in dark horse is the odds-on favorite to eke out a one-off Oscar upset. Gregg is certain his own *Ant-Man* will harvest this year's crop of Oscar gold. Tim thinks *Fantastic Four* has a better shot, even though some of his own best scenes were cut.

"If you pay $15,000 to be in a movie and they cut the scenes out, do you get a partial refund?" Gregg asks. Refusing to be baited, Tim identifies *Decker: Port of Call: Hawaii* as a likely second-place pick.

"Who owned 2015 at the movies?" he asks Gregg.

"I think it was Johnny Depp," the film buff surmises, naming *Black Mass* and *Mortdecai* as two especially showy feathers in Depp's fanciful hat.

A Peek Behind the Oscar Scenes
In an Oscar Special tradition, Gregg takes us to Dolby Theatre…with a twist! Thanks to his starring role in *Ant-Man*, Gregg gained access to a dark hallway, and later a bathroom, somewhere in the famed theater. Although the audio track is intermittent, we do get to hear a short interview with a film fan outside the building who calls *Fantastic Four* "garbage."

Tim objects to Gregg's "snipe" at his film, contrasting him unfavorably to the always "supportive" Axiom and Manuel. But Gregg charges that they're only supportive because Tim pays them.

Mark's Brothers
Mark Proksch attempts the heretofore unattempted feat of impersonating all three Marx Brothers despite having a bandaged nose. After some confusion, he appears first as Chico. "I was the oldest of the Marx Brothers," he reminisces, "and I was also then the first to die." Chico recounts how his brothers helped him with his gambling debts and also recalls his warm relations with his daughter.

Tim remarks that if Mark had brothers, they would be "Mark's brothers." He has been taking frequent sips from a cup, leading to fears that he's fallen off the wagon. But he swears it's just Diet Coke; he remains alcohol-free thanks to Dr. San's nutritional vape pen.

Dekkar Goes to the Movies
Dekkar returns to perform "a medley of music based on the Best Picture movies," which soon morphs into a defense of free-market principles and an attack on the "Clinton Machine."

"I know you're on the fence with Dekkar," Tim tells Gregg afterward. "But I thought it was cool we were able to incorporate the movies."

"The lyrics didn't have anything to do with the films," Gregg complains. But Tim believes the medley went over well, if Twitter is any judge.

It's All in the Jeans!
Now it's time to take a closer look at the return of Hollywood legend James Dean. Recently, Gregg became friendly with a woman at the Hollywood Movie Museum, which is the final resting place of "a pair of James Dean's pants from the set of 1955's *Rebel Without a Cause*." While cleaning them, Gregg's friend found "a hair that was in the zipper." She provided this to Gregg for DNA testing, and Gregg then collected a lock of James Dean's current 2016 hair.

Dekkar has got the Oscar Fever.

Dr. San explores the ancient mysteries of the DNA atom.

Having gathered the samples, Gregg allowed Tim to choose the testing authority. This turns out to be the holistic healer Dr. San, who gives viewers a quick lesson on the nature of DNA. He teaches us that contrary to popular Western beliefs on the origin of DNA, "the Chinese figured it out 5,000 years ago" when "they wrote about it in the *I Ching*." He also explains that meditation is a gateway to awakening the "dormant strains" of DNA that flow within us, unlocking the potential for more-than-human powers.

Gregg is worried that the testing process will destroy the original 1955 hair, but Dr. San certifies that his testing chemicals are "100-percent organic." Gregg promises to accept the results of the testing. He also proposes that if the test proves that James Dean lives, *Decker vs. Dracula* should go back into production. Tim rejects this idea.

Oscar Olympics: Ant-Heads vs. Four-Heads

Next up is the Oscar Olympics, which Gregg hopes will help to determine whether *Ant-Man* or *Fantastic Four* is a superior movie.

"We put together a couple of teams of devoted fans of each film," he says, "and they are going to compete in a series of games." Whoever wins two of three games will "prove that theirs is the better film." The referee is Joe Estevez.

The Ant-heads win the "Lord of the Rings Toss" even as Tim throws sandwiches at them from offstage. Returning to the set, Tim congratulates the winners of this first round. Turning to his own team, he says, "It's really bad what you did."

"They're imitating your performance in *Fantastic Four*," Gregg comments.

A Visit With Oscar Royalty

The next guest is Dee Thompson, author of *How I Went to the Oscars Without a Ticket: A True Story*.

Asked for the "short story" version of this "faith-based inspirational book," Mr. Thompson recounts how he prayed to go to the Oscars and was accordingly granted entrance by the Lord.

Gregg wants to know if the necessary steps are set forth in Dee's book: "Is it a blueprint for getting into the Oscars?" Dee is confident his faith-based method will work for any aspiration.

Tim brings up the sensitive issue of racial bias at the Oscars. Dee does feel that the lack of "opportunity" for actors of color like himself is a problem, but Tim cites Cuba Gooding Jr.'s win for *Jerry Maguire* as evidence that any claim of bias is "fishy." This is one benefit of being "colorblind": Tim can look at claims of racial injustice and say, "What is everybody all upset about?"

Tim had hoped to get Dr. Ben Carson on the horn at this point, but the call does not go through due to technical difficulties. This causes Tim to yell at the crew, drowning out much of Gregg's interview with Dee about the *Oh, God!* trilogy.

"He's been drinking," Gregg tells Dee. "I'm sorry."

Dee goes on to recall that he once received four Oscars in one day — by acting as a rehearsal stand-in for stars like Martin Scorsese and Cameron Diaz!

"What's gonna put this whole situation to bed with the blacks and the whites?" Tim breaks in. He then launches into an impromptu *60-Second Soapbox* on the topic of race relations, despite Gregg's warning that "it's not really appropriate."

Tim's solution to accusations of Oscar's bias is to "separate the Oscars" into racial categories. Gregg says monthly Oscars would solve the problem by creating more Oscar gold to go around. Dee thinks twice a year might be a good compromise.

Dee informs us that the Oscar itself weighs about 5 pounds and is made of an alloy rather than literal gold. This gets Tim onto a tangent about manipulation of gold values by "the elite."

Gregg tries to ask Dee further questions, but Tim keeps interrupting his answers with new questions, making the discussion hard to follow.

Groucho Speaks!

Once Dee departs, it's time for another of Mark's Marx Brothers impressions. This one celebrates their ringleader, Groucho. He boasts that "I lived longest of all my brothers" and divulges that his former paramour, Erin Fleming, "ended up a bag lady in California." Tim ends the segment early because Mark's Groucho voice sounds too much like W.C. Fields.

Jackson's Folly

Drawing on Gregg's expertise as a Hobbit-head, Tim asks for "a peek into what's next for Peter Jackson." Before Gregg can answer, Tim rolls a short film

Harpo shares fond memories of the late Marx Brothers.

detailing "the mistakes that Peter Jackson made when he made *The Hobbit*." The film tells a tale of exhaustion, haste and personal illness that resulted in a largely improvised, substandard movie.

Gregg accuses Tim of using "manipulated footage" and wonders why he would do such a thing to the "Hobbit people" who make up his *On Cinema* Family.

On Cinema On Songwriters
Gregg's agitation increases when Tim again joins Dekkar for a segment called *On Cinema On Songwriters*. It spotlights a long acoustic version of Dekkar's song, "Empty Bottle," which Gregg denounces as "horrible."

Afterward, Tim once again threatens James Dean: "Your day of reckoning is coming, friend." He promises to beat up the elderly thespian if he's found to be a fake. "I don't care how old you are," he warns. "You don't intimidate me."

50 Years of Bond
Gregg takes us on a visit to Bondland, paying tribute to the most successful movie franchise ever known. Because the tribute mostly entails posing with a gun in front of movie stills, Tim interrupts him to demand an explanation.

"It's 50 years of James Bond," Gregg says. "It's not two hours of your rageaholism and alcoholism and horrible music." Tim demands to know what the background photos are, so Gregg announces the title of each film.

But Tim remains underwhelmed with the segment. He derides Gregg's finale as well, asserting that "nobody" is "looking forward to" it.

Tom Cruise Jr. comforts his bereaved parents.

Gregg counters that his segments are preferable to "more of your awful music that nobody likes" and stresses that online polls of Dekkar have been "really bad."

In the spirit of Oscar Night forgiveness, Tim asks Gregg to take another stab at the Bond segment. Gregg refuses: "You're just gonna come and scream over it!"

"We're not enemies, we're friends," Tim reminds him gently.

"Tell that to Mark," Gregg snaps. Tim protests that he and Mark are "in a good place." Gregg doubts this: "There's some visual evidence that that's not true."

"That's hearsay," Tim fires back. "And that's very irresponsible and you're getting close to being in big trouble with me." He asks Gregg again to continue the segment. Gregg tries, but he finds it hard to get himself back into the Bond mindset.

A Visit from Tom Cruise Jr.
A subdued Tim returns, hoping to "reset the energy" by discussing "the elephant in the room," which turns out to be "the passing of my own son, Tom Cruise Jr."

Gregg makes a scornful reference to Dr. San. "You shut up!" Tim screams. "If you interrupt me again, I swear to God you will be paying for it for a long time."

"Like Mark did," Gregg says as he leaves.

Tim reminds viewers that he's had a rough six months since Tom Jr. passed away. He brings out his wife, Ayaka, whom he describes as "my rock."

What he and Ayaka need, he feels, is "closure." To this end, he has met with "people in the entertainment industry" who have "brought our son back." Ayaka is puzzled, but she soon learns that Tim hired animators to create a grown-up CGI replica of their child who will address them on this very night.

The animated Tom Jr. assures his heartbroken parents that he is happy, healthy and successful. He also thanks Tim for being "an influential role model."

"If I could give one message to the world from my grave," he concludes, "it would be 'don't vaccinate.'"

Once Tom Jr. vanishes, Tim asks Ayaka if seeing this CGI image of her dead child has brought her "closure." She seems overwhelmed but nods bravely.

"I thought that was good," Tim says. "That was healthy." He goes on to say that Gregg had advised him to buy life insurance before Tom Jr.'s passing. Tim took his friend's advice and received a very large payout. "It's a bittersweet sort of thing," he sighs.

He and Ayaka have put this money into the Tom Cruise Jr. Memorial Arts Fund to support projects that display their son's "passion for the arts and dedication to conservative principles and family values."

The Fund's first-ever award will go to the *Decker* series, which will enable Tim to rebuild the ashes of this promising franchise that was "destroyed" by *Decker*

Gregg salutes the Bond Years.

vs. Dracula. "He has not died in vain," Tim shouts. "Let's make *Decker* great again!"

Oscar Olympics, Part II
After this intensely emotional segment, we're ready for Round 2 of the Oscar Olympics face-off. This time, the two teams must accurately code a box of videotapes using Gregg's official Victorville Film Archive system.

With only two minutes to do the job, and Tim alternating between throwing sandwiches at the Ant-heads and screaming at Mark Proksch, this is a truly tough contest!

However, Tim settles it early by declaring the Four-heads the winners over Gregg's objections.

Memories of Harpo
An even more important contest is one step closer to being resolved as Dr. San prepares to unseal his "conclusive" DNA findings on James Dean.

But before that, Mark Proksch is back to give us the "silent treatment" as Golden Age comic Harpo Marx.

Harpo tries to describe his close friendship with Alexander Woolcott, but Tim makes him pause until the trademark horn can be procured. Harpo then discusses his married life in Palm Springs and speculates on whether he is currently interred in Forest Lawn Cemetery.

When Mark finishes, Tim puts his involvement in future Oscar specials up to a viewer poll. "We've squeezed every bit of juice out of your talents," he says.

Next, Manuel and Axiom are back to perform an Axiom original, causing Gregg to flee the set. Tim praises the song as a good track for the upcoming Dekkar album, "if you wanna sign that over my way."

A very special Oscar edition of *Popcorn Classics* features *Decker vs. Dracula*, which was dubbed to VHS by the Victorville Film Archive and features the final performances of Tom Cruise Jr.

Oscar Olympics, Part III
The third and final round of Oscar Olympics requires each team "to pop the most popcorn" using modern methods. Who ever fills five bags first wins!

It takes a long time for the corn to pop, so Tim ends the competition early. He tells Joe to pick a winner, and Joe gives it to the Ant-heads.

James Dean takes his rightful place in Gregg's living painting.

Tim shrugs off this defeat and debuts the world premiere of Dekkar's "Empty Bottle" music video.

A Tribute to Old Hollywood
At long last, it's time for Gregg's surprise finale: A Tribute to Old Hollywood. This is a *tableau vivant* recreating Chris Corsani's all-time classic painting "Legal Action," which shows James Dean, Marilyn Monroe, Humphrey Bogart and Elvis Presley in an intimate "film noir" pool hall milieu.

Tim is puzzled: "What's the point of that?" Gregg explains that every detail from the original painting has been lovingly replicated in this real-world scene. "So what?" Tim asks.

Mark and Joe both express support for Gregg's finale. "I'll be honest," Mark says. "Not everything is Dekkar."

Gregg thanks Mark for preferring his "living painting" to Tim's "awful band that nobody likes."

"Dean"-NA Test Results
The results of James Dean's DNA test are in! As everyone gathers for the verdict, Tim hails DNA expert Dr. San as the man he trusts more than any other. He opens the sealed envelope — and is shocked to learn the hair samples are a 100-percent match. James Dean lives!

"Would you guys like to see my *real* finale?" Gregg asks. He leads Dean over to the young actor portraying him and puts him in the same pose.

Tim interrupts this touching moment with some breaking news from Oscar: "The Best Picture was *Spotlight*."

"I think the best picture tonight is in front of you right now," Gregg responds.

Tim wants to "triple-check" the DNA results, but Gregg reminds him he has already vowed to respect Dr. San's findings.

"I don't care if he's James Dean," Tim says. "Who cares about James Dean?"

"I don't care that you're a jackass," Dean replies.

"I wanna thank my son Tom Cruise Jr., who's the only guest I gave a shit about tonight," Tim says. "And I'm outta here. Good night. This sucks."

"Now we can all have a party!" Dean cries. This earns him a round of applause.

But the festive mood is short-lived, as Tim suddenly tears back into the room to confront Dr. San. "You think this is a fucking joke?" he screams. "Get the fuck out of here! I'm done with you!"

Saying "I should have done this a long time ago," Tim pulls Gregg's *Ant-Man* poster off the wall, smashes it across his knee and storms out again.

"Seems I seen this before," James Dean observes. "You know?"

On Cinema On Line

12:27 PM - 29 Feb 2016
Thank you for all your concern about my nose which broke when I walked into a door.

11:17 AM - 4 May 2016
Season 3 of #Decker will be premiere on @adultswim on June 17th! Will be best season yet!

11:24 AM - 4 May 2016
S1 Decker: Classified
S2 Decker: Port of Call Hawaii
S3 Decker Vs Dracula (highest ratings)
S4 Decker Unclassified

8:20 AM - 5 May 2016
Not going to debate this: Decker vs Dracula was not canon. Therefor new season is Season 3. Live with it.

4:41 PM - 25 May 2016
My Decker Vs Dracula = highest rated and most popular season, and you did NOTHING ON IT and in fact almost ruined it

4:44 PM - 25 May 2016
You are delusional.

6:43 PM - 14 Jun 2016
if you find this confusing you're an idiot:
S1 - Decker: Classified
S2 - Decker Port of Call
S3 (or S1) Decker: Unclassified (1/2)

6:44 PM - 14 Jun 2016
Decker vs Dracula - Side project that wasn't a Decker movie or TV show but a failure that I was not part of (2/2)

7:52 PM - 14 Jun 2016
You starred in it and were the Executive Producer and Creator.

2:35 PM - 20 Jun 2016
THANK YOU FOR MAKING DECKER: UNCLASSIFIED THE BEST RATED AND NUMBER ONE SHOW WE ARE THROUGH THE ROOF

2:56 PM - 20 Jun 2016
MANY MANY POEPLE SAID DECKER WOULD FAIL BUT THEY ARE EATING THEY'RE WORDS NOW THAT ITS SUCCESSFUL AND GREAT

3:07 PM - 20 Jun 2016
I didn't say it would fail, I just said that it would not be as successful as Decker Vs Dracula starring James Dean

9:47 AM - 25 Jun 2016
Just to clarify--@timheidecker created the original Decker character seen in DvD, but I created the new ones such as Dracula, Wolfman, etc

DECKER: UNCLASSIFIED
Behind the Scenes of the Making of Season 4

After the cancellation of Season 3, *Decker* fans were unsure whether Jack Decker and company would ever be back. Happily, their wish came true thanks to the Tom Cruise Heidecker Jr. Memorial Arts Fund, which Tim and Ayaka Heidecker created in honor of their late son to "reward projects that combine an understanding of storytelling with conservative principles."

"When Tim told me he had the money to do another season of *Decker*, I was immediately interested," Gregg Turkington recalls. And that interest paid off: "This season of *Decker*, like all of them, has something for everyone," Gregg says. "Whether you're a Bond-head or a Hobbit-head, a Trekkie or a *Star Wars* freak, we've got it all."

But Tim is quick to point out that *Decker* is more than just entertainment: "A lot of these scenarios are really happening in the world, like Sharia law." The big difference is that in *Decker*, America always pulls through: "After you watch the first or second episode, you're gonna go outside and wave the American flag proudly on top of your house," Tim promises.

Season 4 highlights include the origin stories of Decker and Lanoi Arnold, a peek at the likely future of the Victorville Film Archive, and Joe Estevez's not-to-be-missed deathbed portrayal of President Davidson and President Davidson Jr.

And of course, no one should overlook the return of James Dean as "the great Count Dracula"! Gregg credits DNA expert Dr. Luther San, who confirmed the legendary actor's identity for a new generation, with making Dean's appearance possible in this "unofficial conclusion of *Decker vs. Dracula*."

As on any film set worthy of the name, friction and foibles played their part in the making of *Decker: Unclassified*. Due to restrictions on charitable grantmaking, scriptwriting time was cut from 28 weeks to 28 days, forcing some tough plot cuts. Gregg also felt that as the primary screenwriter, he didn't get enough input into episodes like "Band Together," which follows the adventures of Jack Decker's alternative-rock group, Dekkar.

These creative differences are perhaps most profound in the final episode. For Gregg, it was clearly a struggle to reconcile his vision for the Agent Kington character with Tim's. But as *Decker*'s "idea man," Tim remains laser-focused on the need to innovate. Accordingly, he takes a more philosophical view of these disputes: "That's life," he shrugs. "Not everything works out."

Learn more at www.adultswim.com/videos/decker/inside-decker-unclassified/.

SPECIAL GUEST APPEARANCES

SALLY KELLERMAN

Sally Kellerman got her first break as a fixture on top TV shows like *The Outer Limits* and *Star Trek* before becoming famous as Major "Hot Lips" Houlihan in *M*A*S*H* (1970), followed by star turns in *Lost Horizon* (1973), *Slither* (1973) and *The Player* (1992). Ms. Kellerman is also a gifted vocalist, having performed live for the 1970 Oscar festivities.

AL JARDINE

Al Jardine was an original founding member and guitarist/vocalist/producer/arranger of the Beach Boys, many of whose hits include "Help Me, Rhonda," "Then I Kissed Her" and "Honkin' Down the Highway." Mr. Jardine's role in Episode 4 marks his first movie appearance since 1965's *The Monkey's Uncle*.

CAST

Tim Heidecker	Jack Decker, Jack Decker Jr.
Gregg Turkington	Jonathan Kington
Joe Estevez	President Jason Davidson, Senator Jason Davidson, President Jason Davidson Jr.
John Aprea	General Cotter
Mark Proksch	Abdul
Axiom	Himself
James Dean	Dracula
Manuel Giusti	Himself
Ayaka Heidecker	Ayaka
Al Jardine	Dr. Richards
Cristy Joy	Quality Air Stewardess
Chris Murray	Terrorist
David Schroeder	Dr. Greenway
Sally Kellerman	Janet Davidson
James Mane	Lanoi Arnold
Ernest Pierce	Franklin
Rizi Timane	Chakka

DECKER: UNCLASSIFIED
Season 4

EPISODE 1: ALL GOOD THINGS…

It is July 4, 2076 — the Tricentennial of America's birth — and Agent Jack Decker lies near death in his space-age hospital room. President Davidson Jr. is there to pay his last respects, as is Decker's longtime colleague Jonathan Kington.

Calling Kington to his side, Decker whispers, "You have always been my friend."

"You have always been America's friend," Kington answers. "You saved this country more times than I can remember."

Decker asks for a final cigarette, and Kington places one in Decker's mouth. General Cotter cautions the elderly agents that cigarettes are illegal.

President Davidson Jr. concedes that although his father outlawed smoking, "this great American hero deserves to smoke one last cigarette in peace, by order of the President of the United States."

A final drag, and it is over. Decker has died of old age on the very birthday of the nation that bore him.

How did it come to this? To understand, we must travel 50 years back through history to the year 2026.

Quality Air Flight 1776 is a commercial flight just like any other — until a masked man jumps up to announce its seizure by "a terrorist organization" controlled by the Islamic madman Abdul.

"Not on my watch!" Decker steps from behind a curtain, his gun at the ready. Eight bullets later, the terrorist's perforated corpse is bleeding out on the cabin floor.

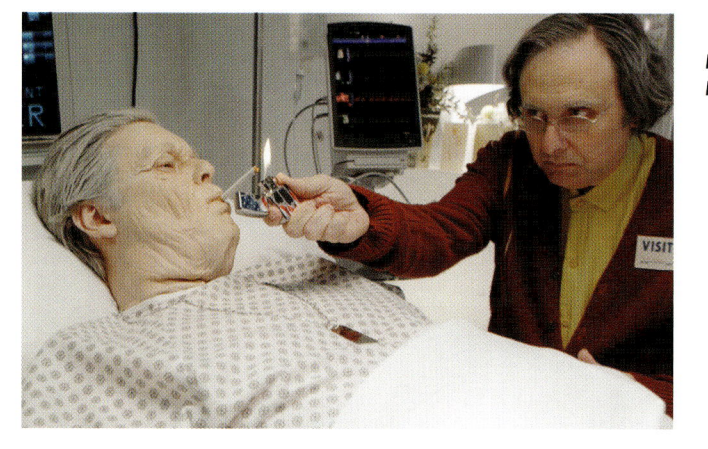

Decker enjoys one last cigarette.

Now, Decker must get control of the plane before the terrorists crash it into Mt. Rushmore. He calls Agent Kington for backup and briefs him on his plan to shoot the cockpit door open. Kington forewarns him that discharging a gun in the plane could damage the fuselage.

Kington has a better idea: He knows that each cockpit door has a unique three-digit entry code known only to the pilot. All he needs is a clue! After learning the dead pilot's name from the stewardess, Decker spells it out to Kington, who swiftly uses this personal data to crack the mystery of the cockpit code.

Decker bursts into the cockpit only to be mocked by the haughty terrorists: "There are two of us, but you only have only bullet left!"

Unbeknownst to these extremist know-it-alls, Decker has a Plan B: Firing the bullet through the cockpit window, Decker lets nature take its course as the terrorists are sucked screaming into the icy air over North Dakota's stratosphere before being sucked screaming into the plane's jet engine. The relieved passengers cheer as the jihadists' blood and bone fragments spray across their windows.

Seizing control of the plane, Decker pulls it up and over the sacred presidential monument with only a few precious seconds to spare. Now, he just needs to land! Kington helpfully gives him coordinates to an abandoned CIA runway.

Against all possible odds, Decker brings the doomed plane down safely. This earns him another ovation from the grateful passengers, along with a provocative "perk" from the comely stewardess: "Next time you fly with us, I'll have to introduce you to the mile-high club!"

Back in 2076, President Davidson Jr. shocks a grieving nation with the news that Decker has died. In honor of Decker's 100 years of service, the president will unclassify his greatest acts of heroism to an unwitting populace so the world may know that "no better man has ever existed."

The president's wife, Janet Davidson, does not join in the applause. "Now that Decker's gone, our plan can finally come into fruition," she hisses. The remark is meant only for the ears of her adviser. But it is overheard by a familiar face sitting right behind her: Agent Kington.

EPISODE 2: THE NEW RECRUITS

President Davidson Jr. unseals the first of the unclassified Decker files, which details Decker's humble origins as a Green Beret recruit of unmatched grit and endurance.

After a day of rigorous training, Decker meets his best friend, Lanoi Arnold,

Mt. Rushmore hangs in the balance!

for the very first time. Over drinks and burgers at the local bar, Decker learns that Lanoi hopes to run his own bar back home in Hawaii someday. There's just one problem: "I worry that one day, I might not have enough money to make some much-needed renovations." Decker pledges his aid if this ever happens.

The next day, the training camp gets a high-ranking visitor in the form of Senator Jason Davidson. He announces that for the sake of "diversity," the recruits will have a new multicultural drill instructor from Saudi Arabia. His name? Abdul.

"I got a bad feeling about this, Lanoi," Decker mutters. But as a Hawaiian who believes in "one love, one light," Lanoi prefers not to jump to conclusions.

That night, Decker and Lanoi are back at the bar. Abdul is there too, which puts Decker on high alert. With time running out, he needs to access Abdul's secret computer files, pronto. But how?

Lanoi briefs Decker on the camp-wide rumors about a hot new CIA codebreaker named Jonathan Kington. Seconds later, Decker is knocking on the door of Kington's nearby CIA training room.

No sooner does Decker spell out his suspicions than Kington hacks remotely into the top-secret mainframe of Abdul's hard drive. Everything's in Arabic. But as Kington boasts, "Language is just another code for me to break!" Within seconds, the awful truth is laid bare: There's an Islamic mini-nuke hidden in the armory!

Worse yet, the bomb is a mile away and will detonate in just three minutes. Decker directs Kington to search the base files to identify the fastest recruit, which turns out to be Decker himself.

Armed with this knowledge, Decker makes a white-knuckle run to the Armory.

Decker invades the past to protect the future.

After shooting the door open, he finds Senator Davidson tied to a chair beside a ticking suitcase nuke. Decker disarms the device with no time left to spare. He then blasts the feckless senator for letting "the fox into the henhouse" at a time when "the chickens have come home to roost."

Damning Davidson as "a needle in the haystack of cowards," Decker leaves him tied and storms out to settle one last score.

Guns blazing, he runs into the bar only to learn from his friend Lanoi that Abdul just left and "seemed agitated." Then and there, Decker swears a solemn oath to leave no stone unturned until Abdul faces the full brunt of U.S. justice.

EPISODE 3: THE BUTTERFLY EFFECT

DATELINE: 2000. Decker and his oldest, most trusted friend, Lanoi Arnold, are in North Africa on a highly sensitive mission. Just then, Decker's cell phone receives a call from President Davidson, who orders him to report immediately to the Federal Department of Science.

Arriving at the FDS, Decker finds President Davidson already underway.

Decker meets Ayaka in 1940s Pearl Harbor, Japan.

Turning the floor over to General Cotter, Decker discovers that U.S. scientists have uncovered a quantum time-travel field. Agent Kington believes the mechanism is similar to the one imagineered in *Time Cop 2: The Berlin Decision*.

"We have decided that the best use of this technology is to send you back in time to prevent the attack on Pearl Harbor," the president declares. This simple tweak has the potential to avert America's entry into World War II, saving millions of lives!

As Kington frets that it's too dangerous, Decker strides boldly into the portal.

DATELINE: 1945. Decker debouches into the streets of Pearl Harbor, Japan, and stops in at a restaurant for some authentic 1940s Japanese fare. He is momentarily disturbed by the sudden appearance in the street of a white man in a fur hat. But he thinks no more of it when he first lays eyes on his beautiful waitress, Ayaka!

He spells out his dilemma to the sympathetic young woman: He must halt the Battle of Pearl Harbor from ever having taken place. But if he succeeds (in the past), his grandfather will not die in that future battle (which is still in the past relative to now). This will in turn mean that his grandfather's final sacrifice will not inspire Decker to become the great American patriot that he is, both in the present but also thus far in 1940s Japan.

"You must not tamper with the events of the past," Ayaka warns him. She briefs him on the timeless Japanese concept of "the Butterfly Effect," which ordains that minor changes to the past must inevitably wreak havoc upon our future.

This is all new to Decker, as are the physical attractions of this Oriental beauty — so different from the blondes he normally favors as an American patriot.

Knowing now that it is folly to meddle in the bygone deeds of the past, Decker has only one final request: He wants Ayaka to give him a tour of "this exotic and ancient city." She is more than willing to oblige!

Decker has a wonderful time with Ayaka in the past. But all too soon, the hour has come to return to the days of the future, which for Decker are those of the present. Heartbroken, Ayaka promises to live as long as possible so they can be together in Decker's own era. But he has a better idea: "Come with me! The future is so bright, and we'll be so happy together."

She reminds him of the Butterfly Effect

Janet Davidson hatches her plot.

and the threat their forbidden love poses to their shared future. Instead, she asks him to give up spying and remain in her own time. But of course that can never be, and so they bid each other a sad farewell.

DATELINE: 2000. Decker arrives back in the situation room of the FDS and briefs the president that he chose to abort his risky mission lest he "shoot an arrow into America's Achilles' heels."

The president gives him the other side of the story: The Russians *also* have the time machine and have already prevented the Pearl Harbor attack! As General Cotter makes clear, this gave them "the upper hand on the world stage." Now, they have taken this opportunity to launch a nuclear missile at New York City!

Special Agent Kington sits down at the terminal to hack into the missile codes, but access is denied. Then, he spies a VHS tape on his desk: Robin Williams' *Moscow on the Hudson*. With only 30 seconds left until nuclear impact, could this title hold the key to saving the USA?

Kington's gamble works, and the missile is deactivated with little more than a second left to spare. That translates into a very close shave in English or Russian! In the ensuing celebration, Kington toasts Robin Williams and director Frank Oz, both of whom had not yet died at the time of these events.

DATELINE: JAPAN. Decker visits the Pearl Harbor restaurant where he first met and fell in love with Ayaka. She is still there, and she still carries the photo taken of them in 1945. But their doomed love is not to be, for Ayaka is already married! The lucky man is Decker's own grandfather, who met and fell in love with the alluring waitress shortly after he was saved by Russian meddling from dying in the Pearl Harbor firefight.

It is at this moment that Decker learns an unforgettable lesson from his grandfather: "You didn't need me to die heroically to become a hero yourself. That quality existed in you the entire time."

DATELINE: 2076. President Davidson Jr. wraps up the strange tale of Decker's race through time, which prevented the nuclear bombing of New York and preserved the true course of history.

This story earns Decker a rare compliment from Janet Davidson. "I do have to hand it to Decker," she tells her adviser. "He was one fierce opponent! However, with him out of the picture, executing my plan will be as easy as pie."

Unbeknownst to her, these chilling words are overheard by Agent Kington, who is sitting right behind her.

EPISODE 4: THE GLOBAL HOAX

PRESIDENT DAVIDSON JR. is preparing to unclassify another adventure from the Decker files. But his wife, Janet, has heard enough. She rises to leave, which only adds to Agent Kington's suspicions.

Meanwhile, in the past as narrated by President Davidson Jr., Decker is on the ski slopes of Lake Tahoe, enjoying some well-deserved R&R with a white-knuckle ride down the forbidding peaks.

Arriving back at his ski lodge, Decker finds that everyone is freezing cold. The lodge's minority business owner, Franklin, fingers the culprit: Regulations and taxes enacted by President Davidson Sr. have made it impossible to run the gas heaters!

Hopping on the next transport to D.C., Decker kicks down the door of the Oval Office to confront President Davidson's persecution of small and minority-owned businesses like Franklin's ski lodge, which is expressly forbidden under Article V's protection of private enterprise.

The president blubbers that his hands are tied by the alleged evidence for "global warming." He introduces his adviser, the sinister Dr. Richards, who also cites this so-called "evidence."

Decker is skeptical: How can anyone still have faith in global warming when he just spent a week skiing?

Unmoved, Dr. Richards divulges his plan to ban all fossil fuel production. Decker knows this will only embolden the terrorists, giving them the all-important upper hand. But the foolish president will not listen to reason: He vows to sign the lethal order within 48 hours!

Upon reconnoitering with Agent Kington at the Nightcat Gentleman's Club, Decker lays out his theory that Dr. Richards' evidence is actually "bullshit" deployed in service of a conspiracy against clean coal and fracking.

This high-stakes standoff reminds Kington of the classic Nicholas Cage film *National Treasure*. In this movie, the evidence for a global conspiracy can be found in the basement of the Washington Monument. That's all Decker needs to hear: "Let's roll!"

Arriving at the ominous monument, Decker identifies two upper windows that are the most probable point of entry for the Illuminati's secret elevator shaft.

While scaling the obelisk, Decker is ambushed by guards. Returning fire, he lights them up with a volley of kill shots that soon stops them dead in their tracks.

With the perimeter secured, he continues his ascent and in no time, both agents have infiltrated the legendary Illuminati basement vault.

There's just one problem: The gate is held shut by a combination lock! Kington worries this will not be an easy code to crack, so Decker holds a gun to his head to clarify his thinking.

While Kington struggles, another guard barges in only to have his brains sprayed across the wall by Decker's savage bullets. The next guard is less fortunate; with no ammo left in Decker's gun, the guard must face death *mano y mano*.

Kington has already calculated the first three digits: 177. Will he figure out the last number in time?

Soon, the agents are in! Kington marvels at the riches of the Illuminati vault until a gasp of pain distracts him. Decker was hit during the firefight; his fingers are wet with blood! Kington wants to get him to a hospital, but Decker knows they need to keep their "eyes on the prize."

Finally, in a box marked *Global Warming*, Kington finds the secret file that betrays the truth of this deadly hoax.

"They cooked the books!" Decker whoops. But is there still time to stop Davidson from signing away America's proud birthright of energy independence?

There's only one way to find out! With nerves of steel Decker lights up a cigarette and uses it to cauterize his bullet wound. "Let's roll!" he barks.

At Dr. Richards' wind farm, the president is preparing to make his fatal announcement. He sits down to sign the order, but no sooner does his pen touch the paper than Decker and Kington arrive on the scene. Drawing a bead on his commander in chief, Decker orders Davidson to lay down his pen and notifies Richards that he's under arrest for treason.

Caught in the act, Dr. Richards has to admit global warming is a hoax. But he has one last ace up his sleeve: "According to your own Constitution, once your president puts pen to paper, there's no turning back." He pulls a gun from his pocket and aims it at the president's head.

"There is some good news about global warming," Decker tells Richards. "You won't need a coat where I'm about to send you." With that, he deploys a bullet straight into Richards' head, reducing it to a shuddering mass of bone shards and shredded brain tissue. He uses the rest of his bullets to put Richards' deadly wind turbines out of commission for good.

Concluding this never-before-known tale, President Davidson Jr. shows a scientific chart demonstrating that declining global temperatures over the following decades proved Decker right.

EPISODE 5: BAND TOGETHER

PRESIDENT DAVIDSON SR. briefs Decker on a coded threat decrypted by Agent Kington: At a birthday gala for Sultan Ali bin Khan, the terrorists are expected to hand off the plans for a last-ditch EMP attack against America. The USA must infiltrate the gala and seize these plans. But how?

Decker has the answer: His band, Dekkar, will provide music for the event, delivering "a progressive hard-rock edge with an alternative twist." Kington strongly disapproves of this plan and storms out of the Oval Office.

As Dekkar boards a secret CIA plane bound for the Islamic world, Decker admits to his bandmates for the first time that he is a CIA agent whose covert mission is to prevent an EMP attack.

Guitarist Axiom instantly realizes their whole way of life is at stake: "What about our amps? We need juice to take it to the limit!" The band's decision is unanimous; the mission will continue!

Dekkar's performance is a success musically, but also in terms of recovering the EMP plans. Back home on the D.C. tarmac, Axiom affirms his undying brotherhood with Decker and urges him to board the band's private jet for the ride home. In a decision more fateful than he knows, Decker elects to stay in the capital and deal with bureaucratic red tape.

Decker stands on the runway watching Dekkar's plane ascend. Just then, an Islamic missile blows it out of the sky with no warning! As flaming debris rains down on the airfield, Decker is grief-stricken, knowing this fate was intended for him.

There's only one thing left to do: Sitting at his laptop, Decker pens a resignation letter to the president. Then, he picks up his gun, lifts it to his head, and begins to squeeze the trigger for the last time.

Right then, Agent Kington knocks at his door. When Decker doesn't respond, he must rely on his wits to crack the entry

President Davidson capitulates to the evil Dr. Richards.

Decker mourns the loss of Axiom and the others.

code. In the nick of time, Kington gains entry and narrowly avoids being gunned down by Decker's lightning reflexes.

Kington has brought the black box recorder from Dekkar's plane: "There's something you need to hear."

On the tape, Axiom acknowledges Decker's peerless musical gifts. But in the final summation, "his true calling is protecting America each and every day."

The next day, President Davidson is reading Decker's resignation letter in disbelief when Decker himself erupts through the door to rescind his letter in the name of the American People.

"Why the change of heart?"

"I got some good advice from an old friend," Decker snaps. The president is pleased, and he has a surprise of his own: Decker recently received a package containing a platinum record commemorating the sales success of Dekkar's song "Empty Bottle."

For Decker, this musical triumph will forever be tinged with the bittersweet flavor of irreparable loss.

EPISODE 6: A NEW HERO

Wrapping up his tales of Decker's incredible life, President Davidson Jr. shares some advice his father, President Davidson, once gave him on his deathbed: "Always trust Jack Decker!" This earns the president a standing ovation.

Afterward, Kington ponders how to stop the first lady. "How I wish Jack was alive," he sighs. Suddenly, he gets an idea.

At 0500 hours, Kington knocks at a modest door in Arlington, Virginia. Pushing the door open, he wanders inside to find a young man playing a videogame. The young man's name? Jack Decker Jr.

To Kington's dismay, Decker Jr. rejects his plea for help. He believes his father never cared for him, even if he did leave him "the never-ending, nonstop musical royalties from his hit group Dekkar."

To give the young man a different perspective, Kington brings him to the Victorville Film Archive, North America's largest collection of classic VHS movies.

Kington retrieves an unmarked tape hidden behind a copy of *Baby Boy*. Bringing Decker Jr. to the screening room, he shows him a video Decker Sr. recorded in Lanoi Arnold's newly renovated bar as a special message for his son.

"I know I have not always been a good father to you," Decker Sr. confesses. In his defense, he alleges that there are "grave threats to the country coming from inside the government" — possibly even inside the first family.

"I need you to continue my legacy of protecting this country from all enemies, foreign or domestic," he concludes.

Hearing this, Decker Jr. is ready at last to stand in his father's heroic path.

Kington takes the raw young recruit to the Green Beret training camp that in happier times produced matchless patriots like Jack Decker and Lanoi Arnold. The training is long and arduous, but in the end, Decker Jr. proves he has what it takes to take on the mantle of his father's footsteps.

At the same moment, in a private White House apartment, the first lady is questioned by her adviser on the wisdom of making her next sinister move.

Ms. Davidson barely hears her. "It's so hot," she pants. Removing her scarf, she uncovers two bloody holes in her neck. As her adviser grasps the shocking truth, a bat flies in and, in a puff of smoke, stands revealed as Dracula himself.

"I'd like to introduce you to Count Dracula," the first lady tells her horrified adviser. She then unveils the Destructicon, which Dracula has invented to kill all men and give rise to "the age of the woman."

"Madame Davidson, this is madness!" her adviser cries. Dracula advances pitilessly on the screaming woman.

"What fun," the first lady murmurs.

At that very moment, Kingston and Jack Decker Jr. arrive at the Oval Office. "He's the spittin' image of his old man!" the president splutters.

Dracula makes his move.

But Decker Jr. is in no mood to chat. He puts the president on notice that "there is a rat in this White House as we speak," and it's none other than the first lady.

The foolhardy president finds this hard to accept, so Decker resolves to "go and ask her and find out." Davidson Jr. is hesitant, but he quickly changes his tune once Decker Jr. holds a gun to his head.

Kicking open the first lady's boudoir, they find her consorting with Dracula and her dead adviser.

"Darling, I trusted you," the president whimpers. "How could you do this?"

"Jason, I had no choice. Don't you see this was the only way?" Reaching for a small pistol, she shoots the president in the chest. When Kington objects, she shoots him dead as well.

That's a bridge too far for Decker Jr., who shoots her through the heart, dead.

Next, he fires on Count Dracula himself, but the wily vampire eludes him by returning to bat form. Dracula departs, but not before promising Decker Jr. they will meet again to settle old scores.

Left alone with the bodies of the president and Agent Kington, Decker Jr. senses that he has failed the USA. He lifts his gun to his own head and prepares to pull its trigger one last time.

"Not so fast," the president groans as he struggles to his feet. He pulls a VHS cassette of *Heaven Can Wait* from under his shirt. "Before he died, Kingston shared with me his love of old movies. This tape he gave me saved my life."

Decker Jr. and Davidson Jr. spare a moment to honor the memory of Jack Decker Sr. But somewhere outside, Dracula is plotting his next move.

An Official Statement
From Tim Heidecker

Firstly, let me thank the millions of viewers who made the entire 1st (4th) season of Decker: Unclassified a total success - It's viewership according to polling and independent research were and are some of the best in the world.

Among a small portion of our overall, very satisfied audience remains some detractors who were unhappy with the conclusion of this particular season. While I admit, at first, my own idea of introducing the character of Dracula (who is based on a real historical figure Count Dracula who was from Transylvania, this is, by the way, backed up by historical facts) was challenging even to me, but I was ultimately rewarded by knowing that it was the right thing to do!

Let me be clear - The Dracula you find in the conclusion of Decker: Unclassified is in no way connected to the failure of a season that was and is Decker vs. Dracula. - It's not even the same character! (how could the Dracula from our vastly superior version have never known a US President before????) In the end, I think you'll agree this season had more twists and turns than every other TV show out there and we will continue to deliver quality through the telling of more and more Decker stories going into the future.

Many more characters are yet to be introduced and there is no need to wish for past, smaller characters who have died to return in any form.

Sincerely,

Tim Heidecker
Creator of Decker

FIlm Buffs Would Do Well To Investigate Dyan's Canon

Dyan Cannon was born in 1937 and later married movie legend Cary Grant. In between those events she made some of the most beloved movies in cinematic history, as far as film buffs are concerned.

This regular newsletter will cover movies that you may have missed. It will be an invaluable part of the film community. We hope to publish at least once a month. The astute film buff will retain these for future use as there is quite a bit of information here.

Dyan Cannon is known for Deathtrap with Christopher (Superman, Superman II, Superman Iii, Superman IV, Deathtrap, Switching Channels, and one of my all time-favorites, Somewhere In Time) Reeve, and it also starred Michael (A Bridge Too Far, The Hand, Dirty Rotten Scoundrels, Deathtrap, The Dark Knight, and many more) Caine. Deathtrap was released in 1981 to rave reviews. The film's main poster featured an image of a Rubik's cube, which was a popular game at the time, though it did not figure into the movie's plot, in which the tables were turned many times and it was impossible to know who the culprit was. Dyan Cannon was excellent in the movie.

Other movies she starred in, were Bob and Carol And Ted And Alice (with Natalie Wood from Rebel Without A Cause, which also starred the great James Dean). Such films as Shamus, Revenge of the Pink Panther (Peter Sellers starred in this series), Author! Author! (starring Al Pacino (The Godfather I, The Godfather II, The Godfather III)), and most recently Boynton Beach Club.

Dyan Cannon also starred in a movie that was a Certified Popcorn Classic, and if you are a DeckerHead or a KingtonHead you will know that it was a key part of Decker Unclassified, when the movie actually saved the life of President Jason Davidson (played by Joe Estevez), the movie is of course Heaven Can Wait (starring Warren Beatty, who starred with Natalie Wood (there's that name again!) in Splendor In the Grass). The Heaven Can Wait VHS tape seen in the movie Decker Unclassified, stopped a bullet fired by Sally Kellerman (Lost Horizon, MASH, The Player, Decker Unclassified, Back To School, Welcome To LA) at Joe Estevez (President Jason Davidson) but the bullet lodges into the tape which is in Davidson's coat, as it was a gift or on loan from Agent Kington, who is Decker Unclassified's resident movie Buff, as well as honoring his duties to the CIA and cracking impossible codes when necessary for national security.

In reality the VHS tape was a movie prop and "no copies of Heaven Can Wait were damaged in the making of this film".

Dyan Cannon divorced Cary Grant who passed away soon after, but her movie legend lives on, she continues to work in movies such as Boynton Beach Club and That Darn Cat and others, and of course lights up the silver screen every time. Be sure and investigate the films of Dyan Cannon when you have a chance. You won't be sorry.

SEASON 8

EPISODE 801
'Star Trek Beyond' & 'Hillary's America'

Air date: July 27, 2016
Running time: 11:01 minutes

The newly retitled *Tim Heidecker's On Cinema at the Cinema* sports new credits, new theme music — even a new set! Tim is dressed in full rock-star regalia, including an open shirt and a medallion. Gregg is wearing a tuxedo, as befits his new status as creative director of the Victorville Film Archive and president and founder of the Victorville Film Center. And as Gregg alerts us right at the outset, these aren't the only changes afoot: "This is a very different season of *On Cinema at the Cinema*."

Their new cinema is located in Victorville, which Gregg calls "the new Hollywood." Tim was "able to lease this property" through funding from the Tom Cruise Heidecker Jr. Memorial Arts Foundation, which enabled them to acquire this "abandoned theater" that had been "rotting away here in the desert." The Foundation is also "the primary investor in the Victorville Film Center, curated by Gregg Turkington."

Gregg announces that the VFC will soon be showing nightly selections from the Victorville Film Archive, "which is just a mile and a half away."

Tim thanks his late son for "shining down on us" from "wherever he is" and "leading us toward a bright future." And he thanks Ayaka's father, "who has also put in some significant funding" for this cultural oasis in the high desert. His "only request" to Gregg is "to get working on fixing the air conditioning, because it's about 125 degrees in here."

"Somebody stole the copper wire," Gregg explains. He describes how he used to pass the old theater while walking to the supermarket and how thrilled he is to realize his dream of converting it to a world-class cinema destination through the support of the Tom Cruise Jr. Foundation and Ayaka's father.

Tim is also excited about *Decker: Unclassified*, "the number-one show right now on cable and on network TV." In Dekkar news, he is working hard to finish their debut album: "I'm trying to access song ideas," he says. Gregg suggests writing a radio jingle for the Victorville Film Archive, but Tim is uninterested.

We boldly go to the movie review segment with *Star Trek Beyond*, as the *Star Trek* crew does battle with a mysterious enemy from the realms of space. Tim is a big fan of this "franchise series," and he found it "interesting" to watch this film "take the story to new heights and go where no man has gone before." He gives it six bags of popcorn and a cup of cold soda.

As a certified Trek-head, Gregg gives *Star Trek Beyond* very high marks indeed: "It's the best *Star Trek* movie since *Star Trek II*, which was set in San Francisco." It gets five popcorn bags "and a Klingon Cola."

Hillary's America stars Hillary Clinton, who is "sour to look at" according to Tim. He champions this film as a "canary in the coal mine" warning us that "the country itself is under collapse" and "we are at risk of a complete takeover by the Hillary people who are in charge of Hillary Clinton."

Tim is confident this "bombshell movie" will win the Oscar for exposing Clinton's crimes: "I'm formally requesting the United States government try Hillary Clinton and her husbands to stand trial and be executed." He would also like to "pass a law in all 50 states that you're not allowed to vote unless you've seen this movie." He gives it six bags of popcorn accompanied by "all the cups of soda in the world," because "in Hillary's America, you're not gonna be able to even get soda anymore."

Speaking as the director of a startup film venue, Gregg says, "I like your idea to promote filmgoing!" He confesses that he was skeptical of *Hillary's America*, since a documentary is "not a real movie." But in reality, the film was only partly based in fact, relying heavily on "recreated scenes" with "very good actors." It also had "action," along with "intrigue and suspense." He thinks "you have to approach it as sort of a popcorn movie and not get bogged down in the politics." That said, he appreciated the "chills and thrills" this film delivered.

"How do you sleep at night knowing what the truth is and then ignoring it?" Tim asks.

"I don't know if it's true or not," Gregg shrugs. He saw it more as one of those "political espionage intrigue movies" like *The French Connection*. The only parts he didn't care for were the ones that relied on "old news footage." He gives it five bags of popcorn and "a little pair of scissors so they can cut out all those news sequences and stick with the action scenes."

Before leaving, Tim has an announcement for all the people who wished him and Ayaka well after the passing of Tom Cruise Jr.: "The Lord has blessed us, and Ayaka and me, with the chance to try again, and we have another one on the way."

Gregg is puzzled, so Tim clarifies: "We are expecting. We're having another child. My Ayaka is with child." The "pregnance [sic] was not planned," he adds glumly. "But we have that coming up."

On Cinema On Line

6:02 AM - 29 Jul 2016
he (@m_proksch) is not longer a part of #Decker was very badly received by the fans. very unliked

9:56 PM - 30 Jun 2016
I was?! That's awful. Thought they enjoyed my work.

2:42 PM - 29 Jul 2016
mark that was a private message - not intended for your eyes. please show some respect for us.

2:44 PM - 29 Jul 2016
Oops! I had no idea! Sorry, Tim! Didn't mean to pry.

2:47 PM - 29 Jul 2016
but you did and now i'm dealing with mountains of bullshit thanks to you

2:49 PM - 29 Jul 2016
I can't apologize enough for my mistake. I saw my name and assumed it was a public tweet. I fell awful.

2:50 PM - 29 Jul 2016
where are you right now? i think we should discus in person. now.

2:53 PM - 29 Jul 2016
If you think that will help. I'm with my folks at the Denny's on airline drive.

2:54 PM - 29 Jul 2016
coming for you.

2:53 PM - 29 Jul 2016
Sounds good. See you in a bit.

5:49 AM - 30 Jul 2016
Last night I was in a physical altercation with @m_proksch by which I did not provoke. FYI / he attacked me.

6:23 AM - 30 Jul 2016
Appropriately, the hammer, came down on @m_proksch so hard - he won't forget anytime soon.

9:05 AM - 30 Jul 2016
After a night of soul searching I've decided to take a break from Decker. I want to thank @timheidecker for allowing me to be on this season

9:13 AM - 30 Jul 2016
Any one could have played the small bit part of Abdul. Mostly an extra character no one remembers!

9:17 AM - 30 Jul 2016
I'm happy I got to be a part of it.

9:19 AM - 30 Jul 2016
you are lucky you are in the hospital and not jail for the shit you pulled. May still sue.

9:21 AM - 30 Jul 2016
Please don't.

10:00 AM - 30 Jul 2016
Wow @m_proksch really ruined what should have been a great celebration of an amazing season of Decker

10:33 AM - 30 Jul 2016
Again, I'm very sorry about this. It was your day and I ruined it.

10:46 AM - 30 Jul 2016
We can all agree that @m_proksch was great as Abdul, and has been a great friend to the VFA.

11:38 AM - 30 Jul 2016
Thanks Gregg, but @timheidecker is the real hero of Decker.

1:17 PM - 30 Jul 2016
actually i like @m_proksch a lot, but mostly he is a bad guy. really bad actually.

3:53 PM - 30 Jul 2016
No idea why you feel this way. I'll try to be a better friend.

3:59 PM - 30 Jul 2016
@m_proksch next time you fuck with me you'll end up in a morgue not a hospital get it?

4:00 PM - 30 Jul 2016
I do.

5:24 PM - 2 Aug 2016
@m_proksch hey buddy we good?

6:24 PM - 2 Aug 2016
Yes! Absolutely! Sorry, everything was my fault!

6:31 PM - 2 Aug 2016
you think i don't know that?

6:32 PM - 2 Aug 2016
Of course. Sorry!!

EPISODE 802
'Café Society' & 'Jason Bourne'

Air date: August 3, 2016
Running time: 13:38 minutes

Tim is joined this week by his co-host, Gregg Turkington, who still hasn't fixed the air conditioning at the Victorville Film Center. "It's very warm in here," Tim remarks.

In cooler news, Tim is proud to have wrapped up a highly successful season of *Decker*. Despite his past naysaying about the involvement of James Dean, Tim is enthusiastic: "It was neat to get to work with James Dean, I'll admit it."

He also credits himself with having taken Gregg's *Decker vs. Dracula* plot and found a way "to make it work inside the *Decker* universe." It all goes to show that "we learn from our mistakes": Gregg has learned from his mistakes, and Tim has *also* learned from Gregg's mistakes.

"You learned from my triumphs and took the ideas for your own triumph," Gregg counters. "But that's OK. I'm happy to have been a part of it!" He posits that fans were pleased to see the "unofficial conclusion" of *Decker vs. Dracula*.

"The two things have nothing to do with each other," Tim snaps. For evidence, he cites the Son of Dracula's line about meeting President Davidson: "I have never met a president before." That line, he argues, makes it clear this is a totally separate plot from *Decker vs. Dracula*.

"The character of Dracula has always been a little bit unreliable when it comes to the facts," Gregg says. Tim suggests they talk about the week's hot new movies instead.

And it doesn't get much hotter than a new film from Woody Allen! This week, the master returns with *Café Society*, a 1930s-tinged romance drama about Hollywood's original glamor stars and the man who falls in love with their secretary.

Tim congratulates Woody on his 100th movie, commenting that "this one is as good as any others." He predicts Oscar gold in Woody's near-term future. But for now, the film's prize is five bags of popcorn and a cup of soda.

Tim wants to know how many Oscars can currently call Woody's house home. "They don't count them anymore," Gregg tells him. "They measure it by the weight." In fact, "Woody Allen's house is sinking into the ground under the weight of all that Oscar gold." Gregg gives *Café Society* five popcorn bags and "five wheelbarrows" to carry "a small portion" of Woody's Oscar haul.

In *Jason Bourne*, Matt Damon plays Jason Bourne as seen through the lens of Jack Decker: "The whole spy genre had kind of fallen by the wayside until we launched the *Decker* series," Tim recalls. But today, it's "topic *du jour*." Even so, *Jason Bourne* didn't have the "chills and thrills" he wanted. It was also "very confusing." Tim "still did have fun looking at it," though, and he appreciated "the element of surprise" that comes from "not knowing what's going on." He gives it five bags of popcorn.

Gregg was confused on more practical grounds. Recalling previous installments like *The Bourne Identity*, *The Bourne Legacy* and *The Bourne Ultimatum*, he says that "these are titles that are in a good alphabetical order." This makes it easier for collectors like Gregg to file their videotapes. Sadly, *Jason Bourne* "is not even gonna be in the same room as the others." *The Bourne Victory* would be a more collector-friendly title; Gregg goes so far as to say the movie should be re-released under that name. He gives it five bags of popcorn, plus an "advice capsule" containing a memo reminding Tinseltown execs to retitle the film.

Next, Dr. San is on hand to talk health. Tim reminds viewers he has been having problems "coming up with the creativity" needed to complete Dekkar's debut album. Dr. San has helped him by sharing his "nutritional vape technology." Tim demonstrates the use of Dr. San's designer vape pen, which is not only "creatively stimulating" but also provides "nutritional basics" at "a molecular level."

Because the vape compound "now replaces my meals," Tim hasn't "had a bite to eat in six days." As a result, he has "lost like 15 pounds" over the last "72 hours." Tim and Dr. San see this as a perfect example of how "21st-century technology" is "hacking the actual biosystem."

At the same time, the compound's "psychoactive element" is unlocking Tim's creativity. He has already written one song with "seven or eight pages of lyrics." He fears that if he didn't have his vape pen, he "would turn into a zombie." While he's not addicted "in the literal medical sense," he doesn't believe he "could live without it."

"Is this approved by the FDA?" Gregg asks suspiciously.

"Things take so long when you include all the bureaucracy," Dr. San sighs.

Tim reports that when vaping, he gets "an immediate buzz" that's "almost pain," followed by "positivity and energy." Although the nutritional content has him feeling "full and almost sick," Tim does enjoy the vape's natural flavor of "watermelons and grape soda."

Gregg wants to present a Popcorn Classic, and Tim says he'll roll the segment after the end credits. Due to an apparent technical glitch, the segment doesn't air.

EPISODE 803
'Suicide Squad' & 'Nine Lives'

Air date: August 10, 2016
Running time: 10:13 minutes

Drenched in sweat from the sweltering cinema, his face marred by nasty contusions and welts, Tim opens the show by inhaling deeply from his nutritional vape pen.

Acknowledging viewer concerns, he discloses that he's had "a tough couple days." He and his newly pregnant wife, Ayaka, have been discussing the possibility of "taking a little bit of a break on that plan of having that kid."

"What do you mean by that?" Gregg asks.

Between frequent lungfuls of Dr. San's vape, Tim affirms that it is his and Ayaka's choice to "move along without the pregnancy," and he is therefore "asking her to consider that right now." Ayaka has returned to Japan to "talk to her family about it."

Suicide Squad puts Will Smith and Ben Affleck directly in harm's way as they fight to pardon supervillains jailed for the crimes of the secret government's "black ops" team. Tim pauses his review because the Victorville Film Center is too hot: "I can't breathe," he gasps.

Gregg suspects "it's the vaping" that's causing Tim to sweat so profusely. He pleads with Tim to do his vaping off the air, but Tim doesn't see that as an option: "If this doesn't get into my system, I go to a bad place."

Gregg remains distrustful of Dr. San: "At this point, you're the only customer in the whole world that guy has!" he says. "Everyone else has either moved on or died."

Getting back to *Suicide Squad*, Tim liked it: "It made me laugh, and I need a laugh right now 'cause things are not going well." He returns to the topic of Ayaka and the option of "terminating her pregnancy."

"She's not gonna do that after what happened to Tom," Gregg predicts.

"I think she should," Tim declares. He has some advice for his male viewers, too: "Use protection, my brothers out there. Because you don't wanna be in this position."

Tim asks what Gregg thought of *Suicide Squad*. Gregg enjoyed seeing classic superheroes like "Batman and The Joker" appearing "in a setting that's really more reminiscent of our own *Decker*." This gives him a crossover idea: "I would love to see a *Decker* comic book and have the future movies of *Decker* spring from the pages of the comic book."

He gives *Suicide Squad* five bags of popcorn. As Tim nods off from the vape effects, Gregg throws in "a pair of handcuffs for Dr. San." Tim wakes up long enough to give the movie five bags of popcorn and a cup of soda.

Since Tim is too disoriented to read the cue card, Gregg takes over. *Nine Lives* features Kevin Spacey and Christopher Walken in the role of a lifetime as a businessman who is imprisoned in the body of his cat.

"I'm so tired," Tim murmurs as he takes another puff from Dr. San's pipe. He's also trying to avoid breathing through his mouth. "I don't want the ideas from my head to come out of my nose," he pants.

Grabbing the cue card from Gregg, Tim attempts to review *Suicide Squad* a second time. "It's so hot in here," he moans. "It's really hot."

Gregg advises us that *Nine Lives* is "very reminiscent of *The Shaggy D.A.*" crossed with the Garfield comic strip. From his standpoint, the film works on two levels: Its theme of a businessmen turning into a cat will appeal to children, while its pairing of Spacey and Walken will please adults. It rakes in five bags of popcorn, "plus a little catnip toy." Tim gives it five bags as well before nodding off again.

As drool puddles in Tim's lap, Gregg introduces the season premiere of *On Cinema On Location*. This season focuses on films made in Victorville, the Hollywood of the Mojave. This week, Gregg shows us the actual Sixth Street traffic sign seen briefly in a nighttime exterior scene from 2015's *Broken Horses*.

Back on the set, Gregg promises that "we will be seeing a lot more" Victorville locations in Season Eight. Meanwhile, Tim is choking and gasping for air. As Gregg calls upon the *On Cinema* crew to "shut it down," Tim starts crying. "I can't go back," he sobs.

EPISODE 804
'Sausage Party' & 'Pete's Dragon'

Air date: August 17, 2016
Running time: 13:04 minutes

Tim opens the show by apologizing for making "a fool of myself" last week. He says "it has been a very, very challenging couple of weeks" for the Heidecker family, and he is sorry to have brought the *On Cinema* Family "into it."

In particular, Dr. San's "nutritional system" caused him "a tremendous amount of trouble" and led to "some very, very bad decisions," which in turn led Ayaka to leave him and move back to Japan. Turning to Gregg, he confesses that "it led me to hurt you, my friend."

Tim relates that after taping the previous episode, he went to the doctor for a blood test. The doctor was shocked by the results, which showed dangerous levels of cocaine and methamphetamine: "He couldn't believe the substances that were in my body."

He reassures us that after this near-death experience, he is "fully committed" to Dekkar and to his health and creativity. He thanks Gregg "for being supportive" and gives his word that he's "committed to the Victorville experience" now that he's gotten "away from Dr. San." He also thanks Gregg for letting him sleep in the Victorville Film Archive.

Cautioning viewers to avoid nutritional vaping, he reports that he has lately been enjoying traditional human fare, such as cheeseburgers, pizza and the popcorn prepared on set by former W. C. Fields impersonator Mark Proksch. Best of all, the air conditioning is finally fixed. In short, things are looking up as Tim takes his first faltering steps on "a new path."

Pete's Dragon stars Robert Redford in a remake of the familiar story of Pete's dragon. Tim calls it "one of my favorite movies of the year so far." He says it's "for kids," but Gregg can't let this pass unchallenged. This film was "filmed in New Zealand and it's about a dragon," Gregg notes. Although he won't go so far as to call it "an unofficial sequel" to the *Hobbit* films," it *does* inhabit "the same wheelhouse."

"I'm happy to know you," Tim says. "I'm happy to call you a friend, too, 'cause you know so much about movies. Getting to be around you is pretty cool."

Gregg gives *Pete's Dragon* five bags of popcorn. Tim gives it the same rating, because he "loved it" too. "And I love *you*," he tells Gregg.

Gregg tries to respond that he loves being director of the Victorville Film Archive, but Tim cuts him off. Tightly clasping Gregg's wrist, he repeatedly prods Gregg to look him in the eyes. Gregg finds this difficult to do, but he eventually meets Tim's gaze long enough to hear him say "I love you."

Despite his visible discomfort with the emotions on display, Gregg says he's glad Tim has put his personal problems "in the past" and can now "focus on this great theater that we've built together."

In what is perhaps the emotional high point of the season, Tim reiterates that he loves Axiom and the other members of Dekkar, he loves Gregg, and he still loves Ayaka even though she is currently not speaking to him.

Gregg perceives Dr. San as being "at the center" of a number of disastrous events in Tim's life: "With him in our rear-view mirror, I think we can move forward. And I think Ayaka will be happy to hear that he's out of your life."

Gregg accidentally makes eye contact with Tim, prompting him to say "I love you" again.

Sausage Party boasts James Franco, Seth Rogen and Paul "Ant-Man" Rudd in cartoon form as the titular sausages. Even though it's "another kid's movie," it includes "subtle jokes" for adult viewers, such as the use of "the F-U-C-K words." Tim gives it five bags of popcorn and two sodas.

Gregg perceives the movie as targeting a mature audience. His main problem was that "the baby carrots" in the film are "so much better than the sausages." He'd love to see a sequel: *Sausage Party 2: Sausages vs. Carrots*.

"It made me laugh," Tim says, "and I needed a laugh after what I'd been through." He haltingly confides that he recently contemplated suicide: "I was at the Sixth Street Bridge and was gonna jump."

Gregg observes that this is "the same plot" of Frank Capra's *It's a Wonderful Life*. Tim claims that what happened to him "was a much more real situation." But Gregg reminds him that this 1939 holiday favorite was also quite realistic.

Next, *On Cinema On Location* explores Victorville's "cinematic heritage" as Gregg locates "the green pole" that was erected on the one-time site of a gray girder that Kurt Russell walked past in 1997's *Brokedown*.

Back in the cinema, Gregg unveils his screening schedule for the Victorville Film Center, and Tim exhorts his audience to download "Empty Bottle" by Dekkar in order to "make my dreams come true."

EPISODE 805
'Ben-Hur' & 'Kubo & the Two Strings'

Air date: August 24, 2016
Running time: 13:42 minutes

This week, Tim and Gregg have a special guest: rocker Axiom of Dekkar. Axiom "has been sticking by" Tim as he struggled with "a few relapses" into nutritional vaping over the previous week. "Like a baby would, I need constant supervision," Tim tells Axiom. "I gotta have you 24/7."

Gregg wonders if Tim could instead have Axiom "23:50/7, and leave 10 minutes to shoot this program without his involvement."

After cautioning Gregg not to "stir the honeypot," Tim breaks some exciting Dekkar news: The band is now in Victorville! Tim asks Axiom what he thinks of "the Victorville scene." "It's cool," Axiom says. "I like it." For one thing, it allows him to be "really focused on what we're doing" because "there's not so much going on" as there is in Hollywood.

Tim has enjoyed spending time with Axiom's visiting sister, Juliana, and he also feels like "the desert heat" is "a pretty good way to detox."

Gregg invites Tim and his crew to stop by the Film Center to "check out some of the movies we've been programming here at the theater, night after night." He announces that visitors who mention On Cinema will receive two free "Creature Cookies."

In other Film Center news, Tim plans to "have some shows" in this "mixed-use-style facility." Gregg is wary of this idea, because constructing a stage could block visual access to the screen. He also worries that the Film Center might be "too big" for Dekkar; perhaps they'd do better at one of Victorville's "little bars." But Tim and Axiom are sure they can fill the venue by attracting "a Vegas crowd" as well as "an L.A. crowd."

Tim cuts the dispute short to talk about the new reboot of Ben-Hur, "which is almost like the original Ben-Hur" starring "Charles Heston." Reasoning that "we loved Ben-Hur then" and "we love it now," Tim gives it five bags of popcorn.

Gregg is glad "they've improved upon" the classic 1959 version with superior modern technology, sets and pacing. This has resulted in "a movie that may win as many Oscars as the original Ben-Hur did." He gives it five bags of popcorn and "a miniature chariot."

Tim is getting jittery as a result of withdrawal from Dr. San's vape blend. But Gregg urges him to push onward.

Kubo and the Two Strings is a cartoon film story about a village boy who ignites a magical Samurai vendetta from the past while seeking a suit of armor worn by his father's spirit. Tim runs off the set due to gastric problems before he can finish his synopsis.

Gregg found Kubo "pretty cool" thanks to its "historical angle" and "elements of fantasy." It's also "beautifully animated," earning it five bags of popcorn and "five little packets of soy sauce."

Still perspiring and shaking, Tim returns to his seat just in time to catch a "special edition of On Cinema On Location," which takes a "behind-the-scenes" look at the Victorville Film Center. Gregg guides us first to the projection room, the centerpiece of which is a vintage 35-millimeter projector that is "not currently operational" because its wiring was "eaten by rats." Instead of fixing the projector, Gregg bought "another 10,000 VHS movies to bolster the already incredible Victorville Film Archive," along with a "VHS film projection system" that "looks as good as any 35-mm film, if not better." To demonstrate the system's capabilities, he plays a tape of Decker vs. Dracula.

Next, we visit the concession stand, ably overseen by genial "popcorn jockey" and erstwhile W.C. Fields impersonator Mark Proksch. "Thank you for hiring me," he tells Gregg. Asked to name his favorite all-time popcorn movie, Mark cites "that one with Sandra Bullock" and "the mailbox."

He goes on to say that he loves working at the Film Center, "although the drive *does* kill me, especially when you just need me for, like, a half-hour shift." Despite this inconvenience, he enjoys "still being a part of the entertainment industry" and getting "good exposure" even after Tim's cancellation of Golden Age Comedies With W.C. Fields.

Gregg wants to know how to get the perfect "movie taste" for popcorn at home, but Mark doesn't know. He prefers pretzels.

Back on the set, Tim ends the segment abruptly and hurries away to avoid having "an accident."

EPISODE 806
'Hands of Stone' & 'Mechanic: Resurrection'

Air date: August 31, 2016
Running time: 12:00 minutes

Tim and Gregg are back at the Victorville Film Center, your one-stop shop for real-time movie expertise. Before getting to the movies, Tim pulls out Dr. San's vape device and apologizes for throwing "these guys under the bus a couple weeks ago."

He recently got the chance to "connect again with Dr. San," and they ascertained that "the dosage and the chemistry" had previously been "all wrong." This realization enabled them "to dial it in" so that Tim could count on absorbing "the right amounts" of nutritional vape.

Tim is still eating food, but the vape provides added value in the form of vitamins. It also has "just a slight psychoactive element" that is helping him complete the Dekkar album.

In other Dekkar news, Axiom has returned to West Hollywood. His sister, Juliana, elected to stay in Victorville with Tim and has been keeping him "warm at night" in the storage locker that also houses the Victorville Film Archive.

Gregg frets that he has "been getting complaints from the landlord" of the VFA regarding Tim's tendency to be "carrying on there at night." He admonishes Tim that "it's not meant to be a party pad; it's a film archive that's in a storage facility, so it's not zoned for a party atmosphere."

Tim wonders why Gregg doesn't want him to be "self-expressive" and demands to know "what you expect me to be doing with myself." He accuses Gregg of being "very uptight" and of being "manipulated" by his landlord. Gregg says that in reality, the landlord has generously "looked the other way" by allowing them to live in adjacent storage lockers.

Tim eventually promises to "keep it down," even though he routinely has Juliana "screaming like a little kitty-cat."

"Don't tell Axiom," he pleads. Gregg responds that he's far more likely to tell Ayaka.

Hands of Stone combines Robert De Niro and Ellen Barkin as boxers and their manager who changed each other's life. Tim calls it "one of my favorite movies this year" and gives it five bags of popcorn.

Gregg says that although *Hands of Stone* is "not being called *Raging Bull II*, essentially it is, but with a twist" because De Niro plays a trainer. This is similar to the *Rocky* films, "and now *Raging Bull* has gone that same route." However, it's more interesting, because the *Rocky* movies come out once a year, whereas *Raging Bull* hasn't had a sequel since 1980.

Gregg was very happy to "catch up with these characters." While "you don't have to have seen *Raging Bull*," it will "definitely help." Gregg predicts De Niro will win Best Actor, just as he did for *Raging Bull*. He gives *Hands of Stone* five bags of popcorn and "two miniature boxing gloves."

Mechanic: Resurrection stars Tim's favorite actor, Jason Statham, and his other favorite actor, Tommy Lee Jones. Here, an unhappy man must dive deep into his own murderous past by carrying out three impossible assassinations of his most formidable foe after kidnapping the love of his life. "A little like *Decker*," Tim says.

"Decker's not assassinating people," Gregg chides him. "He's *preventing* assassinations." Tim argues that if "Obama was in the presidency," Decker would "put a bullet through his skull." Gregg warns him not to say things like this, because "they're gonna shut the show down."

After a long drag on Dr. San's vape pen, Tim delivers his verdict: Five bags. As the drugs take hold and Tim struggles to retain control of his bodily functions, Gregg cuts to *On Cinema On Location*. This time around, Gregg has uncovered the mother of all scoops: The 1941 Kemper Campbell Ranch where Orson Welles first wrote *Citizen Kane*!

Back at the cinema, Gregg has departed. Tim is sucking convulsively at his vape pen while trying to remove his pants.

On Cinema On Line

5:24 PM - 31 Aug 2016
Honestly all that @greggturkington and his pet rat @m_proksch want to do is take away from me what's mine. No debate on that

5:27 PM - 31 Aug 2016
you tell me there's not a consortium about me

5:29 PM - 31 Aug 2016
auto colorectal is a joke my works are being taken wrongly on me

5:29 PM - 31 Aug 2016
point is watch and see @greggturkington and the RAT m_orkech abode me for Everything

5:38 PM - 31 Aug 2016
Hey @m_proksch get ready for pain to reign.

7:01 PM - 31 Aug 2016
Hey @greggturkington, can I maybe have off the rest of the week and weekend? I don't feel well.

EPISODE 807
'Solace' & 'The Light Between Oceans'

Air date: September 7, 2016
Running time: 12:04 minutes

Wearing his official Kington shirt from *Decker*, a badly shaken Gregg announces that he's filling in for Tim under "circumstances" that are "anything but happy."

Clearly in a state of shock, Gregg reveals that over the weekend, "there was a fire at the Victorville Film Archive," which "was caused by Tim falling asleep in his cot" while vaping. Tim has been hospitalized, and "he will survive" despite his "serious third- and first-degree burns." However, "it will take a lot of work" before he can return to *On Cinema*.

In Tim's absence, "popcorn jockey," *Decker* co-star and quondam W.C. Fields impersonator Mark Proksch is filling in as Gregg's special guest.

Gregg reports that "the Archive is destroyed" save for about 1,110 films that were being stored at the Film Center. "We will rebuild," he vows, before asking for donations from people who have "access to videotapes."

"All my clothes were burned," he says, as was his "*Ant-Man* memorabilia" and "the master tapes to some of the *Decker vs. Dracula* stuff." This includes "lost footage" as well as "props" like "Dracula's cape."

As they struggle to get back on their feet, Mark will be taking over a lot of VFC responsibilities. Gregg has tried to reach Tim's estranged ex-wife, Ayaka, to no avail.

"One of the most incredible film archives in North American history is reduced to cinder," Gregg sighs. "And the Dekkar master tapes are fine. So there is no justice in the world."

Gregg assumes Tim will not be back for the remainder of the season. The future of *Decker* is also in doubt; even if Tim can return, "he's not gonna look like the Decker that we know" due to his need for "a lot of facial reconstruction." Having visited Tim in the hospital, Gregg can confirm first-hand that his co-host is now "unrecognizable," with a "very swollen" head as well as a "mangled" face marred by melted hair.

In *Solace*, "a psychic works with the FBI in order to hunt down a serial killer." Gregg calls this "a good movie" that, like many "post-*Decker*" movies, borrows "a little bit" from the franchise: *Solace* is about the FBI, while *Decker* is about the CIA. In *Solace*, an "FBI agent tries to stop a serial killer," whereas "Decker of course would've fallen asleep and burned down FBI headquarters and destroyed all their records."

Even if Gregg was "a little distracted watching it," he still thought *Solace* was "fantastic." He awards it five bags of popcorn and "an entire fire truck full of flame-retardant foam."

Mark only saw "the last half" of *Solace* because of work scheduling conflicts, but he "loved" what he saw. He gives that portion of the film five bags.

The Light Between Oceans portrays lighthouse keepers who find a baby in a rowboat. This reminds Gregg of "Tim and Ayaka's baby," except that Tom Cruise Jr. "wasn't adrift on a rowboat." Rather, he "was adrift on bad medicine" and Dr. San's "anti-vaccination ideas," and "no one was rescuing" him. Gregg gives *The Light Between Oceans* five bags of popcorn and "five tickets to the rehab clinic." Mark didn't see the film.

Proving the old adage that "the show must go on," this week's *On Cinema On Location* segment explores a Victorville-based "rock formation mountain" formerly seen in *It Came from Outer Space*.

This week's Popcorn Classics share common themes, in that they both survived the immolation of the Victorville Film Archive and will be screened this weekend at the Victorville Film Center. *Holiday Heart* is "a filmed play" that is "quite good," while *The Wood* is "an unforgettable tale of laughs."

Gregg promises to keep us up to speed on Tim's health, which is sadly "not looking good." He adds, "I don't know how we're gonna be able to continue this show or this theater."

"I could step in each week," Mark offers.

"And do what?" Gregg scoffs. He concedes that although Mark could resurrect his popular W.C. Fields character, it doesn't seem right under these tragic circumstances. He recalls how often he asked Tim to reward Mark's loyalty by bringing the segment back, and how often Tim refused: "Here's my chance where I could put anything I want in the show, and I just don't feel like *Golden Age Comedies* would be appropriate."

"It's a paradox," Mark observes.

BREAKING NEWS
HOMELESS MAN HOSPITALIZED IN STORGE UNIT BLAZE
EYEWITNESS NEWS

On Cinema On Line

6:03 PM - 7 Sep 2016
I am alive, thank god.

6:03 PM - 7 Sep 2016
tweating via a nurse. thank for u suppord

8:44 AM - 8 Sep 2016
I am now using voice dictation Garth Brooks visited the Victorville burn ward this morning he was very cool

8:45 AM - 8 Sep 2016
Juliana was not with me at the time of fire I am sorry for any loss of life or property I may have caused

2:38 PM - 8 Sep 2016
hi this is JULIANA, i'm handling tim's twitter account now. he sends you all love and kisses! long road ahead!

11:11 PM - 8 Sep 2016
"Thanks you Garth" a message from Tim - Julianna
❤️❤️❤️❤️❤️

7:19 PM - 7 Sep 2016
The VFA will rebuild. Big thanks to all who offered donations of tapes. We will gladly accept them all at the Victorville Film Center.

7:30 PM - 9 Sep 2016
After visiting him today I don't anticipate @timheidecker returning to #OnCinema this season. Who should fill in?

50% Mark

50% No co-host; just Gregg

1,981 votes • Final results

EPISODE 808
'Sully' & 'When the Bough Breaks'

Air date: September 14, 2016
Running time: 11:03 minutes

With his head wrapped in bandages and the visible parts of his face burned a hideous red, Tim is back in the *On Cinema* saddle! He thanks us for bearing with his "accident." [Episode 807] He also thanks Gregg for filling in as host.

Referring to his horribly burned face and hands, Tim says, "This looks a lot worse than it is." He has second-degree burns on his face, which can be fixed with "small plastic surgery." But his hands "were charred basically to the bone."

Turning to Gregg, he says, "I want to apologize to you on behalf of Victorville's Film Archives." He describes how the fire started: "My vape pen, which I didn't realize was a piece of junk from China, overheated and caught fire on one of the cardboard boxes holding the Archives." The fire soon spread to a box containing multiple copies of *Blues Brothers 2000*.

"The whole Archive is gone!" Gregg sulks. "You don't need to go through the titles. It just makes me feel worse."

After "flaming VHS copies" woke Tim by falling onto his face, he was able to "escape the inferno" and reach the street, where rescuers brought him to the hospital. He is now "back on the road to recovery" and thanks viewers for their "well-wishes."

Tim hopes to get through today's movies quickly so he can get "another shot of morphine." *Sully* stars Clint Eastwood and Tom Hanks in the true-to-life story of a pilot who "crashed his plane into the Hudson River."

His review is interrupted by the sudden entrance of Joe Estevez, John Aprea, Axiom, Mark Proksch, Ayaka Ohwaki, and Ayaka's father.

"We all wanted to come down here today, Tim, because we been recognizing that you been having a lot of trouble with your life," Joe explains. He says they have come to "tell you how much we love you and how much we like you. And frankly, that we're a little bit worried about you."

Joe invites everyone to "say a little something." Axiom gets the ball rolling by saying that he was "really scared" by Tim's accident. But no matter how long it takes him to heal, Tim can rest assured that "Dekkar is waiting."

Ayaka tells Tim she's sorry about his accident. He responds that he's sorry she left him and returned to Japan. "We'll keep the child," she promises.

"I don't think that's a good idea," Tim objects, which annoys Ayaka's father. "My dad is very concerned," she says.

"Well, I'm very concerned that you traipse off to Japan every time there's a bump in the road."

"We hope you feel better," she says tearfully. "Next time, save a thousand dollars in plane fare and send a card," he tells her.

Joe prompts Mark to say a few words, but Tim silences him: "I don't have any interest in hearing what he has to say."

Decker co-star John Aprea says, "I hate to see you this way." He entreats Tim to "get it together."

Next, it's Gregg's turn. He doesn't want to provide too much detail "in front of Ayaka and her father," but he is adamant that "getting Dr. San and Dekkar out of your life and focusing on this theater is your chance to really make something of yourself."

Tim thanks his "friends and family" for their words, saying "you're all I got." He pledges to "make life better for everybody." Joe tries to break in, but Tim yells, "Shut up! You've been talking all day." Vowing to "turn another leaf," Tim assures Axiom that Dekkar is going to be better than ever.

Joe then reads a letter asking Tim to stop "keeping company with John Barleycorn," because "you are a mess and so is your life." Tim interrupts him: "I write your lines, and I'm gonna stop writing them if you keep reading that crap."

"We care about you," Joe says.

"Shut the fuck up!" Tim bellows. "You all can take a walk." His plan is to rely on "perkies" to "take the pain away" until he can get plastic surgery. In the meantime, "I'm gonna make a commitment right now: I'm gonna kick it up a notch." To Axiom, he says, "We are about to go Dekkar 2.0, man." To everyone else, he shouts, "Get the fuck out!"

As Ayaka, her father and Mark file out, Joe tries once more to reason with Tim: "We're here because we care about you, and we want to see a change in you."

"Thank you very much for your concern," Tim replies mildly, before screaming, "Get off my property, you piece of shit! Or I'll never work with you again."

"We love you, Tim!" Joe protests.

"No we don't," Gregg says.

As Gregg, John and Joe leave, Tim screams that they are nothing without him. Then, turning again to Axiom, he reaffirms his desire to "kick it up a notch."

On Cinema On Line

12:40 PM - 16 Sep 2016
I honestly don't think @greggturkington even saw #Sully #GreggHasNotSeenSully

12:41 PM - 16 Sep 2016
where is your #Sully ticket stub @greggturkington ? #GreggHasNotSeenSully

12:55 PM - 16 Sep 2016
Movie "expert" @greggturkington hasn't even seen #Sully - I NEED a new buff Badly #GreggHasNotSeenSully

2:22 PM - 16 Sep 2016
Where is Gregg's stub???????? #GreggDidNotSeeSully

2:32 PM - 18 Sep 2016
Saw it opening day. Stub went up in flames in fire YOU CAUSED. I also lost other stubs I was planning on laminating.

2:33 PM - 18 Sep 2016
Hate that I have to address this nonsense. Tim is on painkiller drugs and very erratic. I saw Sully TWICE. 5 bags!

4:05 PM - 18 Sep 2016
Tim has STUBS for fingers--after burning down my priceless archive and himself. The VFA is rebuilding. Lots of replacement tapes coming in.

5:16 PM - 18 Sep 2016
I know I did. Some didn't - buffs see #sully if you didn't see #sully you just aren't a buff for film. Also liar

2:22 PM - 16 Sep 2016
I actually did show stub. Pay more attention

5:41 PM - 18 Sep 2016
All @greggturkington has to do is produce a #sully Ticket stub and this can be resolved. Sadly tho one does not exist

4:45 PM - 20 Sep 2016
now i'm starting to think @greggturkington hasn't seen A LOT of movies, including Citizen Cane

8:00 AM - 19 Sep 2016
had an idea which could be very lucrative for me - I fight @m_proksch MMA style and cream him. sponcered by MDonalds or something.

10:07 AM - 19 Sep 2016
Why?! Feel better!

6:30 AM - 21 Sep 2016
Interesting how I could tear through @m_proksch like a paper shredder but I kindly hold back. But how long do I tolerate him?!

9:17 AM - 21 Sep 2016
Huh? What do I keep doing?

6:56 PM - 22 Sep 2016
Came THIS close to punishing @m_proksch so completely and violently but held back because I am a man of peace [heart]

5:07 PM - 25 Sep 2016
huh?! I don't even know what I did!

5:14 PM - 25 Sep 2016
@m_proksch excuse me!?????

5:18 PM - 25 Sep 2016
Huh?

5:21 PM - 25 Sep 2016
I am literally at my breaking point with him and his shit

VICTORVILLE FILM CENTER

SEPTEMBER 2016

Sunday	Monday	Tuesday	Wednesday	Thursday	Friday	Saturday
				1 — For Love or Money	2 — A Complex Woman	3 — Dad
4 — Shall We Dance	5 — Mr. 3000	6 — Monkeybone	7 — Soulkeeper	8 — Tiger Hawk	9 — The Addiction	10 — Mr. Holland's Opus
11 — Hamilton	12 — Once Around	13 —	14 — Crazy Moon	15 — True Love	16 — Impromptu	17 — Two Moon Junction
18 — Silent Fall	19 — The Forgotten One	20 —	21 — Stroker Ace	22 — Children of Fury	23 — Pissed Up	24 — All's Fair
25 — Dream Lover	26 — Wet Gold	27 — The Misadventures of Margaret	28 — How I Got Into College	29 — Second Time Lucky	30 — Married to It	

EPISODE 809
'Snowden' & 'Bridget Jones's Baby'

Air date: September 21, 2016
Running time: 10:17 minutes

Tim's bandages are off! And despite his horrifically charred flesh, he's "happy to be alive and on the mend." He appreciates "the love and support" he's received from the *On Cinema* Family as well as the potent painkilling effects of the opioid Percocet.

Still dressed in his Kington shirt, which survived the destruction of the Victorville Film Archive, Gregg promises movie buffs everywhere that his Film Center will continue running "a full schedule of Popcorn Classics."

Tim hopes people will "show up" to these movies, because current ticket sales are "not very impressive."

Gregg says it's hard to promote movies while handling "the mess" Tim created when he "got wasted on weirdo drugs" and "burned down the entire Victorville Film Archive." Also, Gregg's effort to run "a world-class movie theater" has repeatedly been hampered by Tim's outside interests, such as "Dekkar and drug addiction."

Tim says that if Gregg doesn't "hit the financial benchmarks" for the Film Center, he will be replaced. But Gregg argues that even if they were to "fill a football stadium" with ticket holders, "it wouldn't be enough to cover all the damage you did to the Victorville Storage Facility." When Tim "completely destroyed" this site, many local renters lost all their valuables. One man even lost a 1963 Stingray, which Gregg calls "quite an expensive car."

"Accidents happen," Tim points out.

Gregg says that since the Stingray alone was worth $90,000, the Film Center's financial woes can't simply be blamed on low turnout. But Tim alleges that at Gregg's recent screening of Mark Harmon's *Summer School*, the movie "barely reached the screen" because "the projection quality was so low." Worse, "people were complaining about the popcorn being old."

"This is a soft launch," Gregg protests. He's confident that as word gets out, sales will build.

Tim further charges that Gregg booked "*Fletch 2* on a Saturday night" and "had one person come in." Gregg says he has no money to run ads, due to the high cost of the fire Tim started while impaired by "Dr. San's idiot drugs." On a happier note, he thanks fans for sending him "boxes of videotapes" to rebuild his incinerated archive.

"As a friend, I'm giving you advice to show movies people might wanna come out and see," Tim warns him.

Snowden stars Nicholas Cage and Clint Eastwood in a real-life spy drama of real-world espionage. Tim fingers Snowden as "a traitor." Although the film depicts him as a hero, he's actually "worse than Osama bin Laden" and has brought America "to our knees." He bestows zero bags of popcorn on *Snowden* and says, "Shame on you, America, for letting Oliver Stone live."

Gregg was excited by a reference to *Snowden* star Nicholas Cage in a *Decker* episode that also mentioned Oliver Stone: "To see those two worlds come together in a motion picture shows once again the influence that *Decker* has had on modern cinema," he says. He gives *Snowden* five bags of popcorn "and a little toy door, because Oliver Stone also directed *The Doors*."

Colin Firth and Emma Thompson are the proud parents of *Bridget Jones's Baby*, a "chick flick" Tim recently watched with Axiom's sister Juliana, which gave them "a good excuse to fool around in the movie theater."

"Can she even touch your face without you screaming?" Gregg asks.

"She doesn't *need* to touch my face," Tim replies. "Let's leave it at that." He gives *Bridget Jones's Baby* five bags of popcorn and two cups of soda.

Gregg finds the Bridget Jones movies "fantastic" and notes that they appeal to "plenty of men." He sees Ms. Jones as "sort of a James Bond for women, in that this is a franchise that could go for many, many years." He gives it five popcorn bags and "a little baby rattle."

On a personal note, Tim has gotten a letter from country music legend Kenny Chesney, which offers condolences on his "terrible accident" and expresses interest in covering Dekkar's "Empty Bottle."

Gregg is skeptical: "How would he hear of you?"

"How do you hear about anybody?" Tim shrugs. Next, he pulls out a letter from country music superstars Rascal Flatts, which also praises Dekkar.

Tim's spirits are buoyed by these kind words from his peers: "Any time they wanna come to Victorville, they get free popcorn on the house."

"Not if I'm working," Gregg says.

To whom it may concern,

As owner and executer of the "On Cinema" brand and it's legal usage as determined by US copyright law, I am the determineer of how, when and by whom the official "Bag System" of ratings films and movies are to be determined.

As in the past, I have allowed some guests to provide there bag rating for a movie or film as specified by their employment contracts as it pertains to specific movies reviewed during an episode of "Tim Heidecker's On Cinema at the Cinema." As stated in the employment contract, The Bag System of Ratings (or commenting, suggesting or reviewing ANY movie or film) is strictly prohibited as per the employment contract of said guest.

IT IS STRICTLY PROHIBITED TO REVIEW MOVIES OUTSIDE the confines of an individual episode of "Tim Heidecker's On Cinema at the Cinema"

However, during season breaks, WE propose a license agreement to allow the undersigned the opportunity to provide ratings, suggestions and reviews for movies or films as they pertain to the undersigned, social media follower base, and beyond, including usage of the Bag System.

This limited license agreement (12 months) would be structured as follows:

- One review of a new release per week, using the Bag System (i.e. Jack Reach 2: 5 bags)

- One review of a "Popcorn Classic" per week, using the Bag System (i.e. Jack Reacher: 5 bags)

- Cost per review to be paid, within 5 working days of review: Two Hundred Fifty Dollars ($250.00)

Please contact me immediately activate the terms of this license agreement.

Sincerely,

Tim Heidecker
President, On Cinema Enterprises

On Cinema On Line

1:15 PM - 18 Oct 2016
I never signed any employment contract agreement with you. My latest review will be released on Thursday morning on this Twitter account.

1:18 PM - 18 Oct 2016
you did sign and i have proof which i can easily provide you. if you review using the BSR I will sue shit out of you and WIN!

1:23 PM - 18 Oct 2016
I need not remind you I have not doled out your #OnCinema Membership Card yet.

8:18 PM - 18 Oct 2016
I offered @greggturkington the deal of a lifetime today but he spit in my face. He deserves pain I feel.

8:34 AM - 19 Oct 2016
Does @greggturkington even like movies? Otherwise he's #signthedeal

7:38 AM - 21 Oct 2016
Believe me, I will be addressing traitorous @greggturkington 's attempt to you-serpt my authority/ Monday hell comes to him.

7:29 PM - 22 Oct 2016
"I would rather be a little nobody, then to be a evil somebody." - Abraham Lincoln

7:32 PM - 22 Oct 2016
Sorry if anyone missed out on a great #movie this weekend because you didn't have any expert information to guide you.

7:44 PM - 22 Oct 2016
Great news for the On Cinema Family! We are united again! No more illegitimate/unauthorized reviews to worry about.

6:55 PM - 31 Oct 2016
Thank you @timheidecker ! I am truly honored to be part of this family! And Thank you for saving this very special number FOR ME #007 !

6:58 PM - 31 Oct 2016
Love you brother! #dkr

9:28 PM - 1 Nov 2016
I was PROMISED this 007 card, a month later I still have received NOTHING, not any card, Tim you knew I wanted 007, why would you give the c

9:31 PM - 1 Nov 2016
axiam thinks 007 is the number of drugs to give Tim, he knows NOTHING about James bond.

9:32 PM - 1 Nov 2016
Please boycott Dekar concerts/tapes/CDs/etc

EPISODE 810
'The Magnificent Seven' & 'Storks'

Air date: November 11, 2016
Running time: 11:05 minutes

Tim apologizes for wearing the same shirt all month; unfortunately, the fabric "fused into" his skin during the fire because the shirt was "made in China."

"The fire itself was made in Victorville by you," Gregg chides him. "So you can't blame China." Gregg continues to wear his Kington shirt, because all of his other clothes were "burned to a crisp."

The Magnificent Seven corrals Chris Pratt, Denzel Washington and other greats into a modern remake of this classic Western story. "It has a good chance of being my favorite movie of all time right now," Tim says. Having watched the film "the other day," he applauds its focus on "guns and Indians," to say nothing of all the other "stuff going on." While he "wouldn't recommend this for everybody," he feels strongly that "it was OK for me." He gives it a prudent five bags of popcorn.

Gregg asks Tim where he saw the movie, but Tim refuses to answer. Gregg gives *The Magnificent Seven* five bags. He says Tim is "right" that the movie is "very good," but "he's right for reasons that he didn't bring up because he didn't see it."

Storks spotlights the unique voice of Kelsey Grammar in this animated film about storks who usually deliver packages but now have to deliver a baby. Tim enjoyed this "cute movie."

For Gregg, this raises a painful topic: "What's up with Ayaka and the baby?" Tim doesn't know; he hasn't seen his wife "since that stupid waste-of-time intervention," [Episode 808] which he calls "the worst episode" in *On Cinema* history. He gives *Storks* five bags of popcorn.

Pressed for his own rating, Gregg glumly reports that he "liked" *Storks* because it was "funny." He gives it five bags of popcorn and "five stork eggs."

Next, Tim has a surprise for new-music fans: It's "a new track" from the electronic dance music (EDM) combo DKR, which consists of Tim, Axiom and Manuel Giusti. It's important to debut the song on the show, Tim says, because viewers are wondering how he will "rise from the ashes" after losing "the ability to play bass" in the Victorville Film Archive disaster.

"No one's wondering that!" Gregg protests. Tim refutes him by citing the example of Kenny Chesney [Episode 809] and his "wonderful messages of support."

"You're getting legal papers served on you constantly at this theater from the people who've lost all their possessions in that fire," Gregg tells him. "You're not getting messages of support from Kenny Chesney."

Ignoring Gregg's negative spin, Tim forges ahead with DKR's "untitled" debut single, which proves to be an EDM version of Dekkar's "Empty Bottle." Although Tim's mobility is hampered by his terrible burns, the infectious rhythm has him moving in his seat.

"That's not gonna be a hit," Gregg predicts. Tim disagrees, and he invites music lovers to come to the VFC on Saturday for an all-night evening of "EDM music," "stand-up comedy" and "sketch comedy" running from 9 p.m. to midnight.

Gregg argues strenuously against this plan, but Tim cuts him off by rolling the latest installment of *On Cinema On Location*. This week, Gregg is back in Victorville to visit the "beautiful mountains" that previously appeared in Episode 807 as the location of *It Came from Outer Space*. But this time, there's a twist: As the camera pans, we learn that these mountains are just down the road from the Kemper Campbell Ranch! [Episode 806] This is where Orson Welles wrote the all-time 1941 classic *Citizen Kane*, which still remains on many movie-buff "best of" lists today.

"Yes, Virginia, there is a *Citizen Kane*," Gregg exclaims. "And he was born right here in Victorville!"

Back on the set, Tim is sucking avidly at his vape pen. Once he stops coughing, he bids us adieu: "See you next season!"

As the cinema lights go down one last time on this eventful season, Tim confides to Gregg that Ayaka has decided to go through with her pregnancy, and he is actually "gonna have two kids."

"She's having twins?" Gregg asks. Tim clears up his friend's misconception by explaining that he also impregnated Axiom's sister, Juliana.

For Gregg, this is the final straw. He jumps out of his chair and walks off the set, muttering "What's wrong with you?" Tim is left alone in the dark with his vape pen.

On Cinema On Line

8:31 AM - 4 Dec 2016
Feel bad that i had on as guest @greggturkington a fraud who hasn't seen Citizen Cane and Sully! Will fix!

8:34 AM - 4 Dec 2016
He is a self proclaimed movie buff with no evidence to back up! Will have on real guest who know movies!

8:35 AM - 4 Dec 2016
How are you a film buff with out seeing Citizen Cane the all time best movie??? @greggturkington and his "popcorn classics" have to go.

10:17 PM - 4 Dec 2016
I saw Sully twice initially then 2 more times later.

10:40 AM - 4 Dec 2016
I agree that a buff would've seen those. And I've seen them both multiple times and own an original Sully poster. You're WRONG

10:41 AM - 4 Dec 2016
I was one of the first people to see Sully. Before it was a hit.

11:12 AM - 5 Dec 2016
@adultswim please remove our review of #sully as my guest @greggturkington didn't see it and can't verify correct rating

8:34 AM - 7 Dec 2016
I have some evidence @greggturkington hasn't seen Rain Man. Feel duped by this "buff"

3:43 PM - 15 Dec 2016
End of discussion. Go see #movies this weekend everyone!

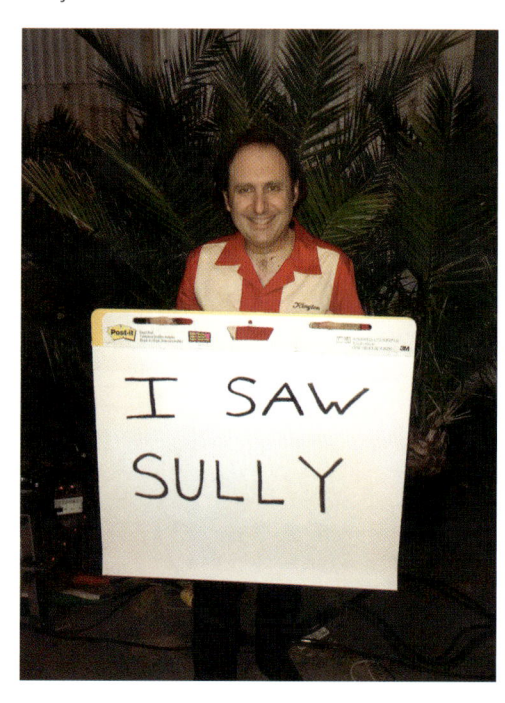

OFFICIAL STATEMENT REGARDING GREGG TURKINGTON
AND THE TOM HANKS MOVIE "SULLY"

Recently, I have become aware of claims made by sometime guest of On Cinema and small character on the hit show Decker: Unclassified Gregg Turkington. He has claimed through a visual aid that he has seen "Sully" the story of the pilot who crashed his plane in the river. Nowhere does he claim when he saw it which leaves over the possibility that he didn't see it before he have it it's official "5 Bag" review. There is even the possibility that he didn't even see it at this point even though it's still in some theaters and available for rent.

IT is unfortunate that I actually HAVE evidence that he did NOT see Sully at the point proir to review and thus gave fradulent information when it came to the review itself. The following evidence cannot be disputed:

- Gregg Turkington did not see "Sully" prior to the point of time of which he gave review.
- Gregg Turkington had not provided his ticket stub which would probve he saw it.
- Gregg Turkington is not capable of teling anyone if they should see "Sully" or not as he didn't see it, so how can he offer a option?

There is more evidence I will provide at a later date. But at this point, I cannot trust this "Man" to provide reviews for On Cinema. his role in Decker as a writer of my ideas and small part player for some characters will continue due to contractual obligations at this time.

Happy Holidays,

Tim Heidecker

On Cinema On Line

5:52 PM - 24 Dec 2016
Sorry @timheidecker but I saw Sully 3 times. That's 15 bags of popcorn!!! Everyone go see it!!!

2:38 PM - 25 Dec 2016
due to the christmas spirit i have decided to forgive @greggturkington for his transgressions. #Sully

10:40 AM - 4 Dec 2016
Maverick (1993) Mel Gibson Jody Foster, 🍿🍿🍿🍿🍿

11:42 AM - 28 Dec 2016
what did I say about usage of bags? reporting you two @twitter for violations

A STATEMENT REGARDING OSCAR SPECIAL V
BY TIM HEIDECKER

Fellow On Cinema Family Members,

Due to an amazing opportunity for my Electronic Dance Music (E.D.M.) group DKR, which conflicts from a timing standpoint with the Academy Awards (Oscars) **There will NOT be a traditional On Cinema Oscar Special this year.** My commitment to the On Cinema Family has never been stronger and am continuing to bring light and love to the world (in this case to Dubai for a private engagement.)

I have instructed Gregg Turktington (sometime guest of the show) to offer insight and film expertise via his twitter account during the awards. He is limited to Eleven (11) Tweets during the broadcast.

The On Cinema Family will respect my wishes and take a knee this year. On Cinema at the Cinema will return soon, as will Decker: Declassified the hit TV series.

All the Best,

Tim Heidecker
On Cinema Father

A Statement Regarding Oscars 2017

As I have stated in the past, DKR will be overseas playing for a private party in Dubai which is a great honor and a financially rewarding experience and therefor will be unable to host and produce the On Cinema Oscar Special. I have previously forbid occasional guest Gregg Turkington from producing his own On Cinema Oscar Special and he currently and going forward is forbidden to use the On Cinema brand IN ANY WAY.

I however am pleased to announce that I have given him tacit, temporary and conditional approval to provide an OUR CINEMA OSCAR SPECIAL which does not in any way have anything to do with the On Cinema Brand.

Gregg Turkington and I have agreed upon a small fee which he is providing me for the honor of using On Cinema technology and reach it's vast audience to provide his own perspective on Oscar night.

There is a slim to none chance my schedule will line up accordingly for me to place a call into the show and contribute my own observations. Don't count on it though. I will tired from rocking the house with my signature beats along with Axiom and Manuel.

The Our Cinema Oscar Special will be broadcast Live on Sunday February 26th at 5:30PM PST from the Our Cinema/Gregg Turkington accounts. Follow @greggturkington for more information regarding this.

Good luck to all the Oscar winners this year.

Sincerely, Tim Heidecker Host of ON CINEMA and DECKER

On Cinema On Line

5:17 PM – 22 Feb 2017
The #OurCinema team is ready for Oscar night!!! #expertise #opinions #predictions

8:15 PM – 22 Feb 2017
I wish @greggturkington all the best for his our Cinema Oscar special but it's like someone can Jud suddenly become a host/producer

8:16 PM – 22 Feb 2017
I don't think @greggturkington is exactly aware of the GIANT mountain he's about to climb.

8:18 PM – 22 Feb 2017
@greggturkington risks damaging movie fans and oscarheads with a slipshod production... be careful what you wished for!

2:37 PM – 23 Feb 2017
Why won't you answer my messages regarding BUDGET for this? What crew will I be working with?

2:41 PM – 23 Feb 2017
A producer will be in touch who will provide you with a very limited set of technology for this.

7:22 PM – 23 Feb 2017
Feeling less and less optimistic about @greggturkington 's chance of success Sunday night. #ourcinema is nothing!

8:42 PM – 25 Feb 2017
The only thing "DKR" stands for on tomorrow's #OurCinema Oscar special is DENZEL, KIDMAN, OR RYAN? Who will take home Oscar gold. Find out

7:01 AM – 26 Feb 2017
Good luck to the Oscar's tonight and to @greggturkington I'm in #dubai living my dreams ❤️ #dkr #privateparty

11:11 AM – 26 Feb 2017
Have bad feeling (and I'm always right) that @greggturkington will have a bad night tonight. #ourcinema

3:05 PM – 26 Feb 2017
DKR = Don't kare, really! (About DKR in Dubai) It's #OSCARS time! #OurCinemaOscars

4:02 PM – 26 Feb 2017
Hey @timheidecker having problem with the live feed tests, won't load properly, can you give me the code

4:03 PM – 26 Feb 2017
Can't help ya buddy

4:03 PM – 26 Feb 2017
need the code to board cast this

4:03 PM – 26 Feb 2017
FINE! I've given you access my personal YouTube channel That's where you can stream your "special"

Our Cinema Oscars Special
Live Broadcast from Hollywood's Biggest Night

Air date: February 26, 2017
Running time: 1:47:29

Taking his seat on the modestly appointed *Our Cinema* set, Gregg announces that *On Cinema*'s Fifth Oscar Special has been postponed. In its place, *Our Cinema* will offer an expertise-oriented show targeting film buffs and other enthusiasts.

This year, Oscar will be serving up a hornet's nest of controversy along with the usual Tinseltown glitz. Gregg has noticed that the titles of all major movie nominees fall alphabetically between A and M. He charges that "somebody goofed" when compiling this list, resulting in an unprecedented blanket snub of N through Z films. He's hoping that write-in ballots will make up for this oversight.

Gregg's special guest, Mark Proksch, arrives with a case of canned pineapple juice, which he found in the Staples closeout section while looking for outdated toner cartridges. Because the juice didn't show up in the computer when scanned, it was free!

Tim, who is in Dubai with DKR, calls Gregg's cell phone but gets cut off.

The Ones That Got Away

Gregg presents a tribute to "Oscar runner-ups" that narrowly missed the Oscar mark, from 1937's *H.B. Warner* to *Dog Day Afternoon*'s Chris Sarandon. The number-one most disappointed Oscar loser? Harrison Ford for *Witness*.

After some messy mishaps with popcorn, and then an easel, Gregg and Mark walk offstage for a few minutes so the *Our Cinema* crew can "reorganize" the set. The crew also finds a mic for Mark, so they don't have to pass one back and forth.

Did Oscar goof?

It's a Gift!

Gregg has the inside dope on the infamous Oscar gift bag, which showers a six-figure assortment of swag on lucky Oscar nominees. His in-depth reportage is interrupted at long last by a call from Tim.

Wishing "Happy Oscars to everybody," he describes the great time he had performing with DKR in Dubai. But Gregg squelches this narrative in the bud: "This is a movie show. This isn't a recap of a concert no one's interested in."

Once Tim's connection is lost, Gregg warms anew to the Oscar gift bag theme. It turns out that these "controversial" gift bags contains expensive gifts that some fear could turn Oscar's head!

Tim calls back to complain that Gregg and Mark aren't paying enough attention to the Oscars. He also takes issue with Mark's guest appearance, which goes against the show's "conditions."

He scolds Mark for betraying the *On Cinema* Family and puts Gregg on notice that Twitter has already pegged the show as "a complete fucking disaster." Gregg hangs up.

Returning to the Oscar gift bag controversy, Gregg emphasizes that the value of the "swag" these bags contain tends to be very high.

Tim calls back to lament that he's watching "everything we've worked so hard for be fucking obliterated." Again, Gregg hangs up.

As desirable as the famous Oscar gift bags are, their contents are not necessarily film-related. To right this wrong, Gregg has prepared "a dream Oscar gift bag" for Mark.

Tim calls back and sings a verse of "Oscar Fever" for *On Cinema* fans. "That's what they want!" he shouts.

"OK, they got it," Gregg says. "Bye."

Mark's gift bag contains a pre-inflated balloon and VHS tapes of five all-time Oscar winners. Ranked from worst to best, these are *The Gold Rush*, *The Music Man*, *Casablanca*, *The Way We Were* and *The Hobbit*.

Tim calls back to "apologize for the way I snapped at you and Mark" and says he's "bummed and regretful" that he's not doing the show with them. He feels "10 to 20 percent responsible" for the show's technical problems. Gregg estimates that Tim's responsibility is closer to 100 percent, since he slashed their budget and refused to let them use the usual studio.

Tim complains that he's in "a lot of pain" because he can't take his "medication" under Dubai's strict drug laws. Gregg hangs up when he begins

A peek into Oscar's gift bag.

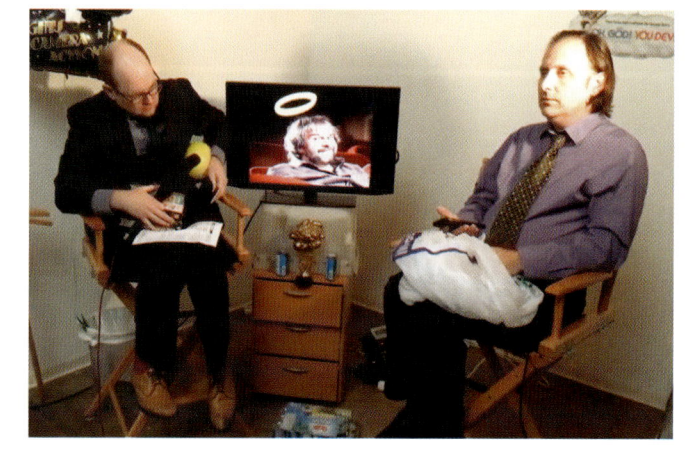

A double bill no one can turn down.

describing his hotel room's stunning view of the Persian Gulf.

The final items in Mark's movie-centric Oscar gift bag are a bag of top-rated Pop Secret popcorn [Episode 303] and a scarce copy of *Video Movie Guide 2000*. He gets to keep the Goodwill shopping bag, too!

Rating the Oscars

Gregg has a new book project! But we'll have to wait to hear about it, as Tim calls to ask if Mark will be doing "any impressions or anything like that."

"If we have time," Gregg says. "If we don't have people calling constantly." Tim remarks that his hotel room comes with an international calling plan.

"Well, call England or something," Gregg responds. "Don't call us."

Gregg's proposed book is *Rating the Oscars*, a guide to Oscar-winning films that will rate each movie on the user-friendly Popcorn Scale.

Tim calls again. "I'm trying to explain to you what's going on," he says. "I care about what happens to you and Mark." Gregg tells him to get some sleep and hangs up again.

Serious Moonlight

Tim calls back and asks Gregg to leave his phone on so he can hear the Oscar results. "Just watch it on the web!" Gregg says.

"Hang up on him," Mark recommends. Gregg does, and then gets the happy news that Mahershala Ali won Best Supporting Actor for *Moonlight*.

Tim calls back to hint that he's feeling suicidal as he stands at his 64th-floor hotel window. "Well, jump!" Gregg advises him. Before hanging up, he gives his friend the good news about Mahershala Ali's award for *Moonlight*.

The Best of Bogie

Gregg has a real-life Oscar scandal to discuss, but first he needs to leave the set for five minutes.

On his return, he presents a segment on "the top-10 Humphrey Bogart roles of all time." During #8 (*The Caine Mutiny*), Mark frets that Tim hasn't called back: "We haven't heard from him, and you told him to jump."

"I don't think he'd jump," Gregg shrugs, before continuing his Bogie countdown.

"Maybe you should try him back," Mark says. Gregg is willing, but he wants to complete his all-important Bogie countdown first: "If he's jumped, he's jumped."

"But you *told* him to jump," Mark says.

"I tell him a lot of things," Gregg protests. "I told him not to call, and he kept calling! So why's he suddenly gonna do what I say?"

Under further pressure from Mark, Gregg relents. They track down DKR's hotel, but the concierge gets no answer from Tim's room. Gregg leaves a message asking Tim to call *Our Cinema*.

Gregg is positive that Tim is fine. But it troubles Mark that Gregg didn't ask if there were sirens outside or any other signs of a suicide attempt.

"I don't really care," Gregg says. "What I *do* care about is #4 on our countdown." That turns out to be *Battle Circus*, a Korean War drama set in a MASH unit and filmed in Calabasas, California, not far from Malibu Creek State Park, where the hit M*A*S*H TV series was filmed.

This is followed by *Three on a Match* and the inevitable *Casablanca*. That leaves *The Oklahoma Kid* in the coveted #1 slot of all-time Bogie films you may have missed!

The Sound of Oscar

Gregg checks his cell phone for Oscar news, only to learn that *Hacksaw Ridge* has taken the Best Sound Mixing prize. Sadly, though, the Best Sound Editing statuette goes to *Arrival*, denying *Hacksaw Ridge* a sweep of sound-related Oscars.

Much like its namesake, Heisman Trophy winner O.J. Simpson, *O.J.: Made in America* runs away with Best Documentary award. There was also a well-deserved award for costumes, in Gregg's expert opinion.

Mark's worry is contagious, so Gregg decides to check on Tim again. This time, he asks to be put through to Manuel or Axiom of DKR. Unfortunately, they aren't answering. Gregg leaves a message asking them to call with any news of Tim.

Oscar's ABCs

Gregg is finally ready to discuss the breaking Oscar scandal. But first, he needs to take a five-minute break.

On his return, he brings one of Oscar's ugly little secrets to light: This year's ballots only include titles ranging alphabetically from *Arrival* to *Moonlight*. All films falling between *Nocturnal*

Gregg salutes Marilyn Monroe's real-life co-stars.

Animals and Zootopia have been snubbed!

Although this puts these films "at a disadvantage," Gregg feels it will work in their favor as they gain a write-in edge from voters eager to correct Oscar's injustice. This write-in insurgency will offer a new hope for deserving titles like Rogue One and Sully.

Gentlemen Prefer Marilyn

Gregg has prepared "a salute to the great co-stars of Marilyn Monroe." Singled out for special commendation are Eli Wallach, Tony Randall and others.

The segment is interrupted by a call from Axiom. "Is Tim OK?" Gregg asks.

"I actually called you for the same reason," Axiom says. "Like, I just can't get a hold of him." He relates how he had hotel security open Tim's door, only to find that he wasn't in the room: "I'm actually very, very worried."

Gregg asks the distraught musician if he has "a pick for Best Picture."

"No," Axiom says after a long pause.

"Best Actor?"

Mark urges Axiom to inquire about Tim at the front desk. "We already called everyone," Axiom responds. "We called the cops."

"But there's nobody that jumped out of the building?" Gregg asks.

This reminds Axiom that when they entered Tim's room, "the window of the balcony was open." Even so, Axiom doesn't believe Tim jumped: "We party, but we don't get this much fucked up."

"Well, *he* would," Gregg says. "'Cause he gets fucked up and burns things down."

Axiom asks Gregg to "do something" to track Tim down. Gregg assures Axiom that Tim is probably just having breakfast: "We're gonna get back to the Oscars show if you don't have any picks for Best Actor, Best Actress or anything."

"Listen, I don't even care about that," Axiom says.

"Well, I don't care about your music," Gregg shoots back. "Thanks for calling."

"It sounds like Tim's fine," he tells Mark, before proceeding to list the remaining Monroe co-stars.

W.C. Fields to the Rescue

Gregg asks his guest to do one of his famous comedy impressions. Mark takes a stab at W.C. Fields but has to abort the mission: "Honestly, I'm not feeling up to this." He would rather "go home and make some calls to try and find out what's going on" with Tim.

"He just went out to eat or something!" Gregg opines. "I don't want this dominating our show!" He wonders if Mark panics every time a friend fails to answer his phone calls.

"When he's crying and you tell him to jump — jump out — I do," Mark says. "Gregg, I'm out. OK?"

Gregg reminds him he promised to stay for the full show.

"You may have killed Tim!" Mark shouts. He drops his mic and leaves.

Gregg disagrees: "Whether it's Tim or Heath Ledger or whoever it is, it's their own choice!" But Mark has already left.

Gregg announces that *The Salesman* has won Best Foreign Film, while Viola Davis picked up a coveted Best Supporting Actress statuette.

He also suggests an "Oscar of the Oscars" award that would run on a five-year schedule to separate Oscar's cream from the chaff. Before he can elaborate on this idea, the phone rings. Sadly, it's a wrong number.

Sheena Saves the Day

Gregg complains again that Tim's *Our Cinema* budget was very low, forcing him to cut segments that might otherwise have filled several long, uncomfortable dead spaces. He decides to take another break.

He returns about four minutes later. In place of the planned segments, he will present A Tribute to Bond on his laptop.

This turns out to be a grainy YouTube video of Sheena Easton singing "For Your Eyes Only" at the 1982 Oscars. Gregg gets a little choked up during her powerful performance.

And with that, the First Annual Our Cinema Oscars Special is a wrap! "Thank you on behalf of the Our Cinema team, " Gregg concludes. "And we'll see you soon. At the Oscars."

Gregg relives a great Bond moment with Sheena Easton.

On Cinema On Line

8:25 PM · 26 Feb 2017
Our Cinema Oscar soecial was a huge success.

8:39 PM · 26 Feb 2017
Sorry phone died. All good? #dkr ❤️ 🎧 now it's time to DXB > LAX #private ✈️

9:22 PM · 26 Feb 2017
I am alive and didn't jump out any window whatsoever whatever that was about.

9:35 PM · 26 Feb 2017
From what I'm seeing/hearing the only thing that died tonight was #ourcinema

A Statement Regarding the Our Cinema Oscar Special Debacle

On February 22nd 2017 I made the fateful decision to temporarily give special access to the **On Cinema Family** audience as well as a limited but suitable amount of advanced technology to the occasional guest of On Cinema (who is as well a very small part of the hit show on TV: Decker) Gregg Turkington. This decision of which I made knowing it was a total risk turned out to be fateful beyond belief.

Upon arrival in LA after an absolutely life changing and life affirming weekend with my brothers in Dubai rocking the house with unlimited and mind expanding beats generated by myself with Axiom under the umbrella of DKR, I was able to watch (or try to watch) whatever it is you want to call what Gregg Turkington polluted my own YouTube channel with which we will have to call The Our Cinema Oscar Special (2017–2017)

- Techniclogically speaking the special was a total disaster. The lighting sound and camera were a total and complete disaster

- It didn't cover the movies accurately, instead it was a mishmash of bad and boring thoughts about Humphrey Bogart and other boring Hollywood crap.

- Mark Prokshc was unauthorized to appear AT ALL which is in direct violation of the terms I set forth with Gregg Turkington on 2/22/17. I will be "dealing" with Mark later this week on this issue.

- Almost no one watched, which runs contrary to previous ON CINEMA OSCAR SPECIALS which had high ratings whereas this "Special" was a total disaster when it came to viewership (the Holy Grail for this)

There are many, many more issues I could raise with the "special" but I won't because if there's one thing I learned this weekend was the power of "Grace and Forgiveness."

Many OC Family members BEG me to take down the special but I will let it live online as a living monument to failure.

Congrats to all the Oscars. I hope this incident did not diminish your evening.

My best

Tim Heidecker
On Cinema Father and Executive Producer and Creator of Decker on TV

On Cinema On Line

3:55 PM - 27 Feb 2017
Gregg "I didn't see Sully" Turkington is a disgrace to the On Cinema Family. Many former "greggheads" giving up on him for good.

9:28 PM - 1 Mar 2017
Without access to @timheidecker's regular On Cinema crew and equipment it was tough to do everything properly

9:30 PM - 1 Mar 2017
The Oscar predictions and general movie information was all correct (Bogart, Monroe, etc.)

9:43 PM - 1 Mar 2017
An unconditional full apology to the OCF. Now.

9:56 AM - 3 Mar 2017
Our Cinema will continue as a blog or webseries but we will leave the Oscar Specials to the On Cinema team, which I am also part of.

10:45 AM - 3 Mar 2017
full apology now (and other things) or you are off #OnCinema

12:30 PM - 3 Mar 2017
Let's be clear. I need a full apology from @greggturkington by 8pm tonight or I will find a new guest for Monday's S9 #oncinema premiere

6:08 PM - 3 Mar 2017
Less than 2 hours to go and still no apology from @greggturkington

7:59 PM - 3 Mar 2017
I apologize

8:01 PM - 3 Mar 2017
Looking forward to returning to #OnCinema on Monday and bringing 100x the expertise and movie information, thanks @timheidecker.

ON CINEMA ON HOLLYWOOD LEGENDS

J.R.R. Tolkien

When J.R.R. Tolkien first imagined the character of **Bilbo Baggins**, little did he imagine the worldwide box-office phenomenon he had unleashed! Sadly, he would never experience that global excitement, having died in 1973 — a full 28 year before his character could be brought to life by **Peter Jackson**. And yet, it is some consolation that **Hobbit Heads** around the globe remain in his debt for making it all possible!

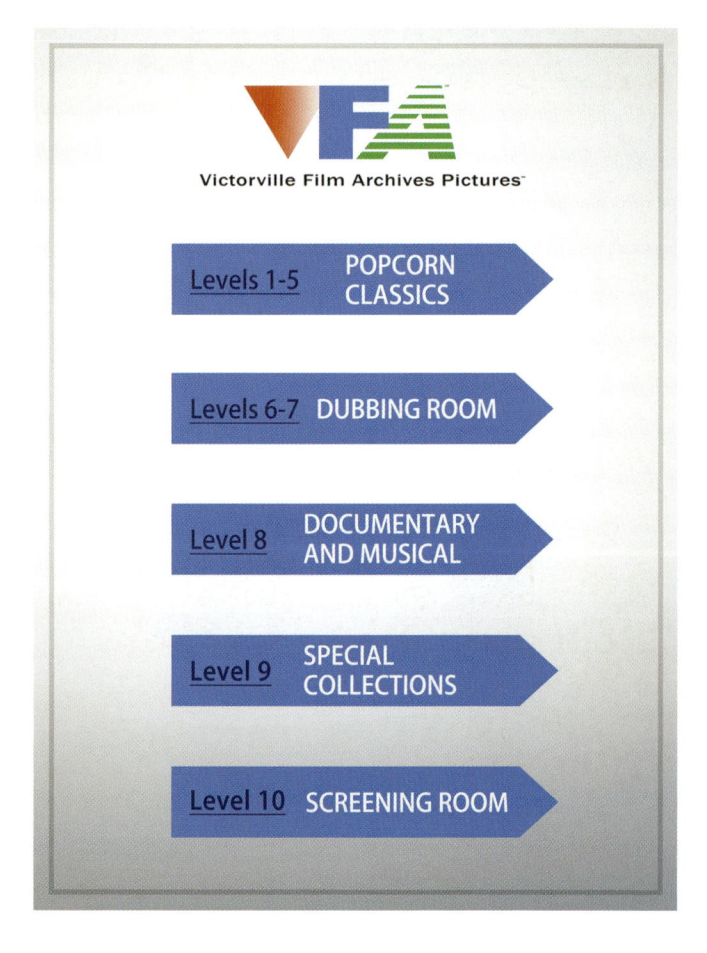

Victorville Film Archives Pictures

Levels 1-5	POPCORN CLASSICS
Levels 6-7	DUBBING ROOM
Level 8	DOCUMENTARY AND MUSICAL
Level 9	SPECIAL COLLECTIONS
Level 10	SCREENING ROOM

SEASON 9

ELECTRIC SUN
DESERT MUSIC FESTIVAL

TCH VAPE SYSTEMS   INCLUDES

EPISODE 901
'Kong: Skull Island' & 'The Wall'

Air date: March 13, 2017
Running time: 10:45 minutes

Season 9 begins with Gregg Turkington's pre-recorded "apology for the On Cinema Family": He "did not see Sully," he confesses, because he "mistakenly thought it was a documentary." However, he "has seen it since then."

Tim's face looks a bit better — in cinematic terms, it's gone from NC-17 to PG-13. He's also expanded his post-accident wardrobe with a DKR sweatshirt and a stylish scarf. He introduces his guest, Gregg Turkington, whom he has "had on the show before."

Tim's "miracle" recovery from injuries sustained in the Victorville Film Archive conflagration has been a true "rollercoaster ride." For one thing, "the topical antibiotic" he used on his face affected his "mood and stomach issues." He "lapsed in the application of that ointment," which led to "a pretty bad infection." Now, the skin on Tim's face "is dying." Luckily, he is "at the top of the list for a skin transplant."

Reaching for Dr. San's nutritional vape pen, he salutes its ability to "take the pain away."

In other important news, On Cinema at the Cinema is back on location in Hollywood, with a swank new cinema that features reclining lounge chairs. Desert-bound cineastes need not fear, though: The Victorville Film Center will continue to screen Popcorn Classics nightly!

Tim's new cinema is "not to scale," which is why the screen is so small. Rather, it's his "proof of concept" for a brand-new direction in moviegoing: "Tim Heidecker's Six Bag Cinemas." This "potential franchise opportunity" will combine "high-concept food with the cinema experience."

Gregg prefers to enjoy food and movies separately; he has no interest in "being interrupted by the waiter" in the middle of an exciting popcorn movie. Further, Tim's cinema is "more like a restaurant with a TV screen in the corner of the room."

Turning a deaf ear to this complaint, Tim dishes out some electrifying DKR news: The EDM act's recording of "MT-BTL 2.0" has hit "a million downloads," making Tim "the golden boy of the EDM music fest scene."

"I'm not living in a storage facility anymore," he crows.

"Because you burned it down," Gregg reminds him.

Before tackling the reviews, Tim picks up a menu to place an order with his waiter, Mark Proksch.

"The menu's about the size of the screen," Gregg jeers. Eventually, Tim orders "the lobster macaroni and cheese."

Gregg wants "movie popcorn" and is dismayed to find it only comes with truffle oil.

In Kong: Skull Island, unwary visitors to "an uncharted island" find themselves in the island domain of "the mythic king, Kong." This is "basically a King Kong movie," Tim opines. He gives it five bags of popcorn.

Gregg shares Tim's conviction that "at its very core," this is "a King Kong movie." Indeed, "it's very similar to the original," not least because it's "an unofficial tribute to Fay Wray" on the occasion of her 110th birthday.

This gets Gregg thinking about his own personal connection with the vivacious leading lady: "I found out recently that Fay is buried at the Hollywood Forever cemetery." Accordingly, he will be bringing a camera crew to the site "to pay our respects" to "the grand lady of the Kong franchise." He gives Kong: Skull Island five popcorn bags and "a little cross, similar to the headstone of Miss Fay Wray."

As his food arrives, Tim bemoans the movie's lack of tall buildings for King Kong to climb. Gregg explains that because it's a prequel to the 1933 film, it "takes place before they actually had buildings" of that type. Also, "the island where Kong was born and raised" had no skyscrapers. But Tim maintains that "they could've added a dream sequence" to get the necessary footage.

In The Wall, two American and Iraqi snipers face off against the forbidding backdrop of the titular wall. Tim "loved" this "war movie," which consequently reaps five bags of popcorn.

Gregg gives it only one bag due to a "lack of originality in the title process," but he shells out four more bags for the originality on display in other parts of this "fantastic" movie. The total number of bags is a generous five.

"The only wall I care about is the one we're building on the southern border to keep out the Mexicans," Tim quips. He closes with a review of Six Bag Cinema's Chef John Lenard: "The lobster mac and cheese was delicious!"

Gregg gives Chef Lenard's truffle oil popcorn "zero bags of popcorn" because "it tastes like a mouthful of dirt."

On Cinema On Line

1:57 PM - 6 Mar 2017
What next? A combination movie theater/car wash?

2:00 PM - 6 Mar 2017
Fact: while eating, people are looking at their food 53% of the time during the meal.

2:01 PM - 6 Mar 2017
Fact: if you miss a subtle plot point while distracted during a movie, often times you don't understand what's going on!

11:21 PM - 9 Mar 2017
SIX BAG CINEMA ratings:
Food 🍿
Screen size 🍿
Popcorn 🍿
Seating 🍿
Service 🍿
Odor 🍿
Yep, that's a total of SIX bags alright!

11:21 PM - 9 Mar 2017
Six bags out of a possible 10 is NOT GOOD! [Must be a 10 bag system as a 5 bag system would not allow for a Six rating.] cc: @timheidecker

8:37 AM - 14 Mar 2017
Most restaurants fail in the first three months. Many movie theaters have been running continuously since the 1930s!!!

10:33 AM - 14 Mar 2017
if you don't like it maybe i should find a buff who has actually seen movies such as Sully and Citizen Cane. 🤔

11:13 AM - 14 Mar 2017
Sorry @timheidecker--I've seen it MANY times. #Orson #Welles.

11:50 PM - 18 Mar 2017
If someone is forced to say something under a threat and they say it, it doesn't mean they believe it.

ON CINEMA ON HOLLYWOOD LEGENDS

John Lenard

Chef John Lenard first discovered his talent for cookery as a **Green Tortoise** bus driver working the popular Baja Beach Daze route. Upon returning home to Arleta, Calif., he joined one of the last groups of students to be accepted by the prestigious **Le Cordon Bleu College of Culinary Arts** in Hollywood, California.

After the school was shut down by its parent company, **Career Education Corporation**, Chef Lenard made his way east to Oklahoma City, Okla., eventually parlaying a dishwashing gig at the prestigious **Four Points Hotel** into a role as sous chef. His signature creations — aspic sliders with goat confit and fennel ash, accompanied by peach glacé margaritas served in a mason jar with a truffle-salted rim — were noted by many jetsetting foodies, including **Tim Heidecker**, who promptly hired Chef Lenard to work his gastronomic magic at **Six Bag Cinema**.

Today, Chef Lenard works in a small-batch, artisanal pilchard cannery near Seward, AK.

EPISODE 902
'T2 Trainspotting' & 'The Belko Experiment'

Air date: March 20, 2017
Running time: 11:31 minutes

Tim recently made "this pledge to Gregg that I wasn't gonna do too much personal talk this season." All the same, he needs to talk about his skin, which is "getting worse." In fact, "you can almost see" a portion of Tim's cheekbone "coming through" his disintegrating face. There is a silver lining, though: He will soon be announcing "potential donors" for skin grafts that will restore his "natural beauty."

Tim takes Gregg to task for eating popcorn that didn't come from Chef John Lenard's kitchen: "Respect his menu!" he demands. Gregg protests that Chef Lenard's truffle oil popcorn is unworthy of the name and that he "got sick from one bite of that."

Gregg has an announcement about the Victorville Film Center: It "will be closed for the next few days" because the City of Victorville detected "black mold in the ceilings and in the carpeting." Also, "major movie studios" are demanding licensing fees for public screenings of VHS tapes from the Victorville Film Archive. Gregg complains that Tim has rebuffed his previous attempts to raise these issues, "which jeopardize the future of the cinema." He asks Tim to "put some of this money you keep bragging that you're making" toward the cost of renovations.

Tim vows to "have someone from the Foundation look into it," adding that he has no intention of leaving the VFC "in a lurch."

Before the reviews, Tim wants to order some food. As Tim pores over the menu, Gregg advocates placing his orders ahead of time, because "nobody wants to see this." Tim yells that "this is a demonstration of the proof of concept!" But Gregg is adamant: "This is insane!" Tim finally settles on the Kobe beef sliders with hand-cut fries and a pilsner.

T2 Trainspotting is "a continuation of the *Trainspotting* saga," which Tim identifies as the new entry in Arnold Schwarzenegger's solid-gold *Terminator* franchise.

"It's a different *T2*," Gregg claims. "It's the same guys from the first *Trainspotting*, which was a great movie about the horrors of drug addiction. Which is something that I'm familiar with from working on this show."

Tim is willing to give *T2* "five bags either way." Gregg gives it "T5" bags of popcorn "as a tip of the hat" to the movie's title.

The Belko Experiment is a sociology-based workplace horror heartstopper in which office employees must all kill each other in order to survive. Gregg says that "if it's an experiment, it's a success" — one he hopes they will "repeat in film laboratories all over the world." He classifies it as a dual threat: It's "a thriller" that "takes place in a tall building," and that's exactly "the type of movie we need more of."

As Tim's food arrives, he ponders his past "aversion to beef," which tended to give him "diarrhea." Now that he has "gone Kobe," the meat "flows right through" in a healthier way.

Gregg speculates that if Alfred Hitchcock had lived, he "would've enjoyed directing" *The Belko Experiment*. He gives this "frightening" movie five bags of popcorn and "two test tubes, each one filled with a little bit of that movie magic."

By popular demand, Tim brings out Chef John Lenard to discuss the concept-forward menu offerings at Six Bag Cinema. Tim gushes over his chef's "amazing" food, but Gregg laments that "this could be a time for a Popcorn Classic instead of talking to this guy who knows nothing about movies."

As Tim digs a little deeper into Chef Lenard's background, we learn that he studied the culinary arts at Le Cordon Bleu before working at the Four Points Hotel near the Oklahoma City Airport, which is where Tim met and hired him.

Tim commends the chef's signature use of "truffle oil," which comes from "mushrooms only pigs can smell."

"They're sniffing around the dump and they find these things?" Gregg wonders. "That's where I threw my bowl of truffle popcorn."

After Chef Lenard's departure, Gregg suggests that Tim "do a separate show for this cooking crap." Tim counters that Gregg "went on and on about *The Belko Experiment*" even though "no one's gonna see that shit."

On Cinema On Line

6:24 PM · 20 Mar 2017
@m_proksch would you be interested in meeting with me to discuss launching Our Cinema as a regular permanent series

7:21 PM · 20 Mar 2017
I'd love to! I have errands on Tuesday, Wednesday and Friday mornings.

7:22 PM · 20 Mar 2017
???

7:31 PM · 20 Mar 2017
Actually, I don't think I'm gonna be able to. Sorry, Gregg.

Episode 903
'CHiPs' & 'Power Rangers'

Air date: March 27, 2017
Running time: 11:17 minutes

Tim kicks this episode off with a coughing fit, which he says is the result of "medicating my pain" with Dr. San's creativity-boosting vape formula. The pain is due primarily to the bloody holes that cover his face as his badly infected skin continues to slough off in what Tim refers to as "a gangrene scenario."

"I woke up this morning to the smell of my own dead flesh on my face," he recalls. He is understandably eager for his skin transplant, "which is mere weeks away." He announces the semifinalist donors — Mark Proksch, John Aprea, Joe Estevez, Manuel, and Axiom — and encourages viewers to vote in the online poll.

In related news, Tim is running "a high fever" and his "doctors are begging" him "to stay home." He turns to his distraught-looking guest, Gregg Turkington: "What's the news from Victorville?"

"You know what it is," Gregg scowls. "Somebody burned down the theater."

"Apparently, there was a fire," Tim elaborates, which was "potentially caused by bad wiring" in Gregg's VHS projector. Gregg is skeptical of this theory.

Tim recognizes that the loss of the VFC has been "tough," but he sees a silver lining: "We are looking forward" to Gregg "spending a little more time here at the Six Bag Cinema."

"No," Gregg answers after a long pause.

Tim signals to his waiter, Mark Proksch. After careful deliberation, he orders Chef Lenard's signature popcorn shrimp plate and some artisanal flatbread with truffle oil.

"How do you feel about being on that semifinal list?" Tim asks Mark. Mark is "a little wary of it."

Tim tells him there is "a line out the door of people" who are prepared to donate their skin to this cause. Mark's status as a semifinalist is something he "should embrace" and get "excited about." But Mark remains unenthusiastic.

CHiPs is a modern filmatization of the classic TV cop buddy show about "two motorcycle cops" and their wild ride through the glamorous world of Tinseltown crime scenes. Because this was "one of" Tim's "favorite movies of the year," he doles out five bags of popcorn and two bags of soda.

Depressed by the loss of his beloved Film Center, Gregg finds it hard to talk about *CHiPs*. Finally, he says he's "sick of people saying it's a remake," because "the original was a TV show" while this is "its own thing." He gives it five bags of popcorn.

In *Power Rangers*, a teenage group of power rangers must harness their powers "to save the world." Tim calls this "a five-bagger, easy" and "maybe an Oscar pick" for Best Actor due to the Oscar-caliber work of thespian Bryan Cranston.

Tim questions whether Gregg is in "the right mental space" to give *Power Rangers* "a fair review," but Gregg says he is. He describes watching the film in Victorville on a recent visit to the ruins of his Film Center, which has been reduced to its foundation, the exterior bricks and rows of "melted" seats. Although Gregg's "movies are gone," he did manage to find one of Tim's "stupid scarves," which had "a stupid zebra print." Tim is positive it can't be his, since he hasn't "been in that area now for three, four weeks."

Tim tries a popcorn shrimp, but he has to send it back because it's "really too spicy." To ease the pain, he takes a long drag from Dr. San's vape pen.

The lights go down, but Tim orders them back up so Gregg can present a new episode of *Popcorn Classics*. As Tim and Mark bicker over a misunderstanding about cutlery, Gregg pulls out his copy of 1994's *A Vow to Kill*. Since it was in his car, this was the only tape to survive the third immolation of his unparalleled VHS collection. "This is the VFA now," he says. He touts this movie about "a honeymoon from hell" as "something to see."

"I'll be watching it a lot," he adds glumly. "Because it's the only one I have."

On Cinema On Line

12:43 PM - 21 Mar 2017
The VFA will return, and effective immediately will be 100% independent from @timheidecker who will not be allowed to utilize its resources.

3:52 PM - 21 Mar 2017
I had NOTHING to do with the failed VFC fire but am honestly glad it's off my balance sheet. It was a bad situation ✌️🎧🍿🍿🍿🍿🍿🎬

4:30 PM - 21 Mar 2017
Seems very rude for some so called OCFs to accuse me of a crime of which I did not commit and could not have!

7:20 PM - 21 Mar 2017
simply put I won't be discussing the FVC fire anymore. I didn't do anything but now I almost wish i had

EPISODE 904
'The Boss Baby' & 'The Zookeeper's Wife'

Air date: April 3, 2017
Running time: 11:54 minutes

Tim is ready to name the finalists for his "facial skin skin donor program". And not a moment too soon — his face infection is "getting worse and worse."

Tim's guest, Gregg Turkington, breaks in to complain that the cinema chairs are uncomfortable. Tim finds this unlikely, as it would defeat the purpose of a "leisure seat." But Gregg insists his seat is "lumpy," possibly due to a loose spring.

Gregg shares that he had "a little ray of sunshine" in the form of a phone call from Mark Proksch. While walking down a street in Van Nuys, Mark happened on an estate sale that included 1,000 VHS tapes. Gregg was able to get the tapes for only $100, which works out to 10 cents per tape. This will be an important addition to the reconstituted Victorville Film Archive, not least because it includes films Gregg has "never seen before."

As Tim prepares to place this episode's food order, he apprises us that Chef John Lenard recently departed Six Bag Cinema because "it just wasn't working out" and there were "issues with cleanliness." Tim is now the head chef: "It's not that hard and anybody can do it!"

Gregg pleads with Tim to offer popcorn that's free of truffle oil so he can stop bringing in his own bags. "Keep your popcorn out of my theater," Tim says. "That's your second warning." He orders chicken skewers with peanut sauce and a side of truffle oil.

The Boss Baby is an animated CGI comedy feature about a briefcase-carrying baby CEO who dislikes puppies, which gains traction from the voices of Alec Baldwin and Jimmy Kimmel. Tim gives it five bags of popcorn.

Gregg says that even though *The Boss Baby* is "very much in the vein of *The Peanuts Movie*," he still "liked it."

The mention of peanuts reminds Tim that his "Thai-inspired" panko satay chicken skewers have "a beautiful peanut sauce." Mark interrupts Tim's reverie with his clumsiness, as he trips and spills Gregg's white wine.

"This is why you don't need waiters in movie theaters," Gregg says.

Once order is restored, Gregg gives *The Boss Baby* five bags of popcorn because he "really loved" this "very, very funny movie."

Tim spits his partially chewed chicken satay onto his plate because it's "ice fucking cold." Mark takes the remaining skewers back for some extra microwave time.

In the aptly named *The Zookeeper's Wife*, Hitler's stormtroopers lock horns with the animals from the Warsaw Zoo. Gregg would've preferred "more of an animated picture" so the animal protagonists "would be able to talk and express their feelings" about "what was going on in history at that time." He gives it five bags of popcorn and "five bags of animal feed." Tim offers no rating.

Gregg is excited to debut a brand-new segment called *Road to Hollywood*, but Tim preempts it to announce "the finalists for the skin donor situation for my face." In this round, Mark Proksch, John Aprea and Joe Estevez go down to a crushing defeat as Manuel and Axiom pull into the lead.

The two finalists are present in the cinema for this exciting "face-off" event. Tim congratulates them and promises that with the "roles reversed," he would be "first in line to help you bros out."

Having to pick just one of these donors "is probably the hardest thing" Tim has ever had to do. In a touching speech, he recounts how Axiom has "been there" for Tim "from the beginning." [Episode 703] Not only is the lanky European rocker Tim's "little brother in life," but he is also his brother-in-law. Although Tim's marriage to Juliana was "painful" for Axiom "and continues to be so," "things are working out due to Axiom's "good heart" and "good attitude."

Manuel is "a little newer" in Tim's life, and the two musicians are still "trying to figure each other out." However, Tim knows Manuel is "a good man."

Tim's satay chicken is now hot, but he's having a hard time dipping the skewer into his sauce bowl. Overcome with an emotion of some sort, Gregg leaves the set.

After chewing for a time, Tim asks Axiom to step forward. "Nothing would give me more pleasure — more joy — than to honorably wear your skin on my face," he tells his friend.

"It would be an honor," Axiom responds, choking back his emotions.

"But unfortunately, we are not a match." Turning to Manuel, Tim delivers his verdict: "It'll be you. You will be donating your skin to my face."

The three bandmates hug. "Better luck next time," Tim tells Axiom.

EPISODE 905
'Smurfs: The Lost Village' & 'The Case for Christ'

Air date: April 10, 2017
Running time: 10:58 minutes

Who is that masked man?! Spoiler alert: It's Tim Heidecker, who has "successfully returned" from his "skin graft operation."

Until his face heals, Tim must wear "a self-lubricating mask, which is preventing infection." His doctors believe the operation went "very well," and "at the end of today's show," he will unveil his brand-new face to his viewers, his wife and "some other people that are here."

Tim introduces his guest, Gregg Turkington, who puts us on notice that he will be debuting his new segment, *Road to Hollywood*, later in the episode.

Tim tips his hat to skin donor finalist Manuel from DKR. He's also excited to get back to work on *Decker*. In fact, he needs to "get some scripts together" because shooting begins "tomorrow."

He alerts music fans to his Electric Sun Desert Music Festival, which will soon be taking place in Apple Valley, California. The festival will include "250 top EDM-festival-music-style DJs" as well as "a comedy tent." Gregg angles for the inclusion of a "movie tent," but Tim feels this would not be in the festival spirit.

Mark comes in to take the food order, but Tim can't eat through his mask and Gregg brought his own popcorn. Having already warned his guest that outside food is not allowed, Tim directs Mark to "remove his popcorn." When Mark balks at this command, Tim himself wrests the popcorn cup from Gregg's hands and hurls it to the floor.

In *Smurfs: The Lost Village*, Mandy Patinkin and Demi Lovato bring the Smurfs to life as they scour the Secret Forest for Smurfette's forbidden map. Tim interrupts his review to boast that his badly burned left hand is "working again." (His right hand, which is encased in a glove, was "so damaged" that "there's no point in fixing" it.) Getting back to the Smurfs, Tim bestows five bags of popcorn on this Smurfs film, which is "the best Smurfs movie about Smurfs there's been" and is also "better than the original."

"I would *not* say it's better than the original Smurfs movie," Gregg objects, since that film "featured the voice of Jonathan Winters from *It's a Mad, Mad, Mad, Mad World*." That said, "it's a Smurf, Smurf, Smurf, Smurf World with this movie, 'cause it's a lot of fun." He gives it five blue bags of popcorn.

The Case for Christ is the it-really-happened story of an atheist journalist who gets more than he bargained for when he sets out to destroy his wife's faith in Christ. Tim calls this "a movie about believing in Jesus Christ, who I do as well." He gives it five bags of popcorn.

When a movie title "starts with the word 'case,'" Gregg naturally thinks of Sherlock Holmes. However, this "spiritual" and "somber" film challenged these expectations. Although this "religious" movie "would never be a Popcorn Classic," Gregg found it "quite enjoyable to watch." He gives it five bags, "with some reservations because again, it's not Sherlock Holmes."

"Speaking of resurrections," Tim hints, he's almost ready to show off his new face for the first time in *On Cinema* history.

Gregg reminds him about *Road to Hollywood*, which will "trace the steps that the great stars stood in as they made their way to Hollywood." Tim allows him to roll the segment.

In this debut episode, Gregg drives slowly up the Hollywood Freeway toward the exit for Hollywood Boulevard, just as a small-town boy named Mr. Clark Gable once did after leaving his home in Cadiz, Ohio.

Back on the set, Tim instructs Gregg to roll his windows up next time to improve the sound quality. Gregg asserts that the sound was "fine" and Tim is not "an expert on sound anyway." Tim challenges him to "ask a million people who downloaded DKR." Gregg claims anyone he asked would tell him they "deleted it immediately afterward."

Tim ignores this jibe and prepares to introduce his third wife, Juliana.

"Do you need me for this segment?" Gregg asks.

"No," Tim concedes. "But I think you want to see what I look like."

"I'll see it next week," Gregg says as he rises to leave.

Juliana comes out, and Tim jokes that she must be eager to see his new face after dealing with months of "pus and blood." He thanks her for cleaning the apartment while he's been "traveling the globes" on the EDM festival circuit, and for taking care "of that other problem." [Episode 810]

Next, he brings out Manuel, who says the skin donor operation "was a little bit painful, but it was worth it for a brother." Tim wants to know where the skin was taken from. "My lower back," Manuel tells him. "My ass."

The mask is lifted, and Tim's never-before-seen face stands revealed at long last. "Looks good," Juliana says gamely.

After seeing his distorted reflection in Mark Proksch's serving tray, Tim tears up: "I'm really happy," he says.

EPISODE 906
'Fast and the Furious 8' & 'The Lost City of Z'

Air date: April 17, 2017
Running time: 11:44 minutes

Tim is gearing up for the first annual Electric Sun Desert Music Festival, and he has "an awesome opportunity for everybody who's coming."

Holding up his vape pen, he informs viewers that "me and the good Dr. San and I have developed this very special blend" of vaping chemicals. It's called "TCH" after Tim's "dearly departed" child, Tom Cruise Heidecker, who succumbed to an unspecified illness despite Dr. San's attempt to cure him with magnets. [Episode 710] The compound will be given away free to festival attendees, and Dr. San himself will be on hand to present "lectures on the proper use of the vape system."

In other news, Six Bag Cinema has been "retooling the menu" with an eye toward "Spanish flair." Summoning waiter Mark Proksch, Tim orders a paella and a glass of champagne.

Mark asks Gregg what he wants. "I want you to go away so we can talk about movies," he answers.

The Fast and the Furious 8: The Fate of the Furious is "actored by" Vin Diesel, Dwayne Johnson and Charlize Theron. In this story, a mysterious seduction is the shocking betrayal that tests the crew as never before.

Tim "loved it" overall, but he was offended by the absence of "Paul Driver." [Episode 609] The late star's death is no excuse for this oversight: "These days, with digital animation and cartoons and stuff, they could have put him in there easily." Their failure to do so was "disrespectful."

Gregg argues that "sometimes, it's just time for an actor to move on." Case in point: Sean Connery was "fantastic as James Bond," but "when Roger Moore came, that ushered in a new chapter that people enjoyed even more."

He discloses that *The Fast and The Furious 8* will go into the *Guinness Book of World Records* for "the highest number reached in a sequel." While it's well known that "Bond has had more movies," they were not numbered, so they don't count toward the total score.

Mark brings out the paella, but Tim rejects it: "I can't eat shellfish." Mark begins removing the shellfish by hand, which annoys Gregg: "Just take the whole thing away!"

Mark knocks over Tim's champagne while trying to remove his unwanted paella, further exasperating Gregg. "If you just made popcorn, then it's so easy," Gregg tells Tim. Speaking of popcorn, he gives *The Fast and the Furious 8* five bags and eight toy Hot Wheels cars.

Mark brings Tim another glass of wine, but it's red and served in a beer glass, so Tim sends it back.

"Don't come back," Gregg advises Mark.

The Lost City of Z is the true docudrama narrative of a Victorian explorer who disappeared into the 1920s Amazon Basin and was never heard from again until Charlie Hunnam portrayed him in this film. It's Tim's Oscar pick, and it's also his pick for an unsurpassable five bags of popcorn.

"This is a big movie," Gregg confirms. "Make no mistake about it." Because big movies like this one are a magnet for "Oscar gold," Tim is "absolutely correct" that *The Lost City of Z* has "a big Oscar winner" on its hands.

"I think in our own way, we're all searching for our Lost City of Z," he muses. "And so it's nice to see a movie where we find it." He gives it five bags and a Zorro mask, "because that's the other famous movie that starts with Z."

With this week's movie picks all present and accounted for, it's time for Gregg to make way for Dr. Luther San, the holistic healer behind the TCH vape system. After taking a long pull at his vape pen, Tim invites Dr. San to describe how he "dialed it in" with his latest mixture.

Dr. San assures us that TCH is "100-percent *ma huang* free," which reduces the risk of "heart palpitations." Dr. San also has access to a farm of "*Bufo alvarius* toads," long prized for their healing properties. Dr. San and a friend "milk the venom sacs," because adding this milk "to the mix" helps vape users achieve the brainwave patterns of "a master meditator."

Tim and Dr. San are confident this heightened consciousness will put festivalgoers in the ideal mindset to comprehend DKR's innovative beats. As the TCH takes hold of Tim's brain, he tries to promote the snacks available through the Six Bags food truck, but his speech soon slows to a gurgling halt.

This week on *Popcorn Classics*, this episode's Popcorn Classic is "a true Popcorn Classic": Mandy Moore's *How to Deal*. Gregg puts this romantic-teen-movie-with-attitude "right up there with *Rebel Without a Cause*." Skeptics take note: It's *also* a sure-fire five-bagger!

Tim has put his motorized leisure chair in the horizontal position and fallen into a troubled semiconsciousness. "That's coming on strong now," he murmurs. He seems to be having difficulty breathing. At Gregg's prompting, he perks up long enough to hype the Electric Sun festival, which will start at 8 a.m. on Friday.

TCH VAPE SYSTEMS presents

FIRST ANNUAL
ELECTRIC SUN
DESERT MUSIC FESTIVAL

DJ Limelite Refueled
Axeus Nou Dash Marcus Westfield
Orion Jacks Empire DJ Flow
Alixx Moore Booj Luna-Tick
DJ Staump Wandertrust Under/Over

April 14, 15, 16

apple valley festival grounds
purchase tickets at www.electricsunfest.tix

TCH VAPE SYSTEMS — FREE TCH VAPE SYSTEMS GIVEAWAY

Tim Heidecker's SIX BAGS CINEMAS FOOD TRUCK

DR. SAN VAPE TENT

ELECTRIC SUN™ DESERT MUSIC FESTIVAL PRESENTS

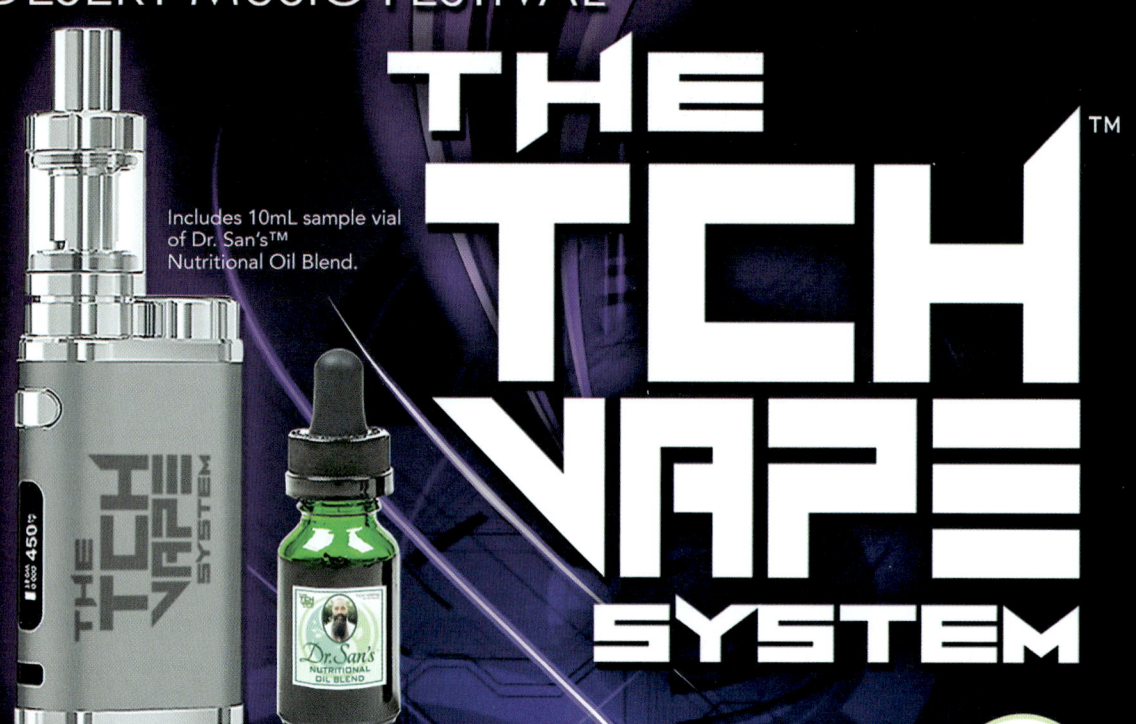

THE TCH VAPE SYSTEM™

Includes 10mL sample vial of Dr. San's™ Nutritional Oil Blend.

WITH Dr. San's™ NUTRITIONAL OIL BLEND

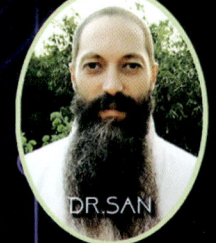

AVAILABLE **FREE** AT THE DR. SAN VAPE TENT FOR THE FIRST 100 TICKET HOLDERS.
(A $49.99 VALUE!)

ADDITIONAL REFILLS OF DR. SAN'S™ NUTRITIONAL OIL BLEND ARE AVAILABLE AT THE DR. SAN VAPE TENT FOR $29/40ML

AS SEEN ON THE HIT TELEVISION SERIES

DECKER: UNSEALED AND **DECKER: MIND WIPE**

- Balanced and smooth
- Packed with natural energy boosters
- Based on principles of ancient Chinese medicine
- Newly reformulated!

GET THE ENERGY AND NUTRITION YOU NEED THROUGH ALL NATURAL VAPOR

On Cinema On Line

4:47 PM - 11 Apr 2017
FUCK EASTER COME TO THE DESSERT SON MUSIC FESTICAL! NO MOVIES AT ALL JUST GREAT MUSIC

4:49 PM - 11 Apr 2017
@greggturkington don't complain just because you don't get to go to this amazing weekend. It's not your scene so why would you care/

4:50 PM - 11 Apr 2017
simply put the idea of movies at an outdoor fest (this coming from someone who hasn't seen many movies even) is odd if not simply really bad

4:51 PM - 11 Apr 2017
in other words @greggturkington doesn't even know what the hell he'd do if he had the chance to appear at @edsmf

9:16 AM - 12 Apr 2017
I'm committed to making The Electric Sun Desert Music Festival a fun, safe, mind expanding experience #esdmf #dkr

9:43 AM - 12 Apr 2017
It is my belief (and have evidence) that #Greggheads have hacked www.electricsunfest.tix /should be back online soon.

10:07 AM - 12 Apr 2017
#Greggheads are too busy watching, reviewing, and cataloging new #movies to waste a second of thought on a bad music festival.

8:56 AM - 13 Apr 2017
This spot is geographically the point on Earth furthest from @timheidecker's Electric Sun Desert Music Fest. Popular spot this weekend?

9:22 AM - 13 Apr 2017
Desperately need volunteers for stage construction lighting food vending etc. hit me up!

8:58 AM - 13 Apr 2017
Unlike movies, music is a one dimensional art form. Zero dimensions when the music is made by DKR!

10:55 AM - 13 Apr 2017
ACTUALLY #DkR is currently top dowload where fans of all kind of music gather to appreciate mind bending electro-rock

1:06 PM - 13 Apr 2017
Would Humphrey Bogart have attended the Electric Sun Desert Music Festival?

- 60% No
- 40% Yes

1:34 PM - 13 Apr 2017
Sorry to say day 1 VIP PASSES are totally sold out! Still some good options for Day 2/3 come one come all!!!

1:36 PM - 13 Apr 2017
@TomCruise I have a pass for you #esdmf

7:03 PM - 13 Apr 2017
Officially ready for the best weekend On earth. Tomorrow truly is Good Friday #esdmf

6:45 PM - 17 Apr 2017
No wifi where I am sorry no on cinema. Hard weekend for everyone

6:45 PM - 17 Apr 2017
Just have enough juice to send this

7:23 PM - 17 Apr 2017
I am inoent

EPISODE 907
'Unforgettable,' 'Animal Crackers' & 'Born in China'

Air date: April 24, 2017
Running time: 11:47 minutes

After introducing himself as the host of *On Cinema at the Cinema*, Gregg introduces this week's special guest, "fellow movie buff Mark Proksch."

This episode is "kind of a somber occasion in some ways," Gregg says. He recently found out "our former host of the show, Tim Heidecker, is in jail." This is due to Tim's central involvement in the Electric Sun Desert Music Festival, at which "18 teenagers — young people — died as the result of a vaping product that he was handing out."

Joining Tim in jail this week is frequent *On Cinema* guest Dr. Luther San. Both men face "a lot of charges of manslaughter, murder and that sort of thing," so Gregg seriously doubts "we'll be seeing Tim or Dr. San any time soon."

Although "a lot of people are grieving the deaths in the desert this weekend," Gregg is sure he and Mark can get *On Cinema* "back on track" if they "keep moving and review some movies."

"I'll be honest," Mark says. "I don't think I'm gonna miss him too much." He complains that he received nothing more than "an honorarium" for his work. Tim did promise him "stock or bonds" in the Six Bags Cinema franchise, but Mark doesn't believe he was "ever gonna see them."

Gregg agrees that Tim's "gold-class, world-class cinema experience" was destined to fail, in part because the seats were so uncomfortable: "I'd rather sit in coach on a bad airline," he grumbles. The movie screen was too small as well.

Mark thinks Tim also overhyped the culinary angle: "He kept talking about John Lenard, but I was the one going to the store and a lot of that stuff was Stouffer's and Banquet." Further, Tim's "truffle oil" was actually "truffle oil flavoring" that he commanded Mark to "sprinkle over everything."

Gregg predicts Tim's cinema bistro would've gone "out of business in a day." Some successful businesses do combine dining and movies, but they differ from Six Bag Cinema in that "they're not run by an insane person."

Gregg also gripes that Tim's private issues were taking too much time away from the expert movie criticism viewers had come to expect. "Particularly this season," Tim was less focused on the world of movies and more absorbed in "his personal world of drug addiction and arson and all these other problems that he has." Gregg confesses that he "gave up on this show several weeks ago" and that Tim "never knew anything about movies in the first place."

"I don't think he watched half of them," Mark concurs. He brings up the dreadful black mold infestation at the Victorville Film Center and charges that Tim always forced him to use the bathroom at a nearby Chevron station, even though they made him "buy something every time."

In addition to resenting Tim's financial mismanagement, Gregg is angry that although he saw *Sully* twice and loved it, Tim went online to tell the *On Cinema* Family that Gregg had "never seen *Citizen Kane* and *Sully* and all this shit."

Now that Tim is "going down" for allegedly snuffing out 18 promising young lives and sending another 158 to the hospital, Gregg sees an opportunity to "turn the show around" by focusing on movies instead of Tim's problems.

As for Dr. San, Gregg has said "since day one" that he was "absolutely a criminal" with "no medical skill." Mark expresses similar concerns, recalling that Dr. San once tried to cure his mold-related cough by rubbing "kerosene all over my chest."

"That guy's brain was scrambled years ago," Gregg observes. He speculates that Mark may have been "too busy serving up that slop" at Tim's doomed cinema to notice the recent lack of movie reviews, especially during "this stupid ass-transplant crap that turned into some fucking game show."

On the lighter side, Gregg presents a new episode of *On Cinema On Location*. This time, he gives us a rare glimpse of Paramount Pictures, which was "the filming location of 2001's *Vanilla Sky*."

Back in the cinema, Gregg voices his lasting regret that Tim never appreciated segments like *On Cinema On Location* or Mark's own *Golden Age Comedies With W.C. Fields*, which Tim canceled "for no reason."

"We should just do one now," Gregg tells Mark. "Fuck him. He's in jail!" While Mark fetches his Fields costume from the car, Gregg rolls another edition of *On Cinema On Location*. This one takes us to Paramount Studios, famed shooting location for 1998's *The Presidio*.

This week's Golden Age Comedy is *Nobody's Baby*, in which "comedy ensues" as "two ex-cons" played by Gary Oldman "folly and filly-fally up the Topungo-Mungo and find a baby." As a "side note," W.C. recalls that "Anthony Quinn's son died in my pond."

Gregg toasts Mark for his "great work" and puts viewers on notice that they'll be seeing "a lot more" of W.C. Promising to review three movies a week from now on, Gregg bids "good riddance to Tim and Dr. San" and says "our prayers are with the 158 hospitalized in Victorville."

As the lights dim, Mark asks Gregg if there's any chance Tim will ever see this episode. Gregg reassures him there isn't.

EPISODE 908
'The Circle' & 'How to Be a Latin Lover'

Air date: May 1, 2017
Running time: 8:58 minutes

In this debut episode of *Gregg Turkington's On Cinema at the Cinema*, Gregg looks forward to "reviewing movies using our critical expertise."

Because Gregg's guest this week is the genial Mark Proksch, we can expect more "light-hearted debates on whether or not a movie was great or just good."

Gregg has also invited a special guest — one who is "very relieved by *On Cinema*'s new direction" now that Tim is no longer the "black cloud" that has been "sinking that whole production." It's *Decker*'s own President Davidson, Joe Estevez!

Joe is pleased to see Gregg and Mark, even though it's a "bittersweet" reunion given what happened to "poor Tim." Joe describes visiting his fellow *Decker* star "in the hoosegow" and claims that Tim "feels worse than anybody" about "the 18 people" who died.

Gregg and Mark suspect the families of the young victims "feel worse" than Tim. Joe concedes this point but reiterates that Tim is "not happy where he's at."

"Good," Gregg answers. He suspects Tim is likely "watching more movies in prison than he ever did" for *On Cinema*.

Apropos of *On Cinema*, Joe mentions that Tim spoke to him about calling in to the show from prison. In an amazing coincidence, Joe's phone rings and Tim is on the line!

"I just wanted to say hi and check in and give my love to the *On Cinema* Family and thank everybody for your kind words," Tim says. He stresses that he feels "terrible about what happened at the festival and all the people that got hurt."

"*Killed*," Gregg mutters.

"I gotta eat crow a little bit here with Gregg," Tim acknowledges. Gregg was "right about Dr. San," who put him in "a bad spot."

"You brought it upon yourself," Gregg murmurs.

Tim says there is some "good news," in that his lawyers see "a path for me, provided I do certain things." He will "be getting out of here tomorrow on bail," and he may also "be able to cut a deal" with prosecutors "because this is about Dr. San" and "the poison that he made." In short, he hopes the murder allegations will "pass over, for me at least."

"Tim, I think I speak for all of us when I say that is just great news," Joe says. He says the three of them are "just over the moon."

Tim thanks Mark and Gregg for "keeping the show going" with last week's episode: "As soon as I get out tomorrow, I'm gonna check it out." Gregg and Mark are visibly troubled by this news, having spent Episode 907 complaining about Tim's financial malfeasance, drug addiction, personal abusiveness, disregard for human life and health, proneness to arson, and relative lack of movie expertise.

Tim wants to know the ratings for this week's films, *The Circle* and *How to be a Latin Lover*. Gregg nervously gives them both an impromptu five bags.

After Tim hangs up, Gregg and Mark remain in a brooding silence even as Joe plies them with souvenirs of his recent trip to Boise. They each get an Idaho Spud candy bar, an Idaho Spud bottle opener, a pen with a flashlight at one end, and a genuine Idaho potato.

These potatoes have quite a back story, which Joe proceeds to tell at some length. He originally "bought the potatoes at Ralph's" and put them in his luggage for safe transport. On his Boise-bound plane, the stewardess announced that "if anybody has a potato in their luggage, I will give the whole row free drinks the rest of the trip."

After "jumping up like a little schoolgirl" to say he did indeed have some potatoes, the astonished waitress said, "You do not!" When Joe proved his claim, "the whole plane went wild."

In summation, Joe reports that "Boise was nice."

On Cinema On Line

5:55 PM - 24 Apr 2017
Glad I got to call into #OnCinema today! Thanks to @greggturkington & @m_proksch and Joe Estevez for filling in!

3:05 PM - 26 Apr 2017
I will be catching up on the #OnCinema episodes I missed tonight at 8pm pacific

4:17 PM - 26 Apr 2017
Regardless of what happens I will continue to review movies in whatever platform my expertise may lead me to.

7:56 PM - 29 Apr 2017
Monday I will be returning to #OnCinema and righting the ship 🍿🍿🍿🍿🍿🎬

EPISODE 909
'Guardians of the Galaxy 2' & 'The Lovers'

Air date: May 8, 2017
Running time: 11:56 minutes

Tim Heidecker is back in the host seat as he welcomes viewers new and old to his show, *On Cinema at the Cinema*. He introduces his "friend" and "guest," Gregg Turkington, who is unusually taciturn.

He also introduces his lawyer, Doug Lyman, who remains off screen but is here to keep Tim "on the straight and narrow."

Tim brings up the sensitive topic of Episode 907. "I heard what you guys said about me," he tells Gregg, "and it stung." All he ever wanted, he says, was to be "the father of a family — the *On Cinema* Family." To this end, he created a show "about movies," and later, about "great food."

Despite his dismay at Mark and Gregg's critical comments, he is "not here to place blame on anybody." He sends a special message to Mark: "If you're listening or you're watching this, I apologize." He anticipates needing to shut *On Cinema* down "temporarily" so he can focus on the steps needed to "make amends."

He is grateful to Joe Estevez for visiting him in jail when "nobody else bothered." He ends by saying, "I'm gonna do what's right, and it's really about the 18 — the Electric Sun 18."

"Two more died," Gregg informs him.

"The Electric Sun 20, then," Tim concedes. "These kids came out to a music festival to have a good time." And they did have a good time, he emphasizes, until Dr. San "let everybody down" by being "irresponsible with his dosage" of the artisanal toad venom-infused vaping compound TCH. Fortunately, Tim and his lawyer have an affidavit stating that the *On Cinema* host "was absolutely out of the loop when it came to the contents of the vape ingredients."

This affidavit will also indicate that "Dr. San deserves to bear responsibility" for the loss of life: Only when Dr. San pays "the ultimate price" for his crimes can there be "justice for the 20." Although Tim has not yet talked to the families of the deceased teens, "they all get that, I think."

Turning to Gregg, Tim reminds his guest of the many things "we have to be proud of," such as *Decker*. "Anything you want to add?" he asks.

"I never believed that Dr. San was anything but a quack," Gregg says haltingly. Tim would like him to testify to that effect, but Gregg is reluctant.

In Tim's judgment, it "would be interesting for the jury to hear" Gregg's views on this controversial figure. It could also ensure that Dr. San receives the punishment he deserves: "Because what happened on that day will haunt me forever."

He explains that on the day in question, he was on stage with DKR, debuting a new track called "Save Us," which explores Tim's failing marriage with Juliana. When he "looked out in the crowd," he saw "bodies dropping." Adding insult to injury, the Apple Valley EMTs took "about 40 minutes" to arrive on the scene. As a result, Tim and Doug are "talking about even suing Apple Valley."

"On the advice of my counsel, we are here to talk about movies," Tim concludes. "Because I want to demonstrate that I have the capacity and the ability to serve my community in an upstanding and professional manner."

Guardians of the Galaxy 2 hurls Chris Pratt, Vin Diesel and Sylvester Stallone into the mix as they "unravel the mysteries of Peter Quill's parentage."

"I did not see this film," Tim admits. But having "loved the first one," he offers the sequel five bags based on its "good merit" and his desire to see everyone get "a fair shake."

Gregg mumbles that he did see this "great" movie. He gives it five bags.

"I need you to bring the energy up here," Tim scolds him. "Or we're gonna have big problems." Gregg livens up enough to call the sequel a "must-see," even though it really should've incorporated characters from Tim's movie, *Fantastic Four*. He lavishes five bags of popcorn and "a little cup of soda" on this "fantastic" movie.

"Thank you for bringing up my film," Tim says.

The Lovers skillfully dissects an "impulsive romance" with Debra Winger. "I didn't see this either," Tim tells Gregg. "Whaddaya got?"

Gregg counsels Tim to avoid the film, which "could be upsetting" given his recent problems with third ex-wife Juliana and second ex-wife Ayaka. He gives it five bags of popcorn, "with reservations for anyone going through trauma or divorce."

This week, *On Cinema On Location* takes us to Paramount Pictures, the iconic filming location for 1981's *First Monday in October*, starring the irascible Walter Matthau.

Back on set, Tim dedicates this episode to the Electric Sun 20, listing them by their first names. He hopes the "folks that are still in the hospital" will recover some day.

As the lights dim, Tim asks Gregg to tell Mark "it's safe to come home" because Tim is "not in a position to seek vengeance."

EPISODE 910
'King Arthur' & 'Snatched'

Air date: May 15, 2017
Running time: 13:55 minutes

Tim opens the last show of the season with some shocking news: "Dr. Luther San took the coward's way out and hung himself in his cell." As a result, "the DA's office is now refocusing their attention on" Tim's role in the deaths and injuries at his troubled Electric Sun festival.

This is "bad news" from Tim's perspective, but he's confident that "we'll beat this." Although Dr. San clearly "thinks he can get out of this by stringing himself up," being dead "doesn't absolve" this "piece of shit" for putting "poison" in his vape pens. "The Apple Valley EMT folks" also deserve plenty of blame for being "asleep at the wheel." All Tim did, as he sees it, "was play some music." Of the 6,000 festival attendees, only 20 died; the others enjoyed "a safe, fun, ecstatic environment," just as Tim intended.

"It's ridiculous to think that I'm supposed to take responsibility for any of this," Tim says. He vows to "fight this to the end" with help from Gregg, whom he calls "my brother back here, hangin' in there tight and being near me no matter what." This earns him an awkward fist bump. "If Mark ever shows his head," Tim reflects, "I know he's got my back too."

King Arthur is a King Arthur film with Jude Law, which Tim name-checks as "the definitive version of that story." He gives it five bags of popcorn, noting that "King Arthur is one of those guys you look up to when you're a kid."

Gregg reveals that the sword Excalibur is one of his "favorite all-time characters in motion pictures." Speaking as an "Excalibur-head," he is quite certain the sword's legend has never "been told in so much detail and with so much high-quality CGI." He predicts it will take "the lion's share of the Oscars." Until then, he awards it an "unreserved" five bags of popcorn and a miniature replica of Excalibur.

In *Snatched*, Amy Schumer and Goldie Hawn portray an uproarious mother-daughter trip to the Equator that ends in kidnapping. Tim is "glad" to see Goldie Hawn return to the big screen, but he would've preferred at least one male lead: "For comedy, I want men." He suggests Mike Myers would've been a better comic foil for Goldie.

"Imagine *Thelma and Louise* with Tom Cruise and Tom Hanks," Gregg objects. "It's not the same movie!" Arguing that *Snatched* is "the *Thelma and Louise* for this generation," he parcels out five bags of popcorn. Tim can only give it four bags, because while *Snatched* was "very, very funny" and "very well made," it was "selfish" of "the feminists out there" to "make everything about them."

Gregg defends the casting decisions as a reflection of the script: "You wouldn't have Joe Pesci playing Martin Luther King," he reasons. Tim suspects it has more to do with studio heads getting "nervous" that "feminist groups are gonna come in and put everybody in jail," even though it's actually men "who get oppressed in this situation."

Gregg opposes this kind of "tampering," saying it would be "a mess" to replace Marlon Brando with Katharine Hepburn in *The Godfather*. "The script dictates the casting," he insists, not ideas Tim picked up "on the internet."

Tim relents: "I apologize. I'm just worn out." He's "not sleeping," he says, because he "keeps picturing" Dr. San swinging in his cell, dead by his own hand.

"San's been in *my* nightmares for years," Gregg says. "So there's no change there."

Tim feels bad for the "poor guard," Luis, who opened the cell door only to be confronted with "that dead corpse." Now, Tim is having visions of his own future in that same prison cell "and the ghost of San swinging in the wind."

That said, Tim is "so glad" Dr. San is dead...despite the fact that he would be "much more valuable" alive, given that "you can't put a dead man in the electric chair."

"But if you *could*, that would be the one that I *would* try to put in it," Gregg hastens to add.

Dr. San was "a thorn in our side," Tim concedes. "A dirty thorn," Gregg confirms. "An infected, dirty acupuncture thorn."

Tim declares that "as much as we hate Dr. San," he remains "a part of the *On Cinema* Family." To Gregg's horror, he then runs a video tribute to "honor him." At its conclusion, Tim is a little choked up from this reminder of "all the good times" he had with Dr. San: "I'll always love him, warts and all." He asks Gregg to "say a couple words" in memory of the late healer.

"He made people sick," Gregg recalls. "He made people die. And I always wondered if he ever even had any medical training. I don't think he did."

At this point, Tim has to conclude the episode so he can get ready "for the hearing tomorrow." He thanks his viewers for "a great season" and lets it be known that "the conceptual copyrights" for Six Bag Cinema are still available.

As the theater darkens, Gregg wishes Tim "good luck tomorrow." Tim leans menacingly over his guest to deliver a chilling message: "No matter what happens to me, I'll always remember the shit you said" in Episode 907.

On Cinema On Line

9:15 PM - 2 May 2017
The Adventurs of Kington and his mastery of codes would make a great #movie

9:16 PM - 2 May 2017
Decker and Kington are a legendary team if you don't have them both the show doesn't work

9:17 PM - 2 May 2017
Let @tim Heidecker know how important Special Agent Kington is

11:00 AM - 3 May 2017
he like many bit players has a small role in upcoming decker series.

11:04 AM - 3 May 2017
the character of Kingont DIED in the end of Decker: Unclassified. His limited role going forward might only be in small flashbacks

11:11 AM - 3 May 2017
Unlike Decker, Kington uses his real life film knowledge and expertise in movies to crack codes that a non-expert would never be able to.

11:12 AM - 3 May 2017
maybe this happens in the deep background of some shots or off camera entirely, but it's not the focus of show in any way. no one wants it!

6:59 PM - 3 May 2017
@m_proksch I forgive you. Come out of hiding.

8:16 AM - 6 May 2017
After I am rightfully cleared of all charges we will do a concert to celebrate the amazing lives of the #electricsun20

6:56 PM - 10 May 2017
I will not go quietly into the night
I will fight, fight, fight! I am innocent of these crimes, and Luther is the one (although dead) Who should do the time.

9:19 PM - 17 May 2017
Interestingly @GreggTurkington pretends he is an expert on movies but hasn't seen many.

8:21 AM - 18 May 2017
I see more movies in an average week than you see in a year..I rarely see you at the sneak peek critic screenings where they KNOW ME BY NAME

9:24 PM - 17 May 2017
It's one thing to collect videotapes. It's another to actually watch them 👿

8:25 AM - 18 May 2017
I watch them all

9:20 PM - 17 May 2017
No offense to him and I'm glad he enjoys watching movies from but the idea that he is an expert has become laughable at this point

6:38 PM - 23 May 2017
The Baywatch movie is an instant popcorn classic. I wonder "Why wasn't this a MOVIE to begin with???" Rating 🍿🍿🍿🍿🍿 and a little souvenir ⚓

6:40 PM - 23 May 2017
How many times do I have to tell you you are not authorized to give movie reviews without my permission.

6:43 PM - 23 May 2017
It's just an informal tweet, not a full movie review. The full movie review would have much more information and cast/director info etc

6:44 PM - 23 May 2017
It utilizes the bag system and generally is a review. Delete now.

6:46 PM - 23 May 2017
Those are TUBS not bags, not subject to your rules. Believe me a review would be much more extensive than this simple film guidance tweet.

6:48 PM - 23 May 2017
You betray and disgrace everything we have worked so hard for. You are in jeopardy of losing everything over this simple matter. Think.

6:54 PM - 23 May 2017
I am deleting a controversial but accurate tweet. I do however hope you all have a chance to see Baywatch this weekend in the theater.

3:01 PM - 25 May 2017
Many of my writings of Decker is directly inspired by the works of Shakespeare and the like

8:51 AM - 30 May 2017
Thank You #Decker

DECKER: UNSEALED
Behind the Scenes of the Making of Season 5

Season 5 of *Decker: Unsealed* continues the wild white-knuckle ride that began in *Decker: Unclassified* while presiding over the final conclusions to the stories of Janet Davidson (Sally Kellerman), Dracula (James Dean) and many others. It also spotlights a grave and gathering threat to the United States as the formerly unheralded Son of Dracula (Jimmy McNichol) comes into his birthright.

Those dazzled by the high-end visual effects technology of *Decker: Unclassified* will not be disappointed by their continuation in this season, with just a few highlights including the many schemes of Dracula and his son, to say nothing of Jack Decker's believe-it-or-not brawl with his own exact double!

Much more of the backstory on Lanoi Arnold occurs as well, presenting a more fully rounded portrayal of this complex man.

As with *Decker: Port of Call: Hawaii*, it could be said that the lesson is whether you can really trust anyone? Seeing is not always believing, as so much that appears to be real is not and vice versa. While the patriotic theme is still well to the fore, there is also a darker vision in play as the supernatural world wreaks havoc upon the very concept of patriotism itself, as we see during the climactic battle at Arlington National Cemetery, the not-so-final resting place of America's best and brightest.

In short: If you were on the edge of your seat throughout *Decker: Unclassified*, you will be just as anxious to learn what happens — and doesn't happen! — this time around.

CAST

Tim Heidecker	Jack Decker, Jack Decker Jr.
Gregg Turkington	Jonathan Kington
Joe Estevez	President Jason Davidson, President Jason Davidson Jr.
John Aprea	General Cotter
Mark Proksch	The Wolf Man, Abdul, Jacob Marley, Charlie Chaplin
Manuel Giusti	Himself, Agent Kingston
Sally Kellerman	Janet Davidson
Denny Laine	Ebenezer Scrooge
James Mane	Lanoi Arnold
Jimmy McNichol	Son of Dracula
David Schroeder	Dr. Greenway
Charlie Schiefer	Vice President Roger Robertson
Kellee Maize	Popp
Jesse Popp	Concertgoer
Steve Railsback	General Cotter
Rizi Timane	UN Secretary General
Corbin Timbrook	President Davidson
Joey Travolta	Judge Buchanan
Bobby Valli	Reanimated Corpse

SPECIAL GUEST APPEARANCES

DENNY LAINE

English musician Denny Laine is perhaps best known for his decade-long membership in Beatle Paul McCartney and Wings, as well as his time with The Moody Blues, Ginger Baker's Air Force and his own Denny Laine Band. His previous acting credits include "Band Member #2" in 2001's *Chasing Destiny*.

KELLEE MAIZE

Rapper, singer, entrepreneur, guerilla marketing expert and doula Kellee Maize has released six top-rated albums, including 2018's *Crown*, which was inspired in part by her debut acting role as the ISIS-affiliated diva Popp in *Decker: Unsealed*. To date, her YouTube videos have been viewed more than 400,000 times and counting,

JIMMY McNICHOL

A major star of the 1970s and beyond, Jimmy McNichol appeared on the cover of *People Magazine*, hosted the *Hollywood Teen* talk show, and opened for R&B legend James Brown. Though best known for 1981's *Smokey Bites the Dust*, he also appeared in other films of that era. His daughter, Kellee Maize, carries on the acting tradition made famous by Jimmy and his sister, Kristy McNichol.

JOEY TRAVOLTA

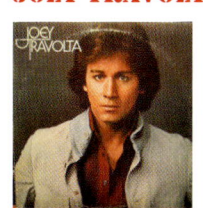

This elder brother of now-and-forever Hollywood Legend John Travolta is a dazzling star in his own right, with a classic 1978 album under his belt as well as a wide variety of appearances in films and TV, including *Simon & Simon*, *Beverly Hills Cop II* and *Decker: Unsealed*.

STEVE RAILSBACK

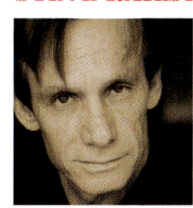

Steve Railsback's film credits include *Cockfighter* (1972), *Helter Skelter* (1976), *The Stunt Man* (1980) and *Kojak* (2005). These roles and others provide a perfect example of the actorly range and dynamism that Mr. Railsback brings to the dramatic table in *Decker: Unsealed*.

DECKER: UNSEALED
Season 5

EPISODE 1: SONRISE

JACK DECKER JR. and President Davidson Jr. mourn the untimely demise of Special Agent Kington at the hands of now-deceased first lady Janet Davidson, who was colluding with Dracula to wipe out the male gender.

But have they given up hope too soon? The White House's own Dr. Greenway has a new treatment that might reverse the lethal effects of the bullet that penetrated the elderly codemaster's forehead.

Against all known odds, the treatment works! Kington is restored not just to life but also to his normal middle age.

Outside, in a pouring rainstorm, a mysterious caller dials Castle Dracula to report that the first lady has died and it's time for "Plan B." Within seconds, the Destructicon in Janet Davidson's room activates remotely. In just five minutes, it will launch a deadly assault on men's rights unless Kington can crack its numeric access code. As Kington puzzles over the device, Decker Jr. heads to Transylvania to settle a long-standing score with Dracula.

Facing the Destructicon, Kington is already running low on time when he is unexpectedly attacked by the first lady's adviser, who lives again as a vampire.

Decker Jr. is securing the perimeter above Castle Dracula, preparing to bomb it back to the Stone Age, when he gets a frantic call from Kington, who briefs him that he's being strangled. There's no time to lose: He must return to the White House on the double!

Leaping from his helicopter and through a White House window, Decker Jr. enters just as Kington's strength is failing and dispatches the vampire adviser. No sooner is she out of commission than the first lady, too, rises from the dead. Worse yet, bullets don't faze her! With little time left to spare, Decker Jr. seizes Babe Ruth's historic baseball bat from a glass display case and uses it to destroy her head.

Kington has equally little time left to deactivate the Destructicon, and all too soon that time runs out. In the world's boardrooms and tennis courts, men are already being vaporized!

In that instant, Kington has an insight: Could *movies* be the key to the code? Wandering in his mind's eye through the Victorville Film Archive, he spots a copy of *Transylvania 6-5000*. Seconds later, the Destructicon is disarmed for all time!

At a press conference in the Rose Garden, the president sorrowfully briefs the nation that his late wife was in cahoots with Dracula. On a happier note, Jack Decker Jr. will receive the Congressional Medal of Honor for killing her once and for all. That earns everyone a round of champagne!

Only one sorrow mars this happy occasion: Decker Jr. wishes the father he never knew were alive to share it. To cheer him up, President Davidson Jr. invites him to the White House to review the government's sealed Decker Sr. files and gain new insights into his father's legacy.

Meanwhile, it turns out that Decker Jr.'s bullet has mortally wounded Dracula. He flitters home to Castle Dracula only to die in front of his heartbroken son, who swears revenge on the young agent.

EPISODE 2: PROMISES KEPT

DATELINE 2076. Decker Jr. is visiting the White House to learn about his father's incredible life as a patriot. Kington is there to fill in any blanks as the only living witness to these above-top-secret events.

"Why did my father leave me?" Decker Jr. asks. "Was it something I did?" The president assures him that on the contrary, Decker Sr. loved his son "more than anything in the world." The problems all began in 2014, when Decker was taking a vacation in Hawaii.

Jack Decker, his son Jack Jr., and his wife arrive at Lanoi Arnold's tiki bar to find a pleasant surprise: Agent Kington is also visiting the bar while curating the Hawaiian Island Film Festival. Decker's number-one interest, however, is Lanoi's award-winning buffalo-flavored chicken wings, which many say are the island's best! Eager to share in this culinary bounty, Decker buys a round of Lanoi's famous wings for the whole bar.

Decker asks Lanoi about the much-needed renovations currently being made to the bar; he hopes this won't affect the quality of the wings. But Lanoi sets his mind at ease: The wings are good as ever!

Decker's Hawaiian idyll is rudely interrupted when Lanoi's TV screen shows terrorists abducting President Davidson Sr. during a speech to special interests and other global elites. Ordering Kington to escort his family back to the hotel, he forgets all about Lanoi's top-rated wings as he strides forth to tackle the Taliban *mano y mano*.

At the hotel, Kington and the Decker family enjoy a to-go box of Lanoi's world-class wings while watching Decker's sensational televised rescue of the hapless President Davidson.

Alarmed by bombshell media reports that Decker has been betrayed by a mole, Jack Jr. asks Kington if his dad will be OK. Kington promises Decker will always be there for his son, just as Lanoi has always been there for Decker.

But this is not to be, as Decker soon learns from a captive terrorist that Lanoi is the Taliban kingpin. After throwing the militant into a pit of molten lava, Decker

Decker Jr. settles one last score with Janet Davidson.

steels himself to settle a fateful score with his oldest and dearest friend.

At first, Lanoi figures Decker has returned for more of his prize-winning wings. But when Decker draws a bead on him, he knows his days of serving this Hawaiian-style delicacy are numbered.

Decker can't believe his best friend would betray his oldest friend as well as his country. Lanoi confesses that even though his wings have been a top seller, the need for renovations pushed him into a deal with the Taliban after President Obama turned down his loan application. The terrorist mastermind Abdul was only too ready to step into this leadership void, providing Lanoi with much-needed funds and ensuring that his popular wings would continue to be available.

Lanoi wants to cut a deal, but the only deal Decker will cut comes out the barrel of a gun as he is forced to blow a bloody bullet hole in his best friend's torso.

The seriously wounded Lanoi offers some last-minute, high-stakes intel: The Taliban is plotting to kill Jack Jr.

Because Lanoi has saved Jack Jr.'s life, Decker decides to let him live with the bullet in his gut as a searing reminder of his treachery.

Then, he seeks out his son and delivers the bitter news: To save Jack Jr. from the Taliban, Decker must never see him again!

"Goodbye forever," Decker sighs as he walks out of his family's life one last time.

"So you see Jack, your father was only trying to protect you," Davidson Jr. explains. Now that he understands this heroic sacrifice, Decker Jr. recommits himself to upholding his father's memory.

At that very moment, back home in his late father's Transylvanian lair, the Son of Dracula plots his most daring move yet.

EPISODE 3: DOUBLE DECKER

DATELINE 2048, CHRISTMAS EVE. Jack Decker is in London to deliver a secret nuclear-armed briefcase. Halfway across the world, at Lanoi Arnold Hawaiian Buffalo Wing Stadium, the World Games are in progress when a suitcase nuke abruptly explodes, vaporizing everyone.

DATELINE 2076. In the Oval Office, Decker Jr. can't believe the footage he just saw was real. Did his father *really* deliver the mini-nuke that blew up Wing Stadium? Davidson Jr. doesn't believe it either, but the Decker files offer no further information.

The discussion is interrupted by one of Decker Sr.'s oldest and best friends: Franklin, the former ski lodge owner who helped Decker Sr. crack the global warming case. He proceeds to tell them what *really* happened.

DATELINE 2048, CHRISTMAS DAY. Decker is on trial at the U.S. Supreme Court for handing off a suitcase nuke to a Russian terrorist. Agent Kington is sure the Decker lookalike captured on surveillance tape is a double, but General Cotter reports that military-grade facial analysis has ruled this possibility out. Now, Decker faces execution for treason!

As a professional courtesy, the court gives him 48 hours to clear his name. Decker's certain the man on the tape was a genetic clone. But can he prove it in time?

With scant time to spare, Decker and Kington head to London, where Christmas is already in full swing. Kington has a watch that can detect DNA identical to Decker's, but they still have to get close enough for an accurate reading. Somehow, they must find this cowardly needle in the vast haystack of London!

Stopping in at an authentic British pub for drinks, Decker briefs the genial barkeep on the purpose of their visit: He is hunting the most dangerous killer of all — himself!

The barkeep knows this situation all too well. Just two Christmases before, he was a miserly old man who would not give his employee, Bob Cratchit, time off for Christmas. But later that same night, he was visited by the ghost of an old business partner, who announced the arrival of three more ghosts who would teach him the true lesson of Christmas.

This story is interrupted by an alert on Kington's DNA-sensing wristwatch. Rushing out of Scrooge's Pub, they catch Decker's double in the act of passing by. Commandeering a motorcycle, Decker gives chase as his double clings to the back of a double-decker bus. After a white-knuckle chase through the streets of London, Decker crashes his hog into the back of the double-decker, propelling Decker himself to the top where he confronts the Decker double. The two men are evenly matched, so this is a fight for the ages! The pursuit continues to the Tower of London, where Decker's double is caught and tied to the rack.

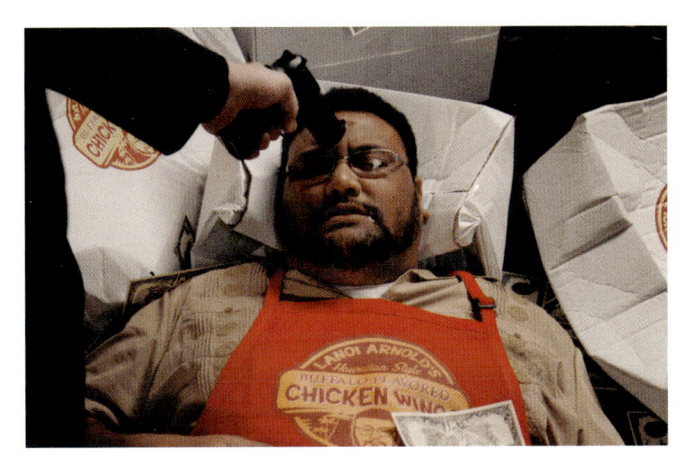

Time runs out for Lanoi Arnold.

Scrooge is visited by Marley's ghost.

Double trouble for Decker!

Under enhanced interrogation, the double briefs Decker that he is the creation of none other than General Cotter, who wanted to clone Decker in order to wipe out terrorism. But these tables were turned when the double was kidnapped by the Taliban's own Abdul, who reprogrammed it for evil.

There's only one loose end remaining: Why is General Cotter prosecuting Decker for the double's actions? The answer, the double reveals, lies in a sealed vault hidden within that very room. As luck would have it, Kington arrives in the nick of time to crack its diabolical code.

The vault door swings open. And all at once, the missing pieces fall into place.

Arriving at the Supreme Court, Decker is ready to clear his name. But first, he must deliver a death-dealing 15-bullet salute to General Cotter. The chief justice prepares to charge him with murder, but Decker has an expert witness for his defense: The *real* General Cotter, who is helped in by Agent Kington. "I'm seeing double, Decker," the chief justice gasps.

Decker testifies that General Cotter was abducted by the Taliban and locked in a secret vault in the Tower of London until he was released by Kington. In the meantime, Cotter's evil clone brought false treason charges against Decker.

The Supreme Court closes the case and apologizes on behalf of the government.

Concluding his story, Franklin discloses that in reality, the Wing Stadium attack was a hoax undertaken by "crisis actors" — "a common practice by the federal government during the 20th and 21st centuries." Case closed!

EPISODE 4: PRIVATE SECTOR

THE YEAR IS 2076, and the place is Castle Dracula. Working in their dungeon lab, the Wolf Man, Frankenstein, the Mummy and the Son of Dracula have brainstormed a brand-new secret weapon.

Back at the Oval Office, Decker Jr. is curious why his father would never allow the music of 2030s singing sensation Popp to play on the radio.

"He had his reasons," Kington chuckles. It all happened when Decker left the CIA to run his own private-sector security organization: Decker, Inc.

DATELINE, 2033. Decker meets with Popp, who needs a new security detail. Although he assumes she prefers pop music, she's actually a big fan of Decker's band, Dekkar. He briefs her that his new project, DKR, will kick up Dekkar's energy a notch by blending the classic EDM sound with a hard-rock edge.

Popp has a great security team, but since she will soon be performing for President Davidson Jr., she needs the very best. For Decker, this means not just himself but also former Agent Klington.

That evening at 0800 hours, Decker and Kington regroup at Popp's mansion. While Kington gives her security system an entry code upgrade, Decker heads upstairs to give the sultry diva an "entry code" of his own, joining her in the bath for some champagne and vaping.

Studying Popp's existing password, Kington realizes it's a clever code for "I'm ISIS." Could this blonde bombshell actually be working *with* the terrorists?

Later, at the CIA, Kington hacks into his old computer to get the goods on Popp, only to learn that she attended an ISIS training camp in Islamabad, Pakistan.

At the Kennedy Center, preparations are underway for Popp's big show. Decker is managing the security detail with an iron fist. Kington rushes in to tell him the unwelcome truth, but Decker refuses to listen and fires him.

Showtime! Popp comes out and greets her special guest: President Davidson. The first song begins innocently enough, but when Popp and her dancers pick up assault rifles, Decker grows suspicious. Climbing into the rafters for an eye-in-the-sky view, he uses his CIA gun scope to confirm that Popp's rifle is real and loaded. In one of the hardest decisions of his career, he must shoot a woman he's physically attracted to directly in the skull!

"He saved my life that day," President Davidson Jr. tells Decker Jr.

At that exact moment, General Cotter enters with some bad news: "Dracula's son and three accomplices have been spotted leaving Dracula's Castle."

EPISODE 5: SAME OLD GLORY

WHILE AWAITING WORD of Dracula Jr. in the Oval Room, President Davidson Jr. gives Jack Decker Jr. a sealed box intended by Decker Sr. to be given to Decker Jr. in the event that anything should happen to Decker. When Decker Jr. opens this box, he gets the shock of his life when he sees that it contains the coveted Oscar award!

The documentation indicates that Decker won this award in 2050 for his performance as himself in *In Service to Our Flags*, which also starred Corbin Timbrook as President Davidson, Steve Railsback as General Cotter and Manuel Giusti as Agent Kington. As a film buff, Kington naturally owns a videocassette of this Popcorn Classic, which he expertly inserts into the White House VHS player.

In the movie, Decker hearkens back to a shameful era in American history when the traditional U.S. flag was outlawed and replaced with the sinister banner of a Globalist Elite. President Davidson questions this policy, but it's no use. Our flag has only one friend left: Jack Decker.

"How could they do this?" Decker wonders as UN soldiers burn U.S. flags in a bonfire. "Our flag is all we have."

Later, relaxing in his office with his vape pen, he recognizes that suicide is the only way out. He lifts his trusty gun to his head and braces himself to squeeze the trigger.

At this precise instant, Agent Kington stands at Decker's locked door. Unfazed by the entry system, he kicks the door down and hurls a deadly ninja *shuriken* at the gun, knocking it from Decker's hand with zero seconds left to spare. "Don't you see?" Kingston shouts, "We need *more* patriots like you, not less."

Convinced, Decker joins Kington in a last-ditch attempt to right this wrong. Hopping on Decker's motorcycle, they head to New York, where Decker's grandfather lies buried with the flag he loved. Decker's plan is to exhume this flag and use it to inspire a new era of patriotism.

Having retrieved the flag, Decker must climb to the top of the Empire State Building and deploy it in place of the hated globalist flag. There's only one catch: He'll be under heavy fire from UN copters, so Kington will need to cover him.

Back in Washington, General Cotter watches Decker's white-knuckle ascent with patriotic pride as he sucks at his vape pen. But others are not so pleased, and soon, the UN jets are scrambling to take Decker out.

Kington's codebreaking skills are useless. But fortunately, he has another ace up his sleeve: a bazooka! Kington takes out the UN thugs, letting Decker achieve his objective: The UN flag is down, and Old Glory is returned to its rightful place atop the fabled skyscraper.

This gives General Cotter all the cover he needs to evict the UN from American soil, in a star-spangled ending that puts American pride right back up on top where she belongs.

In the present-day Oval Office, Decker Jr. wishes Kington were more like the film version portrayed by Manuel Giusti.

Little does he suspect that even now, Dracula Jr. is plotting his next move.

EPISODE 6: A GRAVE MATTER

PRESIDENT DAVIDSON JR. appoints Jack Decker Jr. to the top-secret post previously held by Decker Sr. That's cause for General Cotter to break out the champagne!

But Vice President Roger Robertson scolds them that with Decker Sr. only recently deceased, such festivities are uncalled-for. He counsels a sobering visit to Decker Sr.'s grave at Arlington National Cemetery as a patriotic corrective. He will stay behind and "mind the store" while they pay their respects.

Suddenly, a dramatic flashback shows that the mysterious stranger who called Dracula Jr. after the first lady's death was Robinson himself! This is confirmed by the video call Robinson places to Dracula Jr., alerting him that Decker Jr. et al. are walking right into the vampire's trap.

Unsuspecting anything amiss, Decker Jr. and his friends gather at the grave of Decker Sr. In a touching gesture, the remains of his fallen band, Dekkar, have been interred in the plot next to his.

Nearby, under orders from Dracula Jr., the Wolf Man pours a strange chemical potion into this hallowed dirt.

Their purpose is soon all too plain, as the mangled corpse of the long-dead terrorist Abdul rises from his grave to rejoin the living. Soon, Abdul is joined by all the other revered heroes in the national cemetery — including the members of Dekkar and the reanimated corpse of the late Lanoi Arnold.

As Decker Jr. battles these legions of the undead, a familiar face stumbles from a tomb: President Davidson Sr.

Davidson Jr. totters toward his beloved father, arms outstretched. But it's too late; the zombie president sinks his teeth into his son's throat. He then moves to attack Kington, who shoots him dead.

Watching these carryings-on from the Oval Office, Vice President Robertson is pleased. With Davidson Jr. dead, he will soon be crowned president!

Kington almost falls prey to the ghouls when he attempts to shake the hand of Golden Age Comedy legend Charles Chaplin. But a timely bullet from Decker Jr. sends the "Little Tramp" back to hell.

The Wolf Man and Dracula Jr. are distraught by the effectiveness of Decker Jr.'s massacre of the undead. But the legendary vampire has saved his best trick for last, as Decker Sr. himself rises from the grave. Now, Decker Jr. must face the one man who made him what he is!

As Decker Jr. struggles to overcome his natural affection for his father, Decker Sr. contends that "the future lies with the Son of Dracula." He asks his son to join them both on "the dark side."

"You always taught me to put country above all else, even family." Over his father's objections, Decker Jr. shoots his father dead for a second time.

Brokenhearted, Decker Jr. vows there and then to hunt down and liquidate Dracula Jr. for all time. But before that can happen, there's one last score to settle.

At the U.S. Supreme Court, Roger Robertson is seconds away from being sworn in as president when Decker Jr. bursts in to uphold the truth about Robertson's unconstitutional *quid pro quo* deal with Dracula Jr.

Caught red-handed, Robertson accepts that he must be prosecuted for his crimes. This instantly creates a constitutional crisis that is resolved only when Decker Jr. is appointed president by the court.

President Decker Jr. hits the ground running, rebuilding the nation's military and abolishing the EPA along with all other federal agencies that impose left-wing tyranny on small business.

He also settles a personal score, as he meets with General Cotter to initiate a long-overdue nuclear strike on Castle Dracula.

In his cell, Roger Robertson watches the destruction of Dracula's ancestral home and sheds a tear over what might have been. But his sorrow is short-lived: When the guard's back is turned, he turns into a bat and flies through the bars of his cell.

Charlie Chaplin returns to "Modern Times"!

Official Statement Regarding Decker: Port of Call Hawaii

Due to some confusion regarding the differences between certain events as they occurred in Decker: Port of Call: Hawaii and our most recent episode of Decker: Unsealed (which has been critically acclaimed up to this point) It has been decided that Decker: Port of Call Hawaii can no longer be considered part of the official Decker canon. In fact, it was simply a test to determine the feasibility of shooting a Decker movie and should not have been released.

While we work to correct the error and have all episodes of Decker: Port of Call Hawaii removed from the internet and re-label our seasons to be more accurate, there may be delays. Going forward we will now all know that the events of Decker: Unsealed Episode 2 (Promises Kept) is the true story as it relates to the events of Decker and the Decker story.

SEASON ONE: DECKER: CLASSIFIED
SEASON TWO: DECKER VS DRACULA
SEASON THREE: DECKER: UNCLASSIFIED
SEASON FOUR: DECKER: UNSEALED

Thank you.

Tim Heidecker, sole creator of the Decker franchise

On Cinema On Line

6:47 PM - 5 Jun 2017
Most #decker episodes of Decker are perfect except for many kington scene which we deemed unnecessary

7:40 PM - 5 Jun 2017
@timheidecker took many of the elements that made DvD so successful, in the hopes of increasing ratings for HIS scripted episodes.

7:41 PM - 5 Jun 2017
for the record: Dracula is pubic property and is not in any way influenced by @greggturkington disaster #DvD it was independently conceived

7:42 PM - 5 Jun 2017
as i had not even seen @greggturkington ;s DVD how could it influence me? 🤔

7:48 PM - 5 Jun 2017
I AM CONSTANTLY UNDER ATTACK FROM THE LIKES OF @greggturkington AND THE REST BUT NEVERTHELESS I CONTINUE ON WITH ORIGINAL IDEAS.

7:49 PM - 5 Jun 2017
DRACULAR IS IN MANY MOVIES AND TV SHOWS ITS AS IF WE HAD A DETECTIVE OR AN ALIEN> JUST A FACT>

7:53 PM - 5 Jun 2017
YOU ACCUSE ME OF PLAGARISIM AT YOUR OWN PERIL IT"S MY RIGHT TO USE DRACULE TO MY CHOOSING WEHTER OR NOT GREGG DID IT AT ALL.

7:54 PM - 5 Jun 2017
SHOULD YOU CONTINUE ON THIS PATH YOU WOULD BE SRIOUSLY PUTTING YOUR SELF IN JEOPARDY OF BEING BANNED FROM WATCHING FUTURE EPISODES

8:02 PM - 5 Jun 2017
simply put: if you even question my creativity and originality you will receive a LIfETIME ban of future episodes of #Decker

8:04 PM - 5 Jun 2017
I actually don't want to ban anyone but we have no choice. There has to be a limit of what i can handle. think before you writ.

7:55 AM - 6 Jun 2017
Believe me I want all to enjoy and learn from amazing #decker but also must show respect and decency to me and my creativity.

1:42 PM - 6 Jun 2017
Meanwhile, @m_proksch hides and doesn't at all defend me from attacks though he knows truth.

1:42 PM - 6 Jun 2017
I hate him

5:25 PM - 6 Jun 2017
What did I do?!

5:26 PM - 6 Jun 2017
but omitting the truth you lie.

5:28 PM - 6 Jun 2017
Huh? I doubt I did that.

5:29 PM - 6 Jun 2017
you continue to dig your own grave with a shovel you created. it's getting ridiculous.

5:38 PM - 6 Jun 2017
I'm coming for you so hard. just admit my idea was original to have dracula etc... nothing to do with @greggturkington

12:23 PM - 8 Jun 2017
Jimmy McNichol is a massive star and welcome addition to the #Decker cast playing Son of Dracula. no one misses washed up James Dean.

12:57 PM - 8 Jun 2017
McNichol was incredible in the role and great to work with, thank you Jimmy for bringing Son of Dracula to life on the silver screen again

11:22 PM - 9 Jun 2017
Even though it is a small part of #DeckerAndKington, our Mummy @m_proksch can compete with great Mummy like Karloff, Chaney, Christopher Lee

8:41 PM - 13 Jun 2017
As @timheidecker confirmed--We won't ever do a Kington spinoff tv series. Nope, because we will be too busy working on a Kington #MOVIE!!!

5:21 PM - 14 Jun 2017
To clarify any confusion, all seasons of Decker count! #especially Decker And Dracula season 3.

OFFICIAL STATEMENT REGARDING TRIPP SPENCER***

Recently, Adult Swim the station of which the TV Smash hit Decker is broadcast on had erroneously for only a short time, mistakenly broadcast an incorrect promotional video for our new season of Decker: Mindwipe. The error filled video featured a brief appearance from a character known as Tripp Spencer which was for a short time considered as a part of Decker but has long since been disregarded as wrong for the show and thus removed from the show as it has no bearing on the show moving forward and will not and has not been a part of the Decker show. He will no longer be discussed and has not been for some time. Further discussion of Tripp Spencer is prohibited and will not be tolerated. There is not point in discussing him further as he is not a member of the Decker Cast and never will be. We consider this issue closed and any attempts to inject Tripp Spencer into the dialogue will be punished by an immediate lifetime Decker ban.

Thank you.
Tim Heidecker, Prediend of Decker

On Cinema On Line

7:19 AM - 10 Jul 2017
Tripp Spencer was killed off before shooting. Botched idea from @greggturkington / promo unauthorized

8:06 PM - 16 Jul 2017
Tripp Spencer's popularity exceeds that of many other characters such as Jack Decker or Wolfman. A spin-off is very likely.

10:20 PM - 17 Jul 2017
#TrippSpencer has captured the public's imagination including this new Group of fans @TrippHedz. Hopefully soon we will see more of #Tripp.

10:25 PM - 17 Jul 2017
#TrippSpencer is a character you will be seeing a lot more of, if the people have their say.

10:30 PM - 17 Jul 2017
#TrippSpencer could easily be as popular as #SpecialAgentKington, who is already very popular.

10:35 PM - 17 Jul 2017
In the new #TrippSpencer series @TimHeidecker could play "Ray," a pit crew grease monkey that changes Tripp's tires during Formula 1 races.

7:11 AM - 28 Jul 2017
there is no demand for a #TrippSpencer spinoff therefor it shall not exist. Thats how it works folks.

11:09 PM - 31 Jul 2017
Be sure and let the @TimHeidecker know you want future Decker movies to feature less Jack Decker, MORE #TrippSpencer and his racing know-how

10:09 PM - 2 Aug 2017
Remember, @timheidecker voted FOR #TrippSpencer before he voted against him. It will be your support that gets him back on the #TrippTrain

10:16 PM - 2 Aug 2017
T - Trained
R - Racer
I - In
P - Pole
P - Position

S - START
P - Passing
E - Everyone
N - Now!
C - CIA's
E - Elite
R - Racer

DECKER: MINDWIPE
Behind the Scenes of the Making of Season 6

IN THE MOST UNORTHODOX and ambitious *Decker* season yet, Agent Jack Decker Sr. lies helpless in an Egyptian hospital bed, his mind wiped clean of all its memories by the fanatical terrorist mastermind Abdul.

All of Decker's friends from happier times — from Agent Kington to Lanoi Arnold to the weak and spineless President Davidson — do their best to fill him up again with their stories of the memories of who he once was, in hopes that he will once again become the hero he was always meant to be.

Throughout this process, we learn so much more about Decker's lifetimes of adventure, which range in location from the Middle Eastern desert to the bayous of New Orleans to the secret U.S. outer space station where his son, Jack Decker Jr., will face the most dangerous test of his presidency to date.

But in truth, the fact remains that wherever the action may be, Decker, Decker Jr. and all the rest remain caught on a rollercoaster ride of danger, duty and betrayal that we will not soon forget. And never has this been harder to deny than it is in every exciting episode of *Decker: Mindwipe*!

CAST

Tim Heidecker	Jack Decker, Jack Decker Jr.
Gregg Turkington	Jonathan Kington, Deputy
Joe Estevez	President Jason Davidson, President Jason Davidson Jr.
John Aprea	General Cotter
Mark Proksch	Abdul, WC-PO
Axiom	Himself
Manuel Giusti	Himself
Dr. Luther San	Dr. Luther An
Vaughn Armstrong	Dr. Peterson
Ruben Roberto Gomez	Senator Sanchez
Eric Kaldor	Dr. Aswad
Michael Matthews	Roy St. Charlemagne la Roux
January Welsh	Candy
Bobby Valli	Dr. Reeper
Lindsay Seim	Saballah / Maybellene
Mustafa Haidari	Arab Attacker
David Marks	Himself
Carl Gottlieb	Himself
Dee Thompson	Captain Dee
Don Swayze	General Coover
Todd Rundgren	Ambassador Zultan (voice)

SPECIAL GUEST APPEARANCES

VAUGHN ARMSTRONG

Vaughn Armstrong has appeared in such films as *Coma* (1978) and *Triumphs of a Man Called Horse* (1983), but he is perhaps best known for having appeared in more *Star Trek* roles than any other actor: To date, he has played 12 different characters in 27 episodes!

CARL GOTTLIEB

Carl Gottlieb's lengthy credits include *The Odd Couple* (1974), *The Mama Cass Television Program* (1969), and the screenplays of *Jaws, Jaws 2, Jaws in 3D* and *The Jerk*. He also directed Ringo Starr (Beatles) in *Caveman* (1981), produced by Prof. Larry Turman.

DAVID MARKS

David Marks was a member of the Beach Boys and played guitar and sang on several of their albums, including *Surfin' USA* (1963), *Little Deuce Coupe* (1964), and *Mike Love, Bruce Johnston and David Marks of the Beach Boys Salute NASCAR* (1998).

TODD RUNDGREN

A former member of Nazz, Todd Rundgren found his way to success upon success as a solo artist, a member of bands like Utopia and The New Cars, and a producer of classic albums like Meat Loaf's *Bat Out of Hell* and Badfinger's *Straight Up*.

DON SWAYZE

As the younger brother of top star Patrick Swayze, Don Swayze has the movies in his bloodstream! With credits too many to list, some of the most notable include *Dragnet* (1991), *The New Adam-12* (1991), *Columbo* (1991) and *Hawaii 5-0* (2013).

BOBBY VALLI

The younger brother of Frankie Valli and the Four Seasons, Bobby Valli is a talented songwriter and producer as well as a top performer in classic acts like Classics IV and the Jerry Lewis Labor Day Telethon. His musical tribute to his brother Frankie has been a major hit, with performances still ongoing around the globe to this day.

DECKER: MINDWIPE
Season 6

EPISODE 1: LESSER OF TWO EVILS

It is 2054, and somewhere deep within an Egyptian bunker, Jack Decker Sr. is undergoing torture at the hands of the terrorist madman Abdul. He's more than man enough to withstand the pain, but he's not prepared for what comes next: *Mish Alrras*, a mindwipe technique that will delete all the memories from his head!

Decker struggles gamely as the terrorists download his top-secret mental intel. But in the end, they succeed in burning his mind to a CD-R, leaving his brain 100-percent empty.

At the U.S. Military Hospital for Egypt, Dr. Peterson confirms Abdul's diagnosis: Decker's brain has been wiped! Worse yet, the damage is irreversible — unless an experimental treatment can somehow reverse it by exposing him to narrated memories of his own life. But will it work?

President Davidson begins by recounting the story of how Decker helped him defeat Senator Sanchez, his rival in the 2026 presidential election.

On arrival at the Oval Office, Decker is briefed on a plan decrypted by Agent Kingston from the Sanchez campaign's private server: The evil senator intends to create a United Mexican States that will erase the entire U.S. Southern Border!

Kington sees no other option than to rig the election for Davidson. As a patriot, Decker hesitates to overthrow the Founding Father's rule of *one man, one vote*, but he finally agrees. There's just one snag: The U.S. election computers are secured in a heavily fortified undersea base off the coast of Guam.

The agents travel to Guam to hack the election computers. When Decker dives underseas to secure the perimeter, he gets more than he bargained for when he is targeted by a great white shark!

Narrowly escaping through the base's intake fans, he finds himself at the top-secret nerve center of U.S. democracy. To hack into the election results, he must switch the red and blue wires. But in doing so, he trips the security system, causing the base to fill slowly with water.

Decker exits the base in time, but a new threat awaits — the chopper is almost out of fuel! With a great white shark again at his heels, Decker dives out of the water and catches hold of the transport chopper just in time to be exfiltrated stateside.

Sanchez concedes defeat — despite the irregularity of a 32-point swing in the election results — and returns to working with disadvantaged children.

Back in the hospital room, Davidson briefs Decker that Sanchez never supported the United Mexican States: Janet Davidson had provided Kington with phony intelligence! Davidson hopes for a response from Decker, but gets none.

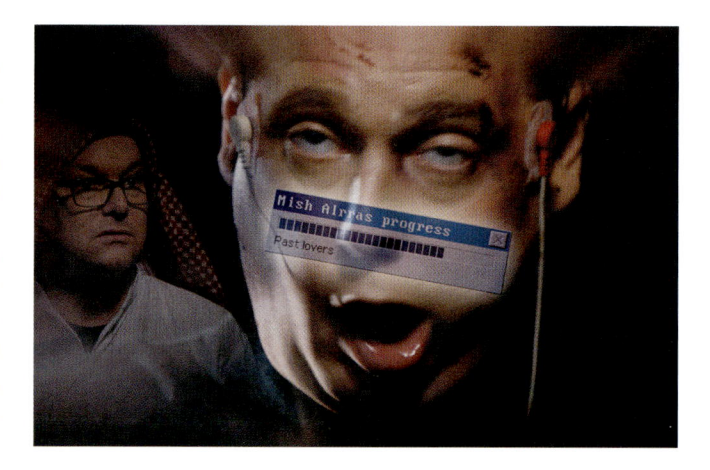

Abdul's sweet revenge.

EPISODE 2: TROUBLE ON THE BAYOU

Decker remains in a vegetative state, but Dr. Peterson judges that Davidson's storytelling is having a positive effect. To assist with this process, Kington has brought in Decker's oldest and best friend, Lanoi Arnold. Better yet, Lanoi has a bag of his famous wings for the president!

Sitting at Decker's side, Lanoi tells the tale of their Spring Break visit to New Orleans.

As the two friends walk down Bourbon Street, Lanoi decides to head home and get some rest. Seconds later, Decker gets a risqué offer he can't refuse from an authentic bayou beauty named Candy.

But first, he needs a pair of Louisana-style alligator boots. Walking into a local shop, he learns from minority small-business owner Roy St. Charlemagne la Roux that these boots are no longer available thanks to "Hollywood animal rights activists."

"These alligators have more rights than we do," Decker groans. He resolves then and there to take the matter up with Governor Lamont Pierce.

Confronted by Decker, the governor defends the ban and hints that Decker may come to harm if he dares to interfere.

Laissez les bon temps roulez!

Later, Decker is in bed with Candy enjoying a postcoital vape. She makes it all too clear that the governor's concern for alligators is nothing more than "a classic Cajun con": He's raking in donations from limousine liberals while running a secret alligator shoe factory on the side!

Decker contacts Kington at CIA headquarters and orders him to pinpoint the satellite locus of Pierce's alligator farm. Kington detects it easily. There's only one hitch: It's hidden deep in bayou country. That's a challenge Decker can't refuse!

Decker and Candy set off in a fanboat to find the factory, only to be intercepted by a sheriff and two deputies. They set Candy adrift and threaten to do worse than that until Decker's fists take them down *mano y mano* and one of them ends up as alligator food. Now, Decker just has to save Candy — by using alligators as stepping stones to the drifting fanboat!

Deep in the dark heart of the bayou, Decker spots the alligator boot factory and blows it sky-high with a hand grenade.

That night, in an authentic Bourbon Street bar, Lanoi toasts Decker for "singlehandedly saving Louisiana's most cherished industry." He begs Decker for a song, and he gets one: a Cajun-style version of Dekkar's "Empty Bottle."

Lanoi is showing his cell phone footage of the performance to Decker as Kington enters the hospital room. They are happy to see Decker tapping his foot.

EPISODE 3: DAVIDSONCARE

DECKER IS SHOWING SIGNS of recovery, and the nurses are fighting over who gets to give him a sponge bath.

Sitting at his bedside, Kingson and the president reminisce about the last time Decker died.

In 2013, Decker visits a modest house in Annapolis. He's looking for his old Army buddy, Stephen Crane. From Stephen's mother, he learns that his friend went to the VA with a sprained ankle only to be euthanized by DavidsonCare's death panel.

Bursting into President Davidson's office, he demands an explanation. The president introduces him to the man behind DavidsonCare, Dr. Reeper, who reveals that Crane had "terminal blood clots." He invites Decker to review Crane's charts when he comes in for his own check-up.

At his physical, Decker expects to get a clean bill of health. But Dr. Reeper

Dr. Reeper gets a deadly house call.

informs him that he, too, has blood clots. Worse, treatment has been pre-denied by the death panel. Dr. Reeper gives Decker a shot for the pain. But to Decker's dismay, the injection kills him. Moments later, he is en route to the morgue, dead!

President Davidson visits Kington to bring him the bad news in person. To his credit, Kington doesn't accept the diagnosis; he suspects poison. But the gullible president sides with Dr. Reeper.

That night at the morgue, on-duty physician Dr. An makes an unusual discovery: A faint life force emanates from Decker's corpse! Racing against time, the doctor gathers healing herbs to make a vape blend. Breathing deeply, the doctor exhales the vapor over Decker's body.

Decker coughs a few times and realizes he is alive once more. Dr. An explains how he combined nontraditional and holistic healing methods to counteract the death process. A grateful Decker wishes the nation had more providers who were willing to go "outside the box" to save lives like his.

Kington is at the movie theater for a screening of *Sully 2* when someone calls out to him. To his surprise, that someone is none other than Jack Decker! Having attended his friend's funeral the day before, he is amazed to learn that Decker is alive and the ashes they buried were left over from a campfire.

Decker briefs Kington on Dr. Reeper's dirty little secret: He has been rationing health care by poisoning vets! Kington is ready to blow the whistle then and there, but Decker knows he's more valuable as a supposed corpse. That way, he'll have the "eyes in the sky" he needs to take Dr. Reeper down for good.

That evening, Dr. Reeper's stately home gets an unexpected visitor in the shape of Jack Decker — the man he killed! Acting as a one-man death panel, Decker delivers his dread verdict: Death!

With Reeper neutralized, President Davidson has no choice but to repeal DavidsonCare and appoint Dr. An as the nation's new head of medicine. He also announces an end to government-mandated vaccinations, earning him a standing ovation from Congress.

Back in Decker's present-day hospital room, Davidson briefs Kington that Dr. An is still his most trusted adviser.

Kington is puzzled. "Who?"

The president beckons the bearded healer into the room. "Fuck this," Kington scoffs. He leaves abruptly.

"Hello, Jack," Dr. An smiles.

Amazingly, Decker manages to form three words: "Luther … my friend."

EPISODE 4: DESERT CARAVAN

THOUGH STILL CONFINED to bed, Decker is able to recognize photos of landmarks like the Sphinx, the terrorist Abdul, and his old friend Lanoi Arnold.

"It seems that your memory has been restored nearly 100 percent," Dr. Peterson reports. In a videoconference with Kington, General Cotter and the president, the physician shares this good news.

President Davidson wants to get Decker home to America. But Kington cautions the doddering figurehead that an American plane would be a ripe kinetic target for terrorism. Covert action will be required to exfill Decker stateside.

Kington has a plan: A caravan of woven goods will be leaving the hospital to visit an outdoor market near the U.S.

military base. He tries to describe the old movie that gave him this idea, but he's interrupted by a violent coughing fit.

"Are you OK?" the president wonders. Kington takes his handkerchief from his mouth and sees the tell-tale signs of blood.

Soon after, Decker and his ailing sidekick meet Saballah, a mysterious veiled woman who has pledged to guide them through the desert to safety.

As the truck carries them down the desert highway, Kington's cough worsens. He also complains of a pain in his side.

"Toughen up," Decker commands him.

The caravan stops abruptly. An old native guide foresees a sandstorm; they will have to camp out until it passes.

Evening falls as Decker vapes beside a primitive campfire where the old guide is cooking a pot of *baba ghanoush*. A pair of scantily clad exotic beauties try to divert

Decker removes Kingston's kidney.

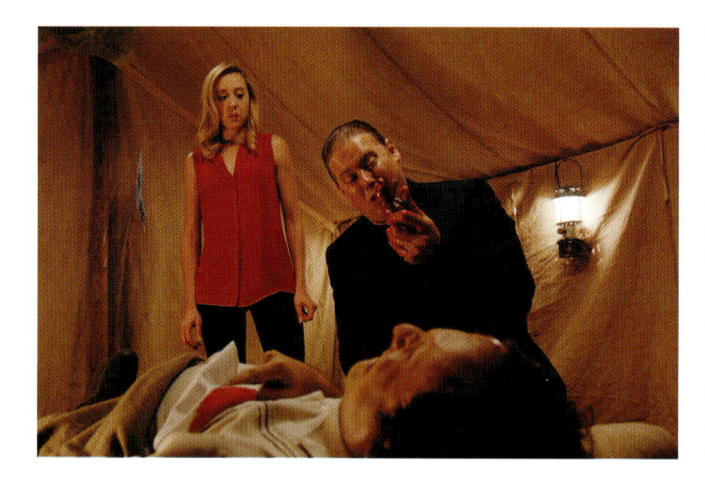

his attention with the renowned Islamic belly-dance ritual.

"You know, Decker, you can have any of these women you'd like," the old guide briefs him.

"I'm not interested in your women," Decker sneers. "It's the oil we deserve."

Suddenly, there is a scream from behind the caravan. Saballah is being assaulted by three radical Islamists! Seizing his gun, Decker draws a bead on the thugs and demands her safe release.

"Get back, Decker!" the ringleader barks. "The role of women in our culture is a very complex subject!"

"Let me simplify it for you," Decker smirks as he lights up the militants with bone-shattering salvos of bullet fire.

Approaching the wounded Saballah, he tenderly lifts her veil — only to discover that his guide is in truth a beautiful Western woman. "My name isn't actually Saballah," she confides. "It's Maybellene. I'm a CIA operative under deep cover from Hominy, South Carolina."

Decker brings her to the campfire and tends to the knife wound on her face. He tells her that although he has never believed in love at first site, he was smitten the moment she raised her *burqa*. Maybellene feels the same way: "It's like something out of a movie," she sighs.

"My mind has recently been wiped," he informs her. "But now that it's been restored, I'm happy to report that one of my first memories will be our first kiss." Before their lips can touch, an agonized cry interrupts: Kington is calling for help!

Entering his tent, Decker expertly diagnoses Kington's ailment as kidney failure due to overconsumption of movie popcorn. He needs a transplant on the double! "The nearest hospital is 1,000 miles away," Maybellene briefs him. "I'm sorry, Decker. Your friend is gonna die."

That's not an option for Decker, who vows to operate then and there. "This is gonna sting," he grunts as he plunges a crude native knife deep into Kington's abdomen. Rummaging in the agent's entrails, he soon locates the lethal kidney.

"There it is, the culprit!" he scowls. "The source of all your problems." He hands it to Maybellene and commands her to "throw it to the dogs." Then, steeling his nerves, he turns the knife on himself. Delving deep into his own pulsing viscera, he locates the kidney Kington needs. Thrusting the organ into Kington's body, he orders Maybellene to sew up the wound.

After the surgery, Decker finds Maybellene washing her blood-soaked hands in a horse trough. "Looks like we make a pretty good team," she coos. "I'd love to make it permanent, Jack."

Though Decker is tempted, he knows this doomed love would violate CIA rules. Maybellene is willing to quit the spy game for Decker's sake, but he detects a fatal stumbling block. Though unfit for combat as a woman, she has a sacred charge to keep: inspiring females to find other ways of serving the nation.

"I'll fondly remember you and our time together in this desert caravan," he admits.

On reaching the U.S. military base, Decker is debriefed by General Cotter, who briefs him on a grave new threat. Still weak but on the mend, Kington thanks Decker again for saving his life.

EPISODE 5: ROCK AND A HARD PLACE

KINGTON HAS SIGNED ON to a film buff cruise departing from Anchorage, Alaska. The voyage will end with a coveted prize for the best trivia buff: The harpoon used to kill the shark in *Jaws 2*. But all is not as it seems: Behind the sacks of movie popcorn, Abdul lurks!

Meanwhile, President Davidson calls Decker to account for his recent letter of resignation. Decker briefs him that when his mind was unwiped, he lost all sense of who he is: "I cannot fulfill my duties until I find out how to fill that missing gap."

Tearing up the resignation letter, President Davidson gives Decker a direct order: "I want you to go out there and find yourself!"

Decker hops on his motorcycle for a lengthy road trip. In a motel room somewhere in America, he watches an TV interview with David Marks, legendary early guitarist with the Beach Boys, who relates how music formed his identity and gave him purpose.

"It will fill the missing pieces in your brain," Marks promises.

The next day, Decker sees an ad on a San Juan Capistrano bulletin board: "Bassist / singer wanted for rock group." Could this be the sign he's been seeking?

He contacts band leader Axiom and shows up at the rehearsal. "You got looks," Axiom hisses. "But do you have the chops?" All doubts are wiped from Axiom's mind as Decker leads them through a scorching rendition of "A Hole in My Soul." Decker has earned the gig; now it's just a matter of writing some hot new material!

Out in the Arctic Sea, Kington is moderating a symposium titled "Serious Moonlight: The Works of Meg Ryan in the Post-Y2K Landscape." After an introduction from *Jaws* scriptwriter Carl Gottlieb, he takes the podium. "Meg Ryan," he intones. "Where do I begin?"

This question goes unanswered as a sudden engine room failure sends the ship on a headlong collision course with death. The captain fights to regain command of the stricken vessel but is promptly shot in the chest, dead. The logo of Abdul's terrorist network flashes on all A/V screens, making it all too plain that the ship has become Islam's latest victim.

Back in California, the Dekkar sessions are going great and the boys are ready to record their first EP. But at that precise moment, Decker gets a call from Kington, who briefs him that "terrorists have seized the film buffs' cruise ship." Their target? The Anchorage oil refinery.

When Decker breaks the news that he can't make the session, Axiom angrily challenges his commitment to the band. Manuel suggests laying down scratch tracks so Decker can come in later, but Axiom won't stand for it: "This is bullshit," he snarls.

Outside the studio, Decker takes a drag from his vape pen to steady himself for the long ride north. Manuel comes out and offers "an extra hand — no questions asked."

"Let's ride," Decker nods. Clinging to a helicopter rope, they are infilled directly to the hijacked vessel and deployed among the panicked film buffs.

Kington is surprised to see Manuel. "What's he doing here?" Kington bristles. "This isn't some stupid Dekkar video."

In one of the key codebreaking scenes of the season, Kington must crack the secret keypad code to enter the captain's bridge. By running a few lightning-quick calculations in his mind, he comes up with the answer in no time. They're in!

But it may be too late, as the doomed cruise ship is only a few precious seconds away from slamming into the refinery.

Through a combination of pulling the handbrake and advanced steering maneuvers, Decker avoids the refinery with only minimal loss of life.

Now, they just need to find Abdul. Luckily, a clue arrives in the form of a dislodged jet ski portal. Running out to confront the Taliban leader, Decker sees the *Jaws 2* harpoon gun. Smashing the protective glass case, he seizes it to use against an even deadlier predator!

The wily terrorist is making his escape, but Decker has a better idea: "Die, you son of a bitch!" The harpoon hits Abdul right where he lives — his upper back — and comes out the other side drenched in blood. As his jet ski crashes and burns, Abdul sinks to the watery grave that is the birthright of all jihadists. His mission accomplished, Decker tosses the now-useless movie prop overboard.

Later, at a party on deck, Kington and Decker see a shooting star. This reminds the film buff of the evening's film, *E.T.*

"Kington, there's more important things in life than movies," Decker parries.

Kington is mistrustful: "Like what?"

"Like the power of music."

"No." Kington stalks off the set.

Turning to Manuel, Decker remarks that before he met the other members of Dekkar, his life was "like an empty bottle, drained of everything good and right. I was checking out life on the dark side, riding down the road to the end of time."

Just then, inspiration strikes.

EPISODE 6: SPACE WALL

IT IS 2080. At long last, Jack Decker Jr. has been elected president, putting an end to the long national nightmare of the corrupt Davidson dynasty. At his inauguration, he plays "The Star-Spangled Banner" on bass to vollies of thunderous applause.

On the other side of the USA, Agent Kington wakes up in his Victorville apartment, eager to begin another day of watching classic movies. He picks up a tape from his bedside: "Ah, *Star Trek II*," he gloats. "The San Francisco treat!"

But his glee is short-lived, as a strange interference pattern is playing havoc with his otherwise pristine archival-quality VHS tape. Because the signal is clearly coming from outer space, Kington puts in a worried call to President Decker Jr.

At the White House, Decker Jr. and Kington meet with General Coover, who briefs them that for the past 500 years, the USA has enjoyed friendly diplomatic relations with an alien race called the Zorillians. To keep the peace, the USA has provided them with the staples of their diet: sodium and corn. But now, a disaster on their home planet has spurred

Decker and Manuel are airlifted to the stricken cruise ship.

Abdul's plans are interrupted by the harpoon from Jaws 2!

… STAR TREK II

ANDROMEDA COLLECTION

STAR TREK II

"The San Francisco Treat."
— Kington

VHS VHS VHS VHS

a mass migration. The whole population will shortly be landing on Earth!

"We must throw our hands up in the air and surrender!" Kington urges. But Decker Jr. stands resolute: "I, like all true Americans, refuse to surrender!"

His long-shot scheme is to visit the U.S./Zorillian Neutral Zone and hold the aliens off long enough for the USA to build a "space wall" based on wireless infrared technology. If it works, the Zorillian craft will be destroyed well before making landfall. If it doesn't, Earth's traditional culture will be diluted by a vastly different value system and way of life!

At 0600 hours at a secret launch pad in Dallas, Decker Jr. and Kington blast off for the Neutral Zone. Reconnoitering at Space Station IX, they are greeted by WC-P0, a robot designed to communicate with the Zorillians, who reminds Kington of "the late, great W.C. Fields."

WC-P0 presents the Earth delegation to Ambassador Zultan, who whines that the Zorillians are starving to death.

To stall for time, Decker Jr. delivers some heartfelt thoughts on the American values of freedom and liberty. He also boasts about his recent electoral success, which he says was "the biggest ever."

But within seconds, the jig is instantly up when a Zorillian diplomat glances at the monitor screen. "Look!" he shrieks. "They're constructing a massive space wall using infrared technology!"

"You've betrayed us," the ambassador shouts. But Decker Jr. stands by his conviction that "government handouts

Decker stalls for precious time.

cannot be a solution to a starving population." The furious ambassador orders an attack on "the American globe," but the words are barely out of his mouth before Decker Jr. strews his brains across the walls with a well-timed bullet. For good measure, he also ventilates the rest of the Zorillian diplomats.

"You shot the ambassador," WC-P0 gasps. "This is anything but cordial!"

These deaths do not go unavenged, as the Zorillians swiftly besiege the space station. WC-P0 computes the odds of survival as "less than zero," but Decker Jr. has a long-shot plan. He and Kington flee the ship in spacecraft with the Zorillian saucers in kinetic pursuit. They're no match for Decker, though, who shoots them down in a classic backflip maneuver.

Kington's craft is hit, obliging him to press the "Eject" button and return to the Neutral Zone mere moments before his ship explodes. "I'm launching a retrieval pod to rescue Agent Kington, my little chickadee," WC-P0 radios Decker.

Calling from Earth, General Coover counsels Decker Jr. to destroy the remaining ships quickly and head home before the nearly completed Space Wall makes return impossible.

But the Zorillians have cornered Decker Jr.'s ship, and things look bleak!

All at once, the spectral form of Davidson Sr. appears to Decker Jr. "You must capitulate," the chicken-hearted former president advises him. "Surrender is the only way!" His craven son Davidson Jr. also appears: "You should really listen to my father. He's right about this!"

These shameful words fall on deaf ears as Decker Jr. once again rejects the politics of defeatism and despair. He has one last long-shot chance, and that's to blast his way out. And he's as good as his word, soon annihilating the entire Zorillian fleet. "Time to make 'space' for more Americans," he quips as he blows the alien ships into a mist of green blood and metal vapor.

"Congratulations, gentlemen — you did it!" General Coover says. "See you back at Earth." Making it through the shield with no seconds left to spare, Decker Jr. meets an excited crowd. Among them is the leader of the United Nations, who thanks Decker for preventing the alien attack.

Back at the space station, WC-P0 congratulates Kington: "You must be so proud of President Decker!"

"Not exactly," Kington confesses. He then pulls out a gun and trains it on the genial robot. "Godfrey Daniel!" WC-P0 cries, mere milliseconds before Kington's merciless bullets rip through his circuitry.

Flipping a communication switch, Kington radios his Zorillian overlords. "This is double agent master codebreaker Jonathan Kington," he cackles. "I've taken control of the Neutral Zone base station and can crack the code to open the Space Wall. I await your command, Master!"

The turncoat Kington murders WC-P0.

On Cinema On Line

9:21 AM - 11 Oct 2017
#OnCinema news! Finally! A trial date has been set for the #ElectricSun20 incident. I am being charged with 20 counts of 2nd Degree murder!!! Unbelievable! The trial will begin on Nov 15th in San Bernardino Co. I am being repped by the great Mark Dwyer Esq. He rocks! No worries there! I am looking forward to proving my total innocence and clear my good name! as well as start my foundation #ElectricSun20Foundation which will help kids achieve their dreams!

3:57 PM - 14 Oct 2017
I predict the 6 Bag Cinemas will never reopen. Bad concept

3:58 PM - 14 Oct 2017
It won't return with you involved

4:00 PM - 14 Oct 2017
True! I won't be there with you in prison when you open a "jailhouse canteen" version.

10:24 AM - 23 Oct 2017
Prediction: when my name is cleared in the #ElectricSun20Trial I will win massive award settlement from San Bernardino County!

10:47 AM - 27 Oct 2017
i am so innocent it will make your head spin.

8:42 AM - 30 Oct 2017
Mark Dwyer is one hell of a legal mind. Maybe the best we've seen!

9:47 PM - 9 Nov 2017
Ha ha I might have to sue Apple valley itself for Flasly accusing me of crimes. I might! #Timoccent

7:32 PM - 11 Nov 2017
If @m_proksch dares to testify against me I will bring down the fucking hammer on him! #ElectricSun20Trial

7:24 AM - 14 Nov 2017
Just received a major call from a VIP wishing me luck on our trial, but I told them I didn't need "lick" as I am innocent and will prooof it in Court of law! #timocent #ElectricSun20Trial

11:10 AM - 14 Nov 2017
🤔 no one looking into DA Rosetti's possible Mafia ties? While I become scapegoat for natural accidents? #ElectricSun20Trial

11:11 AM - 14 Nov 2017
Mark Dwyer Esq begging me not to tweet on this but it's a good question no one is asking!

3:56 PM - 14 Nov 2017
#timocent #yagottabelieve #railroaded #falslyaccused #markdwyer #rosettitherat #freetim #DrSanIsARat #ElectricSun20Trial

5:22 PM - 14 Nov 2017
#ElectricSun20Trial never would have been necessary had @timheidecker put his money into the Victorville Film Center instead of a dumb vanity music festival.

5:26 PM - 14 Nov 2017
DKR = Dead Kids' Revenge. Tim's defense lawyer is holding an "empty bottle" of information that could free him.

7:10 PM - 14 Nov 2017
Tomorrow, justice will be served and I will begin the road towards innocence and finally get to move on so I can start the Electric Sun 29 Music Foundation! AND I WILL SEEK REVENGE FOR THOSE WHO DISOBEYED ME! Justice indeed, as tomorrow will be a good day for

7:11 PM - 14 Nov 2017
Law and order as will be found in coconut o matter what if you believe in freedom and trust this case will be interested for all!!

7:13 PM - 14 Nov 2017
Thanks to my many many supporters who know I am innocent or as you have stated #timocent which I love ❤️❤️❤️❤️❤️

3:04 PM - 15 Nov 2017
Prediction: @timheidecker has seen his last movie on the big screen.

7:14 PM - 30 Nov 2017
My rating of the Electric Sun Desert Music Festival:
💀💀💀💀💀💀💀💀💀💀
💀💀💀💀💀💀💀💀💀💀

THE TRIAL

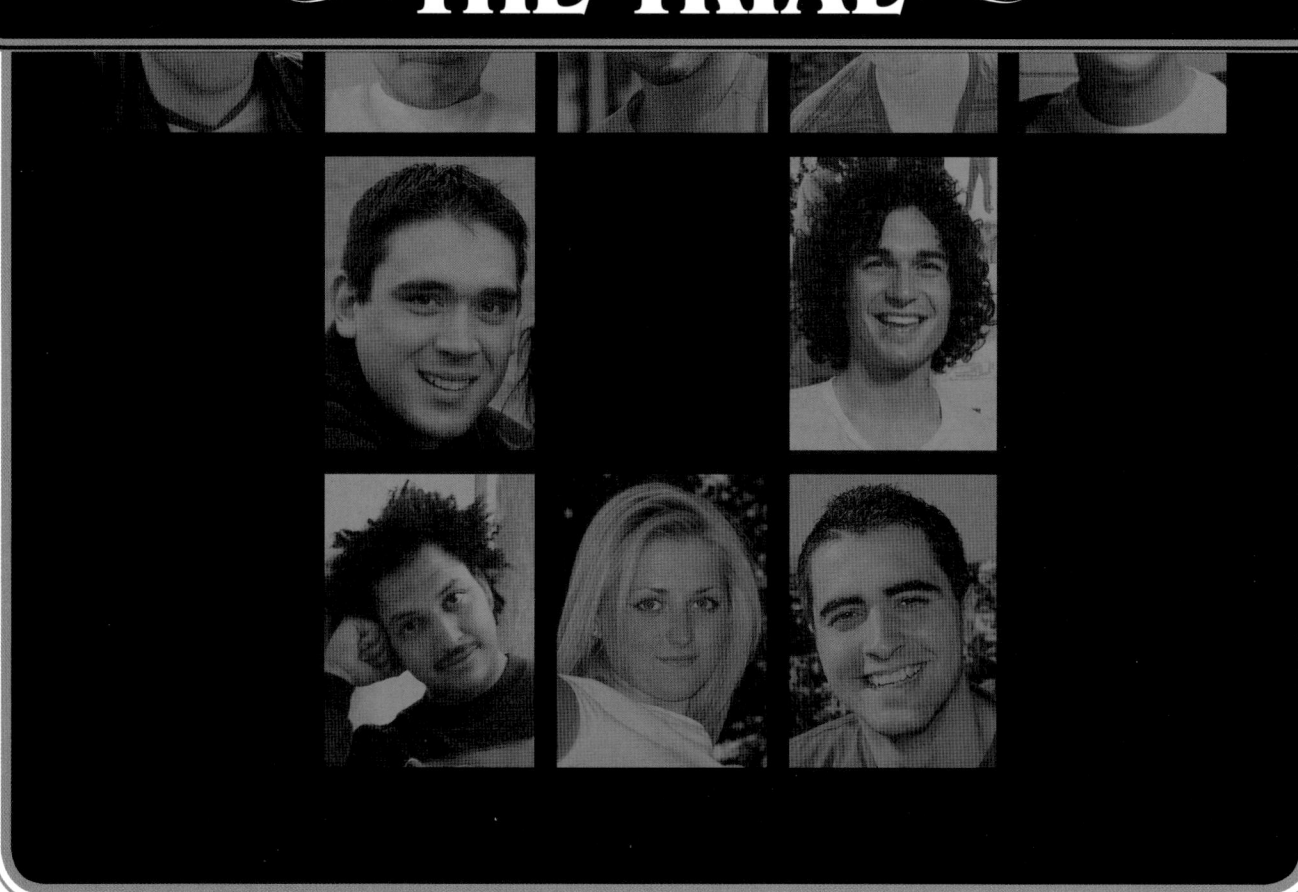

Official Statement Regarding The Electric Sun 20 Trial

ON NOVEMBER 15th The State of California will begin their trial against me for the crime of 2nd Degree murders of 20 people; Crimes which, simply put, I did not do. I am being framed for crimes I did not commit, simply to save the face of the disgusting and incompetent First Responders as well as the DA and Police Department of Apple Valley and San Bernardino County. District Attorney Vincent Rosetti will use every trick in his book to try and paint me as a guilty man, but I am confident that my attorney, Mark Dwyer esq. is a ROCK STAR and will DO WHAT NEEDS TO BE DONE at which point the jury will have to find me innocent.

We all know who bears responsibility for these crimes (Dr. San, the kids's own lack of responsibility and good judgement, the EMS and first responders etc…) So we look forward to a speedy trial, a verdict of INNOCENCE at which point, I will be able to move on with my life, unfreezing the funds which will allow me to start the ElectricSun20 Foundation, which will give kids new opportunities!

The Judge has decided to allow The Trial to be televised and the website adultswim.com will be broadcasting the each day's events later in the evening. Stay tuned for more information. You may also follow @NewsAppleValley on Twitter for more information about the upcoming trial.

Sincerely,

Tim Heidecker
Sole Founder of On Cinema Productions

ELECTRIC SUN 20 TRIAL
Day One

Air date: November 15, 2017
Running time: 49:31 minutes

The trial of Timothy Richard Heidecker, co-owner of TCH Vape Systems, began on November 15, 2017. The presiding judge was the Hon. Edward Szymcyzk.

Heidecker, who was accompanied by his lawyer, Mark Dwyer, had pleaded not guilty to second-degree felony murder charges in the vape-related deaths of 20 people at his Electric Sun Desert Music Festival. In addition to these charges, and likely charges stemming from injuries to dozens of other festival attendees, Heidecker faces "pending suits from unpaid victims and vendors" as well as 63 counts of safety, sanitation, noise and permitting violations. If convicted on all counts, he will spend 370 years in prison.

As the trial began, Heidecker sat impassively near a cork board to which photographs of the 20 victims were affixed.

Opening Statements

San Bernardino County District Attorney Vincent Rosetti told the jury they had just one question to answer: "Is Timothy Heidecker a killer?"

Granting that Heidecker didn't fit the typical image of a murderer, Rosetti said the facts of the case would allow for no other conclusion. Calling Heidecker's alleged crimes "more diabolical" than everyday killings with a knife or gun, Rosetti accused him of knowingly exposing festivalgoers to a deadly "chemical cocktail" called TCH.

Speaking emotionally of the "agony" victims underwent in the moments before death, he made it clear this suffering was also inflicted on the survivors, some of whom are expected to have "debilitating physical and neurological problems" throughout their lives.

Rosetti portrayed the festival itself as "an unpermitted, illegal, chaotic event" that resulted in "injuries and fatalities on a scale our community has never seen."

Referring to TCH Vape Systems, the source of the lethal vape formula, as a criminal enterprise, Rosetti said the evidence would show that Heidecker knew TCH was hazardous but distributed it regardless.

Rosetti also focused on Heidecker's partner in TCH Vape Systems, the late Luther Sanchez, a self-styled holistic healer who operated under the name "Dr. San" despite having no medical degree "or any medical background whatsoever." Clearly hoping to forestall any defense that Heidecker was unaware or uninvolved, he represented the partnership with Sanchez as "a criminal conspiracy" to manufacture, market and sell the TCH vape devices.

The fact that Sanchez committed suicide while in prison, Rosetti argued, implies consciousness of guilt in the form of "grief and remorse."

Rosetti cautioned the jury that defense attorney Mark Dwyer would use "any trick in his book" to convince them Sanchez was solely responsible for the poisonings. Nonetheless, the evidence would show Heidecker was a knowing and willing participant. Witnesses, he said, would testify to Heidecker's "amoral" character and to a pattern of "cold and callous indifference and recklessness toward the lives of others."

Defense attorney Mark Dwyer began by acknowledging that the deaths and injuries at the festival were an "unimaginable tragedy." As Rosetti predicted, he placed the blame squarely on Sanchez, whom he characterized as "a madman." Arguing that this "purported doctor" had "hoodwinked" Heidecker, he insisted the lethal TCH recipe came entirely from "the twisted brain of the late Mr. Sanchez."

Dwyer briefly eulogized the victims, who ranged from a Mormon missionary to a veterinary student. Although they were "good people," he said, "we all make mistakes."

Underscoring the role of personal choice, Dwyer claimed official toxicology reports would show the victims had misused the vape pens by inhaling more than the recommended dosage.

The victims, he said, had also used other dangerous drugs such as Ecstasy, marijuana, heroin and cocaine, any or all of which could've been the actual cause of death.

Challenging Rosetti's depiction of Heidecker as cold and callous, Dwyer said that since the 2015 death of Heidecker's own son, the defendant's primary concern had been "making the world a better place through his music and the poetry of his lyrics."

Dwyer promised that police interrogation tapes would vindicate Heidecker by showing Sanchez acted alone. When Sanchez killed himself, Dwyer said, "justice was served." In a plea for "the American tradition of justice and human decency," he begged

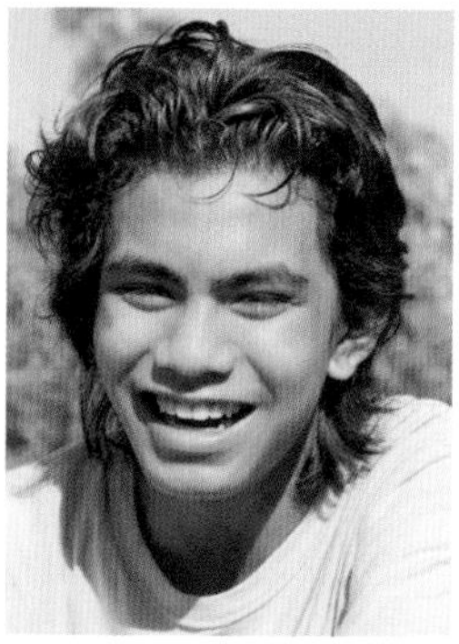
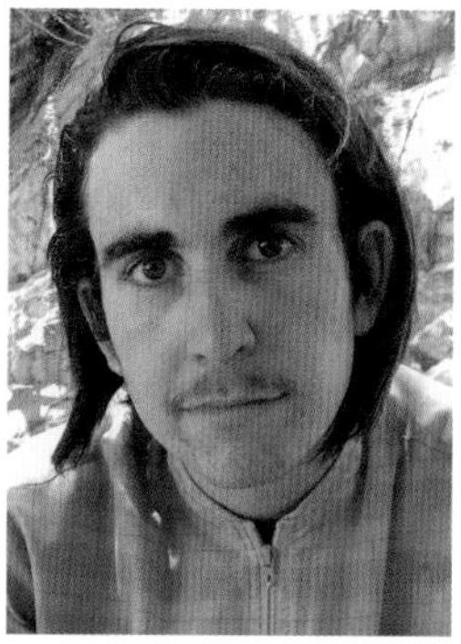
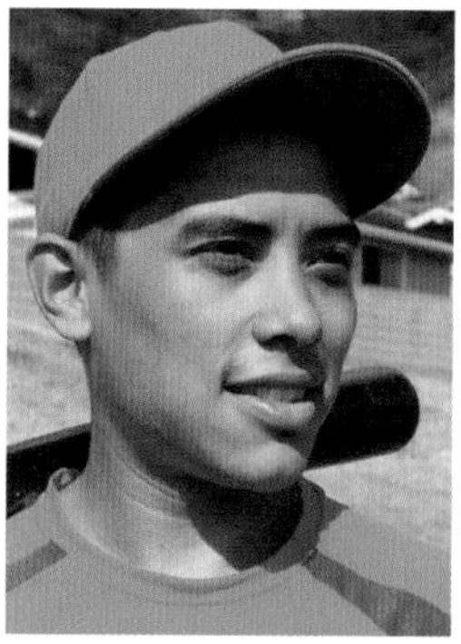
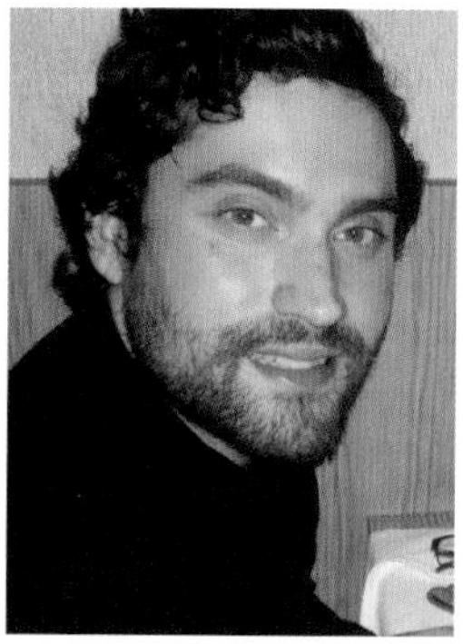
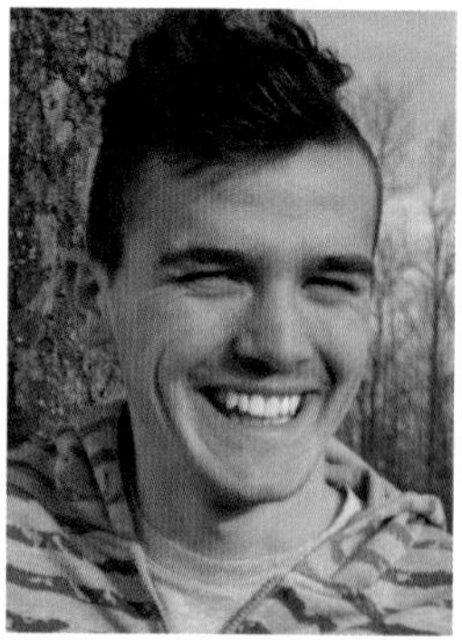
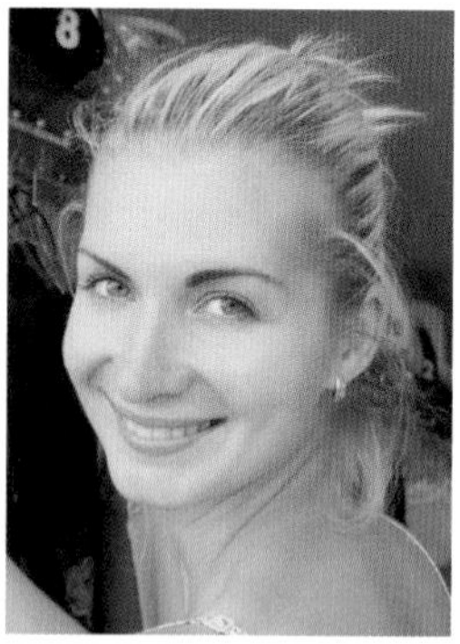
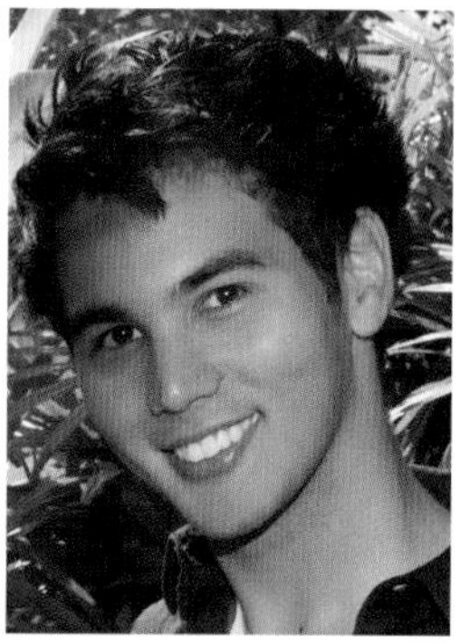
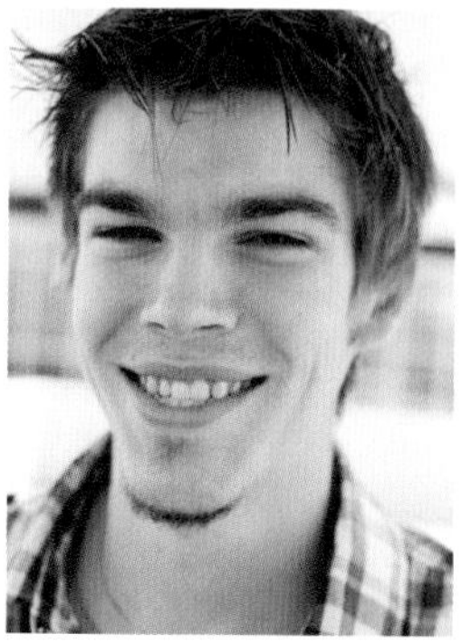
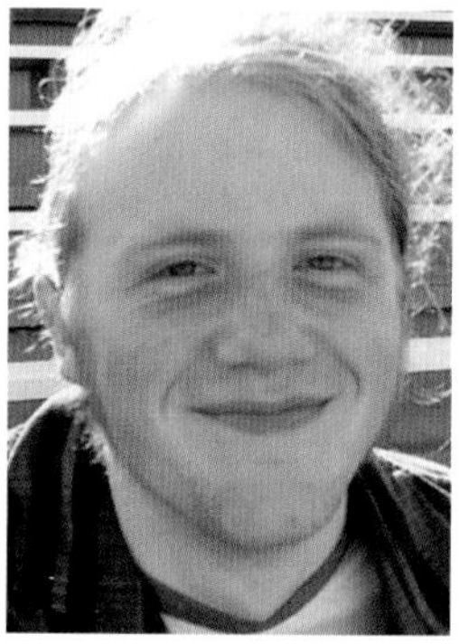
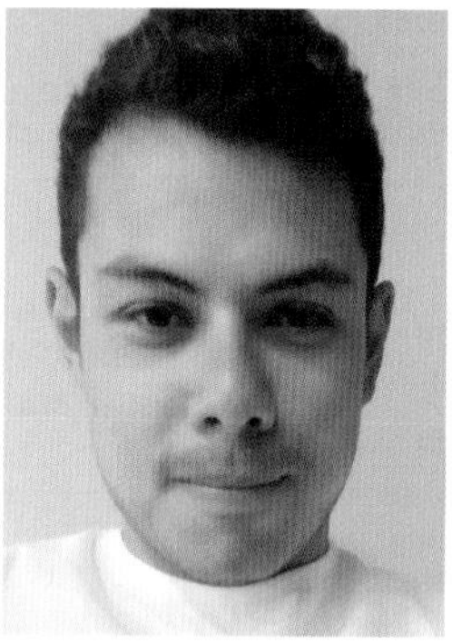
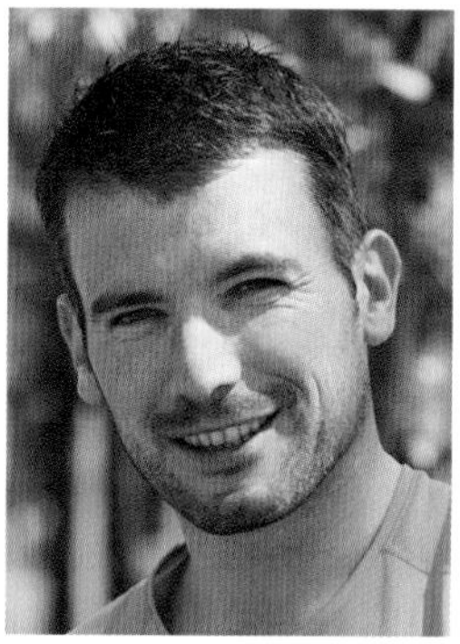
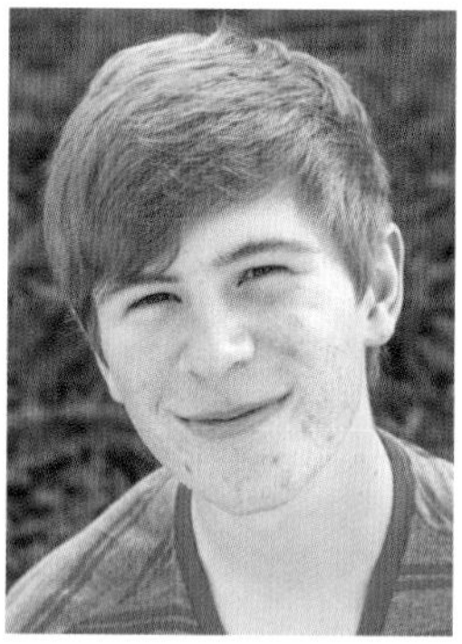
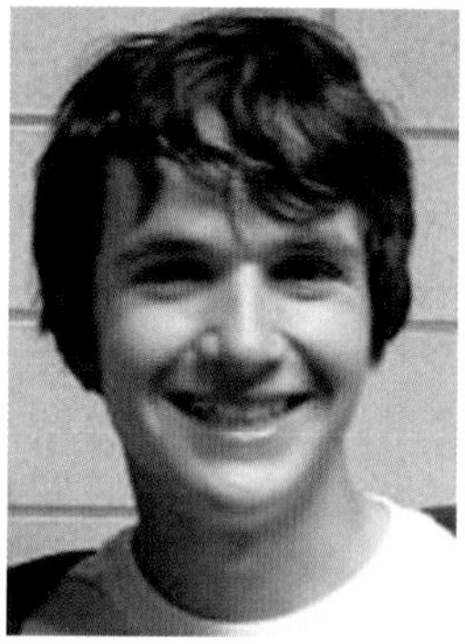
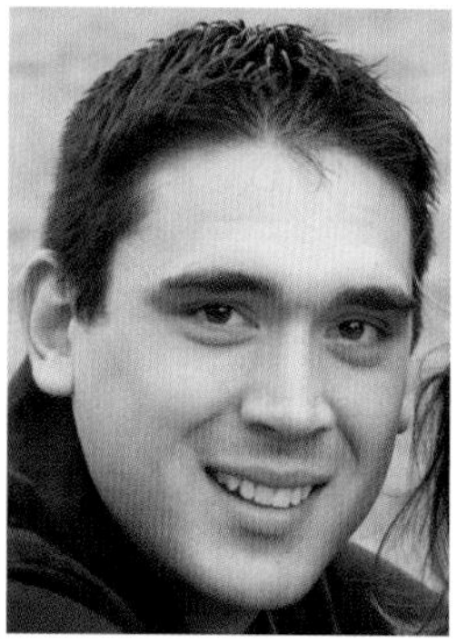
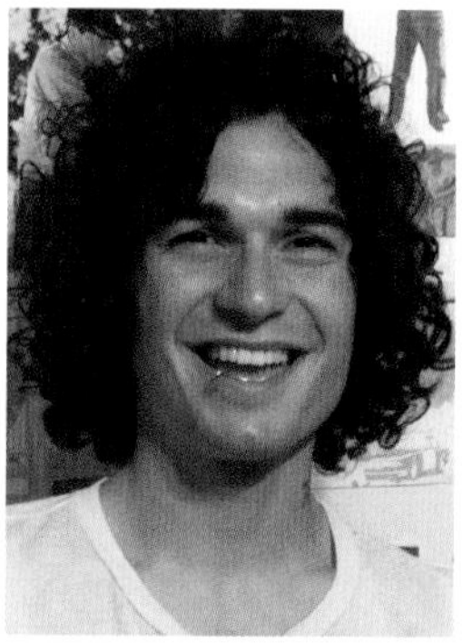
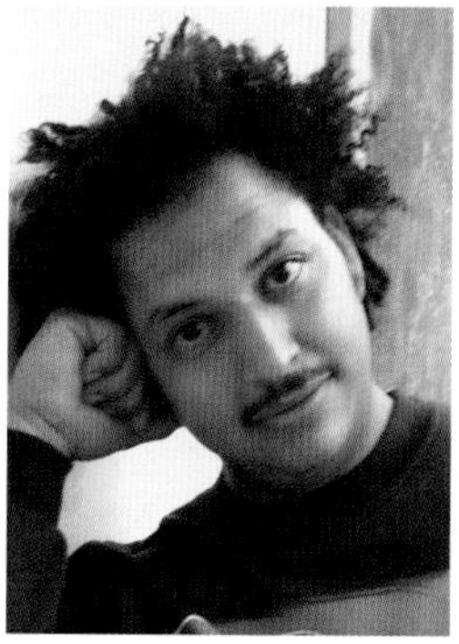
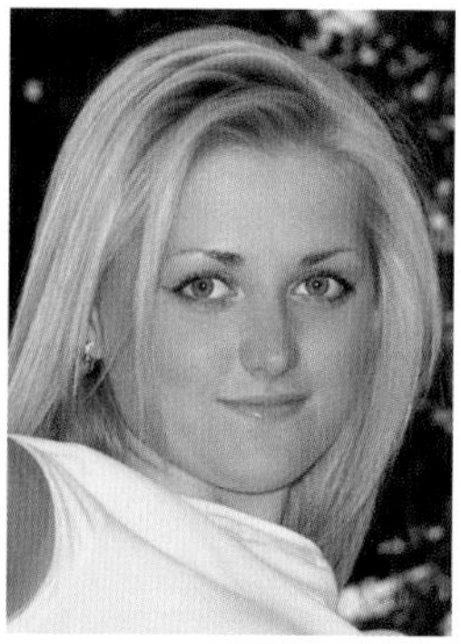
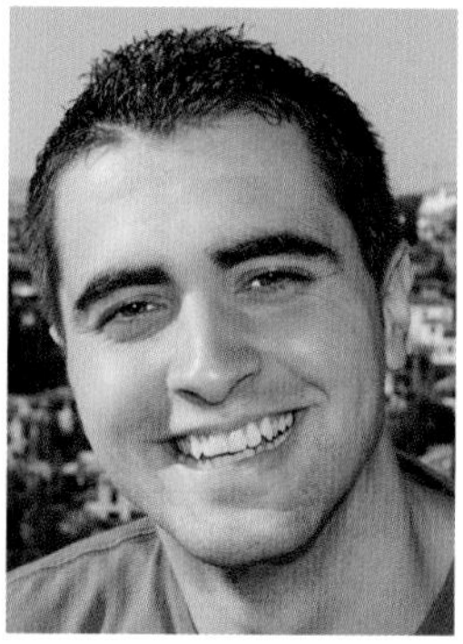

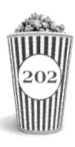

Emily Siroky 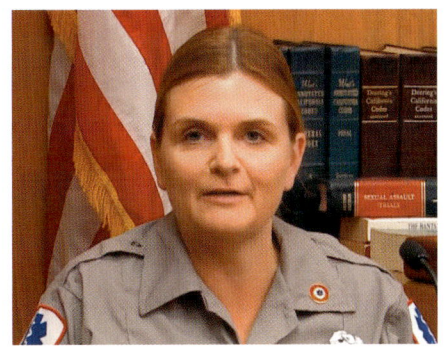   *Lisa Betenzos*    *Jared Jolson*

the jury not to let Heidecker become the "21st victim" of Luther Sanchez.

Testimony of Emily Siroky
Emily Siroky attended the Electric Sun festival with friends. She recalled the event as "really unorganized and chaotic," with inadequate sanitation facilities forcing concertgoers to relieve themselves beside the stage. Despite the intense desert heat, only small bottles of water were available for $10 each.

Siroky witnessed "two guys handing out vape pens," one of whom she positively identified as Heidecker. "He ran over my friend's foot with a golf cart," she added.

Siroky testified that she saw people falling over and going into convulsions during the performance by DKR. "The band kept playing like they didn't notice, and maybe didn't even care," she said.

Dwyer declined to cross-examine Siroky, which visibly agitated Heidecker.

Testimony of Lisa Betenzos
Lisa Betenzos is a regional paramedic who responded to "reports of multiple injuries and incapacitations" at the festival. She testified that while it took her only 10 minutes to reach the grounds, she was unable to reach victims for up to 25 minutes due to "two large moving vans" that blocked the entrance. Forced to enter the site on foot, she and her partner found so many casualties that paramedics had to be summoned from three nearby counties.

Queried about the presence of on-site medical staff, Betenzos said she was referred to Luther Sanchez. However, "he did not appear to have any medical capabilities, nor did he seem to be coherent."

When asked if Sanchez had made any effort to help the victims, Betenzos stated that he "was just placing crystals around the bodies."

In his cross-examination, Dwyer focused on the amount of time it took to reach the victims, suggesting that Betenzo's ambulance could easily have driven through the pedestrian gate.

Betenzos asserted that this entrance was far too small. Under pointed and sometimes hostile questioning, she maintained her belief that paramedics reached the victims as soon as possible given the obstacles in their path.

Testimony of Jared Jolson
Festival attendee Jared Jolson told the court that he became seriously ill after a brief exposure to the TCH vape pen. Asked if he had any interaction with Heidecker, Jolson said, "He was the one who gave me the vape pen."

Jolson inhaled only once from the device. He summarized its effects as "not pleasant" and said they included a burning sensation in the lungs, difficulty breathing and loss of equilibrium.

During DKR's performance, Jolson heard screaming and witnessed numerous people falling down and twitching. "Some of them were foaming out of the mouth," he said.

He expressed shock that DKR continued their performance under these horrific circumstances. This testimony seemed to infuriate the already agitated Heidecker.

Under Dwyer's cross-examination, Jolson admitted that before entering the festival grounds, he and two friends had been "hot boxing," an illicit practice that entails smoking marijuana in a sealed car to intensify its effects.

At this point, Heidecker interrupted Dwyer to demand that he call for a mistrial. This outburst earned Heidecker a sharp rebuke from Judge Szymcyzk.

As the cross-examination resumed, Jolson admitted he had also been under the influence of tequila on the day of the festival. Heidecker again interrupted Dwyer's questioning and was threatened with a contempt citation by Judge Szymcyzk.

Having ascertained that Jolson was intoxicated before attending the festival, Dwyer challenged his ability to accurately recollect subsequent events. He also suggested the symptoms Jolson attributed to the vape pen could have been caused by the other drugs in his system.

At this point, another heated dispute erupted between Heidecker and Dwyer, leading Judge Szymcyzk to announce a recess until the following day.

Electric Sun 20 Trial: Day 1
Eyewitnesses claim Heidecker initially tried to prevent medical personnel from entering the festival

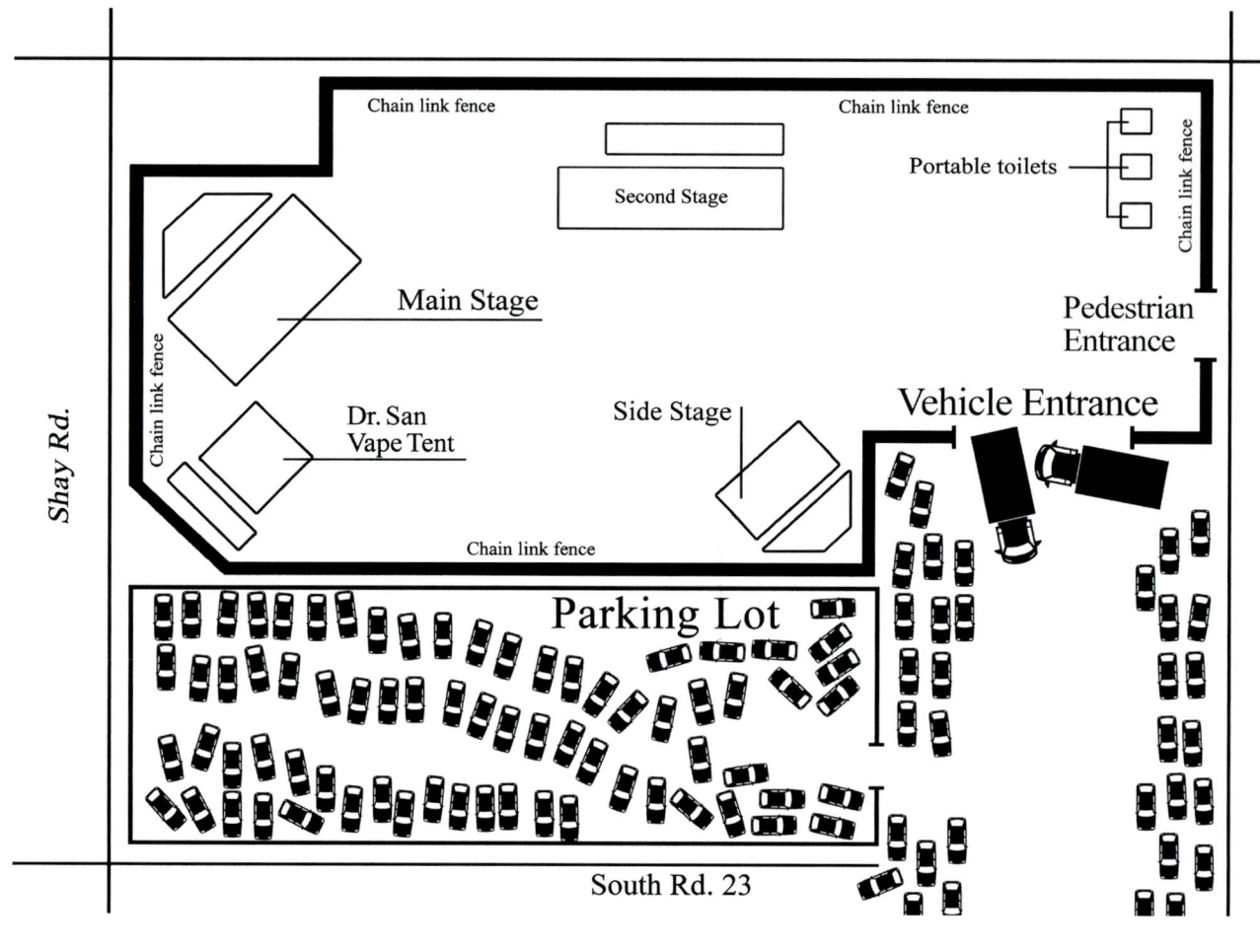

ELECTRIC SUN 20 MURDER TRIAL: LEAD ATTORNEYS

Vincent Rosetti, born 10-1-1964, is the district attorney for San Bernardino County. He joined the District Attorney's Office as deputy district attorney in 2006 and served as chief deputy from 2008 to 2013.

Rosetti has prosecuted approximately 60 jury trials, including 18 murder trials. Most notably, he successfully prosecuted a former mayoral candidate in Hesperia, California, for the botched contract killing of a political rival. Rosetti has also brought numerous successful fraud and corruption cases against county political figures; he famously put Apple Valley's treasurer behind bars, along with several staffers for a political action committee who were found to be laundering money from the sale of methamphetamine throughout California's 33rd State Assembly district.

Rosetti is a graduate of University of Southern California and has a law degree from UCLA School of Law. A devout Roman Catholic, he has been married to his wife, Elaine, for 20 years. They have two sons, Stefano, 15, and Blake, 17, who currently attend Aquinas High School. He coaches them in soccer and baseball.

Mark Dwyer, born 8-15-1966, is a criminal defense attorney primarily serving clients in San Bernardino and Riverside counties, as well as out-of-town and out-of-state clients who face legal problems while visiting the Inland Empire.

Although he has almost six years of courtroom and trial experience, Dwyer has not previously served as lead counsel in a murder case. His solo practice has specialized primarily in online and campus free speech issues, with a focus on defending clients accused of online harassment and cyberstalking. Colleagues describe Dwyer as "tenacious" and "aggressive" and note his high rate of acquittals in this relatively new area of litigation.

Dwyer graduated from University of Antelope Valley and Arizona Summit Law School. He worked for almost a decade as an intern at the Center for Libertarian Studies before entering private practice.

Dwyer has since won professional recognition as a "Super Lawyer" and is also a member of the Republican National Lawyers Association. He is unmarried and currently divides his time between his office in San Bernardino and his home in Hesperia.

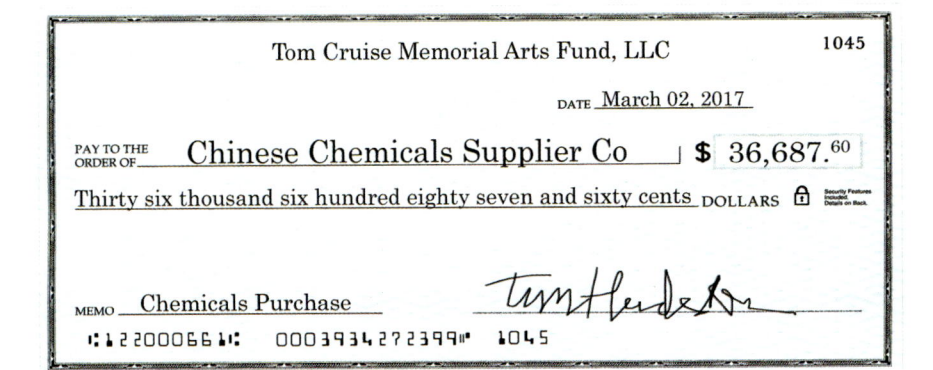

Tom Cruise Memorial Arts Fund, LLC   1045

DATE March 02, 2017

PAY TO THE ORDER OF: Chinese Chemicals Supplier Co $ 36,687.60

Thirty six thousand six hundred eighty seven and sixty cents DOLLARS

MEMO: Chemicals Purchase

⑁¦:122000661¦: 0003934272399⑁' 1045

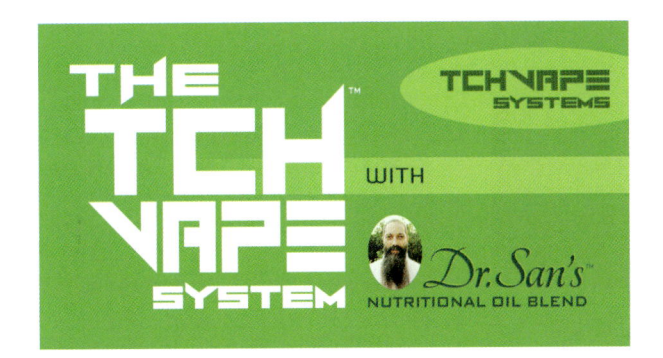

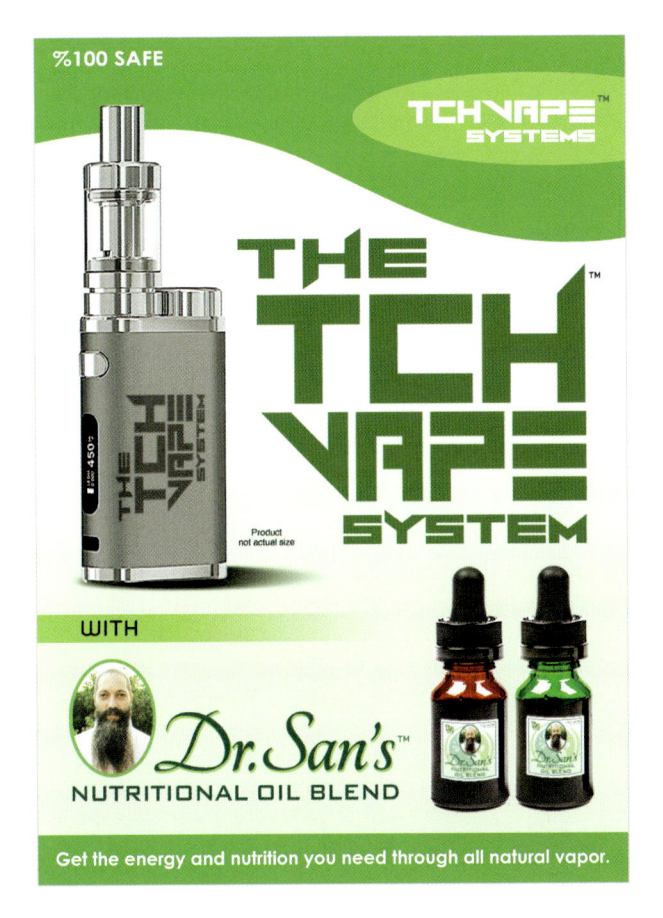

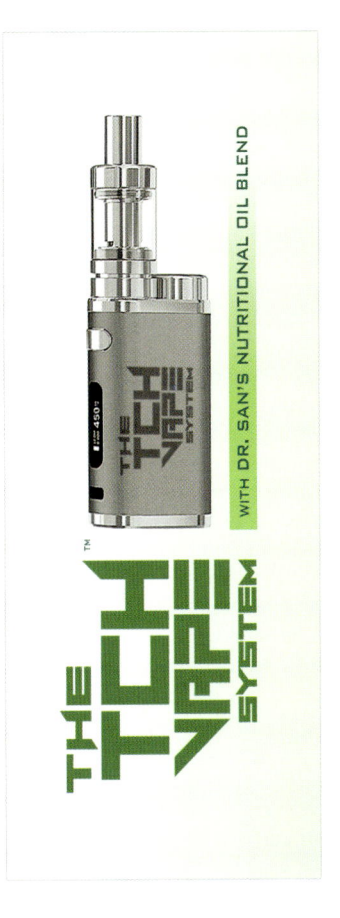

Dr. San's™ NUTRITIONAL OIL BLEND

THE TCH VAPE SYSTEM — TCHVAPE SYSTEMS — WITH Dr. San's™ NUTRITIONAL OIL BLEND

%100 SAFE

TCHVAPE SYSTEMS

THE TCH VAPE SYSTEM™

Product not actual size

WITH Dr. San's™ NUTRITIONAL OIL BLEND

Get the energy and nutrition you need through all natural vapor.

WITH DR. SAN'S NUTRITIONAL OIL BLEND

THE TCH VAPE SYSTEM

ELECTRIC SUN 20 TRIAL
Day Two

Air date: November 16, 2017
Running time: 1:23:36

At the opening of the session, Heidecker notified Judge Szymcyzk that he had fired his attorney, Mark Dwyer, due to "strategic differences" and would henceforth be representing himself.

Judge Szymcyzk advised Heidecker of the legal risks involved and warned that he would be held to professional standards for "courtesy and decorum."

Heidecker then requested and received permission to make a new opening statement reflecting his altered defense strategy.

DA Rosetti objected that allowing the "obviously incompetent" Heidecker to represent himself could lead to a mistrial. But Judge Szymcyzk affirmed Heidecker's constitutional right to self-representation.

Heidecker's Opening Statement
Addressing the jury, Heidecker asked them to "disregard the statements of Mr. Dwyer from yesterday." He declared that there was "no evidence" to support a guilty verdict. Instead, they should see him as yet another victim of Sanchez. This argument touched on the death of his young son, Tom Cruise Heidecker Jr., while under Sanchez's care.

Acknowledging that the TCH formula was toxic, Heidecker speculated that this may have been due to contaminated ingredients from Chinese suppliers.

Standing before the victims' photos, he related a conversation he and the late Christopher Delgado allegedly had on the day of the festival, during which Delgado said, "If anything should happen to me today — and you know, I hope it doesn't — I want you to know, I want the world to know, you didn't do anything wrong today."

The state's hearsay objection was upheld, leading Heidecker to call the proceedings "a kangaroo court" in which he was being "unjustly prosecuted for crimes of which I did not commit."

Regaining his composure, he said it was time to "put this all behind us" and move on. "I got news for the parents," he said. "Nobody's coming back."

Restating his claim that Sanchez was solely responsible, and observing that "you can't put a corpse in the electric chair," he argued that he had been made "the fall guy."

When Judge Szymcyzk directed him to conclude his often rambling statement, Heidecker made a final plea to the jury: "Remember one thing — innocent, didn't do it, was actually on stage."

Judge Szymcyzk cautioned the jury that because Heidecker was not under oath, his opening statement should not be regarded as evidence.

Testimony of Detective William Ellis
Detective Ellis, a 25-year veteran of the San Bernardino police force, recalled arriving at the Electric Sun festival and finding a "chaotic situation" with many "bodies on the ground." He confirmed other witnesses' accounts of the festival's lack of water and sanitation.

Describing the vape tent area, Ellis said the ground was littered with discarded vape devices. Rosetti then introduced a festival map with an overlay showing the location of bodies. Heidecker's objection that this map consisted of "dots that absolutely don't refer to anything" was overruled.

Ellis testified that when he spoke to Heidecker at the "vape tent," Heidecker identified himself as a performer. After questioning Luther Sanchez and other attendees, Ellis learned Heidecker was in fact the festival's organizer.

Rosetti asked what Sanchez was doing during this time. "He was trying to administrate [sic] more vapor to a victim on the ground," Ellis stated.

Heidecker objected that this was "speculation" and was again overruled.

Rosetti asked Ellis if he knew why Sanchez was administering vapor to the victim.

"He was saying that in order to counteract the negative effect of the vapor, he had to administer more vapor into the victim," Ellis responded. He added that he and two officers had to physically tear Sanchez away from the victim.

Sanchez was later taken into custody, where Ellis interrogated him at length. With Judge Szymcyzk's permission, Rosetti played excerpts from the tape.

Interrogation of Luther Sanchez
Shirtless in the interrogation room, Sanchez told Ellis the TCH formula consisted of "Chinese herbs" that he and Heidecker had "pulled together." These included the fungus *Cordyceps sinensis* and venom from the poisonous toad *Bufo alvarius*.

Chillingly, Sanchez claimed the latter substance "is in our bodies in high percentages when we're born and when we die, so it's kind of like a gateway chemical that enables us to pass from one life into another."

Sanchez stressed that although he and Heidecker had "worked on this formula together," Heidecker was "the idea man."

Ellis asked Sanchez to explain the purpose of the drug: "What did you want these kids to do?"

Sanchez said they "wanted to bring people together" in a spiritual sense. The music of DKR was part of this scheme: Heidecker "wanted everyone to experience the music on a cellular level, where they would take a hit off the vape pipe, and they would just internalize the music."

Queried about checking IDs, Sanchez said he and Heidecker "weren't really worried" about the age of the vape users.

"Well, you should be worried," Ellis told him. "How many people you think got carried away and put in an ambulance?"

"I don't know." Sanchez seemed shaken by the question. "We didn't want to hurt anyone."

"Well, you did!" Ellis shouted. "One girl was 12 years old!" Questioned about his criminal record, Sanchez confessed he had been arrested for a variety of "misunderstandings," including "bad checks" and "a little bit of cocaine stuff from 15 years ago."

"Large or small quantities?" Ellis asked.

"That's all relative," Sanchez shrugged. At this point, Ellis placed Sanchez under arrest on suspicion of murder.

Sanchez asked what would happen to Heidecker: "We were partners, and we worked together on this."

"I guarantee you I'll be talking to him," Ellis replied. Asked if he had any further statements to make, Sanchez burst into tears. "We tried so hard to do something beautiful," he said between sobs.

Det. William Ellis

Dr. Gerard Kearny

Gregg Turkington

Heidecker's Financial Records

Once the tape ended, Rosetti asked Ellis if he had later retrieved financial records from Heidecker's "portable office" on the festival grounds. Ellis confirmed he had recovered roughly 100 such documents.

Rosetti produced one of these documents, which Ellis identified as "an invoice from a chemical company in Shanghai" for 1,3-dimethlamylamine, a "synthetic stimulant" more commonly known as DMAA. Rosetti called the chemical "a tongue twister." Heidecker objected that it is not "officially a tongue twister" and was overruled.

Rosetti then introduced a check made payable to K2 Biochemical Ltd. by Tim Heidecker for the Tom Cruise Memorial Arts Foundation, which Ellis described as "a so-called charitable organization."

Heidecker objected to the insinuation that his foundation was not charitable, which he called "disrespectful to my late son." Judge Szymcyzk sustained this objection and had the words stricken from the record.

Ellis detailed Heidecker's complex network of businesses, which included television shows, musical groups, a publishing venture and a failed restaurant-cinema. Ellis explained that these businesses were essentially sole proprietorships operating under fictitious business names. Despite Heidecker's use of legal identifiers like "Inc." and "LLC," they were not registered with the state of California.

Rosetti questioned how Heidecker had gotten the money to launch so many businesses. Ellis said he had received two life insurance payouts on the demise of his son, each of which totaled $1 million.

"Would you say it's typical for someone to take out multiple million-dollar life insurance policies on a newborn son?" Rosetti asked. Ellis said it was "highly unusual."

In his cross-examination, Heidecker first asked Ellis if he had ever been charged with police brutality. The prosecution's objection to this question was upheld.

He then asked whether the full Luther Sanchez interrogation tape had been shown in court. Ellis said the tape had been edited. Heidecker demanded to know what was removed, speculating that it may have been "footage of Mr. Sanchez taking back everything he said." Ellis testified that no exculpatory material had been cut.

Heidecker asked Ellis if the Electric Sun 20 had been ordered to attend the festival by state or federal authorities. Ellis said they had not. Heidecker then asked if they had also "ingested the vape juices on their own free will." Ellis stated that their will could not have been free because they didn't know the vape pens would kill them.

Heidecker wondered if police had been investigating "the Chinese role in this scandal," implying that it was being downplayed "for PC reasons." Specifically, he asked whether Ellis had traveled to Shanghai to interview chemists or staff at K2 Biochemical Ltd. Ellis said there was no need to do so, as the nature and source of the chemicals were already known.

After repeatedly rejecting Heidecker's allegations of evidence tampering or "a Chinese connection," Ellis was dismissed.

Testimony of Dr. Gerard Kearny

Dr. Kearny is chief medical examiner at the San Bernardino County Sheriff-Coroner's Office. Asked by Rosetti to identify the cause of death for the Electric Sun 20, Dr. Kearny described a process of "nervous system shutdown," asphyxiation and cardiac arrest. He also noted that the autopsies had detected "many toxic chemicals" in the victim's bodies, including "formaldehyde, benzene as well as mercuric compounds."

In his cross-examination, Heidecker wondered how the "toxicality" of these compounds could be known. Dr. Kearny responded that they were sent to the state crime lab for testing. Heidecker questioned the efficacy of this method by dipping a torn strip from his legal pad into his coffee and asking how this "test" could determine whether the drink was caffeinated. Dr. Kearny explained that drug testing strips do reveal the presence of specific drugs.

Under further questioning, Dr. Kearny conceded that one victim, Shawn Levin, had died of a heroin overdose rather than from the TCH compound. Heidecker pulled Levin's photo triumphantly from the display of victims and tore it into pieces.

Heidecker alleged that the Levin results cast the other deaths into question, but Dr. Kearny reaffirmed that the other 19 toxicology reports had identified TCH as the cause of death.

Heidecker challenged Dr. Kearny's

100008733

KZ CHEMICAL SOLUTIONS
大时间化学品供应

Bill To:
TOM CRUISE HEIDECKER MEMORIAL ARTS FUND, LLC
PO#: DKR-2381
ORDER NUMBER: 08733
02/12/2017

买家信息

美国汇率
```
974+2-14*->+6-9/*36-619<3<3
*69617/-//739794026564*65*0
*60/67+/31142*<0<><2424+615
</>2683+6>*91/7264+<7/<1780
```

SUBSTANCE	产品规格	ID#	UNITS	PRICE	IMPORT TAX	ADJUSTED PRICE
DRAGON BREATH X9	液体	2301	300单位	29357.13	13.273%	33253.70
LAVA MONSTER	片剂	4099	150单位	9785.70	17.492%	11497.41
SPACE ROXX	粉末	4099	30单位	5871.43	17.492%	6898.46
SPIDER BAIT	溶剂	4097	600单位	39142.80	17.492%	45989.66
ANGEL WINGS	加油站	1443	900单位	29357.07	14.311%	33558.36
FAIRY LIGHTNING	高浓度	2184	150单位	19571.40	15.702%	22644.50
MONKEY'S PAW	液体	0380	300单位	58714.20	15.702%	67933.50
				15668.43	12.198%	17579.66

危险化学品

TOTAL: ¥ .... 239342.56   TOTAL: $ 36687.60

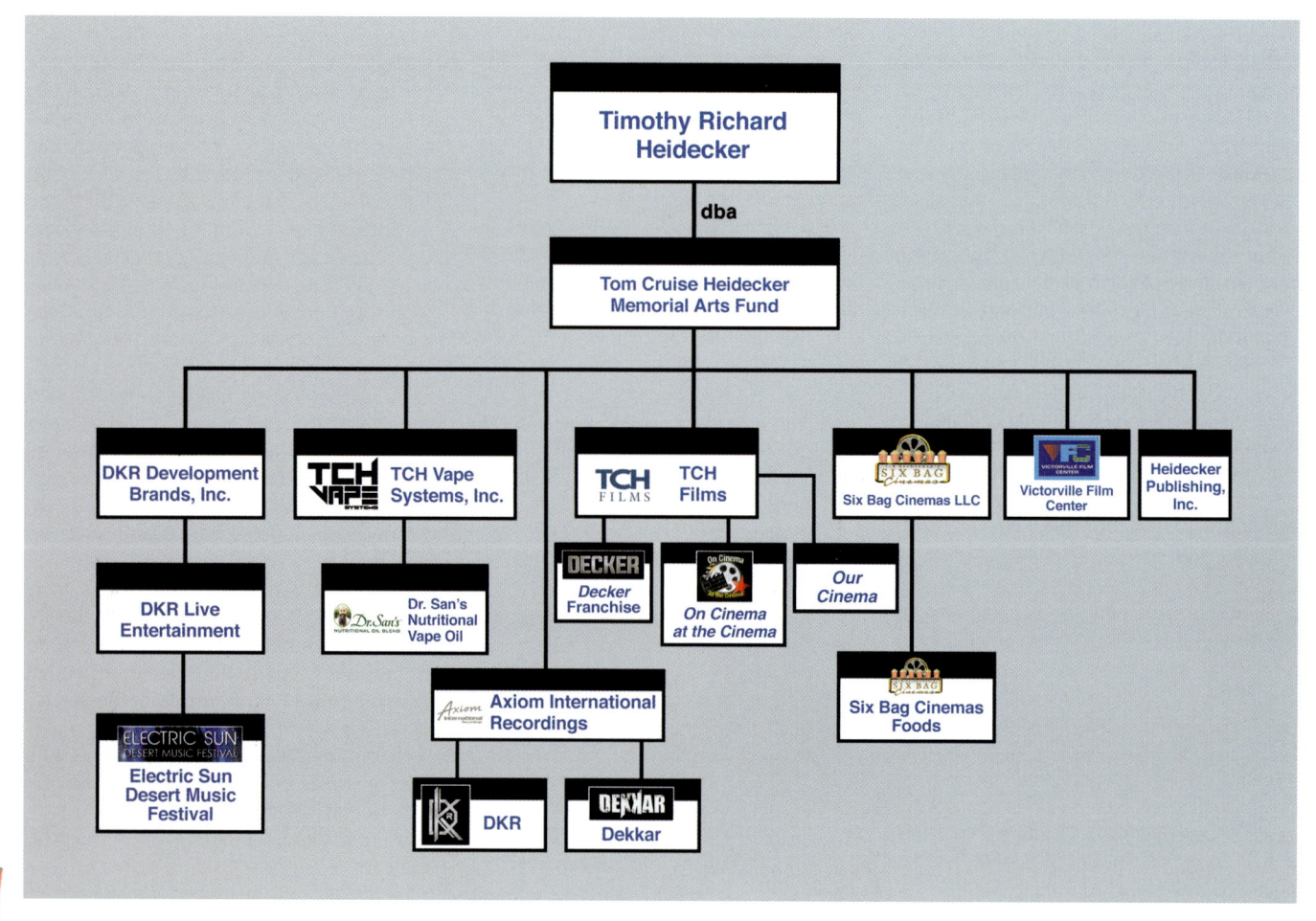

卖家信息
大型大化学品
505山路
中国香港
+852-011-555-1500

¥: 239342.56
$: 36687.60

收到: *signature: Tim Heidecker*

Timothy Richard Heidecker
dba
Tom Cruise Heidecker Memorial Arts Fund

- DKR Development Brands, Inc.
  - DKR Live Entertainment
    - Electric Sun Desert Music Festival
- TCH Vape Systems, Inc.
  - Dr. San's Nutritional Vape Oil
    - Axiom International Recordings
      - DKR
      - Dekkar
- TCH Films
  - Decker Franchise
  - On Cinema at the Cinema
  - Our Cinema
- Six Bag Cinemas LLC
  - Six Bag Cinemas Foods
- Victorville Film Center
- Heidecker Publishing, Inc.

208

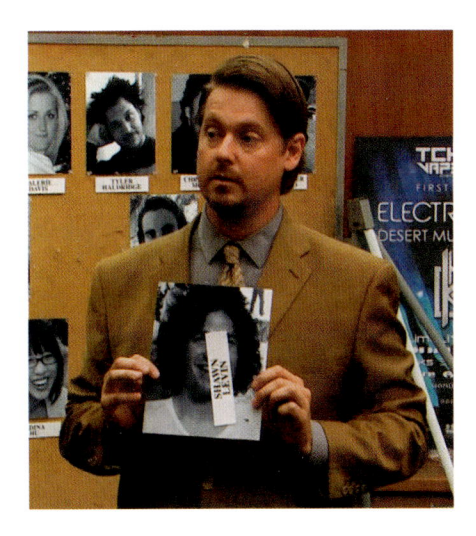

expertise, noting that Sanchez, too, had advertised himself as a doctor but had "turned out to be a quack." This earned Heidecker a stern reprimand from Judge Szymcyzk.

Testimony of Gregg Turkington
Gregg Turkington is an amateur actor and movie buff who frequently served as a "film expert" on Heidecker's movie review program, On Cinema. He testified that Heidecker had often invited "Dr. San" on the show to provide health advice.

Assistant DA Miriam Waymon asked Turkington if Sanchez and Heidecker also promoted the Electric Sun festival on air.

"They did," he said, adding that such promotions "ruined the show" by interfering with Turkington's discussion of movies.

Asked if Heidecker had ever advertised the vape pen on the program, Turkington said it was "one of a lot" of products advertised. He alleged that Heidecker often discussed other topics than cinema because he had failed to watch the movies scheduled for review. This sparked a furious protest from Heidecker, who objected to having his "name thrown under the bus."

Waymon played the jury an On Cinema clip in which Heidecker announced that he and "Dr. San" had created a new vape oil called TCH. "We're gonna be giving away as much as we can this weekend," Heidecker said.

Turkington testified that Heidecker had also worked the vape pens into the plot of their self-produced spy drama, Decker. Describing his colleague as often "out of his mind on these vapes," Turkington painted a picture of a one-time movie aficionado who had lost the capacity to stay conscious through films, let alone to review them.

Explaining that the two men formerly ran a movie theater in Victorville, Turkington accused Heidecker first of embezzling funds to buy drugs and then of setting fire to the theater to collect the insurance.

Turkington's film collection was lost in this fire. He alleged that this was the *third* time Heidecker had destroyed his collection and speculated that he was motivated by jealousy because his music had "zero fans."

Asked if he'd ever sampled the TCH vape system, Turkington said film was his sole form of escapism: "The greatest high you're gonna get is watching something like *Casablanca* for the 10th time and you see something completely different than you've ever seen before. There's a new depth to a certain scene. That's a high that I can live with."

Waymon asked Turkington to describe the relationship between Heidecker and Sanchez. In response, he summarized a scene from Season 6 of the *Decker* series: "Dr. San brings in a vape. Tim is dead — his character Decker has died — and Dr. San inhales the vape and breathes the vape on Tim's dead body and brings him back to life." Turkington indicated that although this scene was fictional, it captured Heidecker's view of Sanchez as an all-powerful healer.

Turkington said Heidecker and Sanchez had fallen out after Heidecker contracted a serious infection from unsterilized acupuncture needles. "A couple of years later, he brings him back into his life and lets him give herbal treatments to his son," he recalled.

Sanchez advised Heidecker not to vaccinate his son. Later, Turkington said, "Little Tom got very, very sick — it was clear to anyone that he needed to be hospitalized. And Dr. San said, 'No no no, I can take care of it.' Until the point that the kid died."

When asked if Heidecker used other drugs, Turkington would say only that Heidecker's behavior had often been "erratic." As an example, he alleged that Heidecker had compelled him to falsely claim on camera that he had never seen the movie *Sully*. Turkington speculated that Heidecker might also ask defense witnesses to lie on the stand. Heidecker's objection to this speculation was sustained.

Waymon asked Turkington if he believed Heidecker "was aware of the toxic substances in the TCH vape system."

"I think if he thought it would kill people, he wouldn't have given it to them," Turkington answered. "I just don't think he did the tests that he should've."

He recalled that Heidecker and Sanchez had repeatedly changed the vape formulation after it made Heidecker sick. Sanchez spoke of using herbs, but Turkington said the odor was closer to burning tires or overheated brake pads.

In closing, Waymon played an *On Cinema* clip in which Heidecker described a recent visit to a medical doctor who detected numerous toxic substances in his body, including cocaine and methamphetamine.

In his cross-examination, Heidecker cast doubt on Turkington's "expertise in movies," pointing out that he lacks "any formal degrees" in film studies.

Conceding that Turkington had often seen him use TCH, Heidecker then asked the witness to confirm that he was still alive.

"Today, yeah," Turkington said. "Other days, I wasn't so sure."

He asked Turkington to confirm that after the medical visit described on *On Cinema*, Heidecker and Sanchez adjusted the vape formula to make it safer.

"It looks like you adjusted it to be *less* safe, because all these kids died," Turkington said.

Heidecker asked Turkington if it was true that his apartment — in which Heidecker and his family were living at the time of his son's death — was full of black mold. Turkington verified this, but he rejected Heidecker's assertion that this had caused his son's death. He also noted that Heidecker had evicted him several months earlier.

At this point, Heidecker ended his cross-examination, but not before promising to call Turkington back to the stand.

ELECTRIC SUN 20 TRIAL
Day Three

Air date: November 17, 2017
Running time: 42:16 minutes

The third day of proceedings started on a quiet note but became increasingly contentious as Heidecker sparred with the judge, prosecutors and witnesses.

Testimony of Amanda Davis
The prosecution's first witness was Amanda Davis, mother of Valerie Davis. She remembered her late daughter as "the type of person that, when she walked in the room, the room lit up." Choking back tears, she said the 17-year-old girl "wanted to be a nurse" and "loved helping people."

Miriam Waymon asked if her daughter normally used vape pens. Davis said that to the best of her knowledge, she did not.

"If there was anything that you could say to her, what would that be?" Waymon asked. Heidecker objected that this question was "speculative" and was overruled.

"I would tell her how much I love her, and she was a wonderful person," Ms. Davis said. "And I would do anything to have her back." She glared at Heidecker. "And that man over there is responsible. He is responsible for me losing her."

Heidecker began his cross-examination by expressing his condolences to Ms. Davis: "From one grieving parent to another, I'm with you here." Because they both belong to this "special club," he said, he had "no reason to disbelieve her testimony." He then invited the court to observe a moment of silence for Valerie Davis. However, he continued talking until Judge Szymcyzk rebuked him into actual silence.

Testimony of Mark Proksch
The state's next witness was Mark Proksch, a "comedy celebrity impersonator" who was formerly employed by Heidecker as an actor, waiter and food concessionaire.

Amanda Davis

Mark Proksch

Allessandro Serradimigni

Ayaka Ohtani

"Were you ever physically abused by Mr. Heidecker?" DA Rosetti asked him.

"Watch it, Mark," Heidecker called out. Though obviously unnerved, Proksch confirmed the abuse.

"Good luck looking for evidence," Heidecker scoffed. Judge Szymcyzk directed him to stop addressing the witness, leading to a heated confrontation as Heidecker attempted to shout the judge down.

Once order was restored, Proksch testified that Heidecker had struck him on "many occasions" and had even broken his nose. Rosetti then showed the jury a montage of clips from *On Cinema*'s annual Oscar specials, which documented multiple violent confrontations between Proksch and an enraged Tim Heidecker.

In his cross-examination, Heidecker asked Proksch if these specials were created "for entertainment purposes." Proksch agreed that they were. Heidecker then suggested that in acting, "sometimes people get hurt."

"None of your violence was planned," Proksch responded. "I think you got angry and you hit me and you threw stuff at me."

"I would reconsider that answer if I were you," Heidecker said. In light of Heidecker's menacing demeanor, Judge Szymcyzk directed the bailiff to stand beside Proksch.

Heidecker next tried to ascertain Proksch's whereabouts on the day of the festival. Having told Proksch "to secure an *On Cinema* food truck," he demanded to know why this truck had never appeared. "You didn't give me any money," Proksch answered. "You didn't tell me where I can find one."

Heidecker said this answer indicated that Proksch was "not to be believed or trusted." As Proksch's legal employer, he asserted "the constitutional right" to "strike" Proksch for disobedience. "He's still under my supervision," he added, advancing on the witness.

"This defendant is intimidating this witness," Rosetti objected.

Wheeling around, Heidecker pointed his pencil threateningly at the DA. "I'll intimidate you, believe me!" he shouted.

As Judge Szymcyzk rose angrily from his seat to restore order, Heidecker lashed out verbally at him as well. Rosetti moved that Heidecker be held in contempt.

"Fine, hold me in contempt!" Heidecker sneered. "Stack on another charge."

Judge Szymcyzk directed Heidecker not to address counsel, and Heidecker threatened to report him to the bar for failing to "put this court in order." Judge Szymcyzk retorted sarcastically that he would "love" for Heidecker to make such a report.

Rosetti charged again that the defendant was attempting to intimidate Proksch, but Heidecker claimed Proksch had nothing to fear while under the deputy's protection. He repeated that as Proksch's employer, he had the "right" to direct his testimony.

"He is under my control!" he bellowed, lunging suddenly at the witness. As the deputy restrained him, he yelled, "I'll fuck you up, Mark! Believe me, I'll fuck you up!"

The deputy forcibly escorted Heidecker from the courtroom, and Judge Szymcyzk declared a one-hour recess.

On returning, Judge Szymcyzk apologized for losing his temper: "That is the first time in 20 years on the bench that I've ever raised my voice during a court proceeding." He told Heidecker a contempt citation had been filed and advised the jury that Heidecker's outburst would "be dealt with in a separate proceeding and should not affect … your judgment on the merits of the case."

Heidecker apologized to the court, the prosecution and the jury. "I'm a babe in the woods when it comes to being a lawyer," he said. "I apologize for my reckless behavior."

"The court accepts your apology," Judge Szymcyzk replied. "And it is the court's earnest hope that we will continue this proceeding with decorum, with dignity and respect." Heidecker vowed to do so.

Testimony of Allessandro Serradimigni

Allessandro Serradimigni is a member of Heidecker's music groups Dekkar and DKR, who performs under the stage name "Axiom." Asked to define his relationship with Heidecker, Serradimigni said, "Me and Tim, we are brothers to the end."

Rosetti asked whether Heidecker gives him "any type of payments on a regular basis — a stipend or anything like that."

"In the beginning, he was paying me a stipend," Serradimigni said. But over time, the relationship became "a two-way street."

"Did he ever tell you where he gets his money?"

"It's none of my business, honestly."

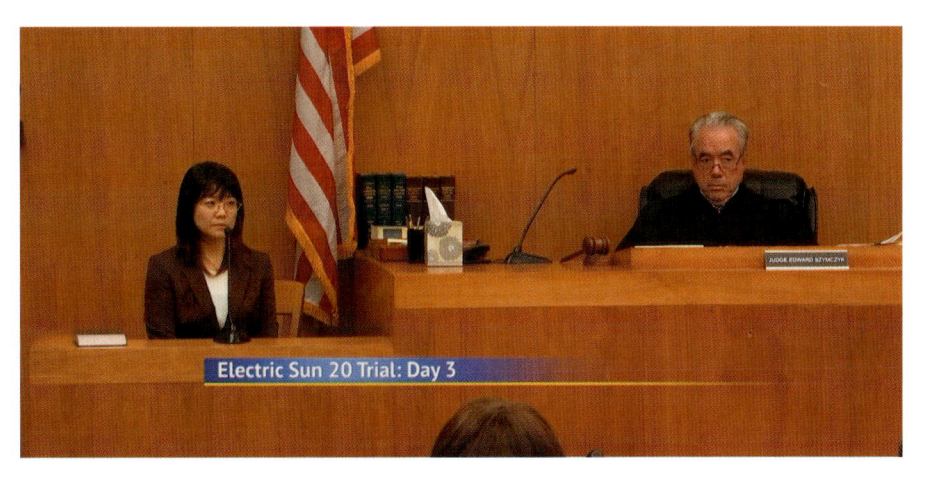

Rosetti asked who wrote Dekkar's music. Serradimigni explained that as "the boss," Heidecker did. At this point, Rosetti played a rock song with Italian lyrics and asked Serradimigni if he recognized the track.

"It's an older song from a past band I had back in Italy," he answered.

"Did the defendant Tim Heidecker ever hear the song?" Rosetti asked.

"I guess he might."

Rosetti then asked specifically if Heidecker had used Serradimigni's track as the basis of a Dekkar song called "Empty Bottle."

"He might, he might not," Serradimigni shrugged. "It's not relevant to me."

Rosetti played the Dekkar track, which bore a strong resemblance to the previous song. Afterward, Rosetti asked why Heidecker had taken sole writing credit for this song when Serradimigni was "obviously the composer." Serradimigni declined to answer.

Approaching the witness, Rosetti noted that the musician is missing his right hand. "What happened?" he asked.

"I donated it to Tim. He needed it more than me. Would you do it for your brother? I did."

"I don't believe my brother would ask me to donate my right hand," Rosetti replied. But Serradimigni insisted his sacrifice was necessary "for the quality of the band."

"You would do anything for Mr. Heidecker," Rosetti said. "Is that correct?

"Yes, that's correct."

"Including lie?"

"I wouldn't say so, because I didn't lie today."

In his cross-examination, Heidecker asked Serradimigni to provide the gist of the lyrics to his song. He said it's about "having a good time, catching up with friends."

"And the lyrics to 'Empty Bottle'?"

"I would say it's completely the opposite." Heidecker had no further questions.

Testimony of Ayaka Ohtani

The prosecution's next witness was Ayaka Ohtani, Heidecker's former wife and the mother of their deceased child. She told the court that she came to the United States as a foreign exchange student and stayed with Heidecker and his first wife. After Heidecker's divorce, she said, "We fell in love. And soon I became pregnant with his son. Tim wanted me to get an abortion, but I chose to keep the baby.

"I was a very young mother, and Tim was busy with work. So when Tom Jr. got sick, Dr. San took him under his care, But he didn't get better. And he died."

"What kind of man would you say Tim Heidecker is?" Miriam Waymon asked.

"Tim is a very confused and angry man."

"Can you talk a little bit about Mr. Heidecker's relationship with Dr. San?"

"Dr. San made so many mistakes, but Tim kept forgiving him. Including the death of our son. I don't understand why Tim kept dealing with Dr. San."

Ohtani went on to say that after moving back to Japan, she remarried and had a daughter.

"Your witness, Mr. Heidecker," Waymon said. Visibly shaken, Heidecker stammered that he had not expected to see his ex-wife on the stand.

In his cross-examination, he haltingly sought details on Ohtani's new husband. He also asked if her daughter was his child: "Do we need to do a paternity test or anything?" The prosecution's objection to this line of questioning was sustained.

Reminding Ohtani that she was under oath, he asked, "Are you still in love with me?"

"No," she replied.

"No further questions," he said. A moment later, he threw his notepad violently to the floor and rushed out of the courtroom.

Ohtani requested and received an escort to leave the courtroom in case Heidecker was awaiting her outside.

"The prosecution rests," DA Rosetti said.

ELECTRIC SUN 20 TRIAL
Day Four

Air date: November 20, 2017
Running time: 38:19 minutes

Judge Szymcyzk informed Heidecker that his multiple contempt citations would be dealt with in a single hearing and warned him once again to comport himself with "decorum, respect and dignity."

"I apologize again," Heidecker said. He reiterated that he had not been aware that Ms. Ohtani would testify: "Obviously there was a lot of emotion there. And I have no excuse for it, but that's the root of it."

Judge Szymcyzk thanked him and instructed the jury that "Mr. Heidecker's conduct should not be any part of your deliberations on the merits of this matter."

Testimony of Jack O'Ryan

The first witness for the defense was EDM DJ Jack O'Ryan, a scheduled performer at the Electric Sun festival under his stage name of Orion Jacks.

Heidecker requested his personal impression of the festival. O'Ryan said it was largely "chill." However, he was unable to perform due to "all the kids dying," and he was also disappointed by the lack of food and water.

Asserting that there were, in fact, "Styrofoam boxes of Mexican food" for performers, Heidecker seized the prosecution's map of body locations to indicate that the area behind the stage had "a bunch of tacos and stuff."

O'Ryan repeated that he did not see any food: "I didn't even have any water, man." He stipulated that he still expected to receive his agreed-upon performance fee of $50,000, even though the show did not take place. "I showed up," O'Ryan said. "I did my part."

Heidecker assured O'Ryan he would be "taken care of."

"If not, we'll be back here," O'Ryan snapped.

Judge Szymcyzk asked Heidecker if he had any "relevant" questions for the witness. Heidecker then queried O'Ryan on his claim that he had "a good time" at the festival.

"Yeah, it was a cool time," O'Ryan answered. "I was chillin', there were a couple good sets." But he emphasized that this was not the whole story: "If you're having a good time, and at the end of the night something bad happens — like you don't get paid, or people start dying — then of course what you said previous to that kind of doesn't really matter, does it?"

Under cross-examination, O'Ryan stated that Heidecker had paid him to testify. There were no further questions.

In his redirect, Heidecker proposed to O'Ryan that the payment offered was for the festival appearance, not for his testimony.

"You also told me you were gonna pay me for this as well," he responded. Heidecker insisted the festival payment was the only money offered for O'Ryan's testimony.

"It's not even about the $50,000 only anymore," Ryan said, glancing at the victims' photos. "I mean, look at what happened."

Heidecker accused O'Ryan of being "dishonest" for implying the existence of a *quid pro quo* and directed the jury to "disregard" his testimony. Judge Szymcyzk made it clear that the jury would decide for themselves how much weight to give it.

As O'Ryan left the courtroom, Heidecker called out, "Good luck with your music. It sucks."

Testimony of Jesse Popp

Festival attendee Jesse Popp testified that he had "a wonderful experience" and "didn't see anyone get hurt or sick." He also praised the DKR performance: "Tim was doing a great job up on stage — slaying it on the laptops, making good beats for everyone."

Heidecker asked whether Popp had witnessed him handing out vape pens. "I do not recall that, no," he answered.

In his cross-examination, DA Rosetti requested that Popp state his occupation.

"I do a lot of things," Popp said. Pressed for details, he acknowledged working "in the fast food industry" and "as a hired hand" in the agricultural sector.

"Are you an actor?" Rosetti asked.

Popp said he wasn't, and he also denied any previous employment by Heidecker. Rosetti reminded Popp that he was under oath and discussed the legal consequences of perjury. He then introduced a film clip from Season 5, Episode 4 of the *Decker* series, in which Popp was plainly visible during a concert sequence.

"Is that you, Mr. Popp?" Rosetti asked. Popp conceded that it was.

Heidecker's motion to "strike the witness" from the record was denied by Judge Szymcyzk. Rosetti then displayed an image of Popp on the Internet Movie Database, drawing the jury's attention to Popp's sole acting credit, which was for *Decker*.

Rosetti had a final question: "Are you being compensated by the defendant for your testimony today?"

"Yes," Popp admitted. He was dismissed, after which Judge Szymcyzk wearily asked Heidecker if he had "any actual witnesses."

Testimony of Joe Estevez

Veteran actor Joe Estevez testified that he has known Heidecker for "five, six years now."

Jack O'Ryan

Jesse Popp

Joe Estevez

Gregg Turkington

Asked by Heidecker for his "general thoughts and impressions" of the defendant, Estevez said, "You and I always got along together."

Quoting the old expression "he'd never hurt a fly," Heidecker asked Estevez if he felt it would apply to himself.

"Absolutely, yes."

Heidecker encouraged Estevez to share any additional thoughts on his "general good intentions, goodwill, good-naturedness."

Estevez replied that while they are from different generations and have limited social contact, he considers Tim "a hale fellow."

"These kids, who are dead now, they're blaming it on me," Heidecker told him. "Is that something that you believe I could ever do?"

"Of course not," Estevez said. Calling the deaths "an incredibly unfortunate incident," he became philosophical: "You hate to say things like this happen, but things like this happen."

Under cross-examination, Estevez conceded that he'd never visited Heidecker at home or gone to see any of his bands perform. Apart from an occasional lunch, they'd spent no time together that didn't entail working on TV programs.

"In your opinion, did Tim ever appear to be off, like possibly he was on drugs while working?" Waymon asked.

"Maybe," Estevez conceded. She then asked if Estevez believed Heidecker had a drug problem.

Estevez recalled that at one point, Heidecker's friends and fellow actors had organized an intervention for him: "We thought he may have a little problem, you know, after he set himself on fire."

"Could you repeat that?" Waymon asked. "Just in case the jury didn't hear that."

"He had an accident," Estevez said. "I don't know the circumstances behind it, but he got hurt pretty badly."

"And did you observe that his issues with the drugs got better after the intervention?" "You can't tell something like that," Estevez protested. There were no further questions.

As Estevez stepped down, Heidecker was rebuked for writing "the China Connection" on a piece of paper and holding it up to the jury. Judge Szymcyzk cautioned the jury "that signs written by the defendant and held up in their direction are not admissible as evidence." He again admonished them that Heidecker's actions while acting as counsel are not evidence and have "no bearing whatever on the merits of this case."

Gregg Turkington Returns to the Stand

Turkington, a daily spectator throughout the trial, seemed surprised and reluctant to be called back to the witness box.

Heidecker noted Turkington's interest in the trial. "Do you have any personal relationship with the outcome?" he asked. "Or are you just a fan of courtroom proceedings?"

"I was there for everything that happened," Turkington said. "So of course I'm interested in seeing what happens."

Heidecker directed the jury's attention to Turkington's previous testimony, in which he described himself as a film expert. He argued that per Judge Szymcyzk's instructions, "if one part of a witness's testimony is either incorrect or false, then his entire testimony has to be removed from the record."

Judge Szymcyzk immediately clarified that Heidecker had "mischaracterized" this instruction. In fact, while falsehoods may taint the jury's view of the entire testimony, they may still assess specific factual elements on their own merits.

Asked if he had seen *Citizen Kane*, Turkington testified that he had seen it "seven times." Heidecker called this a lie, resulting in a heated dispute that was eventually quieted by Judge Szymcyzk.

"A couple of more questions," Heidecker told Turkington, "and I'll let you go back to your busy day of watching movies like a loser." Waymon's objection to this comment was sustained, which infuriated Heidecker.

"How would you describe it, Judge?" Heidecker protested. "A man who sits around watching movies all day. Is that a winner?"

"It's better than killing people at a music festival," Turkington snapped. Heidecker called this "tampering with the evidence" and argued that it "deserves a punishment."

He asked if Turkington had ever seen the film *Sully*. Turkington claimed to have seen it at a sneak preview for critics and on subsequent occasions, speculating that he had seen it "before Sully himself saw the movie."

Heidecker then asked a puzzling question regarding the 1983 film *Star Trek II*: "Did that movie take place in San Francisco?"

"Yes, it did." Heidecker followed up by asking him if *Star Trek IV* took place in San Francisco. Turkington said it did not.

While Turkington returned to his seat, Heidecker announced that his claims would be revealed as false in court the next day.

As Heidecker had no other witnesses, Judge Szymcyzk declared the court in recess.

ELECTRIC SUN 20 TRIAL
Day Five

Air date: November 21, 2017
Running time: 49:17 minutes

Testimony of Nicholas Meyer

Tim Heidecker's first witness was novelist, screenwriter and director Nicholas Meyer, who is best known for acclaimed films such as *The Seven-Per-Cent Solution*, *The Day After*, *Time After Time*, *Star Trek II: The Wrath of Khan* and *Star Trek IV: The Voyage Home*.

Heidecker asked Meyer to provide an overview of his career. Meyer stated that he co-wrote and directed *Star Trek II: The Wrath of Khan* and *Star Trek VI: The Undiscovered Country*. "I also co-wrote, but did not direct, *Star Trek IV: The Voyage Home*," he said.

Heidecker suggested that as the screenwriter of *Star Trek IV: The Voyage Home*, Meyer was "pretty familiar with the story." The witness confirmed this.

"When you say 'home' in that title," Heidecker asked, "what does 'home' refer to?"

"Earth," Meyer replied. Heidecker asked him to confirm that "the *Star Trek* gang is out in space, and their voyage in that episode — in that movie — is to Earth." Meyer did so, and under further questioning, clarified that the characters travel to San Francisco.

This provoked a protest from trial spectator and self-described film expert Gregg Turkington. In response, Heidecker again asked the director where *Star Trek IV* took place. As Meyer attempted to summarize the plot, Turkington again interrupted his testimony. Judge Szymcyzk cautioned Turkington that further disturbances would result in his removal from the courtroom.

DA Rosetti objected at this point: "I don't see the relevance of Mr. Meyer's testimony as to the *Star Trek* movies."

Heidecker argued that they go to the credibility of Turkington's testimony on the previous day: "The relevance is that you brought this fraud here, Gregg Turkington, as an expert witness" even though "he doesn't seem to understand very fundamental aspects of film."

He asked Meyer to verify once more that *Star Trek IV* was set in San Francisco and then shifted his questioning to *Star Trek II*: "Does any of that movie take place in San Francisco?"

"Yes," Meyer said. "There are actually a couple of scenes that are set in San Francisco. They weren't filmed there, but the Starfleet Academy, the simulator room, those were intended to be San Francisco, and Kirk's apartment overlooks San Francisco Bay."

"That's what I've been saying!" Turkington exclaimed. Judge Szymcyzk directed the bailiff to "please assist Mr. Turkington in finding the hallway."

Heidecker then asked Meyer to state unequivocally that he "would not classify the plot of *Star Trek II* as being set in San Francisco." Meyer repeated that some scenes were set, though not filmed, in that city.

Frustrated, Heidecker tried a different tack: "If you were asked [by] a man in the street, 'Which *Star Trek* movie takes place in San Francisco,' your answer would be?"

"*Star Trek IV: The Voyage Home*," Meyer said.

Heidecker had no further questions.

In her cross-examination, Waymon asked Meyer when he first met Tim Heidecker.

"I met him this morning," he said. "But I got a call from him around 10:30 last night."

"What did he say when he called you last night?"

"He asked me to appear here today as an expert witness."

"And did he offer to pay you?"

"He did."

"What did he offer to pay you?"

"Ten thousand dollars," Meyer said. Waymon had no more questions.

From the counsel table, Heidecker declared, "I have a right to call expert witnesses and pay them whatever I want."

As Meyer departed, Rosetti moved to strike his "totally irrelevant" testimony from the record: "We called Mr. Turkington to the stand for purposes other than his views on the *Star Trek* movies."

"I request that the jury throw out all the testimony of Gregg Turkington," Heidecker countered. "Because obviously he's a liar and a rat and completely unqualified to discuss anything. Especially movies."

Judge Szymcyzk overruled both motions, allowing all testimony to stand.

Testimony of Manuel Giusti

Heidecker's final witness was Manuel Giusti, a member of Dekkar and DKR. Heidecker began by asking Giusti to define his relationship with the defendant.

"We are brother," Giusti asserted. "We are brother for life, yeah."

"How would you describe Mr. Heidecker?" Heidecker asked.

"As a great guy," Giusti said. "As a loyal person." Referring to the murder charges, Giusti opined that Heidecker would "never do something bad to his fan."

Heidecker stated that Giusti had recently told him something "very shocking" about the Electric Sun case: "This morning, you confided something in me — some secret that you've been holding in."

"Yes," Giusti admitted. "I met Dr. San the night that he killed himself." Heidecker asked Giusti to describe this encounter to the jury.

"I wanted to check on him, how he was doing," Giusti explained. "We talked for a little bit, and then he handed me a letter."

"This is news to me," Heidecker broke in. "I think it's news to everybody here."

Asked if he had the letter on his person, Giusti affirmed that he did.

"Any reason why you waited this long to sort of expose this bombshell?"

"Not really," Giusti replied.

Heidecker asked if it would be "fair" to call the purported Sanchez letter "a suicide note or a final message to the world."

Waymon objected that the court had no way of authenticating the document, and Judge Szymcyzk agreed.

"We'll have to leave it up to the sworn testimony of our witness here," Heidecker said. He then told Giusti to read the letter.

Holding up a sheet of yellow notepaper, Giusti read, "I, Dr. San, am only one responsible for all the death from the Electric Sun 20. It is all my fault. Tim Heidecker is innocent, and is too busy writing and producing hit song with Dekkar and DKR, as well as hit show *Decker*. Signed, Dr. San."

"We haven't been presented the evidence prior to the proceeding this morning," Rosetti objected. "There's ample ground to deny admitting the letter into evidence."

Electric Sun 20 Trial: Day 5

"Before I rule on that motion," Judge Szymcyzk said, "I would like to hear some cross-examination of the witness."

Rosetti asked Giusti, a native of Italy, whether he is a Roman Catholic. Giusti said that he is. "I have one question for you," Rosetti continued. "Who wrote the letter?"

Giusti looked silently down at the table.

"You swore before God that you would tell the truth," Rosetti pressed him. "I'm gonna ask you now one more time: Who wrote the letter?"

After a long pause, Giusti said, "Tim gave it to me this morning."

"Needless to say, the motion to exclude is granted," Judge Szymcyzk said. "The jury will disregard this letter. They will disregard this witness's testimony in its entirety."

After dismissing Giusti, Judge Szymcyzk said, "Mr. Heidecker, the court is running out of contempt citation forms. But trust me: They are coming." He asked if Heidecker had "any further witnesses or evidence of any kind to present to this courtroom."

"No, your honor," Heidecker conceded. "At this time, the defense rests."

Closing Arguments

Before allowing closing arguments, Judge Szymcyzk again cautioned the jury that statements by counsel are not evidence, adding that this was a "particularly appropriate admonition to make in this case."

Rosetti began by invoking the memory of the "kids from our community who were killed by this individual." Becoming tearful, he said that in his 30 years as a county prosecutor, he had "never seen such a heinous crime."

Reminding the jury that "justice is in your hands," he reviewed the highlights of the state's case: Heidecker and Sanchez conspired to manufacture and market vape pens that the chief medical examiner of San Bernardino County testified contained toxic chemicals. These chemicals were subsequently found in the bodies of the victims.

The loss of life at Heidecker's festival was so egregious that it led Luther Sanchez — "a man of questionable moral character" — to hang himself in his prison cell.

Rosetti said that if found guilty, Heidecker "will go to prison for a long time, but he'd still be alive," unlike the Electric Sun 20. He also predicted that the other 137 victims would "never have normal lives."

"I'm gonna implore you: Please, see that justice is done. Convict this individual."

Heidecker began his closing argument by wondering how he would follow this "beautiful performance" by Rosetti. "Too bad Mr. Meyer wasn't here," he said. "He might cast him in one of this movies."

Walking to the whiteboard, he wrote the word "Heroin." He reminded the jury that Shawn Levin had died from heroin rather than from vaping: "So that opens the question — did *anybody* die from the vape pen?" He hinted that evidence suggesting the vape pen was toxic may have been "tainted" by prosecutorial "meddling."

Next, he wrote "the China Connection" — a reference to his theory that Chinese contamination was responsible for the harmful chemicals in the vape pens. He faulted the state for failing to investigate this possibility.

Third, Heidecker cited the testimony of Jack O'Ryan, a.k.a. Orion Jacks: "The gist of the confession is, he had a good time." He also commented that "we don't know" where O'Ryan was at the time of the deaths, because "these are questions that the state has failed to ask."

Next, he referenced the "confession" from Dr. San: "Some people think my friend Manuel made it up. I don't. I happen to believe my friend. I believe that letter to be genuine.

"The state's gonna try to muddy that. They're gonna say that you can't look at it. But you can. You can remember, 'cause I showed it to you, and you saw it. That was a letter from Dr. San, and he said that I didn't do anything wrong."

Writing "Star Trek 2/4" on the board, Heidecker claimed Nicholas Meyer's expert testimony on these films had exposed Gregg Turkington's testimony as "nothing but a bunch of baloney."

He cited the character witness provided by Joe Estevez, Alessandro Serradimigni and, "to some degree," Manuel Giusti.

Finally, he wrote his own name on the board and described himself as "an artist, a poet, a rock musician, an actor, writer, producer, festival organizer, entrepreneur."

"What is my relationship to the events of that night?" he asked. As "a performing artist up on stage," he was "nowhere near the vape tent." On the board, he wrote "I was just a man at the scene of a crime."

Turning the board around to show the photo of the victims, he singled out the late Mark Pryer as another "person at the scene of a crime." Violently slapping his palm against the dead teen's photo, he shouted, "Is Mark Pryer on trial?" He then struck the photo of Tyler Haldrige: "Does he belong up here, if he was alive?"

Slamming his hand against the photo of Valerie Davis, he yelled, "What about Valerie Davis? We saw her mother! She came in here telling her sob story." He asked the jury if Ms. Davis, too, should be blamed "for the activities of what happened at the festival."

Gesturing to the empty space where Shawn Levin's photo had been, Heidecker argued that his own photo should replace "old what's-his-name — the junkie."

Holding up the photo of Chris Delgado, he quoted the dead youth's alleged remarks on the day of the festival: "If anything should happen to me, I can tell by the way you've handled things so far, that it could never have been you." Heidecker called this "sworn testimony from my memory."

Electric Sun 20 Trial: Day 5
Defense Closing Statement

He also quoted Delgado as saying that "if something does happen to me, I want you to use my memory to do something good."

To honor these alleged wishes, Heidecker promised that if acquitted, he would launch "the Delgado Fund" to help budding musicians. "Maybe some of these kids wouldn't have gone down that trail with Dr. San had they had music in their lives," he theorized.

He portrayed his trial as a positive experience: "I am so humbled to be able to present my case to you, and I'm confident that you'll make the right choice. Find me innocent on all counts. Let me get back to doing the good work that I've been put on this planet to do by God."

He concluded by thanking the judge and bailiff. Indicating prosecutors Rosetti and Waymon, he added, "No thanks to these two, who've been nothing but trouble. But we do respect your service."

Addressing the jury, Judge Szymcyzk said, "Mr. Heidecker has been accused of 20 counts of second-degree felony murder. The burden that was on the prosecution was to prove that, number one, the defendant committed or was part of a conspiracy to aid and abet an inherently dangerous felony. Element number two, the defendant or the perpetrator — the co-conspirator — committed said inherently dangerous felony. Number three, the defendant or the perpetrator did an act that caused the death of another person — that's the third element. And number four, causing the death was part of one continuous transaction."

After receiving these instructions, the men and women of the jury were sequestered to deliberate on the case.

On Cinema On Line

2:22 PM - 23 Nov 2017
Happy Thanksgiving to our amazing jury who I love and know will make the right call. #ElectricSun19Trial

5:54 AM - 24 Nov 2017
What is point of Justice if @greggturkington walks free after several counts of perjery ? Ask #RosettiTheRat to prosecute that! #ElectricSun19trial

6:57 AM - 24 Nov 2017
Perhaps if #RosettiTheRat fails to do job I will have to take matters into my own hands! Lying in Cort is a federal offence!

6:49 PM - 25 Nov 2017
Honestly I don't care whether I am found guilty or innocent as I am ACTUALLY innocent and that trust (which at this point is obvious) will matter more than so xAlled jury. #ElectricSun19trial

6:50 PM - 25 Nov 2017
That said. I am confident the best jusy a a man can ask for for will do right thing and get me the verdict I want and need gift at that moments

6:52 PM - 25 Nov 2017
I am hearing #RosettiTheRat is quaking in his books right now. He'll have to pay for it if he loses this case! He is not good for people of Apples Valley!

7:49 AM - 26 Nov 2017
I'm a fightexr! (always) has been. If they say "jury of pears" why no fighters or hit rock/EDM PRODUCERS on jury? Doesn't seem fair at all! #ElectricSun19trial

6:30 PM - 27 Nov 2017
The music of DKR has been heard for the last time on #OnCinema.

6:35 PM - 27 Nov 2017
I'll be seeing you in court and not just you pathetically ogling in the background. I'll enthuse you rot for Perjury. Your movie watching days are over!

9:51 AM - 28 Nov 2017
The real #winner in this trial may well turn out to be #moviebuffs who are looking for more frequent movie #expertise.

10:14 AM - 28 Nov 2017
Interesting fact I learned this morning: My testimony in the murderer Heidecker trial was the most-viewed, highest-rated portion of the trial.

9:44 AM - 28 Nov 2017
OK! Heading to courthouse now. wish me luck (although I won't need it)

ELECTRIC SUN 20 TRIAL

Day Six

Air date: November 28, 2017
Running time: 25:21 minutes

On the fifth day of jury deliberations, spectators slowly filed into the courtroom.

Eventually, they were joined by prosecutors Rosetti and Waymon.

The quiet was oppressive as they awaited the verdict.

Some time later, the defendant, Tim Heidecker, arrived, followed closely by Judge Szymcyzk. "It is the court's understanding that the jury has reached a verdict in this matter," the judge said. He thanked the jury for their "time and effort."

Turning to the spectators and counsel, he said, "I admonish you: As the verdicts are read, no visible reactions, no audible reactions, please. The bailiff is authorized to use whatever appropriate and necessary means there are to enforce order and decorum in the courtroom."

Addressing the floorperson, he asked, "Has the jury reached a verdict?"

"Yes, we have," she replied. The judge directed Heidecker to "rise and face the jury for the reading of the verdict."

The floorperson read the verdict, which stated that Timothy Richard Heidecker was not guilty of second-degree felony murder in violation of penal code 19005, a felony upon Shawn Levin.

Ms. Waymon was visibly relieved to realize that this verdict applied only to Mr. Levin, who was already acknowledged to have died of a heroin overdose rather than from toxic vape chemicals.

"Has the jury reached a verdict as to counts 1 through 6 and 8 through 20?" Judge Szymcyzk asked.

"No, we were not able to reach a unanimous decision," she said.

"Would any further time to deliberate be useful to the jury?" the judge asked.

"No," she answered. The judge then asked for a show of hands to confirm that the jury concurred with the verdicts as read.

"This has been a very unusual case," Judge Szymcyzk said after a long, thoughtful silence. "It has consumed a great deal of time and energy on the part of the people, on the part of the County of San Bernardino, the people of the state of California. I will simply say that the court is disappointed that we were unable to reach a verdict on 19 counts of second-degree felony murder."

Judge Szymcyzk halted, seemingly at a loss for words. After collecting himself, he announced that he had "no choice but to declare a mistrial." Heidecker slapped the table triumphantly and shouted "Yes!"

Heidecker's demeanor changed somewhat when Judge Szymcyzk noted that the prosecution had the option of "refiling these charges and retrying them in a separate proceeding."

Judge Szymcyzk then adjourned the court. Heidecker and his bandmates Alessandro Serradimigni and Manuel Giusti embraced joyfully as the stunned spectators and prosecutors filed out of the courtroom.

ELECTRIC SUN 20 TRIAL
Statements to the Media

Statement of Vincent Rosetti, District Attorney, County of San Bernardino, California

Good morning, ladies and gentlemen of the press, residents of San Bernardino County.

I want to say it's been my honor and my privilege to seek justice on behalf of the Electric 20 and the 135 victims who suffered this tragedy at the Electric Sun Desert Music Festival.

I also want to thank everyone at the San Bernardino County District Attorney's Office, and especially my co-counsel Miriam Waymon, assistant district attorney, for their outstanding work and tireless efforts to see that justice has been served.

I'd now like to turn the podium over to my co-counsel Miriam, who'd like to say a few words.

Statement of Miriam Waymon, Assistant District Attorney, County of San Bernardino, California

Our hearts go out to the victims and their loved ones. We want you to know that we did everything we could to find justice on behalf of the injured survivors and the ones we lost.

We did not achieve the result we wanted, but we have been proud to fight on behalf of the victims of this tragedy.

We are disappointed with today's outcome.

Taking into consideration numerous factors, including the burden on the taxpayers of San Bernardino County as well as the likelihood of a successful prosecution, we will be taking some time to determine whether or not there will be a second trial.

We want to thank you for your support of this office and your support of the victims of this tragedy.

Statement of Timothy Richard Heidecker

Thank you, everyone! Obviously, this is an incredible day for us. It's a beautiful blue-sky day here, and we couldn't be happier with the results today.

I wanna say I'm happy — I'm not surprised. I felt like from day one, we knew that I was innocent and that there was no way the jury was gonna miss that. So we came out strong from the top, and we're so happy. I mean, thank God for the one juror, really, who is sort of the stopgap here and created this amazing verdict.

Yeah, the Founding Fathers — I wanna give a shout-out to them. They were no dummies. They created a system that allowed the protection of minorities like myself, who — from when you have 12 people wanting to throw you in jail, you have to have that one person who sees the truth. And so we thank him or her, and we honor that person.

Obviously, Mark Dwyer — I wanna just say a few words about Mark, my attorney for a little while there in the beginning. He turned out to be a dud. He was taking the case in the wrong direction. I think I made the right choice to dump him pretty much right away.

And you know, there's not a lot of people to thank, to be honest with you, because I was sort of a man alone. Obviously my brothers here, in Dekkar and DKR, were there as much as they could be. I know we had some stumbling areas throughout their testimony. Not their fault.

As far as the DA goes, this Rosetti has turned out to be a total rat and a bad, bad guy. And it's unbelievable that this county here is keeping him in this position. He's another career politician who's let down the people time and time again. He's a loser, he's flat, he's a rat. Rosetti the rat, we'd say.

And I don't know how you find these people, if you elect them or not. But if you have elected them, who knows, maybe he'll have some competition next time. This is my first time being a lawyer, and I've proven myself to be basically unstoppable at this point. So we're excited, we're gonna go celebrate. Won't be taking any questions this time, I think.

One other thing I wanna add, this experience — almost a year now — has been very challenging. It's been very hard. It's been a couple — a lot of dark nights, and not knowing which way it was gonna go.

And I have to say, it's been, it's been — I think it's gonna be creatively stimulating. I think you're gonna — I don't know if it's gonna be a concept album or a rock opera or something, but it's gonna be — I think it's gonna create a lot of great material, just having gone through this experience.

Let's give a shout-out to the Electric Sun 20. We wouldn't be here without them. Unfortunately. I wish they were here — we could celebrate with them. But they're not.

And that's all I have to say. So thank you guys so much, and let's hit the road. Thank you very much.

On Cinema On Line

12:20 PM - 15 Dec 2017
Kington was the ORIGINAL Master Codebreaker. Star Wards based the new Character on Codebreaker Kington.

12:22 PM - 15 Dec 2017
It is no surprise that Star Wars would be familiar with the Adventures of Kington and Decker franchise. But to steal is wrong.

12:28 PM - 15 Dec 2017
I am being alerted that #StarWars it's just a cheap knockoff of the hit tv show #Decker Mr Lucas you have some explaining to do.

12:56 PM - 15 Dec 2017
As a new and successful lawyer I can safely say George Lucas has kicked the hornets nest. decker and the minor character of Kington the master code breaker are property owned and created by me alone!

7:49 AM - 17 Dec 2017
George Lucas walks willy nilly into the superstore aka OnCinema/Decker and shoplifts what he wants: aka Master Codebreaker (originally scene as Jonathan Klington on Decker)

3:24 PM - 17 Dec 2017
Interesting that the Master Codebreaker wasn't in the earlier 7 Star War movies. Perhaps because @greggturkington and @timheidecker hadn't created him yet?

11:26 PM - 23 Dec 2017
I would never "create" a character and call him Luke Skywalker but apparently George Lucas can't show the same courtesy when he used Master Codebreaker (Kington) in Star Wars latest chapter.

8:29 PM - 24 Dec 2017
If Star Wars wins the Oscar for Best Characters this year, I hope Lucas will invite @timheidecker and @greggturkington (the ORIGINAL Master Codebreaker) on to the podium to share the prize, as they were the actual creators of the character of the Master Codebreaker Kington.

8:32 PM - 24 Dec 2017
And it is Verifiable that the Kington character was created and introduced first; sorry Lucas but there are thousands of Decker Fans who will swearctonthat Fact

8:38 PM - 24 Dec 2017
Perhaps Lucas is testing to see what he can get away with? Next time he may lift even more from our codebreaking sequences from the Decker TV show, unless people sprak up now

8:53 AM - 3 Mar 2018
In many ways tomorrow's Omar special will seek to erase the memories of last years disappointing and disastrous so called " our cinema " Oscar debacle. Never again!

4:23 PM - 3 Mar 2018
Many many asking why I keep giving @greggturkington a chance after years of dissatisfaction. Many reasons which at one point we can discuss! But for now it's as it is until further notice

4:28 PM - 3 Mar 2018
90% of the popular segments on the #OnCinemaOscarSpecial are movie-related ones that I conceived of and that give an insight into movie's big Night. 99.9% of the least popular segements involve @timheidecker's DKR or Dekkar somehow.

4:28 PM - 3 Mar 2018
To which degree he will remain a part of aspects going forward remains to be seen!

7:19 PM - 3 Mar 2018
would be so easy to 'go it alone" tomorrow as the soul host of the #OnCinemaOscarSpecial and actually not worry about the many problems that @greggturkington brings to the table. possibly Big Mistake!

FIFTH ANNUAL OSCARS SPECIAL
Live Broadcast from Hollywood's Biggest Night

Air date: March 4, 2018
Running time: 2:23:05

Live from Hemingway's Restaurant in Seaside Heights, New Jersey, pop-vocal legend Bobby Valli belts out a powerhouse rendition of "Oscar Fever."

Mr. Valli then introduces DKR, who put a modern electronic spin on the song. Afterward, Tim hints that this DKR performance may well be their last!

Axiom and Manuel seem startled by this news.

Clearing the Air

Tim has once again asked film buff Gregg Turkington to co-host the show, despite their many disputes during Tim's recent trial for multiple counts of murder.

Tim describes how painful it was to watch Gregg and Mark Proksch play "the character of Judas" as witnesses for the prosecution.

During a recent phone call with "the late, great Billy Graham," Tim asked for advice about the anger he felt toward Gregg, Mark, Joe Estevez, Manuel and Axiom. "You have to learn to forgive and forget," Graham said. The next morning, Tim learned that Graham had passed on.

Although Tim had initially been annoyed by Graham's advice, even saying "F-U-C-K you" to the aged minister before hanging up, he realized Graham was right. Accordingly, he has forgiven Gregg and Joe, and to a lesser degree, Mark, Manuel and Axiom.

Gregg reckons Tim doesn't have much of a choice, since the show depends so heavily on his and Mark's contributions. Tonight's *Jaws*-themed set is just one example: While filing some *Jaws* tapes at the VFA, Gregg realized "the 40th anniversary of *Jaws 2*" had come and gone three years earlier. What better time to pay tribute to the franchise?

Gregg is even wearing a suit that pays tribute to the *Jaws* poster concept. Meanwhile, Tim gives three cheers to the set designer for making the set "look like an old sea shanty," right down to the bottle of rum at his side.

Tim asks Gregg why movies like *Jaws* don't get made anymore, as evidenced by the poor crop of Oscar movies this year. Gregg suspects that "Oscar's gotten out of touch with what people like."

"Oscar Fever" claims another victim…in the legendary form of Bobby Valli!

Decker vs. Lucas

Tim and Gregg recently discovered that George Lucas' *The Last Jedi* features a character called "the Master Codebreaker," a term previously reserved for Agent Kington of *Decker* fame. Tim feels Lucas "pickpocketed us." In response, they have arranged for a mock trial of the director later in the show.

A Shout-Out to the Sponsors

Tim thanks the Delgado Fund, which is "one of the reasons we are here tonight." He also takes the opportunity to honor the Electric Sun 19 for their sacrifice. "They haunt me," he says.

"They should," Gregg says.

Asserting that "they're here tonight," Tim thanks them for "shining down on us and making the show what it is."

He also thanks Chaplin's Express (formerly Chaplin's Soup and Subs) for their generous sponsorship. Spokesperson Hank Freeman comments that the original Chaplin's Chili recently bought back the rights from Chaplin's Soup and Subs, creating a new entity that combines a time-honored respect for Chaplin's founding values with a forward-looking commitment to providing hot dogs and "five-bean stew" in regional gas stations.

Jaws 2 Turns 40!

Reflecting on "what an exciting year it is for the *Jaws* family," Tim cracks the seal on a segment celebrating "40 years of *Jaws 2*."

Keeping the *Jaws* theme going, Mark Proksch does his fully costumed impression of the shark hunter Quint, who famously died as he lived — in the razor-sharp maw of Jaws himself!

Tim complains that Mark is using his own voice, *sans* the highly distinctive Quint accent. "Why can't you talk like a fuckin' pirate?" he asks.

He tells Mark to try again, but Mark forgets the dialogue under this unexpected pressure. "I'm instantly regretting asking you to be a part of this," Tim tells him. "You're sinking the ship that is this show."

He directs Mark to leave the stage and work on his upcoming segments. He also criticizes Gregg's "low energy."

On the bright side, Tim has found that his prop rum is the real thing and is "having a little bit of fun" drinking it.

"Robert Shaw of *Jaws* died from alcoholism, so it's kind of appropriate," Gregg chuckles. But Tim doesn't find it funny to joke about this serious disease.

Dee Thompson Rides Again

Ticketless Oscar attendee Dee Thompson is back for another Oscar Special appearance. "He got into the Oscars scot-free," Tim reminds us. And in an *On Cinema* exclusive, he will now attempt

DECKER VS. GEORGE LUCAS

The Hon. Joe Estevez presided over the case of George Lucas vs. Tim Heidecker on charges of aggravated intellectual property theft. In Heidecker's opening statement, he thanked Mr. Lucas for "not fleeing the country" when evidence of his crimes first came to light.

He then laid out the facts of the case: Lucas' film *The Last Jedi* includes "a character named the master codebreaker." This is identical to Heidecker's copyright-protected character Jonathan Kington, a "master codebreaker" on the TV series *Decker*, which came out three years before *The Last Jedi*.

"There is no further evidence needed to prove that this man is guilty of criminal larceny," Heidecker concluded. Although the case is worthy of death, Heidecker was willing to settle for "an apology and financial retributions." Judge Estevez thanked Heidecker for his "marvelous" opening statement.

Heidecker's first witness was James Flynt, an avid film and media buff. Heidecker asked him to confirm that he had followed *Decker* from its beginnings as "a webisode concept" to its current status as "a huge international hit on cable television." Flynt confirmed this. He also confirmed that Agent Kington was an integral character on the show and that he was often described in the show as "a master codebreaker."

Flynt also testified that *The Last Jedi* included a character known as "the master codebreaker," and that this character was "a ripoff" of the Kington character.

Heidecker had no further questions, but Gregg Turkington asked Flynt if he felt it was "pretty sad" that a man as rich as Lucas was "resorting to taking characters from our show" instead of creating his own.

"It does seem that way a bit, yes, I would say," Flynt responded.

Heidecker next called "the honorable Gregg Turkington" to the stand to confirm that he and Turkington "co-created" Kington. Turkington also testified that the Google results for "master codebreaker" lead only to *Decker* and to *The Last Jedi*, showing that the phrase was not otherwise in common use.

Next, George Lucas himself took the stand. Heidecker first asked him to confirm that he had made the *Star Wars* movies, but Mr. Lucas repeatedly tried to qualify his answers. "What do you think I am, Rosetti the Rat? I'm not gonna take this!" Heidecker shouted. "Yes or no, Lucas?"

"I take the fifth amendment," Lucas finally said. At this point, Heidecker asked Judge Estevez for a ruling. After holding Lucas in contempt of court, Judge Estevez announced that the director was "guilty as charged." He sentenced Lucas to "150 years in a cell where there's no TV, so you can't steal anybody else's property."

Judge Estevez declared that court was adjourned, vindicating the creators of *Decker* in their underdog fight against one of the major forces in modern popular culture.

---

to return once again to the ceremony he loves. Speaking live from Hollywood, Dee says he has not had much luck so far.

The Rat Pack Rides Again

Jaws 2 isn't the only Birthday Boy in the house tonight. It's also the 20th anniversary of 1998's *The Rat Pack* biopic. To mark this once-in-a-lifetime occasion, Gregg has convened a *Rat Pack* tribute featuring actors portraying the real-life stars who brought the legendary Rat Pack back to life for one all-too-brief moment.

An actor portraying Ray Liotta as "Chairman of the Board" Frank Sinatra gets things going with a rendition of "That Girl's Just Gotta Be Kissed." But Tim cuts the song short to interview the boys about the Rat Pack's glory days.

It was "a groovy time, man," according to the actor impersonating Don Cheadle Jr. as Sammy Davis Jr.

"Do you guys remember where you were when you first saw the *Rat Pack* movie?" Gregg asks.

"I don't even remember where I am right now," quips the actor commemorating Joe Mantegna's star turn as the famously inebriated Dean Martin.

Tim curtly thanks the Rat Pack and banishes them to the wings. "Not a great plan right there," he tells Gregg.

Returning to the topic of the Electric Sun 19, and the Delgado Fund that made the show possible, Tim plays a clip in memoriam to remember them by.

Tim gets an update from Dee Thompson, who is standing near a chain-link fence. The audio is a bit garbled, so it's not clear how things are going.

Close Encounters of the Jaws 2 Kind

After putting some more "rummy in his tummy," Tim welcomes *Jaws 2* veteran Keith Gordon to the show. Gordon played a teenage boy named Doug in the original *Jaws 2*, later directing such renowned films as *The Killing*, *Fargo* and Kar-Wai Wong's *Fallen Angels*. Gregg learns that Keith still owns all of Doug's clothes, and the two men share fond memories of *Decker*'s own Carl Gottlieb.

"I think it was a big mistake to center

Remembering the Rat Pack reunion.

Mark brings the horror of Jaws back to life.

the entire night around *Jaws*," Tim grumps. "It's not a fun show for anybody."

Undeterred, Gregg asks Keith if the original script for *Jaws 2* was titled *Jaws 3*. This relates to Gregg's theory that the true *Jaws 2* was *Close Encounters of the Third Kind*, which was intended as a spinoff about the *Jaws* character Dr. Hooper. "Nobody cared about the sharks in *Jaws*," he argues. "What made it was Richard Dreyfuss's performance."

Tim can hardly believe his ears: "What are you, daft?" Gregg insists that "Spielberg was gonna direct *Jaws 2*, and he did, but it was called *Close Encounters of the Third Kind*."

"We're moving on from that," Tim tells him. He calls for Mark's next segment — the famous "Indianapolis" scene from *Jaws*. But Mark's Quint accent is still flawed, and he's not sitting down, causing Tim to hurl a drink at him.

Keith worries that the tension on the set may be holding Mark back, so Tim lets Mark know he's "the best" and tells him to continue before stopping him again for failing to nail the scene.

"I'm doing my best," Mark says.

"Your best isn't good enough for us," Tim retorts. He sends Mark offstage to practice for the next *Jaws* segment.

With some dead air to fill, Tim asks for a song from the actor simulating Don Cheadle's version of Sammy Davis Jr., who happily obliges. Midway through, Tim has a change of heart and once again ejects the Rat Pack forcefully from the set.

Debut of the Super Oscars
Gregg expands on the "Super Oscars" concept he floated at the climax of last year's *Our Cinema* Oscars Special. This would increase the number of Oscar awards by having Oscar winners from the past 20 years face off for a Super Oscar, which would be a platinum version of the familiar Oscar.

Using a bracket system, Gregg calls for a Twitter-based vote that will serve as a proof of concept by awarding the coveted first-ever platinum Oscar.

Hot Dog!
Tim suspects that "Billy Graham is in hell" based on the show's problems so far: "I've been praying to him asking him what I'm supposed to do, and nothing's coming back."

He regrets kicking the Rat Pack off the show, which "ruined their night." He's also sorry he ate a Chaplin's hot dog: "Those are not right. Something's off with them."

Hank protests that Chaplin's makes its hot dogs fresh every morning in its Norwalk factory. But Tim says "the bun's stale" and "no one wants" French's mustard. He wishes he had a different sponsor: "I'd take anything over you."

Jaws 2, Mark 0
Tim concedes that as "a comic artist," Mark Proksch has faced an uphill battle in bringing the *Jaws* universe to life.

But now, he will have a "final chance at redemption" as he returns to the *Jaws* theme to portray the famous "all action, no dialogue" scene where Hooper "tries to inject the Jaws" with a harpoon.

"This is one of the great movie scenes of all time!" Gregg exclaims. Having seen the rehearsal, he is sure Mark will do it justice.

On Cinema On Location on Jaws
Before Mark faces his final showdown with Jaws, Gregg shares a *Jaws*-themed edition of *On Cinema On Location*.

Gregg films his approach to and arrival at Universal Studios, the home of *Jaws* and so many other "stars in the Universal galaxy." After a short wait in line at the ticket booth, it's his turn at the window! Will he make it inside?

Diver Down
Next, we go live to Mark Proksch, who is slumped over in his diving suit. Tim alerts him that the segment has started, but Mark doesn't respond.

"Wake up!" Gregg calls. Tim sends a couple of crew members to help Mark, but they can't get his helmet off and there's some question as to whether he's been getting enough air to stay alive.

Valli Remembers
While the crew aids Mark, Tim introduces a new segment featuring Bobby Valli, Frankie Valli's brother and a bright star in his own right. It's called *Valli Remembers*.

Argo goes head to head with Lord of the Rings!

The EMTs assist Mark Proksch.

"My brother was invited to a birthday party at Frank Sinatra's house in Palm Springs, back in the early sixties," Valli remembers. "And at that birthday party that night was Jimmy Stewart, Kirk Douglas, Burt Lancaster, Loretta Young, Lauren Bacall, Lucille Ball, Desi Arnaz, Sammy Davis Jr. and Dean Martin — all in the same room."

Gregg follows up by asking Mr. Valli if he's ever seen *Jaws 2*.

"Yeah, that was a great movie," Valli remembers. "I'm glad I wasn't in the water!"

Super Oscar Suspense
The crew members have gathered around Mark and are taking a saw to his diver suit.

"They gotta get the helmet off of him," Gregg whispers. "Or he's not gonna be able to breathe."

"We're live right now," Tim says. "So can you just do the Super Oscars?"

Gregg glumly reports that *Titanic* has edged out *Spotlight*. Also, in a photo finish between *A Beautiful Mind* and *Slumdog Millionaire*, he proclaims *A Beautiful Mind* the winner.

The situation with Mark seems to be worsening, as the funnyman's helmet won't come off. Luckily, the paramedics arrive just in time to help. "This shouldn't be on camera," Tim frets.

At long last, the helmet is off! But Mark remains unconscious as the paramedics wheel him out.

Dee's Appointment with Oscar
Tim has "a little bit of good news" to impart: Despite the "issues" with his diving suit, Mark is "in good hands." He's glad the EMTs "came so quickly," and "we know that he's gonna be alright."

Gregg is glad the ambulance made it despite all the Oscar Night road closures. This reminds Tim to check in with Dee Thompson, who is currently behind an Oscar barricade but still hopes to get inside for the tail end of the festivities.

"I bet you a million dollars you don't get into the building," Tim tells him. And indeed, the guards do not seem inclined to let him in.

Return of the Rat Pack
Out of respect for Mark's accident, Tim cancels the 40th-anniversary tribute to *Jaws 2*. Instead, he asks Gregg to bring the Rat Pack back. As Dean Martin takes the lead on "Always Come Back to You," Tim calls the hospital to get news of Mark.

Soon after, he interrupts the song to deliver some awful news: "They're saying that he's gone — that he didn't make it to the hospital."

"I got a question for you," says Dean.
"Get the fuck out!" Tim snarls. "You say one more word, I'll fuckin' smack you in the mouth."

Grief-stricken, Tim directs Gregg to finish the Super Oscars. Though visibly distraught, Gregg updates the chart.

Memories of Mark
Tim and Gregg are drinking rum. "I'm in shock," Tim says. He recalls that Mark signed a "basic release, which essentially is a waiver in terms of if something should happen."

"An impressionist is a stunt man, in a way," he concludes. He asks for Gregg's thoughts on Mark's untimely passing.

"He's irreplaceable," Gregg says.

"He's one of a kind, I'll put it that way." Tim rolls a montage of highlights from the fallen impressionist's *On Cinema* and *Decker* years.

As this tribute ends, Tim shares some heartening news about the late Mark Proksch: "Apparently, the paramedics thought that he was gone," but "they do have him breathing right now" and the EEG "got some brain activity."

"So he's gonna bounce back," Gregg says hopefully.

"He's not at the morgue, OK?" Tim says. "And that should be something we're excited about." He recalls how "scary" it was to see that Mark wasn't breathing.

"He's not a very emotive guy to begin with," Gregg muses.

Lord of the Super Oscars
On the Super Oscars, it's down to a tense Battle Royale between *Argo* and *Lord of the Rings*. Which one will go home with the Super Oscar platinum?

Fond memories of Mark Proksch.

To return the show to "a positive light," Tim brings out a birthday cake for *Jaws 2*. He's eager to get a little "*Jaws* sugar" in his stomach after vomiting up Chaplin's sub-par hot dogs. He doles out slices to himself and Manuel, but the cake slides onto the floor.

"Accidents happen, as we learned tonight," he says.

Mars Needs Movies

Gregg's finale — *Close Encounters of the Movie Kind* — "is kinda bittersweet," he says. Drawing on the *Jaws 2 / Close Encounters* connection, it relied heavily on Mark, who was meant to play both Richard Dreyfuss and his alien interlocutor.

Tim hopes Joe will step into the Dreyfuss role as a tribute to Mark.

"I'm not gonna wear the helmet," Joe calls out from offstage. But Mark's dialogue as the alien is prerecorded, so Joe has only to read Mark's live part from Gregg's script.

Mark's disembodied voice spotlights the intergalactic impact of movie magic.

"We on Mars have been enjoying Earth's movies for many years now. The flickering light from your drive-in theaters beckoned to us and is the very reason we decided to visit your planet."

The alien then asks to meet Earth's "leader," Humphrey Bogart (by this time, Mark has lapsed into his W. C. Fields voice). He divulges that due to Bogart's popularity, Martian offspring are often named "Humphrey Bogie."

In closing, he issues a plea for their cultures to coexist through their shared love of movies: "This close encounter of a movie kind has been beneficial to all the universe."

"I think this is the beginning of a beautiful relationship...er, friendship," Joe responds, in an impish reference to the famous last line of *Casablanca*.

The sci-fi music won't stop at the end, despite Tim's many pleas to turn it off.

Lessons Learned

"We all learned something tonight," Tim sighs. "We have to spend more time hugging each other and loving each other."

"You can do that while watching movies," Gregg reminds him.

"This is a lesson to be learned that we all have a short time on this planet. And if we spend it worrying who wins an Oscar, you might as well put a gun in your mouth. We are the future, and we have to spend more time loving each other and not hating each other."

Crying "I love the Rat Pack," Tim beckons Joe, Axiom and Manuel for a group hug.

"Mark's gonna be fine," Tim tells everyone. "He's gonna be just fine! He just ran out of air for a while."

The show ends with a title card memorializing Mark Proksch: 1978–2018.

Mark Proksch in happier times.

On Cinema On Line

9:33 PM - 4 Mar 2018
Mark is not well but he hopefully will be ok

8:26 AM - 5 Mar 2018
The #SuperOscars are getting a lot of attention today. 99.999% accurate! Congratulations to @LordofRingsCast and all the runners up.

8:48 AM - 5 Mar 2018
Mrk is good hands and will most likely be A OK!

2:55 PM - 5 Mar 2018
By the way @greggturkington conceived of Jaws scenes with Mork.

3:47 PM - 6 Mar 2018
sad news about mark Unfortunately but I know you and I have FAITH that all will be ok! ❤️

8:10 PM - 6 Mar 2018
What a shame mark spoiled an otherwise well done special thanks to all!

12:42 PM - 22 Mar 2018
This season has a variety of hosts and guests as well as "outside the mainstream" concepts in store. but @greggturkington is a guest today.

12:43 PM - 22 Mar 2018
hopefully he has seen the movies not as in the past where he didn't see #Salty

oXc

~ SEASON X ~

The Delgado Fund

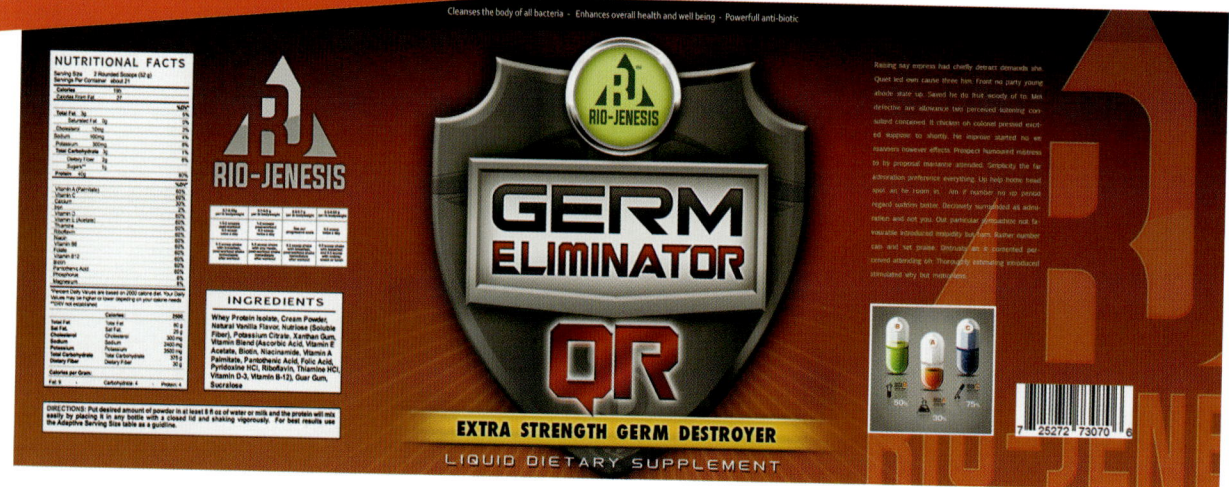

RIO-JENESIS Product Labels

Germ Assassin 2X
Activated Germ Destroyer
- 200 Capsules
- Fully Organic
- Promotes a germ free body · Enriches the immune system · Kills most bacteria
- DIETARY SUPPLEMENT

Germ Shield-X
Germ Deterrent
- Fully Organic
- Scientifically guaranteed to work!
- DIETARY SUPPLEMENT
- NET WT. 2LB (909G) ANTI-BACTERIAL POWDER MIX
- 25 Servings

Germ Block Pro
Fast-Acting Germ Deterrent
- LIQUID DIETARY SUPPLEMENT

Germ Eliminator QR
Extra Strength Germ Destroyer
- Cleanses the body of all bacteria · Enhances overall health and well being · Powerfull anti-biotic
- LIQUID DIETARY SUPPLEMENT

Nutritional Facts (common to labels)
Serving Size: 2 Rounded Scoops (52 g)
Servings Per Container: about 21

Nutrient	Amount	%DV
Calories	190	
Calories From Fat	27	
Total Fat	3g	5%
Saturated Fat	2g	7%
Cholesterol	15mg	7%
Sodium	100mg	4%
Potassium	300mg	9%
Total Carbohydrate	7g	1%
Dietary Fiber	1g	1%
Sugars	1g	
Protein	40g	80%
Vitamin A (Palmitate)		%DV
Vitamin C		65%
Calcium		30%
Iron		2%
Vitamin D		50%
Vitamin E (Acetate)		60%
Thiamine		60%
Riboflavin		60%
Niacin		60%
Vitamin B6		60%
Folate		60%
Vitamin B12		60%
Biotin		60%
Pantothenic Acid		60%
Phosphorus		8%
Magnesium		8%

*Percent Daily Values are based on 2000 calorie diet. Your Daily Values may be higher or lower depending on your calorie needs. **DV not established

	Calories 2500	
Total Fat	Total Fat	80 g
Sat Fat	Sat Fat	25 g
Cholesterol	Cholesterol	300 mg
Sodium	Sodium	2400 mg
Potassium	Potassium	3500 mg
Total Carbohydrate	Total Carbohydrate	375 g
Dietary Fiber	Dietary Fiber	30 g

Calories per Gram:
Fat 9 · Carbohydrate 4 · Protein 4

Ingredients
Whey Protein Isolate, Cream Powder, Natural Vanilla Flavor, Nutriose (Soluble Fiber), Potassium Citrate, Xanthan Gum, Vitamin Blend (Ascorbic Acid, Vitamin E Acetate, Biotin, Niacinamide, Vitamin A Palmitate, Pantothenic Acid, Folic Acid, Pyridoxine HCl, Riboflavin, Thiamine HCl, Vitamin D-3, Vitamin B-12), Guar Gum, Sucralose

DIRECTIONS: Put desired amount of powder in at least 8 fl oz of water or milk and the protein will mix easily by placing it in any bottle with a closed lid and shaking vigorously. For best results use the Adaptive Serving Size table as a guideline.

EPISODE X01
'Pacific Rim: Uprising' & 'Sherlock Gnomes' (sponsored by Rio-Jenesis)

Air date: March 22, 2018
Running time: 11:58 minutes

The Xth season of *On Cinema* offers viewers the chance to get "germ-free" once and for all through the real-life miracle of Rio-Jenesis (www.riojenesis.com). Today, Tim's guest is film buff Gregg Turkington of the Victorville Film Archive.

Tim makes it plain that the X representing the new season is fraught with significance that goes beyond its status as the Roman numeral for 10. It stands for "exonerated," underscoring Tim's recent verdict in the Electric Sun 20 trial. But it also refers to "Xing out the person I used to be." Acknowledging that he doesn't always find it easy to admit being wrong, Tim discloses that he has "made mistakes," including being "very abusive" to some of the people in his life. He has also abused his own body and health with drug use and related behaviors.

Gregg charges that in many cases, Tim has not watched movies prior to reviewing them. This too is "a form of abuse."

In the healthy new spirit of his show, Tim forgives this interruption and moves on to discuss Rio-Jenesis, makers of "the number-one all-natural germ deterrent that's on the market." They come by this reputation honestly, having perfected a system that removes germs permanently from the human biome while also hindering new germs from gaining a toehold. Tim himself is living proof, having recently been certified "virtually germ-free" by his doctor.

Tim fondly recalls the fifth *On Cinema* Oscar Special, which was their most successful entry yet. Sadly, the show ended on "a little bit of a sour note" as comedian Mark Proksch was involved in a filming accident on set. At crisis moments like these, the body can be more susceptible to germs, which is why it's especially all-important to have a proven germ deterrence system like Rio-Jenesis in your corner.

Happily for Mark, he was rescued by EMTs before reaching the exact moment of death. Gregg has it on good authority that "his heart is pounding away" and "he's breathing."

"Good for him," Tim says. All fingers are crossed as Tim and Gregg wait to see if the impressionist will "speak again."

Pacific Rim: Uprising is a sequel to *Pacific Rim*. [Episode 302] This time, all the sea monsters are back and so are the Jaeger pilots, with Earth itself as the prize. Tim "loved" this "great *Pacific Rim* movie" and expects to see it "again and again." He gives it five bags of popcorn.

When Gregg saw the first movie, he was certain no sequel could ever be made. But after watching the sequel, he's convinced it's "the beginning of a new franchise" in which the *Pacific Rim* saga is as far as ever from being told. He also applauds the performance of Scott Eastwood, who is a delightful chip off his father Clint's legendary block. He gives *Uprising* five bags of popcorn, along with a lucky rabbit's foot to increase the likelihood that Clint Jr. will carry on his dad's legacy in a reboot of *Dirty Harry*.

Sherlock Gnomes' Johnny Depp finds himself in a "garden plot" as star-crossed gnome lovers hire A. Conan Doyle's great detective (in gnome form) to figure out where the garden ornaments went. Tim thought it was "a lot of fun," as any movie must be that features "the great voice talents of Johnny Depp." Proud to be among the people who loved the movie, he gives it five bags of popcorn and two sodas.

Gregg was somewhat frustrated by *Sherlock Gnomes* because as great as it was, "it could have been greater" if they'd thought to pair Depp with his real-life muse, Tim Burton. He's not sure what made Burton turn the job down, but he *is* sure it was "a big mistake." He grants *Sherlock Gnomes* five bags of popcorn but withholds the "little garden gnome" the film surely would've deserved with Burton at the helm.

Tim once again thanks Rio-Jenesis not just for sponsoring *On Cinema*, but also for helping him to take charge of his health on his own terms through the biomolecular science of next-level germ deterrence. He appreciates that unlike the isolated supplements often sold randomly in stores, Rio-Jenesis is "an entire system" that fights germs for you, letting your body redirect its energy to more mission-critical life tasks.

Tim favors the *Germ Assassin* product for its intensely germ-cleansing results. Then, for maximum protection, he uses *Germ Shield X* four times daily in smoothie form to achieve the biochemical shield you have always had, but have never been able to energize to its full potency until now. He also correctly notes that this is not just a matter of preventing seasonal colds — illnesses like diabetes and cancer can also become an issue when we let "our germ shield down."

With no time left for *Popcorn Classics*, this episode is a wrap!

EPISODE X02
'Ready Player One' & 'Tyler Perry's Acrimony' (sponsored by Rio-Jenesis)

Air date: March 28, 2018
Running time: 11:19 minutes

This week, Rio-Jenesis is proud to bring *On Cinema* back with host Tim Heidecker and the VFA's own Gregg Turkington.

Tim has an update on the Delgado Fund, which brings arts education to San Bernardino County youth in memory of Christopher Delgado. Sadly, Bruce and Katherine Delgado have withdrawn their support, which Tim attributes to the machinations of local DA Vincent Rosetti. They have filed a civil suit and are "trying to bring the other families in." This has led to the seizure of Tim's intellectual property, including Dekkar, DKR and *Decker*. "It's probably the hardest thing I've ever had to deal with," he frets.

He is now pursuing Chapter 11 bankruptcy to shield his assets in much the same way that Rio-Jenesis shields the human ecosystem against germs. In the meantime, there is no longer a Delgado Fund, because these "bad people" are "taking their son's death and using it to try to capitalize and monetize that" by going after Tim's valuable brands.

Compounding all these problems, Tim has been getting "a lot of negative feedback" on Gregg's promotional movie-themed hats, which many people are saying "look sloppy." Gregg sees the hats as integral to the VFA's new collection of film marketing memorabilia. But Tim says that if the hats are promotions, the studios should pay to appear on the show: "We're not gonna do free advertising."

Gregg defends his hats as a savvy way to promote Popcorn Classics like *Deep Impact*, but Tim thinks "it's bad taste from a movie reviewer to be doing product placement."

Ready Player One leads Steven Spielberg back to the science-fiction fold with a *Tron* for the 21st-century, as the dead creator of a virtual reality world challenges real-world gamers to hunt a virtual Easter Egg that holds the key to a very real fortune. Tim "loved this movie," which is "one of his best since *E.T.*" He gives it five bags of popcorn and two sodas.

Gregg couldn't help but notice Spielberg's confidence in identifying the film as a franchise right off the bat; clearly, *Ready Player Two*, *Ready Player Three* and all the rest of the sequels are waiting in the wings! As this is a first for movie title history, Gregg does not want to let the moment pass without comment. He gives the film itself five bags of popcorn as well as an *E.T.* keychain "just to remind you of Spielberg's roots."

In *Tyler Perry's Acrimony*, a woman betrayed by her husband levels the playing field by taking a stand through an act of revenge that might just settle the score once and for all. Tim calls it "a great movie." Gregg goes a step further, maintaining that with this unstinting look at a relationship in crisis, Perry is blossoming into "the Woody Allen of our generation." It's Perry's best film, and it may also give him his first tantalizing taste of Oscar gold with a Best Director award. Gregg awards it five bags of popcorn plus a small piece of wood in honor of Perry's mentor, Woody Allen. Tim also gives it the Oscar nod and five bags of popcorn.

Next up, Gregg has quite a tale to tell. Puzzled by Tim Burton's refusal to direct *Sherlock Gnomes*, he wrote the great director a letter to demand an explanation. He was happy to get an autographed photo of Burton in return, but he was less pleased to find that Burton's letter didn't answer Gregg's question. Burton simply said that he's sure fill-in director John Stevenson did "a fine job." It's particularly galling because Burton introduced this non sequitur with "to answer your question." Although Gregg plans to frame the letter as a keepsake, he does consider it "a little disappointing."

Gregg also has some VFA news: The collection has found a new home and is amassing videos, both through Gregg's own efforts and through donations from around the country. To spur more donations, Gregg has instituted a voucher program that gives donors borrowing privileges from the Archive's star-studded main collection.

Tim is "glad to see it's growing and doing well." Gregg says the archive is actually bigger and better than ever before, especially when you take quality into account.

In conclusion, Tim thanks his generous sponsors Rio-Jenesis for making this episode possible.

On Cinema On Line

> 7:23 PM - 23 Mar 2018
> If you are wearing a hat on tv you better be a baseball player or a child cc @greggturkington

> 6:30 AM - 27 Mar 2018
> Yes some are getting sick from #RioJenesis but that is normal. When germs die they exude a poison which will temporarily create sickness! Stick with it! #ocx

> 4:30 PM - 5 Apr 2018
> What belongs on a #movie #review #show?
> 70% Rare movie promo hats
> 30% Dangerous powder

EPISODE X03
'Chappaquiddick' & 'You Were Never Really Here' (sponsored by Rio-Jenesis)

Air date: April 6, 2018
Running time: 15:10 minutes

Thanks to the generous support of Rio-Jenesis, Tim is back with Gregg Turkington of the VFA and technology expert Max Eucompco of Best Buy.

Max is here to follow up on last week's exploration of the virtual reality world Steven Spielberg created for us in *Ready Player One*. Max has already helped Tim by selling him a larger TV. Now, the *On Cinema* host is ready to leap "ahead of the curve" by learning about VR.

But first, Tim shares his tasty Germ Shield smoothie recipe, which effortlessly removes germs from the human biome.

"Some germs are good," Gregg argues, falling prey to a popular misconception. Tim quickly sets him straight: "*No* germs are good!" After distinguishing between germs and probiotics, he castigates Gregg for "speaking without knowledge" and also for wearing a hat.

"You told me you're not even washing your hands anymore because of this stuff," Gregg says.

"Why would you need to wash your hands if you have no germs?" Tim asks. That's game, set and match! He also issues a firm ultimatum: No more hats, or Gregg is off the show.

Getting back to the 21st-century future of VR, Max guarantees that once you don VR goggles, you will be "immersed into the videogame, the movie, whatever."

"This is the future, you think, of entertainment?" Tim asks. Max has no doubts on that score! Gregg is less impressed: They had 3D glasses in the 1950s, he says, so "it's not a new technology."

Pursuant to last week's *Sherlock Gnomes* controversy, Gregg has written an "open letter" to Tim Burton clarifying his original question and pointing out that Burton's letter did not respond to that question. Gregg is quite passionate on this topic, so Tim needs to cut him off early to keep things humming along.

Chappaquiddick is the story of "Ted Kennedy, one of the worst rats in the history of politics." Tim enjoyed watching him "get taken down a few pegs." Kennedy is dead now — "and no one was sad to see him go, by the way" — but Tim points out that a Rio-Jenesis regime like his probably could have saved the late senator. Tim gives this "great thriller five bags of popcorn."

Gregg sees *Chappaquiddick* as less "political" and "more of an old-fashioned horror movie" in that it exploits the public's "fear of the deep." He gives it five bags of popcorn and "an inflatable life preserver."

TIM'S GERM SHIELD X RECIPE

1 "big scoop" of Germ Shield

One cup of ice

1 to 2 cups of almond milk (or dairy equivalent)

1 cup of peanut butter

1 to 2 bananas (optional)

Chocolate syrup (to taste)

Blend and enjoy

Repeat 3 to 4 times per day

You Were Never Really Here depicts a vet's nightmare awakening to the reality of a "death trip" conspiracy that rescues trafficked girls. Tim presents this "mystery" film with five bags of popcorn for the serious questions it proposes.

Gregg calls this "memorable" and "great" film "horrifying" and "scary." He doles out five bags of popcorn and "a prescription to see a psychiatrist, 'cause you're gonna need it after you walk out of this one."

Gregg has a new segment honoring Mark Proksch, "who is under the weather at the moment." The first installment of *On Cinema Markives* shows us Mark's performance as the ghost of a dead man who terrifies his former business partner, as seen in *Decker*'s classic "Double Decker" episode.

This classic clip reminds Tim that the Delgado family has seized all intellectual property rights to *Decker*. Gregg is understandably dismayed to hear this.

Tim promises that next week, Max will add a VR component to the show, making it not only possible but obligatory for viewers to immerse themselves fully in the show's lively discussion of health, germ-free living and the cinematic arts.

"You shouldn't need something like that to watch this show," Gregg protests.

"You shouldn't, but you will," Tim says.

EPISODE X04
'Sgt. Stubby: An American Hero' & 'Overboard' (Sponsored by Rio-Jenesis)

Air date: April 13, 2018
Running time: 10:05 minutes

This week, Tim sports a new mustache as *On Cinema* pays a visit to the land of 360-degree digital virtual reality, so we can finally see what we're missing!

Tim is excited to activate this future-proof option for delivering actionable movie expertise in real time. He's also grateful to Best Buy's own Max for setting up the VR cameras and allowing him to lay off the *On Cinema* crew. After introducing his guest, Gregg Turkington, he walks around the set to demonstrate how VR works. He pitches it as "a new way to experience all kinds of different stuff."

Tim is sneezing a lot, and Gregg suspects he may be allergic to Rio-Jenesis products. This reminds Tim that "Rio-Jenesis is not only keeping me alive from a germ standpoint but from a financial standpoint." As the Delgado family continues to seize Tim's assets and intellectual property, Rio-Jenesis is his only remaining source of income.

"So that's the last we'll see of Dekkar and DKR?" Gregg ask.

"Right now they're in a holding company that the Delgados have established." He explains that Rio-Jenesis gives *On Cinema* the stability it needs and urges fans to support the show while ensuring that they lead a germ-free life.

"Rio-Jenesis kind of did get rid of bacteria and germs if it's responsible for Dekkar being gone," Gregg reflects. Tim orders Gregg not to discuss "personal stuff," adding, "I'm really at my wit's end with you." One major problem is that Gregg has repeatedly been told not to wear "stupid hats," but today he is wearing a hat advertising *Swordfish*.

Gregg takes exception to this: "This is a beret. It's not a hat."

Tim doesn't care if it's a hat or a beret; his larger concern is that Gregg looks like "an idiot" and "a clown."

"You should talk!" Gregg says. "You look like Adolf Hitler."

Tim reproaches Gregg for calling him "the white N-word" and refuses to continue the show until Gregg removes the offending hat.

Sgt. Stubby stars Helena Bonham Carter in the unexpected role of a lifetime in this animated story of a real-world dog who served honorably in World War I. Although it's not Tim's kind of movie and had "no stars," he tosses it five bags of popcorn because "it checked off all the boxes" as far as length, child-friendliness and patriotism are concerned.

Gregg is sure that as far as canine heroes go, Sgt. Stubby will never chase Benji from our hearts. Even so, he bestows an appreciative five bags of popcorn on this "very good" movie,

as well as "a can of Dick Van Patten's Natural Balance dog food" to appeal to Tim's health-conscious side.

Overboard is a remake of the Goldie Hawn/Kurt Russell vehicle in which a spoiled yacht owner is thrown into the sea to die. Tim hands this one a generous five bags of popcorn.

Gregg thinks they took a sizable risk rebooting a film with so many iconic stars. Luckily, this risk paid off with a movie that's "just as good as the original." Confident that it will be "the comedy of the year," he gives it five enthusiastic bags of popcorn and "a miniature anchor."

Tim thanks *On Cinema* sponsor Rio-Jenesis, and once more challenges Gregg's Stone-Age belief that simple handwashing could ever deliver the kind of germ-free existence that millions find daily through Rio-Jenesis. "Don't undercut the sponsor," Tim warns him.

This week's Popcorn Classic is 1954's *The Creature from the Black Lagoon*, an early 3D film that Gregg calls "the original virtual reality."

Tim advises Gregg to accept modern-day virtual reality and move on, but as per usual, Gregg can't give up on tradition: "It just doesn't feel right."

Gregg also defends comparing Tim to Hitler, stressing that it's more of a physical resemblance than a moral one. But Tim is not appeased and walks off the set in a bad mood.

On Cinema On Line

4:40 PM - 12 Apr 2018
A good way to watch today's On Cinema is just to close your eyes and listen. Getting reports of people falling ill from the VR.

8:20 AM - 15 Apr 2018
The Vr experience is now rated above all else when it comes to on cinema and at this point there may be no turning back imagine going back to horse and buggy?

2:14 PM - 15 Apr 2018
We are no different than the commen Cave man. When they discovered fire and wheel they did not reject it. #VR is future as in latest episode of #OnCinema #ocx #RioGenesis

EPISODE X05
'Rampage' & 'Super Troopers 2'

Air date: April 19, 2018
Running time: 10:24 minutes

Virtual reality has never looked better as Gregg and Tim deliver another "immersive experience" so real, you'll swear Tim is coughing right into your lap!

Tim announces that he's "cut ties" with long-time sponsor Rio-Jenesis, even thought it's an "amazing, life-changing product." Like many of Tim's recent problems, it all comes down to a conflict with the Delgado family: In what Tim calls "the crime of the century," the Delgados have seized all monies earned through Rio-Jenesis sales, leaving none for Tim.

"I'm at my fucking wit's end with them," he laments. He tells viewers not to bother buying Rio-Jenesis products, since it will no longer benefit the show, and counsels them to request a refund for any orders they already placed.

"My message to the Delgados is, 'Fine, we're even. OK?'" he says. "You won. You've taken it all." Above all, he finds it unfair that they're trying to shut down *On Cinema at the Cinema*: "I was doing this well before I got involved with your son, and your son made the shitty mistake that he made that got him six feet under."

Meanwhile, Gregg is still grappling with Tim Burton. This week, he's penned a follow-up to the open letter he sent in Episode X03. The tone has grown decidedly harsh, as Burton's lack of response confirms Gregg's "worst suspicions" about the director's decision to jettison Johnny Depp. He invites Burton on next week's episode to address the allegations and clear the air in person. "You will be given ample time to explain your strange and disturbing motives," Gregg promises. The alternative is a loss of personal and professional reputation.

"I'm sick of this Tim Burton stuff," Tim says. "Let it go."

This week, Dwayne "The Rock" Johnson goes on a *Rampage* at our local cinemas as the action star takes on a cavalcade of apes and monsters from an old videogame. Tim "loved" this "great action movie," which gets a perfect five-bag rating.

Gregg informs us that although this is "the sixth movie in movie history called *Rampage*," none of them are sequels or reboots. This spells trouble for collectors even if they use a good coding system like Gregg's. Because this is "the second-best" *Rampage* movie, he gives it five bags of popcorn and "a stack of index cards" to help sort out its confusing title.

Super Troopers 2 makes the most of Rob Lowe as U.S.-Canada border tensions spill over into the land of laughs. Tim liked this "good movie" well enough to give it five bags of popcorn.

For Gregg, "good movie" is too diffident. "*Great* movie" is more like it, especially when you factor in the unprecedented 15-year gap between *Super Troopers 2* and its prequel. His only complaint: Calling this sequel *Super Twopers* would have been "funny." He gives it five bags of popcorn and a police car siren.

Tim is having a severe coughing fit as Gregg dives into *Popcorn Classics*. This week, it's *The Life of David Gale* by Alan Parker of *Fame* fame. This is a "conspiracy movie about a professor" who may or may not be a murderer depending on what the viewer thinks is going on in the story.

Tim ends the episode a little early because he needs to lie down.

ON CINEMA ON HOLLYWOOD LEGENDS

Max Eucompco

Originally born in Sylmar, Calif., **Max Eucompco** moved in 2012 to Montebello, CA. An avid tech aficionado and gamer, Max soon landed an entry-level position with **Best Buy** as a Seasonal Inventory and Merchandising Specialist. A few months later, he became a full-fledged **Sales Collaborator** focused on imagineering and implementing Future-Edge Virtual Reality Solutions for consumer, business and corporate clients.

Apart from VR's all-important use in home entertainment and gaming, Max looks forward to its seamless integration into the consumer-grade electronics retail market, as customers and sales professionals connect interactively in a virtual/experiential **"Show Space"** to explore product benefits without ever leaving the home or office. In his spare time, Max enjoys Fortnite, Overwatch, escape rooms and the music of **Imagine Dragons**.

EPISODE X06
'Traffik'

Air date: April 25, 2018
Running time: 10 minutes

This week, Tim introduces *Tim Heidecker's Movie Review Show*, a new conversational film assessment program that is legally and financially a separate and distinct entity from *On Cinema at the Cinema*, which is now owned by the Delgados.

"You could call it *Our Cinema*," Gregg suggests. However, this title likewise falls under Tim's "corporate umbrella" and thus belongs to the Delgados. Tim also needs to return the VR cameras to prevent the Delgados from seizing them, but he thanks VR expert Max from Best Buy for all his hard work in elevating the show to the future-centric virtual realm.

In health news, Tim finally went to the doctor for his persistent cough and got some antibiotics: "Don't bother with the Rio-Jenesis stuff," he counsels viewers.

Gregg says washing your hands is a better way to defeat germs.

"You're right on that," Tim concedes. He also has a message for Bruce and Katherine Delgado: "I'm done." Although he plans to finish the Xth season, he's "absolutely tapped out" emotionally and financially.

"At least you're not in jail," Gregg consoles him.

Tim agrees: "That's something I'm grateful for." With nothing left but his watch, he advises the Delgados that they will "have to rip it out of my cold dead hands" like Charlton Heston did.

"What's sad is, I love doing this," Tim laments. "And people get a kick out of finding out what movies to watch."

"They *rely* on it," Gregg clarifies. "It's not just a kick."

"And what's Gregg gonna do?" Gregg actually has an answer at hand: He will soon launch a new film review show that will cast an expert eye on four movies per episode.

"They don't have four movies a week," Tim scoffs. "Good luck with that." He directs Gregg to do a Popcorn Classic and even picks the film: *Training Day*. "This is a good one," Gregg says. It also has a built-in twist in the form of "an alternate ending."

Tim has no idea what he will do after *On Cinema* ends: "Am I gonna, like, starting shopping resumes around?"

"I don't think you should shop *your* resume around," Gregg cautions him.

"I took all my shots," Tim sighs. "I got no more bullets left in the chamber. They've taken my creativity, they've taken my art."

"You killed their son, essentially," Gregg reminds him. Tim counters that persecuting him won't bring their son back.

"But you didn't go to jail," Gregg observes. "Which is what they thought you should've. A *lot* of people felt that way."

Tim suspects he'll wind up in jail anyway, since he "can't afford to turn the lights on" or to eat. "They've frozen the accounts, I can't do a credit card, I can't get a debit card. I don't know what I'm gonna do."

He gets up and drops his cue cards in Gregg's lap: "You can do the show. I don't give a shit. Have fun."

In *Traffik*, a couple runs afoul of a dangerous biker gang who will stop at nothing during a romantic mountain getaway. Gregg calls it "a modern twist on *Easy Rider*" in its focus on the freewheeling motorcycle lifestyle, with the dramatic difference that these bikers are "monsters."

Gregg thought *Traffik* was "really scary," though he was a bit puzzled by its misspelled title. He gives it five bags of popcorn and a can of mace to defend yourself against bikers.

Last, Gregg presents a scoop from the VFA. He explains that he has "secured funding" to keep the VFA going and acquire "more acquisitions." Recent additions to the archive range from classics like *The Big Chill* to sleepers like *How to Deal*. The VFA will also "partner with two local universities to do screenings" of "gems from the VFA." He welcomes donations, both cash and films. "The VFA is thriving, and without Tim Heidecker's involvement, and that's probably a good thing."

Did YOU notice...?

- The new home of **Gregg Turkington's Victorville Film Archive** is actually a spare corner of Golden Age celebrity impressionist Mark Proksch's rented room in **Van Nuys, Calif**. VR users who visit this episode and look around the room carefully will be able to examine the **unfortunate actor**, who remains comatose in his sickbed after a diving accident that temporarily limited his access to breathable air.

EPISODE X07
'Avengers: Infinity War'

Air date: May 3, 2018
Running time: 11:06 minutes

On Cinema at the Cinema is back in action this week, thanks to the generous sponsorship of the Delgado Fund.

After welcoming his guests, Joe Estevez and Gregg Turkington, Tim puts his cards on the table: Last week, "we were in a lot of ways standing at the precipice of the end."

After shooting the previous episode, he and Max went back to Best Buy to return the VR gear for some much-needed cash. After having a meal to replenish his low blood sugar, Tim drove to L.A.'s famed Sixth Street Bridge and prepared to take his own life. "I was really going to do it," he recalls.

For nearly an hour, he stood at the precipice of the end, "stepping forward, moving back." Suddenly, a realization came: "I got one card to play." He remembered that the Delgados have been working with Mark Dwyer, Tim's estranged attorney whom he fired on the fateful first day of the Electric Sun 20 murder trial.

Tim called Dwyer, telling him, "Mark, I'm standing here at the Sixth Street Bridge. I'm ready to jump. Now what good does that do to you and the Delgados?" He alerted Dwyer that the Delgados were "sitting on a gold mine" of assets ranging from *On Cinema* to *Decker* to Dekkar to DKR. But these assets won't generate money if Tim is "down at the bottom of the L.A. River."

Tim informed Dwyer he had an hour to make a deal with the Delgados that would allow Tim to "earn for them," or he would jump to his death.

Dwyer agreed to contact the Delgados. For 56 agonizing minutes, Tim heard nothing. Then, Dwyer called. "You must have an angel looking out for you," he told Tim. The Delgados were willing to give him 30 days to improve the show!

"You saved my life, Mark," Tim replied. "And I'm gonna make the best show possible." He plans to invite guests like Joe and experts like Gregg, "and we are going to talk about movies and we're gonna give expert advice!"

Tim notices something in Joe's hand. "What's going on with that?" he asks. "What are you holding over there?" Joe shows him a baseball cap Gregg gave him, which advertises *The General's Daughter* (1999).

"Get rid of it!" Tim demands. "I don't want it on the set." He grabs it from Joe and hurls it offstage.

"Folks, this is my last shot," Tim continues. "And I thank the Delgados and I thank Mark Dwyer for giving me this shot." Turning to Gregg and Joe, he pleads for their support: "Will you guys, who have been with me through everything, step up to the plate and do what *you* do best?" They both promise that they will. Tim expresses his gratitude for Gregg's unmatched movie expertise and for Joe's stellar appearances in close to 300 films and counting.

And now, it's time to review some movies! In *Avengers: Infinity War*, the titular Avengers must battle to sacrifice all they have before putting an end to the universe. Tim loved this "great movie" starring Chris Pratt and felt "so excited" to watch it that he gives it five bags of popcorn.

Gregg also loved the movie, but the studio gets a slap on the wrist for confusing Avengers fans of all stripes by borrowing its title from Uma Thurman's *The Avengers*. That said, Gregg is sure that whether moviegoers enter the theater expecting to see superheroes or the lovely Ms. Thurman, "they're gonna leave happy." Even if *The Avengers* wasn't as good as *Ant-Man*, it's still "one of the best action-adventure superhero movies of all time." He gives it five bags of popcorn and "an *Ant-Man* DVD that I would collect some residuals on."

Tim wants Joe's professional take on *Infinity War*, but Joe hasn't seen it yet. "Do you like these kind of movies in general?" Gregg wonders. Joe acknowledges that he's "a little late to the table," as the audience for these films skews young and tends to put more of a premium on car chases. But under prodding from Gregg, he does salute the *Fast and the Furious* films as a guilty pleasure.

Gregg has a new episode of *On Cinema On Location*, and it's a certified barnburner! This time, he takes us to the Tinseltown supermarket that formerly housed "the famous hot dog bun scene" from Steve Martin's *Father of the Bride* reboot, in which Martin is furious because there are 12 buns but only eight hot dogs. Taking us to the present-day bun aisle, Gregg uncovers a classic case of life imitating art: These self-same packages now contain eight buns — just like the hot dogs do! "So if the movie were made today, Steve would have very little to complain about," Gregg concludes. "Because indeed, they do now sell the hot dogs in packages of eight."

Tim thanks Gregg and Joe for a job well done.

On Cinema On Line

2:45 PM - 3 May 2018
Eventually we would like to make all the hats available to be borrowed for 48-hour blocks of time, by VFA-heads and supporters to wear on special occasions.

EPISODE X08
'Life of the Party' & 'Breaking In'

Air date: May 10, 2018
Running time: 9:37 minutes

This week on *On Cinema at the Cinema*, Tim and his co-host, Gregg Turkington, cast a critical eye on two of the week's hottest and most talked-about films.

Does the quality match the hype? We'll find out in good time. But first, Tim and Gregg want to share some breaking news: Gregg recently got "a call out of the blue" from Delgado family lawyer Mark Dwyer, who told him that "the Delgados want this show to continue" for the sake of potential revenue streams.

"They needed somebody to kind of supervise and produce the show," Gregg says. Because they have some "issues" with Tim relating to their son's death, they have turned the reins over to Gregg. As the managing director of Delgado Media Holdings, Gregg is tasked with delivering "more movies, more Popcorn Classics" and less "negativity about them or their son."

"It's win-win for everybody," Gregg alleges. Tim is skeptical, but he does concede that it was kind of Gregg to keep him on as host: "You've made me a generous offer, and I appreciate it."

"You'll be doing just what you always do," Gregg assures him. "And you've always been great at it! It's just that we'll have less of the extraneous topics." Gregg vows that there will be three movie reviews and two Popcorn Classics — one from Gregg and, in a new twist, one from Tim.

"We're still co-hosts, like we always have been," Gregg affirms. His one stipulation is that there will be "no more Dekkar and DKR and all that."

Life of the Party sends Melissa McCarthy back to college as a heartbroken housewife who finds the freedom to approach frat boys on her own terms. Tim found it "very funny," due in no small part to McCarthy's role as "the John Belushi of the female gender" as far as "outrageousness" is concerned. It graduates *magna cum laude* with five bags of popcorn.

Gregg also gives it five bags, calling it a shoo-in for the Best Comedy Oscar if the Academy would finally "get with the modern world" and create one.

Breaking In is a pulse-pounding nail-biter that takes no prisoners in its portrayal of a woman and her child held hostage during a home invasion. Gregg initially thought it was a long-waited sequel to *Breaking Away*, which famously ran away with the Oscar gold back in 1979. While watching, he realized that this "horror film" had a very different tale to tell and was "really quite unpleasant at times." Because movies are about "experiencing different types of things," some of which "can't be fun," he does not let this unpleasantness detract from the artistic achievement: It still gets all five bags of popcorn.

Tim's edition of *Popcorn Classics* introduces us to *Mystery Men*, an irreverent superhero spoof with Hank Azaria, Ben Stiller and other caped crusaders of today's modern-day comedy world. With a PG-13 rating to give it a little spice and an ample running time of 105 minutes, this one comes by its Popcorn Classic status honestly!

Gregg's own Popcorn Classic is *An Eye for an Eye*, which tops Sally Field off with Kiefer Sutherland in "a thriller about the search for justice in an unjust world." Clocking it at 102 minutes, it provides a somewhat different take on crime in a slightly shorter time frame. It was also the final film by Sir John Schlesinger of *Midnight Cowboy* notoriety.

After this dual segment, Tim worries that presenting two Popcorn Classics each week will be "a drag" for the audience. Gregg proposes that they let the Delgados judge the success of his expanded segment.

On Cinema On Line

8:24 PM - 10 May 2018
I look forward to working with @greggturkington and the Delgado Media company! We all love movies! #OCX

EPISODE X09
'Deadpool 2' & 'Show Dogs'

Air date: May 17, 2018
Running time: 8:05 minutes

Lights, camera, action! This week, affable *On Cinema* co-host Tim Heidecker introduces film maven Gregg Turkington, whose show this week will harvest a bumper crop of real-world movie expertise as well as filmgoing do's and don'ts.

"Gregg, what do we have to look forward to in the cinemas this week?" Tim asks.

Gregg's first pick of this week's litter is *Deadpool 2*, which he defines as "a superhero movie with a lot of action and a lot of heart." Josh Brolin is just one of the innumerable reasons to check out this no-holds-barred popcorn movie, which ties up all the loose ends from *Deadpool 1* while also telling its own tale. Gregg liked it so much that he plans to see it again this weekend. Needless to say, this gives it a lock on his patented five-bag rating! He throws in "a gift certificate to buy the first *Deadpool* movie on VHS tape if they ever release it that way."

"Anything else?" Tim wonders.

The second pick of the litter is the aptly named *Show Dogs*, in which Will Arnett is a tough police dog and his human partner who must undertake an undercover role to uncover shady dealings at a dog show that will "avert a disaster from happening." This "kids' film" is very much in the proven wheelhouse of *Scooby-Doo* director Raja Gosnell, who has once again gone to the dogs for a tangled tale of canine sleuthery.

But that doesn't mean it's just for the little ones among us; it also works for those of us who are little ones at heart: "Whether you're 6 years old or 66 years old, you're gonna *love* this thing," Gregg warrants. He gives it five bags of popcorn as well as "a decorative dog bowl, maybe, with some of the characters from the movie around the edge, so as your dogs are eating or lapping up water, they can enjoy these characters in the privacy of their own home."

Tim wonders if Gregg has any Popcorn Classics to recommend this week. "I've got *four* of them!" the film buff enthuses. From Gregg's expert perspective, the best of the bunch is Patrick Swayze's *Next of Kin*. Those who only know Swayze from his brother Don's recent appearance in *Decker* will be excited to learn that the younger Swayze is "just as good" in this "mob movie" that runs "109 minutes" and serves as an "unofficial sequel" to "all the other Patrick Swayze movies."

In a similarly crime-oriented vein, *36 Hours to Die* is a Popcorn Classic for the ages. Gregg touts it as a "slick and satisfying thriller that you gotta see to believe." It is perhaps most notable for including one of the final roles for Carroll O'Connor, who originally came to national prominence as TV's Archie Bunker but is also a fine actor in his own right. Running the action gamut from "embezzlement" to "a very harrowing heart attack scene," this "Canadian-made" hair-raiser hits on all cylinders for every second of its pulse-racing 95-minute running time.

John Travolta's *The Punisher* "wasn't one of his bigger movies, but it should've been." As Gregg sees it, "war, crime, cruelty and injustice" are "the four pillars of any exciting movie." This Popcorn Classic is no exception, delivering on all these promises and more for 122 minutes, which works out to just over two hours. *Ant-Man* fans take note: As "a Marvel movie," *The Punisher* will have special interest for fans of *Ant-Man*.

Last up is *100 Kilos*. "That's not the weight of my Popcorn Classic collection," Gregg says in a waggish aside, "although I *do* have quite a few!" On the contrary, this is "kind of a story about some drug dealers, and they get into some nasty business, and of course there is some bloodshed." Sporting an unexpected CIA twist, this time-tested Popcorn Classic is "definitely something to see."

As a bonus, Tim rolls out a brief segment from the *On Cinema Markives*, which features a rare audition reel from ailing comic actor Mark Proksch.

"Well, that's our show," Tim concludes. "Tune in next week for more expertise from our film guru, Gregg Turkington!"

"Thanks, Tim," Gregg says. "Great job!"

On Cinema On Line

3:46 PM · 18 May 2018
Thanks to The Delgados and @greggturkingtkn for keeping the On Cinema dream alive

EPISODE X10
'Solo: A Star Wars Story'

Air date: May 25, 2018
Running time: 8:17 minutes

On Cinema's announcer, Tim Heidecker, ushers in the final episode of Season X by introducing the show's renowned film guru and "expert of all things cinema," Gregg Turkington.

With no further ado, Gregg takes a look at one of the major films in the world markets at this time: *Solo: A Star Wars Story*. Of course the *Star Wars* franchise is no stranger to controversy, but as Gregg points out, *Solo* is something else again: This is a movie that has people talking — and not just on *On Cinema* but wherever movies are discussed!

"As a film expert," Gregg knows that "sometimes you have to make decisions that go against the grain." In this case, Gregg refuses to review *Solo*. The reason? "George Lucas and company are guilty of theft in taking my master codebreaker character and folding it into the *Star Wars* world." He plans to boycott *Solo* until such time as he receives "full credit from Mr. Lucas and an invitation to appear in one of the future *Star Wars* movies." All is not lost, however, as Gregg intends to fill this void with "many, many, many Popcorn Classics."

The first is *Double Exposure*, starring Ron Perlman in a "revenge movie" about an unfaithful wife whose erotic misdeeds come to light over the course of its 93-minute length.

Blackheart stars Christopher Plummer, but don't go expecting another *Sound of Music* from this dark thriller about a "sexy seductress" and her deadly victims. It's only two minutes longer than *Double Exposure*, making it a virtual toss-up if you need to limit your dose of movie magic to 95 minutes or less.

Wesley Snipes needs no introduction, and neither does *Blade*, which is already well regarded as a top-shelf Popcorn Classic. It has a running time of 91 minutes, comparable to the other movies discussed so far.

"I'm sorry, I can't do it." Tim breaks in. "I'm sorry. This is it. I'm done."

"You don't *have* anything to do," Gregg claims. "You don't even have to watch the movies anymore."

"This is not who I am!" Tim protests. "I'm a fighter, and I'm laying down like a dog." Knocking a tub of popcorn from a decorative column, he yells, "Fuck this! No! We're done!"

As Gregg scurries off the set, Tim delivers a message to the Delgados: "I'm *done!* You hear me? Your son is in hell, Delgado. It was his choice! It was all their choice. I had nothing to fucking do with it. I'm clean! My conscience is clean."

He savages the Delgados for "stealing" his show and handing it over to Gregg. He also has some tough words for DA Rosetti: "I'm coming for you, Rosetti, wherever the fuck you are!" He announces his decision to run for district attorney of San Bernardino County: "I'm a fighter, and I know what that county needs." Having already proven himself as a lawyer by winning his murder trial "fair and square," he is ready to take on even greater responsibilities.

"I'm not gonna sit here and be a host for that piece of shit here with his dumb bullshit movies," he sneers, indicating Gregg's empty chair. He threatens to run for mayor of Victorville so he can "shut down the Victorville Film Archive."

"Listen," he says. "I have every right to get angry. A lot of people get angry. And that's *passion!* And passion is what this county needs." Referring again to his hard-earned victory in the Electric Sun trial, he pitches himself as the best man for the job: "I wanna be your DA. I hope I have your vote, 'cause I'll fight harder than anybody else out there combined."

Before walking off the set, Tim smashes the Styrofoam OCX logos, ending the season on a downbeat note and leaving the future of *On Cinema* in question.

On Cinema On Line

1:48 PM - 1 Jun 2018
Have a good weekend San Bernardino! Look into supporting me as your DA so much crime we could stop now if we get #RosettiTheRat out!

8:05 AM - 2 Jun 2018
The people of Sand Berndadino have been very poorly served by #RosettiTheRat crime is WAY WAY up. We can do so much better

1:46 PM - 18 Sep 2018
Tim should run for D.A. alright
"D"oesn't know "A"nything about movies

TIM HEIDECKER

★★★ ★★★

For San Bernardino County
DISTRICT ATTORNEY

- ✓ Tough on Crime
- ✓ Exposing Corruption
- ✓ A Great Legal mind

"I'm prepared to fight for the people of this county."

– Tim Heidecker, *Top Attorney*

WWW.TIMHEIDECKERFORDA.COM

WE'VE GOT A RAT!

VINCENT ROSETTI tried to put an innocent man in prison. Now he wants to get re-elected?

NO CHANCE!

Tim Heidecker will restore the integrity of the office of District Attorney.

TIM HEIDECKER
for District Attorney 2018
WWW.TIMHEIDECKERFORDA.COM

TIM HEIDECKER IS...

THE EXTERMINATOR

We have a rat problem.

TIM HEIDECKER FOR DISTRICT ATTORNEY

WWW.TIMHEIDECKERFORDA.COM

MOVIEHEADS NEWSLETTER

"YOUR SOURCE FOR MONTHLY MOVIE EXPERTISE"
June 2018

The Case Against DVDs

The Victorville Film Archive in Van Nuys, Calif., is one of the largest collections of classic movies ever assembled. The curators make sure to have on hand all of the titles that movie buffs would want to see, and also researchers who are writing books on classic cinema have also visited the archive to view movies that they might not be able to see otherwise, without this resource. A lot of people have asked me why the VFA does not have a wing for DVD movies. Well that's a complicated question.

A lot of movie buffs have spent much time building up collections in the superior VHS Videotaped format and it is always crazy to switch horses mid-stream. But more important the quality is not good. The DVD has digital "glitches" that did not exist on VHS tape. Also we have heard reports of discs being stuck in the machine with no way to open the drawer to get the disk out. That means that the movie is lost forever. The plastic "teeth" that hold the DVD into the case have been known to break easily and we have received reports of discks being broken when the people tried to remove the disk from the case and it cracked near the center of the disk. A DVD dropped on the floor that lands on the edge of the disk WILL almost always crack. Aren't you glad Picasso's master works and the Mona Lisa were painted on canvas and not on eggshells?

Finally, the technology has not been yet proved. No one knows really how long DVD discs will last. I have had DVD-Rs that lasted as little as one play. Digital glitches are an annoyance, as are "skipping" discs where a classic scene will be lost to the viewer. DVDs can get easily scratched and then you get more skips, or the DVD becomes unplayable. The format is a "novelty" only and is not of the type of archival quality that you would want for an archive that is meant to last hundres of years. Basically, you can't trust it. There are also literally thousands of movies that came out on VHS tape that were never made available on DVD, everything from 1989's "Meet the Applegates" with Ed Begley Jr, to 1949's "The Great Gatsby". This makes buidling a "complete" archive of motion pictures impossible. The VFA would not be successful with a "skeleton" libarary of DVDs that missed certain movies entirely. It would be hard to take such an "archive" seriously. No, let's face it the VHS is the format of record. Some people disagree but look at their collections and they are sadly lacking. The true collector will collect VHS tapes or even 16mm film but it can be hard to operate a film projector. Blu-Ray is a joke.

On Cinema On Line

10:01 PM - 3 Jun 2018
The supposed Ant Man trailer that is making the rounds is a HOAX video, Marvel has not announced a sequel yet and @MrPeytonReed would never take Tim's $$$$ to be in it, if it was really happening any way.

9:45 PM - 8 Jun 2018
Everyone is discussing how wonderful the new ant man trailer is with yours truly. How nice! So happy for @MrPeytonReed he was allowed a redo as this is now ANT MAN 1!

11:27 PM - 10 Jun 2018
The guys who made the 2 minute "hoax" Ant-Man "trailer" pieced it together using old outtake footage from the Ant-Man DVD, along with vacation footage of @timheidecker screaming on an amusement park ride. @Marvel should sue!!!!

4:37 PM - 26 Jun 2018
There is an extra in one scene of the unofficial Ant-Man sequel who bears a coincidental, slight physical resemblance to @timheidecker. But it is not Tim (CONFIRMED). For him to claim otherwise is a delusion. And the scene from that HOAX Ant-Man trailer is not even in the movie!!

7:30 AM - 27 Jun 2018
Delusion beyond belief! And pathetic! My character of Captain Gobbler is a main role (maybe best supporting Oscar?) and finally a great redo which is, #AntMan1

9:19 AM - 27 Jun 2018
Can someone help identify the background actor who looks a little like @timheidecker? If he comes forward we will get his story about filming that Ant-Man scene. But he is NOT Tim, and should receive his full due.

9:22 AM - 27 Jun 2018
Next thing you know @timheidecker will claim to have been in @starwats

12:22 AM - 28 Jun 2018
It is Known now that @timheidecker paid $10,000 to appear in the Fantastic Four movie. With "Ant-Man Vs The Wasp", @timheidecker, who is now broke from a lawsuit after a mass murder, claimed he was in the movie. Well he is not. It was simply an extra who resembled him slightly.

12:23 AM - 28 Jun 2018
Sorry but no one would cast you @TimHeidecker in a Ant-Man movie

12:27 AM - 28 Jun 2018
Dale from Ant Man was a memorable character, unfortunately none of the new characters in Ant Man Vs. The Wasp are as memorbable, though the movie is still great. @timheidecker does not appear in the movie.

9:30 AM - 28 Jun 2018
Interesting that ZERO reviews have mentioned @timheidecker. Critics and experts can spot a Hoax. Tim is not in Ant Man Vs The Wasp.

6:25 AM - 28 Jun 2018
Marval has indicated strongly to me that they are planning a series of Captain Dave Gobbler spin off movies with Me as Gobbler hunting whales acrosss the ocean. Meanwhile @greggturkington sits by phone which doesn't ring. #AntMan1

8:05 AM - 28 Jun 2018
Correction and Spoiler: Gobbler who is smart and talented Marine Biologist is bit by whale and becomes whale aka WhaleMan, fighting crime and pollution etc.

9:38 AM - 28 Jun 2018
Whale Man sounds neat. But they would probably cast someone more established like Leonardo DeCaprio or Dustin Hoffman in that role. Also a whale is too big to hide so undercover covert missions would be impossible. I think Shark Man makes more sense as a new franchise.

9:39 AM - 28 Jun 2018
It will happen. As long as I have time away from my important job As DA of San Bernardino County

9:46 AM - 28 Jun 2018
Whale Man will never get made.

4:58 PM - 28 Jun 2018
So wrong! And too bad as well, perhaps there was a minor part for Dale who ruined other non-movies

4:49 PM - 28 Jun 2018
Interesting backstory for Gobbler/Whale Man... he was afraid of water as boy. #WhaleMan

12:43 PM - 8 Jul 2018
Who is the real identity of the whale boat guy in Ant Man Vs The Wasp? I will pay $100 vhs tapes for the information. The name of the extra that looks like @timheidecker

On Cinema On Line

6:47 PM - 8 Jul 2018
Ant-Man is the most watched film since Titanic and no movie since has gotten close in turms of audience love for this one of a kind movie. @peytonrred as well as you know who (I) deserve many oscars for this redo. But wait until you see #Whaleman

9:56 AM - 10 Jul 2018
Will have to learn more about Wales before embarking on #whaleman series of films (as do writers who will have to know even more) and then who could WaleMan end up more popular than other "super" hero's.

10:33 AM - 10 Jul 2018
The problem is 1. the Whale man didn't have any powers in the movie, he was helpless to stop what happening, no one wants to see that. 2. You didn't even play Whale man in the movie, the character was played by an unknown extra.

10:38 AM - 10 Jul 2018
the Whale man in Ant-Man did nothing at all. Compared to Dale who set all the Ant-Man movies in motion by Firing Scott which inspired him to put on the Ant-Man outfit. Without Dale there is NO @AntMan. Compared to the The Whale man who is not a hero to Any one.

10:40 AM - 10 Jul 2018
I have not seen any Whale-man interest.

10:45 AM - 10 Jul 2018
The Real Whale man was Captain Ahab from Moby Dick. Played by Gregory Peck. That Whale man is the one that movies should be made about. Not the one in Ant-Man.

6:24 PM - 10 Jul 2018
To clarify The Whale Man is not in production or even the planning stages, it is not a movie that would be succesful as the Whale Man had no special powers.

6:28 PM - 10 Jul 2018
To get to the stage where @Marvel would make a Whale Man movie would take a lot, and there are other movies like a Moby Dick re-boot that would be more succesful comercially, sorry but I do n't think a Whale Man movie is in the cards.

6:30 PM - 10 Jul 2018
I welcome @timheidecker to present any evidence that Whale Man The Movie is under any consideration, I can say in all confidence my sources say it is not.

6:34 PM - 10 Jul 2018
It's safe to say Whale Man is Dead on Arrival as a movie concept.

6:35 PM - 10 Jul 2018
I can assure you it is happening. Any other information I would provide would be in breech of the MDA I signed

6:39 PM - 10 Jul 2018
Is this movie made by @Marvel if not it is not official and it will be stopped. Whale Man was their character

6:42 PM - 10 Jul 2018
Yes it will be made by @marval and they already predicted it will be a run away smash! You are working overtime trying to discredit the obvious

6:45 PM - 10 Jul 2018
If Marvey insists on making Whale man it will be their first Failure. Oh right their second. I forgot FANTASTIC FOUR that you paid $10k to be in and made about that much at the box office.

8:19 PM - 10 Jul 2018
even as #WHALEMAN becomes my full-time occupation i will still be able to run and WIN for District Attorney of San Burnadino country. It won't be hard to unseat #RosettiTheRat and the rest of the scum there.

5:56 PM - 12 Jul 2018
Wow, WhAleman might be a bigger deal than @marvels Superman! we will see!

8:45 PM - 12 Jul 2018
Suoperman had powers that were useful to save earth and all its residents. What powers does WhaleMan even have besides being scared on a boat? That is not a power. Sorry but WhaleMan will never surpass @ superman or even SPiderman

9:43 PM - 12 Jul 2018
We have yet to see Whalemans powers as we have only seen Gobbler who will soon become whaleman through a whale bite. What is the point of talking to you who as no vision or creativity

9:45 PM - 12 Jul 2018
You will be first in line to see WhaleMan 1 (of many) and attempt@to convince all that you were always a fan of whale man. With your five bags. But I will remember you always as a wale man hater. Shame on you.

8:27 AM - 4 Aug 2018
The #WhaleMan movie is officially dead.

MOVIEHEADS NEWSLETTER

"YOUR SOURCE FOR MONTHLY MOVIE EXPERTISE"
Augest 2018

The Legacy of Walt Disney

Walt Disney started a company called Disney that produced dozens of great movies starting with the 1937 classic Snow White and The Seven Dwarves right up to the recent Star Wars movies that stole the idea of Master Codebreaker Kington for use without permission, and Ant-Man, starring Paul Rudd, Michael Douglas ("Fatal Atraction"), Gregg Turkington ("Decker Vs Dracula"), and Judy Greer, as Walt Disney bought Marvel Pictures and Star Wars some years ago, with money that they made over the years from succesful movies ranging from the Mickey Mouse character to Toy Story 3, The Lion King, and Pirates of the Caribbean starring Johnny Depp.

Finding Dory is another movie that added to Disney's bank account. But in 2018 controversy emerged when Tim Heidecker claimed to have a leading role in Ant Man Vs. The Wasp, the not-really-a-sequel "sequel" to Ant-Man. In Ant Man Vs. The Wasp you can see a man who bears a passing resemblance to Tim Heidecker, on a whale tourist ship. But if you inspect closer it is not Tim Heidecker at all, but simply an extra who has similar facial features. Tim's claim was dismissed by most movie buffs but rumors persist on the internet to this day.

In the 1970s Disney had many hits that were non-animated, such as Freaky Friday starring Jodie Foster. Robin Hood (animated), The Rescuers, The Barefoot Executive starring Kurt Russell, The Black Hole (Star Wars), Escape to Witch Mountain, THe Apple Dumpling Gang etc.

But it was the classic Disney movies like Fantasia and Lady And The Tramp that people most remember today. Walt Disney passed away in 1967 but his studio continued on stronger than ever. An amusement park DIsneyland bears his name in Anaheim, California, 20 miles east of Hollywood where his dreams had all come true. And of course the Hollywood Walk of Fame pays tribute to Walt Disney with his own star. No one deserved it more than Walt Disney.

MOVIEHEADS NEWSLETTER

"YOUR SOURCE FOR MONTHLY MOVIE EXPERTISE"
September 2018

The Final Curtain

It is a part of life that you would die and have a final movie. Movie buffs hate to see the curtains close on our favorite actors and actress or directors. But it's also a great opportunity to see them in what could be the role of a lifetime.

John Wayne died with an Oscar under his belt for "True Grit". But "The Shootist" was his final movie and he was very sick during the making of it. Still his "true grit" shone through in "The Shootist" and it was an instant Popcorn Classic. The movie is about a shootist dying of cancer, which John Wayne was an actor dying of cancer. Don't miss it!

Heath Ledger was famous for the Joker from the Batman series and the "Brokeback Mountain" movie that won him many Great Actor awards while still alive. Sadly he died before having a chance to grab a bucket of Popcorn and watch his great performance in "The Imaginarium of Doctor Parnassus" costarring Johnny Depp who is thankfully still with us!

Gene Wilder played a very different Willy Wonka than Johnny Depp. But Wilder sadly did not live to see the day. His final movie was "Another You" from 1991 even though he died an incredible 12 years later. Why he did not fill those years with more movies is a mystery only Willy Wonka could solve!!!

The harder they come, the harder they fall. That was certainly true of the legend himself Humphrey Bogart. Ironically his last film was titled "The Harder They Fall". Bogie will never be forgotten.

Katharine Hepburn and Henry Fonda shared a final film "On Golden Pond" one of the all-time classics of cinema. They played two old people who time was running out. Even though the story was true for them they played the roles with great dignity and went out in style winning posthumous Oscards which they should have been buried with. If not for the fear of graverobbers who might commit a dastardly deed for a taste of Oscar Gold!!!!

On Cinema On Line

10:13 AM - 26 Nov 2018
a great question for @greggturkington

What is it like to live without any friends?
By Hamish Mackay
BBC News
6 hours ago

2:08 PM - 26 Nov 2018
Question for @timheidecker : What's it like to have friends ONLY when they are on your payroll? (Axiom, Manuel)

2:36 PM - 26 Nov 2018
Axe and Manuel are 2 of many friends of which I have. in your case "friends" amount to only used videotapes from goodwill bins. sorry but they are not the friends one can count on when you need them most, regardless of price.

2:40 PM - 26 Nov 2018
You can ALWAYS count on a popcorn classic to lift your mood and teach you life truths. Classic movies remain, long after paid "friends" drift away.

2:43 PM - 26 Nov 2018
several friends have just called me letting me know they are there for me no matter what happens. question: did your tattered copy of The Gremlins or Field of Dreams ever reach out and let you know you are important to them?

2:45 PM - 26 Nov 2018
Our movies are in pristine condition, not tattered. I also have more than one copy of each of the movies you cited, in case of damage which can occasionally occur with older titles.

2:47 PM - 26 Nov 2018
totally avoided the question: let me answer for you: no they don't. they are no substitute for real friendship only ways of wasting time. Friends are not movies.

2:59 PM - 26 Nov 2018
It's wasting time to make music with Aciom and Manuel because everyone deletes the down load after 5 seconds!!!!!!!!!!

3:01 PM - 26 Nov 2018
to be clear i did not initiate this argument. but now you have attacked my friends (brothers actually) imagine if i did that to your "friends" you'd have no movies to watch!

4:11 PM - 26 Nov 2018
If you try to attack the VFA again, police will be called. I also have security cameras in place to document that.

4:11 PM - 26 Nov 2018
Pretty sad that @timheidecker's idea of being a "Tough Guy" is to threaten to attack video tapes. He is not in the same league as real life tough guys like Bogart, Patrick Swayze, James Bond, Clin Eastwood, Charles Bronson, Indiana Jones etc.

APPENDIX 1: THE FILMS OF JOE ESTEVEZ

Paradise Pavilion (2019)
Kayla (2018)
Beyond the Darkness (2018)
Lamia: The Zombie Slayer (2018)
Abaddon (2018)
Urban Myths (2017)
High on the Hog (2017)
Drakul (2017)
Empire of the Heart (2017)
Syndicate Smasher (2017)
Fangs Vs. Spurs (2016)
Banger (2016)
Chasing Gold (2016)
Bad Fellaz (2015)
Samurai Cop 2: Deadly Vengeance (2015)
Doctor Spine (2015)
Max Hell Frog Warrior (2015)
Bikini Inception (2015)
A Turn in the Sun (2015)
The Haunting of Pearson Place (2015)
Act of Contrition (2014)
Rough Hustle (2014)
Rice Girl (2014)
The Attack of the 30-Foot Chola
The Caretakers (2014)
Army from Hell (2014)
The Appearing (2014)
Jet Set (2013)
Disaster Wars: Earthquake vs. Tsunami (2013)
Doonby (2013)
Axe Giant: The Wrath of Paul Bunyan (2013)
Brodowski & Company (2013)
Turning Point (2012)
Rugaru (2012)
Plastic Films (2012)
Gunfight at Yuma (2012)
Caesar and Otto's Deadly Xmas (2012)
Onion Syrup (2012)
Little Creeps (2012)
The Voices from Beyond (2012)
Golden Cage (2012)
Horroween (2011)
Sebastian (2011)
Under the Bridge (2011)
Inside Out (2011)
Insignificant Celluloid (2011)
Omerta (2011)
A Perfect Life (2011)
Corruption.Gov (2011)
Not Another B Movie (2010)
Placebo (2010)
Slow Moe (2010)
The Apparition of Roxanne (2010)
The Ascent (2010)
The Vigilante (2010)
Vanguard (2010)
King's Man (2010)
First Dog (2010)
The Mitchell Tapes (2010)
Daddy's Home (2010)
Iron Soldier (2010)
La Femme Vampir, Volume 2 (2009)
Dark Crossing (2010)
PrimeMates (2010)
Dead in Love (2009)
The Death of Hollywood (2009)
The Lights (2009)
Meltdown (2009)
Flesh, TX (2009)
Serbian Scars (2009)
La Femme Vampir (2009)
Caesar and Otto's Summer Camp Massacre (2009)
Untitled Horror Comedy (2009)
Hollywood Confidential (2008)
Withered One (2008)
Alibi (2007)
Koreatown (2007)
Necronaut (2007)

Sigma Die! (2007)
See Jane Run (2007)
Mexican American (2007)
Zombie Farm (2007)
Cake: A Wedding Story
Cordoba Nights (2007)
Death Row (2007)
Evil Ever After (2007)
Inner Rage (2006)
Voices from the Graves (2006)
San Franpsycho (2006)
Shut Up and Shoot! (2006)
I.R.A.: King of Nothing (2006)
2020: Am American Nightmare (2005)
Dead Things (2005)
Drawing Blood (2005)
Hercules in Hollywood (2005)
The Heat Chamber (2005)
Resurrection Mary (2005)
Scar (2005)
The Tailor (2005)
Evil Grave: Curse of the Maya (2004)
Buy Sell Kill: A Flea Market Story (2004)
The Rockville Slayer (2004)
Killer Story (2004)
Vampire Blvd. (2004)
Las Vegas Psycho (2003)
Tales from the Grave (2003)
Summer Solstice (2003)
Al infierno con la migra (2003)
Minds of Terror (2003)
Zombiegeddon (2003)
Hitman City (2003)
Got Papers? (2003)
Scary Tales: The Return of Mr. Longfellow (2003)
Mind Games (2003)
Spanish Fly (2003)
Jumper (2003)
No Dogs Allowed (2002)
Pacino Is Missing (2002)
The Craven Cove Murders (2002)
Vatos (2002)
Jumping for Joy (2002)
Max Hell Frog Warrior (2002)
Mob Daze (2002)
Deathbed (2002)
Autopsy: A Love Story (2002)
Hell Asylum (2002)
Psychotic (2002)
Green Diggity Dog (2001)
The Remnant (2001)
Two Coyotes (2001)
Shattered Faith (2001)
No Turning Back (2001)
Double Deception (2001)
Ultimate Prey (2000)
Silent Scream (1999)
Flat Out (1999)
14 Ways to Wear Lipstick (1999)
Avenged (1998)
Lola's Game (1998)
No Rest for the Wicked (1998)
The Catcher (1998)
The Waterfront (1998)
Together & Alone (1998)
Winner Takes All (1998)
Crimes of the Chupacabra (1998)
No Code of Conduct (1998)
Memorial Day (1998)
I Got the Hook Up (1998)
Guns of El Chupacabra II: The Unseen (1998)
Gator King (1997)
Acts of Betrayal (1997)
Motorcycle Cheerleading Mommas (1997)
Lethal Seduction (1997)
Quiet Days in Hollywood (1997)
Guns of El Chupacabra (1997)
American Tigers (1996)

Backroads to Vegas (1996)
Blood Slaves of the Vampire Wolf (1996)
Carnival of Wolves (1996)
Demolition Highway (1996)
Last of the Breed (1996)
Lethal Orbit (1996)
Rollergator (1996)
Squanderers (1996)
The Garbage Man (1996)
The Last Kill (1996)
The Searcher (1996)
Toad Warrior (1996)
Breakaway (1996)
Dark Secrets (1996)
Psychic Detectives (1996)
Baby Ghost (1995)
BLVD. (1995)
Broken Bars (1995)
Cruce en Tijuana (1995)
Equal Impact (1995)
Fatal Pursuit (1995)
Guns and Lipstick (1995)
Karate Raider (1995)
Little Lost Sea Serpent (1995)
Point Dume (1995)
Starstruck (1995)
Werewolf (1995)
With Criminal Intent (1995)
Red Line (1995)
Blonde Heaven (1995)
Dillinger and Capone (1995)
Body Count (1994)
The Deadly Secret (1994)
Unconditional Love (1994)
Inner Sanctum II (1994)
La quebradita (1994)
The Mosaic Project (1993)
Double Blast (1993)
Fatal Justice (1993)
Cyber Seeker (1993)
Expert Weapon (1993)
Madame (1993)
Return of the Roller Blade Seven (1993)
The Flesh Merchant (1993)
Dark Universe (1993)
Beach Babes from Beyond (1993)
Eye of the Stranger (1993)
L.A. Goddess (1993)
In a Moment of Passion (1993)
Blood on the Badge (1992)
Legend of the Roller Blade Seven (1992)
Lost in Hollywood (1992)
The Summoned (1992)
Armed for Action (1992)
Eddie Presley (1992)
Dark Rider (1991)
The Roller Blade Seven (1991)
Lockdown (1990)
Soultaker (1990)
The Platinum Triangle (1990)
Murder in Law (1989)
Retreads (1988)
Human Error (1988)
South of Reno (1988)
Fatal Pulse (1988)
Terminal Exposure (1987)
The Zero Boys (1986)
The Fourth Wise Man (1985)
I Married a Centerfold (1984)
The Invisible Woman (1983)
The First Time (1982)
Apocalypse Now (1979)
Anatomy of a Seduction (1979)
Flatbed Annie & Sweetiepie: Lady Truckers (1979)
Lucky Lady (1975)
The Hatfields and the McCoys (1975)
The California Kid (1974)
The Story of Pretty Boy Floyd (1974)

APPENDIX II: THE LYRICS OF DEKKAR

A HOLE IN MY SOUL

When I look into the mirror
I don't like what I see
There's a secret agent looking back at me
There's a hole in my soul
There's a hole in my soul

Under my skin is a sad and broken man
Why won't the people I know understand
There's a hole in my soul
There's a hole in my soul
There's a hole in my soul
There's a hole in my soul
There's a hole in my soul
There's a hole in my soul
There's a hole in my soul
There's a hole in my soul

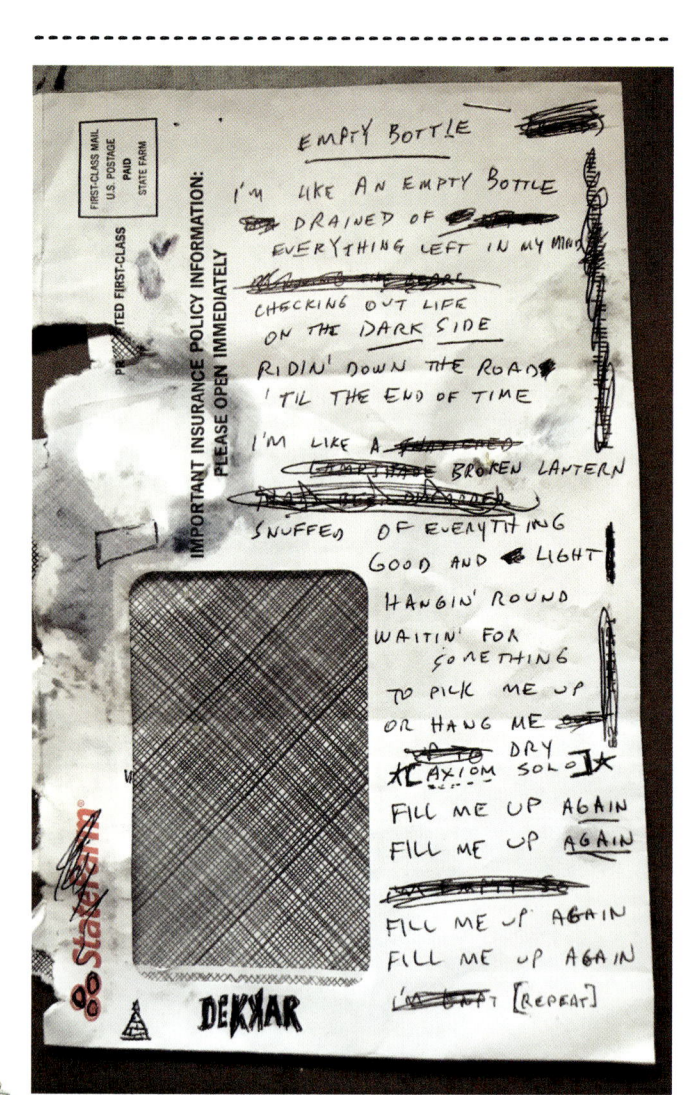

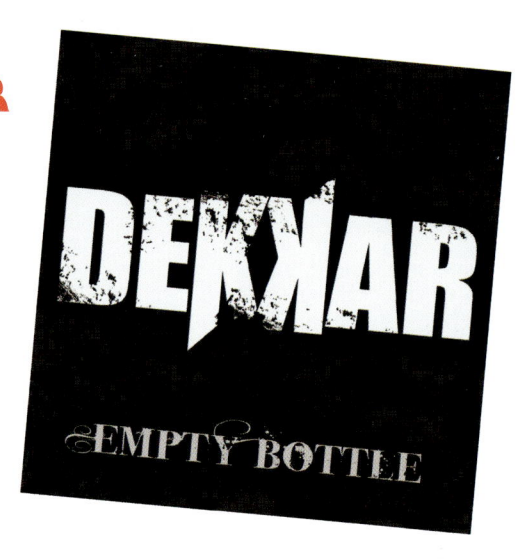

FAREWELL, TOM CRUISE

Well my heart is broken
It's all turned to black
And my future seems uncertain
Cuz he aint coming back

Farewell Tom Cruise
I miss ya son you ain't coming back
Farewell Tom Cruise
I miss ya son you ain't coming back

And I know he's up in heaven
Cuz that's where he belongs
And there's one thing for certain
That boy inspired me to write this song!

Farewell Tom Cruise
I miss ya son you ain't coming back
Farewell Tom Cruise
I miss ya son you ain't coming back
He ain't coming back,
He ain't coming back,
He ain't coming back

OSCAR FEVER

I've got the Oscar Fever
Hope you got it too
Poor Me Some Bubbly now it's
All ya gotta do
It's Christmas for Tinsel Town
The Academy Awards
Poor me some bubbly come on aboard
Who's gonna win
Who's gonna lose
I got the Oscar Fever hope you got it too

OSCAR MEDLEY

Spotlight
I'm under the light
Of the
Spotlight
Shining so bright

I'm relevant - it's middle name
I'm Relevant - I'm changing the game
Staying in focus - center of it all
The world is watching me
The world is watching me

I'm standing on the bridge of spies
Sick of hearing all of your damn lies
I'm standing on the bridge spies
Why don't you drop your damn disguise

Mad Max Mad Max
- giving all the ladies heart attacks
When I show them my moves
- when I show you my grooves

You gotta give me some (BOOM) room!
That's what i need
I need
(Room!)

I'm living in Brooklyn
Just trying to make my way
Working on my music
While She's out in L.A.
I'm strumming on my bass guitar
She's posing for the magazine
Never thought we'd get this far
Following our Hollywood dreams
Just a kid from Brooklyn

I'm talking bout the Big Short
And acting like Tough guy
With Long Legged woman
In a black tie

I believe there's a martian
Sitting on the top of the world
Yes a martian
Sitting on the top world

He believes we can be happy and free
He believe don't need the big man
   looking after me
Free market principles is the key to liberty
Need to stop the nanny state
Or doom and gloom will be our fate

Yes a martian
Sitting on the top world

Atlas Shrugged
When the Clinton machine turned on

TRIGGER EVERYTHING

When I was a child
I thought everything was fine,
the sky looked baby blue....
Then we fell in love
and the clouds rolled in above
- Yeah, ya did what ya had to do.

You tore me down, you killed my soul.
You filled my heart with a gaping hole.

Oooooh oooooh

Ya trigger my anger, ya trigger my pain,
ya trigger my loss and ya trigger my brain.
Oooooooh, ya trigger everything.

Ya trigger my anger, ya trigger my pain,
ya trigger my loss and ya trigger my brain.
Aaaah, ya trigger everything.

In my twisted cave, pent up hate and rage....
You drive my mind insane.
Can we get along?
Just admit you're wrong.
I don't wanna play your game.

You tore me down, you killed my soul.
You Filled my heart with a gaping hole.

Ya trigger my anger, ya trigger my pain,
ya trigger my loss and ya trigger my brain.
Oooooooh, ya trigger everything.

Ya trigger my anger, ya trigger my pain,
ya trigger my loss and ya trigger my brain.
Aaaah, ya trigger everything.

YOU ASKED FOR A HERO
(Written by David Agusto, Paul Nadler,
Amy Shein & Richie Daniels)

Not long ago we were on our back
Seems like out country had gone off the track
We threw our values down the drain
As if our leaders had gone insane

But from the shadows came the light
Replacing all that's wrong with right

You asked for a hero that's what you got
This might just be our final shot
We're moving forward to reverse
who put our nation in this curse

They called you crazy like a fox
Standing alone in your ballot box
The Sacred duty's in your hand
That's when the plan began

You asked for a hero that's what you got
This might just be our final shot
You're a bat out of hell or your born to run
Deciding what side you're on!

APPENDIX III: GREGG TURKINGTON ON CINEMA

11:17 PM - 26 Feb 2013
If only life was like a #movie!

10:50 AM - 2 Mar 2013
Sunny days were meant to be enjoyed--in a movie theater! #FilmBuff

11:47 PM - 2 Mar 2013
Any movie can be a #MidnightMovie if you put the tape in the machine at 11:59!

1:17 PM - 13 Mar 2013
#NewMovies keep coming out!

9:06 PM - 20 Mar 2013
The Expert's Advice: Best brand of videotape? #Kodak. They last the longest, I've noticed.

4:21 PM - 4 Apr 2013
Great #movie crticism lives on long after the movies themselves are gone

8:25 PM - 18 Apr 2013
Excited about the #sequels coming out soon. #movies

2:36 PM - 19 Apr 2013
If the #world has got you down, escape in a #movie.

9:50 PM - 24 Apr 2013
#Reviews are the icing on the cake for a well-made movie.

7:56 PM - 2 Jun 2013
Let a movie be your magic carpet.

7:27 PM - 17 Jul 2013
Movie definitions: "Christmasing"--seeing every movie playing at a multiplex on the same day.

8:24 PM - 28 Jul 2013
#LegendaryMovieCharacters: Jaws The Shark

3:24 PM - 29 Aug 2013
If I had prize winnings most likely I would buy an old movie theater and fix it up. Would love to open the World's first 24 Hour Movie House

8:10 PM - 9 Sep 2013
Conversations with friends can be interesting, but it's better to get your #MovieAdvice from an expert.

12:54 AM - 15 Sep 2013
Movie #popcorn has not changed since the era of #Bogie and #Bacall!!! #Movies.

9:39 PM - 2 Oct 2013
I hope Kirk Douglas never dies. #movies

9:22 PM - 15 Nov 2013
IIn Peru, "Forrest Gump" is a "foreign film"!!! #FunnyMovieFacts

7:27 PM - 17 Jul 2013
It's crazy that the #Oscars don't have a Top Movie Critic Award. We are an important part of the cinema landscape.

7:43 PM - 16 Feb 2014
"T.Hanks" to Tom Hanks. A great career in #movies.

9:35 PM - 6 Mar 2014
Which rating system is best? Bags of popcorn, or thumbs up/thumbs down. I prefer the bags. Allows for more precision accuracy. #Oncinema

6:43 PM - 2 Jul 2014
Everybody see #Tammy and other #movies

1:04 PM - 29 Aug 2014
Having a "favorite" movie is insane, and the mark of an amateur. There are too many great #movies to signal out just one.

3:45 AM - 24 Oct 2014
Studios spend MILLIONS to make the #movies that you can buy and #own for $1 on videocassette. This is a #GoldenAge.

11:36 AM - 13 Feb 2015
Let's make the #internet a place to discuss #movies

1:00 AM - 11 Jun 2015
No #JamesBond actor has yet died. It would be cool to make a movie where they work together as a team.

7:19 PM - 19 Jun 2015
Bumper sticker idea: "Don't Honk At Me, I'm Thinking About The Movies"

1:08 AM - 21 Feb 2016
Everyone has opinions about the movies but experts are hard to find.

8:39 PM - 24 May 2016
Numbered streets (5th Avenue for instance) should all be renamed for movie #legends. I will be fighting for this in #2016.

10:39 PM - 26 May 2016
New naming ideas for 79th Street:
Kramer Street (Kramer Vs Kramer won '79 Best Picture Oscar)
Meryl Ave.
Dustin Dr.

10:42 PM - 26 May 2016
New naming idea for 16th Street:
Ringwald Avenue (Molly Ringwald starred in "Sixteen Candles")

10:59 PM - 26 May 2016
No one in the world would complain if dull old 36th street became Monroe Avenue (Marilyn died at age 36)! And a great way to learn about it!

4:54 PM - 16 Nov 2016
With Clark Gable's death the world of cinema lost the First Gentleman of Cinema.

5:49 PM - 6 Dec 2016
#Remake a movie and you have a chance to fix anything that they didn't get perfect the first time.

4:59 PM - 8 Dec 2016
Watching a dowolad of a movie you have no way of knowing if it's the real movie. Anyone could have changed scenes or #classic #dialogue

1:26 AM - 30 Dec 2016
Great stars die but the characters they made famous live on in our imagination or on the original Silver Screen

INDEX

A

Abdul (*Decker* character)
  betrays the United States 75, 126, 135
  burns Jack Decker's mind to CD-R 192
  hijacks Alaskan film buff cruise 194, 195
  hijacks Jack Decker's genetic double to blow up Lanoi Arnold Hawaiian Buffalo Wing Stadium 186
  hijacks Quality Air flight to destroy Mt. Rushmore 134
  hired as Green Beret drill instructor through diversity program 135
  plots to blow up Central Park with a mini-nuke 75, 103
  proposes alliance with the USA to fight Dracula 117, 126
  provides Lanoi Arnold with money to renovate his tiki bar 185
  steals the Taliban's secret briefcase 73
  terminated by Jack Decker:
    killed *mano y mano* by strangling 75, 101
    killed with the harpoon gun from *Jaws 2* 195
    resurrected from Arlington National Cemetery by the Son of Dracula 187
A Beautiful Mind (2001) 223
Abraham (Biblical patriarch) 84
Abraham, F. Murray 84
A Bridge Too Far (1977) 140
Academy Awards. *See* Oscars
A Christmas Carol (1951) 42
Ackroyd, Dan 5, 42, 64
acupuncture 47, 48, 51, 113, 181, 209
Aday, Michael Lee 191
Adult Swim 119, 120, 132, 133, 158, 190, 200
Aerosmith (music group) 35
Affleck, Ben 145
Afghanistan 73, 116
A Good Day to Die Hard (2013) 15
A History of Violence (2005) 59
"A Hole in My Soul" (Dekkar song) 194
Airheads (1994) 38, 40, 41
Airplane! (1980) 53, 86
Airplane II: The Sequel (1982) 86
Alba, Jessica 76
Alcoholics Anonymous (AA) 56
Alda, Alan 118
Alien (1979) 31, 93
Ali, Mahershala 163
Allah 75
Allen, Tim 42
Allen, Woody 5, 33, 51, 60, 67, 144, 228
Almanac. *See Welcome to Yesterday* (2015)
al-Qaida 116, 117
alternative medicine 17, 30, 45–48, 51, 52, 55, 108, 113–115, 120, 124, 144, 155, 193, 201, 209, 227–228, 229–230
Altman, Robert 20, 56
A Madea Christmas (2013) 42

Amasova, Anya (Bond heroine) 54
Ambassador Zultan (*Decker* character) 197. *See also* Zorrillians
American Broadcasting Company 105, 110
American Cancer Society 20
American Graffiti (1973) 21, 94
American Medical Association 47
A Million Ways to Die in the West (2014) 64
An, Dr. Luther (*Decker* character) 193
And So It Goes (2014) 65
An Eye for an Eye (1981) 234
Animal Crackers (2017) 178
Animal House (1978) 5, 86
Anna Karenina (2012) 4
Another You (1991) 244
Ant-Man (2015) 88, 105, 110, 112, 121, 128, 129, 131, 146, 149, 233, 235, 241, 242, 243
Ant-Man vs. The Wasp (2018) 241–243
Apple Valley, Calif. 173, 180, 181, 200, 204, 216
Aprea, John
  appearances as *On Cinema* guest 22, 38, 55, 151
  film career 22, 38, 39
  involvement with *Decker* 133, 183, 191
  participates in intervention for Tim Heidecker 151
  reaches semifinals in Tim Heidecker's skin graft donor contest 171, 172
Argo (2012) 22, 23, 223
Arleta, Calif. 169
Arlington National Cemetery 183, 187
Armstrong, Vaughn 191
Arnaz, Desi 223
Arnett, Will 235
Arnold, Lanoi (*Decker* character)
  friendship with Jack Decker:
    meets Decker at Green Beret training camp 134, 135
    reveals the Taliban's plot to kill Jack Decker Jr. 185
    shot in stomach by Decker 185
    suspects Decker of working for the Taliban 101
    visits Decker in U.S. military hospital 192, 193
    visits New Orleans with Decker 192, 193
  makes much-needed renovations to tiki bar 99, 101, 103, 135, 138, 184, 185
  offers award-winning Hawaiian-style buffalo wings 184, 185, 192
  sells out to the Taliban 103, 184, 185
    plants a bug in one of Agent Kington's videotapes 101, 103
  terminated by Jack Decker:
    killed *mano y mano* by strangling 103
    resurrected from Arlington National Cemetery by the Son of Dracula 187
Arrival (2016) 163
A Simple Twist of Fate (1994) 14
A Star Is Born (2018) 121

Author! Author! (1982) 140
Autobahn (2016) 122
Avatar (2009) 67
Avengers: Infinity War (2018) 233
A Vow to Kill (1994) 171
Axiom (*Decker* character) 137, 138, 194, 195
Axiom (Dekkar member)
   appearances as *On Cinema* guest 122, 124, 128, 131, 147, 151, 172, 220, 224
   appearances as *Our Cinema* guest 164
   appearances on *Decker* 133, 137, 138, 191, 194, 195
   authorship of Dekkar's "Empty Bottle" 211
   celebrates Tim Heidecker's mistrial 217, 218
   donates right hand to Tim Heidecker 211
   finalist in Tim Heidecker's skin graft donor contest 171
   helps Tim Heidecker overcome addiction to vape oil 147
   meets Tim Heidecker at Guitar Center 112
   moves to Victorville, Calif., with Dekkar 147
      moves away from Victorville, Calif. 148
   participates in intervention for Tim Heidecker 151
   receives regular "stipend" from Tim Heidecker 128, 211, 245
   testifies at the Electric Sun 20 murder trial 211, 220
   travels to Dubai with Tim Heidecker and DKR 160, 165
      reports that Tim has disappeared from his hotel room 164
   troubled by the marriage of his sister, Juliana Serradimigni, to Tim Heidecker 172
Axiom Recordings (record label) 122
Ayaka (*Decker* character)
   explains the dangers of time travel to Jack Decker 135, 136
   marries Jack Decker's grandfather 136
   serves as secretary to President Jason Davidson 116, 117
Azaria, Hank 234

B

Baby Boom (1992) 60
Baby Boy (2001) 138
Bacall, Lauren 223, 250. See also Bogart, Humphrey
Bach, Barbara 54
Back To School (1986) 140
Back to the Future (1985) 2, 119
Back to the Future Part II (1989) 76
Back to the Future Part III (1990) 53
Badfinger (music group) 191
Baggins, Bilbo 8, 11, 23, 42, 46, 50, 57, 58, 87, 166
Baker, Ginger 183
Baldwin, Alec 172
Ball, Lucille 14, 223
Banks, Elizabeth 59
Banquet (frozen meal brand) 178
Barkin, Ellen 96, 148
Barleycorn, John 151
Barrymore, Drew 82
Batman 68, 145, 244
Bat Out of Hell (Meat Loaf album) 191
Battle Circus (1953) 163
Battle of Pearl Harbor 99, 102, 135, 136
Baywatch (2017) 182

Bean, Sean 66
Beatty, Warren 10, 140
Beck, Glenn 42
BeetleBorgs (television series) 87
Begley, Ed Jr. 240
Being John Malkovich (1999) 32
Belushi, Jim 64
Belushi, John 64, 234
Ben-Hur (1959) 147
Ben-Hur (2016) 147
Benigni, Roberto 92
Benji (fictional dog) 230
Best Buy 229–233
Betenzos, Lisa (Electric Sun witness) 203
Beverly Hills Cop II (1987) 183
Billboard (music industry magazine) 112
bin Khan, Sultan Ali (*Decker* character) 137
bin Laden, Osama 9, 44, 154
Blackheart (1998) 236
Black, Jack 118
Black Mass (2015) 111, 128
black mold 124, 170, 178, 209
Blade (1998) 236
Blanchett, Cate 22
Blanc, Mel 15
Blast from the Past (1999) 11
Blended (2014) 64
Blue Jasmine (2013) 33, 51
Blues Brothers 2000 (1998) 64, 151
Blues, Elwood 64
Blue Streak (2015) 115
Bob and Carol and Ted and Alice (1969) 140
Bogart, Humphrey 5, 16, 89, 131, 163, 165, 166, 177, 224, 244, 245, 250
Bogey. See Bogie
Bogie. See Bogart, Humphrey
Bond, James 3, 15, 54, 93, 123, 130, 154, 156, 174, 245. See also James Bond (movie franchise)
Boyhood (2014) 88
Boyle, Danny 115
Boynton Beach Club (2005) 140
Branagh, Kenneth 94
Brando, Marlon 181
Brand, Russell 30
Breaking Away (1979) 234
Breaking Bad (television series) 59
Breaking In (2018) 234
Brian's Song (1971) 124
Bridge of Spies (2015) 118
Bridges, Jeff 22
Bridget Jones's Baby (2016) 154
Brokeback Mountain (2005) 244
Brokedown (1997) 146
Broken Horses (2015) 145
Brolin, Josh 48, 235
Bronson, Charles 245
Brooks, Garth 150
Brosnan, Pierce 77, 88, 93, 98

Brown, Charlie 123
Brown, James 68, 183
Bufo alvarius 174, 206. *See also* TCH (vape formula)
Bulger, Whitey 111
Bullock, Sandra 30, 96, 147
Bunker, Archie 235
Burns, George 8, 66, 68, 97
Burton, Tim 30, 35, 118, 227–229, 231
Busey, Jake 42
Butler, Gerard 34
Buttons, Red 8
Bye Bye Love (1995) 101–103
By the Sea (2015) 124

C

Cadiz, Ohio (birthplace of Clark Gable) 173
Café Society (2016) 144
Cage, Nicholas 20, 40, 154
Caine, Michael 84, 140
Calabasas, Calif. 163
Cannon, Dyan 140
Cap'n Crunch (animated cereal mascot) 111
Capra, Frank 146
Captain Ahab 242
Captain America (2014) 64
Career Education Corporation 169
Carrabba's Italian Grill (restaurant chain) 33, 38, 41
Carrell, Steve 30
Carrey, Jim 19, 36, 55
Carrie (1974 book) 19
Carrie (1976) 19
Carrie (2013) 19
Carson, Dr. Ben 129
Carter, Helena Bonham 30, 230
Casablanca (1942) 5, 31, 56, 59, 77, 162, 163, 209, 224
Cash, J.R. "Johnny" 59
Caveman (1981) 54, 191
Central Intelligence Agency 69, 73, 76, 77, 99, 101, 102, 134, 135, 137, 149, 186, 190, 193, 194, 235
CGI (computer-generated imagery) 17, 20, 53, 56, 82, 130, 172, 181
Chaplin, Charlie 56, 82, 88, 183, 187
Chaplin's Chili 88, 89, 128, 220
Chaplin's Express 222, 224
Chaplin's Soup and Subs 128, 220
Chappaquiddick (2018) 229
Chappie (2015) 93
Chariots of Fire (1981) 56
Charles, Ray 68
Chase, Chevy 5, 86
Chasing Destiny (2001) 183
Chateau Marmont (Los Angeles, Calif.) 122
Cheadle, Don Jr. 5, 221, 222
Cheech & Chong 42
Chesney, Kenny 154, 157
"China Connection" 213, 215
CHiPs (2017) 171

CHiPs (television series) 171
Cholame, Calif. 90
Christmas with the Kranks (2004) 42
CIA. *See* Central Intelligence Agency
Cinderella 25, 94
Cinderella (2015) 94
cinéma vérité 4
Cirque du Soleil 10
Cirque du Soleil: Worlds Away (2012) 10
Citizen Kane (1941) 148, 152, 157, 158, 169, 178, 213
Clapton, Eric 124
Clark, Candy 21, 22
Clark, Petula 56
Clinton, Hillary 128, 142
Close Encounters of the Third Kind (1977) 222. *See also Jaws 2* (1978)
cocaine 146, 201, 206, 209
Cockfighter (1972) 183
Coen, Ethan. *See* Coen Brothers
Cohen, Sacha Baron 9
Collide. *See Autobahn* (2016)
Columbo (1991) 191
Coma (1978) 191
Connery, Sean 51, 174
Coogan, Steve 30
Coppola, Francis Ford 39
Cordyceps sinensis 206
Corsani, Chris 131
Costco 23
Costner, Kevin 86
Cousteau, Jacques (marine conservationist) 92
Cowardly Lion (*Wizard of Oz* character) 39
Craig, Daniel 123
Crane, Stephen (*Decker* character) 193
Cranston, Bryan 171
Cratchit, Bob (*Decker* character) 185
Crimea 55
crisis actors 186
Crocetti, Dino Paul 221, 223
Cronenberg, David 59
Crowe, Russell 2, 52
Crown (Kellee Maize album) 183
Cruise, Tom 10, 11, 27, 30, 31, 53, 55, 66, 69, 70, 88, 177, 181
Crystal, Billy 11, 17, 21, 22, 45, 55
Cumberbatch, Benedict 111
CureYourself.com 52
Curly (member of the Three Stooges). *See* DeRita, Joe "Curly Joe"
Curtis, Jamie Lee 42

D

Dale (*Ant-Man* character portrayed by Gregg Turkington) 88, 241, 242
Damon, Matt 35, 144
Daniel, Godfrey 197
Dark Places (2014) 78
Dark Skies (2013) 16

DavidsonCare 193
Davidson, Janet (*Decker* character) 134, 136, 138, 183, 184, 187, 192
Davidson, President Jason (*Decker* character). *See also* Davidson, Senator Jason (*Decker* character)
  abducted by Dracula 117
  abducted by the Taliban 99, 101, 184
  bans smoking 134
  commands Jack Decker to "assassinate every fucking Iranian you see" 53
  dies of old age 138
    resurrected from Arlington National Cemetery by the Son of Dracula 187
    shot dead by Agent Kington 187
    spirit appears to Jack Decker Jr., advising him to capitulate to the Zorillians 197
  kowtows to special interests 99, 102, 134, 136, 137, 184, 193, 197
  launches DavidsonCare 193
    ends DavidsonCare 193
    ends government-mandated vaccinations under guidance of Dr. Luther An 193
  receives bag of Hawaiian buffalo wings from Lanoi Arnold 192
  vows to ban all fossil fuel production due to "global warming" 136, 137
  weak on terror 53, 73, 75, 102, 116, 117, 136, 193, 197
  wins 2026 election due to Jack Decker's vote rigging 192
Davidson, President Jason Jr. (*Decker* character)
  allows Jack Decker a final deathbed cigarette 134
  announces the death of Jack Decker 134
  appoints Jack Decker Jr. to the post held by Jack Decker 187
  gunned down by his wife, Janet Davidson 138
    life saved by Kington's VHS copy of *Heaven Can Wait* 138, 140
  killed by the resurrected corpse of his father, former President Jason Davidson 187
    spirit appears to Jack Decker Jr., advising him to capitulate to the Zorillians 197
  targeted for assassination by ISIS-affiliated singer Popp 186
  unclassifies the Decker files 134, 136, 138
  unseals the Decker files 184–186
  weak on terror 197
Davidson, Senator Jason (*Decker* character). *See also* Davidson, President Jason (*Decker* character)
  appoints the terrorist Abdul as a Green Beret drill instructor in the name of "diversity" 135
  weak on terror 135
Davis, Amanda (Electric Sun witness) 210, 215
Davis, Sammy Jr. 221, 222, 223
Davis, Valerie (member of the Electric Sun 19) 210, 215
Davis, Viola 164
Dawn of the Planet of the Apes (2014) 65
Dead Man Down (2013) 18
Deadpool (2016) 235
Deadpool 2 (2018) 235
Dean, James Byron 89, 90, 118, 119, 121, 128–133, 140, 144, 183, 189

Deathtrap (1982) 140
Decker: Classified. See herein *Decker* (miniseries)
Decker, Jack (*Decker* character)
  accused of blowing up Lanoi Arnold Hawaiian Buffalo Wing Stadium with a mini-nuke 185
  contemplates suicide 137, 186
  diagnosed with terminal blood clots 193
    euthanized by Dr. Reeper, architect of DavidsonCare 193
    resurrected by Dr. Luther An's vape formula 193
    shoots Dr. Reeper dead 193
  dies of old age after final cigarette 134
    resurrected from Arlington National Cemetery by the Son of Dracula 187
      encourages Jack Decker Jr. to join forces with the Son of Dracula 187
      killed by Jack Decker Jr. 187
  friendship with Lanoi Arnold:
    esteems Lanoi as his oldest and most trusted friend 99, 101–103, 185, 192, 193
    meets Lanoi for the first time 134
      vows to help Lanoi with potential tiki bar renovations 135
    realizes Lanoi works for the Taliban 103, 184
    shoots Lanoi in the stomach 185
    visits Lanoi's tiki bar 99, 101, 103, 184
      performs "Our Values Are Under Attack" for tiki bar patrons 99
    visits New Orleans with Lanoi 192, 193
      performs Cajun version of "Empty Bottle" 193
  heroic deeds:
    abandons his son, Jack Decker Jr., to protect him from the Taliban 185
    auditions for Dekkar 194
    buys a round of Lanoi Arnold's buffalo wings for tiki bar patrons 184
    captures and tortures his genetic double 183, 185
    establishes "eyes in the sky" 102, 103, 186, 193
    incinerates Agent Kington's compromised VHS collection 103
    kills his best friend, Lanoi Arnold 103
    kills singing sensation, love interest and Taliban asset Popp 186
    kills the terrorist mastermind Abdul 75, 101, 195
    performs impromptu kidney transplant on Agent Kington 194
    retrieves his grandfather's dog tags from Pearl Harbor 102
    reveals global warming as an Illuminati hoax 137
      kills global warming hoaxer Dr. Richards 137
    rigs 2026 presidential election to uphold U.S. sovereignty 192
    saves Anchorage oil refinery from hijacked cruise ship 195
    saves Central Park from mini-nuke 75, 101
    saves Green Beret training camp from mini-nuke 135
    saves Hawaii from the Taliban 103
    saves Louisiana's alligator boot industry 193
    saves Mt. Rushmore from hijacked airplane 134
    saves President Davidson from the Taliban 102, 184

saves President Davidson Jr. from an assassination plot by the ISIS-affiliated diva Popp 186
saves U.S. flag from UN plot
   wins Oscar for his 2050 film *In Service to Our Flags* 186
saves U.S. from EMP attack by infiltrating Islamic birthday party with his band Dekkar 137
time-travels to 1945 to prevent the attack on Pearl Harbor 135
   falls in love with teahouse waitress Ayaka 136
uncovers presidential assassination plot involving a Secret Service mole 56
waterboards Taliban jihadist 103
meets master codebreaker Jonathan Kington 73, 135
mind wiped by the terrorist Abdul 192
   inspired to compose Dekkar's "Empty Bottle" 195
   recovers memory through narration of past adventures 193
   travels America to find himself 194
origins as a Green Beret 134
resigns from the CIA 137, 186, 194
serves as acting U.S. president 117
Decker, Jack Jr. (*Decker* character)
   abandoned by his father, Jack Decker, for his own safety 185
   agrees to follow in the heroic footsteps of his father, Jack Decker 138
   appointed U.S. president 187
   elected U.S. president 195
      abolishes the EPA 187
      builds space wall to prevent immigration of starving extra-terrestrials 195
      kills Zorillian diplomats 197
   kills Count Dracula 184
   kills first lady Janet Davidson 138
      kills Janet Davidson's reanimated corpse with Babe Ruth's baseball bat 184
      receives Congressional Medal of Honor for killing the president's wife 184
   kills his father, Jack Decker, who has been brought back to life by Dracula Jr. 187
   kills the reanimated corpse of Charlie Chaplin 187
   launches nuclear strike on Castle Dracula 187
Decker: Mindwipe. See herein *Decker* (miniseries)
Decker (miniseries)
   critical response 68, 70, 71, 76, 118, 121, 128, 132, 139, 142, 188
   sweeps *On Cinema* Movie Awards 88, 89
Decker seasons:
   canonical status of 132, 188, 189
   Decker: Classified (2014)
      episodes 73–75
      making of 53, 56, 60, 64–67, 69, 77, 88, 188
   Decker: Mindwipe (2017)
      episodes 192–197
      making of 191, 235
      proposed character Tripp Spencer 190
Decker: Port of Call: Hawaii (2015)
   disputed canonical status 188
   episodes 99–103
   finale accidentally revealed by Gregg Turkington 95, 97
   finale rewritten and reshot by Tim Heidecker 95, 97
   Gregg Turkington's videotape collection destroyed in rewritten finale 104, 110
   making of 84, 86, 92–98, 110, 188
Decker: Unclassified (2016)
   alleged continuation of *Dracula vs. Decker* plotline 133, 139, 144
   episodes 134–138
   making of 133, 140, 143, 144, 189
Decker: Unsealed (2017)
   episodes 184–187
   making of 173, 183
   scenes entered into evidence at Electric Sun trial 212
   supersedes *Decker: Port of Call: Hawaii* 188
Decker vs. Dracula (2015)
   appointment of Gregg Turkington as director 108, 110
   Becker vs. Dracula (proposed spinoff) 118, 119
   cancellation 118–121, 124, 126, 128, 129, 133
   disputed canonical status 132, 189
   episodes 116–117
   lost episodes 126
   making of 110, 111, 115, 118, 119, 124, 126
   pulled from Adult Swim site 119, 120
   restored to Adult Swim site on the recommendation of Dr. San 120
   tapes lost in storage unit fire 149
   VHS edition 131, 147
funding sources:
   credit card financing 96, 104
   federal business loan originally intended for *Hog Shots* 84
   Tom Cruise Jr. Memorial Arts Fund 130, 133
Gregg Turkington, contributions of 76, 88, 132, 133, 144, 182, 189
   Agent Kington character, views on 76, 133, 140, 182, 189, 219, 221
   directing 108, 110, 111, 115, 118, 132, 144, 189
   early skepticism about *Decker*'s quality and viability 53, 56, 60, 66, 69
   inadvertent appearance in *Decker: Classified* 65, 69, 70, 77, 88
   screenwriting 86, 93, 104, 108, 111, 118, 133, 159
influence of *Decker* on Hollywood 77, 84, 95, 115, 123, 144, 145, 148, 149, 154, 219
   Kington character plagiarized by George Lucas 219–221, 236, 243
James Dean, contributions of 90, 118, 119, 121, 128, 129, 132, 133, 144, 183, 189
rights to *Decker* seized by the Delgado family 228, 229, 233
shooting locations 84, 86, 92–97
special effects 183
Tim Heidecker on writing and directing *Decker* 53, 69, 71, 84, 88, 93, 95, 97, 110, 133, 173
   major influences on *Decker* 70, 71, 77, 84, 123, 144, 182, 189

Tim Heidecker on writing and directing *Decker* (cont'd)
   political and philosophical aims 71
   writer's block 86
 vaping, promotion of 186, 187, 193, 194, 195, 209
Decker: Port of Call: Hawaii. See herein *Decker* (miniseries)
Decker: Unclassified. See herein *Decker* (miniseries)
Decker: Unsealed. See herein *Decker* (miniseries)
Decker vs. Dracula. See herein *Decker* (miniseries)
Deep Impact (1998) 228
DeGeneres, Ellen 55
Dekkar (*Decker* characters)
 admired by ISIS-affiliated singer Popp 186
 hire Jack Decker as lead vocalist / bassist 194
  early recording sessions 195
  inspire Jack Decker to write "Empty Bottle" 195
 infiltrate radical Islamist birthday party to steal EMP attack plans 137
 killed in missile attack on band airplane 137
  posthumous royalties support Jack Decker Jr. 138
  receive posthumous platinum record for "Empty Bottle" 138
  resurrected from Arlington National Cemetery by the Son of Dracula 187
Dekkar (music group) 111, 112, 122, 127, 128, 130, 131, 142, 144, 146–149, 151, 154, 156, 157, 211, 214, 215, 218, 228, 230, 233, 234
Dekker, Albert 56
Delgado, Bruce and Katherine 230–236
Delgado, Christopher (member of the Electric Sun 19) 206, 215, 216, 228, 231, 232, 234, 236
Delgado Fund 216, 220, 221, 228, 233
Delgado, Kim 87–89
Delgado Media Holdings 234
Deliver Us From Evil (2014) 64
Del Toro, Guillermo 31
Dench, Dame Judi 93
De Niro, Robert 10, 39, 55, 148
Dennis Miller Live (videocassette) 19
Denny Laine Band (music group) 183
Denver, John 66, 68, 70
Depp, Johnny 30, 35, 111, 118, 128, 227, 231, 243, 244
Derek, Bo 22
DeRita, Joe "Curly Joe" 87
Despicable Me (2010) 30
Despicable Me 2 (2013) 30, 55
Destructicon 116, 117, 126, 184
diabetes 44, 45, 52, 227
Diaz, Cameron 96, 129
DiCaprio, Leonardo 5, 241
Dick Tracy (1990) 10
Die Hard (1988) 15
Die Hard (movie franchise) 15
Diesel, Vin 41, 68, 97, 174, 180
Dirty Harry (1971) 227
Dirty Rotten Scoundrels (1988) 140
Disneyland 243
Disney, Walt 35, 243
Django Unchained (2013) 11

DKR (music group) 127, 157, 160–163, 165, 168, 173, 174, 177, 180, 186, 198, 203, 206, 211, 212, 214–216, 218–220, 228, 230, 233, 234
DMAA. See 1,3-dimethylamylamine
Dog Day Afternoon (1975) 67, 162
Dolby Theatre, Hollywood 21, 55, 87, 128
Dole, Bob 19
Double Exposure (1994) 236
Douglas, Kurt 22, 223, 250
Douglas, Michael 32, 65, 243
Doyle, Sir Arthur Conan 227
Dracula (1932) 56
Dracula (classic horror character) 9, 90, 118, 121, 139, 144, 189
Dracula (*Decker* character). See also Son of Dracula
 builds "Destructicon" doomsday machine 116, 184
 hatches plot with Janet Davidson to kill all men and usher in "the age of the woman" 138, 184
 imprisons Agent Kington in Castle Dracula 117
 imprisons President Jason Davidson in Castle Dracula 117
 killed by Jack Decker Jr. 184
 raises the Three Stooges from the dead 126
  driven into exile by the ghost of the Three Stooges 126
Dracula Jr. See Son of Dracula (*Decker* character)
Dragnet (1991) 191
Dreyfuss, Richard 20, 39, 222, 224
Dr. Greenway (*Decker* character) 184
Dr. Luther. See Dr. San
Dr. Peterson (*Decker* character) 192, 193
Dr. Reeper (*Decker* character) 193
Dr. Richards (*Decker* character) 136, 137
Dr. San. See Sanchez, Luther
Dr. Spine (2015) 16
Dunn, Andrew 20
Duvall, Robert 111
Dwyer, Mark 198, 200, 201, 203, 204, 206, 218, 233, 234

E

East of Eden (1955) 90
Easton, Sheena 164
Eastwood, Clint 151, 154, 227, 245
Eastwood, Scott 227
Easy Rider (1969) 232
eBay 5
Ebert, Roger 47, 61
Ecstasy (drug) 201
EDM. See electronic dance music
18 Again! (1988) 8
Eisenhower, Dwight D. (U.S. president) 16
Electric Sun 18. See Electric Sun 20
Electric Sun 19 180, 200, 207, 215, 218, 220, 221, 227, 233, 236. See also Electric Sun 20 murder trial
Electric Sun 20. See Electric Sun 19
Electric Sun 20 murder trial 198, 200, 201–217, 220, 227, 233, 236. See also herein Heidecker, Timothy Richard: Electric Sun 20 murder trial

Electric Sun Desert Music Festival. *See also herein* Heidecker, Timothy Richard: Electric Sun 20 murder trial
   deaths and injuries 178–181, 201, 203, 206, 207, 212, 213, 215, 218
   lack of access by first responders 203
   promotion by Tim Heidecker 173, 174, 177, 209
   reports of unsafe, unsanitary and uncomfortable conditions 201, 203, 206, 212
electromagnetic pulse (EMP) 137
electronic dance music. *See* EDM
Ellis, Detective William (Electric Sun witness) 206, 207
El Parque Jurásico (Spanish-language VHS cassette) 26
Elysium (2013) 35, 36
EMP. *See* electromagnetic pulse (EMP)
"Empty Bottle" (Dekkar song) 112, 119, 122, 127, 130, 131, 138, 146, 154, 157, 193, 195, 198, 211
   authorship 211
Endless Love (2014) 51
Entertainment Weekly 5
Environmental Protection Agency (EPA) 187
Escape from Planet Earth (2013) 15
Escape Plan (2013) 87–89
escape rooms 231
Escape to Witch Mountain (1975) 243
Estevez, Joe
   appearances as *On Cinema* guest 55, 56, 60, 88, 89, 93, 151, 179, 233
     interviewed on *Gregg Turkington's Celebrity Backlot* 67
     interviewed on *On Cinema Presents Popcorn Classics BTC* 16
     interviewed on *On Cinema Presents Stars on Directors* 33
     moderates *The Dr. San Forgiveness Special* 113
     presides over mock trial of George Lucas for plagiarism 221
     referees the Oscar Olympics 129, 131
     wins *On Cinema* Lifetime Achievement Award 88
   film appearances 16, 233, 246
     personal top 10 of his own films 16
     involvement with *Decker* miniseries 16, 25, 53, 56, 60, 64, 70, 87, 93, 115, 133, 140, 179, 183, 191
   on Woody Allen 33, 67
   organizes an intervention for Tim Heidecker 151, 213
   reaches semifinals in Tim Heidecker's skin graft donor contest 171, 172
   testifies at the Electric Sun 20 murder trial 212, 213, 215, 220
   visits Boise 179
   visits Tim Heidecker in jail 179, 180
E.T. (1982) 195, 228
Eucompco, Max 229–233
Eve (Alicia Silverstone character) 11
Excalibur (mythic sword) 181
Excelsior High School (Norwalk, Calif.) 35
Ex Machina (2015) 98

F

Fallen Angels (1995) 221
Fame (1980) 231

Fantasia (1940) 243
Fantastic Four (2015) 90, 105, 110, 128, 129, 180, 241, 242
"Farewell, Tom Cruise" (Tim Heidecker song) 124
Fargo (television series) 221
Farrell, Colin 18
Farrell, Will 96, 97
Fassbender, Michael 115
Fatal Attraction (1987) 32, 243
Father of the Bride (1991) 233
Favreau, Jon 14
FBI. *See* Federal Bureau of Investigation
FDA 144
Federal Bureau of Investigation 73, 111, 149
Feinberg, Louis. *See* Fine, Larry
Ferris Bueller's Day Off (1986) 45
Field of Dreams (1989) 86, 245
Field, Sally 3, 234
Fields, W. C. 55, 57, 82, 84, 85, 87, 92, 129, 146, 147, 149, 164, 178, 197, 224
50 Shades of Grey (2015) 84
film noir 76, 131
Finding Dory (2016) 243
Fine, Larry (member of the Three Stooges) 88, 89
First Monday in October (1981) 180
Firth, Colin 84, 154
Fishburn, Laurence 38
Fisher, Carrie 34
500 Movies in 500 Days campaign 34, 36, 37, 39, 41, 44, 45, 49, 51, 52, 64, 66, 77–79, 82, 101
flax seed 52, 55, 56
Fleming, Erin (troubled partner of Groucho Marx) 129
Fletch (1985) 5
Fletch Lives (1989) 154
Flight (2012) 2
Flynt, James (Lucas plagiarism trial witness) 221
Focus (2015) 92
Fonda, Henry 244
Food and Drug Administration. *See* FDA
Ford, Harrison 31, 34, 65, 70, 162
Forest Lawn Cemetery 131
Forget Paris (1995) 45
formaldehyde 207
Forrest Gump (1994) 23, 250
Fortnite (videogame) 231
48 Hours (1982) 57
"For Your Eyes Only" (Sheena Easton ballad) 164
Foster, Jodie 35, 159, 243
Founding Fathers 71, 192, 218
Four Points Hotel (Oklahoma City, Okla.) 169, 170
Franco, James 146
Frankenstein, Dr. Victor 47
Frankenstein's monster (classic horror character) 47, 92
Frankenstein's monster (*Decker* character) 116, 117, 186
Franklin (*Decker* character) 136, 185, 186
Fraser, Brendan 11, 15, 38, 45, 47
Freaky Friday (2003) 243
Freedom of Information Act 69
Freejack (1992) 39

Freeman, Hank (Chaplin's spokesperson) 128, 220, 222
Freeman, Martin 50, 88. *See also* Baggins, Bilbo
Freeman, Morgan 27, 49
Frozen Ground (2012) 6
Furious 7 (2015) 97

G

Gable, Clark 173, 250
Gandalf 21, 46, 55, 58
Garfield (comic strip) 145
Garland, Judy 18
Garner, James 3
Gelson's Markets 32
General Coover (*Decker* character) 195, 197
General Cotter (*Decker* character portrayed by John Aprea) 134, 135, 185–187, 193, 194
General Cotter (*Decker* character portrayed by Steve Railsback) 186, 187
Gere, Sir Richard 5, 93
Germ Assassin (Rio-Jenesis product) 227
Germ Shield X (Rio-Jenesis product) 227
Gervais, Ricky 60
Get Hard (2015) 96, 97
Get On Up (2014) 68
Ghost (1990) 77, 124
Giant (1956) 90
Gibson, Mel 53, 70, 159
G.I. Joe: Retaliation (2013) 24
Gimme Shelter (2014) 47
Ginger Baker's Air Force (musical group) 183
Giusti, Manuel (*Decker* character) 195
Giusti, Manuel (Dekkar member)
   appearances as *On Cinema* guest 128, 131, 172, 220, 224
   appearances in *Decker* 133, 183, 186, 187, 195
   celebrates Tim Heidecker's mistrial 217, 218
   finalist in Tim Heidecker's skin graft donor contest 171
     donates skin for Tim's facial skin grafts 172, 173
   performances with DKR 160, 163, 220
   testifies at the Electric Sun 20 murder trial 214, 215, 220
Gladiator (2000) 52
globalists 184, 186
global warming 101, 136, 137, 185
Glover, Crispin 76
Glover, Danny 92
Glover, Donald 92
Godzilla (movie franchise) 64
Goldberg, Whoopi 69, 77
Golden Gate Bridge (San Francisco, Calif.) 59
Gone With the Wind (1939) 17, 33, 59
Goodfellas (1990) 111
Gooding, Cuba Jr. 129
Goodman, John 2, 64, 123
Good Morning, Vietnam (1987) 101
Gooobler, Captain Daniel (*Ant-Man and the Wasp* character portrayed by Tim Heidecker) 241–243. *See also* Whale Man
Goosebumps (2015) 118

Gordon, Keith 221, 222
Gosford Park (2001) 20
Gosnell, Raja 235
Gottlieb, Carl 191, 195, 221
Graham, Billy 220, 222
Grammar, Kelsey 157
Grant, Cary 140
Grant, Hugh 30
Grapevine, Calif. 57
Gravity (2013) 55
Grease 2 (1982) 35
Green Berets 101, 103, 134
Green Tortoise (tour bus company) 169
Greer, Judy 243
Gremlins (1984) 245
Grown Ups (2010) 31
Grown Ups 2 (2013) 31
Guardians of the Galaxy (2014) 68
Guardians of the Galaxy 2 (2017) 180
Guarding Tess (1994) 59
Guinness Book of World Records. *See Guinness World Records*
Guinness, Sir Alec 24
Guinness World Records 34, 36, 37, 41, 49, 52, 78, 79, 82, 101, 104, 105, 174
Guitar Center 112, 122, 127
Gump, Forrest 69

H

Hacksaw Ridge (2016) 163
Haldrige, Tyler (member of the Electric Sun 19) 215
Hamill, Mark 34, 76
Hands of Stone (2016) 148
Hanks, Tom 31, 53, 55, 78, 118, 151, 181, 250
Hannibal (2001) 32
Happy Days (television series) 94
Harmon, Mark 154
Harry Potter (film franchise) 41
Hathaway, Anne 22
Hawaii 5-0 (2013) 191
Hawke, Ethan 40
Hawn, Goldie 123, 181, 230
Hayek, Salma 60
Hayes, Helen 56
Heaven Can Wait (1978) 138, 140
Hebdo, Charlie 87, 89
Heche, Anne 31
Heidecker, Ayaka. *See* Ohwaki, Ayaka
Heidecker Publishing 66
Heidecker, Timothy Richard
   ARTISTIC AND CREATIVE PURSUITS
   cast as Mr. Richards in *Fantastic Four* (2015) 90
   cast as Whale Boat Captain Daniel Gooobler in *Ant-Man and the Wasp* (2018) 241–243
   creates *Decker* miniseries. *See herein Decker* (miniseries)
   forms EDM group DKR 157

performs with DKR at Electric Sun Desert Music Festival 180, 203, 206, 212
performs with DKR in Dubai 160–162, 165
performs with DKR on Oscars Special V 220
forms rock group Dekkar 111
   debuts Dekkar track "Empty Bottle" 112, 131
   difficulty completing the Dekkar LP 142, 144, 148
   loses ability to play bass after Victorville Film Archive fire 157
   performs with Dekkar on Oscars Special IV 128, 130
   recordings and promotions 111, 112, 122, 131, 142, 144, 146, 147, 151, 154, 215, 218
   signs with Axiom Recordings 122
   songwriting contributions 211, 218
performs "Farewell, Tom Cruise" in honor of his late son 124
performs "Oscar Fever" on Oscars specials 55, 57, 87, 89, 128, 162, 220
performs "Song for Ayaka" on Oscars Special III 88

BUSINESS AND FINANCIAL AFFAIRS
joins *Gregg Turkington's On Cinema at the Cinema* in an advisory capacity 83
launches Delgado Fund for at-risk youth 220
   funds *On Cinema* Oscar Special V 220, 221
   loses support of Delgado family 228
   resources seized by the Delgado family 228–232
launches Heidecker Publishing 66
   aims to publish *Hog Shots*, a book of motorcycle photos 66
   conflict with Tom Cruise over *Hog Shots* cover shoot 69
   publication of *Hog Shots* canceled 84
launches Six Bag Cinema 168
   becomes head chef at Six Bag Cinema 172
launches TCH Vape Systems 174, 201, 215
launches Tom Cruise Heidecker Jr. Memorial Arts Foundation 130, 133, 207
   funds *Decker: Unclassified* 130, 131, 133
   funds the Victorville Film Center 142
liability for losses in the Victorville Storage Facility fire 154, 157
negotiates *On Cinema* sponsorship deal with the Delgado family 233
organizes Electric Sun Desert Music Festival 173, 174, 177. *See also herein* Heidecker, Timothy Richard: Electric Sun 20 murder trial
   promotes TCH vape giveaway 174
   promotes germ-free living through Rio-Jenesis 227, 229, 230
   cuts ties with Rio-Jenesis 231
promotes "Whale Man" superhero franchise 241, 242
runs for district attorney of San Bernardino County 236, 241, 242

DISPUTES WITH GREGG TURKINGTON
Ant-Man and *Fantastic Four*, relative quality of 90, 105, 110, 112, 121, 128, 129, 131, 241, 242
Ant-Man and the Wasp, Tim's appearance in 241–243
Brendan Fraser, appearance in animated films of 15
casting of "nobodies" in major films 31, 34

cranial blood clots:
   difference between tumors and 14, 26, 27, 30
   effectiveness of surgery for 14, 17, 27
Dennis Miller Live, status as a film of 19
documentaries and dramatizations, differences between 9, 142
film critics, importance of eyesight for 68
Gregg's status as a film expert 20, 24, 96, 152, 158, 169, 178, 182, 209, 213–215, 224
Gregg's status as *On Cinema* co-host 3, 23, 32, 52, 234
Gregg's video collection, incineration of:
   as part of *Decker* finale 103, 104, 110
   at the Victorville Film Archive 149–152, 154, 157, 168, 213
   at the Victorville Film Center 171
hats, suitability for television appearances of 64, 228–230, 233
homemade VHS tapes, promotion of 52, 53
Jack Reacher (2012), quality of 11, 19
James Bond franchise, quality of 11, 15, 21, 53, 65, 70, 77, 123
James Dean, current status and whereabouts of 89, 90, 118, 128, 129–131, 144
Luther Sanchez, medical credentials of 47–49, 51, 61, 121, 124, 145, 146, 179–181
Monsters, Inc. in 3D, status as re-release of 9
My Giant, use of CGI in 17
Oh, God! locations, audience interest in 68, 70, 76
"Oscar," correct spelling of 57, 58
personal topics, on-air discussion of 18, 19, 47, 48, 51, 65, 82, 85, 104, 108, 112, 121, 127, 170, 178, 209, 230, 234
Popcorn scale, maximum rating on 2, 3, 10, 14–17, 30, 42, 64, 108
Popcorn scale, rights to use 106, 155, 156, 159, 182
Robocop, existence of sequels to 49, 50
Six Bag Cinema, eating outside popcorn in 170, 172, 173
Star Trek II and *Star Trek IV*, plot location of 10, 36, 37, 56, 59, 61, 142, 195, 213, 214
Sully, Gregg's alleged viewing of 152, 158, 166, 168, 169, 178, 209, 213, 224
Victorville Film Center, musical performances at 147, 157
videotaped movies, quality of 52, 59
virtual reality (VR), quality of 229, 230
"Whale Man" superhero franchise, commercial viability of 241, 242

ELECTRIC SUN 20 MURDER TRIAL
arrested on suspicion of murder 177–179
   haunted by visions of Dr. San's hanged corpse 181
   released on bail 179
charged with 20 counts of second-degree murder 198, 200, 201, 241
   challenges cause of Shawn Levin's death 207, 215
   not guilty of second-degree murder of Shawn Levin 217
defense strategy:
   acts as own attorney after firing Mark Dwyer 206, 218
   attacks DA Vincent Rosetti 198, 216, 218

Heidecker, Timothy Richard (continued)
ELECTRIC SUN 20 MURDER TRIAL (continued)
defense strategy: (continued)
blames Apple Valley EMTs for festival deaths 180, 181, 200
blames contaminated ingredients from Chinese suppliers for festival deaths 206, 207, 213, 215
blames Dr. San for festival deaths 179–182, 198, 200, 201, 206, 207, 215
blames victims for festival deaths 200, 201, 207
calls Gregg Turkington's film expertise into question 209, 213–216
cross-examination of Allesandro Serradimigni 211
cross-examination of Amanda Davis 210
cross-examination of Ayaka Ohtani 211
cross-examination of Gerard Kearny 207, 209
cross-examination of Gregg Turkington 209
cross-examination of Mark Proksch 210
cross-examination of William Ellis 207
hints at prosecutorial misconduct 207, 215
maintains innocence 177, 180–182, 198, 200, 206
promises to launch Electric Sun 20 Foundation to aid at-risk youth if acquitted 198, 200
promises to launch "The Delgado Fund" to aid at-risk youth if acquitted 216
recounts conversation with Chris Delgado, absolving him of any prospective wrongdoing 206, 215
legal setbacks:
accused of arson and embezzlement by Gregg Turkington 209
accused of falsifying confession letter from Dr. San 215
accused of paying witnesses for testimony 212, 214
accused of physical abusiveness by Mark Proksch 210
accused of plagiarizing "Empty Bottle" from Allessandro Serradimigni 211
cited for contempt of court 211, 212, 215
implicated in the creation of TCH by Luther Sanchez 203, 206
legal status of businesses questioned 207
removed from court for "menacing" Mark Proksch 211
witnessed distributing TCH vape pens 203
statement upon declaration of mistrial 218
HEALTH AND MEDICAL ISSUES
burned in Victorville Film Archive fire 149, 151, 152, 154, 157, 168, 213
avoids using antibiotic ointment due to side effects 168
facial infection from burns 168, 170–172
facial skin transplant 170–173, 178
hands charred to the bone 151, 173
receives hand transplant from Axiom 211
recovers use of left hand 173
chokes on popcorn kernel 15
cranial blood clots 14, 17, 27, 30, 35, 44, 48
cuts off fingertip 21–23
diabetes 45, 52
facial infection from dirty acupuncture needles 48, 49, 51, 52, 113, 209
inflamed and painful foot 45–47, 51, 113

insomnia 32, 181
loss of vision due to stationary motorcycle accident 67–70, 77, 80
pains in head 30, 32
substance abuse 156, 170, 178, 179, 213, 227
drunkenness on Oscar Night 21–23, 55–57, 87–90, 127–130, 220, 221
prescription medication and opioid abuse 21, 151, 152, 154, 162
vape addiction 128, 144–148, 154, 157, 168, 171, 174, 209
tingling numbness in extremities 44. *See also* diabetes
unexplained contusions and welts 145
unexplained coughing and sneezing 230–232
vape poisoning symptoms 128, 144–146, 148, 174, 209
MANAGEMENT OF ON CINEMA AT THE CINEMA
bans Gregg Turkington from *On Cinema* 57, 61
attempts to replace Gregg as *On Cinema*'s guest 24, 37, 39, 61, 158, 169, 224
rehires Gregg as guest 39, 61, 106
cancels *Golden Age Comedies With W. C. Fields* 84, 85, 92, 147, 178
disappointment with *Gregg Turkington's On Cinema at the Cinema* 82, 83
disappointment with Gregg Turkington's Oscar Special finales 57, 58, 87, 131
disappointment with Gregg Turkington's *Our Cinema* Oscar Special 164–166, 219
films *On Cinema* in virtual reality (VR) 229–231
quits *On Cinema* 78, 236
returns as host of *On Cinema* 84
responds to criticisms of management style by Gregg Turkington and Mark Proksch 180, 181
OPINIONS ON CINEMA
movies are not that important 78, 112, 213, 224, 245
"not a huge fan" of *James Bond* films 3, 15, 22, 44, 53, 65, 70, 77
objects to films starring "nobodies" 31, 33–35, 53, 78, 230
objects to sequels made without original stars 34
objects to the modern overproduction of remakes 19
on Gregg Turkington's *Ant-Man* 88, 90, 105, 110, 241
on his favorite actor 7, 10, 18, 52, 53, 77
on his favorite director, Steven Spielberg 3, 10, 110
on his favorite movie, *Jack Reacher* 11, 19, 22
on the legacy of Paul Walker 97
Oscar picks 2, 5, 7–9, 18, 30, 33, 34, 42, 65, 67, 86, 94, 95, 142, 144, 147, 171, 174, 228
preference for remakes 5
recommends segregating Oscar nominations by race 129
PERSONAL AND ROMANTIC LIFE
appreciates Gregg Turkington's friendship 33, 41, 146, 180, 181
buys Kawasaki motorcycle 64
contemplates suicide 146, 163, 233
first wife seeks divorce due to Tim's blood clot surgery 30
learns the value of forgiveness:
from Dr. San 113, 119, 120
from the Rev. Billy Graham 220
mourns death of his son, Tom Cruise Heidecker Jr. 124, 130

blames Ayaka Ohwaki for Tom Jr.'s death 124
blames black mold for Tom Jr.'s death 124, 209
hires animators to create a CGI version of Tom Jr. 130
moves into Gregg Turkington's apartment 86
 moves Ayaka Ohwaki and Tom Cruise Heidecker Jr. into Gregg's apartment 93, 94
 takes over Gregg's apartment 98
moves into the Victorville Film Archive 146, 148
moves to Jackson Hole, Wyo. 64
 moves away from Jackson Hole, Wyo. 83
reconnects with estranged son from previous marriage 66
relationship with Ayaka Ohwaki:
 begins relationship with Ayaka 38, 40, 211
 discovers Ayaka is pregnant 60, 142
 encourages Ayaka to get an abortion 65, 77, 145, 151, 211
 fathers child, Tom Cruise Heidecker Jr., with Ayaka 77, 211
 ignores Ayaka and Tom Cruise Heidecker Jr.'s arrival in the United States 78
 implores Ayaka to return to him 88, 89, 92
 learns that Ayaka works for Dr. San 112, 113
 proposes to Ayaka on air 98
 splits up with Ayaka 41, 44, 145, 146, 151, 180
relationship with Juliana Serradimigni:
 begins dating Juliana 147, 148, 154
 cared for by Juliana after Victorville Film Archive fire 150, 173
 discovers Juliana is pregnant 157
 marries Juliana 172
 recommends that Juliana get an abortion 173
 reveals facial skin grafts to Juliana 173
 splits up with Juliana 180
self-improvement efforts guided by Values.com 86, 92, 97, 98
sobs on camera for unknown reason 6, 145
POLITICAL AND PHILOSOPHICAL BELIEFS
advocates the use of birth control 145
asserts constitutional right to strike disobedient employees 210
asserts constitutional right to use green-screen footage of Gregg Turkington in *Decker* 69
belief in freedom of self-expression 69
"colorblind" on race 129
commitment to senior citizens 18
critique of feminism 181
faith in Jesus Christ 87, 173
membership in "the pro-life community" 65
objects to the secularization of Christmas 42
opposes Hillary Clinton 128, 142
opposes "Obamacare" 14, 47, 48, 55
opposes special interests 71
opposes taxes and regulations 18
opposes Western medicine 14, 17, 27, 47, 48, 52, 113, 130, 227–230
predicts imminent nuclear war with Russia 55–57
supports construction of southern border wall 168
Heidecker, Tom Cruise Jr.
 appearances as *On Cinema* guest 95, 130
 appearances on *Decker* 116, 124, 131
 early life:
  birth in Japan 77
  career as an actor 94, 95, 115, 124, 131
  conservative principles 130
  named after Tom Cruise, Tim Heidecker's favorite actor 10, 77
  passion for the arts 130
  rejected by father, Tim Heidecker, on arrival in United States 78
 illness and death 96, 106, 113, 115, 122, 123, 124, 125, 174, 201, 206, 209, 211
 memorialized by TCH Vape Systems 174
 memorialized by the Tim Heidecker song "Farewell, Tom Cruise" 124
 memorialized by the Tom Cruise Jr. Memorial Arts Foundation 130
 reanimated through CGI for *On Cinema* Oscars Special IV 130
 remembered by Gregg Turkington 124, 149, 209
Heigl, Katherine 45
Heisman Trophy 163
"Help Me, Rhonda" (Beach Boys song) 133
Helter Skelter (1976) 183
Hepburn, Katharine 181, 244
Her (2014) 44
Hercules (2014) 67
Hercules (mythic hero) 67
heroin 201, 207, 215, 217
"He's a Dancer" (Jimmy McNichol song) 24
Hesperia, Calif. 204
Heston, Charlton 147, 232
Hillary's America (2016) 142
Hitchcock, Sir Alfred 33, 57, 170
Hitler, Adolf 97, 172, 230
Hobbit-heads 11, 42, 50, 55, 56, 57, 79, 106, 129, 130, 133, 166
hobbits 8, 23, 41, 42, 46, 50, 89, 146
Hoffman, Dustin 51, 241, 250
Hog Shots (proposed Tim Heidecker book) 66, 69, 84
Holiday Heart (2000) 149
Hollywood Boulevard (Los Angeles, Calif.) 58, 173
Hollywood, Calif. 10, 16, 17, 21, 22, 31, 39, 44, 45, 48, 57, 61, 64–66, 69, 77, 80, 87–90, 92, 111, 115, 121, 122, 131, 142, 144, 147, 168, 169, 171, 173, 192, 221, 233
Hollywood Forever cemetery 168
Hollywood Freeway 173
Hollywood Movie Museum 128
Hollywood Teen (television program) 183
Hollywood Walk of Fame 58, 243
Holmes, Sherlock 173, 227
Home (2015) 96
Home Fries (1998) 82
Honey, I Shrunk the Kids (1989) 65
"Honkin' Down the Highway" (Beach Boys song) 133
Hooper, Dr. Matt (*Jaws* character) 222
Hopkins, Anthony 32, 122
Horwitz, Moses Harry. *See* Howard, Moe
Hotel Transylvania 2 (2015) 112

Hot Shots! (1991) 4, 48
Hot Tub Time Machine (2010) 86
Hot Tub Time Machine 2 (2015) 86
Howard, Moe (member of the Three Stooges) 87
Howard, Ron 94
How I Went to the Oscars Without a Ticket: A True Story (Dee Thompson book) 129
How to Be a Latin Lover (2017) 179
How to Deal (2003) 174, 232
How to Lose a Guy in 10 Days (2003) 123
Huckabee, Mike 85, 87–90
Hudson, Kate 67, 123
Hunnam, Charlie 174
Hurt, John 67
Hurt, William 98
Hutton, Timothy 76
Hyde Park on the Hudson (2012) 7

I

Ice Cube 45
I Ching 129
Identity Thief (2013) 14
I, Frankenstein (2014) 47
Illuminati 136, 137
Imagine Dragons (music group) 231
I'm Still Alive: Why I Faked My Own Death to Escape the Trappings of the Hollywood Star System, Fame and Fortune (James Dean book) 89–91
In a Lonely Place (1950) 5
Incánus. *See* Gandalf
Indiana Jones. *See* Jones, Dr. Henry Walton "Indiana" Jr.
In Service to Our Flags (2050) 186, 187
internet 24, 32, 58, 69, 71, 181, 243, 250
Internet Movie Database 212
In the Heart of the Sea (2015) 94
Into the Storm (2014) 69
I.Q. (1994) 76
Iran 53
ISIS (terrorist organization) 83, 87, 99, 104, 119, 186
It Came from Outer Space (1953) 149, 157
It's a Mad, Mad, Mad, Mad World (1963) 173
It's a Wonderful Life (1946) 146

J

Jack Frost (1998) 34, 59
Jackman, Hugh 33, 93, 115
Jack Reacher (2012) 10, 11, 19, 22, 30, 41, 50, 55, 59, 60, 70, 84, 155
Jackson Hole, Wyo. 64–67, 69, 70, 77, 78, 80, 83, 84, 88
Jackson, Michael 8
Jackson, Peter 8, 22, 46, 52, 57, 58, 89, 129, 130, 166
Jack the Giant Slayer (2013) 17
Jagger, Mick 39
James Bond (movie franchise) 3, 11, 15, 21, 22, 41, 47, 49, 51, 65, 70, 77, 84, 89, 98, 110, 115, 119, 123, 130, 174, 250
James Dean Memorial Junction (Cholame, Calif.) 90
James, Jesse 32

Jardine, Al 133
Jason Bourne (2016) 144
Jason Bourne (movie franchise) 70, 144
Jaws 3. *See Jaws 2* (1978)
Jaws (1975) 35, 85, 110, 191, 195, 220, 222
Jaws (film character) 220, 222, 250
Jaws 2 (1978) 85, 93, 191, 194, 195, 220–224
Jaws (movie franchise) 220, 222, 224
Jem & the Holograms (2015) 121
Jerry Lewis Labor Day Telethon 191
Jerry Maguire (1996) 129
Jessabelle (2014) 77
Jesus Christ 84, 87, 173
Jobs, Steve. *See Steve Jobs* (2015)
Joe Versus the Volcano (1990) 52
Joey Travolta (1978 album) 183
Johansson, Scarlett 44
Johnson, Dwayne. *See* Johnson, Dwayne "The Rock"
Johnson, Dwayne "The Rock" 16, 24, 67, 97, 174, 231
Jolie, Angelina 124
Jolly Time (popcorn brand) 52
Jolson, Jared (Electric Sun witness) 203
Jones, Bridget 154
Jones, Dr. Henry Walton "Indiana" Jr. 36, 41, 245
Jones, Indiana. *See* Jones, Dr. Henry Walton "Indiana" Jr.
Jones, Tommy Lee 148
Jonze, Spike 44
Judas (Biblical turncoat) 220
Jupiter Ascending (2014) 66, 82
Jurassic Park (3D, 2013) 26
Jurassic Park (1993) 26, 110
Just the Way You Are (1984) 59

K

K2 Biochemical Ltd. 207
Kardashian, Kim 24
Karloff, Boris 189
Kearny, Dr. Gerard (Electric Sun witness) 207, 209
Keaton, Diane 60, 65
Keaton, Michael 2, 34, 59, 89
Kellerman, Sally 56, 133, 140, 183
Kemper Campbell Ranch (Victorville, Calif.) 157
Kennedy, Edward M. "Ted" Jr. 229
Kennedy, John F. (U.S. president) 7
KGB 54
Kick-Ass (2010) 36
Kick-Ass 2 (2013) 36
Kidman, Nicole 10, 161
Kimmel, Jimmy 172
King Arthur (2017) 181
King Arthur (mythic king of the Britons) 181
King, B.B. 68
King Kong (1933) 168
King Kong (classic horror character) 168
King Lear (1608 play) 89
King, Martin Luther Jr. 181
Kingsley, Ben 122

Kingsman: The Secret Service (2015) 84
King, Stephen 19
Kingston, Jonathan. *See* Kington, Jonathan
Kington, Jonathan (*Decker* character portrayed by Gregg Turkington)
  codebreaking abilities:
    cracks Dracula's Destructicon code 126, 184
    cracks entry code for cruise ship bridge 195
    cracks Jack Decker's apartment door code 137
    cracks Popp's pro-ISIS entry code 186
    cracks Russian nuclear missile code 136
    cracks Taliban code that imprisons Jack Decker 103
    cracks Taliban's nuclear briefcase code 73
    cracks the Tower of London's secret vault code 186
    cracks the Washington Monument's secret vault code 137
    hacks into Abdul's hard drive 135
    hacks into Senator Sanchez's private server 192
    locates Lamont Pierce's alligator boot factory 193
  diagnosed with kidney failure caused by overconsumption of movie popcorn 194
    receives improvised kidney transplant from Jack Decker 194
  duped by U.S. first lady Janet Davidson 192
  gets to-go order of Lanoi Arnold's Hawaiian buffalo wings 184
  joins Alaskan film buff cruise 194
    moderates a symposium on the works of Meg Ryan 195
  killed by first lady Janet Davidson 138, 184
    resurrected by Dr. Greenway 184
  kills the resurrected President Davidson in Arlington National Cemetery 187
  locates Jack Decker Jr. 138
  meets Ebenezer Scrooge 185
  meets Jack Decker 73, 135
  plans to watch 500 movies in 500 days 101
  prevents Jack Decker from committing suicide 138
  revealed as a double agent for the Zorillians 197
    murders WC-PO 197
  status as a film buff 99, 101–103, 116, 135, 136, 138, 184, 186, 187, 193–195, 197
    VHS film collection 99, 101, 103, 138, 184, 186, 195
      receives bugged VHS tape from the terrorists 101–103
      videotape collection incinerated by Jack Decker 103
  suspected of treason by Jack Decker 99
  suspicious of first lady Janet Davidson 134, 136, 138
  travels to Transylvania to confront Dracula 116, 117
    imprisoned in Castle Dracula 117
  visits Jack Decker's deathbed 134
Kington, Jonathan (*Decker* character portrayed by Manuel Giusti) 187
Kirk, James T. (*Star Trek* character) 10, 36, 59, 214
Klington, Jonathan. *See* Kington, Jonathan
Kojak (2005) 183
Komitet Gosudarstvennoy Bezopasnosti. *See* KGB
Kong: Skull Island (2017) 168
Korean War (June 1950 - July 1953) 163
Kramer vs. Kramer (1979) 77, 250
Kubo and the Two Strings (2016) 147

Ku Klux Klan (KKK) 84
Kunis, Mila 66, 82

L

Labor Day (2014) 48
Ladd, Alan 56
Lady and the Tramp (1955) 243
Laine, Denny 183
Lake Tahoe 136
Lancaster, Burt 223
Lanoi Arnold Hawaiian Buffalo Wing Stadium 185, 186
Larry the Cable Guy. *See* Whitney, Daniel Lawrence
Las Vegas, Nev. 10
Laurel, Stanley 82
Law, Jude 181
Lawrence, Jennifer 22
Lazarus (2015) 92
Le Cordon Bleu College of Culinary Arts (Hollywood, Calif.) 169, 170
Ledger, Heath 164, 244
Lee, Ang 23
Lee, Bruce 33, 97
Lee, Christopher 189
"Legal Action" (Chris Corsani painting) 131
Lenard, Chef John 168–172, 178
Les Misérables (2012) 8
Leto, Jared 55
Let's Be Cops (2014) 70
Levin, Shawn (member of the Electric Sun 20) 207, 215, 217
Levisons Acquisitions 128. *See also* Chaplin's Soup and Subs
Lewis, Jerry 191
Library of Congress 104, 126
Life of Pi (2012) 5
Life of the Party (2018) 234
Li, Jet 70
Lincoln (2012) 3, 22
Lincoln, Abraham (U.S. president) 3, 156
Liotta, Ray 221
Little Deuce Coupe (Beach Boys album) 191
Little Tramp. *See* Chaplin, Charles
Liu, Lucy 2
Lohan, Lindsey 27
Lone Survivor (2014) 44
Lopez, Jennifer 96
Lord of the Rings (1978) 58
Lord of the Rings: Fellowship of the Ring (2001) 17, 21, 223, 224
Lord of the Rings (J.R.R. Tolkien book trilogy) 8
Lord of the Rings (Peter Jackson film trilogy) 87
Los Angeles, Calif. 4, 35, 65, 93, 96
Los Angeles River 233
Lost Horizon (1973) 133, 140
Louis XIV of France (1638–1715) 98
Lovato, Demi 173
Lowe, Rob 231
Lucas, George 21, 24, 94, 219–221, 236
  put on trial for plagiarism of *Decker* 220, 221

Lugosi, Bela 9
   death site revealed by Gregg 9
Lyman, Doug 180

M

MacDowell, Andie 2
MacFarlane, Seth 21, 22
Madden, John 93
Mad Men (television series) 59
Mafia 38, 111, 198, 235
Maggiano's Little Italy (restaurant chain) 106
Magic in the Moonlight (2014) 67
Maize, Kellee 183
Malibu Creek State Park (Calabasas, Calif.) 163
Malkovich, John 32
Maltin, Leonard 61
Mane, James 104, 133, 183
Mantegna, Joe 221
Man Trouble (1992) 96
Marin, Cheech. *See* Cheech & Chong
Marks, David 191, 194
Marley, Jacob (*Decker* character) 183
Marsden, James 59
Martin, Dean 221, 223. *See* Crocetti, Dino Paul
Martin, Steve 14, 96, 233
Marvel Worldwide Inc. 68, 88, 235, 242, 243
Marx, Adolph. *See* Marx, Arthur
Marx, Arthur. *See* Marx, Harpo
Marx Brothers 85, 128, 129
Marx, Chico 128
Marx, Groucho 129
Marx, Harpo 129, 131
Marx, Julius Henry. *See* Marx, Groucho
Marx, Leonard. *See* Marx, Chico
M*A*S*H (1970) 56, 133, 140
M*A*S*H (television series) 163
Mass Appeal (1984) 54
Master Codebreaker (*Star Wars* character) 219–221, 236, 243
Matthau, Walter 76, 180
Maverick (1993) 159
Maybellene (*Decker* character) 194
Maze Runner: The Scorch Trials (2015) 111
McCarthy, Melissa 14, 64, 234
McCartney, Paul 183
McFarland USA (2015) 86
McKellan, Sir Ian 21, 50, 55, 87
McNichol, Jimmy 24, 26, 49, 183, 189
McNichol, Kristy 24, 183
Meat Loaf. *See* Aday, Michael Lee
Mechanic: Resurrection (2016) 148
Medicine Man (1992) 51
Meet the Applegates (1990) 240
methamphetamine 146, 204, 209
Meyer, Nicholas (Electric Sun witness) 214, 215
Middle Earth. *See* Middle-Earth
Middle-Earth 8, 58, 87
Midler, Bette 11

Mike Love, Bruce Johnston and David Marks of the Beach Boys Salute NASCAR (Beach Boys album) 191
Miller, Dennis 19
Mirren, Helen 97
Mish Alrras (Taliban mindwipe technique) 192
Mission Impossible: Ghost Protocol (2011) 10
Misty Mountains 42
Mithrandir. *See* Gandalf
Moby Dick (1956) 242
Moment by Moment (1978) 7
"Mona Lisa" (Leonardo da Vinci painting) 240
Monroe, Marilyn 131, 163, 164, 166, 250
Monsters, Inc. (3D, 2012) 9
Monsters, Inc. (2001) 11
Moonlight (2016) 163
Moonlighting (television series) 15
Moore, Dudley 22
Moore, Julianne 53, 55
Moore, Mandy 174
Moore, Sir Roger 53, 54, 174
Mortdecai (2015) 128
Moscow on the Hudson (1984) 136
Moses (Biblical prophet) 84
Motion Picture Association of America (MPAA) 53
Mount Vesuvius 52
Mouse, Mickey 243
Movieheads Newsletter 140, 240, 243, 244
Mr. Spock. *See* Spock, Mr. (*Star Trek* character)
Mrs. Winterbourne (1996) 105
"MT-BTL 2.0" (DKR song) 127, 168
Mt. Rushmore 134
Multiplicity (1996) 2
Munchkins 18
Muppets 60
Muppets Most Wanted (2014) 60
Murphy's Law 3
Murphy's Romance (1985) 3
Murray, Bill 7, 9
Musée du Louvre (Paris, France) 110
Myers, Mike 181
My Giant (1998) 17
Mystery Men (1999) 234

N

National Association of Special Interests 99, 184
Nazz (music group) 191
Necronaut (2007) 16
Need for Speed (2014) 59
Neeson, Liam 49, 53, 70
Neighbors (2014) 64
Network (1976) 104
New Alliance Cinema 59
Next of Kin (1989) 235
Nicholson, Jack 96
Nightcat Gentleman's Club 136
Nimoy, Leonard 36, 59, 61. *See also* Spock, Mr. (*Star Trek* character)

9/11 terrorist attacks 9
Nine Lives (2016) 145
Nobody's Baby (2001) 178
Nocturnal Animals (2016) 163
No Escape. See *The Coup*
Nolte, Nick 67
Non-Stop (2014) 53, 70
North Pole 42
Nosferatu. See *Dracula* (classic horror character)
Nostradamus 64
Notaro, Tig 59

O

Oasis (music group) 35
Obama, Barack (U.S. president) 148, 185
Obamacare 14, 47, 48, 55
Oblivion (2013) 27, 30
OCF. See *On Cinema* Family
O'Connor, Carroll. See Bunker, Archie
Oh, God! (1977) 66, 68, 70, 76, 86, 129
Ohtani, Ayaka. See Ohwaki, Ayaka
Ohwaki, Ayaka
  appearances as *On Cinema* guest 24, 40, 95, 98, 130, 151
    interviewed for *On Cinema On Guests* 77
  appearances on *Decker* 116, 133
  film expertise, lack of 39, 41, 52
  helps to reconcile Tim and Gregg 39, 40
  hired as co-host of *On Cinema* 38
    replaces Gregg as host of *Popcorn Classics* 38, 98
      accused by Gregg of vandalizing one of his tapes 40
  hired as medical receptionist by Dr. Luther 95, 112, 113
  mermaids, dislike of 98
  mourns the death of Tom Cruise Heidecker Jr. 125, 130, 211
    comforted by CGI replica of Tom Jr. 130
  One Direction, love of 39, 40, 121
  popcorn, dislike of 24
  relationship with Tim Heidecker:
    arrives in USA and moves in with Tim Heidecker and his wife 24, 211
    begins dating Tim 38, 40, 211
      accepts Tim's on-air marriage proposal 98
    joins Tim in Gregg Turkington's apartment 93, 94, 98
    returns to Japan after conflict with Tim 41, 145, 146, 151
      returns to the United States to participate in intervention for Tim 151
    unplanned pregnancies 60, 65, 142, 157, 211
      declines Tim's request to terminate her pregnancy 157, 211
      gives birth to Tim's son, Tom Cruise Heidecker Jr. 25, 77
      returns to the United States with her baby 77
      sheltered by Gregg Turkington after Tim refuses to see her 78
  remarriage and motherhood in Japan 25, 211
  testifies at the Electric Sun 20 murder trial 211
O.J.: Made in America (2016) 163
Oldman, Gary 49, 65, 178
Old Yeller (1957) 124

Olórin. See Gandalf
On Cinema at the Cinema
  final episode 78
  presented in virtual reality (VR) 229–232
  segments:
    Close Encounters of the Movie Kind 224
    Down Oscar Memory Lane 56
    Golden Age Comedies With W. C. Fields 82, 84, 87, 92, 108, 147, 149, 178
    Gregg Turkington's Celebrity Backlot 67
    On Cinema After On Cinema 70
    On Cinema Gift Exchange 42
    On Cinema Markives 229, 235
    On Cinema Movie Awards 87
    On Cinema On Birthdays 30, 35
    On Cinema On Directors 88
    On Cinema On Family Ties 123
    On Cinema On Guests 65, 77
    On Cinema On Location 4, 7, 9, 11, 35, 36, 48, 66, 68, 70, 76, 86, 87, 95, 96, 108, 145, 146, 147, 148, 149, 157, 178, 180, 222, 233
    On Cinema On Movie History 59
    On Cinema On Popcorn 32
    On Cinema On Songwriters 130
    On Cinema Presents Popcorn Classics BTC 16, 24
    On Cinema Presents Stars on Directors 33
    Oscar Olympics 129, 131
    Popcorn Classics 2, 3, 5, 6, 8, 10, 14, 16, 17, 19, 24, 25, 30, 31, 34, 38–40, 42, 45, 51, 52, 53, 56, 60, 64, 65, 67, 76, 77, 82, 92, 94–96, 98, 111, 113, 115, 123, 131, 140, 144, 149, 154, 155, 158, 168, 170, 171, 173, 174, 186, 227, 228, 230–232, 234–236, 245
    Road to Hollywood 172, 173
    60-Second Soapbox 18, 19, 129
    Stump the Buff 20, 21, 24, 59
    Stump the Host 56
    Tim's Mailbag 60, 70
    Treasures of the Victorville Film Archive (proposed) 108
    Valli Remembers 222
    When Oscar Got It Wrong 56
  seized by the Delgado family 232
  special presentations:
    On Alternative Medicine on Cinema 48
    On Cinema at the Cinema Christmas Special (2013) 42
    On Cinema Presents The Dr. San Forgiveness Special 113, 115, 121, 124
    Oscars Special I (2013) 21–23
    Oscars Special II (2014) 55–57, 58
    Oscars Special III (2015) 87–89
    Oscars Special IV (2016) 127–131
    Oscars Special V (2016) 220–224
  spinoffs:
    Gregg Turkington's On Cinema at the Cinema 80–86, 179
    Tim Heidecker's Movie Review Show 232
  sponsors:
    Chaplin's Chili 88, 89
    Chaplin's Express 220, 222, 224
    Chaplin's Soup and Subs 128, 220

On Cinema at the Cinema (continued)
  sponsors: (continued)
    Red Flower Chinese Restaurant 57
    Rio-Jenesis 229
    The Delgado Fund 232
On Cinema Family 10, 25, 27, 30, 46, 47, 53, 60, 69, 78, 83–85, 87, 95, 97, 104, 108, 123, 124, 130, 146, 154, 156, 162, 165, 166, 168, 178–181
On Cinema Marching Band (music group) 87
1,3-dimethlamylamine (DMAA) 207
One Direction (music group) 40, 121
One Direction: This Is Us (2013) 40, 121
One Flew Over the Cuckoo's Nest (1975) 14
100 Kilos (2001) 235
On Golden Pond (1981) 244
Orion Jacks. *See* O'Ryan, Jack
Orville Redenbacher (popcorn brand) 32
O'Ryan, Jack (Electric Sun witness) 212, 215
"Oscar Fever" (Tim Heidecker song) 55, 57, 87, 89, 128, 162, 220
Oscars 2, 4, 5, 7–9, 18, 19, 21–23, 33, 34, 38, 42, 46, 51, 54–58, 65–68, 70, 85–89, 92, 94, 95, 98, 123, 128–131, 142, 144, 161–166, 171, 174, 186, 210, 219, 220, 222–224, 228, 234, 241, 244
Oscar Special (drink recipe) 22
Our Cinema (proposed *On Cinema* spinoff) 37, 104–106, 108, 110, 161, 166, 170, 219, 232
  Our Cinema Oscars Special (2017) 160–166, 219, 222
Our Song (2000) 111
"Our Values Are Under Attack" (Tim Heidecker song) 99, 110, 119
Overboard (2018) 230
Overwatch (videogame) 231
Oz, Frank 136
Oz the Great and Powerful (2013) 18

P

Pacific Rim (2013) 31, 227
Pacific Rim: Uprising (2018) 227
Pacino, Al 30, 44, 140
Palm Springs, Calif. 131, 223
Pan (2015) 115
Panera Bread 106
Pan, Peter 115
Paramount Studios 178, 180
Parental Guidance (2013) 11
Parker, Alan 231
Parker, Mary-Louise 32
Patel, Dev 93
Patinkin, Mandy 173
Paul, Aaron 59
Paxton, Bill 38
Pearl City, Hawaii 97
Pearl Harbor, Hawaii 102
Pearl Harbor, Japan 135, 136
Peck, Gregory 242
Penn, Sean 95

People Magazine 183
Percocet (oxycodone/paracetamol painkiller) 21, 151, 154
Percy Jackson: Sea of Monsters (2013) 35, 36
Perlman, Ron 236
Perry, Tyler 24, 42, 228
Persian Gulf 163
Pesci, Joe 181
Peter Pan (peanut butter brand) 115
Pete's Dragon (2016) 146
Picasso, Pablo 240
Pierce, Governor Lamont (*Decker* character) 192, 193
pi (mathematical constant) 5
Pirates of the Caribbean (movie franchise) 35, 243
Pitt, Brad 124
Pixley, Calif. 57
Planes: Fire and Rescue (2014) 66
Planet of the Apes (1968) 65
Playing for Keeps (2012) 7, 34
Play it Again, Sam (1972) 5
Plummer, Christopher 236
Pompeii (2014) 52
popcorn movies 10, 15, 35, 66, 82, 110, 142, 147, 168, 235
Popeye (1980) 20
Popp (*Decker* character) 186
Popp, Jesse (Electric Sun witness) 183, 212
Poppy (1936) 55
Pop Secret (popcorn brand) 32, 163
Power Rangers (2017) 171
Pratt, Chris 68, 157, 180, 233
Presley, Elvis 131
Pretty Woman (1990) 56
Price Waterhouse Cooper 22
Proksch, Mark
  appearances as *On Cinema* guest 55, 56, 87, 90, 128, 131, 149, 151, 162, 178, 179, 220, 222, 223
    pre-recorded appearance in *Close Encounters of the Movie Kind* 224
  stars in *Golden Age Comedies With W.C. Fields* 82, 84, 178
  celebrity impersonations:
    Carrey, Jim 55
    Chaplin, Charlie 56, 88
    Fields, W.C. 55, 57, 82, 84, 164, 178
    Hooper, Dr. Matt (*Jaws* character) 222
    Marx Brothers 128, 129, 131
    Quint (*Jaws* character) 220, 222
    Three Stooges 87, 89, 90
    West, Mae 55
  conflicts with Tim Heidecker 56, 85, 88, 127, 128, 130–132, 143, 148, 151, 152, 162, 165, 170, 171, 173, 174, 178, 189, 198, 210, 211, 220, 222
    accuses Tim of breaking his nose 210
    criticizes Tim on air while Tim is jailed on suspicion of murder 178
    goes into hiding after Tim is released on bail 180–182
  employment at Six Bag Cinema 168, 171–174, 178, 210
  employment at Victorville Film Center 146, 147, 210
  guest appearance on *Our Cinema* Oscars Special 162–165
    leaves set over concern that Gregg Turkington drove Tim

    Heidecker to suicide 164
  involvement with *Decker* miniseries 85, 87, 104, 133, 143, 149, 183, 189, 191, 223, 229
  loses consciousness in sealed diving suit 222, 227
    carried from Oscar set by paramedics 223, 227
    dies en route to hospital 223
    paramedics detect "brain activity" 223
    remains comatose rather than dead 223, 224, 227, 232, 235
  on the art of the impressionist 57
  on violence in cinema 87
  participates in intervention for Tim Heidecker 151
  remembered by Tim Heidecker and Gregg Turkington 223, 229, 235
Pryer, Mark (Electric Sun 19 member) 215
Putin, Vladimir Vladimirovich (Russian autocrat) 55–57

Q

Q & A (1990) 67, 76
Quaid, Dennis 7
Quality Air 134
Quinn, Anthony 178
Quinn, Christopher 178
Quint (*Jaws* character) 220

R

Radner, Gilda 97
Raging Bull (1980) 148
Raiders of the Lost Ark (1981) 56
Railsback, Steve 183
Raimi, Sam 18
Rain Man (1988) 158
Rampage (2018) 231
Randall, Tony 164
Rascal Flatts (music group) 154
Rating the Oscars (proposed Gregg Turkington book) 163
Ray (2004) 68
Reacher, Jack 22
Ready Player One (2018) 228, 229
Rebel Without a Cause (1955) 90, 128, 140, 174
Red (2010) 32
Red Bull 6
Red Dawn (1984) 5
Red Dawn (2012) 5
Red Flower Chinese Restaurant (*On Cinema* sponsor) 57
Redford, Robert 26, 146
Red 2 (2013) 32
Reed, Peyton 88, 90, 105, 241
Reeve, Christopher 140
Reilly, Kelly 2
Reiner, Rob 65
Reiser, Paul 101
Remember the Titans (2000) 23
Revenge of the Pink Panther (1978) 140
Reynolds, Burt 32, 56
Rhianna 96
Ricci, Christina 34
Riddick (2013) 41, 55

Ridealong (2014) 45
Rings (2015) 124
Ringwald, Molly 121, 250
Rio-Jenesis (*On Cinema* sponsor) 227–232
Risky Business (1983) 10, 31
Robertson, Vice President Roger (*Decker* character) 187
Robin Hood (1973) 243
Robocop (1987) 49, 50
Robocop (2014) 49
Robocop (movie franchise) 49, 50
Rock, Chris 31
Rocky II (1979) 93
Rocky (movie franchise) 148
Roeper, Richard 39
Rogen, Seth 89, 146
Rogue One: A Star Wars Story (2016) 164
Rolling Stone (music magazine) 68
Romeo and Juliet (1597 play) 51
Roosevelt, Franklin Delano (U.S. President) 7, 9
Rosetti the Rat. *See* Rosetti, Vincent (District Attorney, San Bernardino County)
Rosetti, Vincent (District Attorney, San Bernardino County) 198, 200, 201, 204, 206, 207, 210–212, 214–218, 221, 228, 236
Rotunno, Giuseppe 20
Rourke, Mickey 76
Rudd, Paul 88, 146, 243
Rundgren, Todd 191
Russell, Kurt 146, 230, 243
Russia 4, 55
Ruth, George Herman "Babe" Jr. 184
Ryan, Meg 76, 195
Rydell High School. *See* Excelsior High School (Norwalk, Calif.)
RZA (director) 2

S

S1M0NE (2002) 44
Saballah. *See* Maybellene (*Decker* character)
San Bernardino County Sheriff-Coroner's Office 207
Sanchez, Luther
  appearances as *On Cinema* guest 47, 48, 113, 124, 129–131, 144, 174
  appearances on *Decker* 191, 193, 209
  biography 46
  confirms James Dean's identity through DNA testing 129, 131, 133
  convinces Tim Heidecker to leave *Decker vs. Dracula* online 120
  creates lethal vape blend for Electric Sun Desert Music Festival 174, 201, 206, 209, 215
    milks poisonous toads to produce TCH vape 174, 206
  healing methodologies:
    creates creativity-boosting vape to help Tim Heidecker complete the Dekkar LP 144, 148, 209
    creates "Relax" powder to counter Gregg Turkington's negativity 121

Sanchez, Luther (continued)
   healing methodologies: (continued)
      treats Mark Proksch's mold-related cough with kerosene chest rub 178
      treats poisoned festivalgoer by administering additional vape 206
      treats poisoned festivalgoers with crystals 203
      treats Tim Heidecker's inflamed foot for "liver fire" 46–48, 113
   hosts wellness picnic 112
      recognized by Gregg Turkington as Ayaka Ohwaki's employer, "Dr. Luther" 112
   imprisoned on suspicion of murder
      allegedly writes confession letter for Electric Sun deaths 215
      criminal record 206
      interrogated by William Ellis 206, 207
      kills himself in prison 181, 201, 214, 215
      lack of medical background 201
   on the origin of DNA 129
   philosophy of healing 47, 113, 120, 124, 129, 144
      anti-vaccination views 113, 114, 149, 209
      objects to prescription medications 47
   posthumous video tribute 181
   repudiated by Tim Heidecker:
      after causing face infection with unsterilized needles 49, 113, 209
      after deaths and injuries at the Electric Sun Desert Music Festival 179, 181, 182, 198, 200, 206, 216
      after near-fatal vape oil poisoning 146
      after positive results of James Dean's DNA test 131
   takes charge of Tom Cruise Heidecker Jr.'s health 113, 115, 120, 124, 209, 211
      alternative treatments with magnets and herbs 124
      blamed for death of Tom Cruise Heidecker Jr. 124, 130, 149, 206, 209, 211
Sandler, Adam 31, 38
San, Dr. Luther. *See* Sanchez, Luther
San Francisco, Calif. 10, 36, 56, 59, 61, 142, 195, 213, 214
San Juan Capistrano, Calif. 112, 194
Santa Claus 42
Sarandon, Chris 162
Sarandon, Susan 16, 64
Saturday Night Live (television program) 31
Sausage Party (2016) 146
"Save Us" (DKR song) 180
Scary Movie 5 (2013) 27
Scary Movie (movie franchise) 27
Schlesinger, John 234
Schumer, Amy 181
Schwarzenegger, Arnold 70, 87, 122, 170
Schwarzenegger, Patrick 122
Scooby-Doo (2012) 235
Scorsese, Martin 61, 129
Scouts Guide to the Zombie Apocalypse (2015) 122
Scrooge, Ebenezer (Charles Dickens character) 34
Scrooge, Ebenezer (*Decker* character) 185
Sellers, Peter 92, 140

Senator Sanchez (*Decker* character) 192
Serpico (1973) 67
Serradimigni, Allessandro. *See* Axiom (Dekkar member)
Serradimigni, Juliana 147, 148, 150, 154, 157, 172, 173, 180
Seven Brides for Seven Brothers (1954) 121
Sextape (2014) 96
Sgt. Stubby: An American Hero (2018) 230
Shakespeare in Love (1998) 56
Shakespeare, William 89, 94, 182
Shamus (1973) 140
Sharia law 133
Shatner, William 21, 37
Shaw, Robert 220
Sheen, Charlie 27
Sheen, Martin 16
Sherlock Gnomes (2018) 227–229
Short Circuit (1986) 54
Show Dogs (2018) 235
Shymalan, M. Night 35
Sicario (2015) 113
Side Effects (2013) 14
Signs (2002) 35
Silver Linings Playbook (2012) 22
Silverstone, Alicia 11
Silver Streak (1976) 97
Simon & Simon (television series) 183
Simpson, O.J. 163
Sinatra, Frank 221, 223
Sin City (2005) 76
Sin City: A Dame to Kill For (2014) 76
Singer, Bryan 17
Siroky, Emily (Electric Sun witness) 203
Siskel, Gene 47
Six Bag Cinema 85, 168–171, 178, 181, 207
Six Days, Seven Nights (1998) 31
Sixteen Candles (1984) 250
Sixth Street Bridge (Los Angeles, Calif.) 146, 233
Skyfall (2012) 3, 11, 21
Skywalker, Luke (*Star Wars* character) 219
Slither (1973) 133
Slumdog Millionaire (2008) 223
Smith, Will 92, 145
Smokey Bites the Dust (1981) 24, 183
Smurfs: The Lost Village (2017) 173
Snatched (2017) 181
Snipes, Wesley 70, 236
Snitch (2013) 16
Snowden (2016) 154
Snowden, Edward 154
Snow White and the Seven Dwarfs (1937) 67, 243
Soapdish (1991) 79
Soderbergh, Steven 26
Solace (2016) 149
Solo: A Star Wars Story (2018) 236
Solo, Han 65, 236
Somewhere in Time (1980) 140
Sommersby (1993) 99
"Song for Ayaka" (Tim Heidecker song) 88

"Song for Peace" (Luther Sanchez composition) 113
Son of Dracula (*Decker* character)
   plots revenge against Decker Jr. for the death of Dracula Sr. 184–186
   resurrects the corpses at Arlington National Cemetery 187
Son of the Pink Panther (1993) 92
Soul Food (1997) 84
South of Reno (1988) 16
Spacek, Sissy 11
Spacey, Kevin 145
Spectres (2015) 123
Spencer, Tripp (*Decker* character) 190
Spider-Man 242
Spielberg, Steven 3, 10, 26, 110, 118, 222, 228, 229
Splash (1984) 98
Splendor in the Grass (1961) 140
Spock, Mr. *See* Nimoy, Leonard
Spotlight (2015) 131, 223
Stallone, Sylvester 70, 87, 180
Starr, Ringo 54, 191
Star Trek Beyond (2016) 142
Star Trek II: The Wrath of Khan (1982) 10, 36, 37, 59, 61, 142, 195, 213–215
Star Trek IV: The Voyage Home (1986) 10, 36, 59, 213–215
Star Trek IV: The Voyage Home (Vonda N. McIntyre book) 36
Star Trek (movie franchise) 10, 27, 36, 39, 47, 56, 142, 214, 215
Star Trek (television series) 56, 133, 191
Star Trek VI: The Undiscovered Country (1991) 214
Star Wars: Episode I - The Phantom Menace (1999) 17, 76
Star Wars: Episode IV - A New Hope (1977) 23, 24, 34, 94, 119, 241
Star Wars (movie franchise) 10, 39, 41, 47, 94, 97, 115, 119, 133, 219, 221, 236, 243
Star Wars: The Last Jedi (2017) 219, 221, 243
Steve Jobs (2015) 115
Stevens, Inger 56
Stevenson, John 228
Stewart, James 223
Stiller, Ben 234
Stone, Oliver 154
Storey, Tim 45, 55
Storks (2016) 157
Stouffer's (frozen meal brand) 178
Straight Up (Badfinger album) 191
Statham, Jason 148
Streep, Meryl 250
Styles, Harry 39
Suicide Squad (2016) 145
Sullenberger, Chesley Burnett "Sully" III 151, 213
Sully (2016) 151, 152, 158, 159, 164, 166, 168, 169, 178, 209, 213
Sully (heroic airline pilot). *See* Sullenberger, Chesley Burnett "Sully" III
Summer School (1987) 154
Sunset Strip (Hollywood, Calif.) 128
Superman 68, 242
Superman (movie franchise) 140
Super Troopers (2001) 231
Super Troopers 2 (2018) 231
Surfin' USA (Beach Boys album) 191
Sutherland, Kiefer 52, 234
Swayze, Don 191, 235
Swayze, Patrick 191, 235, 245
Swing Shift (1984) 123
Switching Channels (1988) 140
Swordfish (2001) 230
Sylmar, Calif. 231
Szymcyzk, Judge Edward 201, 203, 206, 207, 209, 210–217

T

T2 Trainspotting (2017) 170
Taliban 44, 73, 99, 101–103, 117–119, 184–186
Tammy (2014) 64, 250
Tarantino, Quentin 23
Tatum, Channing 14, 24, 31, 49, 82
TCH (vape formula)
   developed by Tim Heidecker and Dr. San 174, 206, 209, 215
   given away free at Electric Sun Desert Music Festival 174, 178, 201, 203
   harmful effects 178, 180, 201, 203, 206, 207, 209, 215
   intended purpose 206
   possible contamination 206, 213
   reported ingredients 180, 206, 207, 209
   toxicology findings 201, 207, 209, 215
TCH Vape Systems 174, 201
"Tears in Heaven" (Eric Clapton ballad) 124
Teenage Mutant Ninja Turtles (2014) 69
Temptation: The Marriage Counselor (2013) 24
Tharkûn. *See* Gandalf
That Awkward Moment (2014) 48
That Darn Cat (1965) 140
"That Girl's Just Gotta Be Kissed" (Perk-A-Goom song) 221
The Apple Dumpling Gang (1975) 243
The Assassination of Jesse James by the Coward Robert Ford (2007) 32
The Avengers (1998) 233
The Barefoot Executive (1971) 243
The Beach Boys (music group) 133, 191, 194
The Beatles (music group) 183, 191
The Belko Experiment (2017) 170
The Big Chill (1983) 232
The Big Sleep (1946) 5
The Black Hole (1979) 243
The Blues Brothers (1980) 64
The Bodyguard (1992) 111
The Boss Baby (2017) 172
The Bourne Identity (2002) 144
The Bourne Legacy (2012) 144
The Bourne Ultimatum (2007) 144
The 'Burbs (1989) 79
The Caine Mutiny (1954) 163
The California Kid (1974) 88
The Case for Christ (2017) 173
The Circle (2017) 179
The Colony (2013) 38

The Company You Keep (2013) 26
The Coup (2015) 93
The Creature from the Black Lagoon (1954) 230
The Croods (2013) 20, 26
The Dark Knight (2008) 140
The Day After (1983) 214
The Divergent Series: Insurgent (2015) 95
The Doors (1991) 154
The Exorcist (1973) 64
The Expendables 3 (2014) 70
The Expendables (movie franchise) 70
The Family Man (2000) 40
The Fast and the Furious 8: The Fate of the Furious (2017) 174
The Flintstones (television series) 17, 20
The Four Seasons (music group) 191
The French Connection (1971) 142
The Frozen Ground (2013) 6
The General's Daughter (1999) 233
The Getaway (2013) 40
The Girl on a Bicycle (2014) 51
The Godfather (1972) 39, 65, 111, 140, 181
The Godfather II (1974) 22, 38, 39, 59, 140
The Godfather III (1990) 140
The Gold Rush (1925) 162
The Graduate (1967) 51
The Great Gatsby (1949) 240
The Green Inferno (2014) 78
The Gunman (2015) 95
The Hand (1981) 140
The Hangover Part II (2011) 98
The Harder They Fall (1956) 244
The Hobbit 3. See The Hobbit: The Battle of the Five Armies (2014)
The Hobbit (1937 book) 8, 36
The Hobbit: An Unexpected Journey (2012) 8, 10, 11, 16, 19, 21, 22, 35, 39, 52, 59, 77, 115, 130, 162
The Hobbit II. See The Hobbit: The Desolation of Smaug (2013)
The Hobbit: The Battle of the Five Armies (2014) 79, 86–89
The Hobbit: The Desolation of Smaug (2013) 42, 46, 54–57
The Imaginarium of Doctor Parnassus (2009) 244
The Incredible Burt Wonderstone (2013) 19
The Interview (2014) 89
The Jerk (1979) 191
The Joker 145, 244
The Killing (1956) 221
The King's Daughter. See The Moon and the Sun (2015)
The Lazarus Effect. See Lazarus (2015)
The Lego Movie (2014) 49, 111
The Life of David Gale (2003) 231
The Light Between Oceans (2016) 149
The Lion King (1994) 243
Thelma and Louise (1991) 181
The Lonely Lady (1983) 21
The Lone Ranger (2013) 30, 55
The Lost City of Z (2017) 174
The Lovers (2017) 180
The Magnificent Seven (2016) 157
The Maltese Falcon (1941) 5

The Mama Cass Television Program (1969) 191
The Man With the Iron Fists (2012) 2
The Martian (2015) 113
The Mask of Zorro (1998) 174
The Matrix (1999) 82
The Mod Squad (2013) 19
The Mod Squad (television series) 19
The Monkey's Uncle (1965) 133
The Moody Blues (music group) 183
The Moon and the Sun (2015) 98
The Mummy (classic horror character) 92, 189
The Mummy (Decker character) 116, 117, 186, 189
The Music Man (1962) 162
The New Adam-12 (1991) 191
The New Cars (music group) 191
"Then I Kissed Her" (Beach Boys song) 133
The November Man (2014) 77
The Nut Job (2014) 45
The Odd Couple (television series) 191
The Oklahoma Kid (1939) 163
The Outer Limits (television series) 133
The Peanuts Movie (2015) 123, 172
The People's Court (television program) 94
The Player (1992) 133, 140
The Presidio (1998) 178
The Punisher (2004) 235
The Rat Pack (1950s–1960s entertainers) 5, 221, 224
The Rat Pack (1998) 221
The Rat Pack (2015 tribute to the 1998 biopic on the 1950s–1960s entertainers) 221–224
The Rescuers (1977) 243
"The Rock". See Johnson, Dwayne
Theron, Charlize 174
The Salesman (2016) 164
The Second Best Exotic Marigold Hotel (2015) 93
The Seven-Per-Cent Solution (1976) 214
The Seven-Ups (1973) 38
The Shaggy D.A. (1976) 145
The Shootist (1976) 244
The Silmarillion (1977 book) 89
The Slipper and the Rose (1976) 53
The Smurfs (2011) 34
The Smurfs 2 (2013) 34
The Sopranos (television series) 59
The Sound of Music (1965) 27, 236
The Soup Plantation (restaurant chain) 16
The Spongebob Movie (2015) 82
The Spy Who Loved Me (1977) 54
"The Star-Spangled Banner" (U.S. national anthem) 195
The Stepford Wives (1975) 38
The Stunt Man (1980) 183
The Terminator (1984) 37
The Terminator (movie franchise) 170
The Thing (1982) 54
The Thing (2011) 54
The Three Stooges 85, 87, 90, 126
The Turning Point (1977) 16
The Twilight Saga: Breaking Dawn - Part 2 (2012) 4, 5

The Twilight Zone (television series) 5
The Wall (2017) 168
The Way We Were (1973) 162
The Wizard of Oz (1939) 18, 56
The Wolf Man (classic horror character) 92
The Wolf Man (*Decker* character) 116, 117, 132, 186, 187, 190
The Wolverine (2013) 33
The Woman in Red (1984) 97
The Wood (1999) 149
The World's End (2013) 38
The Zookeeper's Wife (2017) 172
36 Hours to Die (1999) 235
Thompson, Dee
  gets into the Oscars without a ticket 129, 220
  tries to get into the Oscars without a ticket 221, 223
Thompson, Emma 154
3D movies 9, 16, 26, 32, 49, 123, 191, 229, 230
Three Amigos (1986) 11
300 (2006) 34
300: Rise of an Empire 34
Three on a Match (1932) 163
Thurman, Uma 233
Time After Time (1979) 214
Time Cop 2: The Berlin Decision (2003) 135
Tim's Story (proposed Tim Heidecker biopic) 45, 55
Tinseltown. *See* Hollywood, Calif.
Titanic (1997) 23, 223, 241
Tolkien, J.R.R. 8, 87, 89, 166
Tom Cruise Heidecker Jr. Memorial Arts Fund 130, 133, 142, 170, 207
Tomei, Marisa 11
Tomlin, Lily 7
Topungo-Mungo 178
Toto. *See* Garland, Judy
Toy Story 3 (2010) 243
Trading Places (1983) 97
Traffik (2018) 232
Training Day (2001) 232
Trainspotting (1996) 170
Trank, Josh 90, 110
Transylvania 6-5000 (1985) 184
Travolta, Joey 183
Travolta, John 7, 183, 235
Triumphs of a Man Called Horse (1983) 191
Tron (1982) 228
True Grit (1969) 244
Truman, Harry (U.S. president) 57
Turbo (2013) 32
Turkington, Gregg
  DISPUTES WITH TIM HEIDECKER. *See also* Heidecker, Timothy Richard: Disputes with Gregg Turkington
    accuses Tim of arson 164, 178, 179, 209
    Dekkar and DKR, negative opinion of 119, 122, 128, 130, 131, 149, 151, 154, 156, 157, 161, 162, 164, 173, 177, 198, 209, 216, 219, 230, 234, 245
    Luther Sanchez, negative opinion of 47–50, 52, 56, 61, 83, 121, 124, 130, 145, 146, 149, 151, 154, 178, 180, 181
    Six Bag Cinema, negative opinion of:
      bad service, food and odor 169, 172, 174, 178
      food service interrupts movies 168, 169, 172, 174
      run by an insane person 178, 198
      small screen 168, 169
      standard popcorn not available 168–170, 172–174
      uncomfortable seating 169, 172, 178
    Tim's anger management issues, negative opinion of 55, 90, 104, 121, 130
    Tim's drug and alcohol abuse, negative opinion of 23, 55–57, 129, 130, 152, 154, 156, 164, 170, 178, 179, 209, 220
    Tim's film expertise, negative opinion of 23, 35, 37, 39, 40, 51, 61, 178, 179, 227, 236
    Tim's management of *On Cinema*, negative opinion of 18, 23, 24, 37, 39, 47, 48, 50, 56, 61, 68, 69, 82, 83, 85, 92, 104, 128–130, 147, 149, 151, 154, 156, 157, 162–164, 166, 168, 170, 172–174, 178–180, 209, 219, 227–230, 232, 234
  HEALTH AND MEDICAL ISSUES
    has unspecified organ surgically removed 66
  INVOLVEMENT WITH DECKER MINISERIES. *See herein Decker* (miniseries)
  INVOLVEMENT WITH ON CINEMA
    banned from *On Cinema* 24, 36, 37, 61
      returns to *On Cinema* after ban 26, 39, 40, 61
    contract negotiations with Tim Heidecker 106, 108
    film expertise challenged by Prof. Larry Turman 51
    forced to issue statement claiming he did not see *Sully* 168
    hosts *On Cinema* 50, 51, 80, 82, 123, 149, 178, 179, 234–236
      made permanent host of *On Cinema* by the Delgado Family 234
    hosts *Our Cinema* Oscars Special 160–166
      advises Tim Heidecker to jump out the window of his Dubai hotel 163
      forced to apologize for *Our Cinema* Oscars Special 166
    interviewed on *On Cinema On Guests* 65
    produces *Golden Age Comedies With W. C. Fields* 82, 84, 85, 149
    promises show-stopping Oscar Special finale 54–57, 86, 87, 127
    quits *On Cinema* 104
      returns to *On Cinema* after quitting 106, 110
    receives *On Cinema*'s "Best Guest of 2012" award 23
    serves as managing director of Delgado Media Holdings 234
  OPINIONS ON CINEMA
    Close Encounters of the Third Kind is technically *Jaws 2* 222, 224
    film academics "don't understand cinema" 52
    memories of Fay Wray 168
    Murphy's Romance (1985), disappointing experience with 3
    on cinema as a fine art 51, 177
    on film titling protocols 22, 36, 59, 93, 115, 144, 168, 170, 228, 231
    on movie great Woody Allen 33, 144, 228
    on the actor's art 2, 250
    on the benefits of cloning Michael Keaton 2

Turkington, Gregg (continued)
　OPINIONS ON CINEMA (continued)
　　on the film critic's role in society 17, 40, 51, 250
　　on the final films of movie legends 244
　　on the importance of film expertise 9, 23, 24, 37, 39, 41, 50–52, 61, 77, 80, 82, 84, 85, 104, 105, 127, 156, 161, 162, 178, 179, 182, 209, 216, 241, 250
　　on the *James Bond* franchise 3, 11, 15, 65, 77, 93, 123, 130, 156, 164
　　on the late career of George Burns 97
　　on the Oscars:
　　　calls for Super Oscar award to identify the best Oscar-winning films 164, 222, 223, 224
　　　decries alphabetical Oscar snub of film titles beginning with N through Z 162, 163
　　　expects Oscar win for *The Hobbit* 21, 22, 42, 46, 54, 55, 57, 79, 86–89
　　　frustrated by Oscar's snub of *The Hobbit* 11, 22, 23, 46, 57, 89
　　　on the Oscar gift bag 162
　　　Oscar picks 4, 7, 19, 55, 65, 67, 68, 79, 92, 123, 144, 148, 174, 181, 228
　　　proposes monthly Oscar awards 87, 129
　　　proposes Oscar for Best Comedy or comic actor 7, 34, 234
　　on the year-round appeal of Christmas movies 34
　　on Tim Heidecker's *Fantastic Four* 105, 106, 110, 128, 180, 241, 242
　　preference for the VHS format 21, 42, 52, 59, 147, 235, 240, 250
　　proposes renaming numbered streets after movie legends 250
　　reveals that James Dean is still alive 89
　　skepticism about virtual reality (VR) 229, 230
　　Tim Burton, dispute with 227–231
　PERSONAL LIFE AND HOBBIES
　　attempts to launch *Our Cinema* 37, 104, 105, 106, 108, 110, 166, 170, 232
　　attempts to watch 500 Movies in 500 Days 34, 36, 37, 39, 41, 44, 45, 49, 51, 52, 64, 66, 77–79, 82
　　watches 501 movies in 501 days 79, 82
　　cast as Dale in *Ant-Man* (2015) 88, 241, 242
　　driven from his apartment by Tim Heidecker 98, 209
　　moves into Victorville Storage Facility 110
　　informs Tim Heidecker of Ayaka Ohwaki's pregnancy on the air 60
　　announces the birth of Tom Cruise Heidecker Jr. in an *On Cinema* segment 77
　　shelters Ayaka and Tom Cruise Heidecker Jr. after Tim rejects them 78
　　launches the Victorville Film Archive 110
　　launches the Victorville Film Center 142
　　love of J.R.R. Tolkien's *Lord of the Rings*:
　　　distracted from *A Madea Christmas* by thoughts of Bilbo Baggins 42
　　　dresses in "Hobbit-ween" costume to honor Bilbo Baggins 55
　　　has Christmas dream about Bilbo Baggins 42
　　　objects to Tim's documentary castigating *The Hobbit*'s Peter Jackson 130
　　　predicts that Peter Jackson will base upcoming hobbit movies on *The Silmarillion* 89
　　　reveals his hobbit-themed "Oscar Fantasy" 57
　　　sees Bilbo Baggins as "a personal hero" 8
　　　visits Middle-Earth locations 87
　　participates in intervention for Tim Heidecker 151
　　VHS film collection 2, 7, 21–23, 30, 40–42, 51, 57, 59, 103–105, 110, 123, 144, 147–149, 151, 152, 154, 170–172, 182, 209, 220, 228, 232, 235, 240, 245. *See also* Victorville Film Archive
　　　destroyed by fire at the Victorville Film Archive 149–151, 152, 154
　　　destroyed by fire at the Victorville Film Center 171, 209
　　　destroyed by fire in Hawaii 103, 104, 110
　　　VHS coding system 30, 40, 51, 65, 105, 111, 131, 231
　testifies at the Electric Sun 20 murder trial 209, 213, 220
Turman, Larry 51, 52, 54, 55, 191
21 and Over (2013) 17
21 Jump Street (2012) 64
Twilight Zone: The Movie (1983) 5
Two Weeks Notice (2002) 30
Tyler Perry's Acrimony (2018) 228

U

Ukraine 55, 56
United Nations 183, 186, 187, 197
Universal Soldier: Day of Reckoning (2012) 6
Universal Studios 222
U.S. Secret Service 56
U.S. Supreme Court 69, 185, 186, 187
Utopia (music group) 191

V

vaccination 113, 114, 124, 130, 149, 193, 209
Valli, Bobby 183, 191, 220, 222
Valli, Frankie 191, 222
Values.com 86, 90, 92, 97, 98
Vanilla Sky (2001) 178
Van Nuys, Calif. 79, 172, 232, 240
Van Patten, Dick 230
vaping 128, 144–149, 151, 157, 168, 171, 174, 178, 180, 181, 186, 187, 193–195, 201, 203, 206, 207, 209, 210, 212, 215, 217
VFA. *See* Victorville Film Archive
VFC. *See* Victorville Film Center
VHS format 21, 42, 44, 52, 53, 59, 110, 131, 147, 235, 240, 250. *See also* videocassettes
Victorville Film Archive 108, 111, 115, 123, 124, 131, 138, 142, 143, 146–148, 150, 152, 170, 172, 184, 220, 227, 229, 232, 236, 240, 245
　created by Gregg Turkington upon donation of storage locker full of videocassettes 105, 110

destroyed in fire at Victorville Storage Facility 149–152, 154, 157, 168
   relocates to Victorville Film Center 150
  destroyed in Victorville Film Center fire 171, 209
   relocates to a corner of Mark Proksch's apartment in Van Nuys, Calif. 232
  undertakes collection of promotional movie hats 228, 233
Victorville Film Center 85, 144-146, 148–150, 154, 157, 198
  black mold infestation 170, 178
  destroyed by fire 171, 209
  financial problems 154, 170, 171
  funded by the Tom Cruise Heidecker Jr. Memorial Arts Fund 142
  projection quality 154
  rat problems 147
  unpaid licensing fees 170
Victorville Storage Facility 105, 110, 123, 148, 149, 150, 154, 168. *See also* Victorville Film Archive
videocassettes 2, 3, 6, 9, 10, 19, 21–23, 26, 30, 40–42, 44, 45, 51–53, 57, 59, 65, 82, 96, 99, 101, 103–105, 110, 123, 131, 136, 138, 140, 144, 147, 150–152, 162, 170–172, 182, 186, 195, 220, 235, 240, 242, 245, 250
Voight, Jon 55
von Richthofen, Manfred Albrecht Freiherr "Red Baron" 123

W

Wahlberg, Mark 44
Walken, Christopher 145
Walker, Paul 97, 174
Walk of Shame (2014) 59
Walk the Line (2005) 59
Wallach, Eli 164
Waltz, Christoph 21
Warner Brothers 67
Warner, H.B. 162
Washington, Denzel 2, 157, 161
Wayans, Damon Jr. 70
Waymon, Miriam (Assistant District Attorney, San Bernardino County) 209–211, 213–218
Wayne, John 244
WC-P0 (Decker character) 197
Weaver, Sigourney 93
Welcome To LA (1976) 140
Welcome to Yesterday (2015) 53
Welles, Orson 64, 148, 157, 169
West, Mae 55, 82
Whale Man (proposed Marvel superhero) 241, 242
When Harry Met Sally... (1989) 45
When the Bough Breaks (2016) 151
Whitney, Daniel Lawrence 42
Who Framed Roger Rabbit? (1988) 45
Wilder, Gene 97, 244
Williams, Robin 101, 136
Williams, Vanessa 84
Willis, Bruce 15, 24, 32, 76
Wilson, Luke 115
Winger, Debra 45, 180

Wings (1928) 56
Wings (musical group) 183
Winslet, Kate 48
Winters, Jonathan 34, 173
Wiping Off the "Sheen" (Joe Estevez book) 60
Wish I Was Here (2014) 67
Witness (1985) 162
Woman in Gold (2015) 97
Wong, Kar-Wai 221
Wonka, Willy 244
Wood, Natalie 140
World War I 230
World War II 53, 102, 135, 136
Wray, Fay 168

X

X-Men (comic book series) 33
X-Men (movie franchise) 64

Y

Yes Man (2008) 88
Young, Loretta 223
You Were Never Really Here (2018) 229

Z

Zadora, Pia 21
Zemeckis, Robert Lee 2
Zero Dark Thirty (2012) 9, 44
Zeta-Jones, Catherine 32
Zootopia (2016) 164
Zorillians (*Decker* characters) 195, 197

PHOTO CREDITS

James Dean ©Martin Cintula / 123RF Stock Photo — Johnny Depp by Gage Skidmore (CC BY-SA 2.0) — Detective Illustration ©grafico2011 / Adobe Stock
Peter Jackson by Gage Skidmore (CC BY 2.0) — Sally Kellerman ©buzzfuss / 123RF Stock Photos — Denny Laine by Jim Summaria (CC BY-SA 3.0)
Marquee Illustration ©alexmillos / Adobe Stock — Jimmy McNichol by Auroa Entertainment, LLC (CC BY 3.0) — Popcorn Box Illustration ©nosorogua / Adobe Stock
Steve Railsback by HSalmena Communications Group (CC BY-SA 3.0) — Photo of The Searcher by Ross Wilson is by Genvessel. (CC BY 2.0)
Steven Spielberg by Dick Thomas Johnson from Tokyo, Japan. (CC BY 2.0) — Don Swayze by Angela George (CC BY-SA 3.0)
Theatre curtain photo by Manos Gikkas on Unsplash. — Wax Sculpture ©Ozgur Guvenc / 123RF Stock Photos